KU-264-426

Scotland

Scotland

A HISTORY FROM EARLIEST TIMES

Alistair Moffat

BIRLINN

Coventry City Council	
BEL*	
3 8002 02243 014 6	
Askews & Holts	Oct-2015
941.1	£25.00

First published in 2015 by
Birlinn Limited
West Newington House
10 Newington Road
Edinburgh
EH9 1QS

www.birlinn.co.uk

Copyright © Alistair Moffat 2015

The moral right of Alistair Moffat to be identified as the
author of this work has been asserted by him in accordance
with the Copyright, Designs and Patents Act 1988.

All rights reserved.
No part of this publication may be reproduced,
stored or transmitted in any form without the express
written permission of the publisher.

ISBN: 978 1 78027 280 1

British Library Cataloguing-in-Publication Data
A catalogue record for this book is available from the British Library

Typeset by Iolaire Typesetting, Newtonmore
Printed and bound by Bell & Bain Ltd, Glasgow

In memory of Hannah Moffat – the story of Scotland
she will always be part of

Contents

✻

List of Illustrations   ix

Acknowledgements   xl

Introduction   xiii

 1 The Collisions   1
 2 The Pioneers   8
 3 Caledonia   28
 4 Alba   45
 5 Old Gods and the Edge of Heaven   76
 6 The Nation of the Scots   100
 7 The War for Scotland   151
 8 Scotland Remade   184
 9 An Imperfect Union   230
10 Rebellious Scots   270
11 North Britain   316
12 Imperial Scotland   363
13 Scotlands   410

Envoi   487

Bibliography   491

Index   505

List of Illustrations

✳

1. The Ness of Brodgar, Orkney.
2. Burnswark, Roman siege works and catapult platforms.
3. Nails being excavated at the legionary fortress of Inchtuthil.
4. Athur's O'on, the probable dedicatory temple of the Antonine Wall.
5. St Columba's Shrine, Iona.
6. Eileach an Naoimh, the Garvellachs, the best preserved early monastic site in Scotland.
7. The baptistery at Hoddom, Mungo's see while in exile from Strathclyde.
8. The Aberlemno stone.
9. Burghead, a Pictish royal centre.
10. The great Pictish fortress at Dunadd.
11. David, from the St Andrews Sarcophagus.
12. Dupplin Cross.
13. The Runes of Maes Howe.
14. Temple Pyx.
15. Glasgow Cathedral.
16. Alexander III, from the Wriothesley Garter Book.
17. Edward I receives the homage of Scotland.
18. Doune Castle.
19. Bishop Elphinstone's tomb, outside King's College Chapel, Aberdeen.
20. Ardtornish Castle, site of the signing of the Treaty of Westminster-Ardtornish.
21. The possible Viking Age canal at Rubh an Dunain, Skye.

22. A page from the Carver Choir book.

23. The Great Hall of Stirling Castle.

24. Tyndale's New Testament.

25. George Wishart being burned alive.

26. John Knox.

27. The North Berwick Witch Trials of 1591.

28. Culross Palace.

29. A Solemn League and Covenant.

30. Kelso, as depicted in Slezer's *Theatrum Scotiae*.

31. Bernera Barracks.

32. Culloden, painted by Paul Sandby.

33. Surveying the Highlands.

34. Adam Smith, by Alexander Stoddart.

35. Mavisbank, possibly William Adam's greatest achievement.

36. James Craig's plan of the New Town in Edinburgh.

37. Henry Dundas' house at 36 St Andrew Square, Edinburgh.

38. James Hogg in his shepherd's plaid.

39. Walter Scott's Scott's death mask.

40. The *Comet* speeds past her competition on the Clyde.

41. David Octavius Hill's painting of the 1843 General Assembly.

42. Balmoral Castle.

43. St Andrews fisherfolk, photographed by David Octavius Hill and Robert Adamson.

44. The Forth Rail Bridge under construction.

45. Keir Hardie.

46. Municipal pomp and pride – Glasgow City Chambers.

47. Glasgow School of Art, Charles Rennie Mackintosh's masterpiece.

48. The Glasgow Rent Strike, 1915.

49. The German High Seas Fleet steams to surrender in the Forth.

50. Eric Liddell running in his characteristic style.

51. Hugh MacDiarmid.

52. The independence referendum of 2014.

Acknowledgements

T his was a big project and I needed the patience and help of the team at Birlinn more than ever. My thanks to Hugh Andrew, Jan Rutherford, Andrew Simmons and Anna Marshall, and to my editor, Patricia Marshall. Once again, Jim Hutcheson has designed a superb cover. My agent, David Godwin, also has great patience as well as tact. Thanks to all.

As I was writing the last chapters of this book, my granddaughter, Hannah Moffat, died and my son and his wife and our whole family were shattered by a grief beyond all our experience. The image of her little wicker-basket coffin will stay with me to the end of my days. This book is for the wee lass we were never allowed to know but will never forget.

Alistair Moffat
July, 2015
Selkirk

Introduction

✳

SITTING ON THE STEP outside my office on a sunny summer evening, when a peace seems to settle, I sometimes think I can see all of Scotland's history. Not through an effort of imagination but in the ways in which the five or six hundred generations before us left their marks on the land.

The shape of our little valley was scarted out by slow-motion primeval drama, by the rumble of the glaciers of the last Ice Age as they began to groan, crack and splinter, grinding out the river courses, shearing off cliff faces, rounding the distant hills of the Ettrick Forest and depositing the fertile soil where plants, trees and animals would come to thrive. On the flat valley floor, on the banks of the burns and on the slopes to the south stood the great Hartwood, the Deer Wood. After the ice shrank back and the land began to green, native trees carpeted Scotland with the Wildwood, a temperate jungle that reached up to the flanks of the highest hills and mountains. Willow scrub, birch, Scots pine, alder and ash were amongst the first to take root and they still grow well in the Hartwood, often on the regimented edges of Alaskan sitka. And the deer are still in the forest – velvety, perfect, skittish little roe deer flit into the shadows and disappear in a moment. This year, a hind nested in the Crow Wood behind my office, where each evening the birds bicker and squabble over the best roosts. In the morning's grey dim and at dusk, she brought out two leggy fawns to graze the grassy fringes by the track.

The pioneers, the first to come north after the ice, saw much of what I see. Like the deer, their shadows flitted through the Wildwood, barely rustling the leaves of the six thousand autumns, winters, springs and summers when their descendants hunted and gathered a wild harvest across prehistoric Scotland. At the foot of the slope near my office there is a small standing stone. Twenty years ago when the old orchard by the burn was a tangle of nettles and willowherb, I fell – or rather skidded – over it. The stone was lying flat, recently tumbled, having kicked the earth out of its socket. With a shovel and a fencepost, I managed to lever it upright and now it stands approximately where it did. Perhaps it is not ancient, perhaps it is a boundary marker near the bank of the burn, but it is mysterious – something raised for a forgotten reason by nameless people a long time ago.

Fertile, free-draining and sheltered, the little valley was home to generations of hunter-gatherers and then settled communities of early farmers. From the dark furrows of my neighbour's newly ploughed fields, I have picked up a few beautifully knapped flints and what looks like part of an axe-head. And, further down the valley, a spring plough skinned the stone lid off a cist and, for the first time in four thousand years, the sun warmed the dust and bones inside. To the east of where I sit rises the Deer Park and, in the green folds of the hill, there are scooped-out depressions that offer welcome shelter from the west wind. When a sugar-dusting of snow falls, they are easy to see. Perhaps they were shielings where herd-laddies kept watch on beasts summering out on the higher pasture.

No conjecture swirls around the identity of those who arrived in the valley at the end of the 1st century AD. The thud of hooves, the jingle of bridles and the rhythmic tramp of marching soldiers announced that the Empire had come north. About three miles to the west of where I sit in the evening are the grassed-over banks and ditches of Oakwood Fort, built by a cohort of 500 men, a mixture of cavalry and infantry under the overall command of the great general, Agricola. Watched by the hostile native kindred – the Selgovae – squads of imperial soldiers dug ditches, built ramparts and laid out roads and a signal station. Through a depression in the ridge of the Deer Park, the men at Oakwood could look east and see the signal station built on the summit of Eildon Hill North, above the sprawling supply depot at Trimontium. For only one generation, 20 years, the Romans marched up and down our little valley, filing intelligence reports, skirmishing with the war bands of the Selgovae, laying down the controlling framework of a new province for the Empire. But then in AD 100, the Emperor Trajan withdrew troops from Britain for his invasion of Dacia, modern Romania, and the frontier was pulled back to the line of the Tyne and Solway. And perhaps in triumph, the Selgovae war bands burned the wooden gate towers at Oakwood.

Ownership of a gentler sort was discovered on one of the sheep walks in the Deer Park in 2003. Part of an ogham stone was recognised. Ogham was a strange and ancient tree language which formed its letters like the branches or twigs of a tree cut in straight lines like runes but arranged on either side of a central trunk. Usually spelling out personal names, probably the marks of the ownership of land, the earliest ogham stones were carved in Ireland in the 4th century AD. The finding of a stone so far east in Scotland is striking – perhaps evidence that Gaelic-speaking chieftains were carving out holdings in the centuries after the fall of the Roman Empire in the west, the centuries known as the Dark Ages.

Not far from where the ogham stone was picked up, a ditch runs up the slopes of the Deer Park and across its summit. In places, the ditch has been hacked out of the hard whinstone rock that lies close to the surface of the rough pasture. An immense labour, the ditch and the bank on its eastern side must have demarcated an important boundary. By the early 12th century, it was certainly used as part of a fence. On top of the bank, what was known as the park pale was built. *Palus* is the Latin word for 'a stake' and it later came to mean a row of stakes, a fence – the phrase 'beyond the pale' derives from it. Since a badly frightened deer can jump an eight- or nine-foot fence, the pale had to be high and the ditch immediately in front of it made it even higher. Hunting was an obsession with medieval Scottish kings and the Deer Park lay next to a royal castle at Selkirk and at the eastern end of the vast game reserve known as the Ettrick Forest. In early winter, deer-herds drove pregnant does into the park where they could be fed through the hungry months. Once they had dropped their fawns in the spring, the does and their young were released back into the forest. It was a traditional use of the hill that lasted into the middle of the 20th century when deer were still kept there, browsing the rough pasture.

West of where I sit, backlit by a setting sun, the fields rise gently towards an eminence that looks down over the confluence of the Rivers Ettrick and Yarrow. Below it there is a place name that remembers bands of men who rode north in search of riches and land. The Hartwood burn suddenly splashes over a very picturesque waterfall known as the Motte Linn and it remembers what was once a motte-and-bailey castle built on the hill above at the behest of Norman adventurers, many of whom were granted land by David I of Scotland in the first half of the 12th century. An old, well-made track leads up the flank of the hill and, especially on horseback, it is easy to see the nettle-covered remains of the outer bailey, its ditch and the higher mound of the motte that once rose up behind the palisade. No record of the lord who caused this earth and wooden castle to be built has survived but, when the sun dipped behind Huntly Hill and food and drink were served to him and his retainers, they probably described the landscape around them in Norman French.

Gurgling past the little standing stone at the bottom of the garden, the Common Burn marks the southern boundary of the farm and it took its name from the common land owned by the burgh of Selkirk. From the 16th century onwards, these large holdings gradually shrivelled as surrounding lairds encroached but, every year, a long cavalcade of horsemen and -women ride the bounds to the north of the town and every forty years or so, they trot along the southern bank of the Common Burn to check that no boundary markers (like the little standing stone?) have been moved. With a standard-bearer carrying the town flag, the common riding stirs ancient memories. From a distance, they look like a squadron of light cavalry. Which is exactly what they used to be.

No such suspension of disbelief was needed on the morning of 13 September 1645. If I had been looking south from my house, I would have seen an awesome sight. During the civil war fought all over Britain and Ireland, the Scottish army led by General David Leslie surprised the Royalists and the Marquis of Montrose at Philiphaugh, west of Selkirk. In the early morning mist, he sent about 2,000 cavalry troopers through our little valley, perhaps keeping to the metalled surface of the old road leading to Oakwood Fort. They moved quietly around Howden Hill and, while Leslie led the rest of his army in a frontal assault, the cavalry attacked the rear of the Royalists and scattered them. Philiphaugh was a savage, sadistic rout with much unnecessary slaughter excused by fundamentalist piety.

The greater part of the landscape of the valley was much altered after 1645. The fields, the thorn hedges, the shelterbelts of hardwoods, the steadings, the big houses and their policies are not old. After the middle of the 18th century, the pace of agricultural improvement quickened and shaped much of the countryside we see now and believe to be traditional. One of the most important catalysts was drainage and below where I sit in the evening stretches the 35-acre Tile Field. It is billiard-table flat because it was scraped for clay and at the western end stood a tile works. Its kilns were fired by the trees of the Hartwood and the clay puddled in a pond formed by the Common Burn and the Hartwoodburn. Bright orange drainage pipes were laid and they brought much more land into cultivation. Modern deep ploughing has sliced into much of this back-breaking labour, destroying and clogging the drainage system. Now winter rain lies in large pools on the Tile Field and swans nest by the side of the old pond, its waters now undisturbed by the bustle of manufacture.

As the sun dips behind Howden Hill and the lights twinkle in the kitchen, another day slows down to its close. Shadows gather in the Crow Wood, the birds flock in, wheeling over the treetops, cawing and screeching at each other, and a fox barks in the distance. As night settles and I switch off the lights in my office, it occurs to me how seldom we have the time to reflect on the transit of our lives. As we worry about tomorrow, about what's next, we perhaps think too little about the days that have gone, about our past. But it is only the past that makes tomorrow, nothing else, and it is our shared past that makes us who we are – that makes Scotland.

The industrialisation and urbanisation of the last three centuries have changed the landscape dramatically, sometimes obliterating the ancient footprints of our ancestors. But their story can still be seen, written on the land, and it can be understood and told. The history of Scotland should never be thought of as remote but rather a deeply personal matter, the only really worthwhile context against which we can see our short lives under these big skies. The story of this remarkable little nation on the north-west edge of Europe belongs to all of us and it matters to all of us.

The Collisions

✵

FIRE AND ICE MADE Scotland. For hundreds of millions of years, the molten core of the Earth has been pushing up through fissures in the outer crust, the land we live on and the ocean bed. This ancient, continuous process was only recently discovered by accident. When, in the middle of the 19th century, it became possible to send messages along a telegraph wire, scientists reasoned that it might also be feasible to shrink geography dramatically and lay an undersea cable to link Britain and North America. Communications that took weeks to deliver by ship might be relayed in moments.

In December 1872, HMS *Challenger* sailed from Portsmouth with a group of scientists on board. While exploring the bed of the Atlantic Ocean for the best route for the course of a new cable, the team, led by a marine zoologist from Edinburgh University, Charles Wyville Thomson, came across a very substantial undersea ridge approximately halfway between the Irish coast and Newfoundland. More like a range of mountains, it turned out to run the whole length of the Atlantic, occasionally breaking the surface in the shape of islands such as Tristan da Cunha, Ascension Island and the Azores. Iceland is the largest. Along the axis of the ridge is a very deep rift valley and this was found to be the place where magma or molten rock from the inner crust of the Earth, the asthenosphere, comes to the surface. In the chill depths of the ocean, it immediately cools and forms new crust or lithosphere. The Mid-Atlantic Ridge is part of a 29,000-mile-long system of ridges found under all of the Earth's oceans.

Known as 'seafloor spreading', this phenomenon makes the land we live on dynamic, moving it and the bed of the ocean very slowly. Each year the Mid-Atlantic Ridge shifts the crust between half an inch and one and a half inches, about the same rate at which fingernails grow. This long network of oceanic ridges and also fault lines found on land – such as the San Andreas Fault in California – moves vast segments of the Earth's surface known as tectonic plates. Depending on definitions, there are seven or eight plates and, as magma rises from the fiery core of our planet into the Mid-Atlantic Rift Valley, it moves the continents on either side of the ocean. Through a process known as subduction, tectonic plates also move very slowly under each other, eventually slipping into the asthenosphere. The Farallon Plate pushed up the southern ranges of the Rocky Mountains many millions of years ago but it has now slid deep into the Earth's mantle. Subduction has the effect of equalising, of keeping the total of the surface of the Earth the same.

More than five hundred million years ago, different parts of Scotland's familiar and beloved geography lay far distant from each other – some were attached to huge continents, some were splintered fragments and still others lay submerged on the bed of an ancient ocean. Lying between three palaeocontinents, Laurentia, Baltica and Avalonia, was the great expanse of the Iapetus Ocean. Larger than the Atlantic, it was beginning to shrink as tectonic movement shaped and reshaped the crust of the Earth. By 410 million years ago, the Iapetus Ocean had closed completely and much of what became Scotland had risen out of the prehistoric sea and been welded together into one of the most geologically distinct places on our planet. Scotland is therefore the deposit of a series of slow-motion, ancient collisions. And, throughout our prehistory and in more modern times, these collisions and the angles at which they hit would remain central to an understanding of our nation and its people. Our history is written in our rocks just as surely as it is in monastic chronicles, census returns or the stones and bones of archaeological digs.

The most important collision, symbolically and historically, was with England. Much of what was to become Scotland lay on the leading edge of Laurentia while England was attached to the shores of Avalonia. As the great palaeocontinents welded both of these landmasses together, the harder rocks that made up Scotland ground against the softer strata of northern England, buckling and corrugating them. This process forced the coal and iron seams close to the surface and, in this way, our geology made West Cumbria and Tyneside a gift of their traditional industries.

As these enormously powerful forces moved the crust of the Earth, forming and reforming continents, smaller bits sometimes sheared off. Known as terranes, they drifted across the planet over millions of years. When Laurentia, Baltica and Avalonia moved closer, four very different terranes were ground together to make the distinctive shape of Scotland. Forged deep in the molten inner crust, Lewisian gneiss was pushed upwards to make the Western Isles, Coll, Tiree, Iona, the western peninsula of Islay known as the Rhinns and part of the Atlantic coastline. Gneiss is old – one of the most ancient rock formations found anywhere in the world.

To the east and south, thick strata of Old Red Sandstone were laid down and north of the Great Glen its most spectacular monuments are the Torridon Mountains and the singular peak of Suilven. Durness Limestones overlay much of the Old Red Sandstone and they are solid proof that these terranes were once attached to the coastline of ancient Laurentia. At that time the palaeocontinent lay south of the equator and the limestone and sandstone were beach deposits that contained fossils, evidence for some of the earliest life forms. The Old Red Sandstone also underlies some of Scotland's most fertile farmland – the Moray coastlands, Aberdeenshire, parts of the Central Belt and much of Berwickshire.

LIZZIE

In the mid 1980s, at a quarry in Bathgate, a fossil hunter, Stan Wood, found the remains of a small lizard-like creature which he thought might be old. Perhaps a little predictably, he called it 'Lizzie the Lizard'. In fact, Stan had found a fossil that was 338 million years old, the oldest reptile remains ever found anywhere in the world. At about 20 centimetres in length, Lizzie was not large but she was successful – if she was a she. Once the find had been confirmed, matters became a little more formal as the fossil was renamed Westlothiana lizziae. *She lived near an ancient freshwater lake and hunted for smaller creatures who had the misfortune to live nearby.*

The north-east to south-west orientation of the Great Glen marks the angle at which one terrane collided with another. Below it, the Central Highlands were built from different rocks, thick strata of shales, limestones and sandstones. Known as the Dalriadan and Moine formations, they made the Cairngorms as the Earth convulsed with volcanic eruptions.

South of the Highland massif, Scotland's geography becomes even more abrupt. Along a line from Stonehaven down to the southern shores of Loch Lomond, the mountains suddenly give way to green valleys and ranges of low hills. This is the Highland Boundary Fault, where another collision took place. The Dalriadan and Moine mountains were pushed against what became the Midland Valley, a rift valley of a very different character, now the Central Belt. Again, the angle of the collision runs north-east to south-west. Formed originally in tropical latitudes, the valley was once home to vast, dense forests and swampland. Many millions of years ago this terrane began to move northwards and, as the trees and other tropical plants died and fell, they laid down strata of organic carbon. Much later these would become Scotland's coalfields.

Running from Ballantrae in South Ayrshire to Dunbar in East Lothian, the Southern Upland Fault once again follows the characteristic orientation of Scotland's geography. Below it lie the rolling hills of Galloway and the Borders and, in the lower-lying river basins, some of the most fertile farmland was laid down.

Some way to the south of the Southern Upland Fault lies a fascinating geological relic. On the west coast of the Isle of Man, near the hamlet of Niarbyl, the cliffs of a small cove have running diagonally across them a thin, greyish-white seam of rock. It is visible for only a hundred metres or so before it disappears into the waters of the Irish Sea but it is a memorial to the making of Scotland. Known as the Iapetus Suture, it marks the precise place where the vast continents of Laurentia and Avalonia collided, having welded the four terranes together. And it too runs north-east to south-east, just as the modern border between England and Scotland does.

Sixty-five million years ago, the Mid-Atlantic Ridge was a tectonic seam in the middle of a single, huge palaeocontinent known as Pangaea. Scientists hypothesised that North and South America once fitted neatly into Africa and Europe like a geological jigsaw before the ridge very slowly began to prise them apart and allow the Atlantic Ocean to form. What eventually became Scotland, and Britain and Ireland, was pushed towards the east. As the Atlantic filled and the crust of the Earth was stretched and thinned, magma broke through to form a line of huge volcanoes whose remains can be seen in the dramatic shapes of St Kilda and Ailsa Craig. Over five million years, the skies darkened and thunder boomed as unquantifiable amounts of ejecta flew into the atmosphere and thick ash clouds drifted across the land and the ocean. Ben More on Mull once roared and erupted but perhaps the most spectacular volcanic landscape in Scotland is on Skye.

SKYESAURUS

Two hundred million years ago, the Jurassic period began. Also known as the Age of Reptiles, it lasted for aeons, until 140 million years ago. The Isle of Skye was patrolled by plant- and flesh-eating dinosaurs and their fossilised remains are preserved in the Jurassic sediments found along the east coast of the Trotternish Peninsula. One of them was huge. Cetiosaurus *stood ten metres in height but it was less terrifying than some of the others who stalked the island. It ate only plants. Probably as a result of a catastrophic meteor strike which ushered in a long nuclear winter when vegetation and animals perished in the sunless cold, the dinosaurs died out about 65 million years ago.*

The gentle slopes and scarps of the Trotternish Peninsula and of north-west Skye were once the lava fields of a huge volcano that spewed magma up from the inner crust of the Earth. The magma chamber, the boiling caldera of the volcano, was towering, rising to more than six thousand feet. Erosion has sheared and planed it but its ruins are still tremendously impressive. They are the jagged mountains of the Black Cuillin and the rock known as Skye gabbro is the legacy of the millions of years when the Earth shuddered and boiled.

Fire forged much of Scotland's landscape but, in much more recent times, ice scarted, ground and bulldozed the rocks and soil into their familiar shapes. We live in an inter-glacial period, a brief interval between Ice Ages. For the last 2.4 million years, in the era known as the Quaternary Period, much of the surface of the planet has periodically been buried beneath ice sheets and glaciers.

Relatively recently, around 24,000 BC, the weather began to worsen once more. Storms blew and snow fell and lay on the hilltops all year. Over a short time, perhaps only one or two generations, the temperatures fell steeply and Scotland quickly became uninhabitable. The last Ice Age was beginning. Vegetation shrivelled and died as more snow fell and the animals that depended on it fled south. Our species, *Homo sapiens*, had certainly reached Europe before the ice came and perhaps some explorers had crossed the land bridge across the Channel and the North Sea to walk to the farthest north-west, to stand on the edge of the ocean, the edge of beyond, and gaze at the endless horizon. But, as the cold gripped the land and the ice sheets formed, all trace of those who may have been the first to see Scotland was erased.

Nothing and no one could survive in the savage sub-Arctic climate. The ice formed into domes, huge hemispherical mountains around which constant storms blew. On the summits of the ice domes there appears to have been permanent high pressure and clear skies. For thousands of sterile years, Scotland lay sleeping under a blanket of ice as the sun shone on a dazzling white landscape of devastating beauty. So much water was locked up in this frozen world that the levels of the world's oceans were lowered and so heavy were the domes that they pressed down hard, crushing the crust of the Earth under them.

Around 14,000 years ago, the ice cap that covered Scotland slowly began to crack and splinter. The weather was warming once more and, over a short time, glaciers rumbled over the landscape and began to change it. As it moved, the ice smoothed rock, bulldozed debris and soils, scraped out corries and watercourses and deepened valleys to form the freshwater and sea lochs of the Highlands. In the Midland Valley, glaciers moving from west to east struck the hard volcanic rocks that Stirling and Edinburgh castles sit on. This forced the glaciers to divide and leave behind the classic crag and tail formation that allowed towns to be built in the eastern lee of the rocks. When the ice began to melt, it created torrents of such tremendous force that they could make melt-water flow uphill, especially under or in the ice, from one valley into another. Glaciers deposited debris such as erratic rocks or ridges of gravel and soil known as eskers. As the sun shone and the air warmed, Scotland was stirring, beginning to awake.

But it turned out to be a false dawn. Only a few hundred years after the thaw, an ecological disaster was waiting to burst on the world. In northern Canada, a vast freshwater lake, far larger than all of the Great Lakes combined, had been held back by ice dams. As these slowly melted, water from what came to be called Lake Agassiz spilled southwards to help carve out the Missouri and Mississippi river systems. But some time around 10,500 BC a mighty roar was heard as the ice dams to the north of the huge lake crashed down to release a mega-flood. Its path has been traced as a giant tsunami raced through the Mackenzie River basin out into the Beaufort Sea, through the Davis Strait and into the North Atlantic. Within 36 hours of the dams falling, a vast cubic tonnage of freshwater had stopped the warming currents of the Gulf Stream in their tracks, turning it back south before it could reach the shores of Britain and Ireland. Temperatures plummeted, snowstorms blew once more, a vast ice dome formed over Ben Lomond and animals and people fled south.

What geologists call the Loch Lomond Stadial and historians the Cold Snap lasted for about a thousand years. The North Atlantic eventually regained its salinity and the conveyor effect once more brought the warm waters of the Gulf Stream northwards. In a process known as climate flickering, the melt may have been rapid, perhaps in the span of only a handful of generations. When the land warmed, the first colonists were plants – hardy willow scrub, crowberry and birch came. They were followed by ash and hazel, then oak, elm and pine. With the weight of the ice lifted, the land began to rebound and rise, keeping pace with the level of the seas as they filled with melt-water.

As the trees grew and seeded more growth, Scotland's Wildwood spread and offered cover for all manner of animals migrating north. The aurochs, the giant wild cattle with a seven-foot horn spread, browsed the shoots and grasses, red and roe deer came, wild boar snuffled through the undergrowth and elk flitted amongst the greenwood shadows. It may be that smaller animals were the earliest arrivals – martens, polecats, squirrels and stoats skittered through the canopy. In the streams, rivers, lochs and seas, fish teemed, the mighty salmon amongst the first, waterfowl built their nests and otters and beavers fished and swam. Predators also entered the Wildwood and brown bears, wolves and lynx prowled through the trees. And they were followed by the most deadly predator of all, our ancestors, the first settlers, the pioneers who walked into an unknown land after the ice.

2

The Pioneers

❋

THROUGHOUT THE millennia of ice, many of those who would become our ancestors sheltered from the biting winds and the bitter cold in steep-sided valleys on either side of the Pyrenees. These were the Ice Age refuges and their people have left a remarkable record of their lives as they shivered through the harsh winters and cool summers. More than 350 caves have been discovered in south-western France and northern Spain where immensely talented and mysterious prehistoric artists have left paintings on the walls. Almost all are of animals – the Ice Age fauna such as reindeer, wild horses, the aurochs, cave lions and red deer. While storms blew outside and the world of ice froze the landscape still, painters worked in the black darkness. Lit only by the flicker of torches, they mixed red, yellow and black ochres to create frescoes of charging bulls, galloping horses and fleeing deer. And, even though it is ancient – amongst the oldest works of art ever found – their work is not primitive. When Pablo Picasso saw the paintings in the cave at Lascaux in south-western France after the Second World War, he declared that in the last 20,000 years artists had learned nothing.

The caves appear to have been temples, places where mysteries were enacted, where the animals that were central to the lives of the peoples of the refuges were brilliantly memorialised. Only visible in firelight in their great subterranean chambers or by torchlight in narrow passages, the paintings almost certainly played a part in unknowable rituals as the moving shadows of worshipper-hunters were projected on to the walls amongst the herds of bison or deer. Perhaps the paintings were a means of recognising an absolute dependence on the animals, central to ceremonies involving dance, song and music designed to ensure that the annual migrations did not cease and that the herds would once more thunder through the steep-sided valleys on their way north to summer pasture. Those migrations brought the herds to ambushes, to narrow places or river crossings where hunters could get close and wound or kill many animals. In the late 19th century, the dances and rituals of the Plains Indians of North America were recorded. They wore headdresses and imitated the behaviour and movement of the bison they depended on and enacted rituals to bring them back after the hungry months of the winter.

For many millennia, small populations of hunter-gatherers subsisted in the frozen landscape. The highest peaks of the Pyrenean ranges were encased in a brilliant white ice cap that was lit by the sun all year round. That horizon was a constant reminder that the climate could be even harsher. Down in the deep valleys, the refuges were sometimes shielded and bielded by dense stands of pinewoods whose branches will have bent low, loaded with snow. On windless days when the smallest sound echoed across the frozen rivers, the animals of the Ice Age searched the ground for food. Woolly rhinoceros, with their vicious horns, snuffled and rooted for the bitter grass. The aurochs, their horn spreads swaying, browsed amongst the trees and, on the valley floor, mammoths plodded on the gravel terraces, their long and dense hair brushing the lifeless ground.

Watching for weakness or older animals struggling to withstand the cold, predators patrolled the valleys. Cave lions, panthers, hyenas, wolves and bears waited. But our ancestors will have rarely ventured out in the extreme cold of the Ice Age winter. Instead, small family bands lit fires at the mouths of their refuge caves, huddling for warmth, depending for most of their food on what they had dried and stored from the wild harvest of the summer to last through the long winter darkness. The constant demand for firewood meant that their ranges were wide and the lack of seasoned wood will no doubt have been a compelling reason for hunter-gatherer bands to move on.

When the ice at last began to melt, life may have changed very quickly – and erratically. Climate flickering meant that thaws could be followed by colder periods and, after the chill certainties of the centuries of ice, that will have caused hardship. The seasonal migrations of the herds they depended on will have been disrupted and those who preyed on them will have suffered more than confusion when migrations ceased or took different routes. But, when the ice first shrank back about 14,000 years ago, the herds of reindeer and shaggy wild ponies moved ever further northwards, perhaps quickly, over the span of only a few generations. Unable to evolve as fast as the climate was changing, raising temperatures and altering their feeding habitat, these cold-adapted animals chased the chill temperatures of the moving ice frontier and the open tundra and grasslands on its margins. And, in turn, they were chased by the bands of hunters who depended on them. The retreating cold pulled the herds north and they pulled our ancestors behind them.

BEST FRIENDS

It used to be thought that men and women began to domesticate wolves after the end of the last Ice Age but recent discoveries of 33,000 canine fossils in Belgium and Siberia strongly suggest that this happened much earlier. The great value of domesticated dogs was in hunting. Armed with spears and later with arrows with flint points, hunters could not hope to bring down prey, especially large animals like mammoths, bison and wild horses, with a kill shot. But they could wound them. That is when a pack of dogs became important. They could track and pursue a wounded animal, make its heart pump faster so that it lost blood faster and, when close to exhaustion and fighting for its life, the mammoth or bison could be finished off by a band of hunters with spears. At that point, wolf dogs were helpful in that they could drive off scavengers such as lions and leopards. Good friends – and perhaps another reason why we out-competed Neanderthals.

At Howburn Farm near Biggar in South Lanarkshire, archaeologists made a startling discovery: clear evidence of the earliest pioneers to see Scotland after millennia under the blanket of ice. Some time around 12,000 BC, perhaps right up against the melting ice sheets, a band of hunters set up shelters on the lower slopes of the Black Mount overlooking the upper reaches of the valley of the River Clyde. Excavators found more than 5,000 flint artefacts, points made for spears and blades and burins made for other uses, evidence of the hunting gear needed to bring down horses or deer and process the carcasses. The concentrated pattern of these finds suggested to archaeologists that the flint-knappers worked in oval-shaped tents probably made from hides. No organic material was discovered and the very early date of the encampment at Howburn has been derived from artefact typology, the comparison of characteristic tanged flint points with others of exactly the same manufacture found at sites in northern Germany and southern Denmark that certainly date to the same period.

The hunters at Howburn may have been an expedition from the south, sent out in early spring or late autumn to intercept herds migrating to or from summer pasture further north. Some of the flint appears to have come from Yorkshire, and other nodules may have been picked up on the way to the encampment. Perhaps the reindeer and shaggy ponies followed the course of the Clyde and crossed it somewhere south of Biggar at a place where the spearmen could get close enough to ambush them. Archaeologists have identified points probably notched for hafting on to wooden spears, blades made as scrapers for cleaning the hides of slaughtered animals and burins for piercing them so that they could be sewn together with sinew cords.

The finds at Howburn are nothing short of sensational but they surely cannot be unique. Others bands walked into Scotland after the first ice melt following their prey and somewhere, as yet unnoticed, more evidence of the first pioneers will come to light to give a clearer picture of the lives of these early, temporary visitors. There can have been no greater disruption than the shock of the Cold Snap, as skies darkened once more, temperatures plummeted and the ice returned. As the snow drove people south, there may have been conflict. Refugees from the north cannot have been welcome in the ranges of the warmer south.

There exists slight and uncertain evidence of this new life in Scotland. Summer expeditions may have sailed north just as the Cold Snap was beginning. In 1993, an arrowhead was picked up in a freshly ploughed field in the Rhinns of Islay, the westernmost part of the island. It dated from as early as 10,800 BC and others, less well recorded and located, were found in nearby Jura and Tiree. It seems that part of the Atlantic coastline was ice free at that time and that mountain peaks, such as the Paps of Jura, poked through the ice sheets. Known as nunataks, these peaks could have acted as summer seamarks for the hunters in their curraghs, the hide boats almost certainly used throughout prehistory in the west of Scotland. Perhaps similar risky expeditions sailed north during the Cold Snap to bring back seal meat or other kills to refugee communities in the south forced to scrabble a meagre living on the margins of the ranges of those more established. And perhaps the memory of the buried lands of the north lived on through the thousand years of ice.

When the Gulf Stream began to warm Scotland once more, around 9,500 BC, the thaw appears to have come quickly. What also pulled people north was the changing pattern of migration. As the temperatures rose sharply, cold-adapted animals such as reindeer could not adapt fast enough. With their thick coats and particular diet, the herds needed to chase the cold as it moved northwards. And those bands of hunter-gatherers, our ancestors, who depended on these animals followed. The speed of the advance can be measured by a remarkable discovery in the caves at Creswell Crags, south of Sheffield. Rather than create paintings, artists had engraved the outlines of animals on the rock walls (there is some evidence that they were also painted). One of the engravings is of an ibex, a species of wild goat with extravagant, clearly recognisable long horns. When the artist was working at Creswell, there were no ibex in Britain. He or she was relying on memory, recent memory.

HOPS, HOPES, HOLMS, HAMS, HAUGHS, DEANS, LAWS AND LEAS

Scotland has its own vocabulary for the landscape created by the ice. A 'hop' or 'hope' is a high valley and an example near Stow in the Borders also produced a surname. A 'hoppringle' was a rounded or ring valley and it was applied as a place name to the example near Stow. Hoppringle was eventually shortened to the name Pringle, now principally known as a knitwear brand. Laws are rounded hills rather than peaks. And the name of the town of Huntly remembers an ancient feature – a lea or clearing where hunters waited for prey to be driven towards them. A 'hirst' was a wooded knoll and an isolated, tall tree that stood on its own and perhaps served as a landmark is what the name 'pirnie' or 'pirn' means. It derives from Old Welsh. The word 'holm' is Old English for a meadow and Langholm simply means the long meadow. Its equivalent in Scots is 'haugh'. The Old English 'ham' can mean a house or, more usually, a village and a 'dean' is a small valley or declivity, so, for example, Dryden is a dry dean, one without a burn. A 'sike' is the opposite – a declivity with a burn running through it.

The cave paintings of the western Ice Age refuges on either side of the Pyrenees are not all anonymous. Some carry signatures of a sort. One haunting discovery in 1994 suddenly brought our ancestors very close. A painted cave was discovered in the Ardèche Gorge in south-western France and one of the first images to show up in the head torches of speleologists Jean-Marie Chauvet and his companions was not a charging aurochs or a cave lion. On a whitened limestone wall near the entrance to the cave, he saw a series of handprints in red ochre. Judging by the height of the prints and their size, they were made by a man who pressed his hand into ochre and then on to the limestone wall. He appeared to have a broken or arthritic pinkie and Chauvet and his friends found the same distinctive handprint elsewhere in the cave. Was he the artist who painted some of the animals? It seems likely.

And it also seems likely that many Scots are directly descended from the hunter-gatherer communities of the western refuges. Very recent ancestral DNA research shows that more than 40 per cent carry markers from the mitochondrial DNA haplogroups identified as H, H1 and HVO, all of which originated amongst the people of the painted caves. Each of us carries a great deal of information in our DNA but two small parts of our genomes are especially informative about ancestry. Men carry a Y-chromosome marker inherited from their fathers and their fathers before them, away back in time, and they also inherit mitochondrial DNA, or mtDNA, from their mothers and their mothers, again away back in deep time. Women carry only mtDNA but they pass it on to their children of both genders. So, men carry mtDNA too but can only pass on their Y-chromosome marker, their fatherline, to their sons. In the act of reproduction, when the 6 billion letters of DNA we carry are passed on, tiny errors of copying are made. These are known as DNA markers and both their origin and the date when they arose can be calculated. Therefore, it is possible to say with considerable certainty that more than 40 per cent of all Scots, men and women, carry the DNA of the people of the painted caves. It is a remarkable continuity, something that brings the nameless people of prehistory out of the shadows.

Faint memories of these ancient migrations can be found in unlikely places. When Abbot Bernard of Arbroath helped compose the letter to Pope John XXII that became famous as the Declaration of Arbroath, he began with the origins of the Scots and Scotland. Part of his purpose in writing to the pope was to achieve diplomatic recognition for the regime of King Robert I and to do that he needed to establish that his realm was unique and distinct from England. In a flowing passage of myth–history involving Greater Scythia and the Tyrrhenian Sea, the abbot wrote that the Scots had long dwelt in Spain before sailing north to claim their place amongst nations. An Irish origin legend, the *Book of the Taking of Ireland*, also remembered invaders from Iberia.

More concrete were the marks left on the land by those pioneers, amongst the first to come north after the ice. Most left little trace as they moved through the Wildwood, following tracks made by browsing animals, paddling their coracles and curraghs on rivers and lochs. A chance discovery at Cramond of a camp of hunters who came ashore on the banks of the River Almond shows how faint a trace most of our ancestors made. The holes made by the whippy green rods of a bender tent, probably covered in hide, were found and the organic evidence around it allowed archaeologists to date the encampment to the 9th millennium BC. But, not far to both the east and the west of Cramond, two sites with something altogether more substantial have recently come to light.

In the autumn of 2002, archaeologists investigated what at first seemed like an unpromising field at East Barns, near Dunbar. A local limestone quarry was about to bite into the land and there had been several scattered finds of flints nearby. What quickly came to light was sensational, nothing less than a substantial prehistoric house that dated to the centuries around 8,000 BC, the earliest yet found in Scotland. Unlike the flimsy green rods of the bender shelter by the River Almond, the East Barns house had been built to last. About 30 sturdy posts, some of them entire tree trunks, had been rammed into holes dug in an oval-shaped arrangement and canted inwards like a tipi to form a broadly conical shape. The timber frame was covered with turf and bracken, perhaps even timber walling, a hearth laid down and this large house could easily accommodate six to eight people snugly sheltered from the snell winds blowing off the Firth of Forth. It all spoke of permanence, a house that directly contradicted the conventional sense of hunter-gatherers as transients, bands of people constantly on the move, barely rustling the leaves of the Wildwood, the only marks they left behind being discolorations on the soil where fires had been lit.

More than permanence, the East Barns house also signified ownership or, at least, customary rights. It is difficult to imagine the extended family who went to all the labour of cutting the trees, trimming them, dragging them to the site, digging the postholes and heaving the structure upright allowing others to hunt and gather on their home range. And East Barns was an enviable place to live in prehistory. There was fresh water close at hand, a rising hinterland for summer and autumn hunting and the harvesting of fruits, roots, berries, fungi and all the bounty of the Wildwood. The seashore was close and it could supply food all year round in the shape of crustaceans and fish and seabirds' eggs in spring. And, in 2012, it turned out that others also believed that the shores of the Forth was a desirable place to live. The people of East Barns had distant neighbours.

During construction work for the new road bridge across the firth, a second house of a very similar design and date was found. In a field at Echline, near South Queensferry, another oval pit, seven metres in length, was uncovered. From charred hazelnuts, another winter staple, and other organic material, the structure was dated to c. 8,000 BC and it may have been even cosier than the house along the coast at East Barns. Several internal hearths were found and around the site thousands of bits of flint and flint debris came up, many of them used for cutting tools and arrowheads. The discovery of both of these fascinating sites was prompted by construction and quarrying – which begs the obvious question of how many other prehistoric houses might be lying under unpromising fields.

Equally fascinating is the question of who built them. There stood another, very similar, house at Howick on the Northumberland coast. But, when its builders were hard at work, they were not planning to live on the shores of the North Sea. Around 8,000 BC, it barely existed. Instead, a vast subcontinent lay to the east of Britain, not so much a land bridge as a huge area in its own right, with its own culture and perhaps its own way of building houses. Known as Doggerland after the Dogger Bank, formerly a range of hills towards the north of the now-submerged subcontinent, it was home to thousands of hunter-gatherer bands who fished its rivers and lakes and stalked prey in its woods and estuaries. The population probably exceeded that of prehistoric Britain. So heavy had the ice-dome over Scandinavia been that it pushed up the crust of the Earth to the south and so much water had been locked up in the ice that the level of the world's oceans dropped dramatically. Even after the Ice Age ended, the northern shores of the subcontinent stretched beyond Shetland. The only place where land did not rise out of the sea was the Storegga Trench, a deep channel off the Norwegian coast.

The finds at Howburn Farm made a fascinating and telling link that reached right across the subcontinent of Doggerland. In the absence of organic material, archaeologists made comparisons between the flints knapped in the tents on the slopes of the Black Mount and others found in northern Germany and southern Denmark, probably also belonging to bands of reindeer hunters. This not only supplied a secure date of c. 12,000 BC but also showed how contact and cultural exchange took place across the wide plains of Doggerland. The drowned land is the missing piece in the jigsaw of early prehistoric Europe.

THE FIRST SCOTS

In the 1,000-year period between the first retreat of the glaciers and their brief return c. 11,000 BC, bands of hunters came to Scotland, most likely on summer expeditions. Probably in pursuit of herds of wild horses or reindeer on their annual migration to the fresh grasslands of the north, groups of these people camped at Howburn in South Lanarkshire. There, archaeologists have found more than 5,000 flint artefacts that resemble others found in Europe that can be securely dated. It may be that the Howburn hunters walked across Doggerland, the great subcontinent that was submerged under the North Sea. Or, more likely, they were Doggerlanders from the warmer valleys south of the Dogger Hills. But, when what prehistorians call 'the Cold Snap' brought back the ice, no one ventured to Scotland for about 1,000 years.

Doggerland was enormously influential in Scotland's prehistory but, for obvious reasons, very little archaeology has been possible. Nevertheless, it allowed pioneers to walk dry shod to settle in what was a peninsula at the north-western edge of Europe, and those ancient journeys are again remembered in our collective ancestral DNA. Migration from the east is more noticeable in the distribution of Y-chromosome markers. M423 is old and some of the ancestors of those Scots who carry it walked across the plains of Doggerland to settle in prehistoric Scotland. And a group of what might be termed Germanic and Scandinavian Y-chromosome markers are much more emphatically present in the east than the west. Those who carried them arrived over a long period, certainly during the time of the Anglo-Saxon incursions and the coming of the Vikings from the 9th century onwards, but also many millennia before that.

Patterns of early settlement began to shape the cultural map of Scotland. There are obvious and substantial geographical differences between the east and the west – most of the low-lying fertile land drains to the North Sea coasts, the climate there is generally drier and movement overland is easier. A glance at the map confirms all of that. But DNA strongly suggests that the peoples of the east and west had different origins and that is much less obvious. The western seaboard was, in part, settled by migrants from Iberia and south-western France and they often came by sea. There is a clear set of staging posts marked by a shared lexicon. Celtic languages were once spoken in Spain and are still whispered in Galicia, Breton clings on in Brittany, Cornish is being revived, Welsh thrives, Manx survives, Irish is constitutionally enshrined and Scots Gaelic hangs on, just. But once these cousin languages were very widely spoken down the Atlantic seaboard. Now they are the faint footprints of ancient migration routes.

While the accidental nature of discovery should not be allowed to force Scotland's early narrative into a particular form, it does seem likely that the pioneers preferred to live around the coasts. Far to the west of the shores of the Firth of Forth and the earliest sites at Cramond, Echline and East Barns, archaeologists sailed to investigate promising finds on the Hebridean island of Rum. At the head of Loch Scresort, at Kinloch, forestry workers had reported sizeable caches of worked stone, mostly chips of hard rock, and a beautifully made barbed and tanged arrowhead unearthed by ploughing. More than 150,000 small bits of stone were ultimately counted at Kinloch and most came from Creag nan Stearnan, a mountain on the northwest coast of the island. Known in English as Bloodstone Hill, its hard, flint-like stone was what had brought the hunter-gatherers sailing up Loch Scresort in the millennia after the ice.

Flint is rare in Scotland but it was a vital resource for the pioneers. They needed to quarry nodules of Rum bloodstone, a close geological cousin to flint, so that it could be knapped into cutting tools, scrapers, spear points and arrowheads. At the 'factory' site at Kinloch, flintsmiths tapped and chipped the nodules into tools that were often very beautiful, even delicate, but razor sharp. What the forestry workers had found was the debris of manufacture. And archaeologists found enough organic material to date the encampment on Rum to around 7,000 BC.

On a much less substantial scale than the houses at Echline and East Barns, tipis were raised, conical arrangements of long branches from hazel, birch and willow trees that grew in the shelter of Kinloch Glen. Once these had been staked in a rough circle in the ground and lashed together at the apex, the tipis were covered with hide and caulked to cut down the draughts. Although Kinloch looks east to Morar and the mainland, with its back to the Atlantic breezes, storms will sometime have blown in off the ocean and swirled around Rum.

The flintsmiths may have used their boats in the construction of their tipis. Still built in south-west Ireland, seagoing curraghs employ similar simple technology. A frame of whippy green wood is lashed together and a hide hull is then stretched over it. The skins of three or four adult red deer were enough to make a curragh and when sewn together and caulked, they formed an excellent craft. The benches for rowers or paddlers were used as thwarts to stiffen the structure and the curragh was so light that it could easily be carried by two men. With a draught measured only in inches, this apparently flimsy boat sat on the waves like a seagull, rising and falling.

Made as they were from entirely organic materials, the remains of prehistoric curraghs have never been found but there can be little doubt that they were widely used 9,000 years ago along the Atlantic seaboard. Whenever they could, the pioneers travelled on water. Curraghs were fast, especially running with the tide, and they could carry cargo. If a portage between lochs or rivers was necessary, they were easy to carry and, if the weather worsened, they could be turned upside down to make a watertight shelter. In high contrast to modern land-based perceptions, the earliest Scots understood Scotland from the sea, its lochs and rivers. It was probably seen less as a landmass with a scatter of islands offshore and more as a series of related shorelines. That was, in large part, because the shore was a good place to live, where the bounty of the land and of the sea met, and a curragh increased the reach of a hunter-gatherer band dramatically, extending their ranges much further than the distance men and women could walk.

Other, gossamer traces of the pioneers have been brought to light on the islands south of Rum. Hearths were found on Jura and an immense amount of flint debris on Islay. Two of the most eloquent discoveries concerned food. The raised beach at Staosnaig on Colonsay also faces east but, some time around 6,700 BC, it was thought to be a windy place. Probably on a summer expedition, a band of hunter-gatherers scooped out a sandy depression to make a shelter that would not need a high-pitched roof. After they had stowed their curraghs with a precious cargo, they filled the pit with something surprising. Archaeologists found hundreds of thousands of charred hazelnut shells, more than they could count. Nearby were smaller pits where the nuts had been roasted.

Colonsay was a prehistoric hazel orchard. Too far from the mainland to be inhabited and pillaged by hungry squirrels, hazel trees grew in abundance and each autumn pioneers came to harvest the nuts. Roasting not only improves the flavour of hazelnuts, it also allows them to be mashed into a nourishing paste which keeps through the winter. But, at some point, the gatherers appeared to act directly against their own interests and one year they did something very strange. After they picked the little nuts, they seem to have cut down and even destroyed many of the trees on Colonsay. Perhaps it was a religious act, something linked to the filling of the scooped shelter with shells, a way of returning the trees and their wild harvest to nature. Certainly it was not the act of a community who were starving. In the millennia after the end of the Ice Age, the weather appears to have been generally warmer and more settled. Perhaps the islands of the Hebrides and the Atlantic seaboard were lands of milk and honey where the sun often shone and nature was generous.

The waters around the islands were certainly rich in fish and shellfish. Linked to Colonsay at low tide, the little island of Oronsay revealed a remarkable prehistoric story, a story told by rubbish. Around the shoreline of this low-lying, undulating island, archaeologists discovered five huge middens. Resembling the sort of grassy hummocks seen on links golf courses, they appeared at first to be unremarkable. But once the sandy turf had been cut away, hundreds of thousands of shells came to light – discarded shells of mussel, clams, oysters, razors, limpets and scallops. And amongst the jumble of debris were fish bones, bits of antler – and human remains.

From the abundant organic material, archaeologists were able to date the middens to the millennium between 5,300 and 4,300 BC. Analysis of the fragments of human bones showed that the rubbish collectors lived on a marine diet that also included seabirds and seal meat. The nearby islands of Colonsay, Islay, Jura and Rum were all visited or inhabited by bands of hunter-gatherers before 5,300 BC and after 4,300 BC but during the millennium when the middens were piled up, they appear to have been deserted. It seems that Oronsay was permanently settled and perhaps the small island was the centre of a seaborne band's range, the place to which hunting and gathering expeditions returned.

Antler bone and fragments of tools fashioned from antlers were found in the middens and they offer a sense of the purpose of a prehistoric hunting trip that set out from Oronsay. In Gaelic, Jura is rendered as *Diura* and it means 'Deer Island'. It may well be that the Oronsay band hunted there for something essential to their marine lives. Antlers and venison were no doubt useful and welcome but the hide of a big animal like the red deer of Diura was essential for the building and maintenance of seagoing curraghs. In order to fish the inshore waters as well as mount expeditions to Colonsay, Islay and Rum, the deer pelts were needed to make new boats and repair old ones.

Oronsay is very small, less than two miles across at its widest point, and yet it has been shown conclusively that its band of hunter-gatherers moved around it in a clear, seasonal cycle. A brilliant analysis of fish bones found in the five middens demonstrates that each was filled at a different time of year. Perhaps it was the migration patterns of birds, fish or even a change in the direction of the prevailing wind that prompted the band to uproot their shelters and move. But over only a few hundred yards? It is a baffling discovery.

Perhaps the middens were not seen as heaps of discarded rubbish. What society now throws away in such volume and classifies as refuse is a modern concept. It may be that the middens represented something much more significant – that they had a spiritual role in the lives of the hunters and that those who piled them up over fifty generations moved around their island because of some unknowable religious impulse. Archaeologists made a haunting discovery that lends a little weight to this conjecture. Amongst the shells and fish bones of one midden, human fingers had been deliberately placed on seal flippers. This powerful note of identification with the natural world, the association of the fingers and flippers, may point to a sense of an afterlife, one where the souls of the dead swam with the seals in the deeps of the world.

Such chance discoveries can be tantalising. The stones and bones of archaeology can offer insights into what prehistoric pioneers did and how they lived but very rarely give more than a fleeting glimpse of how they saw the world.

The population of early Scotland during the first five or six millennia after the ice is a matter only for speculation but it is likely to have been very small. At the time of the Oronsay middens, it may be that fewer than a thousand pioneers beached their boats on the shores of Scotland and hunted the Wildwood. Another estimate raises the number to between 1,500 and 2,000 in all. In an age before contraception and when life was short, the average size of an extended family band may have been six to eight people, including infants. This is of course conjecture but, if the estimates are not wildly out, then a number of tentative conclusions are possible.

If 1,500 hunter-gatherers lived mainly around the coasts of Scotland c. 5,000 BC, then there may have been only 200 or so family bands – and they may well have been in regular contact. Each will have needed wide ranges, especially for the collection of firewood, and, if the Oronsay band sent expeditions to Jura, Islay, Colonsay and Rum, that territory need not have been exclusive to them. For example, the deer kill on Jura required to sustain the curraghs of one band will not have been so large that the herds could not have been preyed on by others. In fact, the exploitation of such resources, the production of flint being the other prime need, may have been the occasion for bands to meet, probably in the autumn. Teenage children needed to find partners and all knew that they could only safely do that beyond their own family group.

THE SENIORS' MOMENT

For several millennia our species, Homo sapiens, *was not alone in Europe. Neanderthals competed with our ancestors but about 30,000 years ago, our ancestors appear to have triumphed and Neanderthals gradually died out. Recent research suggests that the reason for this was grandparents. Until c. 28,000 BC, most people died before they were 30. However, a survey of ancient remains showed that for every 10 young Neanderthals who died between the ages of 10 and 30, only four older adults lived beyond the age of 30. By contrast, for every 10 of our species who died young, between 10 and 30, there were 20 who lived beyond the age of 30. This appears to have been a critical development. Grandparents could pass on important knowledge such as where water could be found or where the best hunting and gathering was. This became a virtuous cycle and, the more seniors who survived, the better their family bands did and, since Neanderthals – for whatever reason – did not see the same numbers live longer, they died out.*

In the context of such sparse populations, it is not surprising that few signs of burial or the disposal of bodies have come to light. From such scant remains, it is difficult to build up a picture of what hunter-gatherers looked like. But a comparison with a fascinating find in the south of England might help. In a cave in the Mendip Hills known as Aveline's Hole the first and, thus far, the only hunter-gatherer cemetery was recognised. Dating to around 8,000 BC, the time when the sturdy houses were being built at Echline and East Barns, a group of 21 people had been buried and the analysis of their skeletons was very revealing. Their average height was about five foot and all were slightly built. The lack of wear on their teeth suggested that few lived beyond their late twenties and some, even at that age, suffered from arthritis.

Now, these discoveries predate the Oronsay middens by three millennia but skeletons from more recent prehistory allow some informed guesswork. On Orkney, a chambered tomb at Isbister, the Tomb of the Eagles, was found to have been in use between 3,100 and 2,400 BC. The bones of about 400 people were found inside and an analysis suggested that the average height of men was about 5 foot 7 inches and women about 5 foot 3 inches. Although they were much thicker-set than the people found in Aveline's Hole, the Isbister skeletons showed that they had suffered badly from various forms of arthritis and also did not live much beyond 30 years. Leaving aside the question of their musculature for the moment, it seems sensible to assume that the hunter-gatherers of the Atlantic coasts were small, wiry and that they looked young.

Key to the construction of curraghs was the invention of the bone needle and the art of sewing with sinew or other organic cord. The same skills also made clothes and, contrary to the cliché of grunting cavemen running around in ragged, flapping animal skins, hunters almost certainly wore close-fitting garments made from buckskin. It was important when hunting not to be impeded or wear clothing that was loose and could catch on a branch or twig while stalking prey. The look of our ancestors probably more resembled that of the forest Indians of the Eastern United States, their long hair braided to keep it from blowing in their faces and their slim frames covered by leggings and tunics of soft and supple hide. The caves of the ancestral Ice Age refuges also showed a deep understanding of colour and it would be surprising if that evaporated with the passage of time. This may have been passed on and clothes decorated and even perhaps paintings made which have not survived.

THE LAST GLACIER

During the latest Ice Age, Scotland was covered by thick ice sheets and crushed by huge, spherical ice domes. By 9,000 BC, the glaciers had rumbled over the landscape, the ice had at last melted and plants grew. The Ice Age had ended. Except in one place. High in the Cairngorms, in the remote Coire an Lochain, a glacier formed some time in the last 500 years, probably at the height of what was known as the Little Ice Age. Discovered by scientists at Dundee University, it may have melted as late as the 18th century. The glacier was not large, measuring about four or five football pitches, but its existence shows how cold Scotland became, especially in the period between 1650 and 1790. There may have been other small glaciers in the remote corries of the Cairngorms. Global warming means that there is little chance of the ice returning soon. But scientists believe that it will inevitably return.

At a lay-by on the road around the southern shore of Sullom Voe on Shetland, evidence of an ecological disaster that overtook prehistoric Scotland can be clearly seen. Sandwiched in the dark brown of the roadside peat is a white band of what is known as pelagic sand that had been swept up from the bed of the sea. It washed onshore all down the eastern coasts of Scotland when a huge tsunami hit sometime around 5,800 BC. Deep in the Storegga Trench off the coast of Norway, a vast submarine slide convulsed the bed of the North Sea when it disappeared under a tectonic plate. It may have been an area the size of Scotland. As the sea rushed in to fill the sudden vacuum, the tide receded extremely rapidly, revealing great expanses of the seabed. Moments later a faint rumble was heard and then a giant tsunami raced across the sea at 300 miles an hour with an 80-foot-high leading wave and crashed onshore in Shetland, sweeping away many settlements, surging far inland. Down the east coast, the leading wave was more than 30 feet high as it roared up and over beaches, snapping trees like matchsticks, depositing white pelagic sand. At least one hunter-gatherer encampment at Inverness was inundated and probably many others. If the sparse population of eastern Scotland did indeed live mainly on the shore, they will have suffered badly. But not as badly as their distant neighbours further east.

The Storegga tsunami of c. 5,800 BC almost certainly saw the submergence of much of Doggerland. By 4,000 BC at the latest, only Dogger Island may have survived, the higher ground that is now the Dogger Bank. As the tsunami roared, those in the north of the subcontinent may simply have been swept away and those in the south may have been able to salvage something before they sailed east and west to find dry land.

When the North Sea finally broke through the English Channel to link with the mighty Atlantic and isolate Britain, it only did so in a literal sense. Britain and its islands were not cut off from the Eurasian landmass and migration across the sea and the channel continued. And, in their seagoing craft, probably made from tree trunks and different from the curraghs of the Atlantic west, migrants brought the seeds of revolutionary change to Scotland.

In 1976, an aerial survey over Deeside identified a pattern of crop marks in an otherwise unremarkable field close to the riverbank at Balbridie. At first, archaeologists believed they had come across the outline of a hall, perhaps from the Anglo-Saxon period, a place where warriors caroused and feasted, where fires crackled and tales the like of *Beowulf* were told. The rows of postholes traced a structure that was certainly large enough to accommodate

50 or 60 and it measured 85 feet long and 43 feet wide. When the original depth of the postholes was ascertained, archaeologists calculated that the hall probably stood 30 feet high at the roof ridge – an impressive building that spoke of power and prestige.

But, when the site began to turn up organic material, grains of wheat and barley, the archaeologists were stunned when the radiocarbon dates came back. This was no Anglo-Saxon feasting hall but something far older, a structure that had been raised more than four millennia before. Balbridie Hall had been built some time between 3,900 and 3,700 BC. And it was a startling monument to the greatest revolution in human history – the coming of farming.

Balbridie was made by new people, immigrants to Scotland who had sailed the North Sea and eventually made landfall on the eastern shores of Scotland. The remains of similar halls have been found in southern Holland, the great river valleys of northern Germany and as far east as Poland. The migrants were farmers and, when they crossed the sea, they brought cereal seeds and domesticated animals with them. How this was managed in what must have been small craft is a mystery but these perilous journeys did happen. Balbridie is remarkable but not unique (there are similar sites in England) and aerial photography has discovered two other halls in Scotland. Both on the banks of rivers, one stood at Claish Farm near the River Teith and the other on a terrace above the Tweed near Kelso.

These extraordinary buildings, so impressive from the outside, had restricted access and appear to have been cellular inside rather than being the shell of a large space, like an Anglo-Saxon feasting hall. Probably used to store grain but not to overwinter animals, their design suggests mystery, an unknowable spiritual purpose. In any event, the halls did not last for there is clear evidence that both Balbridie and Claish were burned down around 3,200 BC.

At around the same time, skilled stonemasons began to build a series of structures on Orkney that would shape religious belief over the whole of prehistoric Britain. The Standing Stones of Stenness, the Ring of Brodgar, the houses at Skara Brae and the tomb at Maeshowe are all justly famous and very striking but a discovery was made in 2002 that proved to be even more remarkable and cast all of these in supporting roles. Between Brodgar and Stenness, by the side of the road that connects them across the narrow isthmus with Harray Loch on one side and Stenness Loch on the other, is a low hummock known as the Ness of Brodgar. When the extended site was granted World Heritage status by

UNESCO in 1999, archaeologists undertook a systematic survey of the area. Using the techniques of geophysics, or ground-penetrating radar, they discovered that the hummock was not a grass-covered glacial moraine but entirely man-made. Under the turf, shadowy images could be made out of a network of stone walls, paths and the outline of many buildings.

LAKE ORCADIE

Orkney was born in a loch. About 400 million years ago Scotland was very mountainous, with ranges of sharp peaks, rather like the modern Alps. Around the fringes of the palaeocontinent to which Scotland was attached were several freshwater basins and it was in one of these that Orkney began to form. Around Lake Orcadie, the fringing mountains began to erode rapidly as rivers cut through them and deposited huge volumes of mud and sand. Fossilised in the deposits are the remains of the fish that swam in the lake. Some were armour-plated, many of them very large. Now in the middle of Orkney's Mainland, Lochs Harray and Stenness are fringed by the monuments left by prehistoric farmers and encircled by the low, pillowy hills formed by the mud and sand: the concentric circles of history.

Two massive walls, more than 110 yards long, had been built right across the isthmus from the shores of one loch to the other. And, at 14 feet in height, it was a formidable barrier, screening completely a complex of no fewer than ten temples, the largest extending to an area of 80 feet by 65 feet. Like the hall at Balbridie, it was immensely impressive from the outside but had a restricted interior with room for only a small group of people. In the excavation season of 2010, the diggers made a discovery that changed perceptions of prehistoric buildings. They found a stone slab with traces of red, yellow and orange pigment still discernible. It appears that individual stones in the walls of the temple buildings had been painted, creating a checkered effect. Like the creators of Greek and Roman temples and sculpture, but many millennia before, the Orcadian builders had painted their sacred structures – a striking contrast with the sober grey, lichen-covered megaliths of the stone circles.

The great temple at Ness of Brodgar is the largest non-funerary structure in Europe and seems to have been the focus of a hallowed landscape, a huge religious complex between the lochs at Harray and Stenness, a place where people processed, worshipped and made music in rituals now completely lost. And these landscapes and the individual monuments in them were the first of their kind in Britain. The creation of sacred enclosures that marked off the inside from the temporal outside, the holy of holies from the world beyond them and the circles that became known as henges were invented in Orkney. Brodgar and Stenness were raised before the stones were erected at Avebury and at Stonehenge. It appears that a messianic figure or group of figures may have created a new way of worship on Orkney, a directing mind who invented rites that involved whole communities in massive communal work programmes. At Brodgar, stones were definitely brought there from different parts of the archipelago as though each community was contributing and there is a sense of the megaliths as representatives.

What is clear is the impossibility of these huge and sophisticated projects without the ability of farmers to grow and rear surpluses. The millions of man-hours needed for work that did not produce food or, indeed, anything tangible were enabled by the fact that prehistoric Orkney was fertile and the farming economy not primitive but efficient. These were the farmers' monuments.

Ancestral DNA offers a sense of a dynamic, changing and perhaps brutal society. Hunter-gatherer communities were very small and grew extremely slowly. One persuasive reason for this is diet. The wild harvest of roots, fruits, berries, meat and other items that needed mastication to be digestible were not suitable for infants and their soft baby teeth. It is persuasively conjectured that this depressed the birth rate because infants were breastfed for much longer by hunter-gatherer mothers whose milk was a prime source of protein. When women are nursing, they are generally unable to conceive and that meant a long birth interval, perhaps four or five years between new babies. Given that women died young in prehistory, usually before they reached the age of 30, and had a fertile life of only 15 or so years, they will have had only three children at most, not all of them surviving to adulthood.

When cereals were grown around the great hall at Balbridie and in the small, dyked fields of prehistoric Orkney, the birth rate rocketed. This happened because of the invention of something very like porridge. When ripe or charred grains were mashed into a pulp with water or animal milk, the result could be spooned into the mouths of hungry toddlers. It was nourishing and filling and allowed mothers to wean them off the breast more quickly. This in turn much reduced the birth interval and many more babies were born in the short lives of women. Ancestral DNA studies show this process at work.

KURGANS

In a brilliant new analysis of ancient DNA, scientists have discovered that farming came to Europe in at least two waves. The second took place around 4,000–5,000 years ago and migrants are now thought to have come from the wide steppe lands of the Ukraine and Southern Russia. There, a prehistoric culture began to raise great mounds or kurgans *over burial chambers that contained the remains of powerful people. Farming is believed to have brought a new language to describe a new culture. Known as Proto-Indo-European, it is the mother tongue of almost all European languages and the reason they are so similar in structure and vocabulary. Elements of the speech of our hunter-gatherer ancestors may be preserved in the Basque language of south-western France and north-western Spain.*

Across Scotland (and the rest of Britain, Ireland and much of Western Europe) the dominant Y-chromosome DNA haplogroup is R1b, at a very high frequency of 72 per cent of all men. It appears to have arrived with a second wave of farming immigrants, the groups known as the Beaker People. Their grave goods included fine pottery described as beakers. The origin of R1b has been dated to the middle of the 3rd millennium BC and its rapid spread to every corner of Scotland is testament to the vigour of men who passed it on to their many sons. And the reason for that success and the evidence of what may have been a violent takeover by new immigrants are also found in the graves of the Beaker People. In a burial discovered at Culduthel in Inverness, archaeologists found eight beautifully crafted tanged and barbed arrowheads and a bone bracer or wrist guard studded with gold rivets. A significant number of other similar burials containing archery equipment and metal objects have been found across Britain. The takeover of the Beaker People and the dramatic expansion of the R1b markers may have been the result of the deadly exercise of archery skills and the use of metal weapons. By the end of the 3rd millennium BC, the carriers of R1b had come to dominate prehistoric Scotland and shape its distinctive culture.

3

Caledonia

✳

IN AD 43, ELEPHANTS plodded through Colchester. Brought to awe and amaze all the natives who saw them, war elephants had been carefully ferried across the English Channel by a Roman expeditionary force. It was a moment of high drama, of powerful political symbolism. Led by Aulus Plautius, the legions had crossed what they called the Ocean, swept aside the armies of the kings of southern Britain and extended the Empire to the northern limits of the known world. And, to hammer home the dominance, the reach of Rome, the Emperor had commanded war elephants to come north from Africa, from the southern limits of the known world.

Imperial politics had also persuaded the Emperor to ride in triumph into Colchester, the capital place of the defeated Cunobelinus, Shakespeare's Cymbeline, King of the Catuvellauni. Famously dragged from behind a curtain in the chaos after the assassination of the crazy Caligula, Claudius had been placed on the throne by the Praetorian Guard. After a difficult two years and the suppression of a serious rebellion, this most unlikely of emperors badly needed to assert himself and build a political power base. The traditional means of achieving that was conquest, the extension of the Empire and all the prestige and material gain that would bring. Julius Caesar had crossed the Channel twice but had also retreated twice. Claudius would achieve more than the Divine Julius – his armies would come, see and they would conquer. A new province would be added to the Empire.

The English Channel represented a tremendous psychological barrier, the stormy, unpredictable, unknown ocean on the edge of the world. Legionaries and their generals were much happier marching on solid roads than bobbing about on the swells and the tides. There had been mutinies on the embarkation beaches at Boulogne. But, in AD 43, the transports crossed and it was done.

PYTHEAS AND THE *PERIPLUS*

An intrepid adventurer with an eye to commerce, Pytheas was probably the first to circumnavigate Britain. He wanted to create a periplus, *a route guide for traders, especially those keen to buy British tin. He also gave the nation its name. From the Greek colony of Massalia, modern Marseilles, he arrived on the Channel coast of Gaul or France some time in the 320s BC. When Pytheas asked the natives what the inhabitants of the island across the sea were called,* 'Pretannikai' *was how he rendered the answer. It means 'the People of the Tattoos'. Clearly the ancient Britons had clung on to the habit of body decoration while the Gauls had not. Pytheas called the whole of the largest island* Pretannike *and this was adapted by the Romans as* Britannia, *'Britain', 'the Tattoo Nation'.*

Even though Claudius was in Britain for only 16 days, the invasion was a triumph, an episode that was remembered and celebrated. On a triumphal arch erected in Rome in AD 51, an inscription recounted that the Emperor had received the submission of no fewer than eleven British kings. One of them had also travelled a long way. A 4th-century history of Rome's emperors compiled by the historian, Eutropius, listed amongst Claudius's achievements that 'he added to the Empire some islands lying in the Ocean beyond Britain which are called the Orkneys'. To add weight to these revealing pieces of epigraphic evidence is a chance archaeological find. At Broch of Gurness, a site of very high status on Orkney Mainland, a Roman amphora was found. Not only was it of a type that had become obsolete after AD 60, it was used as a container for a fancy liqueur consumed by aristocrats. Taken together, these fragments offer a fascinating glimpse of native British politics in the 1st century AD.

Communications and effective diplomacy were clearly involved in orchestrating the submission of the King of Orkney. Given the brevity of Claudius's stay in Britain and that the sea journey from Orkney to Colchester might have taken up to a week, there had to have been prior contact (perhaps with gifts of fancy wine in the hold of a ship). Roman diplomats must have negotiated the submission of the king well before Claudius and his elephants plodded into Colchester. And if, as Eutropius noted, Orkney became part of the Empire (and that is what submission meant – a client status), why? The Roman legions and their fleets had landed far to the south, almost 800 miles away, and they can have presented no immediate threat. Perhaps a deal was done. In exchange for the propaganda value of having the king of the islands at the ends of the earth bow before Claudius and so demonstrate his unparalleled reach and power, Rome agreed to support the Orcadians against their more immediate neighbours on the Scottish mainland or to reward them in a more material way. Now that is clearly a conjecture but not unlikely.

Who were the neighbours of the King of Orkney? Using source materials probably gathered in the 1st century AD, the Greek geographer Ptolemy compiled a detailed map of Britain and Ireland in the 2nd century AD. To a modern eye, it looks very strange. Scotland north of the Tay is not plotted as being north of the river and the firth. Instead Ptolemy has bent the map through 90 degrees so that Scotland points to the east. Used to the warmth of the Mediterranean, neither he nor his fellow Greek geographers believed that human beings could possibly survive in latitudes further north than 63 degrees. And so Scotland was distorted to fit.

The detail on the strange map strongly suggests that the data had been derived from a circumnavigation of Scotland, for much of it is coastal. Ten islands, seventeen rivers, seven capes, three bays, sixteen towns or settlements, seventeen kindreds and four other places are named. Many of these have come down to us. *Aebudae Insulae* is clearly the ghost name of the Hebrides, the letter 'r' seeming to have intruded later from a scribal error. *Malaios Insula* is Mull and its meaning of 'Lofty Isle' probably comes from the extinct volcano of Ben More. Very eloquent is *Rerigonium*, a name plotted near modern Stranraer. It translates as 'Very Royal Place' and its importance was recalled in the very early poetry of the Welsh Triads. Bards sang of three national thrones of Britain and one lay at Penrhyn Rhionydd in the north. Rendered in Old Welsh, Ptolemy's *Rerigonium* would be precisely Rhionydd, with Penryhn a reference to the peninsula to the west of Loch Ryan, part of the Rhinns of Galloway – all cognate names. The Very Royal Place of the 1st and 2nd centuries AD probably became one of the capital places of the Dark-Age kings of Rheged, a polity now lost in the mists of the long past.

What is striking about the kindred names and much of the geography of Ptolemy's Scotland is the profusion of animal references. The King of Orkney ruled the *Orcades*, the 'Boar Islands'. In the north-west lay the territory of the *Caereni*, the 'Sheep Folk', in Easter Ross were the lands of the *Lugi*, the 'Raven People', and far to the south-west in Argyll and the Kintyre

Peninsula were the *Epidii*, the 'Horse Kindred'. In a fascinating continuity, the clan name of MacEachern originated there and, translated from Gaelic, it means 'the son of the Horse Lord'. Animals appear to have been revered as totems and the kindreds who took their names probably identified with them and their natures.

Ptolemy's informant may have been someone on imperial business. In AD 83, the great historian Plutarch was in Delphi when he met a man, Demetrius of Tarsus, on his way home. Demetrius had been commanded by the Emperor Domitian to sail around the north of Britain to gather information, make observations and perhaps a map. He told Plutarch of a gloomy journey amongst deserted islands, some of them named after 'daemons' or heroes. But he came ashore on one which was the retreat of holy men. Demetrius does not use the word 'druid' but it may be that he made landfall on Iona. Long before the coming of Columba, it was a sacred isle whose correct name was *Iova*, 'Yew Island'. Like Hebrides, Iona is the result of a later scribal error. Iova is what Columba's saintly biographer, Abbot Adomnan, called it and the ancient trees and their shaded groves had a close association with the druids.

Demetrius was impressed by the holy men and their powers of divination. When a great storm raged out over the Atlantic, lightning crackling, thunder booming, they told him that it was a sign that one of their pantheon of gods, the Mighty Ones, had died. It is a memorable image. If Demetrius did indeed make a map, then that or his journal of the expedition may have fallen into the grateful hands of Ptolemy. The patchwork of territories noted by him were given Greek versions of their Celtic names. By the end of the 1st millennium BC and probably long before that, the kindreds of what would become Scotland spoke dialects of a Celtic language. But it was not Gaelic. Across most of Britain, what might best be described as Old Welsh was used to describe the land and the lives of those who farmed, fished and hunted under the big skies of the north. Gaelic crossed the North Channel in the 4th, 5th and 6th centuries as war bands from Ulster colonised Argyll and founded the famous kindreds of Dalriada. Old Welsh seems to have developed into Pictish, a language that has survived almost exclusively in place names and personal names (no one can now utter a sentence in Pictish) and it may have hung on into the early Middle Ages amongst isolated speech communities.

EAGLES AND EMPERORS

Perhaps because of its size, its longevity – hen birds in captivity have been known to live for more than 100 years – and its stern gaze, the eagle is a symbol of power in many cultures. As the standards that marched in front of Roman legions, the gold eagles were first adopted by the great republican general, Gaius Marius, when he campaigned against the Persians in the east. The great birds were revered by the Persians and the Romans imitated this. The heirs of imperial pretension in more modern times copied the Romans. Two of the eagle standards carried by Napoleon's regiments at Waterloo have recently been brought to Scotland for an exhibition. Both the German and Russian emperors had eagle banners and these dynasties also adapted the title of Caesar as Kaiser and Tsar. Perhaps the owner of the original would have smiled. Caesar was famously bald and the name was ironic – it means 'hairy'.

In the decades following Claudius's flying visit in AD 43, the Roman Empire began to creep northwards. After the appalling slaughter of the Boudiccan rebellion, the provincial administration preferred, where possible, to cultivate client relationships with native kings and queens. When the Brigantian federation of the Pennines was absorbed, the reach of Rome lengthened. By AD 73, the legions had advanced as far as the southern foothills of the Cheviots but were then abruptly withdrawn to campaign against the Silures in south Wales.

Publius Cornelius Tacitus did not live up to his cognomen, his last name. If he had, Scotland would have had to wait a long time for her first historian. Tacitus means 'the Silent One'. In reality, he was eloquent, a distinguished lawyer, orator and senator and the author of the *Agricola*, a biography of his father-in-law. Appointed Governor of the province of Britannia, this determined and ruthless soldier was commissioned by the Emperor Vespasian to bring the whole island of Britain into the Empire. Tacitus chronicled the campaigns in Scotland between AD 79 and 84 and offered the first written, clear, albeit partial, picture of people and events in the north.

Behind the reports of military advance, road- and fort-building, lay a strategy for conquest. When the legions had attacked Venutius, a rebel leader of the otherwise compliant Brigantes, at his fort at Stanwick in Yorkshire in AD 70, historians had noted that he had 'help from outside'. This probably referred to war bands riding south from the Southern Uplands and Galloway through the hill trails to join the defence against the invaders. The kindred known as the *Selgovae*, 'the Hunters', ranged across the ancient expanse of the Ettrick Forest, the tract of wild land extending west from Selkirk to Annandale. Their warriors probably fought and died on the ramparts of the hillfort at Stanwick and brought themselves to the notice of Rome.

When Agricola and his general staff planned the advance north, they divided the invasion force of three legions and several regiments of auxiliaries in order to execute a pincer movement. One group struck through the western ranges of the Cheviots to reach the Tweed near Melrose and their line of march eventually became the great Roman and medieval artery of Dere Street. The western force followed a route north from Carlisle that became the modern A74 and the effect of these deployments was to surround the Selgovae with roads and a network of forts. This was a classic strategy, a vital means of exerting effective military control.

The western advance also divided the Selgovae from another kindred which had probably sent warriors south to the aid of Venutius. This was the *Novantae*, the people whose kings may have ruled from Rerigonium, the Very Royal Place on Loch Ryan. Ultimately a west–east link, a road, was built through what is now the vast Craik Forest to reach Teviotdale. And the fort at Oakwood could also communicate with Trimontium, the depot built on Dere Street near Melrose. It was an outpost in a hostile landscape. To the east lay the territory of a people Ptolemy called the *Otadini*. It was a mis-rendering of *Votadini*, a name that probably meant something like the 'people of Fothad', a deity or a founding ancestor or both. This kindred grew the cereals and reared the animals that the invaders' quartermasters needed to buy to feed the hungry legionaries and auxiliaries and so they were treated as friendly clients. Forts were built in Berwickshire nevertheless, as well as roads, one following the coast close to where the modern A1 runs.

When Vespasian died in AD 79, his son Titus succeeded and Agricola halted the invasion to await new orders. 'Onwards!' was the message from Rome, and in AD 80 the legions set about consolidating their gains and preparing to move westwards against the Novantae. Having reached the Rhinns of Galloway and perhaps Rerigonium, Agricola could see the shores of Ireland in the distance. Probably on the basis of intelligence gleaned from the local kindred, Tacitus noted that his father-in-law made the optimistic judgement that the whole island might be held with only a single legion.

In September AD 81, Titus suddenly died, perhaps in suspicious circumstances, and his younger brother Domitian succeeded. To establish himself, like Claudius, the new emperor reckoned he needed quick military success and the prestige that would bring. He looked for it in Scotland. Agricola's governorship was extended for a further three years and his general staff began to plan an advance beyond Bodotria, the Firth of Forth, into the land they called *Caledonia*.

FINGER NUMBERS

An older generation of Scots used to count differently. For example, instead of saying 24, they would say 4 and 20. This is a memory of 20-base counting and it is probably Celtic in origin, perhaps refined by the developing techniques of farming and herding. It was important to know how many cows or sheep you owned and to be able to count them. In Scots Gaelic 20-base arithmetic is still very much in use – fichead *is twenty and forty is* dha fichead *or two twenties and 80 is* ceithir fichead *or four twenties and so on. There are relics of a similar system in French where 80 is* quatre-vingts. *The English counted differently. They used a 10-base system, probably from the Roman model. Their numerals were based on the fingers. One finger held up was I (one), two held up was II (two, not eleven) and five was V, the angle made by the thumb and the forefinger. Ten was X, the two index fingers crossed. While the confusing business of adding and subtraction was eventually replaced by the adoption of Arabic numerals, the 10-base basis survived and is now widely used in Scotland. Only the Gaels hold to the old ways of reckoning.*

Having become a romantic synonym for Scotland and the title of one of the more likely candidates for a national anthem, the name of Caledonia is interesting. It originally referred to a kindred whose territory probably lay in the Perthshire glens. Place names whisper an ancient presence at Dunkeld, the dun or fortress of the Caledonians, and the great peak of Schiehallion between Loch Rannoch and Loch Tay may have marked a boundary. A shape-shifter, seen from different vantage points, the name means the Magic Mountain of the Caledonians. The kindred itself was not named for an animal totem like the Epidii or the Lugi but instead seems to derive from a characteristic of either the people or the wild landscape they inhabited. A Celtic root that means something like 'hard', *caled* is also found in the name of Kirkcaldy although the Fife town lies some distance to the south. No doubt some would prefer Caledonians to mean something like the 'Hard Men'. Perhaps it does.

Invaders often misapply the names of the first peoples they encounter in a strange land. When the armies of the tsars were pushing the limits of the Russian Empire east beyond the Ural Mountains, they came across the Sabir nomads and named the vast hinterland of Siberia after them. Something similar may have occurred when Agricola led the legions north and they ran into resistance from the Caledonians.

Tacitus wrote that, when the imperial army advanced beyond the Forth, it was 'as if into another island'. In the 6th millennium BC, the waist of Scotland had been even narrower as higher sea levels bit inland as far as Aberfoyle and Loch Lomond had been a sea loch. Whale bones have been excavated in the Forth Valley. By the time the signifers (standard-bearers) lifted the legionary eagles and the centurions led the imperial army into Caledonia, the retreating seas had left an even more formidable barrier. Stretching to the west of Stirling lay Flanders Moss, a string of treacherous bogs navigable only by those who knew the paths, and it was no place for armies. The wild upcountry of the Lennox, Kilsyth and Gargunnock Hills also discouraged movement. The only access road ran in the shadow of the sentinel castle rock of Stirling, where the route to the north began to climb towards the Ochil Hills. In a 7th-century epic poem known as the *Gododdin*, the inheritors of the domain of the Votadini warriors came to a battle muster 'from beyond Bannauc', a name that survives in the famous Bannock Burn. In his account of the campaigns of Agricola, Tacitus recognised a profoundly important internal frontier, one that divided Scotland for many centuries.

The Empire struck north in AD 82 and, according to Tacitus, 'enveloped the states situated beyond the Bodotria [Forth]. Because there were fears that all the peoples on the further side might rise and the land routes be threatened by an enemy army, Agricola reconnoitred the harbours with the fleet. What is clear from this is a good understanding of the logistics and strategy needed for a successful invasion of the north of Scotland. This, in turn, depended on intelligence and perhaps the contacts established with the Orkney kings in AD 43 were still in working order. In any event, the use of the fleet was a key tactic, one informed by a knowledge of the coastal geography of the north. In what may be the earliest written description of the Atlantic seaboard to survive, Tacitus wrote beautifully of the rugged, indented coastline and its sea lochs: 'Nowhere is the dominance of the sea more extensive. There are many tidal currents, flowing in different directions. They do not merely rise as far as the shoreline and recede again. They flow far inland, wind around, and push themselves amongst the highlands and mountains, as if in their own realm.'

FIRSTS AND SECONDS

The 60-base system of dividing up our hours was devised by the Babylonians. Their hours comprised sixty 'firsts' and each first had sixty 'seconds'. Latin replaced the first with minutes and passed that on to English but the Babylonian seconds ticked on. The Celts of early Scotland did not reckon time in the same way. They associated years with events – the year of the great flood or the year of the sparse grass. This method of dating can still be found in the Gaelic lexicon where words like aimsir *(pronounced 'amashir') and* tide *(pronounced 'cheedje') mean both time and weather. It took many centuries for the Roman months to catch on but they are very similar all over Western Europe. Their names make sense only when it is remembered that the Roman year began in March – September is the seventh month, October the eighth, November the ninth and December the tenth. Most of the others derive from Roman gods or deified emperors.*

The summary of events supplied by Tacitus implies that the enveloping of the states north of the Forth was a matter of routine and that all went according to plan. In fact, the IX Legion was almost wiped out in a surprise night attack in the Angus glens when the Caledonian war bands stormed their camp. Help arrived in the nick of time and, when reinforcements attacked at daybreak, Tacitus described their arrival in a memorable phrase, 'At first light the standards gleamed.'

As the legions and auxiliary regiments moved north, they stripped the lands of their enemies like locusts. A force of around 20,000 men and perhaps 5,000 hungry horses, they foraged for food and were probably also supplied by the Roman fleet from natural harbours like the Montrose Basin. When the soldiers dug overnight marching camps, they sometimes simply swept away native villages if they lay on what was considered to be a good defensive site. At Cardean in Angus, such characteristic ruthlessness has been discovered by archaeologists. Under the Roman remains, they found the outline of roundhouses and, far from being primitive, draughty hovels, they could be snug and easy to maintain.

Traces of roundhouses have been found all over Scotland, often marked on the Ordnance Survey as 'hut circles' and dating to the 1st millennium BC and later. A circular drystane wall was built, sometimes up to chest height, and an umbrella-like arrangement of roof timbers rested on the wall head. Lashed together or keyed at the apex, this conical structure was roofed with turf or bracken or both. A roundhouse had only one door and, to catch the morning sun, it usually faced east. Dark inside, these buildings were used for shelter, storage, cooking, sleep and warmth. Most work, such as weaving or sewing, that needed good light was done outside. At the centre of the roundhouse was a down hearth, a circular kerb of flattish stones laid around the fireplace, and it was the focus. Used for cooking and heat, the flames and embers warmed the families who sat around it – and probably slept around it in wintertime. They used low benches because roundhouses had no chimneys or smoke-holes and standing up could be eye-watering. But the constant cone of smoke and carbon dioxide produced by the ever-burning fire was important. When sparks spat and spiralled upwards, they were prevented from setting the roof alight by the carbon dioxide and simply snuffed out before they could reach the thatch or dry, blackened bracken. Roundhouses could be large – some even had two floors – and, when well maintained, they made warm and homely dwellings.

Probably in the summer of AD 83, a year after the attack on the IX Legion, Agricola led his army north once more, hoping to force the Caledonians into a pitched battle. It seems that the kindreds of Scotland beyond the Forth had come together to form a confederacy. Almost certainly because of the tremendous destruction to farmland and the harvest caused by the Roman advance as well as a powerful will to resist conquest, they began to muster a combined army. Intelligence reports told Agricola that he might be granted his wish because the Caledonians were massing at a place in the far north known as *Mons Graupius*, 'the Graupian Mountain'. Yet another scribal error has given us the modern name of Grampian. It was September and no time should be lost. Agricola brigaded together the legions and hurried north. Here is Tacitus's account:

So he came to the Graupian Mountain. It had already been occupied by the enemy. The Britons were, in fact, in no way broken by the outcome of the previous battle: they were awaiting either revenge or enslavement. They had at last learned the lesson that a common danger could only be warded off by a united front. By means of embassies and alliances they had rallied the forces

37

of all their states. Already more than 30,000 armed men could be observed and still all the young men and famous warriors, whose 'old age was still fresh and green', each man wearing the decorations he had won, were flowing in. Now, one was more outstanding among their many leaders for his valour and nobility, Calgacus by name, faced the assembled multitude as they clamoured for battle.

The first Scot to be named in the historical record, Calgacus was more of a title or a nickname. It means 'the Swordsman'. It appears that he had been appointed by the confederates as their general. Had he been a king, it is likely that Tacitus would have said so. Perhaps his title was something like the Old Welsh *Gwledig* or 'Warlord'. Calgacus faced his warriors because Tacitus was about to follow classical convention and put a battle speech in his mouth. A work of the imagination, it nevertheless contained some ringing phrases. The Caledonians were 'the last of the free', the peoples at the ends of the Earth and, as soon as Calgacus completed his exhortations, battle was joined.

The most persuasive location for the Graupian Mountain is the singular hill of Bennachie near Inverurie in Aberdeenshire. Around the natural amphitheatre of its lower slopes a drama unfolded as the Caledonian warriors charged the disciplined ranks of Agricola's army. Many of them rode in chariots, most carried long sabres more suitable for the slashing cuts of cavalry warfare and they held small shields useful only for parrying blows. By contrast, the tight, grinding, stabbing, relentless, close-order advance of the Roman auxiliaries and legionaries was much more effective. Tacitus talked of a great slaughter with more than 10,000 Caledonians falling at the battle of the Graupian Mountain and in its immediate aftermath. Victory left Agricola poised to consolidate and to begin the road- and fort-building needed to bring the new territory into the Empire. But politics in Rome and a flaring frontier rebellion on the Danube pulled troops eastwards and thwarted his plans. Writing '*Perdomita Britannia et statim missa* (Having been conquered, Britain was straight away given up)', Tacitus was indignant. The legions marched south. At Inchtuthil, not far from Perth, a huge legionary fortress began construction but it too was quickly abandoned. Its most tangible relic was a buried cache of one million nails.

The Romans hid them not only because they knew that Caledonian smiths might beat them into swords but also because the ebb and flow of imperial power might send the legions back north. The nails could also have been beaten into ploughshares for it seems that the lands beyond the Cheviots may have become comparatively populous in the 1st century AD. Perhaps as many as 500,000 lived in what is now Scotland. This mirrors an estimate made by medieval historians for the year 1100 and, since agricultural methods and climate appear to have altered little in the intervening millennium between then and the battle at the Graupian Mountain, that may be a sensible conjecture. If so, that means an average population density of 40 per square mile in the Lowlands and less than half of that number in upland pastoral regions. Around 1st-century AD sites, such as the fort on Traprain Law in East Lothian, aerial photography shows traces of a busy agricultural landscape.

Using all of his experience of farming, the distinguished archaeologist Francis Pryor has hypothesised that prehistoric Britain was principally a pastoral society, an economy that depended on stock rearing as its staple. Cereals were grown only on a small scale in garden-like fields and, even though society depended on the output of farming, the wild harvest of fruits, roots and berries continued. A blocked drain of the 2nd-century AD Roman fort in Bearsden lends support to this view. No doubt with a fine scientific disregard for the nature of what they were analysing, archaeologists were able to discover a sense of the everyday diet of the Roman soldiers stationed there. They ate little meat but with cereals they cooked a version of porridge and added some flavour and seasonal variety with wild berries and fruit.

Francis Pryor also makes much of the frequency of markets in prehistoric Britain. Stockmen are very conscious of the dangers of inbreeding in their flocks and herds and will have regularly sought to find new bloodlines amongst the animals belonging to their neighbours or, preferably, farmers even further afield. Even now, stockmen know their beasts very well and are able to identify them as individuals, knowing exactly what their breeding is. Sheep were much more extensively reared than cattle or goats, argued Pryor, because they offered three yields – wool, milk and ultimately meat.

These important observations were made by an archaeologist whose experience was mainly gained in the south of England but they are likely to apply even more readily to the style of early farming north of the Tweed. There is much linguistic and cultural support for Pryor's views. The Celtic tongue of the Caledonians and the kindreds of Scotland below the Forth is rich in the vocabulary of stock rearing. The lexicon of colours, for example, applied to cattle and other animals is far wider than the range of adjectives available in modern English. This ability to describe a beast accurately was important in matters of ownership and breeding. And perhaps it is more than amusing to note that the most extravagant term of endearment in Gaelic survives as *m'eudail*. It means 'my cattle'.

BAWBEES

Although coinage was invented by the Mesopotamians and developed by the Egyptians and Greeks, the Romans were the first to create an economy based on the exchange of money. Minted c. 300 BC, the first coins were related to an older measure of wealth – livestock. The Latin word pecunia *is from* pecus, *the word for 'cattle', and gives us the English word 'pecuniary'. Money drove the expansion of the empire as hard as political ambition and Julius Caesar transformed his vast debt of 25 million* denarii *when he conquered and exploited Gaul. His adopted son, Augustus, made himself the richest man in the world. Trade with the imperial garrisons on the Antonine Wall and Hadrian's Wall introduced money into the early Scottish economy although it is unclear whether or not internal cash exchange replaced barter. Roman coins have been found as far north as the Hebrides, on North Uist, and many hoards of coins, silver and sometimes gold, have been found. These were almost certainly bribes to keep the peace or the settlement of transactions to buy supplies. When the empire in the west disintegrated in the 5th century, the use and exchange of coin ceased in Scotland and the rest of Britain.*

The recorded observations of outsiders should of course be treated with some caution but, for Scotland in the 1st century AD, they are all that is available. Tacitus's *Agricola* offers the earliest description of geography, politics and people and is worth quoting at length:

As to what human beings initially inhabited Britain, whether native-born or immigrants, little has been established, as is usually the case with barbarians. Be this as it may, their physical appearance is varied, which allows conclusions to be drawn. For example, in the case of the inhabitants of Caledonia, their red-gold hair and massive limbs proclaim German origin . . .

All the same it is plausible on a general estimate that the Gauls [from modern France] occupied the adjacent island. You can find their rites and religious beliefs. The language is not much different . . .

Their infantry is their main strength. Some of their peoples also engage in battle with chariots. The nobles are the charioteers, their clients fight for them. In former times the Britons owed obedience to kings. Now they are formed into factional groupings by the leading men. Indeed there is nothing that helps us more against such very powerful peoples than their lack of unanimity. It is seldom that two or three states unite to repel a common threat. Hence each fights on its own, and all are conquered.

The climate is miserable, with frequent rain and mists. But extreme cold is not found there. The days last longer than in our part of the world, the nights are bright and in the most distant parts of Britain so short that you can hardly distinguish between evening and morning twilight. If clouds do not block the view, they say that the sun's glow can be seen by night. It does not set and rise but passes across the horizon. In fact, the flat extremes of the earth, casting a long shadow, do not project the darkness, and night falls below the level of the light of the sky and the stars.

The soil bears crops, apart from the olive and the vine and the other natives of warmer climes, and has an abundance of cattle. The crops ripen slowly but shoot up quickly. The cause is the same in both cases, the abundant moisture of the land and the sky. Britain contains gold and silver and other metals, the booty of victory . . .

Much of this is elegant (especially the description of gloaming) and self-explanatory, if a little snooty – the view down the nose of a superior Roman senator. But his reference to the red-gold hair of the Caledonians has a fascinating resonance in the light of new genetic research. Children fortunate enough to have red hair require both of their parents to be carriers of the recessive gene variant. Many have the variant without themselves having red hair and it may be passed on for generations before it appears in a child. A recent study shows that one region of Scotland has the highest per capita incidence of carriers in the world. In the south-east, the Lothians and the Borders, 40 per cent have the red hair gene variants and in other regions it is only a little lower. Immigration in the millennia since the 1st century AD (especially in the Northern Isles, the Hebrides and the North-West where only 29 per cent carry the variant) may well have diluted the number who have the recessive gene variant and, when Tacitus was writing, there may indeed have been many Caledonians with red-gold hair. This would have been striking to a man from the Mediterranean where red hair is relatively rare.

The chariot-driving nobility of the Caledonians have left two eloquent sorts of architectural memorials. On the Northern Isles and around the Atlantic seaboard the monumental remains of brochs rise in the landscape. At Mousa on Shetland one of these beautiful drystane towers stands more than 40 feet tall, close to its original height. Brochs have no windows, a single door and, while their mass is formidable, they seem not to have been defensive structures but buildings designed to impress or even overawe. Most are found in coastal locations and were built between the beginning of the 1st century BC and the end of the 1st century AD. It is thought that specialist work gangs of itinerant masons sailed around the northern and western shores raising these remarkable and sophisticated structures for the local nobility, rather in the way that big hooses were built on newly aggregated estates in the later 18th century.

Equally spectacular were Scotland's hillforts, although they were almost certainly not forts. Ditches and banks topped by a wooden palisade, these could be vast, a long rampart circling the summits of singular hills, far too long to be defended except by an unfeasibly huge garrison. Amongst the largest and most impressive are two neighbours, the forts dug on White Caterthun and Brown Caterthun near Brechin, in Angus, but 90 per cent of these structures lie south of the Forth. Perhaps the most spectacular occupies the top of Eildon Hill North in the Borders. First enclosed some time around 1,000 BC, it was used intermittently until the arrival of the Romans (who desecrated it with a signal station on the summit). But what is very surprising is the fact that the outlines of 300 hut platforms have been found in a location where there is no spring, no source of water except from the sky. The function of the fort is therefore unlikely to have been defensive or residential. Perhaps Eildon Hill North was the expression of political and spiritual beliefs – in a society that probably did not make that distinction. A king or a priest-king had sufficient authority to command the many thousands of man-hours needed to dig the ditch and raise the rampart and, at important turning points of the stock-rearing year, he may have summoned his people to climb the hill and occupy the huts that lie just below the summit. There they worshipped, perhaps directing their prayers up to the sky gods in long-lost rituals, perhaps they listened to the law laid down and paid tithes to their rulers.

Such turning points in the year may have been those that were remembered in the old Celtic calendar. *Imbolc* was later Christianised as the Feast of St Bride at the beginning of February but it marked the time when ewes began to lactate in anticipation of spring lambing. *Beltane* followed on 1 May and it signalled the start of the movement of flocks and herds to upland pastures, the ancient journey of transhumance. *Lughnasa* is still celebrated on 1 August in rural Ireland and it was the time when summer-grass-fattened beasts were sold for slaughter or breeding. In Scotland it is known as Lammas. And on 31 October, Halloween, was the festival of *Samhuinn*, the end of summer. These were also fire festivals when bonfires blazed on the summits and rituals were enacted in their crackle and glow. One of them still is a fire festival, only five days later than the original date, when an effigy of Guy Fawkes goes up in flames.

MOONTIME

The Romans used sundials, candles marked for the hours and sand-filled hourglasses to measure time. The natives of early Scotland used their eyes. For the passage of a day, farmers looked up at the sun and its position. But for the transit of days and what we now call months, they used the moon and its phases. These are commonly called new, crescent, half, gibbous (more than half) and full. When Native Americans are given the washed-out old line of 'many moons ago', it does at least bring an authentic touch to routine westerns. It is very likely that early Scots used a similar phrase to mean a long time ago. The full moon near to the autumn equinox can often last longer than usual. Which is convenient since it allows farmers several light nights, extra time to bring the hairst hame, *the harvest home.*

When Antoninus Pius succeeded Hadrian as emperor, he too needed the prestige of military glory to underwrite his credentials. And, like Claudius, he chose to make conquests in Britannia. Within months of his accession in 138, the legions had been ordered to reoccupy the territory won by Agricola 50 years before. Like Hadrian, the new emperor built a wall (although the frontier zone extended into Perthshire and Fife), and this time a much shorter and more modest version was thrown up between the Forth and the Clyde. But its garrison looked north from its turf ramparts for only a generation, between AD 142 and 163. It was during this period that the informative drain at Bearsden fort was blocked.

Once the Romans had withdrawn once more from Scotland and the frontier settled back on Hadrian's Wall, the kindreds of the north began to develop their military reach. The rich Roman province to the south was an attractive target for raiders and imperial frustration boiled over in the early 3rd century when the great warrior-emperor, Septimius Severus, led a vast army across the wall. Based at the legionary fortress at York, he planned what was probably a genocide. Here is the relevant passage from the Greek historian Dio Cassius: 'The Britons [meaning the Caledonians] having broken their agreements and taken up arms, Severus ordered his soldiers to invade their territory and put to the sword all that they met, adding the Homeric quotation that "they should let nobody escape, not even the children hidden in their mothers' wombs".'

SPITTALS AND WICKS

The Romans introduced Christianity to Britain, probably through soldiers who had been converted elsewhere in the empire. As it spread in the centuries after the garrison left, religious place names proliferated. Variants of Kirkhill, Clerklands, Prieston and others are found all over Scotland. One of the loneliest is Spittal of Glenshee. This derives from the Latin word hospitium. *Rather than anything medical, it referred to a place where travellers, especially pilgrims, could rest and find shelter. Names also record the overlaying of one culture with another. The Old Welsh word for a steading or a farm is* tref *and the watershed hill of Soutra is from* Sulw Tref, *'the farm with the wide view'. From its summit, North Berwick and the shores of the Forth can be made out. The* wick *part of Berwick meant 'an outlying farm', a name introduced by the Angles who came in the 7th and 8th centuries.*

The kindred known as the *Maeatae* were a principal target but their king, Argentocoxus (it means 'Silver Leg', perhaps a reference to his wearing greaves in the Roman style) appears to have met Septimius Severus and the Empress Julia Domna to negotiate. The second Scot to be named in the historical record, Argentocoxus was lucky. In AD 211, Severus died and his son Caracalla 'made treaties with the enemy, evacuated their territory and abandoned the forts'. With the imperial throne beckoning and his brother Geta to deal with, Caledonia was a minor matter and Caracalla hurried south to Rome.

For almost a century, there were no reports of war in North Britain. Perhaps internal conflicts flared between kindreds or Roman control and bribery were effective. But, in 296, a new name appeared. Roman sources reported that war bands of a people called the Picts had broken through or sailed round Hadrian's Wall and invaded the province of Britannia as far south as Chester.

4

Alba

THE MODERN BORDER between Scotland and England is not new – it began to settle along the watershed ridges of the Cheviots and the eastern reaches of the Tweed almost a thousand years ago. But its increasingly emphatic nature tends to distort, corral, even limit our thinking about how our history unfolded. Too readily we underplay the influence of events and developments in northern England, especially the 300-year period when Hadrian's Wall was patrolled by garrisons. Like the Germanic kindreds to the north of the Rhine frontier and the warlike, horse-riding nomads from the steppes who reined in their migrations when they reached the Danube, the peoples north of the Cheviots lived for many generations in the shadow of a colossus. All at the same time, Rome was a succulent prize, ripe for raiding; its armies were feared, especially in close-quarter fighting; its engineers could construct daunting fortifications and throw mighty bridges across the Rhine and Danube; its glittering cities were wonders of the world with basilicas, aqueducts and theatres; and its emperors ruled over most of that world. The colossus influenced all of its neighbours but, for the people of the land that would become Scotland, the Empire's most profound and enduring legacy was established not by the relentless tramp of the legions but through the adoption of the cult of what was seen as a Roman god.

For more than two centuries after the death of Christ, the religion that took his name was only one of a number of oriental cults to make converts in the towns and cities of the Empire. But serious and systematic persecution began under the Emperor Decius, who ruled from AD 249 to 251, and continued sporadically until the opening years of the 4th century. After the blood of the early martyrs was spilled, small groups of deeply pious men (and some women) fled the towns of the provinces of Judaea and Egypt to form small communities of hermits who became known as the Desert Fathers. Many settled in the harsh conditions of the Scetes desert west of the Nile Delta. Led by figures such as St Anthony the Great, they were the founders of Christian monasticism (the term derives from 'one-ness', the wish to worship and pray alone) and their teachings reached the west, becoming extremely influential, especially in Scotland and Ireland, by way of France. St Martin of Tours had been a soldier in the imperial army but, having declared his faith in the late 4th century, he founded the monastery at Marmoutier in the Loire Valley. In the absence of deserts, the monks saw the dense forests as a barrier against the world, a place where they could be undisturbed and where they could seek a more perfect communion with God. In the centuries following Martin's foundation, communities of monks sought lonely islands and headlands on the coasts of Ireland, Scotland and northern England where the sea took the place of deserts. The most spectacular is surely Skellig Michael, a series of stone beehive huts built on the rocky sides of the peak of an undersea mountain in the Atlantic off the coast of south-west Ireland. The most famous are probably the island monasteries of Iona and Lindisfarne.

After the Emperor Constantine's edict made Christianity the state religion, its popularity soared, especially in the towns and cities. And Christianity became closely identified with Rome, the Latin language and notions of order and hierarchy. In a symbolic sense the Bishop of Rome as the leader of Western Christendom replaced the Emperors who had moved their capital to Constantinople. The earliest known British martyr was St Alban, a Roman officer accused of sheltering a priest during the time of the persecutions of the late 3rd century. The town of Verulamium eventually housed his shrine and took his name. The new beliefs crept north through the movement of soldiers and others and, along the length of Hadrian's Wall, they and their families worshipped quietly until official recognition in 312. At the western end of the land wall, there seems to have been a flourishing and well-organised Church in the old Roman city of Carlisle. The most persuasive evidence for this comes from an unlikely source.

Carlisle or Luguvalium (named for the Celtic god, Lugh) was the site of a fort and a depot for Hadrian's Wall before it gained the status of a *civitas* or 'tribal capital' for the kindred known as the *Carvetii*, the 'Deer People', in the early 4th century. A series of tombstones shows that veterans from the Wall garrison retired to live there and it appears that they brought Christianity with them.

Some time around 430, a band of Irish slavers sailed far up the Solway and raided inland. Amongst others, they abducted a young man called Succat or Sochet and sold him to a landowner in Ireland. The boy became a shepherd but, after several years of solitude in the hills with his flocks, he escaped and made his way to Gaul, modern France. There he became a Christian celebrant of some kind, perhaps taking monastic vows, perhaps at Marmoutier. When he came back home to Carlisle around 440, Succat had taken the Roman name of Patricius or Patrick. After another period of religious instruction, he decided to return to Ireland on a mission of conversion, perhaps on the initiative of the Church in Carlisle.

In a brilliant analysis, Professor Charles Thomas has shown that Patrick's family owned a small estate near the village of Greenhead, about 15 miles inland from Carlisle and not far from Hadrian's Wall. In his *Confessio*, the great saint of Ireland also wrote that his grandfather, a man called Potitus, had been ordained as a priest and his father, Calpurnius, had been a deacon of the Church and a *decurion*, an elected official in the local government of a Roman city. It seems that, at the end of the 4th century, Carlisle was a flourishing town and the focus of a vigorous, expansionist Christian Church, a place that survived the departure of the last vestiges of the Roman administration in Britain around AD 410. Its urban infrastructure appears to have been maintained at least until 685 when St Cuthbert visited and was given a tour of the town walls and saw the marvel of a working Roman fountain. Even later chroniclers of the 12th century wrote of Carlisle's paved streets and architecture still standing that bore Latin inscriptions. What seems very plausible is that the town was home to an active and expanding Christian Church, probably a bishopric, and it acted as base for the conversion of the north of Ireland – and of southern Scotland.

Made around AD 450, the Latinus Stone is the oldest Christian monument yet found in Scotland. The Latin inscription reads: 'We praise thee, o Lord! Latinus, grandson of Barravados, aged 35, and his daughter, aged 4, made a shrine here.' It is not a tombstone but the commemoration of the foundation of a shrine or a monastic retreat. Above the inscription are the faint traces of a chi-rho symbol. These are the first two letters of Chrestos, the Greek version of Jesus's name and they were carved in a style common across the Eastern Roman Empire. The man who paid for the stone and perhaps the shrine associated with it was not only the first Christian in Scotland whose name has come down to us, he was also someone who had it rendered in a Roman style. Two generations after the fall of the province of Britannia and the consequent military irrelevance of Hadrian's Wall, the link between Christianity and the memory of the Empire was still powerful.

The Latinus Stone was found at Whithorn in Galloway, the site of Scotland's earliest known church. Indelibly associated with St Ninian, it was first known as Candida Casa, the White House, because it had been built in stone and probably lime-washed. About 25 miles to the west at Kirkmadrine, there are three more inscribed stones, probably from the early 6th century. They commemorate two bishops, Viventius and Mavorius. The name of Kirkmadrine is a version of the Church of St Martin, a very early dedication to the much-admired St Martin of Tours that was shared with Candida Casa at Whithorn.

HOLYROODS

In Scots the Haly Ruid *was the cross on which Christ died and our history is punctuated by representations of it. The Ruthwell and Bewcastle stone crosses are amongst the earliest and their erection by Anglian elites not only shows how far their culture had come from their days as pirates on the Northumberland coast, they are also beautiful objects in their own right. Their carvings were once much brighter, all of them painted in the Irish tradition. The Black Rood of Scotland was perhaps more Presbyterian, before its time, in that it was a fragment of the True Cross (there were many across Christendom) brought by St Margaret when she fled to Scotland and married Malcolm Canmore. It was kept in a black case and, in 1296, Edward I took it back south, along with the Stone of Scone. In 1328 the Black Rood was returned but lost again at the disastrous Battle of Neville's Cross in 1346. With many of the relics of St Cuthbert, it was destroyed during the English version of the Reformation when Durham Cathedral was ransacked. But the name of Holyrood lives on as shorthand for the Scottish Parliament.*

Ninian is a shadowy figure, his name a Latin version of Ninya, but he was probably sent by a bishop at Carlisle to minister to existing Christian communities in Galloway some time around 500. He may have taken some of the relics of St Martin of Tours with him to establish a shrine at Whithorn. The earliest notice of his mission of conversion is to be found in

The Ecclesiastical History of the English People, written in the early 8th century by Bede of Jarrow, a truly great scholar.

> The southern Picts, who live on this side of the mountains, are said to have abandoned the errors of idolatry long before this date [AD 565] and accepted the true Faith through the preaching of Bishop Ninian, a most reverend and holy man of British race, who had been regularly instructed in the mysteries of the Christian faith in Rome. Ninian's own episcopal see, named after St Martin and famous for its stately church, is now held by the English, and it is here that his body and those of many saints lie at rest. The place belongs to the province of Bernicia and is commonly called Candida Casa, the White House, because he built the church of stone, which was unusual amongst the Britons.

Bede was a Northumbrian and his purpose was to write a history which foregrounded the achievements of Northumbrian kings and saints. Their war bands penetrated deep into Galloway in the 7th century to take over Ninian's see. But his reference to the southern Picts appears to be confusing. It may well be that the saint travelled far to the north of Whithorn to preach amongst the kindreds of southern Caledonia. There are certainly many venerable dedications to him in Central Scotland, Fife, Tayside and Angus. Always precise about Northumbrian kings and saints, Bede was sometimes vague about the native British and it may also be the case that he was simply using the term 'Pict' generically to mean those who lived north of Hadrian's Wall. The description was applied to warriors who tattooed their bodies and those who raided as far south as Chester at the end of the 3rd century may have sailed or ridden from Galloway, the Tweed or Clyde Valleys or from the Lothians.

Christianity crept up and over the watershed hills north of Carlisle in the late 5th century. Stones inscribed with Latin dedications have been found in Liddesdale and a large Christian cemetery discovered on the site of Edinburgh airport was dated to AD 485. All over the Lothians so-called long-cist burials were dug in the late 5th and early 6th centuries. The old beliefs, what Bede called 'the errors of idolatry', took centuries to fade but, just as Patrick did in Ireland, it seems that missionaries like Ninian concentrated their efforts on converting the leaders of pagan communities. And it appears that they were successful.

After the fall of the province of Britannia, Old Welsh-speaking kindreds formed themselves into kingdoms with recognisable identities that were ruled over by named individuals who led their warriors into battle. Their narratives are fragmented, episodic and often reconstructed from epic poetry written down centuries after it was composed or genealogies that were sometimes contradictory, often vague. These men were kings less in the sense of controlling territory inside boundaries, more in building and maintaining interlocking bonds of loyalty fed by success in war and the booty it brought.

The Novantae of Galloway and the Carvetii of Cumbria appear to have coalesced into Rheged, a kingdom hinged around the shores of the Solway. Its most far-famed king was Urien, a name that derived from Urbgen which means 'born in the city', almost certainly in the city of Carlisle. He and his son, Owain, led war bands against the Germanic invaders who had begun to settle in enclaves on the Northumbrian coast. Perhaps piratical at first or mercenaries engaged by the imperial authorities in the dying decades of the province of Britannia, these were Angles and Bede noted that their first king was Ida and that he built a fortress on the spectacular seamark rock at Bamburgh.

THE SON OF DESTINY

Y Mab Darogan, 'the Destined or Prophesied Son', is a fascinating figure in Welsh language culture. A man would come, sang the bards, a hero who would lead the armies of Wales and the Celtic nations of Britain and drive the Anglo-Saxon invaders back into the sea. Llywelyn Mawr, the last Prince of Wales, was thought to be such a man, as was Owain Glyndwr, a princely figure who led a rebellion against the English in the early 15th century. The Welsh bards also sang of the Gwyr Y Gogledd, *the 'Men of the North', and some were thought to be heroic. Arthur is a figure with strong links to what is now Scotland and Owain ap Urien certainly ruled the old kingdom of Rheged after the assassination of his father in the late 6th century. They too were thought to be Sons of Destiny.*

Urien led a coalition of native British kings, certainly from Rheged and probably from Gododdin, the kingdom that developed from the Votadini and was based in the Lothians and the Tweed Basin. They attacked the heirs of Ida and laid siege to the tidal island of Lindisfarne some time in the 580s. But the coalition was suddenly shattered and the Angles broke out when

Urien was murdered on the orders of Morcant Bwlc, a prince who may have ruled on the Tweed over a client kingdom called Calchvynydd, the Old Welsh name for Kelso. Here is the entry in a chronicle known as the *History of the Britons*, an eccentric collection of records and myths compiled by a monk known as Nennius: 'But while he was on the expedition, Urien was assassinated, on the initiative of Morcant, from jealousy, because his military skill and generalship surpassed that of all the other kings.'

The abortive siege of Lindisfarne was followed, a decade or so later, by vengeance of a sort. King Owain of Rheged attacked Fflamddwyn, the Flame Bearer, an Old Welsh nickname given to Aethelric, another descendant of Ida. Here is a passage from the bard, Taliesin, that gives a sense of the atmosphere of the times:

> When Owain slew Fflamddwyn,
> It was no more than sleeping.
> Sleeps now the wide host of England,
> With the light upon their eyes,
> And those who fled not far,
> Were braver than was need . . .
> Splendid he was, in his many-coloured armour,
> Horses he gave to all who asked,
> Gathering wealth like a miser,
> Freely he shared it for his soul's sake,
> The soul of Owain, son of Urien,
> May the Lord look upon its need.

Owain ap Urien became part of the fabric of a remarkable, half-forgotten bardic tradition that lasted until the Tudors and the 16th century. He was hailed as a Son of Prophecy, *Y Mab Darogan*. Their bards never allowed Old Welsh speakers to forget that their kings once ruled in London and, as Anglo-Saxon incursion intensified after the defeats of the 6th century, they sang of the coming of a Redeemer, a Son of Prophecy who would expel the hordes of the Sais, the hated English, and drive them back into the sea that brought them. But, after the brief vengeance of Owain, what seems to have been a pivotal battle was fought at Catterick in North Yorkshire. This time, the alliance of Celtic kings was led by Yrfai map Golistan, Lord of Edinburgh, against the Angles who had established the kingdoms of Bernicia and Deira in Northumberland, Durham and North Yorkshire. His name shows that battle lines could be blurred, for Golistan, Yrfai's father, is a Celticised version of Wulfstan, clearly someone of Germanic origin. Perhaps he had fought as a mercenary for the Gododdin kings.

The battle at Catterick or Catraeth in 600 was a catastrophic defeat, a turning point in the history of Dark Age Scotland. It was recorded by Aneirin, the great bard of the Gododdin court at Edinburgh, who recounted the epic tale of warriors, their mead drinking, their comradeship, their honour, their battle splendour and the tragedy of their terrible defeat. He claimed to be one of only three survivors as the rapids or cataracts of the River Swale ran red with British blood.

> The retinue of Gododdin on rough-maned horses like swans,
> With their harness drawn tight,
> And attacking the troop in the van of the host,
> Defending the woods and the mead of Eidyn . . .
> The men went to Catraeth, they were renowned,
> Wine and mead from gold cups was their drink for a year,
> In accordance with the honoured custom.
> Three men and three score and three hundred,
> Wearing gold torcs,
> Of that hastened out after the choice drink,
> None escaped but three,
> Through feats of swordplay –
> The two war dogs of Aeron, and stubborn Cynon;
> And I too, streaming with blood,
> By grace of my brilliant poetry.

Elsewhere in the great, even brilliant, poem of the Gododdin, Aneirin referred almost casually to a very significant difference between the armies. The men who went to Catraeth called themselves *Y Bedydd*, 'the Baptised'. And, in the fateful year of 600, their enemies, the Angles, were *Y Gynt*, 'the Gentiles' or 'the Heathens'. It was not only a conflict between rival kings but also a contest between light and darkness, between the faithful followers of the Roman Church and those barbarians who had overthrown the Empire.

In the summer campaigning seasons immediately following the slaughter on the River Swale, these heathen war bands pressed home their advantage and raided and ranged far into the lands of the Gododdin kings. At Degsastan in 603, almost certainly Addinston at the head of Lauderdale, the Bernicians were led by a charismatic king. Aethelfrith was known by his enemies as *Am Fleisaur*, 'the Trickster', and, at Degsastan, the site of one of the most complete and dramatic hillforts in Scotland, his warriors defeated the allies of the Gododdin. These were the Gaelic-speaking raiders of Dalriada, another kingdom established by incomers. For generations, they had been settling on the coasts of Argyll. Led by Aedan mac Gabrain, the Gaels were the descendants of immigrants from Ulster and, for a time, the kindreds on either shore of the North Channel knew all of this small sea kingdom as Dalriada. It was to become very influential in the story of Scotland.

By 638, Din Eidyn had become Edinburgh as the great fortress on the castle rock fell to the kings of Anglian Bernicia. By that time, they had united with Deira, created a joint monarchy and converted to Christianity. After a period in exile at the court of Rheged, Edwin succeeded Aethelfrith the Trickster and Bede wrote about his baptism at Pallinsburn, just over the border near Cornhill. The burn took its name from St Paulinus, the sort of Roman Christian missionary the chronicler of Jarrow admired. Normally very scrupulous, the great scholar omitted to mention that, during his exile in Rheged, Edwin had been converted and baptised by Rhun, the brother of King Owain, and probably Bishop of Carlisle or Whithorn. The ceremony at Pallinsburn was evidently a mass baptism and Edwin may have consented to undergo another cold dunking to encourage his leading men to follow him into the faith. Under Edwin and his successors, what grew into the vigorous kingdom of Northumbria encompassed the Tweed Basin, Galloway and the Lothians as far west as Stirling Castle rock. The Angles brought the English language – what eventually became Scots – and, over the four centuries when their kings ruled over the most fertile and valuable part of early medieval Scotland, their culture became embedded and very influential.

After the dramas and reverses of the early 7th century, the realms of Gododdin and Rheged faded from the map. But one of the early post-Roman Celtic kingdoms of Scotland survived much longer, lingering in memory well into the Middle Ages. Dumbarton Rock is spectacular, a volcanic plug rising steeply on the north-eastern bank of the Firth of Clyde. Its summit fortress commanded the sea roads and also glowered over the River Leven as it led inland to Loch Lomond and the Vale of Leven. The oldest name is *Alt Cluith*, 'the Rock of the Clyde', but Gaelic speakers from Ireland rendered it as Dumbarton, *Dun Breatainn*, 'the Fort of the Britons', those who spoke Old Welsh. When the county council was established in 1889, the replacement of the 'm' with an 'n' remembered the antiquity of Dunbartonshire.

The Rock of the Clyde appears to have been a focus for one of the kindreds plotted on the 2nd-century map of Scotland made by Ptolemy. He called them the *Damnonii*, the 'People of the Deeps'. Cognate with Devon in the south-west of England, the name is probably a reference to a seagoing culture around the shores of the Clyde. Place names more than hint at the borders of this ancient polity. At the head of Loch Lomond, as the road climbs up to the watershed in Glen Falloch, there stands a singular, massive boulder. It is known as the *Clach nam Breatann*, the 'Stone of the Britons', and it marked a frontier with the Gaels of Dalriada. Lomond itself derives from the Old Welsh *llomon*, a 'beacon', and fires were lit on the slopes of the great mountains when hostile ships sailed down the loch to attack Alt Cluith. At the head of Loch Goil, there is another boundary stone, *An Clach a Breatunnach*, and below it is Blairlomond or Beacon Field. A line of Gaelic place names that include the word *criche* or *crioch*, meaning 'border', connect these stones and also run down the Toward Peninsula to the shores of the Firth of Clyde opposite Bute. But perhaps the most strategically important frontier posts were on the islands of the firth. A ring of coastal fortresses have been identified by the late Elizabeth Rennie, the archaeologist, on Bute and the Cumbraes. The latter is a modern calque that simply means the 'Islands of the Britons'. The Welsh term *Cymry* was coined in the post-Roman period and it comes from *combrogi*, a word that usually translates as 'compatriots' and carries unmistakable overtones of *cives Romani*. It has bequeathed to modern maps Cumbria and the Cumbraes.

The first substantial figure to emerge from the shadows of Dark Age Dumbarton is King Rhydderch Hael, Riderch the Generous. As the bards never ceased to sing, gift giving was a prime virtue of monarchs. Riderch reigned some time between AD 570 and 600 and his war bands were at the disastrous siege of Lindisfarne. But it is his relationship with the great saint of Alt Cluith and Glasgow that is more widely remembered. The story of Kentigern shades in and out of myth-history but some things are certain. His name is a Gaelicised version of *Cynderyn*, something akin to *Ceann Tighearna* or 'High Lord', a title rather than a name. Jocelyn of Furness's life of the saint recounts his semi-legendary beginnings as the love-child of Princess Thenu of Lleddiniawn, an early rendering of Lothian. Miraculously escaping the wrath of her royal father, the boy was raised at the monastery of Culross on the Forth by St Serf. He was given the term of endearment of *Mwyn Gwr*, 'Dear One', and this morphed into Mungo. What his given name actually was has seeped out of the narrative.

According to Jocelyn, Kentigern founded a monastery or a church on the banks of the Molendinar Burn, a tributary of the Clyde in what is now Glasgow. For some reason, he then fled south, probably to the community at Hoddom in Dumfriesshire. There, archaeologists have uncovered the remains of a baptistery where the saint might have performed the rituals. When he returned to the Clyde at the invitation of King Riderch, Kentigern's piety attracted many followers and the community by the Molendinar grew. *Familia* is a versatile Latin term often applied to such groups and some topo-nymists now believe that *Clas-Gu*, an Old Welsh version of 'Dear Family', is the origin of the place name of Glasgow.

Riderch's kingdom survived long after the Anglian surge across the Tweed and into the Lothians. In 731, Bede wrote of the Britons of the Clyde, 'Where there is a city of the Britons highly fortified to the present day and called Alcluith . . . the city of Alcluith, which in their language means the Rock of the Clyde, because it lies next to the river of that name.'

The persistence of the kingdom was surprising. Later known as Strathclyde, it briefly expanded into Cumbria and was still regarded as a distinct entity in 1018 when King Owain and Malcolm II fought against the Angles at Carham on the Tweed. As the old kingdom faded towards the end of the 11th century, its cultural echoes continued to resonate.

When clans began to form in the north and west, the Galbraiths estab-lished themselves on the island of Inchgalbraith in Loch Lomond, part of the ancient territory of Strathclyde. They probably still spoke a dialect of Old Welsh for their Gaelic surname means 'Foreign Briton' and their claimed name father was Gilchrist Breatnach, Gilchrist the Briton. Like Owain and the last of his dynasty, the Galbraiths adopted the boar's head as their emblem. Other clans whose lands bordered them, such as the Colquhouns, the MacArthurs and Clan Lennox, made similar ancestral links. But perhaps the most surprising and enduring link with the British past is the survival of the ancient system of counting in Old Welsh. In the Lakeland fells and in the Ayrshire Hills, shepherds continued well into the modern period to reckon the size of their flocks in the tongue of the Strathclyde kings. It has gone now but antiquaries once heard men count from one to ten as *yinty, tinty, tetheri, metheri, bamf, leetera, seetera, over, dover, dik.*

Galbraith was not the only Scottish surname to remember the long-lasting kingdom of the Clyde. The great hero of the Wars of Independence, William

Wallace, was probably born at Elderslie near Paisley, not far from Alt Cluith. In Gaelic Uallas is how his name is rendered and it means Welsh-speaker or Briton. It seems that the Gaelic warriors who fought alongside Wallace at Stirling Bridge and Falkirk knew him as Uilleam Breatnach, William the Briton. But memories were fading fast when James MacPherson, the literary embellisher of the 18th century, wrote this elegy for the kings on the Rock of the Clyde.

> I have seen the walls of Balaclutha,
> But they were desolate.
> The thistle shook its lonely head;
> The moss whistled in the wind.

Scotland between the Roman walls, sometimes known as the Intervallum, was a place where different cultures competed as kings and their war bands contended for power. Across Galloway, the Tweed Basin, the Lothians and the valley of the Clyde two different languages described the landscape, transmitted ideas and sang of glory and defeat. But north of the Antonine Wall, two more speech communities would vie for dominance and one would determine Scotland's political direction into the Middle Ages.

Hostage exchange as a guarantee of loyalty and obedience was a widely used facet of politics in 5th-century Ireland and Scotland. Lesser kings gave hostages, usually family members, to more powerful kings and the number held at the courts of the mighty was eloquent about just how mighty they were. Tradition holds that the first High King of Ireland reigned in the middle of the 5th century and that he was Niall Noigiallach, Niall of the Nine Hostages, the ruler over nine sub-kingdoms. These may have included the five provinces of Ireland and four more hostages sent across the North Channel from subkingdoms in what is now Scotland.

Powerful men in the past not only commanded warriors, they also exercised privileges of another sort over women, willing or unwilling. Studies of ancestral DNA have revealed a process known as social selection whereby kings, leaders and magnates had sex with several, often many, different women. In this way they passed on their Y-chromosome DNA to many descendants. And there were few kings who passed it on to more than Niall Noigiallach.

In 2006, the extraordinary genetic legacy of the High King was identified by scientists at Trinity College, Dublin. Niall's Y-chromosome lineage, labelled R1b-M222, turned out to be very common indeed in Ireland, carried by no fewer than 20 per cent of all men. Weighted heavily to the north where 40 per cent of Ulstermen have it and fading to the south where between 10 per cent and 15 per cent of Leinstermen carry the DNA marker, it shows how remarkably influential social selection can be. R1b-M222 is also found in 7 per cent of all Scotsmen but only 1.8 per cent of Englishmen and its transmission traces the arrival of the Gaelic language and culture in the west of Scotland.

The energetic Niall Noigiallach reigned some time in the middle of the 5th century and some of his descendants sailed the North Channel to settle in Argyll. The old Gaelic version of the name remembers the coming of warriors from Ireland, as, according to a later bard, *Earra-Ghàidheal* means the 'Coast of the Gaels'. And writing in the 730s, Bede recorded what sounds like a series of events, a mixture of invasion and colonisation that still survived in memory: 'As time went on, Britain received a third nation, that of the Irish: they migrated from Ireland under their chieftain Reuda and by a combination of force and treaty, obtained from the Picts the settlements that they still hold. From the name of this chieftain, they are still known as Dalreudians, for in their tongue dal means a division.'

His rule may have bridged the North Channel and, in the early years of the Dalriadan kingdoms, they included coastal areas of eastern Ulster. Other kindreds followed Reuda and his war bands and a sense of their military and civil organisation has survived in a very unusual document. Compiled in the middle of the 7th century, the *Senchus Fer nAlban* or the 'History of the Men of Scotland' is a form of census, a muster roll of warriors who appear to have fought in the style of marines. It lists three major kindreds in the territory of Argyll and the basic unit of assessment was the *tech* or 'house' (*taigh* in modern Gaelic). Here are the details:

Cenel nOengusa (the Kindred of Angus on Islay) 430 houses
Cenel Loairne (the Kindred of Lorne in Lorne and Appin) 420 houses
Cenel nGabrain (the Kindred of Gabran in Kintye) 560 houses

These houses may have resembled crofts or small farms and they varied in size. The Islay houses were thought to be smaller. But each group of 20 techs was bound to provide 28 oarsmen, enough warriors to row two seven-bench seagoing curraghs. If all had been mustered at once, the kindreds of the *Senchus* could put to sea a powerful fleet of 140 curraghs carrying a force of almost 2,000 marines. The *Senchus* is a remarkable document for the times. Perhaps other British and European kindreds organised themselves along similar lines but their records have not survived.

The *Senchus* is also an early outing of the Gaelic word for Scotland. *Alba*, pronounced 'Alapa', was first used by Ptolemy in the 2nd century AD when he wrote it as 'Albion'. The name was applied to the whole island of Britain and, although obscure, its use lasted long enough for Napoleon to complain of 'perfidious Albion' and, by the late 19th century, the founders of football clubs in Stirling, West Bromwich, Brighton and elsewhere also incorporated it in the names of their teams. Used by the Irish Gaelic-speaking settlers in western Scotland, it may simply have been a straightforward adoption of Ptolemy's term for Britain, the larger island, but its derivation is intriguing. *Alba* stems from the Indo-European root word for 'white' and perhaps for those who approached across the English Channel, the first sight of land was the chalk-white cliffs of Dover. Or more fancifully, the Irish may have used the name of *Alba*, 'White-Land', because of the snow-capped mountains they could see rising up beyond the shores of Argyll.

In the first sentence of his great history, Bede wrote of 'Britain, formerly known as Albion' and does not use the term again. Later, he turned to the mission of St Columba who certainly did know of a place called Alba:

> Columba arrived in Britain in the ninth year of the reign of the powerful Pictish king, Bride son of Meilochon; he converted that people to the Faith of Christ by his preaching and example, and received from them the island of Iona on which to found a monastery. Iona is a small island, with an area of about five hides according to the English reckoning, and his successors hold it to this day. It was here that Columba died and was buried at the age of seventy-seven, some thirty-two years after he had come to Britain to preach. Before he came to Britain he had founded a noble monastery in Ireland known in the Irish language as Dearmach, the Field of Oaks [Durrow, in County Offaly in the centre of Ireland – in fact, the name means the 'Plain of Oaks'], because of the oak forest in which it stands. From both these monasteries Columba's disciples went out and founded many others in Britain and Ireland; but the monastery on the isle of Iona, where his body lies, remains the chief of them all.

Bede did not know of *The Life of St Columba* completed at the end of the 7th century by Adomnan, one of the saint's successors at Iona. This wonderfully vivid and well-written hagiography enshrined Columba's fame, helped create his cult and exaggerated his role in the Christian conversion of Scotland. Others sailed from Ireland with the Word of God but the work and sacrifice of Saints Maelrubha, Comgall and Moluag have been largely forgotten. They had no hagiographers but place names sometimes commemorate their coming. St Donnan was martyred on the island of Eigg by 'robbers of the sea' with 52 of his fellow monks and his hermitage on the tiny island of Eilean Donan was obliterated by a romantic and famous castle. Kildonan was the site of another church founded by him, probably in the early 7th century.

THE COLOURS OF MARTYRDOM

An early Irish text of the 7th or 8th century listed three colours of martyrdom. Red martyrs were those who shed blood through violent death, such as those who were slaughtered by the Viking raiders. White martyrdom was used to describe the severe asceticism of those monks who shivered in sea-girt hermitages, separating themselves from companionship and spending a life in prayer and meditation to bring themselves closer to God. Using the Gaelic word glas, *meaning 'blue', 'green' and sometimes 'grey', the Irish text talked of another martyrdom, one of denial, of fasting or mortification of the flesh. Monks immersed themselves in freezing water or lay on beds of nettles or·hazelnut shells, in search of salvation.*

Columba was an Irish aristocrat, reputedly the great-great-grandson of Niall Noigiallach. Perhaps he carried the Y-chromosome marker of R1b-M222, although his piety probably prevented him from passing it on. He did pass on the monastery on Iona and the abbots who followed were all early princes of the Church who inherited its property. The usual Irish Gaelic term for an abbot is *comharba* and it can also mean an 'heir'. In Adomnan's *Life*, a striking theme was the business of copying, writing and illustrating gospels – an activity that underlines the early belief in the power of the Word of God as a physical object. Above all, Christianity was seen as a religion not concerned with images but with the book. It seems that a dispute over Columba's copying of a gospel in Northern Ireland was a contributory factor in his departure across the North Channel. And this dispute over copyright may indeed have led to fighting.

What sparked such passion was the iconic nature of the gospel books. Illuminated manuscripts were made less to be read than to be revered, opened on the altar and worshipped as the sacred Word of God. Famously, the Book of Kells, probably begun on Iona, contains many errors in the text; one page has been copied twice and it was never completed. But that mattered much less than its sumptuous decoration and its tremendous power as a sacred biblical text.

When Columba and his small band of followers rowed their curraghs to Iona, they carried with them the Irish tradition of copying. As conversion proceeded, the Word of God was needed by new congregations and foundations so thousands of Irish monks laboured over their pages to meet demand. Between AD 450 and 850, they made more than half of the biblical commentaries which survive in Europe from that time. And, in doing so, they also established the defining shape of cultural transmission. Throughout the classical period, books were written on scrolls but the fact that the gospels were copied on to calfskin meant that opened books were rectangular in shape. A huge investment, two hundred calfskins were used in the creation of the Book of Kells. The younger the calf, the whiter and smoother the skins and it was not uncommon for foetuses to be aborted to feed the demand for perfect vellum (the Old French word for a calf is *vélin*). And an international trade in pigment began between the Mediterranean and Ireland and the Atlantic coast of Scotland. The gorgeous ultramarine blue, ground from lapis lazuli from Afghanistan and used for the illuminated capitals and the so-called carpet pages of the great gospels, was probably the farthest travelled. Folium was extracted from Mediterranean sunflowers and gave a spectrum of pink to purple while a bright red called kermes was made from dried and crushed insects from Southern Europe and North Africa. Merchants carrying these small, light and valuable cargoes sailed amongst the Hebridean islands to supply the monks with colour.

As an aristocrat and a politician, Columba's mission and the foundation of his monastery (the equivalent Gaelic term of *diseart* makes a clear link with the Desert Fathers, a reference to the early Christian hermits of the near east) on Iona was bound up with his relationship with the Dalriadan kings. The singular rock of Dunadd, near Kilmartin in Argyll, is not only dramatic but also naturally defensible with sheer cliffs on three sides and a steep approach on the fourth. A 1st-millennium fortress was built on the crag by the River Add and the flat and boggy moorland surrounding the site added to its great strength. Most of the rampart is now tumbled down but a steep path still climbs through the narrow gateway to reach the summit. Carved into the rock are the remains of ancient ritual. Often filled with rainwater, a footprint and a basin were probably used in the coronation ceremonies for new kings of Dalriada, or for the kindred that held Southern Argyll, the Cenel nGabrain.

In 574, Columba almost certainly took a leading role in the anointing or sanctifying of King Aedan macGabrain. Perhaps the ritual involved some form of baptism. Or it may be an invention. In his life of the saint, Adomnan may have made up the tale as a handy precedent and justification for the close involvement of the abbots of Iona in Dalriadan politics. If it really happened, it was the first such blessing made at a coronation in British history.

In any event, Columba certainly sailed home to Ireland with King Aedan in 575 to attend the Convention of Druim Cett where they met Aed mac Ainmuirech, High King of the Ui Neill kindreds of Ulster. He may have been a cousin of the saint, a link that will have encouraged Aedan to have Columba at his side. It seems that the Dalriadan kindreds paid tribute and may have sent hostages to Irish kings. Aed and Aedan agreed that the Dalriadan fleet would be mobilised in support of the Ui Neill in time of need but that no tribute was owed. And warriors would only be summoned to join the Irish host from those territories of Dalriada in Ulster.

After his defeat at Degsastan in 603, the chroniclers had little to say about Aedan except to report his death, probably in 609. As high king of the Dalriadan kindreds, he was succeeded by his son, Eochaid Buidhe and, in a note of delayed triumph, Bede wrote that Degsastan marked a historical turning point because 'from that day until the present no king of the Irish in Britain dared to do battle with the English'. But others did.

There exists nothing like the *Senchus Fer nAlban* or the great epic of the Gododdin to commemorate the Pictish kingdoms of Scotland. Instead there are stones. The landscape of northern and eastern Scotland is studded with the sites of deeply enigmatic symbol stones. Sometimes human figures are carved on them and very occasionally a narrative can be made out but most of the stones show a series of symbols such as z-rods, crescents, v-rods, what look like combs and mirrors and a double disc that might be interpreted as a stylised chariot. Several recognisable animals were carved – snakes, wolves, bulls, eagles, salmon and what might be bottle-nosed dolphins. But there are no inscriptions in the Pictish language. The distribution of the stones across Scotland is usually linked to that of 'pit-' place names such as Pitlochry or Pittodrie (this prefix is from one of the very few identifiable Pictish words – *pit* for 'a portion of land') to give an impression of the territories ruled by Pictish kings.

When Bede wrote of Columba, he noted that the *diseart* – a place set apart for religious contemplation – on Iona had been the gift of a presumably pious Pictish king. Further up the Atlantic seaboard, archaeology confirms that Skye had once been a Pictish island. But the distribution of stones and pit- names plot a more easterly location for what might be called Pictland. In the late 7th century, it stretched from the Northern Isles to the shores of the Moray Firth, around the Mounth and down through Angus, the Mearns, Tayside and Perthshire and on into Fife. By that time, there appear to have been seven Pictish kingdoms or provinces. An Irish tradition sometimes associated with Columba lists the descendants of *Cruithne*, the Gaelic word for 'Pict', as the progenitors of the kingdoms.

> Seven of Cruithne's children divided Alba into seven divisions,
> the portion of Cat, of Ce, of Cirech, children with hundreds of possessions,
> the portion of Fib, of Fidaid, of Fotla, and of Fortriu.
> And it is the name of each man of them that is on his land.

In his superb *The History of the Celtic Place-Names of Scotland*, W. J. Watson combined this text with a 12th-century version to compile this list of Pictish provinces or kingdoms:

Cirech (also spelled Circenn), Angus and the Mearns
Fotla, Atholl and Gowrie
Fortriu, Strathearn and Menteith
Fib, Fife with Fothreue
Ce, Mar and Buchan
Fidaid, Moray and Easter Ross
Cat, Caithness and S.E Sutherland

The first or principal portion of each province was held directly by a king, a *regulus*, while the smaller territory was ruled on his behalf by a sub-king. Some have survived into the modern period and one these, Angus and the Mearns, illustrates the structure of Pictish royal power. Sub-kings became *mormaers*, meaning 'great stewards'. Deriving from the Latin *maior*, it was eventually rendered as 'mayor'. This term is cognate to Mearns and an alternative might be 'the Stewartry'. The king of Cirech or Angus controlled the Mearns through a sub-king who was ultimately demoted to mormaer or great steward. The shadow of this relationship lasted into the 20th century with the larger county of Angus and the smaller Kincardineshire.

Bede noted that Columba arrived on Iona during the reign of King Bridei map Maelchon and Adomnan added that the saint visited his court somewhere near Inverness in AD 565 on a mission of conversion (which did not succeed). Important courtiers attended the Pictish king, amongst them the King of Orkney. Not described as a sub-*regulus*, he may have held sway over Shetland or Caithness. But Bridei was certainly paramount for Adomnan wrote of hostages held at the fortress near Inverness and described the king as '*rex potentissimus*'. It may be that this most powerful man was the High King of the Pictish provinces north of the Mounth, the point north of Stonehaven where the Grampian massif almost reaches the North Sea, and that he controlled Ce, Fidaid, Cat and Orkney.

Towards the end of the 7th century, Pictish royal power south of the Mounth settled on the high kingship of Fortriu, or Strathearn and Menteith. In the 8th and 9th centuries, Pictish kings were always styled as Kings of Fortriu just as Irish High Kings were always Kings of Tara. But how the less exalted saw themselves is elusive – the evidence for the doings of kings is sparse and for the lives of ordinary people, even sparser. No written records, except those kept by outsiders, survive even to hint at how the mass of the people, almost all of them farmers, understood the world. Certainly, by the later 7th century, the elite were Christians but a sense of the pagan past that might have lingered much longer amongst the ordinary people of Pictland – and a sense of identity – might be seen on the symbol stones.

Intended to be read and to be meaningful to a non-literate society, these stones seem to have been set up as boundary markers and memorials. Amongst the earliest are carvings of animals, about ten clearly identifiable species, and these were probably a link with some of the kindred names plotted on Ptolemy's map of the 2nd century such as the Lugi or Raven People or the Epidii, the Horse Masters. He noted a place called Tarvedunum on the southern shore of the Moray Firth, at Burghead. It means the Bull Fort and, around the remains of the impressive Pictish sea fortress on the headland, carvings of bulls have been found. It may well be that the stones marked the capital place of the Bull People. Others remembered the lands of the Dolphin People, the Eagle People and the Salmon Folk and so on. No clear pattern emerges but that may be a consequence of accidental survival. About 200 Pictish symbol stones have been recognised but farmers seeking handy slabs of dressed stone for gateposts or lintels may have hidden or destroyed hundreds more.

FORTRIU

It is often mind-clearing to upend the conventional historical wisdom, and in the case of Pictish history there have been considerable recent convulsions. The kingdom of Fortriu, what was usually possessed by any Pictish king with a claim to paramountcy, is long believed to have been in the south, below the Grampian massif, amongst the provinces found in what is now Perthshire, Tayside, Fife and Angus, probably in Strathearn. But recent scholarship has suggested a radical relocation north of the mountains. Not only do some now believe that Fortriu, and hence the centre of the Pictish kingdom, was to be found in the Moray coastlands, but they also judge that the Battle of Dunnichen was fought near Kingussie. The latter seems unlikely. There is a very detailed relief carving on a high status stone of a battle between Anglian warriors and Picts at Aberlemno, a long way south of Kingussie. There is also the logistical issue of King Ecgfrith's unfeasibly extended lines of communication and supply. To reach the forces of King Bridei at Kingussie, Ecgfrith would have had to lead his men through little known and hostile country where the danger of ambush loomed around each corner. As to the location of Fortriu, there are good arguments for and against. But this radical relocation might have more to do with the perceived imperatives of Academe. As one historical knight once remarked, the younger members of his discipline are often tempted to murder their fathers. Figuratively speaking, of course.

The symbols themselves are harder to parse but they may hark back to a pre-Christian past. In the 1st millennium BC, part of religious observance was the ritual depositing of metal objects, the most precious items people could own, in watery places. Thousands of pieces of metal have been discovered preserved in anaerobic bogs and at the muddy bottom of rivers and lakes all over Scotland. Duddingston Loch in Edinburgh appears to have had a jetty built out into the deeper water where priests in some unknowable ceremonial threw away swords, dirks, spears and other iron objects so that they could not be retrieved. The weapons were often slighted, that is, bent or even broken. This may have represented some sort of obeisance to the water gods but, however that may be, the practice makes a clear link with the symbols on Pictish stones. For example, the v-rod has been interpreted as a broken arrow, the z-rod as a broken spear and the so-called tuning fork as a slighted sword. Other items such as circular metal shields, impractically heavy, have been found in places in Scotland, most notably near Yetholm in the foothills of the Cheviots, and these are also represented in the lexicon of symbols.

THE DUPPLIN CROSS

Dated to around AD 800, the cross was later moved from a hillside near Forteviot (thought to be a central location in the kingdom of Fortriu) to the shelter of St Serf's Church in Dunning. At 2.5 metres, it is impressive and beautifully carved, but its principle focus of interest is the inscription. Some of it is illegible but the phrase 'Custantin Filius Fircus' *can be made out. This allows the cross to be dated to the reign of Constantine I, the son of Fergus, from 789 to 820, and it serves as one of the few fixed, datable points in Pictish history. It is also an indication of a society developing a royal and hierarchical shape, moving away from the emphasis on the Pictish tribal provinces and their rulers.*

Carved on the stones, these metaphorical sacrifices were intended to be seen and understood as offerings in propitiation to a pantheon of ancient gods who were not necessarily benign and, as such, may have been acceptable in a developing Christian context, certainly more acceptable than the old ceremonies of deposit. Later stones sometimes have a cross on one side and the old v-rods and z-rods on the other. Perhaps this juxtaposition tracked a process of religious transition. Also intended to be seen and read, tattooing not only gave the Picts their nickname, it was also a visible means of marking allegiances and identity. And it may be that some of the designs on the stones were replicated on the bodies of warriors or even kings.

At Aberlemno stands one of the most impressive and informative of all of these stones. Walking up the path into the churchyard, the visitor is greeted by a massive slab with what is usually known as a Celtic cross carved in high relief. There is a hole bored through in the top right-hand angle of the cross and it is flanked by beautifully fluid representations of Pictish animals. On the other side, facing the wall of the church and not immediately visible, is a record of one of the turning points of Scotland's history.

In the afternoon of Saturday 20 May 685, a Northumbrian cavalry force was drawn into a trap in a landscape that has largely disappeared. Near the town of Forfar the ruins of Restenneth Priory overlie an earlier monastery founded by Pictish kings. It was probably seen as a diseart, a place apart from the world because it was surrounded on three sides by a lake that was drained in the late 18th century. Loch Restenneth lay to the east and south of the old diseart and, in the Pictish language, it was probably known as *Linn Garan*, the 'Crane Lake'. To the west was a narrow piece of land and beyond it another loch, Loch Forfar, which has also been drained. Between the two bodies of water and the boggy ground at their edges, a troop of Pictish cavalry pretended to retreat. And spurring on their horses, scenting a quick victory, a force of about 500 warriors led by King Ecgfrith of Northumbria gave chase – and rode into a trap where they were confronted by ranks of infantry commanded by the King of Fortriu, Bridei mapBili.

These two men, adversaries from what were two distinctive cultures, were in fact cousins. Bridei was the son of Bili, King of Alt Cluith, and his mother was a daughter of Edwin who had succeeded to the throne of Northumbria half a century before the battle at the Crane Lake. There were also cultural as well as dynastic links. From what scholars can deduce, Pictish seems to have been a dialect of the P-Celtic group of languages, almost certainly intelligible to the kings on Dumbarton Rock. The people of Pictland did not share a language with the Northumbrians but there may have been a more political connection. It appears that the Kings of Fortriu paid tribute to the Angles and what almost certainly brought Ecgfrith and his cavalry north was default, the refusal of Bridei to continue to send tribute to Bamburgh. Bede related what happened next: 'For in the following year King Ecgfrith, ignoring the advice of his friends and in particular of Cuthbert, rashly led an army to ravage the province of the Picts. The enemy pretended to retreat, and lured the king into narrow mountain passes, where he was killed with the greater part of his forces.'

The stone in Aberlemno churchyard adds welcome detail to that brief account. It shows three ranks of Pictish infantry, probably drawn up on the slopes of Dunnichen Hill, as they wait for the charge of the Northumbrian cavalry. Holding up his spiked shield high and carrying a sword, the warrior in the front rank is supported by his comrade behind him who pushes out his spear beyond the first rank so that he can stab at the enemy. Behind both of these men stands a third warrior, apparently in reserve. Horses will wheel away from a solid phalanx of infantry who stand fast and close up quickly if men fall and gaps appear. Bridei lured the Anglian cavalry to fight on ground of his choosing, a narrow place where he could not be easily outflanked and surrounded. The Aberlemno Stone shows that the Pictish infantry did indeed stand fast for in another scene their cavalry chase a fleeing Northumbrian, his shield thrown away. And in the bottom left-hand corner a figure, probably Ecgfrith, is shown lying dead and being pecked at by the symbol of battlefield carnage, a raven.

The victory at Dunnichen, or in early English, Nechtansmere, or in Old Welsh, Linn Garan, the Crane Lake, was a pivotal moment, famous in two languages perhaps because it influenced their spread. The juggernaut of the Anglian advance was halted and rolled back to south of the Forth. Having established an Episcopal see at Abercorn in West Lothian and having fortified Stirling Castle Rock, Northumbrian kings were forced to abandon these gains permanently. Bede was unequivocal about the consequences of Ecgfrith's defeat at the Crane Lake: 'Henceforward the hopes and strength of the English realm began "to waver and slip backward ever lower". The Picts recovered their own lands that had been occupied by the English, while the Irish living in Britain and a proportion of the Britons themselves regained their freedom which they have now preserved for about forty-six years. Many of the English at this time were killed, enslaved, or forced to flee from Pictish territory.'

Had Dunnichen been lost and the Pictish kingdom badly weakened, the character of Scotland might have been different with Anglian influence stretching far further north. Indeed, there might have been no Scotland at all for Bede seemed to imply that the Gaels and the Britons were also paying tribute to Ecgfrith. Instead, Scotland entered the 8th century as four distinctive and independent cultural zones – the Gaelic-speaking kindreds of Dalriada in the west, the Old Welsh-speaking kingdom of Alt Cluith/Strathclyde on the Clyde, the Northumbrian territory in the Lothians and the Tweed Basin and Pictland north of the Forth.

As the 8th century opened, Pictland appeared resurgent, its rulers vigorous. Bridei was succeeded by his brother Nechtan who reigned between 706 and 724 and probably established himself as Rex Pictorum, High King of all the kindreds north and south of the Mounth. After he abdicated to retire to the peace of monastic life, perhaps at the foundation on the windy headland at St Andrews, years of turmoil followed and the old king put on his war gear once more to lead warriors into battle. In 728–29, Oengus, a contender for the throne and a prince with a Gaelic name, was victorious at a place called Monith Carno, almost certainly the Cairn o' Mounth near Fettercairn. That this was a zone of contention between the kings of the northern and southern Picts is recalled in an old place name. In the 10th century, the area where the Grampian Mountains almost meet the North Sea was known as *Claideom* – the 'Swordland'.

Oengus I emerged as Nechtan's successor and, by 736, his war bands were riding west into Dalriada. In that year, he captured the citadel of Dunadd and his brother, Talorcan, scattered a Dalriadan army nearby on the shores of Loch Awe. Dynastic politics pushed and pulled at the web of allegiances in the west and with the intervention of Teudubr, King of Strathclyde, the Picts had been driven back eastwards by 750.

What all these convulsions meant to the farmers who worked in the fields and the shepherds who drove their herds and flocks up to the high pasture each spring on the ancient journey of transhumance can only be guessed at. When kings and their war bands came, destruction often followed in their wake and the smoke of burning homesteads blew in the wind. Unless they were surprised, sensible farmers and their families will have fled into the hills and high ground where their beasts were summering and where they might keep them out of the sight of foraging horsemen. No one willingly stood in the path of raiding war bands. In any case, what happened on the battlefield probably did not affect the lives of farmers. They paid in kind to whichever lord had power over them and, if incomers wished the land they hoped to control to retain its productivity, they did not trail too much destruction and death in their wake.

What mattered were bonds of loyalty. When Oengus and his men rode up Kilmartin Glen after reducing the fortress at Dunadd, they were not invading and occupying Dalriadan territory in a modern sense. What they hoped to achieve was an expansion in their network of loyalty and dependency. Military success bred more success because it attracted warriors to the standard of the victors and their ability to dole out gold, gifts and privileges. And borders rarely meant what they mean now as power ebbed and flowed and allegiances changed.

It seems that tribute was often paid in cattle. And it is likely that much of Scotland north of the Forth depended on a pastoral economy. Cereals were certainly grown in the small inbye fields but were for human consumption only. Cultivated year in year out like large garden plots, these fields were mucked in the winter by beasts brought down from the upland pasture in late autumn and fed on whatever dry forage farmers had been able to cut in the autumn. Nevertheless, the fertility of the inbye must have fluctuated and needed management.

At Yeavering, near Wooler in Northumberland, archaeologists have uncovered some evidence of the role of cattle as tribute. The excavations of Brian Hope-Taylor and his teams revealed an extensive Northumbrian royal complex, a series of halls, a remarkable wooden structure nicknamed the grandstand, which was probably used for meetings and audiences with the king, and also large corrals. These enclosures were probably where incoming tribute cattle were penned and where some were subsequently distributed to important royal supporters – members of the *comitatus*, the war band and of the household. Cattle raiding was also an integral part of warfare and the battle at Degsastan was probably fought around the wonderfully well-preserved fort at Addinston in Lauderdale because its high ramparts were useful as a defended corral for reived cows.

Aethelfrith, the Northumbrian victor at Degsastan, had been a pagan but his successors saw the political advantages of Christian conversion, as well as the spiritual advantages, no doubt. In the 8th century, kings in Scotland appear to have valued the close involvement of the Church, often acting with the advice of bishops and indeed being themselves genuinely pious. If King Nechtan took holy orders of some kind at St Andrews, it appears that he or his successor may also have contributed something more enduring – a spectacular testament to the cultural vigour of their kingdom.

In 1833, a gang of gravediggers began work somewhere between St Rule's Tower and the ruins of St Andrews Cathedral. Only seven years before they pushed their shovels into the turf, the debris of the tremendous destruction wreaked on the great church and shrine of Scotland's patron saint by the zeal of the Reformation had been finally cleared away and the ancient precincts began once more to receive burials. As they dug down, the workmen came across a series of stone fragments. Some were large and carried remarkable relief sculpture – a man dressed in what looked like Roman robes killing a lion with his bare hands, a mounted hunter in pursuit of lions and a huntsman on foot as well as much beautiful decorative carving. No one appeared to take much notice of what had been lifted out of the ground. In 1836, the Rev. Dr Dibdin arrived, announced that the sculpture was Saxon and promptly removed a fragment for display in a museum in York. On 19th December 1839, the *Fife Herald* reported: 'So lightly were these priceless relics prized at the seat of the oldest University in Scotland, that for 6 years they lay tumbled about as if of no interest or consequence to anyone what-ever.' Or of much value. But gradually what the gravediggers had unearthed began to be recognised for it was.

The St Andrews Sarcophagus is not only a stunning example of Pictish art showing international influences from the Eastern Mediterranean as well as links with the art of Northumbria, it was also built as a shrine, one of the earliest indications of the growing importance of the early monastic foundations on the headland. In 747 the Irish annalists listed Tuathalan as the Abbot of Cinrigh Monaid. The place name was later rendered Kinrymont, an early name for St Andrews and it indicated royal associations. Meaning 'At the Head of the King's Moor', it is a reference to the promontory upon which the early churches and the later medieval cathedral were built. The moor or, better, the muir, a term that meant rough, uncultivated ground rather than a bog, stretched south to Crail and the shores of the Forth. It may have been an early royal hunting reserve where parties of aristocrats rode out after the wild boar. The area was later known as the *Cursus Apri*, the 'Boar's Raik' or 'Boar's Range' and the hunt is commemorated in the village name of Boarhills.

This beautifully made, sumptuously decorated sarcophagus appears to have been commissioned to house the remains of the body of a king rather than a saint. It may have been the wish of the pious Nechtan to be laid to rest in this massive stone coffin, protected by the lion killer (thought to be King David of the Old Testament) and revered by his subjects. Perhaps his monkish piety had made him a saint as well. But scholars believe that the more likely candidate was Oengus I. Shrines such as the St Andrews Sarcophagus were intended as an attraction for worshippers and especially pilgrims, for people who would come to touch it and, through that physical contact, have sanctity or *virtus* transmitted directly to them. The sick hoped to be cured, the sinful shriven. The tomb says something about the innate sanctity of kingship, something that persisted long after the medieval period and is remembered in the habit of common people wishing to touch the hem of royal robes. It must also be significant that the St Andrews sculptor included no Pictish symbols in the design, no z-rods, crescents or discs, and, if these were understood as relics of the pagan past, that connection might have been unwelcome in the precincts of the church at the head of the king's moor.

The style of the garments carved for the King David figure is thought to reflect *imitatio imperii*, a wish for Pictish and other British kings to bask in the afterglow of the glory of imperial Rome. In 789, names began to make more of that link when Constantine I became King of Pictland. Twenty-two years later, he also became King of Dalriada, the first to reign over both Picts and Scots. Names hint that a process of political and cultural unification had been under way for some time. In the list of Pictish provinces, two have clear Gaelic origins. Atholl is a modern version of *Ath Fotla* and it meant

'New Ireland' while Gowrie has a link with Gabran, the father of Aedan macGabrain, King of Dalriada at the end of the 6th and beginning of the 7th centuries. And rendered as *Causantin* in Gaelic, Constantine himself may have had origins in the west. His father was Fergus and, in 820, his brother succeeded Constantine as Oengus II.

Events would also push the focus of royal power further east – events that changed Scotland and Britain dramatically. On 8 June 793, the Vikings sailed out of nowhere and attacked the monastery on Lindisfarne. This is the entry in the *Anglo-Saxon Chronicle*: '793. Here terrible portents came about over the land of Northumbria, and miserably frightened the people: there were immense flashes of lightning, and fiery dragons were seen flying in the air. A great famine immediately followed these signs; and a little after that . . . the raiding of heathen men miserably devastated God's church in Lindisfarne by looting and slaughter.'

IRISH VIKINGS IN EAST LOTHIAN

Half-forgotten kings and ancient alliances that led nowhere were lit by a surprising discovery at Auldhame in East Lothian in 2005. The skeleton of a young man was found with grave goods that suggested a person of high rank and, in particular, there was a belt that spoke of links with the Ui Imar dynasty. These were Viking kings who ruled on both sides of the Irish Sea and who had designs on the kingdom of York or Jorvik. Their route from Ireland across the narrow waist of Scotland took them past the shores of East Lothian. King Olaf Guthfrithsson defeated his enemies at Limerick and then moved to make good his family's claim on York. King Owain of Strathclyde became his ally and Olaf married the daughter of Constantine II of Scotland. He had power in Northumbria and, in 941, attacked the communities at Auldhame and nearby Tyninghame, places associated with St Baldred. When he died in the same year, he may well have been buried in the sacred ground (no doubt having many earthly sins that needed cleansing) walked by the saint. And archaeologists may just have found his body.

When sea lords roared at their oarsmen to row hard for the shore and rasp up the keels of their dragon ships on the shingle beach below the monastery, the monks will have fled for the safety and sanctuary of God's holy church. There the shrine of Cuthbert, the great saint of the north, would surely protect them. But as Viking warriors hacked with their axes and smashed down the doors, the defenceless, terrified monks will have been appalled at the impiety. These raiders were pagans, defilers of the sacred ground where Cuthbert walked and the place where he knelt to pray. The Anglo-Saxon chronicler wrote of slaughter and the looting of the church's treasures, the ransacking of places so revered that they had needed no protection except God's. The shock of this first contact reverberated around the shores of Britain and Ireland. Monastic annalists came to call the Northmen the Sons of Death.

What drove these bands of men to sail 'westoversea' in search of plunder is not well understood. Perhaps it was population pressure, with too many mouths needing to be fed by too little farmland. Perhaps raiding up and down the jagged Norwegian coast became a way of life for dispossessed seagoing warriors in a violent society where goods and lands were grabbed. In Old Norse, what happened at Lindisfarne was known as a *strandhogg*, a 'beach raid', and perhaps these were common in the fjords in the late 8th century. If they were, it was therefore only a matter of time before sea lords looked west across the open expanses of the North Sea and wondered what lay over the horizon.

In the centuries before compasses, sextants and charts, navigation was not a precise science. But Britain presented a long, 800-mile target, difficult to miss for those who could use the sun, the moon and the stars to guide them on a course set to the south-west. The beach raid on Lindisfarne is unlikely to have been a matter of happenstance. Earlier, unrecorded crossings were probably made. Shetland lies only 200 miles from the Norwegian coast – two days sailing before a westerly wind. A sense of adventure, a wish to discover what lay beyond the sea may seem like overly romantic motives for these dangerous voyages across the open water, out of the comforting sight of land, but not implausible. And part of the reason the Northmen sailed west to burst into the history of Scotland and Britain was because they could.

In the elegant shape of the dragon ships, the feared and famed *dreki*, the Vikings built the first, fast seagoing vessels of northern Europe that could also penetrate inland, sliding up rivers and sea lochs. Sleek and with a shallow draught, the longships were so called because of their shape, usually more than 130 feet, and they were stronger and better built than any other ship afloat. Their narrow shape and a powerful side rudder, the steerboard (the origin of starboard), helped the *dreki* ride out storms and their draught meant that they sat on top of the roiling waves like a seagull. With a normal complement of thirty oars and a billowing square sail, the sea lords could call for rates of knots through the water and, much more slowly, these beautiful craft could go into reverse. Their double-ended construction and side rudder meant that, in shallow rivers, the danger of being stranded on sandbanks was much reduced.

The Vikings have left a more enduring legacy than the annalists' entries or even the dense scatter of Norse place names across northern landscapes. In at least 100,000 Scotsmen the Y-chromosome DNA of the Vikings lives on. As might be expected, their direct descendants make up a high percentage of the male population of Shetland (29 per cent), Orkney (25 per cent) as well as Caithness and the Outer Hebrides. Small groups of men who came ashore in small boats began to settle in the Northern Isles and the archipelago of the inshore Atlantic seaways. Some women came from Norway and Scandinavia but most often these sea raiders settled to become farmers and took native women as their partners. That pattern is the reason for the DNA legacy of the Vikings being most obvious in male lineages.

After the reverberating shock of the attack on Lindisfarne, the deliberately isolated and vulnerable communities of the west were plundered repeatedly. A year after the church of St Cuthbert was ransacked, the communities founded on Eigg and Skye and in Applecross by St Donan and St Maelrubha suffered and in 795 the Sons of Death steered their dragon ships into the narrow Sound of Iona and drove them up on to the beach below Columba's great foundation. Sea lords must have gathered intelligence and known not only where the religious communities could be found but also gained a sense of their wealth and importance. Iona had become a focus of pilgrimage and, consequently, was rich and the home of many sacred treasures – and the Vikings knew that. They came back in 798 and 802 for what the monks had managed to hide and, in 806, the Sons of Death slaughtered 68 of the community of brothers and lay workers. The massacre may have taken place at the sandy inlet now known as Martyrs' Bay. It was time to leave and the Abbot Cellach was forced into the difficult decision to abandon Columba's sacred island and, in 807, work began on a new monastery safely sited inland in Ireland.

The impact of the raids in Scotland, Ireland and around the rest of Britain is well recorded, certainly where Viking fleets attacked monasteries. What is not well understood is the impact of the raids in Norway, the deeply indented coastline of fjords from where the sea lords set sail. When raiders arrived home bearing all manner of shiny, bejewelled, precious portable loot, eyes will have widened and it must have seemed to those at home that westo-versea there lay a land of plenty. If indeed population pressure drove men to go raiding, the results may have persuaded many to leave permanently and settle. By the middle of the 9th century, the Northern Isles, the Hebrides and much of the Atlantic seaboard had fallen under the control of a people who knew them as *Hjaltland, Orkneyjar* and *Sudreyjar*. Scandinavian Scotland would retain a clear identity for many generations.

FURLONGS, BOLLS AND ELLS

A relic of the old imperial system of measurement, the furlong was an eighth of a mile, 220 yards, 660 feet, 40 rods or 10 chains – most of which was introduced to Scotland by Anglian farmers. The Old English word furh *meant 'a furrow' and, when attached to 'long', it signified the length of a furrow in one acre of a ploughed field. Acres were not football field-shaped but long strips designed to improve drainage. The term* shotts, *often found in Scotland, indicated a group of adjacent furlongs. For Anglian farmers, the rod was the basic unit and it was reckoned on the Old German foot which was about 10 per cent longer than the 12 inches of the modern foot. These measurements lasted much longer in Scotland where the Scots mile was 10 per cent longer than the English mile until the 19th century. An 'ell' was a long yard, more than 36 inches, and it lasted until the 20th century when it was still in use in the Borders textile mills. Weavers were paid by the ell. A 'boll' was a measure of flour or unmilled grain and a quarter of a boll was a 'firlot'. Not a furlong. Simple.*

The process of Viking settlement was the last great migration. Over the succeeding centuries others would come and make significant impacts on Scotland's history but, by comparison, these incomers arrived sporadically and in small groups. In the 9th century, Bede's list of the peoples of North Britain, the Picts, Britons, Angles and Scots, was augmented by the peoples contemporaries knew as Northmen and their language of Norn replaced Pictish and would continue to be spoken in the Northern Isles until the 18th century. Shetland is closer to the coast of Norway than it is to the Scottish mainland and it remains closer in less obvious ways.

At the outset of the 9th century, Scotland did not yet exist and nor was it inevitable. Many different paths lay open. Our history could have moved in a different direction – given a series of different interactions between people and events, modern Scotland could have understood itself in Norn and been known as Vikland – or perhaps as Pictland or Alba or North Anglia or Yr Hen Ogledd, the Old North. But, to understand how history moved in the way that it did, it is very important to observe how these five different speech communities and political entities interacted. And it is equally important not to look backwards and confect a story of how one triumphed over the other, of how one group forged a nation out of the defeat of others. It did not happen in that way. Our nation is the sum of Scandinavian Scotland, Pictish Scotland, Irish Scotland, English Scotland and British Scotland.

5

Old Gods and the Edge of Heaven

※

OR THE DEVOUT Christians of the Dark Ages hallowed ground was not a cliché or a convention but an active belief. Land sanctified by the presence of a great saint like Cuthbert or Columba had thereby been invested with tremendous power. Those who were fortunate enough to be buried in the sacred soil of a monastic precinct would have their mortal sins, the sins of their flesh, cleansed and purified. Lindisfarne and Iona are also inherently spiritual – places apart from the world, islands on the edge of beyond, where it seems easier to contemplate and to pray.

After Abbot Cellach had established the new community at Kells in County Meath, he resigned his office and returned to Iona to die and be buried there a year later. Diarmait was installed as his successor, and bearing the shrine of Columba, he too went back to the sacred island. In 825, its power also drew Blathmac. An Irish nobleman and warrior, he had been a late but passionate entrant into holy orders. What happened to him, his horrific fate at the bloody hands of Viking raiders became notorious – a story that shivered around the monasteries of Western Europe. It was recorded by Walafrid Strabo, the Abbot of Reichenau in southern Germany.

Knowing that the sea raiders would return to Iona, Blathmac and a group of monks resettled the monastery and it seems that, by doing so, they actively sought martyrdom, to die for Christ at the hands of heathens on the ground hallowed by his saint. When lookouts warned of approaching dragon ships, Blathmac told those whose courage wavered that they could escape 'by a footpath through regions known to them'. He and his brothers waited, no doubt praying at the altar. At dawn the raiders attacked, broke in and cut down all of the monks except their leader. When Blathmac refused to reveal where Columba's shrine was hidden, the Vikings became enraged and 'the pious sacrifice was torn limb from limb'.

Such savagery was not uncommon and sometimes it had a grisly ritual significance as a sacrifice to Odin. Here is a later record of the appalling ceremony of the blood eagle as Earl Einar defeated Halfdan at the end of the 9th century on Orkney: 'Afterwards Earl Einar went up to Halfdan and cut a spread eagle upon his back, by striking his sword through his back into his belly, dividing his ribs from the backbone down to his loins, and tearing out his lungs.'

Recent historiography has tended to play down the violence of the Vikings and it has become fashionable to focus on their social, economic and cultural impact. But there is no doubting the shock of the attacks even though it was amplified by an outraged sense of desecration as heathen warriors hacked monks to death and plundered their sacred treasures. And the violence was no opening storm. The blood eagle was carved on the backs of enemies well into the 11th century.

DNA studies on Orkney hint at genocide. Scientists have so far been unable to detect any significant genetic signal from a male Pictish population that predates the 9th century. It looks as though the archipelago was comprehensively taken over in the decades following the raid on Lindisfarne. Native farmers appear to have been slaughtered or cleared off their land and forced to leave the islands. The distinctive M17 DNA marker of the Vikings persists very powerfully in the modern male population and it has an enhanced presence amongst old Orcadian surnames such as Isbister, Clouston, Rendall, Flett and Foubister. Most men who carry them are the direct descendants of the raiders who sailed out of the sea mists to seize the land and settle.

Skaill lies on the eastern shore of Orkney Mainland and the sandy, gently sloping beach below the township may have been first landfall for ships sailing westoversea. It is a common Norse place name amongst the islands of the archipelago for it means a hall, usually the hall of a sea lord built where there is good land. Sandside Bay is a safe place to beach longships as well as the rounder, more tub-like merchant vessels the Northmen knew as *knarrs*. Behind the bay stretches the sort of green and gentle farmland typical of Orkney, fertile and capable of producing cereals, pasturing milker cows and ewes and sustaining a substantial community.

When archaeologists discovered the remains of the Viking *skali*, the hall, it turned out to be a solid, well-insulated structure. Inside a long rectangular stone skin, the interior had been lined with turf to block the gaps and prevent the whistling winter winds from penetrating the snug interior. Heat and light glowed from a very large hearth in the middle of the hall and, as in the roundhouses of prehistoric Scotland, smoke created an upper layer of carbon monoxide which will have snuffed out sparks spiralling up to the dry roof beams and turf thatch. Not that much wood will have been burned – it was too precious. Trees were rare on windy Orkney, even as early as the 9th century, and the red-gold, earthy glow of peat will have warmed those sitting near the hearth.

Along each long side of the rectangular hall raised benches were used for sleeping, storage, sitting and, in the long winter darkness of the far north, for the telling of tales. The sagas of the Northmen are famous and usually much later versions of the great epics of the oral tradition but their richness suggests a rich cultural hinterland, an immense shared store of stories and lore. Bards were known as skalds and some very vivid skaldic fragments survive. Here is the tale of the beginning of a spring voyage from Norway.

Vestr fork of ver,
En ek Vithris ber
Munstrandr mar.
Sva's mitt of far,
Drok eik a flot
Vith isa brot,
Hlothk maerhtar hlut
Mins knarrar skut.

[Westoversea I came
With me I carried
The sea of Odin's breast.
Such is my profession.
At breaking of the ice floes
I dragged my oak ship to sea.
I loaded my vessel's hold
With its cargo of praise.]

The structure of these tales of adventure and daring, many of which were as long as the Orkney dark, was designed to aid recollection. Short four- to six-syllable lines (better appreciated in the Old Norse version) recited in the steady beat of regular metre brought the lines to mind almost without conscious effort. Where effort was sometimes required, it was amongst those sitting listening around the fire glowing in the hearth of the *skali*. Skaldic poetry and the sagas are peppered with kennings, word puzzles intended to amuse but also to mystify. For passages to make sense, listeners had to pay attention and unravel the kennings as they went along. In the fragment above, the sea of Odin's breast is the mystical mead which the Norse god once stole and its intoxicating power gave the gift of poetry. Perhaps a jug of mead or ale was passed around the hearth at Skaill as a skald warmed to his work.

Perhaps more credibly than the recent portrayals as peace-loving farmers given to the occasional violent spasm, a little knowledge of the Viking love of language and inventive metaphor rounds out the picture of the Sons of Death. Here is a very beautiful description of sailing in the open sea in a dragon ship – the monster of the mast and the wolf of the willow are kennings for the wind whose sharp teeth bite at the hull and Gestil's Swan is a sea god.

> Before the stem of the prow-beast
> The hostile monster of the mast
> With his strength hews out of file
> On ocean's even path.
> With it the chill wolf of the willow
> With its gusts files away,
> Showing no mercy to Gestil's Swan,
> Over the stem, before the prow.

Once the archaeologists at Skaill had painstakingly cleared away tons of sand to discover the remains of the Viking hall, their survey picked up traces of an earlier Pictish settlement close by. It was a poignant reminder of how history always involves change and loss and, in the case of Orkney, a near-complete extirpation. One of the few but perhaps the most obvious remnants of a pre-Norse past is the name – the islands of the Boar People, Orkney.

If, as seems almost certain, the incoming invaders enslaved some of the defeated Pictish population, they did no more than was usual in 9th-century Britain and Ireland. War captives had real value as slaves who could work the land in return for shelter and food. What mattered in Celtic society in particular was that these men and women had no claim on the land. The cultural convention of partible inheritance, whereby all of the recognised sons of lords, legitimate and illegitimate, were entitled to a share of their property, meant that holdings were broken down into ever smaller units over time. In Wales, this became a chronic problem. By contrast slaves could inherit and own nothing and their use was probably much more widespread than the exceedingly sparse sources allow. Once Viking raiders had become settlers in the Northern Isles and the Hebrides by the middle of the 9th century, they began an organised trade which met the market demand for slaves – *thrall* is the Old Norse term and it survives in the phrase 'to be in thrall to someone'.

Dublin became a depot, a place where war captives and those simply kidnapped by raiders were brought for sale. Instead of slaughter, slavery became a big business for Viking sea lords. Not only was there demand in Scotland and Britain, the Frankish successor kingdoms of Charlemagne's empire, the Eastern Roman Empire ruled from Constantinople and the Muslim Caliphate of Cordoba all employed large numbers of slaves. The appetite for Christian slaves in the courts of the Caliphs and their Emirs acquired a cruel twist as captive men were sometimes gelded to make them more attractive and manageable.

DNA also provides strong evidence of the traffic of slaves in the opposite compass direction. The characteristic early British Y-chromosome marker of R1b-S145 is found at a significant frequency of 5 per cent of all Norwegian men and is specifically concentrated along the western seaboard. In the regions of Trondelag, More and Romsdal, and Hordaland, the region around Bergen, the proportion rises to between 12 and 19 per cent of the modern population. The genetic bias is definitely Irish and Scottish with clear examples from a Pictish subgroup. What these statistics mean is a substantial traffic in slaves back across the North Sea and they also chime with one of the few scraps of documentary evidence. Here is an entry dated 789 from the *Anglo-Saxon Chronicle* of what may have been an even earlier contact than the attack on Lindisfarne: 'In this year King Beorhtric married Offa's daughter Eadburh and in his days there came for the first time three ships of the Northmen (from Hordaland) and then the reeve rode to them and wished to force them to the king's residence, for he did not know who they were; and they slew him. These were the first ships of the Denisc men which came to the land of the English.'

To achieve such a presence in the modern population of Hordaland, the slave trade across the North Sea must have gone on for some considerable time. It may be that Vikings had established a base in Orkney or Shetland in the decades before the recorded attacks at the end of the 8th century and had begun to take back captives from Orkney and the north of Scotland to serve in the halls and fields by the fjords.

Largely unnoticed by history, perhaps so much a part of everyday life that it was not worthy of comment, the slave trade and the use of the Dublin market continued well into the 11th century. And it was also the destination for the captives of English slavers. Here is a poignant passage from the *Life of St Wulfstan, Bishop of Worcester*, compiled after 1095, that describes what must have been a common enough sight.

> There is a maritime town called Bristol, which is on the direct route to Ireland, and so suitable for trade with that barbarian land. The inhabitants of this place with other Englishmen often sail to Ireland for the sake of trade. Wulfstan banished from among them a very old custom which had so hardened their hearts that neither the love of God nor the love of King William could efface it. For men whom they had purchased from all over England they carried off to Ireland; but first they got the women with child and sent them pregnant to market. You would have seen queues of the wretches of both sexes shackled together and you would have pitied them: those who were beautiful and those who were in the flower of youth were daily prostituted and sold amidst much wailing to the barbarians.

Slaves in 9th century Scotland will have looked little different from their masters and it is likely that their living conditions were very similar. And, in contrast with the United States in the 18th and 19th centuries, those who were unfree were indistinguishable. Estimates of population in the early medieval period are little better than informed guesses but, as noted earlier, a figure of about 500,000 is not unreasonable. Almost all were farmers. Those who did not work the land were a tiny elite of lords and princes, their war bands and households and the more exalted of the clergy. No towns existed north of Carlisle and the closest to any sense of urban living were the settlements around power centres such as Dunadd, Alt Cluith and Edinburgh Castle Rock and also the huts that clustered close to major religious foundations. Near St Andrews excavations of a large cemetery at Hallowhill have turned up the skeletal remains of a young population whose life expectancy did not often extend beyond the age of thirty. Little had changed since prehistory.

Society looked young and, in an age before contraception, women could expect to be pregnant for much of their adult lives. No records exist to indicate this but it is likely that child and infant mortality was high. Nevertheless, many young children will have been seen around the flocks and herds, helping, yelling and running with a stick in their hands or out in the woods and the wild land looking for birds' eggs in the spring or gathering fungi and picking berries and hazelnuts in the late summer and autumn. As the *Senchus Fer nAlban* hinted, farms or 'houses' were individual units and probably resembled Highland crofts more than the later farms. These were single homesteads whose people cultivated the inbye fields, whose beasts grazed the outbye and who might have shared a common or muir where peats, brackens, wood and turf sods might be cut. Muirs were generally tracts of open upcountry land where beasts from a group of homesteads might be pastured in common from spring to autumn while the lowland fields were rested or cultivated. Aerial archaeology has spotted early medieval farms with what appears to be a steading, several buildings that might have included byres where milker cows might be tethered and fed, and some storehouses. The definitions of the *Senchus* appear to have persisted into the 13th century in the Lennox where a 'house' was defined as one from which smoke issued, the farmhouse.

A legacy of partible inheritance may well have been that neighbours were often relatives and, in turn, that probably meant the consolidation of kindred groups who claimed territory from an early date. All farming was mixed farming. It had to be. Markets certainly existed but these were usually annual or biannual events where cattle and other beasts were traded to avoid inbreeding or simply sold on or more likely bartered. Like 19th- and 20th-century Highland crofts, early medieval households needed to be self-sufficient – able to grow enough cereals to make porridge and bread, gather enough roots, fruits, fungi, berries and birds' eggs in a wild harvest, fish and hunt (although bigger game would become increasingly a lordly preserve), tend milker cows, nanny-goats and ewes, comb sheep and goats for wool and slaughter the occasional bullock, pig or wedder. Archaeologists have identified far more cattle bones than any other domesticated species and not only were the herds probably paid as tribute, they were also a widely accepted measure of wealth in an economy where little cash circulated.

Scotland in the 9th century looked different. But there was no fabled Caledonian Forest carpeting the landscape. For millennia, people had depended on supplies of wood for fuel, tools, weapons and building materials and the rights to woodland would be carefully preserved in later documents. And there was much more wasteland. Before widespread drainage came in the 18th and 19th centuries, flat land, especially on valley floors, was often wetland, boggy terrain that could be dangerous as well as useless for agriculture. Hunters who knew the paths through the likes of Flanders Moss, west of Stirling, could trap wildfowl, gather eggs in the spring and catch eels and other game but some areas remained largely impenetrable for centuries. Invading armies preferred to wade the Solway fords rather than risk the treacherous Solway Moss to the east.

THE WET ROAD

Since the days of Agricola and the legions, invaders of Scotland who took the western approach often got wet. Edward I died at Burgh-on-Sands because his army was about to get wet in 1307 as they prepared to attack Scotland. The reason they and many other armies and war bands camped on the Solway shore lay farther to the east. At the neck of the firth, around the outfall of the River Sark and the Esk, was the dangerous Solway Moss which was very difficult to cross. Avoiding the moss involved a long detour to the east so it was preferable to cross by the Solway fords at low tide. Those coming from the south used an ancient standing stone as a seamark to keep them on the right course. Along the flat horizon of the northern shore, the rounded lump of the Lochmaben Stane could easily be seen and it kept men on the right course across the wet road.

The colours of early Scotland were entirely natural. Almost all buildings were constructed with materials that lay close at hand – timber, turf, bracken and local stone. There were no wide tarmacked roads, only tracks and the rare, grassed-over Roman roads. Very few buildings of more than one storey existed – only small houses bedded down into the landscape for shelter. To those who climbed a high hill to look out over the landscape, all that would have signalled the presence of human beings were the columns of smoke drifting through the thatch of homesteads.

Most farmers, and especially their children, spent time supplementing their diet with what they could trap, gather or catch. And there is a wonderful, timeless poem in Old Welsh that gives a pungent sense that hunting and gathering never died. Instead, it was woven into the fabric of the seasons. Here is a free translation:

> Dinogad's speckled petticoat
> Was made of skins of speckled stoat:
> Whip whip whipalong
> Eight times we'll sing the song.
> When your father hunted the land,
> Spear on shoulder, club in hand,
> This his speedy dogs he'd teach,
> Giff, Gaff, catch her, catch her, fetch!
> In his coracle he'd slay
> Fish as a lion does its prey.
> When your father went to the moor
> He'd bring back heads of stag, fawn, boar,
> The speckled grouse's head from the mountain,
> Fishes' heads from the falls of Oak Fountain.
> Wherever your father struck with his spear,
> Wild pig, wild cat, fox from his lair,
> Unless it had wings it would never get clear.

Scotland's climate began to warm in the 9th century, the beginning of a climatic optimum that lasted until the early 14th century. The treeline began to creep up the flanks of hills and mountains and, as growing seasons lengthened, the population probably also began to creep up. High-altitude woods provided the likes of Dinogad's father with more fruitful hunting grounds as Scots pine and oak created cover for both red and roe deer, wildcats, pine martens and wild boar. The huge wild cattle known as aurochs may still have browsed the upland leaves and bushes and perhaps bears still prowled in their shade. On the open moorland, black and red grouse, partridge and capercaillie nested while wolf packs still howled around flocks and herds. Rats did not arrive in Scotland until the 12th century and that probably allowed many more cliff- and ground-nesting birds to thrive. And although rabbits crossed the Channel with the Romans, the familiar wild species did not flourish in Scotland until the 13th century.

The names farmers and others gave their places tell a story of change, movement and consolidation. Their pattern across Scotland reflects immigration or, in the case of Pictland, the stamp that the earliest peoples left on the land. The pit- names of Eastern Scotland and the Gaelicised versions of others, such as Perth, allow a sense of the territory of the Picts or, at least, they territory they held longest. The same is true of the north and west where, despite many centuries of Gaelic, almost all of the place names of the Isle of Lewis, for example, are Norse in origin. This was a consequence of takeover, incomers wanting no ambiguity about who owned what. When a lord or warrior known as Hoedda came north to East Lothian from the Anglian settlements of the Tweed Basin, Northumberland or perhaps further south, his settlement on the banks of the Tyne became Hoedda's Tun or Haddington. And, if there was an old name, it was submerged by the tide of history. While many of East Lothian's place names remember the coming of the Angles in the 7th century and the fall of the Kingdom of the Gododdin, the pattern is patchy. The great citadel of the Old Welsh-speaking kings on Traprain Law kept one of its ancient names – the *tref* for 'settlement' and *bren* for 'tree', giving the Treestead. Other well-known names in southern Scotland survived in their Old Welsh form – the likes of Peebles, from *pybyll* for 'shielings', and Kelso, from *Calchvynydd*, 'Chalk Hill'.

In classrooms and even lecture theatres for more than a century, Kenneth macAlpin was welcomed as bringing some certainty and the beginnings of continuity. Hailed as the first king to unite Picts and Scots, he was the dynast, the founding figure from whom generations of successors down to Alexander III would claim descent and his reign supplied a blessed relief from the misty confusions and doubtful doings of unpronounceable rulers of vanished kingdoms. Scotland could begin. Here, at last, was a fixed point, a place to start a reassuring march of history towards a Scotland with familiar frontiers, a Scotland ruled by kings and queens, a national destiny set in train the moment macAlpin had a crown set on his head. The reality is, of course, much more interesting.

After the martyrdom of Blathmac, Donnan and doubtless others, the Vikings began to settle along the Atlantic seaboard. At first they set up what were described in Irish Gaelic as *longphortan* or 'ship camps'. Little more than riverside stockades at mooring points, these were certainly established at Dublin and elsewhere in Ireland as bases where crews could overwinter and also eventually trade in goods and slaves. There exist no records of a *longphort* being set up in the Hebrides or in the sea lochs of the mainland but, if the DNA evidence of the early traffic of people from Scotland and Ireland to Norway is suggestive of contact before 793 and the attack on Lindisfarne, then raiders could easily have operated over long distances from ship camps set up on Orkney and Shetland. In any event, the Vikings certainly exerted pressure in the early 9th century on the rulers of the Dalriadan kindreds and there is an unmistakable sense of the shift of political focus eastwards to Pictland and north-eastwards to the shores of the Moray Firth. But there was little respite, for it seems that the sea lords were intent on pursuit, a sustained campaign on an increasingly significant scale.

Here is an important entry in the *Annals of Ulster*: '839. The heathens won a battle over the men of Fortriu and Eoganan, son of Oengus, and Bran, son of Oengus, and Aed, son of Boanta, and others almost innumerable fell there.' Although very little is known of what came to be called the Battle of Strathearn (even its location is uncertain), the crushing defeat appears to have decapitated Pictish leadership, killing their royalty and many of their nobility. If the sea lords sailed a fleet of dragon ships up the Tay and disembarked a substantial army to attack Fortriu, the centre of Pictish royal power, their victory was not followed up by occupation or settlement. But that may not have been their strategic purpose. The names listed in the annalist's entry suggest that Dalriadans fought at Strathearn and their defeat may have opened up the west to Viking control and eventual settlement. And this apparently pivotal battle also opened up opportunities for Kenneth macAlpin.

Despite later efforts to legitimise his seizure of power by inserting him into royal genealogies, little is certain about macAlpin's origins. He carried a Gaelic name, probably rendered by contemporaries as Cinaed macAilpin, and was said to have been born in Iona in 810. But the name may in fact have been a title. Cognate to *Cunedda*, which in Old Welsh means 'Great Leader', Cinaed may have been awarded because of reputation. Posthumously the new king was known as *An Ferbasach*, 'the Conqueror'. Once he had conquered, a suitable royal lineage was soon rattled up and it showed Kenneth's father, Alpin, as a king in Dalriada. Other sources suggest that this was unlikely. What does seem plausible is that the king of Picts and Scots was indeed a Gael, probably descended from the Cenel nGabrain and certainly a warlord who could command – and eventually succeed. But he was not the first Gaelic-speaking king to rule in Pictland. Nechtan and Oengus I almost certainly brought the two kingdoms together long before 843.

After the disaster at Strathearn, probably as a warlord in Dalriada, Kenneth contended for the vacant throne of Pictland and, although his reign is formally dated from 843, he probably only prevailed over the last of his rivals in 848. Once established as undisputed king, he brought the relics of St Columba (and perhaps the Brecbennoch, the Monymusk Reliquary) from vulnerable Iona over the mountains to be safely kept at the monastery at Dunkeld. And he may also have had the *Lia Fail*, the Stone of Destiny, heaved on to a cart and transported east. Tradition held that it that had been brought from Dalriada in Ireland many generations before. Perhaps it was removed from the citadel at Dunadd. It was certainly placed on what became known as the Moot Hill at Scone, the place where Scottish kings would be crowned until the 17th century.

Kings continued to be crowned elsewhere in Scotland, beyond the mountains to the north of Scone. While bards and seannachies attempted to legitimise Kenneth macAlpin's claim to the united throne as they sang of his glorious descent from the hero kings of the Cenel nGabrain and myth-historical progenitors such as Fergus Mor macErc, others traced their line back to a rival Dalriadan kindred, the Cenel Loairn. This dynasty's claims are often ignored or forgotten – because they ultimately failed and became one of history's many losers – but the for the descendants of Kenneth I, their pretensions seriously threatened the southern dynasty for more than four centuries. These were the Kings of Moray.

The Cenel Loairn, the Kindred of Lorne, based in Appin, Morvern, Mull, Lorne and the south-western end of the Great Glen, disputed the high king-ship of Dalriada with the Cenel nGabrain of Kintyre and the south and they sometimes succeeded. But the aggression of the Pictish kings, Nechtan and Oengus I, drove the kindred from their ancestral homelands. It seems that the men of Lorne faded from history and after 736 no mention of them is made in Argyll. Their kings and their war bands appeared to vanish.

In fact they migrated. Recent scholarship has presented a convincing sequence of events that culminated in the establishment of the Kindred of Lorne as the Kings of Moray. In the face of persistent pressure from the warriors of Nechtan and Oengus, the Gaelic-speaking Dalriadans moved up the Great Glen to the mouth of the Ness and gradually fanned out to take control of the old Pictish provinces north of the Mounth: Ce (Mar and Buchan), Fidaid (Moray and Easter Ross) and perhaps part of Cat (Caithness and south-east Sutherland). The kingdom of Moray was far larger than the modern county and local authority and compassed all of the fertile southern coastlands up to the foothills of the Grampian massif as well as reaching the Atlantic seaboard and Skye.

A careful analysis of royal genealogies has identified a series of coherent and chronologically correct links between the kings of Moray and the

Kindred of Lorne and, by the 11th century, these men were claiming the high kingship of Scotland using these ancient lineages as support for their pretension. The most famous was also the most successful. King Macbeth ruled Moray before he deposed the descendants of Kenneth macAlpin and, from 1040, reigned over Scotland for 14 years. It could be argued that he and his line had a better claim.

Like many new rulers before and since, King Kenneth led his war bands on campaigns to seize plunder and build prestige. Nothing underpinned authority, especially if it was shaky, better than military success. The chroniclers relate that he and his men invaded Saxonia six times, by which they probably meant the Scottish territories of the Anglian kingdom of Northumbria. His warriors captured the monastery of famous saints, Cuthbert, Aidan and Boisil, at Old Melrose and they burned the hall and settlement at Dunbar.

According to *The Chronicle of the Kings of Alba*, which appears to have begun its entries in the 840s, Kenneth macAlpin died of the effects of a tumour on 13 February 858, at his palace of Cinnbelachoir, a lost place name which probably lay near Scone. The crown was passed on not to the king's eldest son, through the more familiar system of primogeniture, but according to the Celtic traditions of tanistry. In both Irish and Scots Gaelic, the Tanaiste was the heir apparent but certainly not necessarily the eldest son of a monarch. In Ireland, this man was elected or had gained the support of the *derbfhine*, all those descended in the male line from a common ancestor, usually a great-grandfather or a great-great-grandfather, reaching back four or five generations. The advantage of this process over primogeniture, which insisted on the succession of the eldest son whatever his suitability, was that those fittest to rule usually gained the kingship. The disadvantage was that many men could make a credible claim and contend for the throne and the consequent internecine squabbling was often very destructive and protracted.

Tanistry crossed the North Channel in the sea curraghs of the kindreds of Dalriada and, as Kenneth macAlpin established his dynasty, it was accepted as the mechanism through which the kingship of Alba was passed on. In the century and a half before Malcolm II acceded in 1005, it was more usual for brothers, cousins and grandsons to succeed than the sons of a macAlpin king. And even after that time, tanistry was still sometimes used. Malcolm II attempted to introduce primogeniture and also the right of succession for those who descended from kings through the female line. He himself had only daughters.

It took more than a century for the old Irish practices to fade. Malcolm

III Canmore designated his eldest son, Edward, as his heir but, after his early death, the king's brother, Donald II Ban took the throne and held it until 1097. When Edgar, Malcolm's eldest surviving son defeated his uncle, he had the old man blinded and imprisoned. This was not only an act of cruelty but also a response to the tenacity of traditional Celtic kingship and its supporters amongst the Scottish aristocracy, many of whom had a direct genealogical interest in maintaining the practices of tanistry. According to the old customs, only a man without physical blemish and in possession of all his faculties could succeed to the kingship and, when Edgar's jailors put out his uncle's eyes, they were also disqualifying him. Tanistry of a less extreme sort still persists in Ireland where the Deputy Prime Minister is known as the Tanaiste.

In the summer of 870, lookouts on the ramparts of Dumbarton Rock saw a belly-hollowing sight. A huge fleet of Viking dragon ships, more than two hundred, was sailing around Gourock Point into the mouth of the River Clyde, sailing straight towards the great Dun Breatainn, the Fortress of the Britons. Standing in the prows of their most splendid warships as their captains beat time for banks of oarsmen to pull hard against the current were Olaf, the King of Dublin, and his ally, the feared sea lord, Ivar. They had come to capture the Rock of the Clyde, the kings of Strathclyde and all who sheltered behind the walls on the twin peaks of the old volcanic plug. Here is the entry for 870 from the Irish annals: 'In this year the kings of the Scandinavians besieged Strathclyde, in Britain. They were four months besieging it; and at last, after reducing the people who were inside by hunger and thirst (after the well that they had in their midst had dried up miraculously) they broke in upon them afterwards. And firstly all the riches that were in it were taken; [and also] a great host [was taken] out of it in captivity.' The *Annals of Ulster* added a little detail on the aftermath of the fall of the Rock of the Clyde: 'Olaf and Ivar returned to Dublin from Scotland with 200 ships, bringing away with them in captivity a great prey of Angles, Britons and Picts.' But no Scots.

It seems that Constantine I, who had succeeded his uncle Duncan I as King of the macAlpin realm, may have encouraged, even cooperated in the Viking attack on Dumbarton because, a year later, he asked that the captured King Artgal of Strathclyde be put to death in prison. For the rest there were the miseries of the Dublin slave market, and the novelty of Strathclyde aristocrats as servants or worse will have attracted high prices. Their fate was a function of royal policy. In the decades after the death of

Kenneth macAlpin his successors found themselves surrounded by ambitious Scandinavian interests. To the north, the Norwegian Earls of Orkney were asserting themselves on the mainland, taking control of Caithness and eating into the domains of the kingdom of Moray. That was not an immediate problem for Constantine and those who ruled from Scone but the activities of the Norwegians in the Hebrides and Dublin were.

The splendidly named Ketil Flatnose was a Viking sea lord with power in the Hebrides and strong links to Norway. The equally splendidly named Aud the Deep-Minded was his daughter and had been given in marriage to the same Olaf who led the attack on Dumbarton Rock. But all had not gone well and the Queen of Dublin left her husband (who may have taken at least two brides from native Irish royal families) to join her father. It appears that Ketil and Olaf became sworn enemies and that, in order to pursue his vendetta, Flatnose recruited war bands who became feared as the Gall-Gaidheil. These were men of mixed Norwegian and Hebridean ancestry who were believed by monastic chroniclers to be even more rapacious than the first Viking raiders. They rampaged in Ireland and Scotland in the 850s from their bases in the Hebrides and the south-west of Scotland, the region that took their name. Galloway is from *Gall-Gaidheil* (in fact it comes from the genitive case as in *Tir nan Gall-Ghaidhealaibh*, the 'Land of the Stranger-Gaels') and their settlement there gave rise to a substantial Gaelic-speaking community that persisted until the modern period.

In 857, Olaf of Dublin defeated Ketil Flatnose and his feared warriors and turned his acquisitive gaze on mainland Scotland, the lands beyond the Viking possessions in the north and west. The *Annals of Ulster* recorded that, in 866, Olaf combined the war bands of Irish and Scottish Vikings 'when they plundered all the territories of the Picts and took their hostages'. In the same year, the Anglian kingdom of Northumbria and its lands north of the Tweed and in the Lothians were taken over by the so-called Great Heathen Army of the Danes as part of its invasion of England. The macAlpin kingdom was beset on all sides and Constantine was forced to act.

The taking of Dumbarton Rock may be seen as consequence of his survival strategy. In conniving in the fall of Strathclyde and by securing the death of King Artgal, he took sides in the Scandinavian divide. The Dublin Vikings were Norwegians and the Great Heathen Army and its kingdom of York were Danes. By conceding Dumbarton and accepting – he had little choice – Olaf's hegemony in the west, Constantine could concentrate his resources on dealing with Danish Northumbria to the south. The strategy worked eventually – although not for the king who instigated it. In 877, it seems that a Viking army attacked Constantine's army in the east, probably in Fife. The sequence of events was convoluted but fascinating.

Halfdan Ragnarsson was the brother of Ivar, the one-time ally of Olaf of Dublin and the sea lord who sailed with him to the siege of Dumbarton. A leader of the Great Heathen Army, he had a fearsome reputation for cruelty and led an unsuccessful expedition to attack Norse Viking Dublin in 876–77. It seems that Halfdan's war bands returned to York by sailing up the Clyde and then crossing the narrow waist of Scotland to the Firth of Forth before making their way south by sea to the mouth of the Humber and upriver to their city of York or Jorvik. Sources suggest that this route was travelled several times by armies moving between the two great Scandinavian power centres. Probably at Inverdovat on the southern shore of the Firth of Tay, a Danish army attacked and routed the Scots and, in a memorable phrase, the Irish annalists noted that it was 'on that occasion that the earth burst open under the men of Scotland'. Constantine was either killed there or captured. There is a grisly tradition that cruel Halfdan had the Scots king beheaded on the beach like a common criminal.

For some months after the fight at Inverdovat, the Vikings may have raided in what they will have seen as a leaderless and defeated kingdom but, when Halfdan led another attack on Dublin in 877, he too was killed. By 889, Constantine's son, Donald II, had eventually succeeded and the break-up of the volatile Viking kingdom of York into the two old realms of Deira and Bernicia allowed the Scots to regroup and recover. Danish rule was restricted only as far north as Durham and the buffer kingdom of Bernicia had reverted to Anglian rule from the fortress on the spectacular rock at Bamburgh.

The chronicles of the times were sparse, usually noting only the doings of the mighty, battles, raids, the downfall of kings and exemplary lives of the saintly. Virtually no sense of the lives of ordinary people survives – if such was ever recorded. Documents are silent about the generations of farmers who tended flocks and herds, who ploughed and planted, sowed and reaped the harvest. And yet their toil was the foundation of society, it fed the famous names and was disrupted by the fire and smoke of their wars or blighted by bad weather or disease.

If almost nothing of the texture of the experience of the vast majority of Scots men, women and children who worked their short lives on the land can be found, then at least the framework of agricultural life might be traced. By working backwards from later records of what were clearly ancient institutions and looking at the rich heritage of place names in Scotland, the way in which farming was organised might emerge some way out of the shadows.

Even after the slaughter at Dunnichen in 685, Northumbrian influence still reached across much of Lowland Scotland, extending across the Tweed Basin and the Lothians as well as Galloway and perhaps as far as Ayrshire, Fife and Tayside. The shire or *sgir* became the basic unit of landholding and, in what is now Scotland, it may have existed from an early period – from the 7th century and the first decades of Anglian expansion northwards.

The early shire appears to have contained at least five major elements. At its core stood a shire centre – a hall and a small settlement around it that was occupied by a lord usually described as a thane or a thegn. This man had probably once been a warrior in the royal war band and, at some point, been given charge of a shire by his king. There is a clear sense of the thane as the king's man, acting as his representative or agent in what was seen at first as an outlying royal possession. Amongst other services (and payments), he was usually bound to muster men to fight in the royal host.

In the countryside around the shire centre lay a group of individual farm-steads and in turn, the families who worked them were bound to supply the thane and his household with food rents and services. It is important to realise that these units were much smaller than modern shires. In early Scotland, the likes of Crailshire, Kellieshire, Coldinghamshire, Yetholmshire, Bleboshire and Callendarshire are several examples amongst many. Place names paint a background in the rural landscape. Where ancient shires have been recognised north of the Forth, their farmsteads often bear the Pictish pit- prefix. *Pit* meant a 'portion of land' and later documents appear to quantify this as a 'ploughgate' or 'davoch' – as much land as could be cultivated by a single plough team of oxen. Often also known as an 'oxgang', this unit was, in essence, a farm. In the Lothians and the Borders such outlying holdings were also called 'berewicks', barley farms, a name that has survived in Berwick and its northern counterpart. The families who made these ploughgates produc-tive were mostly bound to the land in some way, although the degree of attachment is rarely clear. Slavery certainly existed.

In addition to a shire centre, its thane and the outlying farmsteads (from Latin, these were translated as 'appendices', a term that became 'pendicles' in Scots), a shire usually had a central church. Many of these are barely traceable on modern maps because they are so old, dating from the coming of Christianity in the 5th century. The word used for shire churches was *eglis* or *egles*, an Old Welsh borrowing from the Latin *ecclesia* and examples are found in old Northumbria at Eccles in Berwickshire and as far north as Monymusk in Aberdeenshire. Its plotting on the map suggests that Bede's report that the Picts were converted in two distinct phases might well be accurate. The old *eccles* name was probably planted near Monymusk in the 5th century, perhaps after the missions of Ninian and others. There appears to be no examples of the place name further north of the Mounth and it may well be that its use had ceased by the 6th century, the time when Bede believed that the Word of God had reached the Picts 'beyond the mountains'.

Most early shires seem to have had a mill where bere and other cereals from the outlying berewicks could be ground into flour in return for a tithe to the thane and later to the church. Ednam Mill in Roxburghshire still turned in the 20th century and, since its rights were carefully protected after the founding of Kelso Abbey in 1128, it clearly had a considerable history before the 12th century. It was probably the mill for the lost shire around Eccles, the original Berwickshire, and the old church (it later became a convent of nuns) lay only three miles to the north-east of the village of Ednam.

The adoption of shire organisation in Fife and, beyond the Tay, in Pictland and beyond the political reach of the Northumbrians, may have been an adaptation of older models with the later addition of a central church. Certainly in north Fife, the cluster of pit- names in the lost shire around Abernethy suggests a cultural fusion of sorts. The Old Welsh term of *maenor* has survived, almost perfectly preserved, in the Manor Valley near Peebles. There, 13 farmsteads stretching south into the sheltering hills were pendicles of a shire centre and an ancient church was dedicated to the obscure 4th-century Roman martyr, St Gordian. A cross by the roadside marks the site of what must have been a very early foundation, perhaps set up by Christians who had walked over the watershed hills from Carlisle. It almost certainly predated the coming of the Angles in the 6th and 7th centuries.

The fifth element of the shires of Dark Ages Scotland was a muir or moor and place names remember shire moors at Sheriffmuir near Perth, Coldingham Muir in Coldinghamshire in Berwickshire, Culross Muir in Fife, Slammanan Muir near Falkirk and several others. These supplied important resources for farmers. Not only were they areas of rough pasture and scrub woodland where peats and bracken could be cut, they were also the upcountry spring destination for the journeys of transhumance, summer grazing for beasts that was essential relief for the inbye fields around the farmsteads.

The distribution of these ancient ghost shires is suggestive of different landholding and farming cultures inside Scotland. Most occur in the east and the Lowlands and, while this may be an impression conveyed by the better documentation associated with better land, it does seem that this form of lordship did not apply in the Highlands and along the Atlantic seaboard. Its penetration looks as though it is a measure of either Anglian takeover or cultural influence in eastern Scotland.

The first half of the 10th century was dominated by the towering figure of Constantine II. Long-lived and lucky, he reigned from 900 to 943 before retiring to become a monk at the community at St Andrews where he died in 952, an old man of more than 70 summers. His achievement was to establish control over much of what became modern Scotland and his ambition was to extend his reach south to the Tyne and across Cumbria. Norse sea lords ruled the Northern Isles, Caithness, parts of Sutherland and the Hebrides and the Kingdom of Moray acted independently but Constantine's hold on central, fertile and valuable Scotland seems to have been secure. By the early years of the 10th century, the kingdom of Strathclyde had been brought into closer union through a mixture of marriage and military muscle. Such consolidation allowed Constantine II to turn his gaze southwards. The north of England, the green fields of the old Kingdom of Northumbria, seemed a greater prize than the rugged lands beyond the mountains.

Like Constantine I, the new king played the Irish Vikings off against the York Danes but, unlike his predecessor, he avoided being killed in the process. In 914 and again in 918, Scottish hosts mustered in the Lothians and followed the old Roman road of Dere Street south over the Lammermuirs to be joined by lords and their war bands in the Tweed Basin before striking through the Cheviots and on down to the ruins of Hadrian's Wall and the tumbled down garrison town at Corbridge. The Roman bridge over the Tyne having long fallen, the road crossed the river by a ford below the walls of the military compound. Early medieval armies often met where it was convenient and Corbridge was a crossroads where the still-metalled surfaces of Dere Street ran south to York and the Stanegate, the Roman road that preceded the Wall, ran east to west. There, Constantine's host fought the York armies twice in four years. In the second battle, in 918, the outcome was confused, perhaps a stand-off. According to the *Annals of Ulster*, it seems that Constantine's host destroyed much of the Norse army but were ambushed by the war band led by Ragnall, the Irish Viking who became King of York. The compiler of the Irish chronicle known as the *Three Fragments* noted the consequences of the battle at Corbridge: 'It was long after this before Danes or Norwegians attacked the Scots, but they enjoyed peace and tranquillity.'

Scone saw Scottish kings crowned for many centuries. Charles II was the last in 1651 and it may be that Kenneth macAlpin was the first in the 840s but it is likely that, even at an interval of eight centuries, the coronations had elements in common. When the Dalriadan kings were forced from Dunadd and their Argyll territories by the Norse fleets, it appears that they brought a hefty piece of cultural luggage across the mountains. The *Lia Fail*, the Stone of Destiny, was said to have come from Ireland, from the sacred Hill of Tara. At Scone, it was placed on top of another mound, what is now known as Moot Hill, and Scottish kings sat on it to be made truly royal.

Gaelic ritual also moved eastwards and Gaelic bards remembered its atmosphere. The place name of Scone is itself a memory of ancient ceremony. Bards sang of *Scoine Sciath-Airde*, 'Scone of the High Shields', probably a reference to the habit of warriors raising up a new king on their shields. As this precarious rite proceeded, another bardic name added a soundtrack. *Scoine Sciath-Bhinne* means 'Scone of the Singing Shields', the shouts and chants of acclamation as lords and warriors roared approval and support for the king raised on the high shields. Here is what John of Hexham wrote about the coronation of Malcolm IV in 1153: 'and so all the people of the land, raising up Malcolm, son of Earl Henry, King David's son (a boy still only 12 years old), established him as king at Scone (as is the custom of the Scottish nation).'

On 13 July 1249, Alexander III was also crowned at Scone. A lineal descendant of Constantine II, his coronation still held to the ancient forms. After the king had been crowned on the Stone of Destiny, *An Ollaimh Righ*, the Royal Bard, stood forward to call down God's blessing and to begin the recital of a vital list, what was called the *sloinneadh*, the naming of the names. Beginning far back in the swirling mists of myth-history, the bard intoned the formula, the steady rhythm of the royal genealogy. This laid down the king's right by blood to rule and it was no straightforward matter at Scone in 900. The Celtic laws of tanistry added many more branches to the royal family tree than the more linear system of primogeniture.

After kings were made and acclaimed on the Moot Hill according to ancient, mostly pre-Christian rite, they were then confirmed and blessed again by an ordained bishop in the church at Scone. Until the outline of its foundations was discovered in 2007, the great medieval abbey appeared to have completely disappeared after it was attacked by the fire and zeal of the Reformers in 1559. But the church in which Constantine's coronation was consecrated will have been much more humble. Nevertheless, he was anointed by the pre-eminent cleric in the kingdom, Cellach, Bishop of St Andrews. He probably followed the Frankish practices established a century before. After the coronation of Charlemagne as Emperor of the Romans on Christmas Day 800 by the Pope in Rome, the church in Western Europe attempted to gain political leverage with the notion of a sacred compact between God and kings. And Constantine carried a famous imperial name, that of a man who had been acclaimed in York by the legions 600 years before, and that along with the ecclesiastical link with the Bishop of Rome will have encouraged him to accept such a formula, in '*imitatio imperii*'.

In 906, the young king and Bishop Cellach were the central players in another ceremony at Scone. Here is the entry from the *Annals of Ulster*: '[They] pledged themselves upon the Hill of Faith near the royal city of Scone, that the laws and disciplines of the Faith, and the rights in churches and gospels, should be kept in conformity with [the customs of] the Scots.'

This declaration can be interpreted as a conscious act of nation-building, an attempt to unify the practices of the Church after the customs of the Scots or the Gaels. And not the Picts. Running alongside this is another important shift. As Pictland faded from the map, the land that Constantine was to reign over for 43 years came, in that time, to be called Alba, now the modern Gaelic term for all of Scotland. Against a background of considerable cultural diversity – across Scotland six languages could be heard: Norse, Gaelic, Pictish, Old Welsh, Scots and, in churches, Latin – the new king wished to weld together homogenous institutions. And Constantine also began to play a significant, even occasionally determinant, role in British politics. He was the first king from north of the Tweed to do so.

Scandinavian leaders in Dublin and York contended for control of northern and central England with their neighbours to the south. After the death of Alfred in 899, the kingdom of Wessex did more than simply survive. His son, Edward the Elder, and his daughter, Aethelflaed, the Lady of the Mercians, sent their war bands to press hard on Danish territory south of the Humber. When Edward established a garrison at Manchester in 919, it was symbolic. He had broken into the old kingdom of Northumbria, what was seen as part of the Danish realm of York. When Edward was succeeded by his son, Aethelstan, the pace of events quickened.

By 927, the new Wessex king had taken York and could claim to have made himself the first king of all the English. At Eamont Bridge, near

Penrith, on the southern bounds of the Kingdom of Strathclyde (which by then included Cumbria) on 12 July in the same year, Constantine II, King Owain of Strathclyde, King Hywel Dda of Deheubarth in Wales and Ealdred of Bamburgh, the Earl of Bernicia, all accepted Aethelstan's overlordship. He styled himself thereafter as *Rex et Rector Totius Britanniae*. A period of peace followed the understandings at Eamont Bridge but, in 934, the King and Ruler of All Britain led an army north to invade and harry Scotland. With four Welsh kings and their war bands in his host and shadowed by his fleet, Aethelstan struck as far north as Dunnotar. Constantine began to look for allies.

Olaf, the new King of Dublin, sealed an alliance with the Scots through his marriage to Constantine's daughter. By 937, he had defeated all of his rival Irish sea lords and he mustered a fleet to sail east to England to reclaim the kingdom of York. Constantine and Owain of Strathclyde and probably King Aralt of Man and several Hebridean sea lords joined Olaf with their warriors and together they came to a place called Brunanburh. Probably fought at Bromborough on the Mersey shore of the Wirral, it was a defining battle in the long war for Britain. Here is an uncharacteristically florid entry from the *Anglo-Saxon Chronicle* that describes the outcome:

> the field streamed with warriors' blood
> When rose at morning tide the glorious star
> The sun, God's shining candle, until sank
> The noble creature to its setting.
> As fled the Scots, weary and sick of war
> Forth followed the West Saxons, in war bands
> Tracking the hostile folk the livelong day . . .
> There lay five kings
> Whom on the battlefield swords put to sleep,
> And they were young, and seven of Olaf's earls
> With Scots and mariners, an untold host . . .

Constantine escaped but the slaughter seems to have been very great. As might be expected the *Anglo-Saxon Chronicle* gloried in Aethelstan's victory as it seemed to establish the idea of England and English hegemony over all of Britain. Imperial pretensions recalled the glories of Rome as the old province of Britannia seemed to re-form. From an opposing point of view, Celtic bards mourned Brunanburh as the last time that the English might have been driven back into the sea whence they came. Six years after his defeat, Constantine abdicated in favour of his son, Malcolm I, and went into seclusion as a monk at St Andrews. It may be that, after a lifetime of war, diplomacy and all the ruthlessness, deceit and savagery that stalks the temporal lives of kings, old and weary, Constantine sought to pray for forgiveness. He seems to have been a genuinely pious man. And more practically, at least to contemporaries, his status as a monk who had made vows and been penitent probably entitled him to burial in the sacred soil around the church at St Andrews and the relics of the great saint who had known Christ.

As their power waxed and spread wider, kings became increasingly fond of ceremony and symbol, the theatre of politics. The *Melrose Chronicle* recorded how the kings of England, the dynasty that had survived the Danish onslaughts on Wessex only four generations before, showed their dominance in an age before mass communications:

> In the year 973, Edgar the peaceful king of the English was at last consecrated king of the whole island, with the greatest honour and glory, in the city of Bath . . .
>
> Some time afterwards, after sailing around northern Britain with a huge fleet, he landed at the city of Chester; and eight under-kings met him, as he commanded them, and swore they would stand by him as his vassals, both on land and on sea: namely Kenneth, King of Scots; Malcolm, King of the Cumbrians; Maccus, king of very many islands; and another five – Dufnal, Sifreth, Huwal, Jacob, Juchil.
>
> With these one day he entered a boat, and, placing them at the oars, he himself took the rudder's helm, and skilfully steered along the coarse of the River Dee, and sailed from the palace to the monastery of St John the Baptist, the whole crowd of earls and nobles accompanying him in similar craft. And after praying there, he returned to the palace with the same pomp: and as he entered it he is related to have said to the nobles that then only could any of his successors boast that he was king of England, when he obtained the display of such honours, with so many kings submitting to him.

With a royal cox steering the ship of state, Edgar chose the location of his brief voyages with care. For almost four centuries, Chester was famous as Deva Victrix, the site of the largest Roman legionary fort and naval base in Britannia. Its ships patrolled and protected the eastern shores of the Irish Sea and its garrison watched over North Wales and the north-west of England. As Edgar's boat glided up and down the river, it passed below the walls of the old fortress and made an emphatic political point. Aethelstan had arrogated to himself the title of *Basileus*, 'Emperor', and Edgar also saw himself as the heir of Rome. Those who rowed him on the Dee only ruled with his consent and at his pleasure.

Nevertheless, it seems unlikely that Kenneth II was forced to bend his back. He and his client king of Cumbria (meaning Strathclyde) almost certainly came to the Roman fortress to reach an agreement with Edgar. Probably in return for the formal acknowledgement of his hegemony 'over the whole island', and more practically over the southern regions of the old kingdom of Northumbria, Kenneth II had his possession of Lothian confirmed. And it also seems likely that the inclusion of Cumbria in the kingdom of Strathclyde was agreed, the frontier reaching down to the Rere Cross on Stainmore.

When Edgar died two years after the theatricals at Chester, there was a disputed succession but neither party seriously considered the partition of the relatively new kingdom of England. And Scotland too became a more solid political reality even though its northern and western fringes remained beyond the reach of Kenneth II and his successors. Reading history backwards can lead to distortion: no outcome was inevitable, borders would fluctuate, dynasties would fail but momentum appeared to accelerate towards the end of the 10th century as a recognisable kingdom of Scotland began to emerge.

6

The Nation of the Scots

✴

THE SARGASSO SEA is indeed wide – 700 miles across – and also long at 2,000 miles from north to south. It lies at the centre of the North Atlantic Gyre, a huge vortex bounded by four ocean currents – the Gulf Stream to the west, the North Atlantic Current to the north, the Canary Current to the east and the North Atlantic Equatorial Current to the south. Moving clockwise around the vortex, these powerful currents deposit marine plants, such as *Sargassum*, a genus of seaweed, and other sorts of natural debris as well as much man-made rubbish, especially plastic. But, by its nature, the Sargasso is also the deposit of climate history. In 1996 the scientist L. D. Keigwin published a fascinating paper which analysed data derived from a radiocarbon-dated box core extracted from the seabed beneath the vortex. It confirmed what had been strongly suggested by documentary and archaeological evidence, namely that the temperature of the ocean had been warmer around a thousand years ago than it is now, about one degree warmer, and also that, 400 years ago, it had been about one degree cooler. These seemingly minor fluctuations had a substantial historical impact on western and northern Europe.

The Medieval Warm Period is conventionally dated between 950 and 1250 and the warmer waters of the North Atlantic allowed the descendants of Aud the Deep-Minded and other settlers in Iceland to sail further north unimpeded by the ice. They discovered and settled in Greenland and the *Saga of Erik the Red* recounts how Europeans made landfall in North America, Vinland the Good, six centuries before Columbus. In 10th-century Scotland, the rise in ocean temperature and the better weather that probably accompanied it not only made sea travel safer, it also warmed the land and extended growing seasons. This in turn prompted the planting of cereal crops further north and the ability to store dried grain initiated a growth in both human and animal populations. And as the longer summers pushed the treeline up the flanks of hills and mountains, the ancient natural harvest of roots, fruits, berries, birds' eggs, nuts and game will have been enriched. Pollen cores substantiate this improvement in the climate and its effects. But sound statistics for a period with such meagre written sources are little better than speculation. However, it is not unreasonable to envisage a Scotland where the sun shone for longer on an expanding agricultural economy and a higher population.

To a modern eye, the wide, flat fields of some parts of Central Scotland, especially around Stirling and in west Fife, may seem like the acme of fertility. And at harvest time when combines lift the cereal crops in a matter of hours, cutting broad straight swathes and leaving behind a scatter of round straw bales, it is easy to think of these fields as always having been productive. But in historical reality, flat ground was usually boggy before the age of agricultural improvement and unusable for cultivation. When drainage depended on the natural fall of the land, small undulating fields were much to be preferred. And some of the most productive and valuable farmland of the early Middle Ages lay in the Lothians and the Tweed Basin, where geology and the glaciers had shelved the largely south-facing ground down towards riverbanks and coastlines. Far enough south to enjoy a longer and warmer growing season, the fields of the south-east were much sought after and fought over.

Part of the kingdom of Northumbria until the 10th and 11th centuries, the Lothians and the Borders represented great gains for the kings of Scotland. After Kenneth II had agreed bonds of suzerainty at Chester with Edgar of England in return for the Lothians, the farmland north of the Lammermuirs and the Moorfoots, his successors began to reach and raid further south to seek control of the Tweed Basin. An ancient place name remembers the much-prized county of Berwickshire (including the settlement and port at Berwick). First plotted in the *Blaeu Atlas of Scotland* of 1654 but in use for centuries before, the name of the Merse is old. Cognate with the early medieval kingdom of Mercia, it meant 'march land' or 'border land'. In the English Midlands, Mercia lay on the southern marches of Northumbria and to the north of Wessex. The shire system was first recorded in Scotland's border country and it was certainly well established as the climate began to warm in the mid 10th century. Scots kings pursued these valuable holdings with persistent vigour and, at the Battle of Carham on the Tweed in 1018, the army of Malcolm II scored a bloody, emphatic and decisive victory over the Earl of Bamburgh – decisive in that it confirmed Scots control of the farms of the Tweed valley.

When the Gaelic-speaking axemen of the Scots king roared their war cries and incited the battle frenzy, the rage fit, they did not charge an army of English spearmen led by an English earl. The warriors who faced them on the banks of the Tweed were Northumbrians, men native to what is only now known as the Scottish Borders, men who spoke an early form of Scots, who would have regarded the host of Malcom I and King Owain of Strathclyde as a horde of invading foreigners. The modern fact of the frontier on the Tweed tends to distort perceptions, characterising Carham as somehow being a moment of liberation, of a welcome inclusion of the Borders into Scotland whose manifest destiny had always been to become Scottish. This way of looking at history backwards misses the reality, the fact that most of the fertile south-east of Scotland had been Anglian in language and culture for the four centuries since the victories of Aethelfrith, *Am Fleisaur*, 'the Trickster'. Law, lordship and farming as well as language resembled that of the communities to the south of the Tweed more closely than those north of the Forth. But, even though the Earl of Bamburgh was defeated at Carham and the incoming Gaelic-speaking lords left a scatter of place names at the likes of Glendearg and Bedrule, the lands lost to the kings from the north would, nevertheless, come to exert a tremendous influence in medieval and modern Scotland.

Two years before Malcolm II and King Owain marched down the Tweed Valley, the England of Aethelstan and Edgar passed into the North Sea empire of Cnut, the king miscalled and ridiculed as 'Canute'. A visionary monarch, he came to rule over Denmark and Norway and drew his most valuable kingdom of England into the Scandinavian world. Suddenly, the realm of Malcolm II became sandwiched between the empire of Cnut and the Norse earldom of Orkney which, by then, reached down to encompass Caithness, the Hebrides and the Isle of Man. But, before history could turn again, the imperial reach of the Scandinavian sea kings evaporated. Within the span of little more than a generation, Cnut's line failed, his empire fragmented and a Wessex king, in the shape of Edward the Confessor, once more sat on the throne of England.

Power did shift north of the Tweed as the dynasty of the macAlpins also faltered after the death of Malcolm II. He was succeeded by Duncan I in 1034, a king who turned his attention north to the lands beyond the mountains, to an unlikely legacy from the days of Dalriada.

The descendants of the Cenel Loairn were a constant and real threat to the macAlpins. In 1032, Malcolm II had blazed through Moray, burning Gillacomgain 'along with fifty of his men'. Not styled as king but rather as Great Steward of Moray, he may have made oaths of loyalty to Malcolm which had not been kept. But vengeance did not wait long as a King of Moray fought his way to fame and literary infamy. There is a terse entry in a chronicle compiled in Mainz by a Scottish cleric, Marianus Scotus, for the year 1040: 'Duncan, the king of Scotland, was killed in the autumn, by his Dux Macbethad, Findlaech's son, who succeeded to the kingship for seventeen years.'

The pivotal battle probably took place at Elgin as Duncan raided in the north in an attempt to subdue 'his Dux', perhaps a Latin version of Mormaer or Great Steward. On the macAlpin king's death, Macbeth seized the crown as of right, a descendant of the Cenel Loairn, the ancient kindred of Dalriada. And, despite his reign being born in blood and despite the indelible stain of Shakespeare's play, it seems that Macbeth ruled over a land at peace after 1040. Certainly the new king was sufficiently secure to embark on pilgrimage to Rome ten years after the battle at Elgin, and it was said that 'he scattered money like seed'. Macbeth's name may offer a glimmer of his character for it is not a patronymic, like MacDonald, rather its literal meaning is 'Son of Life' and it may have been in recognition of his piety.

In the year 1054, the *Anglo-Saxon Chronicle* noted that: 'At this time the Earl Siward went with a great army into Scotland with both fleet and land force; and brought thence much war-spoil, such as no man had gained before; but his son, Osbern, and his sister's son, Siward, and numbers of his housecarls as well as those of the king were slain there on the Day of the Seven Sleepers.'

This forgotten Christian festival was celebrated on 27 July and its events eventually found their way into the text of the great Shakespearean tragedy, albeit in a much-altered version. Later chronicles offered more precision. Siward or Sigurd the Stout was Earl of Northumbria and York, one of the Scandinavian magnates who had acquired great wealth and power under Cnut, and his expedition northwards was an attempt to win back the territories lost at Carham. His fleet sailed into the Firth of Tay and as far inland as the shallow draught of the longships would allow. Andrew Wyntoun's *Orygynale Cronykil of Scotland* reckoned that the sea lords 'passed over Forth, down straight to Tay, up that water the high way, to Birnam to gather whole'. Wyntoun went on to locate the Battle of the Seven Sleepers at Dunsinane, clearly Dunsinnan Hill, a place that figures fatally in the play. There, the ramparts of an ancient hillfort can still be seen and it may be that the battle was, in fact, a siege and that attackers approached through the cover of Birnam Wood. But, even though there was said to be great slaughter and a defeat for the Scottish king, Macbeth survived to reign for a further three years. Siward the Stout died of dysentery a year later.

It may be that defeat at Dunsinane forced Macbeth to retreat north to his Moray heartlands and, in 1057, at Lumphanan in Aberdeenshire, his host faced the army of the future Malcolm III, the king who would be known as Canmore, the Great Leader. It appears that the battle was the culmination of a chase. Lumphanan lies at the northern end of the pass known as the Cairn o' Mount and Macbeth's war band seems to have taken that route after raiding in the south. Pursued by Malcolm III, Macbeth was badly wounded and the prophet, Berchan, related that he, nevertheless, made his way south to Scone, the ceremonial centre of Scotland, the place where new kings were crowned. It seems likely that, as he rode over the high pass and through the fields of Angus and the Mearns, he knew he was mortally wounded but wanted to see his stepson, Lulach, confirmed and anointed in the place of the High Shields, acclaimed by the warriors with the Singing Shields. According to Berchan, Macbeth died when 'he spewed blood on the evening of a night after a duel', almost certainly meaning the battle at Lumphanan. The son of Gruoch, now the Queen Dowager, Lulach became the new High King but he reigned for only seven months. The Irish *Annals of Tigernach* related that, in 1058, 'Lulach, king of Scotland, was treacherously slain by Malcolm, son of Duncan'.

The fact that his stepfather, Macbeth, had a legitimate claim to the high kingship through his descent from the Cenel Loairn appears to have been accepted (and the later charge of usurpation rejected) for the slain king was buried at Iona as were his predecessors and successors.

The house of the macAlpins had retrieved the throne and this pivotal battle, one that would shift the centre of Scotland's historical gravity to the south, was fought at Essie in Strathbogie, not far from Huntly. But the death of Lulach did not mark an end to the ambitions of the Cenel Loairn. In 1085, a man called Mael Snechtai, a fascinating name or title meaning the 'Follower of the Snows', had been hailed as King of Moray. Perhaps he campaigned from a mountain base as he sought the high kingship of Scotland.

While he was still paramount in Scotland, Macbeth welcomed two men who were to be the first of many, men who would change the face of medieval

Scotland. In the struggles between Earl Godwin of Wessex and Edward the Confessor, two Norman knights 'Osbert and Hugh surrendered their castles . . . went into Scotland and were kindly received by Macbeth, king of Scots'. They probably joined the royal host as mercenaries. Across Western Europe and even as far south as Sicily, Norman knights and Norman military innovation were changing the way in which kings and magnates thought about warfare and politics.

Gongu-Hrolf was tall, too tall to ride one of the shaggy, little native ponies used by Viking war bands once they had beached their longships. His name translates as 'Rolf the Walker' and perhaps his stride kept pace with his mounted companions. His ambition certainly outstripped that of most Viking raiders. Born some time in the 860s, Rolf may have been the nephew of a great magnate, Rognvald Eysteinsson, Earl of More in Norway and one of the founders of the earldom of Orkney. In the 880s, he and other warriors seized land along the banks of the Seine in Northern France and Rolf forced the king of France, Charles the Simple, to recognise his right to it. The great empire of Charlemagne was fragmenting and fraying at its edges. By creating Rolf the Walker Dux or Duke of Normandy, the land of the Northmen, Charles was acknowledging no more than a political reality but he was also drawing the Viking and his war bands into a new kind of relationship.

Having ennobled Rolf with the fancy Latin rank of Dux, he made him a royal vassal. The western part of the Carolingian Empire, known as Neustria, had its capital place at Paris and it too was breaking up into smaller units as the old imperial counties of Anjou, Toulouse and Flanders began to act more or less autonomously under their counts. But Rolf and his successors remained loyal to the nascent French monarchy as tenant-in-chief while the structures and nomenclature of what became known as feudalism began to emerge.

In the gloriously eclectic Burrell Collection in Glasgow's Pollok Park, where Renoirs rub shoulders with Ming dynasty china, there is a tiny, beautifully wrought memorial to a profound military and political revolution that rippled through Western Europe after the break-up of the Carolingian Empire. No more than three inches square, the Temple Pyx is a gilded bronze plaque from the early 12th century that shows the figures of three fully armed and armoured knights. Dismounted and fast asleep, leaning over their shields, they are thought to have formed part of a reliquary and may represent King Herod's soldiers. According to the New Testament, they slept while guarding the imprisoned St Peter who stole away in the night.

In such a small object, the sharpness of detail is stunning as the sculptor picked out swords, spears, the characteristic conical helmets with nose pieces and the mail shirts of Norman knights. This equipment and the fighting techniques that went with it developed in north-western Europe and amongst its greatest exponents were the descendants and dependents of the dukes of Normandy. And across Western and Mediterranean Europe, squadrons of Norman knights, armoured like the soldiers of the Temple Pyx, not only changed the political map but also refashioned the agricultural hinterland to sustain their new and dynamic means of making war.

Fundamental was the mail coat or shirt. Although this usually weighed about 30 pounds and was exhausting to wear for long periods, its effectiveness, flexibility and durability could protect a knight from all but the heaviest blows, giving him confidence and initiative in the ruck and confusion of battle. The Bayeux Tapestry is an excellent source for the widespread wearing of mail in a Norman army, but behind it lay what must have been an industrial process. After iron had been mined and smelted, a smith began the laborious work of making a shirt. Modern estimates reckon it took 800 hours to rivet together thousands of links of iron. This, in turn, implies sustained production on a considerable scale.

It is believed that this process began when ingots of iron were pulled out into lengths of wire. These were then wound around a rod of the required thickness to form links which were then cut down one side of the rod and separated. The open ends of these rings, not much larger than a wedding band, were then hammered flat on an anvil before being linked to four other rings and closed with a tiny rivet. Close work such as this was probably done outside for the maximum light but, on darker days or in the winter, the smiddy will have been brightly lit by the flames of torches and the glow of lamps. As a mail shirt was built up, the smith took care to turn the rivets to the outside and, to avoid bunching under the arms, a gap was left. Probably done in a production line with assistants making the links and a smith forming them into the shirt, the creation of this kind of armour must have been not only extended but also very expensive. And yet, in the Bayeux Tapestry, almost every Norman soldier is shown wearing a mail coat.

The early mounted cavalry led by Gongu-Hrolf (if he could find a horse big enough to carry him) and his immediate successors further protected themselves with round shields that were probably light enough to parry blows and to be used as aggressive weapons in their own right. By the time the Bayeux tapestry came to be stitched, design had changed and the mail-clad Norman soldiers all carried kite-shaped shields which were more suitable for mounted combat, the tapering tail covering the left leg if the knight was right handed. And the sharp end could also have been used to jab downwards at an opponent at close quarters. Most men also wore the distinctive conical helmet with the nose piece that could deflect or blunt a blow to the eyes.

What propelled armoured knights into battle and made their impact on medieval warfare so devastating were the destriers, their terrifying warhorses. Always left entire and trained to be aggressive, by kicking out and biting, these stallions thundered into the charge across many battlefields. Probably so-called because they led with the right foreleg, destriers were phenomenally expensive, costing at least eight times the value of a good riding horse. And, unlike a mail coat, they did not last. They grew old, were injured or killed and needed regular replacement. No details survive but there must have been very considerable resources devoted to breeding and feeding these snorting beasts. Medieval farmers understood the principles of selective husbandry and big, aggressive stallions successful in war will have been put to big mares each summer (a risky business in itself) to produce a steady string of spring foals. Even injured destriers could be used to further their breeding lines. And a large annual quantum of agricultural resources will have been needed to sustain this output, grass parks in the spring, summer and autumn and fields devoted to hay-making for winter forage – land that could not used to feed people or pasture animals that could produce milk or were eaten by people.

As the use of armoured knights in warfare became more and more influ-ential, more and more resources were given over to their upkeep – and their retinue. Each knight was usually attended by a squire, a young boy who acted as a servant and a groom, someone who was destined to mount a destrier one day. And they learned the rudiments of horsemanship very early. From the origins of knightly warfare in the 9th century, nostrums such as 'You can make a horseman of a lad at puberty – after that, never', or 'He who has stayed at school till the age of 12 and never ridden a horse is fit only to be a priest', were testament to the importance of an early familiarity with horses. Hunting was seen as a good training ground, the chase across rough country with unexpected obstacles teaching boys to sit tight, and tournaments and the practice of arms helped accustom them to the hurly-burly of combat, sharpening reactions. Saddles with high pommels and cantles were made so that the rider was wedged in and stirrups were ridden long to allow a straight leg to brace the rider for impact.

Couched under the arm, the lance became the knight's primary weapon and as squadrons began the practice of forming up in tight formation to charge in a line, each man spurred his destrier into the gallop. And moments before reaching the ranks of the enemy, they lowered their lances. Such was the impact that a knight risked being catapulted backwards if he was not tight in the saddle and had not pushed his legs forwards against the juddering thud of hitting an opponent. After battle lines had broken up and fighting at close quarter began, knights aimed to swing their slashing swords down on the heads and shoulders of infantry, their height conferring a great advantage. Foot soldiers always aimed to unhorse a knight, hacking at his reins and tack or attempting to hamstring the destrier by cutting at its legs. Since they held a shield in one hand and a weapon in the other, medieval cavalrymen guided their mounts with their seats or their legs. Pricking spurs helped and, when they could grab the reins, powerful, curbed bits pulled on the mouths of the warhorses.

On 14 October 1066, the knights and archers of William of Normandy's invading army eventually wore down the exhausted warriors of Harold II who had formed a shield wall on Senlac Hill, near Hastings. The terrain had been unsuitable for cavalry charges but the death of the English king towards the end of that fateful day appears to have been decisive. After Hastings, Duke William quickly had himself crowned at Westminster on Christmas Day and began to establish control over his new realm. In 1068, the king of Scotland was drawn into taking sides when Malcolm Canmore, no doubt encouraged by his queen, the saintly and Saxon Margaret, gave sanctuary to royal refugees fleeing north. Amongst the Saxon exiles was Edgar the Aetheling, the last male heir of the House of Wessex.

In 1070, Canmore led raids into the north of England, anxious to revive his dynasty's claims to Northumbria and Cumbria at a time when England had been conquered but not yet subdued. When William I found the time to deal with this threat two years later, his mail-clad cavalry drove into the heart of Scotland and, at Abernethy, Canmore was compelled to swear homage to the Norman king, becoming his vassal. This was an important moment. At the heart of the evolving practices of feudalism lay the bond of vassalage, the mutual acceptance of lordship and homage by two otherwise free men. At the ceremony at Abernethy, King Malcolm knelt before him to swear an oath to become William's man, bound to render military service in return for his kingdom of Scotland – which he 'held of' the English king. Although later repudiated and not accepted for much of the 13th century, this bond was to underlie relations between the two nations throughout the medieval period.

Malcolm Canmore's long reign, from 1058 to 1093, saw his realm change radically. From his palace at Dunfermline, he and his Hungarian-Saxon queen saw the incoming tide of Norman influence as men and ambition ventured north and members of their immediate family made links with the new elite in the south. By a mixture of personal piety and political pressure, Queen Margaret had brought the Scottish Church closer to Rome and the Pope and, at the same time, had successfully delivered dynastic strength and continuity with the birth of six surviving sons and two daughters. Between 1097 and 1153, her three younger sons, the macMalcolms, would rule Scotland and her daughter Maud would become the Queen of England, the wife of King Henry 1. Kings Edgar, Alexander and especially David welcomed the arrival of many Norman-French lords, gave them lands, introduced new ways of governing and, perhaps most enduringly, founded great religious institutions, churches, cathedrals, convents and monasteries.

ST MARGARET, QUEEN OF THE FERRY

One of the tantalizingly few women in early Scotland to have any sort of historical presence, this English princess owes much to Turgot, a monk who later became Bishop of St Andrews. His biography was the first to be written about a woman in Scotland. While it recounted charming tales of Margaret reading bible stories to her rough and untutored husband, Malcolm Canmore, and generally civilizing the barbarous Gael, the biography was of course deeply political. Turgot was an English monk and he and his queen wished to see the Church in Scotland move closer to the Church in England and in Rome – and away from the traditional, more independent practices of Celtic Christianity, which looked to Columba and the west rather than to the south. Margaret seems to have been genuinely devout and she established ferries at Queensferry and North Berwick to bring pilgrims across to the kingdom of Fife and the shrine of St Andrew at St Andrews.

Canmore was forced to submit at Abernethy because his warriors were no match for the squadrons of King William's battle-hardened mail-clad knights. But he could still raid. In 1079, Scots skirmishers blazed into Northumbria, penetrating far to the south and the Conqueror sent his son,

Robert Curthose, to secure the frontier. On the north bank of the Tyne, he had the New Castle built, his masons making much use of cut and dressed stone from Hadrian's Wall. Curthose commanded a motte-and-bailey castle to be thrown up quickly on the site of the Roman fort that guarded the Pons Aelius, the bridge over the Tyne named for the Emperor's family. It was defensible by 1080, sitting astride the lowest bridging point of the river. Another of the Conqueror's sons, William Rufus, led a force northwards to secure the western frontier in 1092 when he drove out Canmore's governor from Carlisle Castle, another fortress fashioned from Roman stone.

Amongst the power elite of Scottish society, the old Celtic order was passing – but not without bloodshed. When Malcolm Canmore and his son, Edward, were killed while raiding in Northumbria, his queen was said to have turned her face to the wall and died of grief when she heard the news. Resentment and opportunism bubbled up amongst the native aristocracy and, following the old laws of royal succession, they hailed Canmore's brother, Donald Ban, as king. In 1094, he drove out those Norman knights and their retainers who had come to settle in the north after the conquest.

Having taken Carlisle Castle and inherited his father's suzerainty over Scotland, William II Rufus gave Canmore's son, Duncan, an army and despatched him north to dispose of the Celtic usurper. Success was short-lived. And so was Duncan. Because he had been forced to send Rufus's soldiers back south, the new king was much weakened and, at Mondynes, near Stonehaven, Duncan was killed by the war band of *Mael Petair* (an unusual name, meaning 'Follower of St Peter'), probably the Thane of the Mearns. Now an old man, Donald Ban found himself restored to the kingship. But not for long. In 1097, Duncan's younger brother, Edgar, led another army lent by Rufus and, this time, he was successful – and cruel. Remembering the need for Celtic kings to be unblemished and entire, he had his jailers put out the eyes of Donald Ban, condemning him to a blundering, miserable death two years later in prison somewhere in Angus. Significantly, he was the last king of Scotland to be buried on Iona.

Symbolic, political and defining, the names of kings marked a break with the past. It may have been Gaelicised as *Etgar macMail Choluim* but Edgar was a Wessex name that remembered his mother's Anglo-Saxon heritage and a 10th-century royal ancestor. When he died unmarried and childless in 1107, King Edgar of Scotland was succeeded by his younger brother, Alexander – the first of that name and almost certainly named by the pious Queen Margaret after Pope Alexander II, who had given his blessing to William of Normandy's plans to invade England and also handed him the Standard of

St Peter. More practically, the Pope had also issued an edict to the English clergy to support the Norman Conquest. When Margaret and Malcolm gave their son such a radically different name, it may not only have been an obvious departure from the Duncans, Donalds and Malcolms of the Celtic past but also an endorsement of the seismic changes that were taking place in England, changes that would ripple northwards very quickly. Alexander's younger brother, Margaret's sixth son, was called David, a biblical name and the beginning of a long tradition of Christian names, names from scripture.

Beside an old graveyard on the banks of the River Ury in Aberdeenshire, an imposing, clearly man-made earthen mound rises. The Bass of Inverurie is a monument to the reach of feudalism to almost every part of Lowland Scotland. Built in the middle of the 12th century, it is the motte or mound of a large motte-and-bailey castle, a structure that anchored the new order in the Scottish landscape. These fortresses were developed by the Normans and the Bayeux Tapestry shows men heaping up earth to create a motte at Hastings. The concept was simple – and quickly achievable by small groups or, more likely, a press-ganged local population. The upcast from a roughly circular ditch was piled up to form an upside down pudding basin shape with a flattened platform on its summit. The French chronicler of the early 12th century, Jean de Colmieu, described the construction of the motte-and-bailey castles he saw in the region around Calais. Labourers would make 'a mound of earth as high as they can and dig a ditch about it as wide and deep as possible. The space on top of the mound is enclosed by a palisade of very strong hewn logs, strengthened at intervals by as many towers as their means can provide. Inside the enclosure is a citadel, or keep, which commands the whole circuit of the defences. The entrance to the fortress is by means of a bridge, which, rising from the outer side of the moat and supported on posts as it ascends, reaches to the top of the mound.'

Built a generation after de Colmieu was writing, the Bass of Inverurie is huge and will have taken many thousands of man hours, perhaps as long as six months. Protected by the river and a ditch as well as its height, the Bass was secure against attack from cavalry or infantry. Hides could be slung over the walls of the wooden citadel or keep to defend against fire arrows. Around the foot of the motte was an outer enclosed courtyard known as the bailey and it was protected by a second palisade and a ditch beyond it. In times of peace, this was the heart of the castle where most people lived and worked. Larger baileys like the one at Inverurie had inside their perimeters a hall, workshops, barracks, a chapel and storerooms. The bailey might well have to be abandoned in an attack but the Bass may have been made even more difficult to besiege by a ditch that could be filled with water diverted from the River Ury.

Alexander I began a programme of castle-building in Scotland after he followed his brother on to the throne in 1107. Stirling Castle first comes on record in 1110 but its great rock had been topped by fortresses long before then. Alexander had a chapel dedicated at Stirling and there was almost certainly a royal hall inside the palisade. Stirling may have been a frequent residence for the king for it lay at the heart of that part of Scotland he controlled directly. On his death, Edgar had left instructions that the southern part of his kingdom should come into the possession of his younger brother, David. This arrangement was probably made at the instigation of the English king, Henry I. After 1107, David began to style himself *Princeps Cumbriae*, the 'Prince of Cumbria', the title probably being a legacy of the old kingdom of Strathclyde.

During the dynastic upheavals of the 1090s, caution persuaded David's older sister, Edith, known as Maud or Matilda by her family, to remove herself and her little brother to the court of William Rufus in the south. When he was killed in mysterious circumstance while hunting in the New Forest, Rufus's throne was seized by Henry while his older brother and the rightful heir, Robert Curthose, was away on crusade. After a hurried coronation, Henry consolidated his position by marrying Maud. By 1100 she had status as the sister of the King of Scotland. In the Norman-French milieu of the English court, David macMalcolm had been transformed into David fitzMalcolm and when his sister became queen, his fortunes were also transformed.

Probably as a reward for fighting alongside Henry in battles against his brother, Robert, in Normandy, David was given a lordship in the Cotentin, also known as in the Cherbourg Peninsula. It was a link that would have a long and telling legacy throughout Scotland's history.

When Henry I forced Alexander of Scotland to accept Edgar's bequest of this vast tract of land to David, the whole of the Tweed Basin and the Clyde Valley, he made the young man powerful – but for strategic reasons. Not only did David a control a friendly zone between the two kingdoms, he was also a useful ally. In 1102, the Earl of Shewsbury had rebelled, and after his defeat Henry redistributed his lands to create marcher lordships to protect his western borders from incursion by the Welsh princes. By making his brother-in-law a great magnate in southern Scotland, the English king hoped to create a buffer between him and the ambitions of the king of Scotland to extend his realm into the north of England.

What made the man styled as 'brother of the queen' an even more powerful lord was a remarkable Christmas present. Matilda, the widow of Simon de Senlis, the Earl of Huntingdon, Bedford and Northampton and daughter of Waltheof, Earl of Northumbria, was one of the wealthiest and most widely landed women in England. At the Christmas court of 1113, Henry I gave Matilda to David in marriage. The so-called Honour of Huntingdon made the young man a great magnate in England as well as Scotland and also kept him loyal as a marcher lord in the north. Significantly, Henry I kept the earldom of Northumbria in royal ownership.

One of Earl David's earliest acts was to confirm the possessions of the Cluniacs, an order of reformed Benedictine monks who had founded a monastery in Northampton. Amongst the witnesses to the earl's charter was a man known simply as John the Chaplain. Almost certainly at his instigation, Earl David invited another community of monks from France to found a monastery in the Scottish Borders. From Tiron in the Forest of Perche, south of Normandy, the Tironensians sent 13 monks, emblematic of Christ and the Apostles, to Selkirk and the banks of the Ettrick, close to its confluence with the Tweed. They arrived in 1113 and their detailed founding charter shines a bright new light on a landscape that was changing fast. Before listing the lavish gifts of extensive estates and revenues, it begins: 'David the Earl, son of Malcolm King of Scots, [gives] greetings to all his friends, French, English and Scots, all of whom are the sons of the holy Church of God.'

And at the end, the names of 29 men and one woman are appended as witnesses. In addition to Countess Matilda, Henry, son of the Earl, and Bishop John, there are no fewer than 11 men with Norman-French names, amongst them Robert de Bruis, Hugh de Morville and Robert Corbet, already significant landowners in Scotland. Three of the witnesses are probably Englishmen and only 7 appear to be native Scots while the remainder are difficult to place. It is a cosmopolitan list attached to a precise document endowing 13 French monks with great wealth, land and power.

Described centuries later by James I as a 'sair sanct for the croon', David was thought to be profligate as he founded monasteries and convents across the Borders and later across Scotland. Piety does indeed appear to have been a prime motive. Like most of his contemporaries, David's faith seems to have been absolute and the sole motive noted for the gifts in the charter was 'the salvation of [his] soul' and those of his family and his ancestors. But there were other reasons. Reckoned to be an order with a practical emphasis, the Tironensians were interested in craftsmanship, in husbandry and the operation of an efficient, creative and workmanlike institution. David wanted to develop his great inheritance and see its farming economy flourish under the guidance of literate, educated communities of monks who had international connections.

JOHN CAPELLANUS

One of the most influential men in 12th-century Scotland is also one of the most mysterious. John the Chaplain was David I's closest advisor and an architect of the early Scottish Church. Before he became Bishop of Glasgow, John Achaius (a Latinisation of the Gaelic name Eochaid *– which is odd, since he was almost certainly a Frenchman) brought the first communities of reformed monks to Scotland and Britain when a foundation was set up in 1113 at Selkirk and later moved to Kelso. He then brought more groups of monks to Jedburgh and Lesmahagow. He was probably originally a monk at the immensely influential house of Tiron in France. As Bishop of Glasgow, John fought hard for the independence of the Scottish Church, refusing to submit to the Archbishop of York and travelling to Rome several times to plead the case for St Andrews being elevated to an archbishopric. Recently archaeologists have identified the site of his bishop's palace at Ancrum, near Jedburgh, then part of the diocese of Glasgow. John the Chaplain died in 1147, having seen the beginnings of Glasgow Cathedral rise from the foundations, and he was succeeded by another Tironensian, Abbot Herbert of Kelso.*

In the Selkirk charter, David made sure the new monastery had cash: 'And in Berwick one carucate, and one measure below the church on the Tweed, and half of one fishing, and a seventh part of the [produce] of the mill, and 40 solidi [silver pennies] from the annual tax revenue of the burgh. And in the burgh of Roxburgh one measure [of land], and a seventh of the mills, and 40 solidi from the annual tax revenue, and a seventh part of the fishings.' These are the first references to urban life in Scotland, two towns or burghs that are clearly busy and productive, operating a money economy on some scale, able to generate tax revenues for Earl David. As burghs were founded in the early 12th century, they were royal creations, referred to as 'my' or 'our' places by the king's clerks. And they were new and dynamic, stimulating the agrarian economy by opening up markets. Kings made burghs by granting privileges to groups of merchants and craftsmen. Many were English-speaking incomers, others came from further afield. Burghs were a major conduit for the spread of the northern dialect of English that came to be known as Scots. Mainard the Fleming was appointed by Bishop Robert some time between 1145 and 1150 to supervise the layout and building of the burgh of St Andrews. Several essential elements were involved. There needed to be a market and a market place. Often this simply involved widening the main street sufficiently to accommodate stalls, livestock and other produce and its sellers and buyers. A tollbooth or town house was where tolls or taxes were collected and, at Lauder, a burgh that has retained its medieval shape, the old tollbooth stands at the point where the high street is widest.

Tolls were levied on those who wished to enter the town and bring or buy produce at the market and that meant the creation of boundaries and gates. At St Andrews, the medieval West Port still survives, but in most early burghs only street names remember the control of the movement of merchandise. Medieval Perth had town walls but most boundaries were earthworks, banks and ditches planted with what was known as 'quickset' or thorn hedges making them difficult to penetrate. Houses were generally built with their gable ends on the street frontage and pends led down past them to allow access to backlands, long parcels of land where workshops, storehouses, byres and cesspits were located. Behind South Street frontages in St Andrews, several long backlands have been preserved.

For Earl David, Roxburgh and the port of Berwick were the economic hubs. Now entirely effaced, not one stone left standing upon another, Roxburgh has completely disappeared. Once, its streets bustled with the hum of trade, wealthy merchants endowed its churches, children were taught in its school and the mint master hammered out silver pennies. But in the 14th and 15th centuries history rumbled over the town and obliterated it. Its golden age lasted less than two centuries. With its mighty castle guarding the western approach, Roxburgh was much favoured and frequented by Earl David and, in 1128, after he had become king, he moved the Tironensians downriver to Kelso to re-found their monastery. Kelso Abbey grew into the richest and most influential of Scotland's medieval foundations, with daughter houses at Arbroath, Kilwinning and Lindores and a priory at Lesmahagow.

Wool and hides were what made Roxburgh grow and prosper. Annual, biannual or quarterly fairs, rather than weekly local markets, brought an international trade. As monasteries such as Melrose, Jedburgh, Kelso and Dryburgh organised their great sheep ranches and exploited their English and European links, trade grew quickly. Recently revived, St James's Fair (known in Kelso as Jimie's Fair) had a continuous history from the 12th century until the 1930s, even though the burgh that brought it into being had long disappeared. Its modern descendant is the Border Union Show held at the end of July. Eight centuries ago merchants used to come from England, Flanders and Italy to buy wool and hides at the fair and these bulk commodities were transported downriver to Berwick's quays and the waiting ships. Later records list very large volumes of trade. In the decades before 1286 and the beginning of the depredations of the Wars of Independence, wine, oil, spices, salt, dried vegetables, pots and pans and much else were all landed at Berwick and the holds would have been refilled with hides wool, woolfells (sheepskins), salt herring and live animals. In 1275, two Berwick merchants formed a partnership to export huge volumes to Europe via the port of Hull. Cargoes of hides amounted to 45,000 lbs; 180 woolfells were sent south and 180lbs of sheared wool. What lay behind these numbers was a vibrant and productive agrarian economy in the Tweed Basin, what Earl David had in mind when he began to bring his burghs into being.

When Alexander I died in 1124, the new principles of primogeniture should have ensured the succession of his son, Malcolm. It is ironic that, by taking his brother's throne, David did precisely what Donald Ban did after the death of Malcolm Canmore. It looked like a reversion to Celtic custom but, in fact, it was little more than the exercise of blunt politics. In 1124, Earl David, Prince of Cumbria, had a secure and prosperous power base in his sprawling principality in southern Scotland and his rich holdings in southern England – and, more importantly, he had the support of Henry I.

Malcolm macAlasdair, the son of Alexander, had the support of the north and the King of Moray. Oengus appears to have successfully reasserted his family's dominance and, as the grandson of King Lulach, he himself had a credible claim to the throne. Once David had been persuaded to undergo the rituals of coronation at Scone (His biographer, Aelred of Rievaulx reported that the young king 'so abhorred those acts of homage which are offered by the Scottish nation in the manner of their fathers upon the recent promotion of their kings, that he was with difficulty compelled by the bishops to receive them'.), he attempted to deal with the claims of Malcolm. The chronicler Orderic Vitalis noted that two fierce battles were fought before the rebels retreated northwards.

In 1130, while David was in England at the court of Henry I, insurrection flared once more. At the head of an army raised in Moray, Malcolm and King Oengus moved south. Met at Stracathro in Angus by a royal host led by the Constable, Edward, the rebels were defeated, Oengus was killed and Malcolm fled into the mountains of the west. Moray fell to Edward's advancing army and, in the years that followed, motte-and-bailey castles like the Bass of Inverurie were raised, incoming knights were given land and the old kingdom was secured as part of the realm of Scotland. Rebels and rival contenders from Moray could be cruelly dealt with. A colourful and unlikely rival for the kingship was the Bishop of the Isles, Wimund, who raised rebellion. But, when he was captured in c. 1140, the king ordered that Wimund, his own nephew, be blinded and castrated before being sent far from the north of Scotland to prison at Byland Abbey in Yorkshire. To pacify Moray, David sent Freskin the Fleming north and gave him lands and power around Elgin (his family adopted the style 'de Moravia' which later became Murray), burghs were set up and Urquhart Priory was founded by monks from Dunfermline. With the help of a fleet and a large force of knights sent by Henry I, the supporters of Malcolm macAlasdair were subdued and, in 1134, he was, at last, captured and imprisoned in Roxburgh Castle, far from the mountains.

A year later, David's great patron, Henry I, died. Lacking a male heir, he had designated his daughter, Matilda, as his successor and, in 1127, bound his great magnates in an oath of allegiance to her. One of the first to swear it was David I of Scotland. When Stephen of Blois crossed the Channel and had himself crowned, making civil war inevitable, David, pragmatic as ever, took advantage and invaded the north of England without delay. After two years of raids, negotiations and accommodations with King Stephen, David massed a huge army, perhaps more than 20,000 strong, and marched south into England, into territory he claimed for himself and the Scottish crown.

THE HALIWERFOLC

Literally, 'the People of the Holy Man', this was an early definition of Englishness. The Holy Man was St Cuthbert and his people lived south of the Tweed (although, early in its use, the term may also have referred to some people to the north) and they were later ruled by the Prince-Bishops of Durham. After the Viking attacks on the original centre of the bishopric on Lindisfarne, the monks took St Cuthbert's famously uncorrupted body and his relics with them as they walked around the lands of the Haliwerfolc. They visited Norham, perhaps Jedburgh and settled for a time at Chester-le-Street before work on the shrine and the cathedral at Durham began. These journeys helped establish the idea of St Cuthbert's Land as somewhere that was not Scotland.

By late July 1138, the Scots had crossed the Tyne and were moving deep into the bishopric of Durham, what was known as St Cuthbert's Land. At York, the 70-year-old Archbishop Thurstan hurriedly assembled a council of war where the great magnates of the north appeared to waver, perhaps even panic, at the news of invasion. According to the chronicler Richard of Hexham the old prelate presided over a fragile alliance:

> Archbishop Thurstan of York (who, as will presently appear, greatly exerted himself in this emergency), William of Aumale, Walter de Gant, Robert de Brus, Roger de Mowbray, Walter Espec, Gilbert de Lacy, William de Percy, Richard de Courcy, William Fossard, Robert de Stuteville [attended].
>
> Much irresolution was caused by distrust of each other, arising from suspicions of treachery, by the absence of a chief and leader of the war (for their sovereign, king Stephen, encompassed by equal difficulties in the south of England, was just then unable to join them), and by their dread of encountering, with an inadequate force, so great a host.

The size and reported ferocity of the Scots army persuaded Thurstan and his council to offer terms. Two men whose names would resonate and clash in Scotland's medieval history rode north to meet the Scots king. Bernard de Baliol and Robert de Brus had both sworn homage to David and de Brus had been granted the vast Lordship of Annandale in 1124. But he also held lands in Yorkshire at Skelton, a lordship which lay directly in the path of the advancing Scots. Not for the first time did a Bruce appear to play both sides for family advantage. Aelred of Rievaulx reported a fascinating set of arguments made at the parley. In David's army were contingents of Galwegians – wild Celtic, Gaelic-speaking warriors from the south-west of Scotland renowned for their feral savagery, men Bruce did not admire. 'Therefore I ask you my lord, have you found such fidelity in the Scots that you can safely dismiss the counsel of the English for yourself and your people and deprive yourself of the aid of the Normans, as if the Scots alone sufficed even against the Scots. This reliance in the Galwegians is new to you. Today you are attacking with arms those through whom you have until now ruled, beloved by the Scots and terrible to the Galwegians.'

This speech seemed to summarise the pull of two worlds, what David must have wrestled with personally and politically for much of his reign. He was the son of Malcolm Canmore, An Ceann Mor, the great Gaelic-speaking dynast, but he was also the Earl of Huntingdon, a Normanised knight who had unexpectedly inherited a kingdom and had quickly used all the aspects of the new feudal order – motte-and-bailey castles, the bonds of vassalage, the granting of fiefdoms, the use of armoured knights and the founding of great religious houses and burghs – to effect a revolution in the governance of Scotland. And yet David controlled only the Lowland zone – the Highlands and the Islands, both west and north, were beyond his reach. More than that, the majority of his subjects almost certainly still spoke Celtic languages (although Old Welsh was dying) and lived in a thoroughly Celtic cultural milieu. He had reached an accommodation with the Lords of Galloway and wanted to bring the south-west into his kingdom of Scotland and its army. But every instinct told David that the future lay not with the battle frenzy of its savage warriors but with the modern structures of feudalism.

Aelred had some sympathy with Bruce, 'a worthy old man, belonging by law to the King of England, but from youth an adherent of the King of Scotland', but the parley broke down in rancour and the emissaries returned to Thirsk to report that battle seemed inevitable. The Scots army crossed the Tees and probably moved down the Great North Road, the line of an old Roman road that ran to the east of Dere Street. Meanwhile Thurstan had put steel in the spines of the Yorkshire magnates by summoning God to fight at their sides. Perhaps the prospect of the wild, barely Christian, probably pagan warriors from Galloway had persuaded the wily old bishop that this conflict might be seen as a battle against darkness, a holy mission to defeat barbarians – perhaps even a crusade. The English mustered at York and moved to the north of Northallerton to deploy across a ridge that ran east to west, adjacent to the road that David's army was marching down. At their centre was a battle cart of the type that was common in Italy where it was known as a *carroccio*. Mounted on the bed of the cart, so that they could be seen by all, were the blessed banners of the great minsters at York, Beverley and Ripon. They gave their name to what followed – the Battle of the Standard.

Unusually well documented, the prelude to the fighting was emblematic of how Scotland had begun to unify and emerge, often painfully, from the Celtic past in the opening decades of the 12th century. John of Worcester reckoned that David I's opening gambit was to attempt to take the English by surprise, there being a very dense mist that morning. Richard of Hexham wrote: 'In front of the battle were the Picts [ie the Galwegians]; in the centre, the king with his knights and English; the rest of the barbarian host poured roaring around them. The king and almost all his followers were on foot, their horses being kept at a distance.'

FIFTY SHADES OF GREY, BLACK AND WHITE – AND RED

Street names recall Scotland's monastic orders. In Edinburgh, there are several: Blackfriars Street, the Canongate, Greyfriars, Abbeymount and others. Communities of Celtic monks and nuns had existed for centuries, but when David I brought the Tironensians to found an abbey at Selkirk in 1113, he was the first in Britain to introduce what became known as the reformed orders. Monasteries and nunneries had become lax, even worldly, and men like St Bernard of Clairvaux began to insist that the rule of St Benedict be much more strictly enforced. From the Forest of Perche in Northern France, the Tironensians were known for their industry as well as their piety, and where they had a community, they encouraged crafts and agriculture. Having moved downriver to Kelso, this reformed order founded daughter-houses at Lesmahagow, Arbroath and Kilwinning. Other orders followed, either directly from Europe or from houses set up in England. Cistercians, Cluniacs, Carthusians, Praemonstratensian Canons, Augustinians, Benedictines, amongst them. In the early 13th century mendicant orders were established, consisting of friars who maintained purity through poverty, and instead of owning vast estates, they at first lived by begging. St Francis founded the Franciscans or Greyfriars, St Dominic the Blackfriars or Dominicans, and there were even Red Friars, the Trinitarian order. But they too began to succumb to the generosity of the laity and friaries appeared in Scottish towns. Since their mission was often to preach, they had to be near centres of population. And they too gradually became more secularized.

The Galloway war bands seemed to the English chroniclers like devils, like nothing they had ever seen before. The Celtic habit of fighting bare-breasted (indeed sometimes naked) baffled them. Describing them, the historian and chronicler Ralph de Diceto wrote: 'Men agile, unclothed, remarkable for much nakedness, arming their left side with knives formidable to any armed men, having a hand most skilful at throwing spears and directing them from a distance; raising their long lance as a standard when they advance into battle.'

The men of Galloway had insisted on the right to stand in the front line and lead the army into battle. Aelred adds that 'the second line the King's son Prince Henry arranged with great wisdom; with himself the knights and archers, adding to their number the Cumbrians and Teviotdalesmen . . . The men of Lothian formed the third rank, with the islanders and the men of Lorne. The King kept in his own line the Scots and Moravians [men from Moray]; several also of the English and French knights he appointed as his bodyguard.'

Fighting almost naked, like the tattooed Celtic warriors of the Pictish past or the fables of the *Fenian Cycle*, the Galwegians believed in the sweeping momentum of the all-out charge. David had wanted to use his armoured knights but he had been persuaded otherwise, perhaps wishing to appease his new allies. What happened in the moments before the screaming Galwegians raced across the grass to the English lines may be seen as significant. Drawn from most of what would become the realm of Scotland, from Lowlands, Highlands and Islands, this army roared a war cry. It was *Albannaich*! 'Men of Scotland'! – the men of a nation that, in extremis, still understood itself in a Celtic language. But its power was waning, changing and the charge of the Galwegians failed, as they became impaled on the spears, swords and shields of the knights and men of Yorkshire. Aelred recorded a memorable image: 'Like a hedgehog with its quills, so would you see a Galwegian bristling all round with arrows, and nonetheless brandishing his sword, and in blind madness rushing forward now smite a foe, now lash the air with useless strokes.'

Despite his vast and terrifying host, David was defeated at the Battle of the Standard but 1138 saw neither his ambition nor his fortunes wane. Concluded a year later, the Treaty of Durham conceded Cumbria to Scotland, gave the heir to the throne, David's son Henry, the earldom of Northumbria and confirmed Henry in his possession of the Honour of Huntingdon. Despite the continuing Norse control of the Northern Isles and Caithness, Scotland may be said to have reached its greatest territorial extent as its king's and his son's writs ran to the Tyne and the southern foothills of the Cumbrian mountains. But it was not to last beyond the life of this most capable, revolutionary, astute and unlikely Scottish king.

In the possession of the dukes of Roxburgh and held in the National Library of Scotland, there is a beautifully preserved charter of 1159 that confirmed Kelso Abbey as the rightful owner of vast estates. Two miniature portraits have been painted in the loops of an initial M. It stands for Malcolmus and he, Malcom IV, sits on the right. Clearly a young man, he holds a sheathed sword across his lap and a sceptre in his right hand. Inside the left loop of the M is a bearded, much older man, David I, who holds an unsheathed sword upright and in his left hand an orb. The biblical references are hard to miss. Like the King of Israel and his son, Solomon, these men – although grandfather and grandson rather than father and son – and their royal line ruled by divine right. These are the first and, for many centuries, the best portraits of Scottish kings.

SCOTLAND'S OLDEST BOOK

Glasgow University's Special Collections turned out to contain a gem. A 12th-century manuscript copy of The Consolation of Philosophy *by the late Roman writer, Boethius, was found by Dr Kylie Murray in 2015. When she compared its illustrations and writing style to the foundation charter of Kelso Abbey, compiled in 1159, she found close similarities. The importance of this find is that it makes the Kelso copy the earliest Scottish book that does not deal with religion or the law. Boethius had been arrested for treason by the Ostrogothic King of Italy, Theodoric the Great, and he wrote the book as he awaited execution and mused on philosophy. When it came, his death was said to have been gruesome. A rope was tied around his head and tightened until his eyes bulged out and his skull cracked. The* Consolation of Philosophy *was one of the most copied and read books of the Middle Ages and its presence at Kelso shows an abbey connected to the mainstream of European thought.*

The Kelso charter was given by King Malcolm IV, the successor of David I whose son, Earl Henry, had died young in 1152. The oldest of Henry's three sons was quickly designated as his heir by the king and, at the tender age of eleven, the boy was sent on a tour of the kingdom accompanied by Duncan, Thane of Fife, the magnate who held the traditional right of placing the crown on the monarch's head. It was a show of strength and continuity. Duncan also led a very large escort of soldiers to discourage any outward expressions of dissent. And the point of the capital M was stressed as the touring party visited abbeys and churches – the macMalcolms should succeed one another, with the blessing of the Church and of God.

When David died at his castle at Carlisle on 24 May 1153, Malcolm and his retinue quickly rode to Scone to undergo the rituals of coronation only three days later. Continuity was, it seems, in no way taken for granted. Only twelve years old and a teenager for most of his reign, Malcolm was known as 'the Maiden'. He took no wife and fathered no children, one of the duties of a king. He certainly had a reputation for piety but he may have been gay or possibly impotent. For a year, Duncan of Fife ruled in his stead as 'rector' or regent but, when the young king embarked on his personal rule, it was quickly contested. Malcolm, son of Alexander I, had been freed from a long imprisonment from Roxburgh Castle and he rose in rebellion. What made the son of a recent king of Scots especially dangerous was the support he had from another king, a king in the west – the man known as *Ri Innse Gall*, the 'King of the Islands of the Strangers'.

Somerled the Viking is his traditional name and a guide to his ancestry. In early Norse, *Sumar-lidi* means 'Summer Traveller or Raider' and the attachment of Viking is something of a tautology. The son of a Celtic father and a Norse mother, myth swirls around the origins of Somerled and suggests that it was his prowess rather than his distinguished ancestry that brought him to prominence. The Islands of the Strangers or Foreigners is a reference to the Norse occupation of the Hebrides and, in the first half of the 12th century, this archipelago, the islands in the Clyde and the Isle of Man formed the Kingdom of the Isles. It was a sea kingdom patrolled by navies and marines rather than mounted armoured knights and infantry. Land was granted not for a quota of knights or spearmen but for galleys of eight, ten, twelve or more oars. During the reign of David I, Somerled had made himself master of part of it – Knapdale, Lorne, Argyll and Kintyre – and he may have sent soldiers to join the royal host at the Battle of the Standard. But, by 1156, his own ambitions had turned him from ally to aggressor.

THE HOUSE OF KEYS

Scotland is represented in four parliaments: Holyrood, Westminster, the European Parliament and in the House of Keys, the legislature of the Isle of Man. Its name is from the Manx number, kiare as feed, *'four and twenty' or '24' and it refers to the number of members. They represented the possessions of the old kingdom of Man – 16 members sat for the Isle of Man and 4 each for 'the Out Isles'. The Out Isles refers to Lewis and Skye – and at one time may also have included Harris and the Hebrides and the Clyde islands – which formally passed out of the kingdom in 1266. But the House of Keys refused to accept the loss as permanent and has continued to elect proxy members for the Out Isles.*

The Kingdom of the Isles was ruled from Man by Godred Crovan, Godfrey of the White Hand. As Somerled asserted himself more aggressively and obviously, the king sent the Manx fleet northwards and, on the night of 5 and 6 January 1156, they engaged with 80 galleys rowed by Somerled's marines off the coast of Colonsay. In the fire, confusion, fury and spray of the Hebridean night, Godred's navy was shattered. It was a victory not only for audacity but also for new technology. Somerled's triumph gained him the fertile island of Islay, the granary of the Hebrides, and a place name on its coast offers a reminder of how and why he won in the winter darkness. Dunyvaig is a natural but shallow harbour and its name means the 'Fort of the Little Ships'. Somerled almost certainly commanded a fleet of birlinns – ships that are also known as Hebridean galleys. Smaller than the Viking dragon ships and with a shallower draught that gave them the ability to sail into the rocky shallows and outrun larger vessels whose keels might have been ripped out by reefs, these little ships were also highly manoeuvrable. Instead of the steerboard or steering oar lashed to the stern side of a dragon ship, the birlinns had a hinged rudder attached directly to the sternpost. This enabled an experienced helmsman to turn his birlinn about quickly and also steer it much more accurately – crucial attributes in the ruck of a naval battle. Here is a translation from the 18th-century Gaelic poet, Alasdair macMhaighstear Alasdair that remembers the speed of the little ships in his 'The Birlinn of Clanranald':

> The smooth-handled oars, well-fashioned,
> Light and easy,
> That will do the rowing stout and sturdy,
> Quick-palmed, blazing,
> That will send the surge in sparkles,
> Up to skyward,
> All in flying spindrift flashing,
> Like a fire shower!
> With the fierce and pithy pelting
> Of the oar-bank,
> That will wound the swelling billows,
> With their bending.
> With the knife-blades of the white thin oars
> Smiting bodies,
> On the crest of the blue hills and glens,
> Rough and heaving.

His victory off Colonsay gave Somerled control of the Southern Hebrides and, although Godred retained rule over Lewis, Harris and Skye, his ships had to sail through hostile waters in order to reach their safe harbours. Two years later, Somerled launched another decisive attack on Godred Crovan, defeating him and establishing his control of the whole sea kingdom as Ri Innse Gall. In 1164, the King of the Islands of the Strangers over-reached himself. Anxious that Malcolm IV's great magnates might press hard on his dominions, he led his fleet of birlinns up the Firth of Clyde. Walter the Steward had been granted great estates on the shores of the Clyde and his men were prominent in the army mustered by Malcolm IV to meet the challenge of the Islesmen. In circumstances of confusion, Somerled was killed in a battle fought at Renfrew, probably by a force commanded by Herbert, Bishop of Glasgow. A near-contemporary source relates that, moments before the armies clashed, Somerled was felled 'by a [thrown] spear and cut down by the sword'. A priest was said to have hacked off the Hebridean king's head so that he could take it off as a bloody trophy and proof to his bishop. With the death of Somerled, his marines wasted no time in scrambling aboard their birlinns and setting sail for their fastnesses in the islands of the west.

In the bitter and chaotic squabble over the great Atlantic principality won by this remarkable warlord, it was his early gains, the Southern Hebrides and the coast of historic Argyll, from Glenelg to the Mull of Kintyre, that appear to have been retained by his sons. Ranald was the name father of Clan Donald and the sea kings who became known as the Lords of the Isles, while Dugald was the progenitor of Clan MacDougall and the Lords of Argyll.

Somerled's memorial may be seen as the Lordship of the Isles and its rule by Clan Donald until the late 15th century. But there is evidence that he also attempted to leave his mark on the spiritual as well as the political history of the Hebrides. On Iona, long since abandoned and its glories faded, the little chapel of St Oran, the oldest building on the island, was probably commissioned by Somerled in the hope that its consecration would revive the heritage of Columba and bring back monks and pilgrims to the sacred site of his ancient abbey. But little came of it. The focus of the Scottish Church had shifted decisively to the east, first to Dunkeld and later to a rocky promontory overlooking the North Sea.

Blebo is an ancient name. It derives from *Bladeboig* which, in turn, is a version of *Blatobulgium*. A Latin name conferred by legionary quartermasters in the 1st or 2nd centuries AD, it means the 'Meal Sack Place', a depot where supplies of corn were ingathered and transported to feed Roman legionaries and auxiliaries. The modern village of Blebo Craigs sits on a high shoulder of one of the most easterly hills in Fife and it commands wide views of still-fertile farmland where the ripening corn billows in the August breezes. But it is the view to the east and the vast horizons of the sea that make a traveller pause and, from the 8th or 9th centuries onwards, it caused many to fall to their knees in prayer. They had come, at last, within sight of journey's end. Pilgrims from all over Scotland and much further afield had walked along the Bishop's Road that climbed up to Blebo and, from there, they could gaze upon the turrets and spire of St Andrews, the greatest, largest church north of Durham, the place where the shrine of St Andrew was housed.

An Apostle, a man who knew Christ, St Andrew drew pilgrims in their hundreds of thousands over the centuries of the Middle Ages. Santiago, St James of Compostela in Northern Spain, was the only other destination of similar status in Western Europe. A mere five miles west of St Andrews, Blebo acted as a *statio* – a place where groups of pilgrims stopped to band together for the final, triumphant stage of their journey. They prayed, they sang as they walked on and they hoped that the relics of the man who knew God would hear their prayers, would heal them, store up virtue, absolve them or shorten their time in purgatory.

As bands of pilgrims approached the town, they could see the form of the vast church towering above the single-storey wooden houses. Begun in 1160 during the reign of Malcolm IV, it was cruciform in layout, the nave on an east–west axis with turrets at each end and a great towering spire over the crossing. Behind a precinct wall more than a mile in length, there were the clustered conventual buildings of the Augustinian Canons whose church it was. A cloister and its garden abutted the nave to the south and there were dormitories, a refectory and a guest hall. In the late 14th century, records spoke of granaries, mills, malt kilns, piggeries, barns and byres. Beyond the great church rose the square tower of St Rule, the predecessor of the cathedral. Rule or Regulus was said to have set sail from Patras in Greece (a nation that also claims St Andrew) for Thule, the farthest north, with a few bones of the saint in his possession – three finger bones of the right hand, the upper bone of one arm, a kneecap and a tooth. Mistaking the coast of Fife for Thule, it was said, he landed at St Andrews, where the relics found a final resting place. Much more likely is that the assorted bones made their way north when the kingdom of Northumbria was at its zenith. Acca was abbot of the monastery of St Andrews at Hexham and, at the end of the 7th century, he travelled to Rome where he was probably sold what were advertised as genuine relics of the saint. There is a tradition that he founded a church at St Andrews in Fife in the 8th century and deposited the bones there.

RUBH AN DUNAIN

In 2009 Graeme Mackenzie was thinking about potatoes. Fifty metres from his croft on the Rubh na Dunain, a peninsula at the south-western foot of the Cuillin on the Isle of Skye, lay a likely area of rough grazing. But to make a proper potato patch, it needed draining. Having hired a mechanical digger, the main drain was immediately put to use as the jagged ridge of the Cuillin pierced the clouds blowing in off the Atlantic and rain lashed the coastline. When it faired, Graeme went back to his ditch and noticed something out of the ordinary. Sticking out of the peaty earth was a 10-centimetre iron spike. With a shovel, he levered out the unmistakable shape of an anchor. Forged from iron, it measured more than a metre from top to bottom and a metre across from one curved tip to the other. It had been preserved in the anaerobic conditions of the peat. When archaeologists examined the anchor, it proved to be about 1,000 years old. Graeme Mackenzie had found something that had been stowed in a Viking longship. It turned out not to be a stray find. Aerial surveys of the site revealed the outline of what was probably a Viking shipyard on Skye; a stone-lined canal, a quay and a small inland loch called Loch na h'Airde ('the Upland Loch'). Boat timbers were recovered from the soil and the layout of the canal, quay and loch suggest not only a focus for maritime construction but also a safe haven for ships that needed maintenance. Graeme Mackenzie had been the skipper of a fishing boat, and when he pulled out the anchor, he knew what he had found but could have had no idea that it would lead to the discovery that his croft lay on an ancient shipyard. There is evidence that Rubh an Dunain was used to repair and over-winter the birlinns of the medieval period. It lay in the territory of the Macaskills, the Wards of the Sea for the chiefs at Dunvegan.

However all that may be, St Andrew and not Columba was becoming generally accepted as Scotland's saint by the 13th century. He had been crucified on the *crux decussata*, what became the white diagonals of the St Andrews Cross, the Saltire flag. Compared with Columba, the prestige of

Andrew was much greater and it was to associate him closely with Scotland, and in an appropriately grand style, the great cathedral on the headland was built. Its turrets and spire were visible from Blebo, Largo Law and far out to sea.

At the same time as labourers were digging foundations and cartloads of quarried stone creaked and rumbled towards the site on the headland, Mainard the Fleming was also laying out the street plan of the town, marking off plots and backlands. St Andrews had been newly erected into a royal burgh by Malcolm IV in 1160. The Fleming's plan used the West Door of the cathedral as its focus. Pilgrims walking down the Bishop's Road from Blebo will have approached the West Port of the town (which still stands) and processed east along South Street towards the great church. There is evidence from other places that groups of pilgrims were met, blessed and led to the shrine by a priest and perhaps a novice carrying a cross. Once they had visited the saint's relics, they will have processed along North Street. Wide and straight, these two 'thoroughfares' were in fact nothing of the kind and are very unlike medieval streets. They were processional ways.

The West Door was only swung open on important feast days and on state or episcopal occasions. When those who had banded together at Blebo and the other statios (there was another at Guardbridge where the Eden was crossed), reached the precinct wall, they will have entered the cathedral by a side door. The effect must have been stunning. By far the largest interior almost all of them will have ever seen, its lime-washed walls soaring upwards, the spire even higher, lit by the vivid colours of stained glass, perhaps enlivened by the chant of choristers, made pungent with the smell of incense, St Andrews Cathedral was built to be awe-inspiring as it reached up to Heaven.

It was also designed to be a business that turned over as much cash as it could. Pilgrims paid for candles to be lit for those they had lost and those they loved, pilgrim badges were sold and donations encouraged. St Andrews rose on the bones of the Apostle but its splendour was maintained by the pennies of the pious. Once in the vast nave, pilgrims saw a stone screen behind which the Augustinian Canons in their austere black and white habits said mass. After having passed by the high altar, they came, at last, to the end of their journey. It is lost, shattered by the righteous frenzy of the Reformers, but the shrine of St Andrew, what held that random collection of bones, is likely to have resembled others that have survived. A large rectangular catafalque, it is likely to have been supported and surrounded on all sides by galleries of small arches. Closeness, touching the shrine, mattered very much to medieval pilgrims and many put their heads into the arches that held up the reliquary and prayed that the saint inside, Andrew, the man who knew God, would hear them and grant their fervent wishes.

The cathedral took more than a century to complete and, in the severe gales that howled in the winter of 1272, the west end collapsed. The church was finally consecrated on 5 July 1318, in the presence of King Robert I. By that time, St Andrews was the undoubted focus of the Scottish Church, its bishops becoming archbishops in the 15th century. It was also a symbol of something more prosaic. Even though it took 150 years before it was completed, the building of such a grand, monumental, wealthy cathedral could only have been achieved by a successful medieval economy – the one that David I had begun to put in place two centuries before.

In contrast to that of his elder brother, known as Malcolm the Maiden, the epithet attached to William the Lion implies a high contrast, a warrior instead of a pious, celibate worrier. But, unlike Richard the Lionheart, his contemporary, William the Lion of Scotland, did not acquire his reputation through military prowess or personal courage. Some time after his death, the epithet was attached because of the standard he flew – the royal red lion rampant with a forked tail on a yellow background, now seen as an alternative to the Saltire. William I's long reign, from 1165 to 1214, saw him captured, humiliated, ransomed and challenged by rebellion in the north and the south-west. But, in the sphere of domestic government, he succeeded in furthering the legacy of his pioneering grandfather, David I, and a better, if anachronistic, epithet might have been William the Moderniser.

In late May 1149, on Whitsuntide Eve, a young man knelt at the altar of the chapel at Carlisle Castle. He would keep vigil, praying silently and fasting through the night, and, in the morning, dressed in a vestment that was white for purity and a red robe that symbolised nobility, the young man would hear mass and a lengthy sermon on the duties of knighthood. And then he would undergo the ceremony of the accolade. From the French word *colée*, meaning a 'blow', it was given by a king or a nobleman to the kneeling figure in front of him.

Henry of Anjou rode north to be knighted by a king, by David I of Scotland in his castle at Carlisle. The ceremony of the accolade and the preliminary rituals of knighthood mattered and the young man and the king will have wanted them to be conducted according to custom and in some splendour. But there was, of course, another purpose in the long journey north to the squat castle built inside the perimeter of the old Roman fort.

The son of the Empress Matilda, Henry had come to enlist David's support in the struggle for England with Stephen of Blois. In return, the Scottish king extracted a promise from the young pretender that, if he ever gained the English throne, he would confirm the Scots' possession of Cumbria and the old city of Carlisle and their right to the earldom of Northumbria. By 1154, Henry duly became king and it took him only three years to renege on all of his promises and move the border up the Cheviot watershed and the banks of the Tweed.

Stung by such ruthlessness, William the Lion waited. His chance came in 1173 when the famously quarrelsome Angevins took sides in a bitter family dispute. Supported by their mother, Queen Eleanor of Aquitaine, Henry's sons, Richard, Henry and Geoffrey, rose in rebellion. Mustering his host, William attempted to take advantage and led an expedition into Northumberland. It was a disaster. Near Alnwick, the Scots king was captured by Ranulf de Glanvill and his knights and taken in chains to Newcastle. Then William was subjected to the deepest humiliation for a king when he was paraded through the town of Northampton with his feet tied under the belly of his horse. From there, Henry II ordered that the prisoner be taken across the Channel to Falaise where he was thrown into the castle dungeons. Not since the blinding of Donald Ban had a Scottish king been subjected to such indignities. Worse was to come.

The terms of the Treaty of Falaise were punitive as Henry did not hesitate to press home his advantage on his doubtless miserable and demoralised captive, held well beyond rescue in northern France. William was forced to agree to do homage to the king of England for his kingdom of Scotland, a condition of release that would haunt William's successors for centuries. The Scottish Church was explicitly bound to be subservient, a 'daughter' of the Church in England and its archbishops. Berwick, Roxburgh and Edinburgh castles were to be given up to English garrisons paid for by Scottish taxation. And, perhaps most shamingly, William was instructed to seek Henry's permission before he was allowed to deal with internal rebellions.

The capture and humiliation of the king did indeed ignite rebellion in Galloway. At the Battle of the Standard, the Galwegian warriors may have been repulsed but at least they formed part of the royal host. By the 1170s, they were charging the ranks of the king's men under the command of their ferocious warlord, Gille Brigte. To secure his primacy over the Lordship of Galloway, he had ordered that his brother and rival, Uchtred, be castrated, have his tongue cut out and be blinded. Not surprisingly he died soon after these hideous cruelties had been inflicted. On his release from Falaise and after he had sworn fealty to Henry of England at York, William the Lion led an army into Nithsdale and a motte-and-bailey castle was dug on the eastern bank of the Nith. Across the river, the wild realm of Galloway began and it would be a long time before a Scots king dared to venture west.

As he deepened the penetration of feudalism across the kingdom, the king was much more successful. By the second half of the 12th century, more and more land in the Lowland areas was held in vassalage, the shire system and its sheriffs developed more widely, more castles rose in the landscape, new burghs were erected and the Scottish trading economy had become currency based. Moneyers, generally men who had trained as goldsmiths, set up mints at Berwick, Roxburgh, Stirling and Perth and the Scottish sterling or silver penny was equivalent to the pennies minted by Henry II's masters. By 1250, there were sixteen mints in Scotland.

It may have been as a reaction to the spread of feudalism and the threat to the old Celtic order that Galloway rose in the 1170s but the war bands of the south-west posed less of a problem than the simmering kingdom of Moray. There, men with clear and legitimate claims to William's crown began to gather forces and, in 1181, Domhnall macUilleam, a direct descendant of Duncan II, had gained control of Inverness and the fertile lands to the north and east. For seven years, he defied the king but, by 1187, Domhnall had been killed, his severed head a trophy, and William's soldiers reoccupied Inverness, crushing resistance wherever it was found. It was perhaps at this time the Scots king was given the Gaelic nickname of *Uilleam Garbh*, 'Rough William'.

With the death of England's Henry II, in 1189, and the accession of Richard, the political landscape changed. The Lionheart almost immediately went on crusade and, to raise funds, he agreed to release William from his oath of homage for the sum of 10,000 merks. A unit of account rather than a coin, a merk or mark represented about two thirds of a pound of silver or 160 silver pennies. A huge sum by any reckoning, it nevertheless appeared to the Scots to be a price worth paying. However, the legal quitclaim of Richard was largely ignored by those who came after him and, for four centuries, Scotland was seen by most English kings as an uncooperative northern fiefdom, its fields and farms, especially in the south-east, worth fighting for.

While Richard and his magnates took the cross and sailed for the Holy Land to fight famous battles against Saladin and his armies, relations between England and Scotland settled. It was an interval of peace worth noting, even celebrating, exaggerating. Here is what the chronicler John of Fordun wrote about the relations between Scots and the English in the 1190s: 'Each of the two peoples was thought of as part of one and the same people. Whenever it pleased them, Englishmen on foot or on horseback were able to pass unharmed right across Scotland, both on this side of the mountains and beyond, laden with gold or any other sort of merchandise, and in like manner, Scots [could pass] through England.'

These travellers, no doubt keeping their gold prudently out of sight, rode and walked through a landscape that was very different from today's. It has almost all gone now – the old fields, meadows and muirs where medieval farmers grazed their beasts, tended their crops and went hunting and gathering for nature's seasonal bounty. But there are places where the land can sometimes appear as it once was, where an observer can slip through a crack in time, back to the quiet and green Scotland of eight centuries ago.

Where the road winds uphill from Ashkirk and after cars rattle over the cattle grid, fences disappear and on the plateau between the valleys of the Ale Water and the Teviot in the high Border country, the moorland horizons are often clear. No line of pylons marches, no houses are visible, no fields pattern the hillsides and, as the mist of an early summer morning lifts, it is as though nothing has changed for millennia. Farms down in the valleys summer their beasts on the tracts of coarse grass that stretch away on either side of the single-track road. Cattle browse up to their bellies amongst the tussocks, some tearing at the young shoots of the willow scrub by the sikes and burns. Sheep lawns are nibbled short, lambs are fat and mostly weaned, their muck making the grass grow a luminous lime-green in the same places where generations have grazed the high pasture. Whaups wheel and cry, invisible in the updraughts, and, as the sun climbs to warm the day, the scents of bog myrtle and wild thyme float into the air. Towards Blawearie, walkers may come across a rectangle of big, uncut stones set into the grass. These are likely the founds of a turf-walled shieling, a place where herd laddies summered out with the flocks and the cattle, keeping watch through the long evenings for predators, for beasts in difficulties in boggy ground and making sure their dogs were fed and alert. The months at the shielings were times for fun, tale-telling, singing and what in the Borders is known as 'laughin' an' daffin' when the lassies came up with their yokes and their pales to milk the ewes.

On the very different, much harsher geography of the Barvas Moor, brown and puddled with dark lochans, at the farther end of Scotland, north-west of Stornoway, the quiet blether of steady work can be heard each spring. Neighbours, some of them with access to a tractor and trailer, are cutting a peat bank. All over Scotland people came together for millennia to replenish their fuel supplies in this way. Wood is scarce on the Isle of Lewis but even in mainland regions where many trees grew, their logs were rarely used to provide warmth for ordinary people. They were too valuable. But peat or turf was widely available. Using a long peat iron shaped like a narrow spade and known in Scots as a 'tusker', men would lift out the chocolate-brown slices of rotted primeval vegetation while women stacked them on top of the bank in short stooks so that the summer winds could dry them off. When its colour had lightened and the peat had shed its moisture, trailers and tractors, and before them horses and carts, or ponies or people with panniers, led the precious fuel off the moor and deposited it at each house. Stacking the pieces like brown bricks, they were often built into a house shape complete with a sloping roof to allow rainwater to run off. In Gaelic, this was known as *cruach mhona*, a peat stack. On Orkney and Shetland these were sometimes circular or the peats were arranged in a herringbone pattern so that they could dry quickly after a spell of bad weather.

In the bright days after a sugar dusting of snow, the outlines of medieval fields often show up well. On some of the fairways of the golf courses on the Braid Hills in the southern suburbs of Edinburgh, snow lies in the linear depressions on either side of long ridges. These are the remains of the runrig system of farming – the ridge-and-furrow fields cultivated by teams of oxen pulling the wooden plough, the auld Scots *ploo*. In essence they were a solution to the difficulties of drainage or a lack of it. Often ploughed on sloping land, the raised ridge was where crops were planted and water could drain into the ditches on either side and run downhill to a burn or a water meadow or boggy flat land. Many runrigs were formed in a slight S-shape because of the unavoidable fact that plough teams of up to eight oxen took wide turns when they completed a furrow and were goaded into lining up for the return.

There are other, less obvious relicts of medieval farming to be found in the modern countryside but high, unfenced moorland pasture, the marks of peat-cutting and evidence of the runrig system can be seen in many places all over Scotland. But a sense of the way in which farmers lived, worked together and organised their homesteads has survived in only one place – the crofting townships of the Western Isles and the Highlands. A handful of houses are often strung out in a line at some distance from each other along a road. Each is on the edge or at the centre of small parcel land – the croft

– which they work and cultivate where the ground allows. But all have access to summer pasture, usually upland, and, like peat cutting, it is an activity that brings the community together. Until the late 19th century and even afterwards, croft houses were usually 'blackhouses', built from stone with a door as the sole source of interior light and with a turf or thatch roof.

The cycle of the year changed little for millennia. For medieval subsistence farmers, the winter was an annual challenge to be faced and provided for. Food for people and animals needed to be stored and rationed through the cold and hungry months even though hunting and gathering could supply a welcome supplement to the diet, especially on the seashore where shellfish and crabs could be found most of the year round. Because contact with other communities and transport links were very limited, farmers had to be self-sufficient so far as their land and beasts allowed. There were, no doubt, many local variations but farmland in medieval Scotland tended to be measured in 'ploughgates' or *davochs*, the equivalent in the Highlands and Islands. A ploughgate was reckoned to be 104 acres or thereabouts – an area that could be ploughed by a team of eight oxen in a year. A husbandman or peasant farmer could work a quarter of a ploughgate, 26 acres, as his own smallholding. He was bound to pay taxes or tithes to his lord and also do service in the common army, the medieval host. These obligations aside, husbandmen were freemen who usually cooperated with a small group of other freemen who lived around them in the *fermtoun* or township.

Ploughing, sowing, harvesting and the management of beasts on the summer common were the main areas of regular cooperation. With a mould-board made of wood and tipped with iron and an iron coulter running in front, the auld Scots ploo needed the power of a team of plodding oxen to pull it through the ground, especially heavy ground. It was also labour intensive. The oxen were prodded forward by a goadman while a ploughman held the stilts of the plough to steer it and sometimes another man needed to put his weight on the beam to keep the share in the ground. Behind them walked a group of women and children who bashed down the bigger clods of earth, removed bigger stones and pulled out the weeds not covered with the turn of the furrow slice.

Once the rigs had been harrowed by hand-rakes to make a good seedbed, the oats and barley (often called bere) and sometime wheat seeds (for fancy bread) were broadcast by hand. To save them from being taken by the birds, these were raked in quickly but, even if the seed had been cast by an experienced hand, it could be a wasteful process. If the summer was good, the green shoots would quickly poke through and begin to ripen in the sunshine. Harvest was another communal activity as men moved in a line up the rigs to cut the corn with curved hand-sickles, stopping to sharpen them on whetstones as they went. Behind them, women and children gathered up the corn, banding the yellow stalks into sheaves and stooking them to dry off. Once the ripe ears had been flailed off on a threshing floor, the straw was carefully saved for bedding, flooring and even forage in a hard winter.

The runrig system was unfenced because there was no need. Beasts had been driven up the hill trails to the common in the ancient journey of transhumance where they stayed until after the harvest. Once the hairst was hame, in that evocative phrase that rings down the centuries, the flocks and herds were brought back down off the high pasture so that they could graze the undergrowth on the rigs and refresh their flagging fertility with their muck. Many husbandmen worked a system of inbye and outbye fields. Like modern vegetable gardens, the inbye was always in cultivation and needed regular muck to prevent the soil from falling barren. In the Highlands and Islands, seaweed was sometimes spread so that its nutrients could enrich the soil. In the outbye, a simple rotation was followed whereby rigs might be left fallow for a year or two to recover. Beasts that did not summer out, like milk cows and horses (if a husbandman could afford one), came inbye off the common each evening along green loanings – hedged routes that kept animals off the growing corn. In Scotland many loanings and loans have survived in street and place names.

Fermtouns often organised their runrigs into two or more big areas and again these often survive as place names – Eastfield, Westfield and so on. But much the largest proportion of farmland in medieval Scotland was pasture and the rhythms of stock-rearing a way of life for many. The animals, however, were not seen as a meat crop in the modern sense. Old cows, ewes no longer able to lamb or whatever could not be kept through the winter were killed, preserved and eaten. And, even then, nothing was wasted – hide, bones, sinews for cords, intestines, fat, hooves for glue and horn were all put to domestic use. The best implement for eating porridge is still a bone spoon. Most animals were bred and kept for their produce rather than their meat. Milk, cheese and butter came from cows, ewes and nanny goats, oxen were used for traction and wool could be combed or clipped from sheep and goats for yarn. The size of each husbandman's herd and flock was regulated by *souming*. Derived from the English word 'sum', it involved making sure that the commonty was not overgrazed by too many animals. The calculation was sometimes linked to the amount of arable land each man cultivated. The ditches between the ridges of runrigs came into this reckoning. Known as bauks, they were often densely overgrown with thistles and spikey marsh grass, both of which could make good winter forage when dried. And, if whin or broom grew in the bauks, they would supply decent thatch or be burned for warmth.

The medieval landscape was much more densely settled than the modern countryside. The houses and holdings of husbandmen were neighbours to those of cottars, men who had rights to cultivate only small plots of ground, probably little more than a garden. And there were men with no rights to land, labourers known as 'gresmen' or 'girsemen', who no doubt worked for payment in kind. Attached to the households of some husbandmen as well as lords were *servi* – slaves whose families were also expected to work as part of their servitude.

No matter what their status was, everyone was a hunter-gatherer. Always being careful to respect the hunting reserves of the nobility and royalty, each family supplemented the farmed diet of dairy and cereal products and the occasional piece of meat by trapping wildfowl in the wetlands, by fishing there for eels and other fish, by gathering birds' eggs, fungi (often a job for children whose harvest would have been carefully monitored), wild fruits, berries and roots and, on the seashore, there was a marine bounty to be lifted out of rock pools and dug out of the sand at low tide. Some of the royal and noble hunting estates, such as the vast Ettrick Forest, were huge and, for those who did not respect the forest laws, the penalties for poaching were very severe.

Farmhouses changed little for centuries. Like the Hebridean blackhouse, they were essentially a long rectangle with a hearth, stone or turf walls and a wooden roof-frame covered with thatch through which smoke could seep, a beaten earth floor with straw and wild grasses and herbage to keep smells manageable. Often there would be another door to a partitioned area where a cow and other beasts could be brought in at night or given shelter from the worst of the weather. The writer Alasdair Maclean remembered a blackhouse at Sanna Bay at the tip of Ardnamurchan where a neighbouring crofter, Murdo Macdonald, brought his cow in every evening – 'For thirty years he did this, and there was never a cross word between them.' As families slept around the warmth of the hearth, privacy was impossible in medieval farmhouses and couples must have relied on quiet places out of doors in warm weather. In an age before contraception, women may have delivered children most years and those who survived would likely have been welcome. In the labour-intensive life on farms, more pairs of hands will have been useful.

Such was the way of life for the overwhelming majority of the population of medieval Scotland. The lordly elite who lived amongst the fermtouns and the rigs occupied halls and castles and their military and political lives were sustained by the output of the husbandmen, the cottars, the gresmen, the slaves and their families. So too was the Church. The abbots and bishops behaved like the great magnates they were as the foundations of the macMalcolm kings grew into huge corporations that were widely landed and very wealthy. Increasingly, their estates were run by *conversi*, lay brothers who often lived inside the monastic precinct or on the further-flung possessions of the monastery or church. The rule of the Cistercian order forbade physical work and, for example, at Melrose there is a long range to the north of the abbey church which was occupied by a large group of *conversi*. While the monks prayed, contemplated, worshipped and worked in the scriptorium, the lay brothers oversaw the work on the great granges by the Tweed, the upland sheep ranches and the annual wool clip that made Melrose rich.

HEFT TO THE HILL

To town dwellers, sheep all look much the same. But early farmers knew their beasts well and understood their habits. In particular they knew how a 'hirsel', a small flock of sheep, became hefted to a hillside. That meant that they became attached to a particular patch of pasture and did not often stray far from it. Shepherds still encourage this because it makes their beasts easier to find and manage. Ewes create the heft. Before weaning, lambs stay very close to their mothers, except when they career around in a pack with other lambs – and, even then, they stay close – and, after they have begun to graze, they do not stray far. As the summer population increases and the warmth brings on new grass in the hills (it grows at in temperatures above 5°C and flourishes best in warm and showery weather), the lambs enlarge the sheep lawns, devouring all manner of herbage and pushing back the gorse. Sheep are nature's vacuum cleaners. When generations of ewes become heft to a hill, they scrape out 'bields', places where they can shelter from the wind and the worst storms. And shepherds rarely move them from their hillside.

Most monastic orders followed dietary rules that were strictly enforced, at least at first, and these influenced food production. The meat of four-legged animals was forbidden and so for protein the monks depended on fish, cheese, eggs and poultry. Fish ponds became a feature around abbeys and nunneries and their remains can still be seen. These were known as stews and carp and pike were bred in them. River fishings became important and there were occasionally vehement arguments between monastic communities about who was entitled to which pool or bank. Definitions were stretched. Because they had fishy tails, beavers could be caught and eaten, and because they were believed to be born out at sea, like fish, it was acceptable to eat puffins and barnacle geese, as they fell into the same two-legged category as poultry.

By 1296, there were more than 50 royal burghs in Scotland but their combined population remained small. Many were little more than villages and even the larger towns like Berwick, Roxburgh, Edinburgh and Perth had no more than a few hundred people living inside their boundaries. When burgesses swore fealty to Edward I of England in 1291, there were 84 names listed from Berwick and 70 from Perth. Given the importance of the occasion, few will have wished to be omitted and, if a multiple of four or five is used to include family and servants, then that makes an approximate population of about 400 for Berwick and 350 for Perth.

Most trade was probably local as farmers came to the burgh markets with their produce to barter or pay for manufactured goods, items such as shoes, harnesses, clothes or pottery and other essentials which they could not make themselves. By volume, one of Scotland's most important exports was hide and modern place and street names often recall the existence of a tannery in each of the burghs. Or rather, as far from the houses of a burgh as was possible. With their foul concoctions of dog turds, urine and the other ingredients used to fill the tanning pits, tanneries did not make good neighbours, especially in warm weather.

In the early burghs, neighbours lived cheek by jowl. Most houses were single-storey, 9–10 yards long and 4–5 yards wide, with their gable end on to the street. They were neither robust nor long-lasting. To form the walls, stakes were rammed into the ground and withies woven between them in the same way that hurdle fencing is still made. Clay, mud mixed with straw or turf was slathered or stacked to give the walls some solidity but this method of construction restricted wall height to about five feet. To form the roof, a ridge pole was slung between gable posts or, if they could be afforded, two

A-frames and, to carry the thatch, withies were woven into a series of purlins that rested on the wall heads. Reached by a pend, the door was usually made from planks and it must have been low, forcing men to mind their heads. In the centre of a floor of beaten earth or sand and gravel, there was a central hearth, little more than a circle of flat stones keyed into the ground. Smoke seeped through the thatch.

This form of construction meant a short life of perhaps twenty years before posts driven into the earth rotted and collapsed. But the number of reports of devastating fires in medieval burghs suggests that houses had even briefer lives. Smiddies were likely culprits but sparks from the central hearth may have caused some of the fires. Kept lit constantly for cooking, the fire was the focus of these dark little houses and archaeologists have noticed that big flat stones were sometimes placed so that they projected into the hearth. This was probably where cooking pots sat and seethed in the heat. A near-universal dish was potage. This was a vegetable soup or stew thickened with cereals and sometimes flavoured with scraps of meat and bones. To be eaten with potage, flatbread was made, slapped on hot stones much in the way that nan bread is cooked on the sides of a tandoor in Indian restaurants. Oatcakes were made in a similar way. Hunting expeditions sometimes brought back pigeons or rabbits, and more unlikely fare such as squirrels or hedgehogs were skinned and wrapped in soft clay to bake in the hottest part of the fire.

At the end of the long backlands behind houses in burghs, there was often a byre where a milk cow was kept. Archaeologists working on keyhole sites in Perth have found drains whose contents strongly suggest that arrangement. They also came across one of the central difficulties of town life. There was no communal drainage system and householders often dug cesspits in their backlands and these could be so close to a water supply from a cistern or well that these became contaminated. The widespread brewing of ale was not only a welcome source of calories, it was also proof against an unreliable water supply. Rubbish was dumped indiscriminately outside the boundaries, a habit that will have encouraged rats and other vermin.

Kings rode past rubbish dumps without giving them a second glance. They lived in rat- and mouse-infested halls and chambers and the unpleasant smells, noises and sights of medieval Scotland were as much part of their lives as anyone else's. The modern, gilded, exalted lives of monarchs can be misleading. In 13th-century Scotland, kings, princes and magnates lived close to their subjects. There were no palaces. When the royal court moved around the realm, hauling wagons of gear, wine and other provisions behind them, they set up at royal castles such as Roxburgh, Berwick, Edinburgh and Stirling where they ate their way through the food renders due to the king and then they moved on when the larders were bare. Where no royal castle or hall existed, they might be the locust-like guests of monasteries or great magnates. But the number of documents sealed at their major castles suggests that Scots kings spent much of their time behind their walls.

BOWERS

Until the availability of straight-sawn timber, box beds and partitions, most families slept in a single room. Which made indoor sex awkward for parents. Perhaps abstinence reigned in the winter but as the nights drew out and the weather warmed, mums and dads ventured outside to somewhere shaded and secluded. There, the more romantic men would build a bower, a place of spread leaves and branches, where scented flowers might be picked and entwined. The image is immortalised in the lovely Scottish song 'Wild Mountain Thyme'. Based on a much earlier lyric, it has this verse:

> *I will build my love a bower*
> *By yon clear and crystal fountain,*
> *And all around the bower,*
> *I'll pile flowers from the mountain.*
> *Will you go, lassie, go?*

Nevertheless, rulers appear to have been accessible to ordinary people. The scale of public life in Scotland was small. With burghs little more than villages and the countryside settled in fermtouns, religious foundations and lordly halls and castles, there were few concentrations of population, few places or occasions when great crowds would gather. Statistics for the medieval period are few and generally highly speculative. But, if, as many historians believe, Scotland supported a population of 500,000 in c. 1200, it was widely scattered. And when the outside control of the Hebrides and the Northern Isles is remembered, the number of people who recognised William the Lion as king reduces even further. When the numbers reputedly involved in the Battle of the Standard in 1138 are considered as a proportion of the able-bodied male population, the effect is striking and informative. Leaving aside the areas which did not send contingents to join David I's host of 20,000 and allowing for half of the number of males in Scotland being too young, old or religious (and bearing in mind lower life expectancy), the proportion is high. If 130,000 men could conceivably have been summoned to do service in the common army, 20,000 represents about 15 per cent. Conjectural, certainly, but not unreasonable. And what that meant was something straightforward. Even in a society where movement was usually restricted to localities and communication primitive by modern standards, politics and war affected many families. The ordinary people of the fermtouns did not live in ignorance but understood something of international politics and the ambitions of their kings. Campaigns, raids, treaties, dynastic marriages, rebellions and the question of succession were the business of an elite, without doubt, but the sense of an uncomprehending, ignorant peasantry concerned only with the weather, their crops and beasts is surely not sustainable. Because they affected them directly, matters of politics will have been understood and discussed across all Scotland and by all Scots, regardless of status.

Kings also seem not to have been remote, as modern monarchs are. From the 1130s, Aelred of Rievaulx knew David I personally and, although his biography is entirely uncritical, a hagiography, it is, nevertheless, informative, with some passages carrying the unmistakable whiff of authenticity mixed with exemplary borrowings from other sources. Here is a sketch of King David's dealings with his subjects:

No poor person, widow or orphan, who intended to lodge some complaint, was ever forbidden access to him, but was immediately brought in by the doorkeeper. Even if [the king] was engaged in the most important and pressing business and consultations even with important and select persons, it was all interrupted, and he or she was heard. I also saw with my own eyes, when sometimes he was ready to go hunting, and with his foot placed in the stirrup he was intending to mount his horse, that he withdrew his foot, left his horse and returned to his hall at the voice of a poor person demanding that audience be given to him, and he would not return to what he planned on that day . . . but he heard the case for which he had been called kindly and patiently. It was his custom besides to sit at the door of the royal hall and listen attentively to the cases of poor people and old women, who were summoned on certain days from particular regions wherever they came from, and to strive hard to give satisfaction to each one. For often they argued with him and he with them, when he refused to accept the legal standing of a poor person contrary to justice, and when they refused to give assent to the reasoned argument which he demonstrated to them.

If Aelred is to be believed, then, it seems that deference was minimal in medieval Scotland as ordinary people approached and argued with their king. Towards the end of the 13th century, another conversation between commoner and monarch confirmed this attractive attitude. And, if David was consulted directly by his subjects all over his kingdom, then he will have had command of at least three languages – Gaelic, Scots and French. Perhaps he could write Latin, although his direct contemporary Henry I of England was known as Beauclerc, probably because literate kings were unusual.

When, in 1214, at the age of 16, Alexander II succeeded William the Lion, there was the usual rebellion in the north as the heirs of the Moray kings attempted to exploit a moment of instability. What broke this repeating pattern was the fact that the rebels were defeated by a native warlord, Farquhar macTaggart, acting on behalf of the young king. And despite his youth, Alexander was not slow to exploit instability in England. King John and his great magnates were often at loggerheads, their frustrations not resolved by the signing of Magna Carta, and, between 1215 and 1217, the Scots ran five raids into England in pursuit their king's claims to Northumberland and Cumbria. Remarkably, Alexander II led his forces clear down the length of England to Dover, surely the farthest any Scots invasion ever penetrated. In common with English magnates who wished to depose John, Alexander went to Dover to swear fealty for his lands in England to an alternative candidate for the throne in the shape of Prince Louis of France. But John's death in 1216 and the accession of Henry III prevented history from taking a surprising turn.

Continuity had certainly been maintained in Scotland. William the Lion reigned for 49 years, Alexander would wear the crown for 35 years and his son Alexander III for 36 years. For more than a century, 121 years in all, Scots men and women knew only three kings and many would live out their lives in the span of a single reign. Dynastic stability encouraged long periods of relative peace and, once Henry III had established himself on the English throne, he and Alexander came to an accommodation over macMalcolm claims to estates in England, especially in the north. In 1237, the Treaty of York conceded substantial possessions south of the Border to the Scots king in return for a formal renunciation of his family's claim to the earldom of

Northumberland and to the territory of Cumbria. This, in effect, settled the frontier on its modern line of the Cheviot watershed in the west and the midpoint of the River Tweed from the Redden Burn, near Kelso, to Berwick in the east. To seal the dynastic deal, Alexander agreed to take Henry's sister, Joan, as his queen.

THE ULTIMATE VIKING

Svein Asleifsson was described by the great Orcadian author Eric Linklater as 'the Ultimate Viking'. Although he nominally owed allegiance to the 12th-century Earls of Orkney, Svein appears to have acted completely independently. From his island fastness of Gairsay (and its drinking hall large enough for eighty men), which stands sentinel at the mouth of Wide Firth, the bay at the heart of the archipelago, he set sail for plunder each spring and autumn. Ranging far down the western costs of Britain, the Gairsay longships attacked the coasts of Wales, laid siege to the island of Lundy in the Bristol Channel and took Svein to the Isle of Man to seek a bride so that he could seal a strategic alliance with a Manx sea-lord. In his description, Eric Linklater was only echoing the Orkneyinga Saga *of c. 1200, for its author hailed the Ultimate Viking as 'the greatest man in the Western Lands, either in olden times or present day'. Ancestral DNA research suggests that when the last real Viking died in an attack on Dublin in 1171, his marker carried on – with great vigour. A relatively new sub-type of M17 – S375 – is now prominent in the North Isles of Orkney, on the five major islands north of Gairsay. It is also carried by 30 per cent of men with the surname of Gunn who have taken DNA tests. Tradition, genealogy and history all begin to come together to form a narrative. It may be that the prevalence of S375 on the islands of Rousay, Westray, Eday, Sanday and Stronsay is linked to the well-attested phenomenon of social selection, where powerful men in the past sired many children with different women. In that way their Y chromosome markers were spread widely and quickly, much faster than if they had remained monogamous. And few men were more powerful in 12th-century Orkney than Svein Asleifsson.*

In the second half of the 12th century, Scotia or Scotland came to mean the whole kingdom, *Regnum Scotiae*, and not only the regions north of the Forth. As is often the case, it was a name conferred at first by outsiders but by the 1250s it was being used in royal documents. The old Gaelic term of Alba began to fade into the past.

Language shift is a process rather than an event and, as such, extremely difficult to date. In the absence of written records (which were, in any case, written in Latin), place names are the only indicator. These suggest that Gaelic was never spoken in the Lothians and south-east where the old kingdom of Northumbria understood itself in Early English – what developed into Scots. However, they do not represent conclusive evidence. In the Teviot Valley and south of Kelso, there is a small but dense concentration of hogback tombstones. These were carved by Norse settlers to mark the resting places of important people – lords of some sort – and yet there seem to be no Norse place names in the Teviot Valley.

As burghs were founded in the 12th and 13th centuries, the Scots language spread north to Fife, Lowland Perthshire, Angus and Moray and Gaelic retreated westwards. And yet the place names remembered that it was once the common speech. Usually in compound names, *baile*, Gaelic for 'fermtoun', is found all over these areas and *achadh* for 'field' is particularly concentrated in Moray. In Galloway, where Gaelic arrived in the mouths of the Gall-Gaidheil, the Stranger-Gaels, it also appears frequently. Although it is impossible to be precise about dates, the trend was clear as Scots advanced and Gaelic gradually shrank back into the mountains and the islands.

Alexander II died in the Gaidhealtachd, suddenly on the island of Kerrera in the Firth of Lorne, opposite what is now Oban. In the 1230s, he had subdued Galloway with the help of Farquhar macTaggart and Walter Comyn, the Earl of Menteith and a scion of a rising Scoto-Norman family. After 1235, the Comyns were granted land in the south-west and they held the wild realm for the king. Alexander turned his attention to the Hebrides and the Isle of Man, the kingdom won by Somerled but later controlled by the Norwegians. At first, he offered to buy out their suzerainty but King Haakon seemed indifferent. And so the Scots mustered a fleet to sail north and seize the Norse possessions for the Scottish crown. It was on this expedition that the 50-year-old Scots king died.

Despite the sustained longevity and continuity of the macMalcolm succession, no delays could be allowed and the seven-year-old Alexander III was quickly inaugurated at Scone on 13 July 1249. There exists an illustration of the moment in the ceremony when *An Ollaimh Righ* stood forward to recite the young king's genealogy and thereby assert his right to succeed. Late medieval in origin and probably bound into Walter Bower's great work, the

Scotichronicon, the painting puts a brief speech scroll into the royal bard's mouth. Saying 'Benach De Re Albanne' and rendered as *Beannachd Dé Rígh Albanaich* in modern Gaelic, it meant 'God Bless the King of the Scots' and it harks back to the old Celtic formulae. The style 'King of Scots' or 'Queen of Scots' endured and it may be a memory of Gaelic habits of thought. Clansmen and women thought of themselves as *clann*, children of a name father. Hence Clan Donald. It may be that King Alexander and all those who came before and followed him, such as Mary Queen of Scots, saw themselves as rulers of a people rather than territory.

Behind the boy king at Scone, presumably seated on the Stone of Destiny, although it is hidden by drapery, stand two figures. On the left is Malcolm, Earl of Fife, and he holds what might be seen as a sword of state but, since it has a belt wrapped around it, it is more probably a symbol of knighthood. Next to him is a woman, perhaps the young king's mother, Marie de Coucy. This traditional tableau on the Moot Hill, which is clearly drawn as a mound with a stone cross at its top, disguised a struggle behind the throne. During the first minority for almost a century, two factions of the nobility contended for power and influence and this was to become an insistent theme in the later Middle Ages. Alan Durward, the Justiciar, and his supporters sought the backing of Henry III of England and, after a meeting between him and Alexander at Kelso Abbey, they appeared to be in the ascendant. But momentum shifted soon afterwards when Walter Comyn, Earl of Menteith, had the king seized at Kinross in 1257 and took him into what might now be called protective custody.

When Alexander finally came of age in 1262, he resumed his father's attempts to bring the Hebrides and the Isle of Man into the kingdom of the Scots. A year later, King Haakon determined to resolve the issue and he mustered his fleet at a place that still bears his name, at Kyleakin, the 'Narrows of Haakon', between Skye and the mainland. The Norwegian fleet of at least 120 warships bobbing at anchor, their colours flying, must have been an awesome sight – one that was clearly memorable for those who watched from the shore. Having then sailed south to the Clyde to challenge Alexander, the Norwegian king's fleet was badly damaged in a storm before an indecisive battle was fought on the shore at Largs. What really turned events was the death of Haakon two months later as he over-wintered in Orkney. The Scots took their chance, attacked Caithness and Skye in 1264 and, by signing and sealing the Treaty of Perth in 1266, the Norwegians agreed to give up the Hebrides (but not the Northern Isles) and the Isle of Man for 4,000 merks and a nominal annual payment of 100 merks.

Perhaps Alexander III and his entourage celebrated the accession of these new territories by going hunting. Medieval kings and magnates appear to have been obsessed by the thrill of the chase, by hunting on foot and by hawking. In 1266, King Alexander gave instructions that the deer park laid out for his father at Kincardine Castle should be extended. As places of winter refuge where pregnant does could drop their fawns safe from predators and be fed hay and forage through the hungry months by deer-herds, these large parks and their perimeter pales were thought essential for the provision of sufficient prey in the hunting season. Dozens of sites of deer parks have been identified all over Scotland, most of them associated with a nearby castle. Conveniently close to Stirling Castle, the New Park was created in the 1240s for Alexander II.

Royal and baronial forests were not simply tracts of woodland but closely guarded hunting reserves. In a practice imported with the Norman Conquest, *forestae* were carved out and hedged about by severe legislation in England (poaching was punishable by blinding and castration) as areas where only the king and his lords could hunt game. The New Forest is perhaps the most famous. David I reserved the huge area of the Ettrick Forest, the Pentland and Moorfoot Hills, land around Stirling and several smaller areas further north. Barons set aside thousands of acres in Annandale, Eskdale and Cunninghame. These were not by any means all densely wooded. A hunting reserve was essentially wild land, uncultivated, often upland where trees and scrub would grow up to give sufficient cover for prey animals, such as deer, wild boar and even wolves, to roam. The law protecting these areas was less severe in Scotland and poachers were allowed to keep their manhood and their sight but forced to pay heavy fines.

Alexander III and his magnates went after the animals of the forests in two ways. The more prestigious and knightly was the chase and the most appropriate quarry was the hart or stag. As the king and his party rode through their wild land, in itself a worthwhile exercise which taught riders how to sit tight and react to the unexpected, hunting dogs pursued the hart. There were two sorts of medieval hunting hounds – sight and scent. Scottish sight or running hounds were considered to have great stamina and were exported to England and Europe. They chased the hart until it was exhausted, leading the party of riders to it. Trained not to attack, the sight hounds stopped only when the hart was cornered, at bay. This phrase comes from the fact that an exhausted deer that can run no more and has to turn to face its pursuers will bark or bay. At this point, the king or whoever led the chase would come forward to kill the terrified animal with a spear or a bow.

Scent hounds were known as 'rauchs' in Scotland and, working off a leash, they tracked game. Often the huntsmen followed on foot and, if the rauchs sniffed after the trail of a wild boar, all had to be very wary. A charging boar, its head lowered and its sharp tusks prominent, could be lethal. Scent or sleuth hounds were also sometimes used to hunt people and, in their guerrilla fighting days, both William Wallace and Robert Bruce were tracked by dogs. When a boar or a deer had been found in the forest, huntsmen communicated with their horns, blowing short and long blasts in a now lost medieval Morse code.

Across the map of Scotland there is a clutch of place names ending in the word 'seat' – King's Seat, Arthur's Seat, Abbotseat. Most of these are relics of the second, more practical method of hunting in medieval Scotland – the drive and sett. A semicircle of beaters, making as much clangour as they could, moved through the forest driving frightened game of all sorts before them. Waiting in a place such as a narrow defile where prey could be funnelled towards them were the hunters. With bows, spears, knives and nets, they brought down whatever panicking animals came running towards them. Less glorious and eventful than the chase but much more efficient.

The Scoto-Norman family of the Avenels created a hunting reserve in Eskdale in the south-west. Some time between 1165 and 1168, the monks at Melrose Abbey had been granted the right to take timber from the forest and, in so doing, had disturbed the habitat of sparrowhawks. The Avenels were very unhappy. Hawking was almost as much of a passion as hunting on horseback and, as a short-winged bird that could hunt in woodland, sparrowhawks were much prized and could be caught and trained. Other hawks that gripped the leather gauntlets of medieval aristocrats hunted differently. Peregrine falcons, buzzards and kestrels fly high in the sky, glide and hover in the updraughts, flickering their wings like giant humming birds, scanning the ground for the movement of prey. When they see a rabbit or a mouse, they snap back their wings and drop in what is called the stoop. Peregrine falcons fly very high and drop at an astonishing 180 miles an hour. Hawking was immensely popular with kings and great lords and, ironically, a very beautiful relief sculpture of a hawking party was recently found at Newstead in the Borders. It almost certainly formed part of the fabric of Melrose Abbey.

The reign of Alexander III was seen as a golden age in what seems to have been a retrospective judgement much influenced by the long years of turmoil that came after it. But there does appear to have been a period of prosperity and peace as trade developed and the amount of coin in circulation steadily increased in the 1270s and 80s. And, to foster an atmosphere of cross-border amity between Scotland and England, the young king followed his father's example by marrying into the English royal family, taking Henry III's daughter, Margaret, as his bride. During his long reign (1216–72), the issue of whether or not Henry could claim suzerainty over the kingdom of Scotland was never a source of debate or tension but the moment his son, Edward, succeeded, the atmosphere changed.

It seems that Alexander III had lost control of the great Honour of Huntingdon and, in 1278, he visited the court of his brother-in-law, probably in pursuit of his claim. There are contradictory records of what took place between the two kings. According to English sources, Alexander was said to have sworn fealty to Edward I for his English lands – and, in somewhat ambiguous terms, for his kingdom of Scotland. The English king was said to have reserved his right to receive homage for that. Scottish records tell a different story, stating that Alexander swore homage for his English lands alone, 'reserving [his] kingdom'. At that point, the Bishop of Norwich intervened, saying, 'Let that also be reserved to the King of England if he has right to homage for it.' Alexander was sufficiently self-possessed to reply, 'No one has right to homage for my kingdom for I hold it of God alone.' – a good answer but by no means the last word. The question would be repeated for three centuries.

With two sons, Alexander and David, and a daughter, Margaret, by his queen, the Scots king must have been confident in the continuity of the House of macMalcolm. But, in 1279, Queen Margaret died and, by 1284, his whole family was gone with the deaths of all three children. A crisis loomed. His daughter had married the King of Norway and Alexander had his granddaughter, Margaret, the Maid of Norway, recognised by his parliament as his heir while he cast around for another wife. He had been a widower for ten years and presumably had seen no need to remarry since his 20-year-old son, Alexander, seemed set to succeed. Indeed, the *Lanercost Chronicle*, compiled just across the border at a priory near Carlisle and generally well informed about Scottish affairs, cast a disapproving eye and characterised the king as a very merry widower: 'He used never to forebear on account of season or storm, nor for perils of flood or rocky cliffs, but would visit none too creditably nuns or matrons, virgins or widows as the fancy seized him, sometimes in disguise.'

With the references to cliffs, storms and fancy, this seems like a retrospective judgement but the essence of the entry may be reliable. In any event, Alexander contracted marriage with Yolande de Dreux, Countess of Montfort in her own right and a wealthy, well-connected French aristocrat. When they were married at Jedburgh Abbey in November 1285, the link with France was seen as a deliberate distancing from Edward I and the English royal family. It was probably an astute move politically, diplomatically and perhaps even emotionally. At 21 years old and said to be very beautiful, Yolande de Dreux was no nun or matron. Alexander was 44 – more than twice her age – but the monks at Lanercost at least believed him not to be out of practice at the business of fathering children. Events were to turn out very differently as the royal retinue made their way up Dere Street after the wedding party at Jedburgh and, as they reached the summit plateau of Soutra in November 1285, the winter winds began to blow.

Four months later, on either 18 or 19 March 1286, the king and his council were carousing in the royal hall at Edinburgh Castle, celebrating his marriage to the beautiful French countess. At some point, almost certainly fuelled by Gascon wine, Alexander announced that he was in a mood to see his new queen that very day! The only impediment was that she was not at Edinburgh but in the royal manor at Kinghorn on the opposite shore of the Firth of Forth. The late winter weather was foul – it was dark and the wind was whipping the wave tops in the firth – but the king would not be denied and, despite the protests of his councillors, he and only three squires for an escort had their horses saddled and they clattered out of the gates of the castle to ride for the ferry at Dalmeny.

The wind blew hard, the rain fell and the ferryman was said to have been reluctant to cross but, once gold and silver had glinted, the royal party clambered aboard and soon gained the Fife shore. There they were met by one of the burgesses of Inverkeithing, Alexander le Saucier, a cook in the royal kitchens and a man who was known to the king. A remarkable exchange took place, another example of a lack of deference amongst Scots: 'My lord, what are you doing out in such weather and darkness? How many times have I tried to persuade you that midnight travelling will do you no good?'

Refusing the offer of a bed for the night, his ardour not dampened by the rain and the wind, Alexander III set off along the cliff path to Kinghorn with his squires and two local men as guides. If it was midnight and there were storm clouds full of rain above, then it will have been black dark. Above the steep and rocky cliffs at Pettycur, the king became detached from his small party, perhaps their shouts could not be heard above the roar of the wind. It may have spooked, simply lost its footing or missed a turn on the shore path but Alexander's horse fell and plunged with its rider over the cliffs. On the morning after the storm, searchers found the king's body on the beach below. His neck had been broken. And the survival of his dynasty, the long-reigning macMalcolm kings who had given Scotland such stability, now depended on a little girl, the Maid of Norway.

7

The War for Scotland

✳

ABOUT SIX MILES inland from Berwick, nestled in a wide loop of the River Tweed, the village of Norham is small, beautiful and unexpected. On the higher ground to the east, looking directly over the wide, deep and lazy river at Scotland stand the massive ruins of a great medieval castle. Once a northern bastion of the Prince Bishops of Durham, it was often bombarded and attacked in the centuries after the death of Alexander III. Lying a little way apart, the village is home to another even more ancient monument to the power of Durham. Like a small cathedral, extravagantly out of scale with the scatter of cottages and lanes beside it, stands Norham Parish Church. On the western side of the village, it is set inside a large graveyard, in what looks like an old sacred precinct. Some of the stones by the font come from an earlier Anglian church built on the site in the 9th century but Norham's long pillared nave belongs to the later 12th century. When Viking sea lords repeatedly attacked the Holy Island of Lindisfarne, its monks fled with the body and relics of the great saint of the north, Cuthbert. For a time, they found sanctuary inland at Norham and somewhere in the sacred precinct they buried the bones of a royal saint, Ceolwulf, the Northumbrian king to whom Bede dedicated his *Ecclesiastical History of the English People*. Having abdicated in the middle of the 8th century, the saint entered the monastery at Lindisfarne to lead an exemplary life of prayer and contemplation mixed with a tolerable degree of asceticism. He obtained a dispensation for his brothers to drink wine and beer if they preferred these to water and milk.

In May 1291, another king came to Norham Kirk. Far from saintly, intent on domination and in search of a building large enough to hold hundreds of noblemen and clerics from both England and Scotland, Edward I rode into the sacred precinct. As the May trees blossomed and the spring lambs suckled, the destiny of a nation was to be decided. Less than a year before, the little girl recognised as Alexander III's heir, the Maid of Norway, had sailed the North Sea but, soon after her ship made landfall on Orkney, she died. Scotland was immediately plunged into the uncertainties of an inter-regnum. After the peaceful continuities of the long macMalcolm line, the kingdom was kingless and Edward I had come north to Norham to choose between fourteen candidates, one of them himself.

In the years between Alexander III's death and the death of his grand-daughter on Orkney, Scotland's government had been in the hands of six Guardians – two bishops and four magnates chosen by parliament. It was almost certainly this group who invited the king of England to adjudicate in what later became known as the Great Cause. Their action was perhaps seen as the lesser of two evils. In the event, Edward I did not promote himself as a candidate and the two men with the strongest claims appeared to be circling each other, preparing for civil war. John de Balliol, Lord of Galloway, had developed an alliance with Antony Bek, the Bishop of Durham, and the English king's representative in Scotland. Balliol also began to call himself 'the heir of Scotland'. Meanwhile another magnate based in the south-west, Robert de Bruce, Lord of Annandale, was arming his men, as were his allies, the Earls of Mar and Atholl.

With the nave and aisles of Norham packed with noblemen, abbots and bishops and clerks taking notes, Edward I opened proceedings with a domineering, calculated flourish. Probably speaking in Norman French, he insisted that, before he arbitrated in the Great Cause, one central proposition should be made very clear and be unequivocally accepted. His overlordship of Scotland should be recognised. And instead of laying forth arguments to support this assertion, he challenged the Guardians and their clerical lawyers to provide evidence to the contrary that he was not the legal, legitimate feudal superior of the king of Scotland. The captivity of William the Lion and the Treaty of Falaise loomed out of history to haunt the Scots at Norham. Summary and emphatic, Edward told the Guardians that they had three weeks to respond. And they did. Even though, by any standards, the timescale was ridiculous, the Bishop of Glasgow, Robert Wishart, supplied the only reply possible. To the irritation of the English king, the bishop asserted that, in the obvious absence of a king, there was no one in Scotland with sufficient authority to make such a concession. Edward ignored this circular argument and forbade his clerks from recording it. Brute politics and personal ambition ensured that the claimants accepted English overlordship.

Most of the men who would be king were Anglo-Norman lords who traced their royal descent from illegitimate children of William the Lion and, in one case, of Alexander II. Leaving aside Edward I and Erik II of Norway, the five strongest claims came from: Humphrey de Bohun, Earl of Hereford; John de Balliol; Robert de Bruce; John Hastings, Lord of Abergavenny; and, somewhat unexpectedly and exotically, Count Florence or Floris V of Holland. All except Floris were direct and legitimate descendants of Earl Henry, the son of David I who died before he could succeed to the throne. De Bohun had what was believed by the lawyers to be a powerful claim but he chose not to press it. Because Balliol was descended from Margaret, the eldest daughter of Earl David of Huntingdon, the son of Earl Henry, and Robert Bruce was descended from Isabella, her younger sister, Balliol's claim was thought to be stronger and the feudal laws of primogeniture supported its superiority.

But Floris V would have none of it and put forward what sounds like a deeply implausible argument. He asserted that David I had renounced his right to the throne of Scotland to Floris's ancestor, William, in return for an estate in Aberdeenshire. No copy of any supporting document was immediately to hand to prove this but the Count of Holland's lawyers argued that there must be one – somewhere. And so, no doubt to the consternation of other claimants and almost certainly for other tactical and diplomatic reasons, Edward I granted a ten-month adjournment while Floris's men rummaged around in castles and monasteries in Scotland. Of course, no such document was found although, later on, fakes surfaced.

On 17 November 1292, in the great hall of Berwick Castle, now almost entirely obliterated by the Victorian railway station, Edward I ruled in favour of John Balliol. This decision was nominally arrived at by a jury of 104 auditors, 40 from Balliol's supporters and 40 from Bruce's with the balance made up by 24 English nominees. So powerful was Balliol's case that 29 of Bruce's auditors voted against their man. The reign of King John began with the support of the majority of Scotland's great magnates. But it quickly disintegrated.

In December 1292, in a ceremony of some splendour, King John I of Scotland did homage for his kingdom to Edward I of England at Newcastle. And, in what looks like a test case, the new sovereign's authority was rapidly and publicly undermined. By November 1293, Macduff, the brother of the Earl of Fife, had been tried in a royal court and imprisoned. He appealed over

King John's head to Edward I as his overlord. This, in turn, meant that King John or his representative would have to plead in an English court and, when he refused, Edward sentenced the Scots king for contempt and ordered him to surrender the royal castles of Roxburgh, Edinburgh and Stirling. Balliol's power began to unravel in the face of these belittlements. When the English king demanded in June 1294 that ten Scottish earls and sixteen barons join the royal host to fight in France, events began to accelerate. A parliament held in Stirling a year later removed executive power from King John, who retained only his crown, and transferred the government of the realm to a council of 12 prelates and barons. Neutered politically, Balliol soon found himself utterly humiliated.

Two months after parliament met at Stirling, an alliance was concluded with Philip IV of France, threatening Edward from both the north as well as the south. In March 1296, the Scottish host converged on the ancient muster ground at Caddon Lea near Galashiels and, to counter them, a vast English army of almost 30,000 heavy cavalry, infantry and archers marched north. Little more than 'a ditch and a barricade of boards', the defences of Berwick crumbled in a matter of hours as the English knights charged and their destriers jumped over them and into the streets of the town. Wholesale slaughter followed, including a group of thirty Flemish merchants in their warehouse, the Red Hall, and a blood-soaked signal was sent around Scotland. All resistance to the army of the overlord would be ruthlessly, pitilessly crushed. After only seventeen days, the Scottish host had been scattered at Dunbar and King John captured at Montrose.

In a ceremony usually inflicted on treasonous knights, King John was publically stripped of all that made him a king. Dragged into the market place at Montrose, in front of an audience of noblemen, prelates and common soldiers, and made to stand before King Edward, his knightly girdle was removed. Blazoned with the royal lion of Scotland, Balliol's surcoat was torn off and the royal signet ring pulled from his finger. And then the symbol of his authority, the Great Seal of Scotland, was smashed to pieces on the cobbles. No doubt to a roar of laughter from his barons, Edward I was said to have remarked that 'a man does good business when he rids himself of a turd'.

To buttress the emphatic victory of Edward I and his claims to over-lordship, more symbols made their way south. For at least four centuries, Scottish kings had climbed the Hill of Faith, the Moot Hill at Scone, to

be inaugurated on the Stone of Destiny, the *Lia Fail* that was said to have
come from Ireland, and as 'a sign of the resignation and conquest of the
kingdom', Edward I ordered that it be removed to Westminster, where it
remained for seven centuries. And Scotland's most sacred relic, a fragment
of the True Cross known as the Black Rood of St Margaret, was also taken
and subsequently destroyed when reformers ransacked Durham Cathedral
in 1540. It gave its name to Holyrood Abbey in Edinburgh. Symbols of a
distinctive nationhood had an obvious power and, in 1284, the conquest of
Wales had been made the more absolute when the crown of King Arthur
and another fragment of the True Cross had been summarily carted off to
England, never to return.

On 28 August 1296, Scottish prelates, lords and other persons of substance
were summoned to a parliament at Berwick and compelled to attach their
seals and names to the Ragman Roll, a pledge of loyalty to Edward I. More
than 1,500 Scots acquiesced. Like Wales, Scotland was to become a colony.
Hugh Cressingham was appointed Treasurer and he set up an administration
and exchequer at Berwick. But, in reality, he did not have the resources to
control Scotland (and the location of Cressingham in the extreme south-
east corner of the country suggests that Edward I understood that) and his
writ ran little further than the lower Tweed Basin. Resistance was stirring
elsewhere and it was reported that there were 'conspiracies in very many
parts of the land'.

A year after Balliol's humiliation, his most loyal subject and most famous
supporter entered history, virtually from nowhere. William Wallace's origins
are obscure – and that in itself is significant. What seems certain is that he
was a minor nobleman from Ayrshire, perhaps the son of Alan Wallace,
probably not from Elderslie in Renfrewshire, a later tradition, but probably
a vassal of James the Steward who held large estates in that region. His name
strongly suggests that memories of the old kingdom of Strathclyde had not
faded entirely and, more, that dialects of Old Welsh still clung on around
the Clyde Basin as late as the 1290s. The name Wallace derives from the Old
English *Wylisc* and it meant a 'foreigner', more specifically a 'Welshman'.
At some relatively recent stage, it seems that William Wallace's family were
known as Welsh speakers. Perhaps they still remembered *Yr Iaith Hen*, 'the
old language'.

In May 1297, this minor figure burst into politics and prominence when
he killed William de Heselrig, the English High Sheriff of Lanarkshire. He
was joined in this insurgency by Lord William Douglas and his men and

together they went on to raid the royal town of Scone. At the same time, what initially appeared to be a much more widespread rising flared in Moray. The castles at Inverness and on Loch Ness fell to Andrew Moray, the heir to the earldom, and he was joined by rebels from Aberdeen and the Buchan. Meanwhile Wallace rode to Glasgow to meet Bishop Robert Wishart in his cathedral. Edward I had adopted a colonial approach to the Church in Scotland also, and he insisted that English priests could be appointed to Scottish benefices. This united clerical opposition behind the cause of independence. The *Lanercost Chronicle* offered an English commentary: 'Robert Wishart, Bishop of Glasgow, ever foremost in treason conspired with the Steward of the kingdom, named James, for a new piece of insolence, yea, for a new chapter of ruin. Not daring openly to break their pledge to the king [Edward], they caused a certain bloody man, William Wallace, who had formerly been a chief of brigands in Scotland, to revolt against the king and assemble the people in his support.'

This passage hints at the reasons for the rise of Wallace from relative obscurity. Unlike great magnates like Wishart and Stewart, he had little to lose. His murder of Heselrig had placed him outside the law and shown him as a man who had both courage and the qualities of leadership. Rather than take the lead himself, Bishop Wishart chose to support the bloody man as a focus for popular unrest. But, when Wallace laid siege to Dundee Castle, Edward I realised that he was no mere brigand and ordered John de Warenne, the Earl of Surrey, to muster an army and march north. Messages were sent across the Mounth to Andrew Moray and both rebel leaders were seen as 'commanders of the army of the kingdom of Scotland, and the community of the realm'. This elevation represented a remarkable rise for Wallace as he outgrew both Wishart's and the Lanercost chronicler's estimates. Andrew Moray was much less surprising as a leader, being the heir to an earldom, but his fellow general had emerged from obscurity with no resources except his charisma and prowess. Both men were scrupulous as to their formal status. They acted on behalf of the rightful king of Scotland, King John, and came to be seen as guardians of his realm.

By early September 1297, Earl Warenne and Hugh Cressingham had led their army to Stirling, the hinge of Scotland, its great castle the sentinel watching over the north road, the only road leading north of the Forth. Wallace and Moray had formed up their spearmen and small force of light cavalry on the north bank of the looping, meandering river, on slightly higher ground. They waited and watched. Knowing very well the overwhelming superiority of English numbers – and especially the devastating power of the charge of their heavily armed cavalry in open field, the Scots knew that what seemed like an invitation to pitched battle would be impossible for Cressingham and Warenne to resist. But first their army had to cross the river. There was only one bridge. And it was narrow, made of wood, allowing perhaps only ranks of three men abreast or two horsemen to cross. Wallace and Moray watched and waited.

English overconfidence and incompetence immediately aided the Scots. Sir Richard Lundie, a Scottish knight in English service, advised Warenne and Cressingham that there was another way to cross the Forth and in strength. A mile or so upstream there was a ford where horsemen and infantry could splash cross about sixty abreast. But his local knowledge was ignored. War was expensive, said Cressingham, and they needed to get on with it. On the morning of 11 September, as the Scots watched from their vantage point, many companies of English and Welsh archers crossed the narrow wooden bridge. But they were quickly recalled. Apparently Earl Warenne had overslept and nothing was to happen without his personal oversight. A potential advantage was lost.

When the English army at last rumbled into action, their pennants flying and the hooves of their knights' destriers drumming on the planking of the bridge, Wallace and Moray gave orders that their formations of spearmen should begin to move and deploy. The English chronicler, Walter of Guisborough, later wrote that the Scots waited until 'as many of the enemy had come over as they believed they could overcome'. When that calculation had been made, their captains roared the ranks of Scottish spearmen into the charge and they struck hard and decisively. They cut off the northern end of the bridge, forcing the English back, and then surrounded the cavalry and infantry who had managed to get across. Iron spikes known as caltrops may have been scattered in front of the destriers and, when English knights were unhorsed as their mounts squealed, they were hacked down and cut to pieces. Marooned as a helpless spectator on the southern bank of the Forth, Earl Warenne watched as the standards of his vanguard and infantry went down in the slaughter. The Scots jabbed with their long spears and slashed with their dirks and swords as blood ran into the river. The hated Hugh Cressingham was pulled off his horse and killed and it was said that his body was flayed, the skin used by Wallace to make a sword-belt. As the circle of death tightened, few escaped but in the ruck, Andrew Moray was mortally wounded, dying two months later. Flushed with a famous and unlikely victory, William Wallace was left as sole Guardian of the Realm, a loyal subject of King John.

Stirling Bridge showed that it could be done. The grinding, powerful and battle-hardened English war machine could be stopped in its tracks. Armoured knights, the Panzer tanks of medieval Europe, could be defeated by ranks of humble spearmen but only if they were trained and disciplined. In the *Scotichronicon*, Walter Bower included a fascinating passage that described William Wallace's ruthless and clear-eyed approach to battlefield discipline:

> For he encouraged his comrades in arms towards the achievement of whatever plan he had in hand always to approach battle for the liberty of their homeland with one mind. And as regards the whole multitude of his followers he decreed on pain of death that once the lesser men among the middling people (or in practice those who were less robust) had been assembled before him, one man was always to be chosen out of five from all the groups of five to be over the other four and called a quaternion; his commands were to be obeyed by them in all matters, and whoever did not obey was to be killed. In a similar manner also moving on up to the men who were more robust and effective there was always to be tenth man [called a *decurion*] over each nine, and a twentieth over each nineteen, and so on moving up to each thousand [called a *chiliarch*] and beyond to the top. At length, he himself as preeminent over everyone else was regarded as commander or general, whom all were bound to obey to the death. With everyone harmoniously approving this law (or substitute for the law), they chose him as their captain, and promised to keep the said statute until the succession of a legitimate king.

Distracted by domestic difficulties and events in France and Flanders, Edward I had been forced to trust Earl Warenne to deal with Wallace and Moray. But once he heard of the fiasco at Stirling Bridge, the famously irascible king concluded a truce with the French and began to plan an invasion of Scotland. This time, there would be no mistake but, in the event, Edward needed luck and Scottish misjudgement in order to succeed. By the time they reached the Firth of Forth, west of Edinburgh, the English army was running low on supplies and, in their camp at Kirkliston, a riot broke out as Welsh infantry and archers attacked their English comrades. At that moment, Edward I believed he would be forced into a humiliating retreat, having achieved nothing. But the scouts reported that Wallace had formed up his army near the wood at Callendar near Falkirk, perhaps to pursue and harry the retreating English. Edward I gave thanks: 'As God lives . . . they need not pursue me, for I shall meet them this day.'

Wallace had deployed his disciplined spearmen in four schiltrons, defensive circular formations several ranks deep which bristled with steel-tipped shafts 10–12 feet long, like the quills of a hedgehog. But, unlike Stirling, Falkirk was fought in open field and, once Edward's knights had scattered their supporting archers and companies of men at arms, these formations became static archery targets. Volleys rained down out of the autumn sky, crossbowmen fired bolts at point blank range and slingers peppered them with stones. And, as their ranks thinned, the charges of the armoured knights ripped the schiltrons apart.

William Wallace managed to escape but, in the aftermath of heavy defeat, his authority was much diminished and he resigned his guardianship. After years in Europe on diplomatic missions to gather international support for an independent Scotland, Wallace was captured by the English in August 1305. Following a show trial at which he was not allowed to speak, the famous Guardian of the Realm was condemned to the appalling punishment for treason. Stripped naked and dragged through the streets of London behind a horse and pelted with refuse and worse, Wallace was led to the scaffold and choked at the end of the hangman's rope until close to unconsciousness. Then he was probably tied to an upright hurdle so that the baying crowd could see his agonies. First, the executioner took a knife and cut off his genitals and, after the bloody handful had been held up and cheered, they began to disembowel Wallace. Skilled men working with sharp, specially made knives aimed to keep their victims from going into shock so that could see their entrails burned on a brazier while they still lived. Only then came the merciful release of the block and the headman's axe. Wallace's head was spitted on a pike on London Bridge and his limbs sent for display at Newcastle, Berwick, Stirling and Perth.

The severity of Edward I's conquest and control in the years after victory at Falkirk certainly disaffected some who might otherwise have acquiesced in his overlordship. It is important to recognise that medieval magnates almost always acted in the interests of their families and not in an as yet largely unformed sense of patriotism. The central difficulty for the English conquest was that Edward I never reconciled a contradiction. Many of the great magnates in the south such as Warenne were motivated by what their families might gain in a conquered Scotland. Victory ought to have brought them at least some part of the lands of the vanquished. But, equally, Edward I needed to cultivate the loyalty of the Scottish nobility since he could not hope to hold the nation as a colony without that. That meant he could not seize many Scottish estates for redistribution to his English magnates who brought their men and money to join the invasion armies. They looked for something more enduring than portable loot.

In 1299, King John was released from the Tower of London and allowed to travel to France. He packed some souvenirs. Before he was allowed to take ship at Dover, his baggage was searched and found to contain the Golden Royal Crown of Scotland, a golden seal, many cups and plates of gold and silver and great deal of cash. By 1301, King John had retired to his family estates at Helicourt in Picardy and he took no further part in Scottish politics. The kingdom was effectively kingless once more.

In 1302, Robert Bruce pledged his loyalty to Edward I and was accepted into 'the king's peace'. But, when his father died two years later, Robert inherited the family claim to the Scottish crown and, in 1306, he fled imminent arrest at Edward I's court and began the long journey to Bannockburn. In the Greyfriars monastery in Dumfries, Bruce met John Comyn, his greatest rival for the Scottish crown and, after a fierce argument, killed him. The pace of events began to quicken. Bruce and his supporters rode to Scone and, amidst as much pomp as time would allow (since Balliol had removed the old one, a new crown had to be made), he had himself inaugurated and crowned at Scone in March 1306. His wife, Elizabeth, was sceptical: 'I am afraid, my Lord, that we have been made King and Queen, as boys are made in summer games.' And it began very badly.

After an abortive siege of Perth, Bruce's army was scattered at Methven by an English force led by Sir Aymer de Valence. The new king was forced to flee into the West Highlands. Bruce's queen, their daughter, Marjorie, and his sisters, Christina and Mary, and Isabella, Countess of Buchan (who had crowned the king at Scone) were all captured. Two of the women, Mary and Isabella, were cruelly imprisoned in cages slung over the walls of Berwick and Roxburgh castles for display. Out in all seasons and weathers, they were only allowed inside to use a privy. Bruce's brother, Neil, was also taken and dragged to the scaffold to suffer the horrors inflicted on William Wallace. The sole consolation in these dark times for King Robert and his family was that Edward I, the Hammer of the Scots, died at Burgh-on-Sands near Carlisle in July 1307.

Slowly, the tide began to turn. After minor victories in Ayrshire and

Galloway, Bruce led his men northwards, beyond the effective reach of the English and those sympathetic to them. He captured Inverlochy and Urquhart Castles and then turned to deal with the Comyns, his sworn enemies, in their heartlands. After victory at Inverurie and the defeat of the English garrison at Aberdeen, Bruce had established control of Scotland north of the Tay and, in 1309, he held his first parliament at St Andrews. In the four years that followed, the king's men took all of the strategically important castles – except Stirling. Steadfastly refusing to meet English forces in pitched battle, Bruce gained control of his kingdom by guerrilla tactics. But his brother, Edward, overturned this successful strategy. Sent to besiege Stirling Castle while the king was campaigning in the Isle of Man, he made a pact with the governor, Sir Philip Mowbray. If Edward II did not come to the relief of the castle by midsummer, 1314, it would be surrendered to the Scots. Robert was reportedly furious. His brother had committed him to battle and given Edward II a year to prepare.

Bruce knew which way they would come. They had no other choice. Having mustered an army of almost 20,000 men, many thousands of horses, hundreds of ox-drawn wagons and other assorted encumbrances such as herds of cows and sheep, Edward II's army had to move north on the old Roman road of Dere Street. After more than a thousand winters since the legionaries and auxiliaries made it, its metalled surface still survived and saw a great deal of traffic, especially wheeled carts. Dere Street's northern terminus was probably the Roman fort on the Forth at Cramond and from there another ancient road struck north-west towards Stirling and the old Gask Ridge frontier. Bruce had deployed his army at the New Park, where the highway ran through a medieval hunting reserve. Divided into four battalions or battles, the Scots had been marshalled in retreat order with the vanguard commanded by Thomas Randolph, Earl of Moray nearest Stirling and the sanctuary hills beyond, while Bruce was with the rearguard, closest to what was known as The Entry, where the English army would first approach.

Inevitably strung out for many miles along the length of the Roman road, Edward II's forces were difficult for him to communicate with and to command effectively. He may have intended to make overnight camp on good ground south of the New Park after an exhausting forced march but events soon ran out of his control. The English vanguard were far ahead and, when they sighted King Robert's battalion at The Entry, on the edge of the wooded reserve, Sir Henry de Bohun called for his mounted knights and infantry to halt and form up. But, when he drew close enough to see clearly, de Bohun believed that he could make out a mounted figure who might have been the Scots king. A man whose helmet had a circlet of gold around it and who wore a surcoat blazoned with the royal lion of Scotland was riding up and down in front of the ranks of spearmen on a small grey pony. Adrenalin pumped and de Bohun saw a chance for glory, a chance to kill the usurper and win a battle with a single death. Digging in his spurs, kicking his destrier into the gallop, he couched his lance and charged.

THE MIDDLE AGE

This was a term first used by Christians. The Medium Aevum *was the time between Christ's First and his Second Coming. It is the root of the term 'medieval' and its variable spelling. Apart from the devout, people who lived in the Middle Ages were not aware of doing so. It was not until the 15th- and 16th-centuries rise of humanism in Italy and elsewhere that scholars interested in reviving classical Greek and Roman culture began to think of the Middle Ages in another way. It was the interval between the glittering achievements of Athens and Rome and their own gilded age of developing enlightenment. Partly as a result of the influence of the Renaissance, medieval became a pejorative term. It still is.*

Armed only with a hand axe, on a pony and not a warhorse, Bruce was taken by surprise. His men roared for him to retreat into their ranks. But he did not hear them. With only seconds to react as de Bohun levelled his lance, his destrier thundering across the grass, kicking up clods of earth, the Scots king waited until the English knight was almost upon him. As the point of his lance searched for Bruce's breast, the king suddenly neck-reined his pony to the offside, not allowing de Bohun time to swing his lance over his horse's head. And as the destrier passed, Bruce stood up high in his stirrups and struck a mighty blow to the Englishman's head, killing him instantly.

It was a crazy risk but it set the mood for what was to follow, sending Scottish morale sky high. After this famous incident and late in the evening of the first day of the battle, about 500 English knights circled the Scottish battalions and attacked Thomas Randolph's vanguard. A schiltron of about 1,500 spearmen, well disciplined and determined, they repulsed repeated charges of English knights, reducing them to frustration. They threw maces and swords at the impenetrable ranks before retreating. From the woods of the New Park, Bruce and Douglas had watched the ferocious engage-ment and must have been encouraged. But a battle in the morning was by no means certain. The Scots king may still have been determined upon a withdrawal into the hills west of Stirling.

On the night of 23 June 1314, Bruce convened a council of war beneath the trees of the New Park. In the circle of firelight sat a band of brothers, captains who had fought the long guerrilla war to recapture Scotland's castles and expel English garrisons. Would they risk all of those hard fights, daring escalades and countless episodes of grim determination on one battle? They may have given the English a bloody nose that evening but, down in the carse below the New Park, a huge army was camped, at least twice the size of their own. Two-and-a-half thousand armoured knights on their snorting destriers had not yet engaged and no companies of English or Welsh archers had yet rained death from the skies.

Under cover of the half dark of midsummer, a man slipped out of the English camp. Sir Alexander Seton was a Scot in the service of Edward II and, when he reached the pickets at the New Park, he asked to see King Robert. Explaining that all was dissension and confusion amongst the English commanders, Seton told the council of war that, if ever they were to be victorious, then tomorrow would be the day. No doubt there was discus-sion but soon orders were given for the schiltrons to stand to at dawn and make ready for battle.

As the morning light washed west over the flat carseland on 24 June 1314, Bruce ordered that banners be flown over his four battalions. Crows lifted off the trees of the New Park as trumpets sounded and three schiltrons marched forward in a stepped formation between the Bannockburn and the Pelstream Burn. As drums beat a steady pace, Edward Bruce's men led the way, hugging the left bank of the Bannockburn so that they could not be outflanked. Slightly behind his men came Randolph's battalion and, behind them, the men led by Sir James Douglas.

When the English knights saw the Scots marching downhill in formation towards them, clearly intent on attack, they were quickly armoured and mounted. Without waiting for companies of archers to fire volleys into the Scottish ranks, the Earl of Gloucester led the opening charge. Disorganised and piecemeal, it was a fatal misjudgement. When they engaged with the Scots spearmen, the knights made it impossible for their archers or crossbowmen to fire for fear of hitting English targets. The battle quickly became a close-quarter melee as all of the schiltrons closed with the enemy. So long as the Scots did not break formation, they had a chance of victory but, when companies of English archers got themselves across the Pelstream Burn and began firing volleys from the flank into the ranks of James Douglas's battalion, Bruce reacted immediately. Sir Robert Keith charged the archers with 500 light horsemen and scattered them. Bruce moved with his reserve schiltron to reinforce Douglas and almost imperceptibly momentum began to swing towards the Scots.

Medieval battles were often murderous rucks of hacking, jabbing, pushing and shoving and, when one army began to inch forward, forcing the other to move backwards, there came a tipping point. 'On them, on them! They fail!' A shout went up from the Scottish spearmen. Some fought their way close to Edward II and his destrier and they managed to pull at its caparison. At that moment, his bodyguards took hold of the king's reins and forced him to retreat. Once the English royal standards were seen leaving the field, Bannockburn turned from a battle into a rout. It was then that the real slaughter began. Fleeing men drowned in the boggy pools towards the Forth or were trampled underfoot as panic swept across the Bannockburn itself. Perhaps as many as 10,000 Englishmen died as the disciplined spearmen of the schiltrons broke ranks and gave vent to the frenzy of killing.

It was an unlikely, very famous victory. Bannockburn established Robert Bruce as the rightful king of Scotland. One chronicle noted that the nation was his by right of conquest and the battle showed that with guile, training and luck, the English war machine could be beaten. But it was also a rare victory in the war for Scotland. Many defeats and reverses awaited.

A hero king, certainly the greatest and most successful warrior to sit on the throne of Scotland, Bruce lost no time in pressing home his advantage after Bannockburn. Determined to take Cumbria back under Scottish control, he led an army to Carlisle to take the town and its castle. Squat, solid and unspectacular, it was one of the most secure fortresses in the north, the key to holding North Cumbria and a sentinel close to the Solway fords. Once the Scots had crossed the Eden and surrounded the castle and walled town, much of both built with stones from Hadrian's Wall, they trundled siege engines forward. They made little impression. Ably led by Sir Andrew de Harcla, a local lord, the defence was certainly resolute. But it was much aided by the weather. In the summer of 1315, it began to rain – and, for months, it rarely stopped. The Scots' siege engines sank into the mud and toppled or were impossible to move. Foraging soldiers could find little food in the drenched countryside as crops failed and farms were flooded by rivers breaking their banks. Meandering through a low-lying plain on its way to the Solway, the Eden is particularly prone to spill across the farmland to the east of Carlisle and it may have risen so much in the summer of 1315 that Bruce was forced to lift the siege and retreat northwards. Neither he nor his captains could know it but the Little Ice Age had begun.

THE BATTLE OF ROSLIN

More famous for its elaborately decorated and enigmatic chapel, in 1303 Roslin was also the site of a forgotten battle. Forgotten, that is, except on a map. Around the village are place names which recall the slaughter. Shinbanes Field was the site of burial and the plough has turned up many skeletal fragments. The Kill Burn ran red with blood and, at Stinking Rig, piles of rotting corpses of both men and horses waited for burial. The cause of the conflict may have been personal. On the Scottish side, Earl Sinclair vied with the Englishman, Sir John Segrave, for the hand of Lady Margaret Ramsay and a Scottish force of perhaps 8,000 appears to have beaten off a much larger English force in three separate engagements in the fields around the village. The fact that England and Scotland were sporadically at war during this period might also have had something to do with it.

For almost 500 years, the winters would grow colder, the summers shorter and wetter as farmers struggled to wring a harvest from the sodden ground. Between 1315 and 1317, there was famine not only in Scotland but across Europe. Crops failed for two years and output did not recover fully until 1322. Reports from the English garrison at Berwick spoke of 'many dying from hunger' in 1315 and again in 1316. When foraging parties rode out to commandeer supplies, one had to venture as far east as Melrose, a round trip of almost 80 miles. Perhaps they feared little resistance in the stricken countryside. Populations that had mushroomed in the long, balmy and productive summers of the medieval warm period were savagely reduced as hunger took the young and the old. Chronicles recorded cannibalism and infanticide. The cold was not consistent and there were periods when temperatures rose but the Little Ice Age flickered until the middle of the 19th century. Its depths are remembered in accounts of frost fairs on the frozen River Thames and perhaps most powerfully in the paintings of Pieter Breugel the Elder whose *Hunters in the Snow* (1565) depicted a scene from the winters of the 1560s.

By the time Scotland had at least partly recovered from the famine of 1315–17, her king was growing old by the standards of the time. In 1320, he was 46 and perhaps contemplating his passage to the next world. In 1306, he had been excommunicated, cast out of the Church and condemned to die unshriven, bound for damnation, for the murder of John Comyn in Dumfries. Three letters were written to Pope John XXII which not only asked for the sentence of excommunication to be lifted but also the papal interdict on Scotland to be withdrawn. Only one letter has survived and it has become one of the most famous and most quoted (in translation from the original Latin) texts in Scotland's history. Known as the Declaration of Arbroath, it puts forward a carefully argued and beautifully written case for Scotland's independence from England under the rightful rule of King Robert. John Balliol had died in 1314 but his son, Edward, had a clear and legitimate claim to be King of Scots. Probably the work of Bernard of Kilwinning, Abbot of Arbroath, the Declaration contains this ringing phrase: 'For as long as but a hundred of us remain alive, never will we on any conditions be brought under English rule. It is in truth not for glory, nor riches, nor honours that we are fighting, but for freedom – for that alone, which no honest man gives up but with life itself.'

But it also argues a much more complex point. It makes clear that, if King Robert – or any king – should ever give up the independence of Scotland, then the community of the realm (in effect, the great magnates) had the right to depose him and find another to be their king. Rather than the first glimmerings of democracy, this clause speaks of kingship by consent and also a justification of the replacement of King John with King Robert. Nevertheless, it is a political notion some distance ahead of its time. It was not until 1328 that the papacy allowed itself to be convinced by Abbot Bernard's arguments and the sentences of excommunication and interdict were at last lifted.

By that time, Bruce was ill. Northern English sources were usually well informed about Scotland and the *Lanercost Chronicle* and the *Scalacronica* recorded that King Robert was suffering from leprosy. Since the king continued to rule, hold councils and audiences, this seems unlikely. Lepers were segregated from society and sent to suffer in isolated communities. John Barbour believed that Bruce's constitution had been badly affected by the years of guerrilla warfare – what he called 'cold lying' – during which he and his men hid in remote places bivouacking in all weathers. Whatever his illness, the king appeared to sense that his end was near at hand for he was carried on a litter overland from his old stronghold at Turnberry to St Ninian's shrine at Whithorn. Bruce died on 7 June 1329 and his enduring piety was expressed in one of his last requests. This was recorded in his *Chronicle* by Jean Froissart: 'I will that as soon as I am trespassed out of this world that ye take my heart out of my body, and embalm it, and take of my treasure as ye shall think sufficient for that enterprise, both for your self and such company as ye will take with you, and present my heart to the Holy Sepulchre where as our Lord lay, seeing my body can not come there.'

With dismaying speed all that Bruce had worked and risked so much for threatened to disintegrate. Carrying his king's embalmed heart into battle, Sir James Douglas was killed on crusade against the Moors in Spain. And Thomas Randolph, Earl of Moray, died suddenly in 1332. He had been appointed Bruce's trusted Regent for David II, a child only four years old when his father died in 1329. This moment of instability encouraged Edward Balliol to revive his claims to Scotland and an armada of 88 ships set sail from the Yorkshire coast to carry a small army northwards. Known as the Disinherited, lords who had been forced to forfeit their lands because they had fought on the wrong side at Bannockburn, they won an unexpected victory at Dupplin Moor, near Perth. Even though Balliol was crowned a few weeks later at Scone, he was driven out of Scotland, chased half-naked across the border by supporters of David II.

Much more seriously, Edward III mustered an army and arrived under the walls of Berwick in the summer of 1333. After laying a siege and raiding as far north as Scone, trailing fire and pillage in what seems to have been an exercise in terror, the English king returned to his camp at the mouth of the Tweed. A relieving Scots army marched south and, at Halidon Hill, to the north of Berwick, it formed up in battle order, led by Sir Archibald Douglas. His tactics were a disastrous contrast with the considered choosing of the ground at Bannockburn. Here is an entry in the chronicle known as the *Book of Pluscarden*: 'They (the Scots) marched towards the town with great display, in order of battle, and recklessly, stupidly and inadvisedly chose a battle ground at Halidon Hill, where there was a marshy hollow between the two armies, and where a great downward slope, with some precipices, and then again a rise lay in front of the Scots, before they could reach the field where the English were posted.'

The English archers sent so many arrows into the sky above the floundering Scottish schiltrons that the *Lanercost Chronicle* reported that 'the

Scots who marched in the front were so wounded in the face and blinded by the multitude of English arrows that they could not help themselves, and soon began to turn their faces away from the blows of the arrows and fall'.

It was the first time that companies of archers were deployed in the 'harrow formation' – in wedges which allowed them to shoot to their flanks in order to create a murderous crossfire. So many Scots magnates died at Halidon Hill that initial resistance to Edward Balliol's claim to the crown was feeble. But, in disinheriting his many enemies, this alternative king ensured that opposition continued to bubble. In 1336, Edward I Balliol was deposed by supporters of the Bruce dynasty and, by 1337, Edward III had been distracted by the French king's confiscation of the duchy of Aquitaine and the County of Ponthieu.

Meanwhile the boy king, David II, had been despatched to France into the safe custody of Philip VI. When the returned to Scotland in 1341, he was 17 years old and able to govern in his own right. Within five years, he had invaded England, been soundly defeated at the Battle of Neville's Cross near Durham and taken prisoner. He was to remain in English custody for 11 years. But what must, at the time, have seemed like a disastrous reversal for the kingdom of Scotland soon paled into insignificance.

Bridges and fords across the Tweed were watched night and day and closely guarded and ferry boats were pulled up on the northern banks. No traveller from the south was permitted to cross into the realm of Scotland. In May 1348, the Black Death made landfall in England. Probably carried by Gascon sailors (the pandemic had raged through the English-controlled city of Bordeaux), it claimed its first victims in Weymouth. Fleas on black rats and humans carried what contemporaries called 'the great pestilence' and, once they bit into the bloodstream, symptoms developed very rapidly. Infecting the lymph glands, it converted them into hard swellings or buboes under the arms or in the groin. An agonising death followed in a matter of days. Two other strains were equally deadly. Pneumonic plague was carried directly into the lungs by airborne bacteria and septicaemic plague infected the blood, bringing death even more quickly. In only 500 days, the Black Death had blazed up through the length of England and it may be that as many as half of the population died. It must have been unimaginably shocking, bewildering, as millions died in a matter of only 16 or so months. Countless bodies piled up, tragedy and loss and fear stalked from village to village in an inexorable march of horror, and it must have seemed as though the world was coming to an end.

To the Scots the plague seemed like an opportunity too good to be missed.

Believing it to be 'the foul death of England' affecting only those south of the border, an army mustered at Caddon Lea to invade the land being punished 'by the avenging hand of God'. When the Black Death erupted amongst the pavilions and bivouacs by the side of the Caddon Water, probably brought by mercenaries, the army scattered in panic. The *Scotichronicon* reported that 'in 1350 there was a great pestilence and mortality of men in the kingdom of Scotland, and this pestilence also raged for many years before and after in various parts of the world'.

The overwhelming reaction was to flee, to abandon anyone who exhibited symptoms and almost all of the victims died in great pain – and alone. No comfort could be given by family members and friends gathered at the bedside. It was too dangerous. It is reckoned that perhaps a quarter of all those infected with bubonic plague might have had a chance of survival but, if left to a lonely death, unable to move, marooned in their own filth, many would have perished from thirst or starved to death.

At first, priests seem to have been brave enough to administer last rights. In his account of the first plague year in Scotland of 1349, John of Fordun went on to write in the *Scotichronicon* that: 'In this year it so pleased the Lord that twenty-four professed canons of the house of canons at St Andrews were called from the troubles of this present life, as is the way of all flesh, of whom all except three were priests. They were all men of ample education, circumspect in spiritual and temporal matters, and upright and honourable in their way of life. These plagues occur from time to time because of the sins of mankind.'

It may be that early contact with victims in St Andrews brought the great pestilence into the cathedral's community of Augustinian Canons where it spread quickly. It is likely that the number of pilgrims diminished markedly even though many will have wished to pray hard for the help of St Andrew. Other jeremiads agreed that the Wrath of God was at work. Causes ranged from the laxity of the monastic orders to the habit of fashionable women of 'wearing clothes so tight that they wore a fox tail hanging down inside their skirts to hide their arses'.

With a considerably lower population density than in rural England and its geography of mountains, hills, valleys, sea lochs and firths encouraging the development of isolated communities, it may be that Scotland lost a third to a fifth of its people to the biblical scourge of the Black Death. John of Fordun reckoned that one in three people died. Proximity will have meant that mortality was highest in the towns but since these were little more than large villages, the absolute numbers were relatively small. What also had an impact was fear, an unwillingness to hold or travel to markets and also to worship in common. As the Black Death raged and bodies were carted to mass graves, Scotland was paralysed.

DANGEROUS GERBILS

The ravages of the Black Death were thought to have been caused by the fleas on black rats which came from the east after 1345. The fleas then found local European rats as hosts and that is why there were repeated outbreaks that came to an end with the Great Plague of London in 1665. Researchers in Norway have come up with a different sequence of events. Great gerbils and marmots were hosts of the plague bacterium Yersinia pestis *in Asia and, when sudden climate change took place and the populations of these rodents crashed, the fleas carrying the bacteria needed to find new hosts. Many hopped on to the traders and the camels who travelled the Silk Road and then found their way into Europe by various routes. The scientists at the University of Oslo have found a clear correlation of events – roughly 15 years after each gerbil and marmot population crash in Asia, plague broke out in Europe. Apparently Chinese squirrels are also implicated.*

When recovery came, it was partial and, with recurring outbreaks of plague in 1362, 1379, 1392, 1401–03, 1439 and 1455, Scots must have felt the fell hand of an angry God hovering over the land. As the population fell dramatically in the first visitations and was unable to recover with successive and regular returns, the amount of land under cultivation and in pasture must have declined. There were simply many fewer people to do the day-in, day-out labour needed to farm. Output fell, rents fell and the medieval economy subsided into a long depression. Before 1349 and the beginning of the Little Ice Age in the decades after Bannockburn, Scotland had shown itself as a relatively rich country. The Berwick quays hummed with trade in woolpacks and bundles of hides with Scottish farmers significant suppliers to the European textile- and leather-working industries. A nation that could build great castles at Stirling and Edinburgh, create scores of royal burghs, a vast cathedral at St Andrews and endow the beautiful Border abbeys had substantial disposable income to spend. But after 1349, the telltale signs of an economy going backwards could be detected. The

Scots silver pennies contained much less silver and the equivalence of the pound Scots with the English pound sterling was eroded. By 1400, the pound Scots contained only 30 per cent of the silver that it had in 1296. To 21st-century readers, the picture is all too familiar – exports declined, prices rose and there was a balance of payments deficit with England. In 1409, the Abbot of Dunfermline complained that 'all things are dearer than they were in times past'. As a consequence of two calamities, one following fast on the other, Scotland became a much poorer country in the 14th century and did not begin to recover until the 16th century.

What compounded the devastation of plague and repeated periods of cold and wet weather was Edward III's harrying of southern Scotland. As David II languished impotent in captivity at Odiham Castle in Hampshire, the Borders and the Lothians saw fire and destruction blaze through the farms and villages. But events elsewhere brought relief. Anxious to prosecute a war in wealthy France and secure a settled frontier with his poverty-stricken neighbour to the north, the English king agreed to the Treaty of Berwick in 1357. Its terms dictated a huge ransom for the release of David II – money was needed for the campaigns across the Channel. Scots magnates were forced to accept that a vast sum of 100,000 marks would be paid in ten yearly instalments of 10,000 marks. A unit of account equivalent to about 13 shillings and four pence rather than currency, a mark coin was never minted but for a contracting and impoverished economy a ransom of £66,000 sterling was very onerous indeed. By 1363, the annual instalment could not be raised and there followed a faintly comic series of negotiations.

David II and his retinue rode to London to begin a series of meetings. Astonishingly, he offered to make Edward III or one of his sons his legal heir. On the Scots king's death, the realm would be inherited by whichever member of the English royal family was nominated. David II knew very well that the Scots magnates still cleaved to the spirit of the Declaration of Arbroath and would never accept this proposal. At a parliament held in 1364, they duly rejected the notion that Lionel, Duke of Clarence and third son of the English king, should reign in Scotland after David. King Lionel would not be countenanced. But King David was undismayed and continued to negotiate secretly. The fact that the matter of the outstanding balance of the huge ransom faded into the background must be testament to an astute political operation and to Edward III's absorption in the French wars.

THE LYKEWAKE

In an age before antibiotics, decent drainage and dependable harvests, life in medieval Scotland could be short. When someone died, all of the doors and windows in a house were thrown open, even in winter, to allow the spirit of the deceased to escape. When clocks became more common, they were stopped and not started again until after the funeral. A wake, known as the 'lykewake', was held and it could last several days as neighbours and family paid their respects and offered condolences. Everyone had to be fed and funerals were sometimes very jolly affairs, with drinking and dancing. It was thought important to arrange a good send-off. Expenses could be defrayed by using a coffin with a hinged lid that meant bodies could be borne to the graveside in a proper manner before they were tipped in wearing only a shroud. At a time when death came early and more frequently, such recycling made sense.

After 1364, David II began to take a firm hold of the reins of power and he ruled effectively until his sudden death in 1371. His marriage to Margaret Drummond has been acrimonious and barren and, with his passing, the male lineage of the Bruces came to an end. Another, much more long-lasting dynasty was born when the king's nephew succeeded as Robert II. He was the grandson of Marjorie Bruce, daughter of the hero of Bannockburn and the first Stewart king.

Bannockburn had marked a turning moment for another kingdom in what is now Scotland. From the Butt of Lewis to the Mull of Kintyre and over much of the far northern mainland, kings ruled in all but name. After his great victory, King Robert rewarded the loyalty of Angus Og MacDonald and his Islesmen with the lands of the MacDougalls, a clan which had backed the losing side. The great sea kingdom of Somerled was beginning to reassemble. In 1346, the picture was completed when the last chief of the MacRuaris died and his lands passed to his sister, Amie. She was the wife of John MacDonald of Islay and her territories of Garmoran, the coastline and the islands between Ardnamurchan and Skye, came back into the Lordship of the Isles. For almost 150 years, the royal line of Clan Donald ruled its great Atlantic principality in relative peace and stability as mainland Scotland was convulsed by dynastic conflict and economic upheaval.

In the 1990s, excavations began at Finlaggan, a freshwater loch in the north of Islay, a few miles inland from Port Askaig. There are two islands and they attracted the attention of archaeologists because of their central importance in the government of the Lordship of the Isles. Eilean Mor, the 'Great Island', lies close to the shore and can be reached by a causeway over the reeds and the shallows. Beyond it is Eilean na Comhairle, the 'Council Island', and one of the early discoveries was that this had been an artificial creation formed by centuries of building debris probably resting on piles. It was linked to Eilean Mor by a stone causeway whose remains are still visible just below the surface of the loch. The archaeologists gradually uncovered not only a seat of government but also a place of ceremony where the Kings of the Isles sat in state.

The Great Island was fortified, defended by a ditch and a turf bank faced with stone. Beyond it lay the outlines of twenty or so buildings connected by a series of cobbled roadways and pends. Most were houses and they showed a clear continuity with Norse design. They had characteristic sub-basements, wooden floors resting on joists and timber roofs. There was a chapel, whose gables still stand, and a graveyard around it. Over the centuries, the wind and the rain blowing in off the Atlantic have erased most of the inscriptions and few are still legible. On the western shore of the Great Island, a jetty jutted into the loch and, from it, a wide cobbled road led to the grandest building. The Great Hall of the Lords of the Isles was a stone version of the Viking halls remembered in the sagas. At 20 metres in length, it could host large and lavish feasts and, no doubt, as the fires blazed and the bards sang, tales of prowess were told. No feast will have been more lavish that that given at the inauguration of a new Lord of the Isles. According to tradition, he came to the Great Island dressed in white and ready to place his foot where men of royal MacDonald blood had always placed it, on a square stone where the outline of a footprint had been carved – just as at the summit of the fort at Dunadd in the old kingdom of Dalriada. Holding a white wand for honesty and purity and a sword for power, he was anointed and blessed and his genealogy recited. And after all was done, the new Lord of the Isles feasted with his great magnates and the bards picked up their harps.

At some point in the celebratory week and at regular intervals in the year, council members processed across the 50-metre causeway to the Eilean na Comhairle to discuss matters of state. In addition to the Lord of the Isles, there were four great men of the Clan Donald blood royal – Claranald, MacDonald of Kintyre, MacIain of Ardnamurchan and MacDonald of

Keppoch. They were joined in the small council hall by four other great magnates – Maclean of Duart, Maclean of Lochbuie, Macleod of Harris and Macleod of Lewis. Beside these powerful and widely landed men sat four clan chiefs – MacKinnon, MacNeil of Barra, MacNeil of Gigha and one other who served by rotation. Two princes of the medieval Church no doubt blessed proceedings and they were the Abbot of Iona and the Bishop of the Isles. Until 1334, he had been titled the Bishop of Sodor and Man – that is, of the *Sudreyjar*, a Norse terms for the 'Southern Isles', the *Nordreyjar* being the 'Northern Isles' of Orkney and Shetland. After 1334, Man had passed into English possession.

While policy was discussed and disputes aired in the council hall, the laws of the Isles were administered by brieves, judges whose tenure was often hereditary. It was different in tone from the evolving corpus of Anglo-Norman law in mainland Scotland and had close ties with the law tracts of Ireland. At their core, Celtic codes preferred reparation to judicial revenge. Often taken from a comprehensive tariff system, fines were far more likely to be imposed than hands or heads cut off. Cultural as well as legal links with Ireland stretch back to the 6th century and before then, and one aspect that straddled the North Channel into the medieval period was the concept of honour. Amongst free men in the Isles, *enech* or 'face' was important. An insult was known as *enechruicce* or 'face reddening' and, if the man who had suffered the insult challenged it, a legal process began. If the insulted won his case, the guilty party began a characteristic process. He was expected to use 'the pumice stone' of publically admitting the fault, then 'the water' of payment of a fine and finally 'the towel' of penitence.

Throughout its golden age in the 14th and 15th centuries, the Lordship of the Isles was a force for order and stability. The potential for disorder was much mitigated by the growth of a tradition of seasonal mercenary soldiering. These martial young men became known as 'Gallowglasses' and, as they packed their war gear and sailed south to fight, the Lords of the Isles knew that, each summer, they were exporting trouble.

Gallowglass is from *Gall-Oglaigh*, an Irish term meaning 'Young Foreigner'. Companies sailed to Ireland to fight for kings who were gradually rolling back the invasion of the Anglo-Normans of the 12th century confining them to their pales around Dublin and the other larger towns. Wearing their knee-length mail shirts known as jacks (and further protected by jackboots while horsemen wore jackets, shortened jacks), these regiments of tough and disciplined mercenaries could stand fast in formations against the charge of armoured knights. In the 1500s, an Englishman, Sir Anthony St Leger, admired the fighting qualities of the Gallowglasses, saying, 'These sort of men be those that do not lightly abandon the field, but bide the brunt to the death.' Mercenary soldiering was a significant element in Scottish life and one estimate reckoned that between 1419 and 1424 there were no fewer than 15,000 Scotsmen in French military service against the English in the Hundred Years War – a significant proportion of the total population.

If military adventure beyond the Hebrides and the Atlantic coast made for peace in the Lordship, the consolidation of the Highland clans also owed something to outside influences. Feudal tenure, especially the grants made by Robert I, formalised the holdings of clan chiefs and also their right to dispense justice. But recognitions of this sort by the king heightened an internal tension – one that was to surface centuries later.

The term *duthchas* is difficult to translate but it means something like 'the collective heritage of clansmen and women, their customary rights to land, fishings, upland pasture and other staples' – and, even more simply, 'home'. They paid rents in kind and labour to the chief and his leading gentry, the *daoine uaisle*, and expected protection in return. In this way, a chief's authority and loyalty came from below, from his clan, his children. But, after the granting of feudal charters in the 14th century and afterwards, the competing concept of *oighreachd*, literally 'that which is inherited', came to be accepted more and more. This made it clear that clan lands were owned by the chief and could be passed on by him. Clansmen and women paid rents in return for their land, a much less complex exchange than the ancient bonds of *duthchas*. After the Battle of Culloden and the beginning of the forced emigrations, the Highland Clearances, in the late 18th and 19th centuries, the legality of *oighreachd* was accepted but, as the ships set sail for the Americas, the long traditions of *duthchas* sharpened the pain of leaving.

Many clans claimed great antiquity, lineages that reached back into myth history to name fathers who may or may not have existed. Clan Campbell also called themselves *Siol Diarmaid*, the 'Seed of Diarmaid', an Irish hero wreathed in the mists of legend. Clan Donald also claimed Irish descent from the semi-mythic Conn of the Hundred Battles. But most clans' history really began in the 13th and 14th centuries.

The word *clann* is Gaelic for 'children' and the term clan began to be applied to all those with links, geographical as well as genealogical, with a common name father. The MacLarens are said to descend from Laurence, Abbot of Achtow in Perthshire, and the MacEwens from Ewen, a warlord who flourished on the shores of Loch Fyne, probably in the early 12th century. The clans were by no means culturally homogenous and, broadly, they have five distinct origins. The north and north-west were the lands of the Norse clans – the MacLeods (sons of Ljot), the MacIvers (sons of Ivar), the MacSweens (sons of Swein), the MacAulays (sons of Olaf) and several others such as Clan Gunn. On the mainland were the territories of clans with clear Pictish origins, the most famous being the confederation of Clan Chattan which includes Mackintoshes, MacGillivrays, MacPhersons and other names. To the west lay the glens and straths of the Irish or Dalriadan clans, principal amongst them Clan Donald and its satellites. Clan Campbell probably arose in the Old Welsh-speaking kingdom of Strathclyde for the name is from *Cam-Beul* which means 'Twisted Mouth', possibly denoting people who did not speak Gaelic. The similar origins of the Galbraiths are clearer – their first recorded chief was Gilchrist Bretnach, Gilchrist the Briton, an Old Welsh speaker who lived at the end of the 12th century in western Stirlingshire. And the final group are the most recent and perhaps the most surprising. Encouraged by David I in his long war against the kingdom of Moray, Anglo-Norman families came north in the early 1100s and soon morphed into the likes of Clan Grant (from grand or large), Clan Fraser (possibly related to the French surname Frézelière or the name of an area in Anjou), Clan Menzies (from the place name Mesnières in France), and Stewarts (coming from the Cotentin Peninsula, their ancestor was High Steward of Scotland).

In the centuries when Clan Donald and their fleets of birlinns policed their sea kingdom, there was generally peace in the Highlands and Islands. On the mainland, by contrast, there was deep dissent at the heart of royal government. Robert II's coronation in 1371 was delayed by William Douglas and his armed supporters. It may be that Douglas disputed his right to succeed. English garrisons still occupied the strategically important castles in the south at Berwick, Roxburgh, Jedburgh and Lochmaben and, although he was bound to formally maintain the terms of a treaty with Edward III, the king tacitly encouraged the gradual re-conquest of the Borders. But increasingly his son, John, Earl of Carrick, ignored Robert's authority and, in 1384, the royal council removed their king's ability to govern. By that time, he had attracted the deeply unflattering and contemptuous nickname of Auld Bleary. In what amounted to a coup d'état, Carrick took control. Despite victory at the Battle of Otterburn in 1388, his power began to wane. Badly injured by a kick from a horse and effectively crippled, he could take no part in warfare and Carrick, in turn, was replaced by his younger brother, Robert, Earl of Fife. By the time Auld Bleary died, exiled in Dundonald Castle in Ayrshire, the new king, styling himself Robert III, ascended an empty throne in every sense. His realm was run by his brother and power shifted this way and that for 15 years as the great magnates traded alliance and influence.

In 1396, Robert III did manage to act on his own initiative. His courtiers organised a remarkable event, something that was widely reported by chroniclers in Scotland, England and France. Carpenters and labourers were set to work on the river island in the Tay known as the North Inch to build grandstands and raise pavilions. Just outside Perth, a show was planned, a grisly, gory spectacle that vividly illustrated how a cultural gulf was beginning to yawn in Scotland. Two bands of Highland clansmen would fight to the death in a judicial trial by combat. And, just as in the Roman Coliseum, blood would spurt and lives be extinguished for the entertainment of an audience who would thrill and shudder at the carnage. Lowlanders, their king and his foreign guests would watch Highlanders hack each other to pieces for sport. Clearly seen as inferior beings, babblers of an unintelligible language, they were beginning to be thought of as savages whose feral behaviour somehow represented the past.

The organised slaughter on the North Inch is thought to have been a means of resolving a long-standing territorial dispute between Clan Cameron and Clan Chattan. Each side had selected 30 warriors and, as they entered the arena, King Robert and his guests could see that the men wore no armour or helmets and nor did they have shields. Blows were intended to be fatal. As they formed lines and glared at each other across the grass, each man carried a broadsword or a Lochaber axe, a dirk and a crossbow with only three bolts. As the crowd bayed for blood, screaming for the slaughter to begin, one man lost his nerve, broke away, dived into the River Tay and swam back to sanity.

At a signal, probably trumpeted by royal heralds, each band of clansmen fired three volleys of crossbow bolts at close range. This was a lethal exchange as unprotected flesh was repeatedly pierced. Many men fell, fatally injured, gushing blood as the lines charged, and vicious hand-to-hand fighting began. As the crowd gasped, the wounded were hacked at where they lay, their screams and dying gasps audible in the grandstands. Clan Chattan began to gain the upper hand and, when trumpets sounded and a halt was called, ten of their number were left standing and only two from Clan Cameron. Known as the Battle of the Clans, the frenzy of butchery had seen 38 Highlanders die on the North Inch for the entertainment of the packed stands and pavilions.

A French chronicler, Jean Froissart, summed up the developing cultural divide: 'The manners and the customs of the Scots vary with the diversity of their speech. For two languages are spoken amongst them, the Scottish [Gaelic] and the Teutonic [Scots]: the latter of which is the language of those who occupy the seaboard and the plains, while the race of the Scottish speech inhabits the Highlands and the outlying islands. The people of the coast are of domestic and civilized habits . . . The Highlanders and the people of the islands . . . are a savage and untamed race, rude and independent.'

Divisions of other sorts racked Scotland during the reigns of the early Stewart kings. In 1399, the royal council once again removed the levers of government from their king and first set up his son and heir, David, Duke of Rothesay, as Regent. This displeased his uncle, Robert Stewart, Duke of Albany. He had been Regent earlier in Robert III's troubled reign and he may have had ambitions to succeed. Albany began to move against his nephew and made an alliance with the Douglas family. After being arrested outside St Andrews, David was taken 'mounted on a mule and dressed in a russet tunic', according to the *Scotichronicon*, to imprisonment at Falkland Palace. There he starved to death and his uncle resumed the regency.

In 1406, Robert III at long last died. And, when Walter Bower came to write the relevant entry in the *Scotichronicon*, it appears to have been a merciful release. In what must have been an imaginary conversation with his Queen Annabel, Bower reported that she asked Robert what sort of tomb and epitaph he might like. He is said to have replied: 'Let these men who strive in this world for the pleasures of honour have shining monuments. I on the other hand should prefer to be buried at the bottom of a midden, so that my soul may be saved in the day of the Lord. Bury me, therefore, I beg you, in a midden, and write for my epitaph: "Here lies the worst of kings and the most wretched of men in the whole kingdom." ' While this extraordinary dialogue is unlikely to be literally accurate, it does offer a powerful sense of deep royal disappointment and ill fortune. A dismal end.

What may have driven Robert III to take to his deathbed was the news of the capture of James, his son and heir. So that he might not fall into the hands of the Duke of Albany, the king sent the boy to sanctuary in France. But his ship was boarded by English pirates as it rounded Flamborough Head and they made the young prince captive. Recognising his worth, they handed James over to the authorities and the custody of Henry IV. In no hurry to see him released or ransomed, the Regent Albany allowed the English to hold the heir to the Scottish throne for fourteen years. Acting as though he were in fact king, the duke issued charters in his own name that were authenticated by his personal seal. The legalistic rationale was that James I had not yet been crowned. And he was not likely to be any time soon. When Albany died in 1420, aged at least 80, his son, Murdoch, succeeded to the regency and the rightful king suffered a further four years of captivity. This evidently wilful abandonment was not something James would forget.

Suffering 18 long years of imprisonment, the young man not only had time to store up resentments, he also composed poetry. Raised and educated in an English milieu, James clearly admired the work of Geoffrey Chaucer and his influence is apparent in the *Kingis Quair*, the 'King's Book', one of the earliest examples of Scottish poetry. Probably written in the early 1420s, before his marriage to Lady Joan Beaufort, it is a long poem that uses classical allusion to celebrate married life. Opening with an image of imprisonment, the king looks down from a high window to a garden below where he sees a beautiful woman walking. Smitten with Lady Joan, the author visits the Empire of Venus and the Garden of Minerva. Composed in 379 lines of rhyme royal, a rhyme scheme similar to that used by Chaucer in his *Troilus and Criseyde*, it is the work of a well-educated, cultured and intelligent man. The *Kingis Quair* is the first glimmer of the impact of the Italian Renaissance in Scotland.

Alongside literature, James also learned the martial arts as he fought in the armies of Henry V in France. And, when at last he returned to Scotland in 1424, after a ransom of £40,000 had been agreed, the king acted decisively, even brutally. In the first state executions for a century, Murdoch, Duke of Albany, his two sons and the 80-year-old Earl of Lennox were led out of the gates of Stirling and put to death in front of a large crowd. James appointed his own men to the bishoprics of Glasgow and Dunblane and began to humble the over-mighty magnates. When James returned there were fifteen earldoms and, in the next decade, he reduced the number to eight and only four of them were held by the same families. This ruthless cull began to build a fatal resentment.

Trouble had been developing in the north. In 1411, the Duke of Albany had attempted to secure the vast territories of the earldom of Ross for his second son, John. This ignited immediate opposition from Donald, Lord of the Isles, who, in fact, had a superior title to Ross. With 10,000 Islesmen at his back, the Macdonald prince met the army of the Albany faction at Harlaw, near Inverurie. The preliminaries to this savage battle, known as 'Red Harlaw', were instructive, offering a sense of the growing cultural differences between Highland and Lowland Scotland.

On one side the Earl of Mar marshalled a late medieval army of mounted cavalry, men at arms, spearmen and archers. On the other, the bard, Lachlan Mor MacMhuirich, walked out in front of the great crescent-shaped lines of the clans. He turned to them to recite the *sloinneadh*, the 'naming of the names', the glorious genealogy of the Lords of the Isles and, by extension, of his warriors. 'Sons of Conn of the Hundred Battles, remember hardihood in time of strife.' As the sound of Gaelic echoed across the field, in the hush before war cries rent the air, the name of a Celtic hero from the mists of myth history was used as an incitement to join battle with the Gall, the hated Lowlanders of eastern and southern Scotland, men with no ancestry worth the name and who spoke a 'thin' language.

Harlaw was indecisive. The animosity between the Lords of the Isles and the clan chiefs and the Kings of Scots simmered for more than three centuries as the Stewart dynasty at first attempted to assert themselves in the Highlands and then, when in exile, later relied on the courage of the clans to reinstate them. In 1429, James I summoned 50 clan chiefs to a parliament in Inverness – and promptly imprisoned them. For Alexander Macdonald, Lord of the Isles and descendant of Irish High Kings, and his mother, Mary, Countess of Ross, it was an appalling affront to their dignity to find themselves confined in damp, dark dungeons. Three chiefs were hanged as an example but, when Alexander was released, his fury needed venting and once the royal court had departed, he burned Inverness. But it was a brief satisfaction. Confronting him with a superior force in Lochaber, James I compelled the Lord of the Isles to submit and demanded that he subject himself to more humiliation in Edinburgh. Wearing only his linen sark, this great prince held his claymore by the blade and, before the high altar at Holyrood, offered it to the king. It turned out to be a meaningless ritual for the Islesmen rebelled again in 1431 and twice defeated royal armies in the north.

In the south, James I had different enemies to deal with. He led a large army below the walls of Roxburgh Castle. A formidable fortress built on a long, steep-sided oblong mound near the confluence of the Tweed and Teviot at Kelso, it was of tremendous strategic and symbolic importance. Corroded by 150 years of Border warfare and often occupied by the English, the adjacent town of Roxburgh had withered as the wool and hide trades shrank. But the castle still mattered and, by 1436, it had been extensively strengthened and repaired by its English garrison, determined to hold on to this important enclave north of the Cheviots. The Scots artillery could make no impression on Roxburgh's walls and James was eventually forced to retreat, having achieved nothing and incurred considerable expense. At a council held in October of that year, a curious and prophetic incident took place. As the king attempted to raise more taxes to reclaim territory and take the war into England, Sir Robert Graham, a knight in the household of Walter Stewart, the Earl of Atholl, attempted to arrest him, accusing James I of being a tyrant.

Clearly resentment was building but few could have predicted the dramatic events of the night of 24 February 1437. The king and his family were guests at the Dominican Friary in Perth and, despite lodging in a religious house, were unknowingly in great danger. A conspiracy, led by the Earl of Atholl, Sir Robert Stewart, Chamberlain of the royal household, and the same Sir Robert Graham, was planning to kill the king. Stewart ensured that doors were opened – but servants saw the approach of the assassins and rushed to the royal bedchamber. There was only one door and no other exit but, by tearing up the floorboards, James attempted to escape by slipping down into a sewer. But the outfall was blocked – apparently to prevent his tennis balls from rolling into it – and he was cornered. Graham and the others stabbed the king to death. James's body was dragged off and disposed of. Its remains have never been found.

A badly injured Queen Joan managed to get a galloper away to ride like the wind to Edinburgh and make sure of the safety of her son, the new king, another James. When Atholl, Graham and Stewart were captured, their ends were not quick. All were forced to endure three days of appalling torture and mutilation before a merciful execution silenced their agonies. Known as Fiery Face because of a red birthmark, the six-year-old James II was quickly crowned at Holyrood Abbey and, in a break with ancient tradition, not on the Moot Hill at Scone. Perhaps that location was thought too open and risky in the febrile, uncertain atmosphere following the assassination as the great magnates jockeyed for power while another royal minority began.

Chief amongst the nobility were the Black Douglases but, with the death of Earl Archibald in 1439, their influence began to decline sharply. Sir Alexander Livingstone seized the initiative, placed Queen Joan and her new husband, Sir John Stewart, under house arrest and extracted an agreement that he should have custody of the boy king. Despite this, Livingstone sensed that the Black Douglases might remain a threat. On 24 February 1440, what became known as 'the Black Dinner' took place in Edinburgh Castle. In the king's name, Livingstone invited the young Douglas heirs – 16-year-old Earl William and his 11-year-old brother, David. When all were seated, an ominous dish was said to have been served. A black bull's head, the symbol of death, was set in front of the two boys and, after a summary trial on trumped-up charges, they were murdered in front of the 10-year-old king. Young heirs to great titles quickly learned the brutal realities of power.

In 1449, James II began his personal reign, taking Mary of Gueldres as his queen. He was 18 years old, as was she, but in an age when the transition from childhood to adulthood was abrupt, they were old enough. And ruthless enough. When Sir Alexander Livingstone and two members of his family were arrested, tried for treason and beheaded on Edinburgh's Castle Hill, James showed unhesitating determination to assert himself. But the removal of Livingstone and the enfeeblement of much of the aristocracy under James I left the Black Douglases in a tremendously powerful position, the sole focus for opposition to Stewart rule.

After the murder of Earl William and his brother at the Black Dinner, their great-uncle, James the Fat, inherited all of the vast territories held by members of the wider Douglas family and, when he died in 1443, his five sons united against James II. Most dangerous for the king was the compact made between Earl William, the Earl of Crawford and John of Islay, the Lord of the Isles. Assuring him that he wished to negotiate, the king issued a safe conduct to the Earl of Douglas to attend a meeting at Stirling Castle on 22 February 1452. But, instead of talking, James himself led his courtiers in a vicious attack on William, plunging a dagger into his neck. Mutilated and stabbed more than 20 times, Douglas's body was heaved out of a window and it landed in the garden at the foot of the castle rock. This premeditated, cynical act of betrayal sparked a civil war.

Earl William's brothers, the new Earl James, Archibald Douglas, Earl of Moray, Hugh Douglas, Earl of Ormonde, and John Douglas, Lord of Balvenie, united in open rebellion. But James II had also learned the arts of bribery and coercion. By distributing titles, lands and offices of state, he built a broad pro-Stewart power base and, when the Earl of Crawford defected from the rebel cause, the position of the Douglases began to look shaky. And they were undone by a distant relative. A Royalist army led by the Red Douglas, George, Earl of Angus, met the forces of the Black Douglas at Arkinholm, near Langholm, and decisively defeated them. The Earl of Moray was killed in the fighting, the Earl of Ormonde was executed and their supporters scattered. Douglas lands were forfeited to the crown and the power of this once-mighty family broken. No Stewart king of Scotland would be seriously challenged again for almost 200 years.

Roxburgh remained in English hands. Like Calais, it was a symbol, a threat, a reminder of the claims and ambitions of English kings, and James II was determined that it should be reclaimed. In 1460, he led an army under the walls of the great castle and laid a siege. The king was fascinated by artillery and one of the few fruits of Scotland's alliance with France against the English was the import of European expertise in using the destructive but chancy power of cannon. In the wars against the Douglases, Royalist commanders were granted an advantage 'by the gret gun the quhilk a Frenchman shot richt wele'.

Late medieval cannon had barrels because the skills of coopers were central to building them. Barrels were little more than long tubes made by fastening together wrought-iron strips or strakes and binding them tightly with hoops – like a barrel. James II's army had trundled the great bombard known as 'The Lion' to Roxburgh and the huge gun was dug into a trench on the northern, River Tweed side of the castle where its long walls presented an easier target. But then disaster struck. The Old Scots of one chronicler offers a graphic description of what happened: 'King James hauing sik pleasure in discharging gret gunis past til a place far fra the armie to recreat him selfe in schuiting gret pieces, quhairof he was verie expert, bot the piece appeiringlie, with our sair a charge, flies in flinderis, with a part of quhilk, strukne in the hench or he was war, quhairof (allace) he dies.'

Aged only 29, James fulfilled the prophecy of Thomas the Rhymer that only a dead man would win Roxburgh Castle. A few days after the king had bled to death and after more than 160 years of varying degrees of occupation, Scotland was free of English garrisons. Except for Berwick. The town would ultimately remain in English hands, an anomaly never rectified after the unions of the crowns and the parliaments and an enduring legacy of the colonising instincts of English kings.

8

Scotland Remade

⁂

ALL OF THE FIRST six Jameses succeeded to the throne when they were children and, between 1406 and 1585, there were almost as many years of minority rule as there were of majority rule. Patterns repeated. Regents rose, enriched themselves, rewarded their allies and were usually brought down, their blood spilling on the headsman's block when the young king began his personal reign. James III was nine when his mother rushed him across the Tweed for a hastily arranged coronation at Kelso Abbey. The grandest monastic church in Scotland, it had soaring double crossings and an ornate Galilee porch. With noblemen and prelates gathered in the nave to watch the boy process towards the crowning rituals, it suited such ceremonies of state. In the hope that government by the royal family would forestall the usual reflexes of faction fighting and influence peddling amongst the magnates, Queen Mary had parliament appoint her as Guardian. But the dowager lived on for only three more years, and in 1466 James III was abducted by Lord Robert Boyd of Kilmarnock and held as a virtual prisoner.

In 1469 the king's captors made an unusual foray into what might be called statecraft. Lord Boyd contracted a dynastic marriage between James and Margaret, the daughter of Christian I, King of Denmark and Norway. As surety for the 12-year-old princess's dowry, the archipelagos of Orkney and Shetland fell under Scottish rule. The islands were to be handed back once the dowry was paid in full – and it never was. In 1472, the Northern Isles were formally annexed to the realm of Scotland and the nation at last assumed its modern frontiers.

In the Atlantic west no such bloodless and canny diplomacy would bring the Hebrides and the glens and the straths of the north-west under Stewart control. Ardtornish Castle is a tumbled, grassy ruin on a high promontory that juts out into the Sound of Mull. No road leads to it, no sign even gives it its name and there is no information board to tell its history. It is a forgotten and little visited place. And yet Ardtornish once pulsed with power. Part of a wide network of sea castles, places that needed anchorages or sheltered beaching bays rather than roads to reach them, it looks south-east down the sound to Duart Castle, another fortress on a promontory, and also beyond it to the great castles on the mainland shore near Oban, at Dunollie and Dunstaffnage.

On 19 October 1461, John Macdonald of Islay, Lord of the Isles, High Chief of Clan Donald, attached his seal to a half-forgotten document that could have changed the direction of our history profoundly. He was to become co-signatory to the Treaty of Westminster-Ardtornish, the other being Edward IV, King of England. Its terms divided the realm between the two rulers once the vulnerable boy king, James III, was deposed. Old Scotia north of the Forth would pass into the Lordship of the Isles and the Earl of Douglas would hold the lands to the south. Both would swear fealty to the English king. And it was no idle speculation. On his accession to the Lordship, John of Islay mustered 10,000 soldiers at the windy headland at Ardtornish and 250 war galleys were bobbing at anchor in the sound or beached on the shingle shore of the bay below the castle. But it all fell out differently.

The Treaty of Westminster-Ardtornish was intended as 'a secret league and band', but in 1464 the Scottish crown, by now advised by Bishop James Kennedy of St Andrews, concluded an alliance with Edward IV and the existence and content of the treaty became known. Ten years later, John of Islay was indicted for treason. His position had been weakened further by a series of internecine quarrels and the Macdonald Lord was eventually forced to forfeit his far-flung territories to the crown. Islay became a captive pensioner in the royal household, his dreams of domination no more than gilded memories of glory, and he died at Paisley Abbey in 1492. But the idea of the Lordship lived on and six rebellions attempted to revive it until it finally failed in 1545 with the death of the last claimant to the great Atlantic principality, Donald Dubh. The bards mourned the passing of the royal line of Clan Donald and this famous elegy was composed by Giolla Coluim mac an Ollaimh:

> It is no joy without Clan Donald,
> It is no strength to be without them,
> The best race in the round world,
> To them belongs every goodly man . . .

Brilliant pillars of green Alba,
A race the hardiest that received baptism,
A race that won fight in every land,
Hawks of Islay for valour,
A race with arrogance, without injustice,
Who seized naught save spoil of war,
Whose nobles were men of spirit,
And whose common men were most steadfast,
Chaneil aoibhneas gun Chlann Domhnaill
It is no joy without Clan Donald.

When James III reached his majority he began to develop a more auto-cratic style of monarchy, a style that increasingly grated. In 1469, the king was granted by parliament 'full jurisdiction and empire within his realm' and the head of James began to appear on newly minted coins, the Scottish groat. This assertiveness began to make enemies. James III became ever more unpopular and he had to deal with two ambitious adult brothers prepared to harness growing disaffection. When, in 1482, Edward IV sent an invasion force of 20,000 men to bring fire and sword to Scotland under the command of his brother, the Duke of Gloucester, he was accompanied by Alexander Stewart, Duke of Albany. He had demanded to be known as Alexander IV of Scotland. Tremendously destructive, the English invaders burned beau-tiful Melrose Abbey to the ground and induced the Scottish magnates to arrest James III. They also took Berwick back into English hands, where it was to remain. When the expedition ran out of supplies and money and its commanders were forced to order a retreat south, Alexander IV's claims quickly evaporated and his older brother returned to power. But not for long.

Perhaps not surprisingly, the king had begun to surround himself with men known as 'the familiars', those who owed their position to him alone and had no independent power base. Also James preferred to remain in Edinburgh, perhaps for his own safety, rather follow the traditions of a peri-patetic kingship, travelling the length and breadth of his realm to see and be seen, dispensing justice, maintaining alliances. He had been abducted in open country once before and probably welcomed the security of the walls on the castle rock. The royal marriage had also foundered and Margaret of Denmark had taken to living at Stirling Castle. To compound the family fracture, it seemed that the king favoured his second son, James of Ross, over his heir, the future James IV. Simmering under the surface, these tensions would boil over in a dramatic episode with apparently innocuous beginnings.

Characteristic of the Stewart dynasty was the accumulation of territory into the royal demesne, estates in their own personal ownership, and the harvesting of as much income as possible therefrom. The ancient foundation of Coldingham Priory, perched on the North Sea coast of Berwickshire, had once been a daughter house of Durham, its revenues sent south to the treasury of the Prince Bishops. But, in 1488, James III insisted that these should come to the king. This appropriation was vigorously contested by a powerful Berwickshire family, the Homes, and what began as a disagreement quickly spiralled into rebellion. Older grievances added to the fire and a coalition of Hepburns, Red Douglases, the Bishop of Glasgow and the Campbells of Argyll formed around the Earls of Home. They then enlisted the support of the disaffected heir, Prince James – or perhaps forced the enlistment of his support – and, after some advances and retreats to the west of Edinburgh, battle was joined at Sauchieburn, near Stirling, not far from the site of the battle at Bannockburn. It was said that James III buckled on the sword carried by Robert Bruce.

It did him little good. The king's army was slaughtered or scattered and, once the outcome was clear, the mists of myth history gathered. Mounted on 'a gret grey horse', James III was said to have fled from the battlefield. Thrown by his galloping steed, he was approached by a man impersonating a priest, perhaps to administer last rites, perhaps not. But the false priest produced a dagger and killed the king in what sounds like an assassination, possibly premeditated. More likely, James was killed in the ruck of battle and his body was buried nearby, at Cambuskenneth Abbey. Sixteenth-century chroniclers produced a number of florid, melodramatic versions of events but a more contemporary source noted that 'the king happenit to be slain'. This is either a cover-up for what was clearly an emphatic coup d'état that demanded the death of the hated king or confirmation that James III died in the fighting. His heir, James IV, was said to have been consumed with guilt for his complicity in his father's death and, each year during Lent, he wore a cilice, an iron belt, next to his skin in penance, adding an ounce to its weight with each year that passed since the events that took place at Sauchieburn.

Hallowed tradition revived when the new king sat on the Stone of Destiny to be inaugurated on the Moot Hill at Scone. If a seannachie stood forward to recite his glorious genealogy in Gaelic, James would have understood every word. His command of languages much impressed the Spanish diplomat

Pedro de Ayala. Here is part of a despatch he sent to King Ferdinand and Queen Isabella of Castile and Aragon. It also has something to say about the growth of internal divisions in Scotland:

> The King is 25 years and some months old. He is of noble stature, neither tall nor short, and as handsome in complexion and shape as a man can be. His address is very agreeable. He speaks the following foreign languages; Latin, very well; French, German, Flemish, Italian, and Spanish; Spanish as well as the Marquis, but he pronounces it more distinctly. He likes, very much, to receive Spanish letters. His own Scots language is as different from English as Aragonese from Castilian. The King speaks, besides, the language of the savages who live in some parts of Scotland and on the islands. It is as different from Scots as Biscayan is from Castilian. His knowledge of languages is wonderful. He is well read in the Bible and in some other devout books. He is a good historian. He has read many Latin and French histories, and profited by them, as he has a very good memory. He never cuts his hair or his beard. It becomes him very well.

The hirsute James IV is the first Scots king to emerge from cliché and acquire a distinctive personality. Having succeeded his father towards the end of the 15th century, the period when the Florentine Renaissance was at its fullest flowering, the king appears to have been aware of the gathering pace of intellectual enquiry and artistic innovation across Europe. As a polyglot, language clearly interested James and he was said to have had an experiment conducted to discover if speech was innate or learned whereby two children were sent to the island of Inchkeith in the Firth of Forth to be raised by a mute woman. What language would they speak? Hebrew, the language of the Bible? The conclusion was not clearly reported but it may be imagined.

At Stirling Castle, the king had a laboratory set up, installing an Italian alchemist, John Damian, to experiment with chemicals in an effort to discover the 'quintessence'. Well paid and endowed with the income from the Abbey of Tongland in Galloway, Damian was the butt of attacks by the less well-paid poet, William Dunbar. Probably in 1507, when it was becoming clear that his expensive experiments were failing, Damian announced that he could fly. In fact, he would reach the coasts of France (on his way to Turkey) before a Scottish embassy travelling by more conventional means. On the appointed day, no doubt in front of an expectant crowd that may have included his patron, the king, the Italian mounted the battlements of

Stirling Castle to begin his epic flight to Turkey. He had a pair of wings made from bird feathers strapped to his arms. William Dunbar wrote a ballad whose title recorded what happened next. It was 'Ane Ballat of the Fenyeit [Bogus] Frier of Tungland, How He Fell in the Myre Fleand to Turkiland'. Fortunate to survive the fall, possibly with the help of the dung heap, Damian broke his thigh bone. But his scientific spirit was undaunted. The reason he did not take flight was simple, he explained: the wings were supposed to be made only from eagle feathers but some chicken feathers had inadvertently been mixed in with them.

More reliable and durable were the architectural achievements encouraged and paid for by James IV. Between 1501 and 1541 the old castle at Falkland in Fife was completely redeveloped as a royal palace built in a renaissance style. It resembled a French chateau of the same period and it incorporated a real tennis court, the oldest tennis court still in use anywhere. At Stirling Castle, James had almost all of the present buildings inside the curtain wall constructed or remodelled, including the King's Old Building, the magnificent Great Hall (recently painted white, as it used to be) and the Forework. This complex amounted to a centre for royal government and, for the early part of James's reign, this was run by Archibald Whitelaw, the Archdeacon of Lothian. Serving James III from 1462 and James IV until 1493, he was the king's principal secretary and Keeper of the Privy Seal – and very powerful indeed. All of the paperwork of state passed through his hands, all of the letters and petitions to the king and his replies. All dispatches, warrants and written orders were sent by Whitelaw and his clerks and he himself was sent as part of an embassy to Richard III, the short-lived, ill-fated king of England. Whitelaw's surprising description of Richard, that 'never has so much spirit or greater virtue reigned in such a small body' has famously survived.

As his powers faded and age overtook Whitelaw, James IV appointed a remarkable man to take over the role of Keeper of the Privy Seal. William Elphinstone was a graduate of the University of Glasgow, which had been founded in 1451 at the prompting of James II, and he was one the earliest career civil servants whose actions and achievements have been documented. Some time before 1474, Elphinstone was appointed rector of Glasgow University and, in 1487, he was consecrated as Bishop of Aberdeen. His greatest achievement was the foundation of a university in the town. After receiving its papal bull in 1494 and the appointment of the philosopher and teacher Hector Boece as rector, Aberdeen quickly grew into a vibrant and popular seat of learning, outstripping both Glasgow and St Andrews. Known as King's College (where the main campus still flourishes, two miles from the modern city centre), it began its long and distinguished history of teaching in 1505.

A series of accounts of the lives of Scottish saints and a compilation of the rituals and ceremonies of the Scottish Church, the *Aberdeen Breviary*, was edited by William Elphinstone and it was one of the first books to be printed in Scotland. In 1507, a royal charter had granted a monopoly to Walter Chepman and Andrew Myllar to found a printing press and, under its terms, they should specifically produce 'bukis of our lawis, actis of parliament, croniclis, mess bukis [mass books], and portuus [portable breviaries] efter the use of our Realme, with addiciouns and legendis of Scottis sanctis' and the King would decide what reasonable prices should be for these books. This seems to have been part of a conscious attempt at modernisation and even nation-building, emphasising the differences between Scotland and its much larger neighbour to the south. Sadly the press only lasted two or three years but it did mark the beginning of a long, honourable and occasionally profitable tradition of printing and publishing in Edinburgh. Set up in the Cowgate, Chepman and Myllar did have some success. With the *Aberdeen Breviary* also intending to show how different the Scottish Church was from the English, the output of the new press is tinged with propaganda. But by 1600 others had set up in business and their catalogues brimmed with popular works in Scots as well as grammars and Latin texts.

While printing presses clacked and rattled in the canyon of the Cowgate, shipwrights were hewing, planing and planking vast quantities of timber at Newhaven two miles to the north of the centre of Edinburgh, on the shores of the Firth of Forth. In 1504, James IV ordered the creation of a new harbour, a new haven, and a settlement grew up around the shipyard. There, the king planned the building of a mighty warship, the like of which had never been seen before. It was an extraordinary expression of royal ambition – and confidence.

Know as the *Great Michael*, after the Archangel Michael, the warship was designed as a carrack, a type of three- or four-masted sailing ship developed by the Portuguese as their explorers and merchants ventured down the Atlantic coast of Africa. But they had built nothing on the scale of the massive ship in the specially constructed new dock at Newhaven. The keel was laid down in 1507 and the work was supervised by Jacques Terrell, a master shipwright brought from France or, more probably, Flanders. Robert

Lindsay of Pitscottie was the continuator of *The Historie and Chronicles of Scotland*, 1436 to 1565, a work begun by Hector Boece, the first rector of Aberdeen University and the first history to be written in Scots rather than in Latin. According to Lindsay, the building of the *Great Michael* required 'all the woods of Fife' as well as a great deal of timber imported from Norway and the Baltic. The ship was vast.

Lindsay reckoned that James IV's warship was a spectacular 240 feet in length and 35 feet across the beam. A comparison with Christopher Columbus's *Santa Maria*, the largest of the three ships to cross the Atlantic in 1492, offers perspective. It was only 58 feet in length. To counter the impact of cannon fire, the hull of the *Michael* was ten feet thick and fashioned from the dense wood of seasoned oak. To deliver broadsides, 24 guns were imported from Flanders, probably through Jacques Terrell, and, in the prow of the ship, a heavy bronze cannon known as a basilisk (after the mythological fire-breathing serpent) was mounted and there were two more in the stern. In addition, 36 pieces of smaller artillery could be brought forward to supplement the *Michael*'s tremendous firepower. It was the greatest gunship ever built in Europe up to that time. And, if it was true that the famous bombard known as Mons Meg was winched aboard, then James IV's huge ship carried the largest-calibre gun ever deployed in naval history, including those of the cruisers and battleships of the Second World War.

On board was a crew of 300 sailors, 120 gunners and up to 1,000 marines. All were under the direction of Sir Andrew Wood of Largo. Knighted by the king in 1495, he was later appointed Lord High Admiral of Scotland. What first brought Wood to national prominence were actions that seem close to acts of piracy. With his two fighting ships, the *Yellow Carvel* and the *Flower*, he attacked and captured five English ships off Dunbar in 1489. A year later, retaliation sailed north as an English fleet, under the command of Stephen Bull, engaged with Wood's ships in Leith Roads. When the ships began to exchange cannon fire, word of the sea battle spread like wildfire through the city of Edinburgh and, for two days, crowds stood on the shore at Leith to watch. Despite being outnumbered, the Scottish ships outmanoeuvred and outshot the English and all of Bull's ships were boarded and captured.

Despite Wood's stunning success, the *Great Michael* was not intended for use against the English navy. In 1503, King James had married Margaret Tudor, the daughter of Henry VII and, the year before, had signed the Treaty of Perpetual Peace with England. Instead of looking south, the Scots planned to sail the *Michael* into the Mediterranean at the head of a seaborne crusade to take back the Holy Land for Christendom. Only 50 years earlier, Constantinople and the remnants of the Eastern Roman Empire had fallen to the Ottoman Turks and James wished to turn back the tide of Islam that threatened to wash over Europe. He was a prince who did not lack ambition.

What became known as 'the Auld Alliance' between Scotland and France was first agreed in 1295 and it lasted intermittently until 1560. And its strategic imperatives prevented James IV from taking the cross and sailing his huge gunship to Palestine. Instead, the Royal Scottish Navy was strengthened and its 38 ships included two smaller carracks, the *Margaret* and the *James*. The programme of shipbuilding prompted an arms race and Henry VIII commissioned the *Henri Grace à Dieu*, the *Great Harry*, a ship almost as large as *The Michael*, and also the *Mary Rose*, the 700-ton warship that was famously lifted out of the waters of the Solent in 1982.

MEDIEVAL PERTH

Marks & Spencer's decision to build a new department store in Perth High Street turned out to benefit more than those fond of the provender available in the food hall. The resulting demolition on a large and central site in an old Scottish burgh supplied a golden opportunity for archaeologists. Because more recent buildings overlay them, the archaeology of urban sites is very difficult to get at, but M&S opened a keyhole. Excavations began in 1975, and for two years, a large plot on one side of the High Street was thoroughly investigated. No fewer than 29 buildings were found, and they revealed evidence of a hive of activity. Textiles were woven, leather worked, smiths hammered metal, artefacts were made from horn and from wood. Mostly timber, the buildings were small, except for one. In one of the backlands, a hall measuring 15 metres by 6 metres was found. It had a private room and a latrine at one end. Finds of a gilded spur, mail, an arrowhead and a spearhead suggested that this may have been the residence of a knight. There was even evidence of what people wore in medieval Perth. Apparently 'shaggy mantles' were worn by Highlanders who had come down the glens to the town on the Tay.

Relations with England were deteriorating and the Treaty of Perpetual Peace appeared to redefine perpetuity as it lasted only from 1502 to 1513. When French territorial ambitions in Italy brought conflict with the papacy,

Julius II formed the Holy League with Spain and England against Louis XII. James IV responded by sending the *Great Michael* and many of his new ships south to reinforce his French allies and, to threaten England further, he planned an invasion from the north. It was the beginning of a sequence of events that would end in catastrophe.

When dawn broke on the morning of 10 September 1513, the landscape of hell was revealed. On the gently undulating northern ridges of Branxton Hill, more than 10,000 men lay dead or dying. In the midst of the carnage were the naked, plundered bodies of King James, his natural half-brother, Alexander Stewart, who was Archbishop of St Andrews, George Hepburn, who was Bishop of the Isles, two abbots, nine great earls of Scotland, fourteen lords of parliament, innumerable knights and noblemen of lesser degree and thousands of ploughmen, farmers, weavers and burgesses. It was the appalling aftermath of the battle of Flodden, the greatest military disaster in Scotland's history. The Scots army, 30,000 strong, was the largest ever to cross the Tweed. They enjoyed early success in taking Norham Castle and faced an English army not led by their king. But it ended in spectacular disaster and appalling suffering.

In the grey light of that terrible dawn, sentries posted around the captured Scottish cannon could make out where the brunt of battle had been joined. Below them, at the foot of the slope, ran the trickle of a nameless burn now piled with slaughter, a wrack of bodies, obscenely mangled, broken pike shafts, shattered shields and everywhere blood and the sickening stench of death, vomit and voided bowels. Not all of the bodies were yet corpses. Through a long dark night, the battlefield had not been a silent graveyard. Trapped under lifeless comrades, crippled, hamstrung or horribly mutilated, fatally wounded men still breathed. Bladed weapons rarely kill outright and they were often used to bludgeon men to their knees or into unconsciousness. In the churned mud of the battlefield some men will have lost their footing, fallen and been hacked at before they could get up. Many bled to death, maimed, lacerated by vicious cuts, screaming, fainting and screaming once more in their death agonies. Some will have been put out of their misery by parties of English soldiers scouring the field by torchlight for plunder, but others will have lingered on in unspeakable pain, praying to their God, passing in and out of consciousness. The fury of the battlefield may have been stilled and Flodden Field been awash with death and defeat but all was not yet over.

In an instant, the plunderers looked up and the sentries by the cannon stood to, clutching at their weapons, frantically peering through the morning light. They could hear the rumbling thunder of hoofbeats – and then suddenly riders erupted over Barelees Rig. With 800 horsemen at his back, Lord Alexander Home galloped hard across the horrors of the battlefield and up the slopes of Branxton Hill. They had not come back to Flodden to rejoin a lost battle but to rescue their captured ordnance. And they very nearly succeeded. After a sharp skirmish, the English gunners managed to load and get off a volley at Home's squadron and they scattered.

And so it ended. And the Border horsemen wheeled round and raced out of range. To the north, having crossed the Tweed by the morning of 10 September, the remnants of the defeated Scottish army limped homewards. There appears to have been no organised pursuit for, although between 5,000 and 8,000 Scots had been killed at Flodden Field, the Earl of Surrey's army had also taken severe casualties. But those Englishmen who fell were, for the most part, ordinary foot soldiers. King James himself led the downhill charge of his own battalion, running towards the enemy, and most of his noblemen did the same. They led from the front and, when the grim scrummage of hand-to-hand fighting went against them, the king, his earls and knights were amongst the first to be cut down and killed, unable to retreat, trapped in a murderous, fatal vice. By contrast, the Earl of Surrey and his captains had stationed themselves behind their lines, higher up on horseback and able to direct the flow of the battle, making judgements, issuing orders. Submerged in the ruck of the front rank, James IV and his earls were able to see only what was directly in front of them, leaving the huge Scottish army leaderless.

Lord Home and the Earl of Huntly were in command of the battalion on the left wing of the Scottish army and were the first to engage. The Border pikemen and Huntly's Highlanders drove through the English ranks and a rout was only prevented when Lord Dacre ordered his cavalry to charge into the melee. But, when the king's massive battalion of 9,000 men locked with the centre of Surrey's forces and the English billmen began to turn the battle into butchery, Home and Huntly became detached. Able to rally their men on the higher ground to the south-west, they saw the battle turning against Scotland. In the rear of the Scottish battalions, the less well-armed, less disciplined and much less motivated ordinary soldiers could see the Scottish pikes falling in front of them and their lords and captains going down with them. Many turned away and fled, following Home and Huntly as they led their men off the field in some order.

Flodden was a catastrophe, a defeat on an epic scale that seems in keeping with the epic ambition of the king. His mutilated body was recognised amongst the dead and later taken to London for burial. But no interment ever seems to have taken place and James's remains lay for some time at Sheen Priory in Surrey before being lost in the upheavals of the Reformation. That astute observer Pedro de Ayala understood how the king's character had directly contributed to his death and defeat: 'He is courageous, even more so than a king should be. I am a good witness of it. I have seen him often undertake most dangerous things in the last wars. On such occasions he does not take the least care of himself. He is not a good captain, because he begins to fight before he has given his orders. He said to me that his subjects serve him with their persons and goods, in just and unjust quarrels, exactly as he likes, and that therefore he does not think it right to begin any warlike undertaking without being himself the first in danger. His deeds are as good as his words.'

After Flodden, the Auld Alliance with France turned out to be worthless despite the fact that James IV had invaded England and thereby opened up a second front while Henry VIII was campaigning across the Channel. Instead of coming to the aid of a beleaguered ally, the French did not hesitate to betray Scotland. Less than a year after Flodden, England made peace with France and French support for Scotland ceased immediately. Without any consultation or even foreknowledge, the treaty included Scotland by expressly forbidding any raiding into England – but not English raiding into Scotland. By the standards of any age, it was a breathtaking, cynical sell-out – the abandonment of an ally so recently devastated in a battle fought in a common cause.

At the corner of Edinburgh's Drummond Street and The Pleasance, there stands an enduring and powerful memory of the carnage at Flodden. Almost 20 feet high and very thick, a rubble wall runs up the steep slope from the Cowgate and turns sharply west into Drummond Street. On the corner, there is the outline of a blocked-up archway. This is the longest and best-preserved fragment of the Flodden Wall, a defence quickly thrown up after 1513 around the medieval city. The archway on the corner probably led to a bastion or watchtower and west of it, around the Grassmarket, there are two more substantial fragments and, in the Greyfriars Kirkyard, tombstones have been fixed to a surviving run of the wall.

It failed. In 1544, the Earl of Hertford's expedition breached the Flodden Wall easily and, in 1745, Prince Charles's Highlanders simply rushed in through one of the gates as sleepy guards opened it on the morning of 17 September. But the fortifications did give a good sense of the scale of late medieval Edinburgh. They enclosed a busy, noisy, smelly 140 acres and, until the 18th century, defined Scotland's only city.

After Flodden, royal administration and the law began to concentrate in Edinburgh, also establishing it as a genuine capital city. In 1532, the Court of Session was set up and a busy community of lawyers and their employees buzzed around it. Trade bustled and the guild merchants waxed powerful as they exercised a near monopoly of commerce beyond Scotland.

And yet Edinburgh was very unsuitable for expansion. The herringbone pattern of wynds and closes running down off either side of the long street of Castlehill, the Lawnmarket, the High Street and eventually the Canongate was a consequence of geology and history as the town sheltered in the lee of the castle rock. But this dense concentration of what became increasingly high-rise housing was not close to a substantial source of fresh running water. Wells met domestic needs but late medieval manufacture such as tanning and milling had to be sited on the Water of Leith well to the north. Edinburgh's port at Leith was even further away and a constant traffic of carts rattled their way up and down what is now Leith Walk.

Crammed in the 140 acres behind the Flodden Wall, this burgeoning city still saw itself as a single community. It had only one parish church, at St Giles, and it was not until the 17th century that more kirks were built at the Greyfriars and the Tron. There were fourteen different markets, some, as in Fleshmarket Close and Fishmarket Close, recalled in the names of wynds off the High Street and these drew thousands into Edinburgh every week. In 1500, the town council complained of the 'greitt confluence of sempill peipill' as those who wished to sell or buy or both crowded in through the ports. Herds of animals, many of them no doubt bellowing and defecating, sensing their fate as their noses picked up the scent of blood, were driven into the Cowgate to be slaughtered, butchered and skinned. Brewing sent a sweeter smell into the Edinburgh air as women made ale. Before the expansion and commercialisation of the 16th century, brewing had been a female occupation with 288 women registered as brewers in 1500.

To the south of the city, Flodden had a different, much more destructive impact. As the battle raged at the foot of Branxton Hill, men known as 'banditti', parties of horse-riding thieves from Teviotdale and Tynedale, raided the English army's camp, rifling tents and stealing horses. And, as the baggage train and the remnants of the ruined Scottish army limped northwards across the Tweed, bands of horsemen circled them like vultures. The days of the Border reivers were dawning.

The weakening of central authority in Edinburgh as yet another royal minority began led to a reliance on a more immediate, more local source of protection. A year after Flodden, English raiders rampaged through the Borders, stealing and burning, and farmers were forced to turn to men they knew, men to whom they were often related, to seek help in the gathering storms of the first half of the 16th century. The aftermath of the slaughter of September 1513 was felt nowhere so keenly as in the Borders and Dumfriesshire (and in Northumberland and Cumberland) and, for almost a century, a wide swathe of Britain, almost a twelfth of the landmass, suffered the tramp of armies across its fields and farms and an uncountable series of raids galloped across the hills and valleys as the criminal society of the Border Reivers replaced the rule of law and the exercise of royal authority.

Family was what mattered. Loyalty attached itself to heidsmen, those who were seen as the leaders of surnames, groups of people who were related, who often lived in the same valley, farming land that had been theirs for generations. They were not clans and the heidsmen did not have the authority of Highland chiefs but the likes of the Elliots, Armstrongs, Bells, Charltons, Ridleys, Maxwells and Johnstones were a far more powerful focus than any other. The greatest heidsmen could summon armies, putting thousands of men in the saddle in a morning before striking like lightning at distant targets.

While it became most intense in the 16th century, raiding across the border had gone on for centuries and kings had long accepted that special arrangement were necessary to deal with what had become organised international crime. March Wardenries had been set up, three on each side, and Wardens were mandated to deal directly with each other in particular cases. Truce days were held each year and these were intended to be neutral occasions when disputes could be aired and perhaps resolved. The Scottish Wardenries tended to be passed on down established surnames – the Maxwells often held the west, the Scotts and Kerrs the Middle March and the Homes the East March. South of the line, these tended to be royal appointments for career soldiers (the garrisons on the border were manned by the only regular soldiers in the pay of the English crown), civil servants and occasionally local families. The splendid Sir John Forster was a Falstaffian figure who combined the role of March Warden with a lucrative sideline in cattle raiding and general larceny run from his base at Bamburgh. The English records of

Scottish activity are comparatively plentiful because the Wardens regularly reported back to London, but by far the most informative and apparently the most professional of these men was Sir Robert Carey. Appointed to the Middle March in 1592, he was assiduous about patrolling the middle ranges of the Cheviot Hills, especially in the late autumn and early winter, when many raids were run.

On a September night in 1596, two Scottish reivers had led a routine foray into England, lifting cattle probably from Upper Redesdale. But Jock and Geordie Burn were very unlucky. As they drove their slow-moving, complaining stolen cows through the darkening evening, over the empty wastes of the hills, they and their two henchmen blundered into a patrol led by Sir Robert Carey. Despite the fact that he had twenty troopers at his back, the four reivers fought like furies. Two were killed, one escaped into the night and Geordie Burn was taken prisoner.

Probably imprisoned in Harbottle Castle in Upper Coquetdale (the raid was probably run along the line of the ancient drove road known as Clennell Street), Burn was quickly tried and condemned to death. But, ever sensitive to cross-border diplomacy, Carey did not have the sentence carried out immediately. Instead, he showed a keen appreciation of Border loyalties and sent word to Geordie Burn's patron and protector, Sir Robert Kerr of Cessford, a powerful heidsman. Perhaps the captive could be a bargaining chip – perhaps Kerr could be lured into an attempt to spring him. There was silence. No word came back to Harbottle over the hill trails and Burn realised he was lost, condemned to wriggle on the end of a rope.

Robert Carey was curious. With two guards, he visited Geordie in his cell and made a note of what he said. It was, surprisingly, a confession, and also the only authentic testament left by a Border reiver. 'He voluntarily of himself said that he had lived long enough to do so many villanies as he had done: and told us that he had lain with about 40 men's wives, some in England, some in Scotland, and that he had killed seven Englishmen with his own hands, cruelly murdering them; that he had spent his whole time in whoring, drinking, stealing, and taking deep revenge for slight offences. He seemed to be very penitent, and much desired a minister for the comfort of his soul.'

This catalogue of rape, thuggery and murder was probably routine, the testament of an everyday sort of reiver, not a big name or an especially notorious criminal – just one who happened to get caught. And many men as evil as Burn and worse rode through the valleys on either side of the Cheviots or swaggered in the villages and on market days. Here is an extract from a letter sent by the Bishop of Carlisle to Cardinal Wolsey, Henry VIII's Chancellor: 'There is more theft, more extortion by English thieves than there is by all the Scots of Scotland . . . for in Hexham . . . every market day there is four score or a hundred strong thieves; and the poor men and gentlemen also see those who did rob them and their goods, and dare neither complain of them by name, nor say one word to them. They take all their cattle and horse, their corn as they carry it to sow, or to the mill to grind, and at their houses bid them to deliver what they have or they shall be fired and burnt.' When taken alongside Geordie Burn's 'deep revenge for slight offences', this is a chilling image of a society gripped daily by fear, eyes downcast, not looking directly at any of these criminals strutting in broad daylight without fear of arrest or check of any kind.

In 1521, the Duke of Albany, a cousin of the young King James V, returned from France to take up the office of Regent. His instincts and inclination were immediately to revive the Auld Alliance against Henry VIII's England and a substantial force of French soldiers arrived in Scotland. They left six weeks later having accomplished nothing except the depletion of food and funds. What Albany's Francophilia did achieve was a brutal reaction from England, a spasm of raiding and destruction in the Borders, part of a pattern that added the depredations of international enmity to lawlessness and organised theft.

Thomas Kerr and his brother Andrew (better known as Tam and Dand) held between them a collection of offices and benefits, including the Abbey of Kelso. Such had been the decline of the great Tironensian foundation that a notorious reiver had been able to make himself abbot. Abbot Tam Kerr. And yet he appears to have acted more sensibly in the interests of the Borders than the Regent Albany. Abbot Tam concluded a truce with Thomas, Lord Dacre, Warden of the English West March, at the ancient trysting place at the Reddenburn, a trickle that tumbled from the foothills of the Cheviots to mark where the border joined the midstream of the Tweed. But, when the Regent made it clear that Scotland would align itself with France, that most belligerent king, Henry VIII, ordered the muster of an expedition to trail fire and sword through the Tweed and Teviot valleys.

The raids of 1523 were immensely destructive. In addition to burning hundreds of farm places and hamlets, Kelso was torched and its abbey badly damaged, with the interior being ripped out and lead stripped off the roof to make shot. The young Earl of Surrey, son of the victor of Flodden, was in joint command with Dacre and he was in the habit of sending detailed despatches to London. When the English army reached Jedburgh, Surrey reckoned it a larger town than Berwick and, as well as the beautiful abbey, there were six defensive towers inside the walls. Like those that survive in San Gimignano (and used to exist in other Tuscan towns and cities), it seems that powerful Border families built high towers to defend against attack, probably principally from each other. After vicious street fighting, the young earl reported that Jedburgh was 'cleanly destroyed, burned and thrown down'.

A year after the great raid, Albany returned to France and another welcome truce was quickly concluded with England. Here is a report sent by the commander of the garrison to Cardinal Wolsey from Berwick, now firmly in English hands: 'The confirmation of the peace on the part of the Scots was brought hither by the Abbot of Kelso, the Headsman of the Kerrs of Teviotdale, well accompanied by honest men to the number of 60 persons to whom I made such cheer as I could that day at dinner . . . And because the companions with the said Abbot were Borderers, I bid them to be well accompanied and good cheer to be made unto them. The said Abbot being a sad and wise man, brother to Dand Kerr of Ferniehurst.'

Although it may be seen as a more eccentric abuse than was usual – the heidsman of a surname infamous as border reivers – the reality is that, at the outset of the 16th century, many abbeys, great churches and other religious foundations were in secular hands. James V appointed several of his illegitimate children to ecclesiastical offices – usually those with substantial incomes attached – and his son, Robert Stewart, was not only the first Earl of Orkney, he was also the Commendator of Holyrood Abbey. To hold a benefice 'in commendam' carried the sense of a temporary appointment until a suitable cleric became available although, in practice, suitable clerics rarely were. Another illegitimate son, James Stewart, was Commendator of Melrose and also held Kelso after Tam Kerr died. These once-great houses were in decline and, in the spectacular church at Melrose, the voices of only 23 monks echoed as they sang the mass.

In such an atmosphere, fundamental precepts of the religious life began to fade. Celibacy was increasingly rare amongst the senior figures and the leader of the Scottish Church, Cardinal James Beaton, Archbishop of St Andrews, fathered no fewer than eight children with several different women. His successor and nephew, David Beaton, also had eight children but he at least seems to have remained faithful to his mistress, Marion Ogilvy. Bastard children could be legally legitimised and it is reckoned that, in the early 16th century, 40 per cent of all such were the children of priests.

Decay and dissolution were matched by doctrinal controversy. As happened across Europe, the Catholic Church in Scotland had been periodically threatened by various sorts of heresy but, in 1517, what turned out to be a much more serious and sustained protest began to gather momentum.

HOLY TAIN

Duthac was a local man who achieved great fame as a preacher in the 11th century, and his death was recorded in the Annals of Ulster *for the year 1065. What made him a saint is difficult to discover, aside from a reputation for piety. Tales of miracles developed after his death and his body was said to be uncorrupted. What persuaded people to venerate Duthac may not be clear but he certainly inspired followers. A chapel was built in Tain and it became a sanctuary. This did not discourage a local outlaw who pursued an enemy into the church and overcame the mere technicality of it being a sanctuary by burning it down. Rebuilt by 1360, the church of St Duthac became a focus for pilgrimage, and King James IV visited it every year for twenty years. Like those of many saints, Duthac's remains and relics disappeared in the destructive fervor of the Reformation, but his chapel can still be seen in a graveyard that overlooks the sea.*

In 1516, Johann Tetzel, a Dominican friar, travelled to southern Germany to raise cash for the rebuilding of St Peter's in Rome. He was the papal commissioner for indulgences, the remission of punishment for sins, and his plan was to sell these for cash. 'As soon as a coin in the coffer rings, a soul from purgatory springs' was a jaunty saying attributed to Tetzel. This outraged a German friar and professor of theology. In his 95 theses, Martin Luther objected strenuously to what he saw as the purchase and sale of salvation. Where was faith? Where was piety? According to the custom of the university, he nailed his 95 theses to the church door at Wittenberg and, in a very short time, doctrinal revolt turned into reformation as secular powers began to support Luther's reforms and their effects rippled across the North Sea to Scotland.

One of Luther's most passionate supporters and students was a young Scotsman. Patrick Hamilton was well connected, the great-grandson of

James II, a member of the Scottish establishment and also well educated in Europe's universities. In 1523, aged only 19, he became a member of St Leonard's College at the University of St Andrews and began to preach the heretical precepts of Luther. When Cardinal James Beaton ordered that Hamilton be arrested, he fled to Germany but then returned, it seems, to face his accusers. In early 1528, Beaton had the young man arrested (it was later said that he surrendered on the understanding that he would be released without injury) and he was quickly tried for heresy. Almost certainly to his horrified astonishment, Hamilton was convicted and condemned to die on that very same day. His accusers were anxious that attempts may have been made at a rescue.

Outside the archway that leads under St Salvator's Tower into the old quadrangle, soldiers began to build Hamilton's pyre. Carts brought kindling, wood and tar. It was a wet and dank February day in St Andrews and the wind whistled down North Street. No doubt crowds gathered. Once the wood, twigs and tar had been piled up, the young man was led out in his sark and chained to a wooden stake in their midst. He was to suffer an appalling death by being burned alive and, if ropes had been used to secure him, they would have burned through and released Hamilton. As the rain spattered and the wind blew, the clock tower struck 12 noon. Torches were shoved into the wood around the young man's feet. Smoke swirled around him and the flames began to inflict terrible burns to his legs and lower abdomen. Most heretics who were burned 'quick' (meaning alive and not strangled before the fires were lit) had their lives snuffed out by smoke inhalation but the chill breeze that blew down North Street may have prevented a merciful asphyxiation. Hamilton did not die for six hours of unspeakable agony until the flames finally reached his chest and head.

Few seem to have rejoiced as the heretic perished and it seems that he quickly became a martyr. It was said that one of Beaton's advisors remarked: 'My lord if ye burn any more . . . ye will utterly destroy yourselves. If ye burn them, let them be burned in deep cellars, for the reek of Master Hamilton has infected as many as it blew upon.' His initials have been set in the cobbles in front of the clock tower and students at St Andrews are usually careful to walk around them.

As the smoke cleared and the ashes of Hamilton's pyre were washed and blown away, James V began to take personal control of his government. In the summer of 1529, the young king led what was known as a 'justice ayre' to the Borders. At the head of a substantial force, he rode down the Leader

Valley to base himself at the castle at Jedburgh. The winter before, the reivers had been busy, lifting cattle in Cumberland and Northumberland and these large-scale raids had been so successful that Henry VIII had written to his nephew to ask the Scots king to deal with one man in particular.

The most notorious reiver of the day, a man who could muster hundreds, perhaps even thousands of riders, was Johnnie Armstrong of Gilnockie. James V's courtiers organised a deer hunt in the Teviot Valley and a royal invitation was extended to Armstrong – with a safe conduct attached. Accompanied by only 50 of his men, the reiver rode to meet the king at Carlenrig kirkyard near Hawick dressed in such finery that a startled James V is said to have remarked, 'What wants yon knave that a king should have?' It was the beginning of a famous exchange, one that is very probably apocryphal but its tenor seems to convey a powerful sense of how independent-minded Border heidsmen and their king saw each other.

At a signal, the soldiers of the justice ayre surrounded Johnnie and his entourage and it quickly became clear that the safe conduct meant nothing and that there was no escape. Armstrong shouted to James V, 'King Harry would downweigh my best horse with gold to know that I was condemned to die this day.' What Armstrong meant was that he and his raiders could be servants to the Scottish crown by antagonising Henry VIII and his subjects but he did not know that the English king had asked his royal nephew to deal with the reiver. And deal with him summarily. Armstrong's hands were tied and a noose was looped around his neck and, when he was set on his pony, he made a last plea for mercy. But James V turned his back on him and the rope was tied to a high branch of a 'growand tree' in Carlenrig kirkyard. Johnnie roared in fury, 'What a fool I was to seek grace at a graceless face.' And then a serjeant whacked the pony's backside and the rope snapped tight.

James V could have afforded Johnnie Armstrong's finery several times over for, unlike his predecessors, he managed to increase crown revenues dramatically. An act of parliament enabled his administration to rent out the royal estate and he made sure that taxes were efficiently collected. On the vast hunting reserve of the Ettrick Forest, huge flocks of sheep were run and other sources of income maximised. But perhaps the most lucrative activity was marriage. In 1537, James V married Madeleine, the daughter of Francis I, King of France, in Notre Dame Cathedral in Paris. She brought a substantial dowry but inconveniently, or perhaps conveniently, she died soon afterwards of tuberculosis. A second marriage was quickly contracted and this time Mary of Guise brought another large dowry and it allowed the royal couple to live in some style.

Always on the lookout for new ways to raise cash, James V pleaded poverty and petitioned Pope Clement VII Medici for a portion of Peter's Pence, that part of Church revenue that reverted to Rome. There was, of course, a price, one that bequeathed something enduringly distinctive to Scotland. The papacy had begun to mobilise against the Reformation and Clement VII requested that James V reorganise Scots law to bring it into conformity with Canon law, the legal precepts that governed the Church. The papal strategy was to create as many institutional links as possible with those nations as yet relatively unaffected by the teachings of Luther.

Accordingly, the College of Justice was set up in Edinburgh. Based on a Roman model, complete with senators and other paraphernalia, it was funded by 10,000 gold ducats contributed by Scottish bishoprics and monasteries. There were 14 full-time judges, half of them temporal lords, half ecclesiastics, all governed by a Lord President. This institution turned out to be dynamic and not only did it survive the Reformation, despite its papal roots, it ensured that Scots law began to become distinct from English law. But it was not, as some believe, based on the laws of the Roman Empire but on Canon law, dispensed from Papal Rome.

Fiscally acute and alive to potential sources of income, James may have been, but he stepped much less sure-footedly on the international stage. His affinity with Rome and his personal oversight of the burning of two Protestant martyrs below the walls of Edinburgh Castle made relations with Henry VIII difficult. The latter's marital problems compelled a break with Rome when the Pope refused to grant a divorce from Catherine of Aragon and thereby prevent a marriage to Anne Boleyn. In 1533, Henry set aside papal authority and made himself head of what became the Church of England. Diplomatic channels ran dry as James V refused to meet the English king and Pope Paul III stoked differences with public displays of support, sending gifts to Edinburgh of a golden cap and a ceremonial sword.

Conflict began to crackle across the border and, in August 1542, the Earl of Huntly led 2,000 men to Hadden Rig, east of Kelso. Henry had sent Robert Bowes, Warden of the English East March, north with a force of more than 3,000 but around the hamlet of Lempitlaw, Huntly's men scattered them. This success was soon blighted by farcical failure further to the west.

In 1542, Oliver Sinclair, the royal cupbearer, was given an outfit to match his middling status. It carried the king's livery. Not the most expensive at

£20, it cannot have been as fine as the clothes given to the Masters of the Household. They cost £50. A minor aristocrat Sinclair may have been but it seems that he was a royal favourite. Mistrustful of the great magnates who had manipulated and even imprisoned him and his predecessors, James was given to promoting men who depended for their status absolutely on his patronage. It appears that Sinclair took an unlikely and pivotal role in the events of November 1542.

To press home the advantage of Hadden Rig, a large army of 15,000 to 20,000 was raised and they crossed the Esk Fords into England at Arthuret, now Longtown. It seems that Robert, Lord Maxwell, mustered much of the army and was appointed to command it and Oliver Sinclair was sent from Lochmaben Castle, where James V was in residence, with the royal standard. Apparently the king was too unwell to lead his men. At that moment, the sequence of events becomes blurred and confused. One influential chronicler believed that Sinclair declared, clutching the standard, that he had been appointed commander but the earls and other noblemen in the army refused to accept this and complete confusion ensued. But other reports make no mention of this. In any event, an utter shambles unfolded. The large Scottish army was compressed between the Esk and the trackless reaches of the treacherous Solway Moss by a much smaller but well-led English force. As the English horsemen attacked the ragged flanks of the Scottish army as it splashed across the river, swollen with winter rain, and then wheeled away before charging at another point, morale completely disintegrated. Groups of Scots started to surrender to only two or three Englishmen. Perhaps no one wanted to die fighting for Oliver Sinclair. Many more Scots drowned in the Esk than were killed and 1,200 were made prisoner, including many noblemen and the hapless Oliver.

Solway Moss was a disaster, a shameful, shambolic defeat, and, a month later, at only 30 years old, James V died. Some said he died of shame. Perhaps he did although he had been too sick to lead his men across the Esk. In any event, he left a kingless kingdom and a daughter a week old as his sole heir. Her name was Mary.

What the defeats at Flodden and Solway Moss did was to demote Scotland from a rising European power, ruled by ambitious and vigorous kings, to a northern irrelevance – a pawn instead of a player, at least in diplomatic terms. If the Scots could not supply a credible military threat to England or anyone else, then they could not be seen as a valuable ally; the status of the nation slid and its rulers, regents and royals, became minor figures on the international stage. For the mass of ordinary people, 80 per cent of them peasant farmers, their lives altered little – unless their homes lay in the Borders or the Lothians, in the path of advancing armies. But Scotland was about to undergo a momentous, defining transformation, one that affected everyone who lived north of the Cheviots.

THE MINION

Oliver Sinclair was described as James V's 'minion'. It is an odd description that appears in several accounts of the battle. In the 16th century, it did not mean an 'underling' or 'subordinate' but, deriving from the French word mignon, *it was used as an adjective to mean 'sweet' or 'dainty' or as a noun to refer to someone who was a 'darling' or 'favourite' – not exactly the sort of characteristics that would appeal to an army of hard-bitten Borderers. It may be that 'the king's minion' was the king's lover.*

On the Feast of the Epiphany 1540, sometimes known as Twelfth Night, the January darkness was lit by the blaze of firelight as logs snapped and crackled around the three bays of the fireplace in the great hall of Linlithgow Palace. Candles flickered in the draughts, wine flowed and the household of James V and Queen Mary of Guise waited for the fun to begin. A short play, 'an interlude', had been written by the royal Master of Ceremonies, Sir David Lyndsay. As the king, his noblemen, bishops and burgesses watched, a fictional king took the stage, attended by his courtiers, Placebo, Picthanke and Flatterye. A Poor Man entered and complained of injustices and he was answered by a burgess, a man at arms and a bishop. This interlude was the core of what later became *A Satire of the Three Estates* which was performed in its entirety in Cupar in 1552. Despite the unblinking nature of the attack, it was said that James V laughed out loud when the Church was criticised. The directness of the sentiment and the power of the language are best expressed in the original Scots of the Poor Man's lines:

> Sir, I wald speir at yow ane questioun.
> Behauld sum Prelats of this Regioun:
> Manifestlie during thair lustie lyvfis,
> Thay swyfe Ladies, Madinis and vther mens wyfis.
> And sa thair cunts thay haue in consuetude [by custom].
> Quhidder say ye that law is evill or gude?

Attempts at reform were made and not all priests, friars and prelates behaved as badly as the Poor Man believed. And, soon after the performance at Linlithgow, the habit of concubinage, when a priest and a woman lived together, was forbidden. But James V remained resolutely Catholic and, in the 1530s, ten martyrs had suffered the agonies of being burned quick while very many more who followed the teachings of Luther and the increasingly influential French theologian, John Calvin, fled into exile.

In order to heighten division in Scotland, Henry VIII sent Protestant preachers across the border. One of these made a significant impact. In 1544, George Wishart travelled widely and preached the reformed faith to gatherings at Montrose, Dundee, Ayr, Mauchline, Leith and Haddington. Such open defiance invited reaction and the reformer was arrested on the orders of the leader of the Scottish Church, Cardinal David Beaton. In the cathedral at St Andrews, a show trial began in February 1546 but Wishart's passion and eloquence discomfited his accusers and impressed listeners so much that the great church was cleared when the inevitable verdict was handed down. Outside the gates of the bishop's castle, Wishart's pyre was piled up and a near-contemporary woodcut showed how hideous his death was. Instead of being chained to a stake, the martyr was hung from a gallows by an iron band around his chest and suspended over the flames. From a window in the castle walls, Cardinal Beaton watched.

The horror of Wishart's burning appalled many and, only three months later, a group of Fife lairds broke into St Andrews Castle at dawn on 29 May. As Protestants, some had seen their material interests suffer at Beaton's hands while others were angered at the martyrdom. They made their way to the Cardinal's bedchamber but he had got wind of their coming and barricaded the door. Having set fire to it, the conspirators broke in and, despite his entreaties that he was a priest, they stabbed Beaton to death. They stripped and mutilated the corpse before hanging it from one of the castle windows and then one of the killers 'pished in his mouth'.

The castle was quickly occupied by a force of about 150 men as the Regent, the Earl of Arran, arrived to lay siege to it. It held out through the summer, autumn and winter and, in April 1547, John Knox joined the garrison. He was a devoted disciple of George Wishart. Little more than a month later, a French fleet rounded Fife Ness and dropped anchor off St Andrews. With the threat of a withering bombardment, the occupiers, known as 'the Castilians', surrendered and Knox was sent to France as a galley slave. Not many survived such a fate.

Further south Scotland had seen violence of another sort during what Walter Scott called 'the Rough Wooing'. In the same year as the reek of George Wishart's grisly execution drifted out over St Andrews Bay, Henry VIII gave orders that Scotland should be severely punished. Enraged at the refusal to betroth his son, Edward, to the infant Mary Queen of Scots, and at the signing of a treaty with Catholic France, the English king and his privy council issued an unambiguous edict: 'Put all to fire and sword . . . burn Edinburgh town, so razed and defaced when you have sacked and gotten what you can of it as there may remain a perpetual memory of the vengeance of God.'

It was a tremendously destructive time. In 1545, the Earl of Hertford landed at Coldingham with 12,000 men and many pieces of artillery. By 11 September they had made camp at Kelso to find that about a hundred defenders (including 12 monks) had fortified the great Tironensian abbey. When they refused to surrender, Hertford did not hesitate.

> Whereupon I caused the same to be approached out of hand with ordinance and within an hour a great breach was made . . . [T]he Scots bye and bye driven into the Steeple but the way being so dangerous and of good strength and night being at hand, I decided to leave the assault til morning, setting good watch at night about the house. Which was not well kept what a dozen of the Scots in the dark of night escaped by ropes out of back windows and corners with no little danger to their lives. When the day was come the Steeple was soon assaulted. It was immediately won and as many Scots as were within slain.

Besieged by 12,000 and battered by artillery, the defence of Kelso Abbey seems like a desperate gesture with no hope of success. Hertford moved on, intent on carrying out the terms of Henry VIII's edict to the letter. After the attack on 'the Steeple', probably the eastern crossing, where the high altar stood, he ordered the destruction of the great church. By firing the roof and undermining and toppling the eastern crossing 'so that the enemy may have little use of it', his men cast down most of the fabric of one of the largest and most beautiful buildings of medieval Scotland. Only the western crossing still stands, a monument to the ruthlessness of Henry VIII and the erratic and unrealistic foreign policy of the Scottish magnates. Hertford sent despatches south saying that his army had burned 287 villages, farms and churches across the Borders and beyond. As fire and sword blazed through the countryside, destruction on this scale had not been seen for two centuries.

Bloated and in near-constant pain, Henry VIII died in 1547 and the pressure slackened a little as the attentions of Edward IV were pulled elsewhere. In 1550, the Queen Dowager, Mary of Guise, went to France with a retinue of influential noblemen. After liberal amounts of bribery were ladled out, the noblemen were all persuaded to support a revival of the Auld Alliance. In 1554, Queen Mary became Regent, her daughter, Mary, being only 12 years old, but not too young for a dynastic marriage to be contracted and planned. The Dauphin, the heir to the French throne, Francis, was apparently attracted to Mary and the couple were said to be well matched. The firm prospect of this marriage began to polarise power politics in Scotland.

THE MAKARS

Little is known of the earliest poets writing in Scots, and indeed in Latin, except for their work. Modern poets, or makars, might envy that – the primacy of the work over personality. Robert Henryson was given the title of 'Maister' by William Dunbar when he mourned his death in 1505 in The Lament for the Makars. *It may have signified that Henryson was a graduate of one of Scotland's ancient universities, perhaps St Andrews or Glasgow. He also appears to have been a schoolteacher. But it is his oeuvre that is eloquent. Henryson composed three major narratives: 'The Testament of Cresseid', 'The Moral Fables' and 'Orpheus and Eurydice', as well as several beautiful short lyrics such as 'Robyn and Makene'. In his wonderful translation of 'The Testament of Troilus and Cresseid', Seamus Heaney makes Maister Henryson's words sing once more.*

As an underground movement whose promoters risked hideous deaths for their beliefs, Protestantism and its rise are difficult to detect in Scotland in the decades after Luther famously objected to the sale of indulgences. But there can be little doubt that his ideas and those of other reformers were quietly spreading, their acceptance and understanding fuelled by the availability of William Tyndale's translation of the New Testament into English after 1526. John Knox later claimed that the majority of the populations of eight burghs, those who lived in Ayr, Brechin, Dundee, Perth, Edinburgh, Montrose, St Andrews and Stirling, had renounced Catholicism by 1559. The reality was probably that only Perth and Dundee were overwhelmingly

Protestant. It is inevitably the case that revolutions are sparked by minorities but political events also helped accelerate the pace of change.

When the marriage of Mary and Francis was proposed and agreed, it looked as though Scotland might be relegated to little more than the status of a province of France. For, if Mary died before her husband, when the Dauphin came to rule France, he would also become king of Scotland by right – a Catholic, French king of Scotland.

Styling themselves 'the Faithful Congregation of Christ Jesus in Scotland', a group of influential noblemen signed what was known as the First Band or Covenant. It promised to make Scotland a Presbyterian nation, to resist the influence of France and to oppose the marriage of Mary and Francis. The Lords of the Congregation acted as a political focus for reform but, with Mary of Guise as Regent, they could do nothing to prevent the sumptuous ceremony from taking place at Notre Dame in Paris when the realms of Scotland and France came together in marriage in April 1588.

Mary of Guise buttressed her authority with companies of French soldiers garrisoned in Edinburgh and elsewhere and paid for them by taxes raised from Scots lords, burghs and religious houses. But three deaths in twenty months diverted the course of history in a different direction.

In what seemed like an act of wanton, desperate cruelty, to say nothing of bad politics, Walter Myln was burned at the stake for heresy in St Andrews. He was 82 years old. A former priest at Lunan in Angus, Myln had fled persecution in 1538 for failing to celebrate the Catholic Mass. When he returned 18 years later to preach the reformed faith in Fife, he was arrested at Dysart and imprisoned in St Andrews Castle. For some time, priests attempted to persuade the old man to recant, offering him a comfortable life as a pensioner in Dunfermline Abbey.

Myln clung to his beliefs and his refusals brought him in front of a jury in St Andrews Cathedral – the great church was once more the stage for a show trial where only one verdict was ever handed down. So old and frail was Myln that his accusers feared he would be unable to climb the stairs of the pulpit to face the bishops and the charges laid against him. He began his defence with prayer but he was quickly told to get on with it. There then took place a sequence of events that offered some sense of how public opinion, at least in the towns, was shifting in Scotland.

In order to burn Myln beyond the sacred precincts of the cathedral and avoid polluting the holy ground with the ashes of a heretic, permission was required from the Provost of St Andrews, Patrick Learmonth. He refused it.

Myln's execution was further delayed because the people of the burgh declined to provide wood, coals and rope for the stake. Once the archbishop's men had found what they needed (from a temporary pavilion), an armed guard marched the old man up North Castle Street to Deans Court, safely beyond the precinct but only a short distance from the west door of the cathedral. In a spiteful and petty act, Myln was denied his last words but, before the flames could be kindled, some boys and townspeople intervened. They could not prevent the horror that was about to take place but they demanded that the condemned man be allowed to speak. And what he said was powerful:

Dear friends, the cause why I suffer this day is not for any crime laid to my charge, though I acknowledge myself a miserable sinner before God; but only for the defence of the truth of Jesus Christ set forth in the Old and New Testaments. I praise God that he hath called me, among the rest of his servants, to seal his truth with my life; as I have received it of him; so I willingly offer it up for his glory; therefore as ye would escape eternal death, be no longer seduced by the lies of bishops, abbots, friars, monks and the rest of that sect of anti-Christ, but depend only upon Jesus Christ and his mercy, that so ye may be delivered from condemnation.

After Myln's blackened, charred corpse was removed, the people of St Andrews immediately built a cairn on the site of his pyre. But, in the night, the cathedral clergy came out and removed it, an act that seemed to symbolise the gulf that had opened between the institutions of the Catholic Church and its communicants. Protestant lords moved to protect preachers from arrest and John Knox would later claim that Myln's martyrdom caused 'thousands of his opinion and religion in Scotland' to declare their support for the Reformed Church.

In September 1558, Protestant support broke through in Edinburgh as the traditional procession of the city's patron saint was disrupted and 'the idol of Sanct Giles' was desecrated by being dunked in the Nor Loch. What sparked this outburst was the advertised culmination of that year's procession. When it reached the doors of St Giles, the populace was to witness the public recantation and humiliation of several heretics.

The pace of events began to quicken. On 1 January 1559, an anonymous pamphlet known as the 'Beggars' Summons' was nailed to the door of every friary in Scotland. It demanded that the Greyfriars, the Blackfriars (Franciscans and Dominicans) and other mendicant orders quit their well-appointed houses so that the genuine poor could have somewhere to live. All of the friaries were located in Scotland's towns, where support for reform was strongest. Calling them rich and ungodly, the 'Summons' required that all friars be out by Flitting Friday, 12 May 1559. Only ten days before this ultimatum expired, John Knox returned to Scotland and he seemed to seize the moment. Fired by his passionate preaching, a mob rioted in Perth on the 11 May and the houses of the Franciscans, Dominicans and Carthusians were destroyed. Collateral damage included the loss of the tomb of James I. And, that summer, a band of Protestants attacked another royal site as they fell upon Scone Abbey, for centuries the crowning place of Scots kings, and completely destroyed the church. Perhaps with a touch of affection, Knox called them 'the rascal multitude'.

A second death added more momentum to the cause of reform. On 11 June 1560, the Regent, Mary of Guise, died, bloated by the painful symptoms of dropsy, the build-up of fluid in her body, and French troops quickly abandoned Scotland. Parliament fell under the control of the Lords of the Congregation. Knox was installed as the minister of St Giles, still the focal church of Edinburgh, and, from its pulpit, he preached fearlessly against idolatry. Through her husband, Mary, Queen of France and Scotland, allowed a parliament to be called, making the reservation that matters related to religion should first be referred to them. As noblemen, lords, burghers and prelates travelled to Edinburgh to discuss the issue that was consuming the nation – that of reform – this stipulation was always likely to be ignored.

As those who claimed the right of attendance gathered for the parliament in Edinburgh, the Six Johns set to work. Under the supervision of John Knox, John Winram, John Spottiswoode, John Row, John Willock and John Douglas met to compile 'The Confession of Faith of the Kirk of Scotland'. In only four days, these remarkable ministers distilled into 25 chapters a clear understanding of Protestantism and what it should mean not only for the Church in Scotland but also for the everyday lives of its people. Based on the thinking of John Calvin, 'The Confession of Faith' is an extraordinarily complete manifesto – one of the most radical documents ever to be written in Scotland.

When parliament met in the tollbooth, a ramshackle building next to St Giles that had variously been used as a town hall, a prison and a toll house, 'The Confession' was read out twice, article by article, before being ratified and adopted. In addition, measures were approved to ban the Catholic Mass and to reject the authority of the Pope, 'that man of Sinne'. The English ambassador, Thomas Randolph, 'never saw so important matters sooner despatched'. The Reformation Parliament of 1560 was a master class in political organisation and clarity of purpose and, in a matter of days, it laid the foundations of a new Scotland.

The transformation was, of course, by no means immediate and the aspirations of the new Kirk took generations to come to fruition but a very great deal was, nevertheless, achieved in a short time. The medieval parishes were reformed, at first in towns where the new faith was strongest and eventually in country districts. Kirk sessions of lay elders were appointed and their crucial role was to appoint ministers. Although priests, like Walter Myln, did convert, it took at least 20 years for the universities to meet the Kirk's demand for properly qualified ministers. Many parishes were, at first, in the care of readers – a lesser role and one often filled by converted priests. These men were not always trusted to have abandoned the old beliefs and practices completely, especially since it is likely that parishioners also clung on to the ways of the Catholic Church. Kirk sessions were also expected to demand and enforce godly obedience. This amounted to overseeing the morals of congregations and the elders dealt out discipline for all manner of transgressions. To all intents and purposes, the civil law for ordinary people was administered by the Kirk as it attempted to convert Scotland into a 'Godly Commonwealth'.

ROBERT CARVER

A monk at Scone Abbey all his long life, Carver is Scotland's greatest composer of the 16th century. His experience spanned the Reformation and he probably witnessed the wrecking of the old abbey at Scone by a mob from Dundee in 1559 which had been whipped into destructive fervor by John Knox. Carver was probably born in 1485 and died in 1570. Five of his settings of the mass survive as well as two of his motets (a form of Renaissance polyphony). They are very beautiful and are still performed today. The Carver Choirbook, in which these woks are contained, is held in the National Library of Scotland. The Scottish Reformation achieved a great deal – but much was lost. The stained glass and the decoration of the great medieval churches perished, and their glorious music was silenced.

Central to the new faith was a simple concept – one that would change the nation utterly. The priesthood of all believers was the radical alternative to a dependence on the mumbo-jumbo of priests muttering the Mass in Latin.

In the medieval church, they had occupied a role as mediators between God and their parishioners and they maintained the essential mystery of the Mass. But the new beliefs insisted on a direct relationship. Through a knowledge of the sacred word of God expressed in scripture, believers had no need for a priest or his rituals – if they could read. And, if they could read, then they also accepted responsibility for their own salvation.

The pivotal role of scripture demanded the promotion of mass literacy as a priority in Protestant Scotland. The Godly Commonwealth had to be able to read the Bible and the reformers' noble wish was to establish a school in every parish. This took more than a century to bring about but near-universal literacy, unique in Europe, was a stunning achievement, a departure that defined Scotland for centuries and was the fundamental cause of many of the glittering intellectual breakthroughs that lay in the future.

Poor relief was also to be the responsibility of kirk sessions but its establishment highlighted a chronic early difficulty. The vast wealth, the estates of the monastic houses and the great churches that had accumulated through centuries of gifts and endowments were not passed on to the Reformed Kirk. Instead, a land grab took place. The Crown and many noble families, especially the lordly commendators, seized Church lands and those who rented farms from the abbeys simply retained them as the institutions were dissolved or paid a sum of cash to confirm ownership. For example, the estates of the Dukes of Roxburgh in the Scottish Borders came to include much of the landed wealth of Kelso Abbey. The Reformed Kirk inherited perhaps a sixth of the revenue of the Catholic Church in Scotland and, while it stood in high contrast with the sinful opulence of the Catholic Church, poverty slowed the progress of reform.

In 1560, the first General Assembly met in Edinburgh and it stood at the apex of the government of the Kirk. Below it were the Superintendants, replacements for the bishops (three Catholic bishops converted and remained in office) and 12 were set in authority over what amounted to the old dioceses. All candidates for the ministry were subject to rigorous examination but it took a long time for all 1,080 parishes to be filled. In Lowland Scotland, Reformed clergy were more or less in place by the 1620s. But replacement appears to have been less than ruthless. It was not until the 1580s that, at Kelso Abbey, 'the hail monkis ar decessit'.

Worship changed radically. Much of the pomp and colour of Catholicism was replaced by a new austerity. The wall paintings of scenes from scripture and the lives of the saints in St Giles were obliterated by whitewash, devotional art of all sorts, sculpture, paintings, and stained glass, was removed and such was the fervour of the reformers, the rascal multitude, that much of it was cast down, burned or effaced. Virtually all of Scotland's medieval stained glass was smashed to smithereens, a tragic cultural loss. Instead, the focal point of worship became the sermon, based on scripture, the Word of God, and ministers were instructed to speak loudly – and in Scots. Kneeling before altars was banned and communion took place at long tables, in imitation of the Last Supper. Saints days and feasts, such as Christmas, were no longer celebrated since the Kirk believed that devotion should be constant, undimmed whatever the date. The Reformation was a revolution that changed the character of life in Scotland completely.

In the midst of the intellectual ferment of reform, romance, or at least glamour, made a dramatic entrance. Only a handful of names from Scotland's history are universally recognised and Mary, Queen of Scots, is one. At almost six feet, she was very tall and said to be very beautiful (queens were usually said to be beautiful but the contemporary descriptions and compliments seem to be so detailed as not to be tropes) and she probably towered over John Knox. But he was determined not to look up to her in any other sense. Mary was a Catholic and, in his splendidly titled *The First Blast of the Trumpet Against the Monstruous Regiment of Women*, Knox had made his position clear, railing against the rule of Catholic Mary I of England as well as Mary, Queen of Scots. No punches were pulled: 'How abominable before God is the Empire or Rule of a wicked woman, yea, of a traiteresse and bastard.' But, if he hoped that his righteous, shining faith and the power of his intellect would persuade this slip of a girl (Mary was still only 19 years old) of the error of her idolatrous ways, he was to be disappointed, remarking: 'If there be not in her a proud mind, a crafty wit and an indurate heart against God and His Truth, then my judgement faileth me.'

The Queen was also a widow. Soon after he was crowned, Francis II of France, her young husband, unexpectedly died of an ear infection. This forced an unwelcome choice on the young widow but, in August 1561, her ship tied up at the Leith quays.

There was unquestionably glamour swirling around Mary's return to Scotland and the setting-up of a Renaissance, Francophile court in Edinburgh. Knox muttered that its 'enchantment' was wicked and indeed 'all men are bewitched'. For his attacks, and especially for calling the queen a Jezebel, the great reformer was criticised by the General Assembly – whose members were presumably bewitched and enchanted too.

Even though she remained a Catholic, Mary appears to have been realistic about the attractions of a popular Reformation in Scotland. She agreed to hear Mass only in the private chapel at Holyrood and made no public move to support the restoration of the old faith or resist the rise of the new. Her principal advisors, her half-brother, James Stewart, Earl of Moray, and her Secretary, William Maitland, were Protestants and she seems to have heeded their advice. In the first three years of her personal reign, Mary travelled the length and breadth of the kingdom, showing herself to her subjects. Unlike her mother, Mary of Guise, the new queen did not impose punitive taxation because she did not have to. As Queen Dowager of France, she had a steady income of £30,000 a year and, from the revenues of Church estates claimed by the crown, more cash flowed.

Much more problematic was the issue of a husband and, allied to that, Mary's insistence that she had an excellent claim to the throne of England. Her grandmother had been a sister of Henry VII and, for those who did not recognise Henry VIII's divorce and his subsequent marriage to Anne Boleyn, Elizabeth I was seen as a bastard. She was also childless so, for English Catholics, Mary was a very attractive alternative. Elizabeth I knew that and, in what seems like a deliberately insulting act, she offered her lover, Robert Dudley, Earl of Leicester, as a suitable match for Mary. After the rejection of a number of other candidates, there was an eventual agreement on Henry Stewart, Lord Darnley. Also six foot, he was known by Elizabeth I as 'the Long Lad'. He was tall enough but, more importantly, he was next in line to the throne of Scotland should Mary die. And, if they failed to produce children, Henry would succeed in his own right and could take another consort.

The moment at which the queen's reign began to unravel may have been 29 July 1585, when she and Darnley were married in the private chapel at Holyrood according to the Catholic rite. Elizabeth of England was reportedly furious and, in an act of some petulance, she had Darnley's mother arrested and detained in the Tower of London. She apparently believed that her permission ought to have been sought and she also knew that any child of this marriage would have an even stronger claim to her throne than either Mary or Henry. But what ramped up tension was the armed rebellion known as 'the Chaseabout Raid' led by Mary's half-brother and advisor, James Stewart, Earl of Moray. This quickly fizzled out and its failure may have emboldened Darnley into a moment of fatal rashness. On Christmas Day 1565, he chose to hear Mass at Holyrood and to announce his return to the old faith. Apparently the 19-year-old was seen striding up the High Street declaiming loudly that he had returned Scotland to Catholicism. The General Assembly was in session in Edinburgh at the same time.

It seems that Mary began to turn against her long and loud-mouthed lad at around this time and she relied increasingly for advice on a group of foreigners at court. The most powerful were Catholics. As with all monarchies, access was vital and the Protestant lords were more and more excluded as Mary preferred the counsel of outsiders. Grumbling quickly grew into a fatal resentment. Principal amongst the queen's new advisors was David Riccio, the ambassador of the kingdom of Savoy. Darnley became jealous of this urbane and educated man and, when Mary fell pregnant, he believed that Riccio was the father. The impulsive 19-year-old hatched a crazy plot. On the evening of 9 March 1566, he and several others forced their way into the supper room at the Palace of Holyroodhouse where they knew that Riccio was the guest of the queen. Hoping that the shock would cause her to miscarry, Darnley and his gang stabbed her favourite to death in front of her and her husband left his dagger in Riccio's corpse as a macabre symbol of his anger and defiance. Mary was steelier than her husband knew for she remarked to a courtier that 'it is within my belly that will one day avenge these cruelties and affronts'.

DARNLEY DNA

Henry Darnley's rashness was probably stoked into something worse by his conviction that the baby who would become James VI and I was not his. Perhaps the murdered David Riccio was the father. But ancestral DNA testing has proved that Darnley was indeed the father. The Royal Stewart Y-chromosome marker arose in Sir John Stewart of Bonkyll, who died at the battle of Falkirk in 1298, and it has come down in an unbroken male line to the present day. Richard, Duke of Buccleuch, is descended from James Scott, Duke of Monmouth, the natural son of Charles II, and he carries the marker that arose in Sir John Stewart. Darnley's suspicions were ill founded.

There was no miscarriage. The future James VI was born on 19 June in Edinburgh Castle and his mother declared to Darnley that 'My Lord God has given you and me a son, begotten by none but you. This is the son who will unite the two kingdoms of Scotland and England.' The precious baby was later baptised according to the Catholic rite. By this time, it seems that two Churches claimed loyalty in Scotland. The Catholic Church still claimed many adherents and had been reinforced by Mary's restoration of James Hamilton as Archbishop of St Andrews and the Protestant Church of Knox survived and steadily thrived. But the seeds of more difficulty had already been sown. The ceremony of baptism for Mary's baby was organised by James Hepburn, Earl of Bothwell. There then followed an extended sequence of events which led to great upheaval and eventually to tragedy.

Darnley had been a disastrous choice as a husband but Mary could not divorce him and risk having her son branded a bastard. Another desperate plot was hatched that, amongst other things, would show that the queen continued to make disastrous choices. Suffering from a bout of syphilis, Darnley came to the house at Kirk o' Field in late January 1567. It stood immediately to the south of Edinburgh's Flodden Wall. While Mary danced at a masked ball at the Palace of Holyroodhouse on 9 February, the house was blown up by gunpowder. But the explosion did not kill Darnley. His corpse, dressed in a nightshirt, was found some distance from the smoking ruins of Kirk o' Field. He had been asphyxiated, perhaps by a pillow held over his face. Bothwell was undoubted involved in this plot (he certainly supplied the gunpowder) and the later discovery of what were known as the Casket Letters also implicated the queen. Three months after Darnley's death, the conspiring couple were married. Even though they used the Protestant rites, Mary could not appease the Lords of the Congregation and her popular reputation was by this time in tatters. Crowds chanted that she was a whore and a papist and should be burned at the stake.

Both sides armed themselves and two armies met at Carberry Hill near Musselburgh on 15 June 1567. But no shot was fired, no sword drawn. Instead, negotiations persuaded Bothwell to go into exile (he died ten years later, insane, in a Danish prison) and Mary to accompany the Protestant lords. As the army disbanded and she rode from Carberry Hill, soldiers shouted insults after her. On 24 July, Mary was forced to abdicate in favour of her one-year-old son. He was crowned James VI, the first Protestant king of Scotland, and his mother was sent to prison in a castle on an island on Loch Leven.

The Lords of the Congregation and the Kirk were triumphant. They had deposed a Catholic monarch and would crown a Protestant. When the

General Assembly met in Edinburgh only ten days after the confrontation at Carberry, they set about the consolidation of the Reformed Kirk. With the support of Mary's half-brother, James Stewart, Earl of Moray, and now Regent of the realm, the acts of the 1560 Parliament were finally formally ratified. More cash was found for the setting-up of reformed parishes and the Assembly and Parliament appeared to develop a unity of purpose. If Moray lent political weight, the intellectual driving force behind the second phase of the Scottish Reformation was the new Moderator of the General Assembly, George Buchanan. A historian and a humanist scholar who wrote the most elegant Latin of the age, he exerted profound influence.

Born on a farm near Killearn in Stirlingshire, Buchanan grew up speaking Gaelic and probably a smattering of Scots since his home lay close to the linguistic frontier. In 1520, he was sent to the University of Paris by his uncle, James Heriot, whose family went on to endow the famous Edinburgh school, George Heriot's. Although he was only 14 years old, Buchanan appears to have thrived, embracing all that the great university had to offer but, when his uncle died in 1522, the money dried up and he had to leave. By this time, he was 16 years old and the young student returned to Scotland where he became a soldier, joining the French forces brought to Scotland by the Duke of Albany. Eventually returning to Paris, Buchanan was appointed a professor and he taught, translated and wrote with great distinction. After a series of wanderings and imprisonment in Portugal for his criticisms of the Catholic Church (although he formally remained a Catholic), Buchanan came home to Scotland in 1560 or 1561.

Perhaps because of his ambivalence, certainly because of his erudition, the former professor was appointed tutor to Mary, Queen of Scots, in 1562. Apparently they often read Latin texts together. But when Buchanan at last declared himself Protestant, he began to become closely involved in the practical politics of change. He was clearly able to equate this with his acceptance of the grant of the revenues of the Abbey of Crossraguel in South Ayrshire, a gift from Queen Mary. In the summer of 1567, Buchanan found himself at the centre of history when, even though he was a layman and not an ordained minister, he was appointed Moderator of the General Assembly.

For the immediate future, the abdication of Mary appeared to remove the possibility of a reversion to Catholicism in Scotland and more firmly established Protestantism – more precisely, a version of Calvinism – as the state religion. Just as it had in the centuries before, excommunication was a powerful sanction and the Kirk began to use it, casting people out of the

Godly Commonwealth in much greater numbers as conformity was insisted upon. Beyond the towns of Lowland Scotland and particularly in country districts, Catholicism carried on but the physical fabric of the old Church was being quickly undermined as its buildings were stripped of valuables and stone was robbed or taken over for secular use. But, for practical reasons of continuity, the ruins of many great monastic churches were adapted for Protestant worship. For example, roofs were built over the majestic walls of Melrose and Kelso Abbeys and more readers were recruited from the disbanding monastic orders. George Buchanan had been appointed Principal of St Leonard's College and it began to turn out well-trained graduates for the ministry in small but steady and significant numbers.

As students pored over scripture at the east end of South Street in St Andrews, blood was being spilled in the west as Mary made a last, desperate attempt to cling to power. Sprung from prison on Loch Leven, she rallied an army of between 5,000 and 6,000 and Catholic magnates such as the Earl of Argyll and Archbishop James Hamilton. At Langside, near Glasgow, they were met by a smaller army raised by the Regent, the Earl of Moray, and soundly beaten. Disinclined to surrender once more, the queen had little option but to flee south to seek sanctuary at the court of her cousin, Elizabeth I.

Mary was more than an irritation to the English queen. For English Catholics, she was a very attractive alternative. Elizabeth had no children and, by 1568, she was not likely to conceive and that made her Scottish cousin the heir presumptive. Conspiracies followed Mary around the castles she and her attendants were moved to by her goaler, the Earl of Shrewsbury, and occasionally they flared into possibility. The queen fell in love with the Catholic Duke of Norfolk and plotted with him and the Duke of Alva to overthrow Elizabeth. Arrested for high treason, Norfolk was executed in 1572. Undiscouraged by a clear warning that, if she engaged in any more treasonous activity, she would be indicted and forced to stand trial, Mary continued to plot. In the 1580s, the Spanish threatened invasion and they supported the efforts of a young nobleman, Anthony Babington, to plan the assassination of Elizabeth I and her replacement with Mary. On 7 July 1586, he wrote to the Scots queen, saying that he would rescue her and, astonishingly, Mary replied to him in her own handwriting, agreeing to the plan but stipulating that Elizabeth was not to be harmed. Watched by Francis Walsingham, the great spymaster, the plot was allowed to grow and, when Babington and others were arrested, it was revealed that Mary's letters had been intercepted. She was detained and taken to Fotheringhay Castle in Northamptonshire to await trial.

Mary's letters meant there could be only one verdict but the court had no power to impose a death sentence on a queen. That had to be sanctioned by Elizabeth and it was said that she was very reluctant. Perhaps it is true that she had the death warrant placed in a stack of state papers requiring her signature. Perhaps she did not hesitate.

At about 8 a.m. on the morning of 8 February 1587, Mary was brought by her attendants into the great hall of Fotheringhay Castle. A low scaffold had been set up and many witnesses had gathered around it. Once she had removed her outer garments, all could see that she wore a crimson shirt, the colour of Catholic martyrdom. Before she moved to the executioner's block, one of her ladies tied a blindfold around her head. Here is part of the account written by Robert Wynkfield:

> Then, groping for the block, she laid down her head, putting her chin over the block with both her hands, which, holding there still, had been cut off had they not been espied. Then lying upon the block most quietly, and stretching out her arms cried, In manus tuas, Domine, etc., three or four times. Then she, lying very still upon the block, one of the executioners holding her slightly with one of his hands, she endured two strokes of the other executioner with an axe, she making very small noise or none at all, and not stirring any part of her from the place where she lay: and so the executioner cut off her head, saving one little gristle, which being cut asunder, he lift up her head to the view of all the assembly and bade God save the Queen. Then, her dress of lawn [her wig] from off her head, it appeared as grey as one of threescore and ten years old, polled very short, her face in a moment being so much altered from the form she had when she was alive, as few could remember her by her dead face. Her lips stirred up and a down a quarter of an hour after her head was cut off.

On the instructions of Queen Elizabeth, Mary's clothes were burned to avoid them being seen as relics and her body was embalmed and taken to Peterborough Cathedral to await transport to France. It was a dismal end and one that was perhaps all too predictable. James VI of Scotland was 20 years old when news of his mother's execution reached him. Mary's belief that her son would be king of England and Scotland eventually came true and, when he set up court in London, her son gave orders that Fortheringhay

Castle be demolished and that work should begin on a magnificent tomb in Westminster Abbey for Mary, a mother he had never known.

The years of James's minority had been scarred with what amounted to a civil war in Scotland. Lasting almost 20 years, it began with a series of assassinations and another execution. When the Regent Moray was riding through Linlithgow in January 1570 on his way to Edinburgh, he was shot out of the saddle by a marksman firing from a window in a house belonging to Archbishop James Hamilton. Loyal to Queen Mary and a nephew of the archbishop, James Hamilton of Bothwellhaugh used a French carbine with a rifled barrel for accuracy and his killing of Moray was the first recorded assassination by a firearm. Behind his uncle's house, Hamilton had a fast horse waiting and he evaded capture. His uncle was less fortunate. With other supporters of the queen, the archbishop was captured after a siege of Dumbarton Castle. Convicted of art and part (a peculiarly Scottish verdict that meant he had been an accessory to murder), Hamilton was hanged at the mercat cross in Stirling.

Henry Darnley's father and James VI's grandfather, the Earl of Lennox succeeded Moray as Regent but found himself governing a divided kingdom. Based at Edinburgh Castle, the supporters of Mary called parliaments in her name and were led by her former secretary, William Maitland of Lethington. The Regent held parliaments in the name of James VI at Stirling Castle but he also fell victim to a bullet. In a skirmish with forces sympathetic to the queen, he too was shot. Rumours quickly circulated that the marksman was one of Lennox's own men for it seems that the Regent was shot in the back. The game of fatal musical chairs continued when the new Regent, the Earl of Mar, died in October 1572 on his way home after a banquet given by none other than his successor, James Douglas, Earl of Morton. He lasted much longer before being forced to resign in 1578. But, in that time, he effectively ended support for Queen Mary in Scotland and, a year later, King James VI began his personal rule.

As Regents came and went, the Reformed Kirk had been rewriting its constitution, *The Second Book of Discipline*. The editor of *The First Book* and the acknowledged leader of the reformers, John Knox, died in 1572 after a remarkable career and contribution but one not without its ironies. At the age of 50, a widower, he married Margaret Stewart, a distant relative of Mary, Queen of Scots. She was only 17 but Knox was clearly still vigorous since he fathered three daughters with her. By the summer of 1572, the great preacher's powers were fading and his normally powerful voice was faint as he preached at St Giles. After the installation of his successor, Knox took to his bed and, surrounded by his family and several Protestant noblemen, he died on 24 November. All knew that they had witnessed the passing of a great man.

Two years later, another brilliant, confident, radical thinker emerged to lead the swelling momentum for reform. In 1574, Andrew Melville was appointed Principal of the University of Glasgow and, with others, he set to work on the writing of *The Second Book of Discipline*. An early beneficiary of the drive for literacy across Scotland, Melville learned the rudiments of Latin at Montrose Grammar School before going on to the intellectual ferment that was the University of St Andrews. This revision of Knox and the other five Johns' constitution for the Kirk (the sense of Discipline as they meant it is softened when it is remembered that it also encompassed the notion of followers, as in the Disciples of Christ) established Calvinism ever more deeply and utterly rejected the old hierarchy. There was no scriptural authority for the office of bishop and there would be no bishops in the Kirk. Instead, the governing principle became Presbyterianism – kirk sessions controlled parishes which were organised into larger synods and all met annually at the General Assembly. Scotland was to become a Godly Commonwealth and, in a famous encounter with James VI at his palace at Falkland, Andrew Melville took the king by the sleeve and explained precisely what that meant:

Sir, we will humblie reverence your Majestie always, namlie in public, but sen we have this occasioun to be with your Majestie in privat, and the treuthe is, yie ar brought in extream danger bathe of your lyff and croun, and with yow, the country and Kirk of Christ is lyk to wrak, for nocht telling yow the treuthe, and giffen of yow fathfull counsall, we mon [must] discharge our dewtie thairin, or els be trators bathe to Christ and yow! And thairfor Sir, as divers tymes befor, sa now again, I mon tell yow, thair is twa Kings and twa Kingdomes in Scotland. Thair is Chryst Jesus the King, and his Kingdome the Kirk, whase subject King James the Saxt is, and of whose kingdome nocht a king, nor a lord, nor a heid, bot a member! And they whome Chryst hes callit and commandit to watch over his Kirk, and govern his spirituall kingdome, hes sufficient powar of him, and authoritie sa to do, bathe togidder and sever-alie; the quhilk na Christian King or Prince sould control and discharge, but fortifie and assist, utherwayes nocht fathfull subjects nor members of Chryst.

At the time of the meeting, some time after 1590, Melville was one of what was to grow into a long line of outspoken rectors of the University of

St Andrews and he concluded the lecture by reminding King James, should he be in any doubt about his status in Christ's Kingdom of Scotland, that he was only 'God's silly vassal (in Melville's time 'silly' would have meant 'lowly', 'humble', or 'insignificant' so not such an insult as it appears)'. Perhaps the king sighed and looked longingly to the south where his mother's cousin, Elizabeth I, was held in such reverence that no one would dare speak to her and that tone.

The variety of Scots used by Andrew Melville and by James VI – the association of social class and speech in 16th-century Scotland was different from what obtains now – is no longer spoken in the same manner. But one habit of Melville's way of speaking has survived in a fascinating relict. In Hawick, industrialisation happened so quickly at the end of the 18th and beginning of the 19th centuries that country people moved into the town en masse and preserved their mode of speech. The word *you* in Hawick is pronounced just as Melville said it to the king, as 'yow', rhyming with 'thou' and not 'ewe'. Many other common words have retained this old pronunciation in the south-western corner of the Scottish Borders.

RECTORS

Founded in 1413, the University of St Andrews is Scotland's oldest and, from the first, its leader was known as The Rector. Lawrence of Lindores, a monk, was the first to hold office and, as part of his duties, he arranged for several heretics, Hussites and Lollards, to be burnt at the stake in the streets of the town. Later Rectors have been less active, some of them in the 19th and early 20th centuries failing to visit the university after their installations. Various Liberal and Conservative politicians held the post, including A. J. Balfour, and J. M. Barrie was elected in 1919 but postponed his installation for two years so that he could work on his address to the students. When the day came, Barrie was so nervous that he stood at the lectern for several minutes unable to speak until his audience began to barrack him.

Scots was originally a derivative of the Northumbrian dialect of English brought to the Tweed Basin and the Lothians in the 7th century by invading Anglian war bands. By c. 1500, it had replaced Old Welsh and Gaelic was spoken right up to and beyond the Highland Line. With their emphasis on scripture and the absolute need for literacy amongst the laity, the reformers began to standardise Scots to some extent. This was partly an effect of using English texts like the Tyndale Bible and the increasing tendency for religious books and pamphlets aimed at Scottish readers to be printed in London. By c. 1600, the pronunciation of Scots had begun to be affected by strong Anglicising pressures. The Midland dialect of English written by Shakespeare and used by the London court was slowly accepted as standard.

By contrast, Gaelic was in retreat and itself subject to a change of name and status. Until c. 1500, it had been known as Scots and Scots known as Inglis or English. But, by the early 1500s, Gaelic was increasingly known as Erse or Irish while Scots was called Scots and not English. The irony was that Scots Gaelic had begun to grow away from Irish Gaelic precisely during that period – except in one place. Galloway Gaelic was spoken right across the region, from the Rhinns as far as the banks of the Nith, and also in South Ayrshire or Carrick. It is thought to have been more closely related to Manx and Ulster Gaelic. In 1575, George Buchanan wrote that Gaelic was still the common speech of the south-west but it was slowly dying and, by the end of the 18th century, it had almost completely withered. Only names remember it – place names and the surviving surnames of once-powerful clans such as the Kennedys, the MacLellans and the MacDowalls.

North and west of the Highland Boundary Fault, where the mountains, the lochs and the glens sheltered the language, Gaelic was to survive for much longer. Dialects on the periphery, such as those spoken in Perthshire and Aberdeenshire, were beginning to fade but in the heartlands and on the islands, few had any use for Scots. In 1755, the first year when any statistics are available, 289,798 people had the language – 23 per cent of the population of 1,265,380 – and it is likely that most will have been monoglots.

James VI probably spoke and understood Gaelic and he appears to have had some interest in French. This was much stimulated by the arrival of an exotic visitor. Esmé Stewart was a Catholic, the Lord of Aubigny in France, and apparently extremely good-looking. When he came to Scotland in 1579, he was 38 years old and James VI was 13. The young man developed an immediate passion for the suave and sophisticated Esmé. He, in turn, allowed the young king to kiss and fondle him in public. What happened in the privacy of the royal bedchamber may only be guessed at but the effects of this infatuation were clear in that it closed down access to James. Esmé was created Earl and then Duke of Lennox and, with religious instruction from the king, he converted to Presbyterianism. By now powerful, wealthy and ruthless, Esmé had the Earl of Morton, the former Regent, tried and executed for treason and complicity in the murder of Henry Darnley.

Native noblemen noted this with alarm and, in 1582, in what was known as 'the Ruthven Raid', they kidnapped James VI. After ten months of detention, they forced the king to banish Lennox and he returned to France. It was a fascinating episode, one that was eloquent about the character of the young James. Raised without his mother or father, in an atmosphere of danger and instability, his need to give affection and receive it was extravagantly expressed when he set eyes on Esmé Stewart. He was to be the first of a series of favourites, attractive men who appeared to dazzle and excite James.

Once the king had escaped confinement in Ruthven Castle, a much less wholesome obsession seemed to take hold. He became fascinated by witchcraft and in 1597 wrote *Daemonologie*, a book in the form of a dialogue between two characters, Philomathes and Epistemon. It begins: 'The fearefull aboundinge at this time in this countrie, of these detestable slaves of the Devil, the Witches or enchaunters, hath moved me (beloved reader) to dispatch in post, this following treatise of mine . . . to resolve the doubting . . . both that such assaults of Satan are most certainly practised, and that the instrument thereof merits most severely to be punished.'

This obsession began with a storm. In 1590, James VI was prevented from returning from Denmark with his bride-to-be, Princess Anne, by terrible storms across the North Sea. The admiral of the Danish fleet blamed a witch, the wife of a government official in Copenhagen, for consorting with the Devil who whipped up the seas in an attempt to drown the royal couple. And Scottish witches, a coven that allegedly met in the Auld Kirkyard in North Berwick, were implicated. A sensational trial began and the king took an active part. Agnes Sampson was interrogated by him at the Palace of Holyroodhouse as she suffered horrific torture. Deprived of sleep, she was pinned to the wall of her cell by a witch's bridle, a metal device forced into her mouth that pressed sharp prongs on her tongue and cheeks. After two days of agony, she of course confessed and was burned at the stake.

But, before the North Sea storm whipped up the king's perverted fervour, witchcraft had been recognised as a danger to the Godly Commonwealth. In 1563, the reformers advanced an act through the Scottish parliament outlawing witches and witchcraft on pain of death. In the context of maintaining a thoroughly Christian society in Scotland, it made sense to act against those who might pollute it. And the disciples of Satan presented a real and widely feared threat. All over northern Europe, communities were hunting for witches. In Germany, Benedict Carpzov wrote a textbook on the correct conduct of witch trials and he was involved in the deaths of a staggering 20,000 people convicted of witchcraft.

With the active interest and encouragement of the king, 400 people, most of them women, were accused of being witches in Scotland in 1597. And the hysteria was spreading. Catie Lees of Torwoodlee, near Galashiels, was accused and arrested before being taken to the old tollbooth in Lauder to suffer appalling indignities and excruciating torture. She was to be tried by pricking. Stripped naked, Catie had all her hair shaved off and she was thrown into a filthy cell to shiver and be kept awake for two days. If that failed to produce a confession, she would have had her hands tied and been hung from a beam or a hook. The reason for this was an absolute belief that the power of Satan came from below, from the ground. Once Catie had been lifted off her feet, a witch pricker went to work, probing her naked body with a sharp brass pin, searching for freckles or blemishes that might be the Devil's 'nip' or mark. This was where Satan may have entered the witch's body. Once something suspicious had been identified, the sharp pin was shoved in hard and, if no blood spurted or there was no shriek of pain, then the suspect was clearly a witch. That finding led to only one fate – the complete extirpation of the witch from the Godly Commonwealth by burning.

In 1608 in Edinburgh, a group of eight convicted witches were tied with ropes to stakes to be burned quick or alive. Around the screaming women tar barrels, coals, wood and peat were piled and set alight as a large crowd gasped. The flames burned through the bonds of three of the women and, blackened by dreadful burns, they broke free and ran out of the blaze – only to be caught by the baying onlookers and thrown back in.

This hysterical spasm was not mirrored in the Reformation in England. There, only 500 or so died in fires that raged around the stake in the decades either side of 1600, whereas, in Scotland, more than 4,500 suffered a horrific death. In proportion to the relative sizes of the population, this was a marked difference and the smoke of witches and witchcraft swirled around most communities in Lowland Scotland for at least three generations. The fundamental reason was religious. In Scotland, the reformers had made it a crime simply to be a witch, whereas, in England, it was the act of witchcraft that was illegal. The more open-ended Scottish charge caught up many more – women who were traditional healers, women who were the object of spite in a community or people who were unusual or eccentric in some way.

James VI wrote on other subjects, and one eventually turned out to be even more combustible. In 1598, he committed to paper his thoughts on kingship. They were not those of his tutor, George Buchanan, and, in fact, James burned the great scholar's writings on kingship by consent – that is, the consent of parliament and the landed elite. Since the sending of the Declaration of Arbroath to Rome in 1320, it had been understood that the aristocracy could replace the king if he failed in his duties. James rejected this out of hand and instead posited the notion of the divine right of kings to rule. In his *Basilikon Doron*, he explained to his son, Prince Henry, what that meant: 'First of all things learn to know and love that God, whom ye have a double obligation; first, that He made you a man; and, next, for that He made you a little God to sit on his throne, and rule over other men.' For the Stewart dynasty, this was to prove a fatal manifesto.

After the death of his father William Cecil in 1598, Robert Cecil took over the reins of Elizabeth I's administration as Lord Privy Seal. At 65, his queen was very old for the times and, although her health was not poor, the issue of her successor dominated politics. She would never explicitly name him but James VI had a very strong claim through his mother and grandmother. Writing in code, Cecil sent letters to Edinburgh advising the Scots king on what tone to take with Elizabeth. The promptings were successful and her letters to Scotland show a real warmth. With the death of old friends in 1602, Elizabeth seems to have become depressed and her health began to decline. Preparations were put in hand. And none were more meticulous than those made by Robert Carey. The former March Warden knew that speed was vital, especially if Elizabeth continued to refuse to name her successor explicitly, and he agreed a plan with James VI. The king gave 'a blue ring' to Carey's sister, Philadelphia, Lady Scrope. She was one of the old queen's ladies-in-waiting and constantly in attendance when Elizabeth was finally taken to her bed in March 1603. As soothing music was played in her chamber, the privy councillors gathered and, when Cecil asked if she was content that James of Scotland should be her successor, the queen was said to have made a sign. Perhaps she did.

When death took Elizabeth, Philadelphia Carey took the blue ring and threw it out of a window in Richmond Palace. It was caught by her brother who had been waiting for news in the courtyard below. He immediately mounted a fast horse and rode like the wind for Scotland. Having organised a relay of fresh horses, he arrived in Berwick only 48 hours later, far faster than any official dispatch. But, somewhere north of the town, he fell off his horse and, as he lay on the ground, it kicked him in the head. Spattered with blood and mud, Carey clattered into the inner courtyard of the Palace of Holyroodhouse in the early hours of 26 March and demanded that King James be woken. When the king asked him what letters he carried from the Privy Council, Carey replied that he had nothing except 'a blue ring from a fair lady'. James took it and said, 'It is enough.'

9

An Imperfect Union

✻

JAMES VI WAS ANXIOUS to become James I as quickly as possible. As his household servants scurried about the corridors, apartments, stores and stables of the Palace of Holyroodhouse, packing, fitting out carts, cleaning tack, wondering about their future four hundred miles to the south, the King of Scotland knew that he needed to move rapidly and decisively if he wanted to be safely installed on the glittering throne of the king of England. Carey had been right to ride north with such speed because the conclusion of a long reign can be a time of instability, when other alternatives might present themselves, when dissident factions might seize the initiative, when Catholic plotters might hatch a diversion, when anything could happen.

Only eleven days after James accepted the blue ring, he spoke to a weeping congregation in St Giles Cathedral, promising that he would return home every three years (in fact, he came back once – in 1617 – and that went badly) and then he mounted his horse and rode briskly eastwards on the coast road to his destiny. But, within an hour, the king was forced to stop and dismount. In Musselburgh, his party met the funeral cortege of Robert Seton, the Earl of Winton, who had been one of the rescuers of Mary Queen of Scots from Loch Leven Castle and a lifelong supporter of the Stewart dynasty. Out of respect, King James moved aside, took off his hat and sat on a dyke in silence as the mourners passed.

A day later, Berwick Castle's garrison's cannonade boomed out over the Tweed estuary as the king was welcomed into his new realm. At York, he was given the keys of the city and, in an ironic twist, was lavishly entertained at a house in Buckinghamshire as a guest of Sir Oliver Cromwell. What might have been a dash southwards had turned into a relaxing royal progress and, after taking a month over a journey that Robert Carey had completed in less than three days, James VI came at last to the grand house of Robert Cecil, the second most important man in England. Here is a near-contemporary account:

> Riding slowly, the king came up the great walk; before him the trumpets sounded, and the sheriff of Essex rode with his men. About him were the nobility of England and Scotland, bare-headed, observing no special order, now one, now another, coming up to the king's side and falling back again, according to his highness's pleasure. At the entrance to the first court the whole glorious company dismounted, all but the king. Four nobles stepped to his horse, two before, two behind, and ceremonially laying their hands upon it, brought him forward into the second court. There he himself dismounted; a young man knelt to present a petition, which the king graciously received. He went forward: he came into the court. He saw before him a gathering of the great ones who had invited him: the Chancellor Egerton, the Treasurer Buckhurst, Henry Howard the Privy Seal. At their head, smaller and greater than any, stood the Secretary Robert Cecil, the lord of that house and, under the king, of England. The storm of shouting and cheering went on; the great folk genuflected; on the soft pawing hand of majesty rested the soft-spoken lips of Cecil. The king raised him; together they passed into the house . . . At that point rather than in the later ceremonial entry into London the accession of James was accomplished.

An outbreak of plague prevented parliament from being summoned until the spring of 1604. But at last, on 19 March of that year, Commons and Lords crowded into Westminster Hall to hear what their new king had to say. His vision for the united crowns and kingdoms of Scotland and England was unequivocal: 'I desire a prefect union of laws and persons, and such a naturalising as may make one body of both kingdoms under me your king . . . for no more possible is it for one king to govern two countries contiguous, the one great, the other less, a richer and a poorer . . . than for one head to govern two bodies.'

It seemed that Scotland might disappear, overwhelmed and absorbed by its larger neighbour, much as Wales had been. James wanted to see the separate legal systems made uniform, free trade across the border and to have all Scots born before 1603 naturalised as English subjects. Perhaps taken aback at these radical proposals, the English were not so sure and, in a time-honoured, procrastinating ploy, a commission was formed to 'perfect' James's wide-ranging programme of change. Soundings were to be taken and an Instrument of Union formulated. But this would all take time, it was said – two years, at least.

James VI and I was impatient. In October 1604, he issued a decree declaring himself to be king of Great Britain, Ireland and France. This offended many Englishmen and puzzled more. The counties of Northumberland, Cumberland, Dumfriesshire, Roxburghshire and Berwickshire were henceforward to be known as the Middle Shires and the beginnings of a common currency were put in hand. A twenty-shilling piece was to be minted and called 'a Unite'. None of these measures were adopted.

What did bear enduring and glorious fruit was the granting of a royal licence to build a new theatre in London. The Globe in Southwark was to be home for the company of actors who had been known as the Lord Chamberlain's Men during the reign of Elizabeth I. But, when James VI lent his patronage, they became the King's Men and their most famous member, William Shakespeare, was to be inspired by the new regime to write one of his most political plays, *The Tragedy of Macbeth*. In the royal patent of 19 May 1603, which chartered the King's Men, Shakespeare is listed and, a year later, he and his eight associates were each supplied with four and a half yards of red cloth so that they could take part in the coronation procession in suitable costume.

The optimism of the first two years of the new king's reign was severely shaken by what contemporaries called 'the Powder Treason'. A group of militant English Catholics led by Robert Catesby, which included Guy Fawkes, plotted to blow up parliament when James came to open it on 5 November 1605. Penetrated by the spies of Robert Cecil, the conspiracy was discovered when the Yeomen of the Guard caught Fawkes red-handed in the cellars with a large number of barrels of gunpowder, easily enough to destroy the chamber above. The plot helped create an atmosphere of great fearfulness and a resistance to radical change.

James I's personal inclinations and loyalties also began to stoke resentments. A scion of one of the most notorious reiving families of the Scottish Borders, Robert Carr of Ferniehurst, was one of the king's favourites and almost certainly his lover. James was in the habit of kissing Carr 'after so lascivious a mode in public' and he showered him with gifts, lands and titles. In 1607, the king knighted Carr and then created him Earl of Somerset. After the relative reserve and solemnity of the Elizabethan court, this behaviour raised more than one eyebrow and restricted access to James. Many other Scots had come south in search of preferment and their success sparked more resentment. Anti-Scottishness of a particular sort was a theme taken up by one of the King's Men as he sat down to write about a savage Celtic king in the far north.

Shakespeare skilfully wound together James's fascination for witches and witchcraft with the theme of royal assassination made topical by Catesby, Fawkes and the Catholic conspirators. Wittingly or unwittingly, the tragedy also played to another of the king's obsessions, his concerted attack on Celtic Scotland, what was seen as the barbarity of Gaelic culture. As the lights dimmed and the three witches took the stage in the summer of 1606 with the king in the audience (either at Hampton Court or as part of the revels for the visit of the King of Denmark, his father-in-law), Shakespeare took something of a calculated risk. But he was careful to make Celtic Scotland the dark force in his Scottish play, not the civilised, triumphant, rightful, Lowland King Malcolm.

THE FIFE ADVENTURERS

James VI believed that he needed to encourage the colonization of those parts of his kingdom where savages lived – the Highlands and Islands. In 1597 a company was formed: The Gentlemen Adventurers for the Conquering of the Isles of Lewis. Most of its members came from Fife and they became know as the Fife Adventurers. They had no idea what they were taking on. Just like the English settlers in North America at Jamestown, they made landfall and built a stockade at Stornoway. The natives took exception and Neil MacLeod led his clansmen in attacks on the fort and burned it twice. By 1600 the situation was desperate and the Adventurers sent James Learmonth to find supplies. Not long after it sailed out of Stornoway harbor, his ship was intercepted by the birlinns of Neil MacLeod's half-brother Murdo, and all aboard were slaughtered. Nevertheless, the Fife Adventurers firmly believed that they owned Lewis – though they could never subdue it – and in 1610 they sold it to Clan Mackenzie. As Highlanders, the Mackenzies were better able to deal with MacLeod opposition, and Neil MacLeod was eventually captured and hanged in Edinburgh.

In his own writings, James had made his view of Highlanders plain. Here is a passage from the *Basilikon Doron*: '[Those who] dwell in our mainland, that are barbarous for the most part, and yet mixed with some show of civility; the other, [who] dwell in the isles, and are utterly barbarous, without any show of civility.' If these outlying savages could be brought under control, not only would James's ability to govern his farthest-flung subjects appear effective and impressive, their suppression could only add to the credibility of his English-speaking British project. In 1608, an expedition sailed to the island of Mull where various clan chiefs were invited to board a ship anchored in the bay at Aros. They had been told that a minister would preach an improving sermon but, instead, they were abducted and imprisoned in the Lowlands.

The conditions of release were eloquent about James's intentions. The chiefs were forced to agree to the Statutes of Iona, a mixture of cultural and practical measures designed to promote conformity, to make the Highlands and Islands part of the homogenous British state the king fervently wished to create. Bards and other tradition bearers were banned as were the habits of hospitality and the great banquets where they recited a clan's glorious story. The eldest sons of the chiefs were to be educated in the Lowlands where 'they may be able sufficiently to speak, read and write English'. Not Gaelic. Provision was made for Protestant ministers to preach in the north and the right to bear arms was limited. It was a clear, considered attempt to dismantle the Celtic culture of the north.

With the fall of the Lordship of the Isles at the end of the 15th century, a force for stability and order had withered. What followed was the *Linn nan Creach*, the 'Age of the Forays', a time when clan feuding became widespread and vicious.

Names and the allegiances they signified were everything to Highlanders and James VI and I understood that. On the southern fringes of the Grampian massif and especially in Perthshire, Clan Gregor had been very troublesome. Hard pressed by the loyal and Royalist Clan Campbell, the MacGregors were forced, over time, to become more and more reliant on theft and extortion. Lowland farmers who wanted to keep their cows and not have them stolen by other clansmen were forced to pay blackmail, literally black rent, to the MacGregors in return for protection. In 1604, James intervened decisively and an unusual piece of legislation was enacted. Clan Gregor was to be deprived of the use of the name – it was to be 'altogether abolished' – and those who bore it could be hunted down and killed with impunity and their property seized. The chief of the clan, Alasdair MacGregor, and five of his leading men were brought to the mercat cross of Edinburgh to be hanged for the crime of bearing a surname.

At the other end of Scotland, more disorder required to be dealt with. It is said that the Border reivers invented blackmail and they were certainly adept in the arts of cattle rustling. A year after Clan Gregor was dis-named, James had a Border Commission set up at Carlisle Castle. Lord Hume had been appointed from the Scottish side and Sir Henry Leigh from the English. Both commanded deputies who were professional soldiers. Their methods were direct and summary. Known thieves were simply rounded up, old and new charges trumped up and they were strung up. It was the grisly genesis of what became known as 'Jethart Justice' – the habit of hanging the accused first and then, maybe, asking questions later. On Harraby Hill at Carlisle, Border reivers sang what was cynically called 'neck verse' as a psalm was mumbled moments before the stool was kicked away and the rope snapped tight. There were also mass executions at Dumfries and Jedburgh and, in one year, Lord Hume sanctioned 140 death penalties as 'the nimblest and most powerful thieves in all the Borders' choked on the end of a rope. The heidsmen of the feared and famous surnames could see that this was no routine purge and that history was moving.

By 1610, the criminal society of the Borders had changed. Raids were still sometimes run but those who rode the winter moonlight were fading into the past. Men were no longer permitted to bear arms, ponies worth more than £30 Scots were forbidden and well-known reivers did not strut the streets of Hawick or Hexham. In only seven years James VI and I's commission had deported, hanged or ennobled so many that society was utterly changed.

Absence seems to have been effective. With a ruthlessness that might have been more difficult for a king in Edinburgh to sustain, James asserted his authority in the Highlands and the Borders far more emphatically than any of his predecessors. In a speech to the parliament at Westminster, he summed up his methods – with a hint of surprise behind the bombast: 'Here I sit and govern it [Scotland] with my pen, I write and it is done, and by the Clerk of the Council I govern Scotland, what others could not do by the sword.'

Andrew Melville's estimate of the status of James as 'God's silly vassal' was washed away in the flood of power that swept him to London and the English throne. No vassal, he was Head of the Church of England and the king aimed to bring the Church in Scotland more directly under his control, integrating it into a British Church. Building on what were known as the 'Black Acts' of 1584, when royal supremacy and the authority of bishops were established, James increased their number to 11 in 1610. And the harmonisation of Scottish and English Church law and practice was backed by the new Courts of High Commission.

Having promised to return to Scotland every three years, it was not until 1617 that James saw the Palace of Holyroodhouse again. Perhaps his long absence and the habits of power and deference in England had blunted his feel for the temper of Scottish society, for his announcement of yet more measures towards the creation of a unified Church sparked anger and conflict. Instead of sitting around a communion table in imitation of the Last Supper, communicants were now required to kneel to receive the sacrament. More than the re-establishment of the celebration of Christmas and Easter or the increased power of the bishops, the insistence that congregations should kneel harked back to a popish past and it engendered popular fury. Many refused and, while the Scottish Parliament and the General Assembly belatedly accepted the changes, James was canny enough not to resort to violence to enforce them. He had decided that part of his strategy for ecclesiastical union would be the power of language.

First available in the 1570s in England and Scotland, the Geneva Bible was the most widely used. It was the work of exiled English Protestants and also bore the influence of both John Calvin and John Knox, factors that made the translation popular on both sides of the border. But it was precisely these Calvinist origins of the Geneva Bible that bothered the king and, as a considerable intellectual and linguist in his own right, he also believed that a better version could be made. Accordingly, 47 scholars in Oxford, Cambridge and London translated the New Testament from Greek and the Old Testament from Hebrew. The result was stunning.

In 1969, the philosopher Geddes MacGregor neatly characterised the King James Bible as 'the most influential version of the most influential book in the world, in what is now its most influential language'. Hundreds of wonderfully poetic phrases, such as 'they have sown the wind and they shall reap the whirlwind' (Hosea 8:7) and 'feet of clay' (Daniel 2:33), have found their way into the language and others, such as 'give up the ghost' (Job 13:19), 'salt of the earth' (Matthew 5:13) and 'a law unto themselves' (Romans 2:14), are in everyday use. Regularly read aloud to many millions of people over time, it is not surprising that many of the idioms in this version of the bible created by 'the powers that be' (Romans 13:1) should 'take root' (2 Kings 19:30).

That the king had feet of clay, he was ready to admit. In itself, James's bisexuality was not necessarily seen as a fault – rather, it was the extremes of preferment and generosity that his passions for handsome young men drove him to that caused difficulties. At court, the influence and power of Robert Carr were much resented and, when the young Borderer began to withdraw his affections for the king, those who opposed him saw an opportunity. And then fate took a hand. For convoluted reasons, Carr's wife, Frances, poisoned Sir Thomas Overbury, the Underkeeper of the Tower of London, and she later confessed to her crime. A trial followed and Carr threatened to give details of his relationship with the king in his evidence. As he stood to respond to cross-examination, two soldiers were stationed by his side, ready to muffle his words with their cloaks if he spoke of sleeping with James. In the event, he said nothing and, rather than face execution, he and his wife were sent to prison.

BIBLICAL PHRASES

The King James Bible may be the greatest legacy of the Stewarts. Its translators contributed an immense store of riches to the English language. Here is an alphabetical selection of the best-known phrases that first appeared in it:

A law unto themselves	*Left hand know what thy right hand doeth*
All these things must come to pass	*Let my people go*
All things to all men	*Let there be light*
A man after his own heart	*Milk and honey*
By their fruits ye shall know them	*Money is the root of all evil*
Eat, drink and be merry	*New wine into old bottles*
Eye for an eye	*Out of the mouths of babes*
Fell by the way side	*Put the words in her mouth*
Fell flat on his face	*Seek and ye shall find*
Fell on stony ground	*Set thine house in order*
Fight the good fight	*Suffer fools gladly*
From strength to strength	*The blind lead the blind*
Get thee behind me	*The leopard [change] his spots*
Give up the ghost	*The powers that be*
Holier than thou	*The signs of the times*
How are the mighty fallen	*The skin of my teeth*
In the twinkling of an eye	*The spirit indeed is willing, but the flesh is weak*
Land of Nod	*Turned the world upside down*

A year before this extraordinary sequence of events, James had seen and admired George Villiers, the exceptionally handsome son of a Leicestershire knight. Ever observant and alive to the king's fancies, courtiers who wished to see Carr fall from royal favour began to groom the young man. New and fashionable clothes were bought for him and he was soon made a cupbearer to the king, a position that would allow them to converse. James gave Villiers a nickname, calling him 'Steenie' after St Stephen, who was said to have the face of an angel. The king fell in love and did not trouble to hide it. Steenie was knighted, then made Earl and finally the Duke of Buckingham. His rise was dizzying. In fact, at a meeting of the Privy Council, James invoked an extraordinary biblical justification for this series of extravagant promotions. 'I, James, am neither a god nor an angel, but a man like any other. Therefore I act like a man and confess to loving those dear to me more than other men. You may be sure that I love the Earl of Buckingham more than anyone else, and more than you who are here assembled. I wish to speak in my own behalf and not to have it thought to be a defect, for Jesus Christ did the same, and therefore I cannot be blamed. Christ had John, and I have George.'

Correspondence between the two men was surprisingly frank. In 1623 the 56-year-old king wrote to his 31-year-old lover: 'God bless you, my sweet child and wife, and grant that you may ever be a comfort to your dear father and husband.'

And a letter from Buckingham to the king was very explicit as he wondered: 'Whether you loved me now . . . better than at the time which I shall never forget at Farnham where the bed's head could not be found between the master and his dog.'

James had done his dynastic duty and fathered no fewer than eight children with Anne of Denmark (although only three survived to adulthood). In fact, while the queen was giving birth to their second child, Elizabeth, in 1596, the king was conducting an ill-concealed affair with Anne Murray, the daughter of the Earl of Tullibardine. The eldest child, Prince Henry, died of tuberculosis at the age of 18 and his brother, Charles, became the heir apparent. After reigning over Scotland and then England for almost 50 years, James VI and I died in 1625. Apparently he had been much weakened by a violent bout of dysentery. By this time, the Duke of Buckingham, the beloved Steenie, was at the king's bedside. With him was the new king and, to the surprise and disappointment of many, Charles I kept his father's lover in high office until Villiers's death in 1628.

Steenie owed allegiance to the monarch of three kingdoms. Technically, Charles was Charles I, Charles I and Charles I, the first of that name to rule in England, Scotland and Ireland. At the outset of his reign, he may have regarded his northern and western kingdoms as more settled than England. James VI, I and I had dealt with the Border reivers and the Highland chiefs in summary fashion and he had also found a solution to the disruptions caused by another set of Gaelic-speaking leaders.

Ulster was the most Celtic part of Ireland. The native population were monoglot Gaels and the English invasions had scarcely touched the north of the island. Its name derives from *Ulaidhs Tir*, the land of the Ulaidh, an early Irish kindred who appeared on the maps of Ptolemy made in the 2nd century AD. Much of Ulster later came under the control of the Ui Neill, whose chiefs became the O'Neill earls, and, towards the end of the 16th century, they led resistance to the Elizabethan colonisation. In the Nine Years War between 1594 and 1603, Hugh O'Neill was at the head of a confederacy of northern Gaelic lords but he was eventually forced to surrender. Able to negotiate good terms under the Treaty of Mellifont, he and others, such as Hugh O'Donnell, kept their lands.

At the same time, James VI, I and I's police action against the Border reivers was under way. It gradually became clear to the king of Scotland and Ireland and his council that Ulster might help solve a problem in the Borders and deported Borderers might help solve a problem in Ulster. When Hugh O'Neill and the other native chieftains left Ireland in what became known as the Flight of the Earls to seek Spanish Catholic support for another rebellion, plans for a radical redistribution of land were made. Since 1606, substantial numbers of Presbyterian Scots had settled in the eastern counties of Antrim and Down but James's Lord Deputy in Ireland, Arthur Chichester, began to seize the lands of the departed earls across six more northern counties. Donegal, Coleraine, Fermanagh, Tyrone, Cavan and Armagh were all to be planted with Protestant settlers.

From 1609, a group of principal landowners known as 'the Undertakers' were each granted 3,000 acres on condition that they let farms to English-speaking Protestant tenants. They were to build fortified settlements of 'castle and bawn', the latter a defended courtyard. Irish families were driven to poor land and servile roles around the new plantations. Capital was raised from the livery companies and guilds of the City of London and, when land was granted to them on the western banks of the River Foyle, the town that grew up was called Londonderry. The process was rapid. A survey of 1622 counted 6,402 British adult males in the plantations in the six counties and of these 3,100 were English and 3,700 were Scots. In Antrim and Down, there were a further 4,000 Scotsmen who had settled in the so-called private plantations. Including families, this suggests a very substantial planter population of between 40,000 and 50,000. By the 1630s, this has risen very quickly to about 80,000. The plantation of Ulster was by no means uncontested but it immediately flourished.

A dialect of Scots known as *Ullans* or 'Ulster Scots', still survives and the surnames of many remember Lowland Scottish origins. Most came from the Scottish Borders, Galloway and Ayrshire and names like Armstrong, Bell, Irving, Hume, Murray, Kerr and Burns are common across the province and many were brought by men who rustled cattle on either side of the Cheviots. In County Fermanagh, out of the top five surnames, three are Armstrong, Elliott and Johnston. James VI's Border Commission promoted emigration as a welcome alternative to Jethart Justice and, not surprisingly, many accepted.

SCOTCH IRISH PRESIDENTS

This is a term used mainly in the United States and it means Ulster Scots, a reference to the migrants sent by James VI and I during the settlements known as 'the plantations'. Some of these kept on migrating and, in the USA, a significant Scotch Irish identity built up. No fewer than 13 presidents claimed descent from the Scots who settled in Ulster. From 1829 to 1921, the White House was occupied for only 25 years by men who were not Scotch Irish. The first Scotch Irish president was Andrew Jackson, who was said to be 'as tough as old hickory' – and 'Old Hickory' became his nickname. He was followed by James Polk, James Buchanan, Andrew Johnson, the great Civil War general, Ulysses S. Grant, Chester Arthur, Grover Cleveland, who served two non-consecutive terms, Benjamin Harrison, William McKinley, Theodore Roosevelt, Woodrow Wilson, Richard Nixon and Jimmy Carter. He was the last to claim a Scotch Irish lineage. Bill Clinton was born William Jefferson Blythe and he has family links with the Scottish Borders through the Blythe lineage.

While his father had used Protestantism to dilute and defuse Catholicism in the north of Ireland, Charles I appeared to do the opposite in Scotland. Soon after his coronation as King of England, he promulgated the Act of Revocation which was designed to repossess all of the Church lands granted to the nobility after the Reformation. This immediately made enemies out of a group that would have been ready to support the new king. He also began to introduce religious practices which aroused serious fears of a return to

Rome and popery and the sort of conformity with the Church of England that James VI and I was anxious to see. But his son was far less diplomatic and eventually fatally dictatorial.

Charles I of England and Ireland waited eight years before he was crowned king of Scotland. After many postponements, the new king came north with a vast retinue of 3,000 which included a detachment of 350 fully armed soldiers, his entire household and 150 English noblemen and their servants. It was reported that 200 carts pulled by 1,000 horses were needed for this baggage as one of the most extravagant royal tours ever undertaken rumbled into Edinburgh. Followed by all that grandeur and wealth, the last thing Charles looked like was a Scottish king. Because Scone Abbey, the time-honoured locus for coronations, had been destroyed by bands of reformers in the 1560s and 1570s, it was decided that the ceremony would be held in the Chapel Royal of Holyrood Abbey. It too had been badly damaged but the nave and its vaulted roof were intact and much of the old fabric was restored in the months before the royal procession reached Edinburgh.

THE BLESSING OF BURNTISLAND

On 10 July 1633, a storm blew over the Firth of Forth and sank a treasure ship. Or at least that is the belief of some local marine archaeologists. King Charles I was touring Scotland (long) after his coronation and his domestic servants loaded his silver plate and other valuables on to a wooden ferry known as the Blessing of Burntisland, *bound for Leith. It may also have carried treasure valued at £100,000, equivalent to a sixth of the entire Scottish exchequer at the time. In 1998 Mr J. Longton of Burntisland located what he believed to be a wreck on the seabed about a mile south-west of the entrance to the harbour, in a mooring area known as Burntisland Roads. Using dowsing techniques and a pendulum, he was convinced that there was something on the bed of the firth but was met with the usual scepticism. Then a naval vessel,* HMS Roebuck, *also reported the discovery of an anomaly in the exactly the same location. The site is now protected and awaits investigation.*

Portraits of Charles by the great Flemish painter, Anthony van Dyck, were hung along the Royal Mile and it was said that wine flowed freely for the watching crowds as the coronation procession made its stately way downhill from the gates of Edinburgh Castle to Holyrood. And, as the ceremony began, it became clear that a political statement was being made. Having appointed William Laud as Archbishop of Canterbury, a zealous conservative determined to drive back the tide of Puritanism in England, and not being bound to tradition at Scone, the king had decided that his crowning would not lack colour. Bishops dressed in gorgeously decorated copes had processed down the High Street and the Canongate and, when they entered the Chapel Royal, there was a great deal of kneeling before the altar. To many Presbyterian Scots who lined the streets and to those of power and influence who saw the ceremony, it must have seemed that a return to what amounted to Catholicism was imminent. The day before, Charles's French queen, Henrietta Maria, had had a Mass said for her at Holyrood. At best, the coronation was enormously insensitive and, at worst, it was a statement of intent. By being crowned in Edinburgh according to the Anglican rite, Charles appeared to be promoting the unification of the Church of England with the Church in Scotland. What happened next left no one in any doubt.

On Sunday 23 July 1637, at St Giles, a stool flew through the air. It was thrown at the head of James Hannay, the Dean of Edinburgh, as he began to read from the new *Book of Common Prayer*. It had been largely the work of Archbishop Laud, despite the fact that he had no authority in Scotland and no minister had been consulted in its compilation. The high Anglican tone in a deeply Presbyterian nation sparked immediate trouble. Jenny Geddes was a street stallholder with a Sunday sideline as a 'waiting woman', someone who would arrive early at a service to keep a place at the front for whoever paid them. As she hurled her stool at Hannay, Jenny was reported to have roared at him, 'De'il gie ye colic, the wame of ye, fause theif; daur ye say mass in my lug!' The stool led to a riot, the congregation walked out, the Edinburgh mob organised itself and the first steps were taken down a fatal path that would lead to war between the king and many of the people of his three kingdoms.

The reality was that the riot at St Giles was planned and orchestrated. Two years before Dean Hannay ducked, it had been announced that the *Book of Common Prayer* was being compiled and it would be introduced in Scotland despite the objections of many influential people. But events in Edinburgh's High Street almost ran out of control. When David Lindsay, the Bishop of Edinburgh, climbed into the pulpit to quieten the women, he was shouted down as a 'Wolf', 'Beastly belly-god', 'the spawn of the Devil' and 'a pest on God's Kirk' and bibles were thrown at him. The Provost of Edinburgh summoned his constables and they cleared the women out of the kirk. But the disruption continued as they hammered on the doors and threw stones at the windows.

When the service ended and the nervous congregation tried to leave, the Bishop of Edinburgh was jostled but managed to get into his coach and, despite a shower of stones, the driver was able to control the spooking horses and escape. The Provost of Edinburgh was not so fortunate. He too was stoned and only his constables firing over the heads of the crowds prevented his serious injury or perhaps even his death. But he and his bailies were besieged in the city chambers by the baying crowd and, remarkably, perhaps even incredibly, the Lord Advocate began to negotiate with its leaders. In what smacks of prior agreement or at least premeditation, he suggested that the rioters set up a committee to treat with the Privy Council. Riots broke out all over Lowland Scotland as what became known as 'Laud's Liturgy' was read from pulpits and the royal councillors had little option but to suspend its use in kirks. The atmosphere was electric and a moderate minister, Robert Bailie, wrote, 'The whole people think Popery is at the doors. I think our people are possessed with a bloody devil . . . I think I may be killed and my house burnt over my head.'

By October, Scotland had become dangerously unstable and ideas that amounted to rebellion flickered through the febrile air. In December, the Lord Advocate's proposed committee had, in effect, become the government of the nation, having staged a coup d'état. What were known as the Five Tables were set up. These consisted of noblemen, burgesses, ministers, lairds and an executive committee. It was essentially a parliament, a government brought into being by popular will without the king at its head. When news reached London, Charles I found it difficult to comprehend what had happened and, instead of attempting to negotiate, he issued a proclamation demanding obedience. Even more forcefully than his father, he believed in the divine right of kings to rule; accordingly, they were accountable only to God, not some Edinburgh rabble. This imperious attitude had the effect of concentrating the dissenting minds and, in February 1638, the Five Tables met at Greyfriars Kirk in Edinburgh and they promulgated a document that turned Scotland's history in a singular direction. What became known as the 'National Covenant' was signed.

Drawn up by two leading intellectuals, Alexander Henderson, a minister, and Archibald Johnston of Warriston, an Edinburgh lawyer, this document was revolutionary. Despite its protestations of loyalty to Charles I, it made his kingship conditional on his maintenance of Presbyterianism in Scotland. If he did not fulfil this duty, then he could be legitimately removed. In essence the National Covenant was based on earlier documents, such as the godly band of the Lord of the Congregation and the 1581 Confession of Faith signed by James VI, but its insistence on 'the true worship of God' over all other considerations was powerful and plainly stated. All innovations since 1580, such as the introduction of bishops, were rejected and to sign the Covenant was not rebellion but a simple acknowledgement that Christ was the head of the Church in Scotland. That meant that the king could not impose anything or attempt to control the kirk.

Copies of the National Covenant were sent all over Scotland for signature, and by May 1638 only the Highlands and the north-east had not come over to the Covenanting cause. Scotland was, according to the terms and sentiments of this famous document, different. Like the Israelites of scripture, the Scots were a covenanted people for there now existed a covenant between them and their God. And what may have been left unstated in the seemingly endless multi-clause sentences, but was nonetheless very clear, was an absolute belief that his Scottish subjects did not accept Charles's I's claim to rule by divine right.

Behind the locked doors of Glasgow Cathedral in December 1638, the first General Assembly of the Church of Scotland to meet for 20 years was convened. Despite the fact that the Marquis of Hamilton had persuaded King Charles to give formal permission, the ministers, kirk elders, lairds, noblemen and burgesses who crowded into the nave made sweeping changes. In the presence of the King's Commissioner, they summarily banned Laud's Liturgy and the Courts of High Commission, and there were henceforth to be no bishops in the Kirk. They were deposed and excommunicated. All of this was done in the name of 'Christ's Crown and Covenant', and no consideration was given to the wishes of the king. The two sides were now on a collision course.

Copies of the National Covenant had been sent abroad so that those Scotsmen who were fighting as mercenaries could sign it. Described by a contemporary as 'the auld, wee, crooked soldier', General Alexander Leslie had organised a signing by a regiment of Scots under his command in Germany. News came with the Covenant, and it seemed to Leslie that war was coming in Scotland. In late 1638, ships carrying companies of battle-hardened Scottish soldiers docked at Leith with the auld, wee, crooked soldier on board. Immediately Leslie began to organise.

Charles I had not called a parliament to Westminster for 11 years and, even though he needed it to vote him funds to make war on the Scottish rebels, he dared not issue a summons to the Commons and the Lords. Instead, his captains were forced to muster at York a poorly trained and poorly equipped force of about 20,000 men to march north. When they reached Berwick, scouts reported that General Leslie had led an army of only 12,000 but had fortified Duns Law, just to the north of the town, about 15 miles west of Berwick.

Robert Baillie was Principal of Glasgow University and he had enlisted in the Army of the Covenant as a chaplain. Clearly a thoughtful, erudite man, Baillie left a fascinating, unique description of the camp on Duns Law as well as a powerful sense of the soldiers of the Covenant, of a godly commonwealth that had gone to war to defend its right to seek salvation by its own means and to defeat a king who believed with equal fervour that his right to rule was given by God and that he was responsible only to God.

It would have done you good to cast your eyes across our brave and rich hill, as oft I did, with great contentment and joy. I furnished to half a dozen good fellows muskets and pikes, and to my boy a broadsword. I carried myself, as the fashion was, a broadsword, and a couple of Dutch pistols at my saddle; but I promise, for the offence of no man, except a robber by the way; for it was our part alone to pray and preach for the encouragement of our countrymen, which I did to my power most cheerfully. Our hill was garnished on the top, towards the south and east, with our mounted cannon, well near to the number of forty, great and small. Our regiments lay on the side of the hill, almost round about: the place is not a mile in circle – a pretty round rising in a declivity, without steepness, to the height of a bowshot; on the top somewhat plain; about a quarter of a mile in length, and as much in breadth, as I remember, capable of tents for 40,000 men. The colonels lay in canvas lodges, high and wide; their captains about them in lesser ones; the soldiers all about in huts of timber, covered with divot or straw. Our colonels were for the most part noblemen . . . our captains for the most part barons or gentlemen of good note; our lieutenants almost all soldiers who had served overseas in good charges. Every company had, flying at the captain's tent door, a brave new colour stamped with the Scottish arms, and this motto, FOR CHRIST'S CROWN AND COVENANT in golden letters. Our general had a brave royal tent but it was not set up; his constant guard was some hundreds of our lawyers, musketeers, under Durie and Hope's command, all the way standing in good arms, with cocked matches, before his gate, well apparelled. He [Alexander Leslie] lay at the foot of the hill in the castle [Duns Castle] . . . Our soldiers were all lusty and full of courage, the most of them stout young ploughmen; great cheerfulness in the face of all . . . Had you lent your ear in the morning, or especially in the evening, and heard in the tents the sound of some singing psalms, some praying and some reading scripture, you would have been refreshed: true, there was swearing and cursing, and brawling, in some quarters, whereat we were grieved; but we hoped, if our camp had been a little settled, to have gotten some way for these misorders; for all of any fashion did regret, and all did promise to contribute their best endeavours for helping all abuses. For myself, I never found my mind in better temper than in all that time I came from home, till my head was again homeward; for I was as a man that had taken my leave from the world, and was resolved to die in that service without return. I found the favour of God shining upon me, and a sweet, meek, humble, yet strong and vehement spirit leading me all along; but I was no sooner in my way westward, after the conclusion of peace, than my old security returned.

Surrounded by regiments of lawyers, by psalm-singing and scripture-reading ploughmen ready to fight and die for their beliefs – and by soldiers who swore! – the righteous but apparently reasonable force of Baillie's faith in the Covenant is very striking. He and the men on Duns Law were engaged in holy war but they were also led by a very experienced and canny professional soldier. Alexander Leslie had been promoted by King Gustavus Adolphus of Sweden to the rank of Field Marshal in the Thirty Years War that raged across northern Europe. He had spread his small band of veterans across the whole army and, as Baillie noted, each company was stiffened not only by a lieutenant or ensign but also two sergeants who had fought in Germany. By fortifying Duns Law, a singular hill with a commanding view south over the lower Tweed Basin, Leslie had stalled Charles I's advance into Scotland and forced a stand-off. In a novel tactic, one probably learned during his years as a mercenary general anxious to keep his men alive, Leslie invited Royalist officers to dinner in Duns Castle before suggesting that they inspect his well-organised army and the fortifications on the hill behind. The leaders of Charles I's forces wisely concluded that they should return to the safety of Berwick and, instead of battle, there was negotiation.

In what is known as 'the Pacification of Berwick', Archibald Johnston of Warriston spoke on behalf of the Covenanters. On 18 June 1639, he agreed what was essentially a ceasefire. Johnston conceded that the radical decisions of the General Assembly held in Glasgow Cathedral should be set aside but that another Assembly and a Parliament should convene in Edinburgh a year later. The 1640 Parliament turned out to be even more radical, bringing into being what was essentially a new set of constitutional arrangements. The Five Tables were replaced by a Committee of Estates controlled by the nobility, the lairds and the burgesses but with no place for ministers. Parliament did not recognise the king's right to prorogue it and, by the Triennial Act, it had the right to meet every three years whether the king summoned it or not. And the Scottish Parliament also asserted its right to vet membership of the Privy Council and the judiciary. This was a model soon to be adopted at Westminster.

THE AULD, WEE, CROOKED SOLDIER

Such was the penchant for nicknames amongst soldiers that Alexander Leslie, created the Earl of Leven by Charles I, was unable ever to shake off his. But it appears to have been bestowed with affection, and also in recognition of a long life at the sharp end of many campaigns. A Field Marshal in the armies of King Gustavus Adolphus of Sweden and Lord General of the Army of Both Kingdoms (England and Scotland) during the Wars of the Covenant, Leslie had a meteoric rise from unlikely beginnings. The bastard son of a captain of Blair Castle in Perthshire whose mother merited a cursory description as 'a wench of Rannoch', he made himself the most successful mercenary soldier of his generation and found himself at the centre of power in the mid 17th century. He is probably remembered by this old nursery rhyme:

> *There was a crooked man and he walked a crooked mile,*
> *He found a crooked sixpence upon a crooked stile.*
> *He bought a crooked cat, which caught a crooked mouse.*
> *And they all lived together in a little crooked house.*

After the agreement made by Johnston at Berwick had bought some time, Alexander Leslie took the opportunity to muster what amounted to the first professional army to campaign in Britain since the time of the Roman legions. On his departure from Sweden, he had negotiated with the *Riksråd* or State

Council to have 300 Scottish officers decommissioned from the Swedish army as well as more than a thousand hardened soldiers. As compensation for arrears of pay, the Swedes supplied the departing Scots with batteries of cannon and many muskets. Not only was the Army of the Covenant well led, it was well trained and well equipped. And the forces of Charles I, based on the medieval levy, would be no match for the Scots.

At the end of August 1640, Leslie led his men across the Tweed into England and they quickly reached the strategically vital crossing of the River Tyne at Newburn. With the exception of the bridge at Newcastle, which was in Royalist hands, it was the lowest crossing point before the sea and there was a bridge as well as a ford. What made Newburn strategically vital was the coal trade – the collier ships that made their way from the staithes (loading jetties) on the Tyne down the North Sea coast to supply London with fuel. And Leslie knew that if he could get his army across at Newburn and attack the walled city of Newcastle from the south, he would gain a great advantage.

Charles I's commanders knew that too but they simply did not have sufficient forces to counter Leslie's advance. With only 3,500 men, the Royalist army was vastly outnumbered by the 20,000 Scots who were massing on the opposite bank of the river. Leslie's gunners set up their Swedish artillery on the higher ground north of the Tyne and in the tower of the church of St Michael and, after a barrage rained down shot on the men led by Lord Conway, the Scots crossed the ford and smashed through the earthwork defences. The Royalist soldiers scattered. The Army of the Covenant quickly swung eastwards along the southern bank of the river to Gateshead, opposite Newcastle. As the cannon were once more deployed, the city wisely surrendered.

Newburn was the first action in what used to be miscalled the English Civil War. In reality, the conflict between Charles I and his subjects caught fire in all of his three kingdoms. The defeat on the Tyne would eventually force the king to recall the English Parliament and it sat for 20 years during an extraordinary period of history when a Scottish general would win a crucial battle on Marston Moor to turn the course of the war, a king would be executed and a British republic founded.

One of Leslie's most effective commanders, a soldier who was with him at Duns Law and Newburn, was also a man who embodied an uneasiness felt by many at the pace and scale of change that was overtaking Scottish and British society as Parliaments and Assemblies asserted themselves over kings. James Graham, who would become Marquis of Montrose, was very well educated, a former 12-year-old student at Glasgow University who read extensively through the classics and who later graduated from St Andrews University. A signatory of the National Covenant, he proposed that the army should wear blue bonnet ribbons and blue sashes, the colour of militant Protestantism ever since. In 1639, Montrose was despatched with a small force to the north-east, the only part of Lowland Scotland not to come over to the Covenanter cause, and he captured the Royalist Marquis of Huntly and took the city of Aberdeen.

After the signing of the Pacification of Berwick, the young soldier was part of a delegation who visited Charles I. He may have been impressed. Montrose was vehemently opposed to bishops in the Kirk but he also believed in the secular power of royalty. Despite misgivings, disagreements with the aggressively Presbyterian Clan Campbell and some abortive attempts at reconciliation with an obdurate king, Montrose fought with distinction as his men forced the crossing of the Tyne at Newburn. But, in May 1641, he was summoned before the Committee of Estates, charged with plotting in favour of Charles I and imprisoned in Edinburgh Castle.

The Covenanter stranglehold on the coal trade and the need for money of Charles I forced him to come north to Edinburgh to seek a settlement. Between August and November 1641, he agreed to virtually all of the radical measures passed by the Parliament the year before. The Presbyterian Kirk, bishops having been emphatically rejected, was recognised and the Triennial Act approved. In addition, Charles was forced to pay for the maintenance of Leslie's army at Newcastle, a tremendous burden, and a rare concession to him was that Royalist supporters in Scotland, men such as Montrose, should be released from custody.

In order to honour the agreement to pay the Scots army, the king called what became known as 'the Long Parliament'. But the price of the funds requested from Commons and Lords at Westminster turned out to be too high as the dominant Puritan faction insisted on measures, some of them echoing those of the Edinburgh Parliament, which would have removed much of Charles's authority. In early January 1642, the king attempted to have five members of the House of Commons arrested so that they could be charged with treason. He failed and, fearing for the safety of his family, left London. After touring the country to marshal support, Charles I had the royal standard raised at Nottingham in what was effectively a declaration of war on the English Parliament.

For a year, the fortunes of war favoured neither side in England. Battles were indecisive or won and lost in equal measure. But, when it was believed that the Royalist armies would be reinforced by regiments of Irish Catholic troops, the Parliamentary party decided to seek the aid of the Scots and commissioners were sent north to Edinburgh. Within only ten days, they had agreed to an extraordinary document. The Solemn League and Covenant pledged Leslie's crack Covenanter troops to the Parliamentary cause in return for creating 'the firm peace and union' of England and Scotland. This involved the complete extirpation of popery and not only the maintenance of Scottish Presbyterianism but also its adoption in England and Ireland. The Calvinist Church of Scotland was to become the Calvinist Church of Great Britain and Ireland. And there would be no bishops in the English Kirk either. So desperate were the English commissioners for the help of the tough Scots mercenaries that they agreed.

In January 1644, the 20,000-strong Army of the Covenant crossed into England once more and began operations around the Royalist city of York. Prince Rupert of the Rhine, the famously dashing nephew of the king who had also fought in Germany during the Thirty Years War, was in command of the Royalist forces. According to a typically ambiguous and vague dispatch from Charles I, the prince believed that he had been ordered to engage the Parliamentary forces in pitched battle. At Marston Moor, General Leslie deployed what had become the Army of Both Kingdoms, and since the Scots were the largest contingent, he had been appointed commander-in-chief. It was a wise decision. Always observant and opportunistic, Leslie (by now ennobled as the Earl of Leven) kept his men in readiness throughout the July day on which the armies met. He had moved quickly to occupy Marston Hill. Only 100 feet high, it nevertheless gave the old general the precious ability to watch as his enemy moved and deployed over the flat Vale of York below.

By the time the York garrison had arrived to reinforce Prince Rupert, it was evening before the Royalist army had finally drawn up in battle order. The sky darkened and a series of sharp rain showers blew over the moor. And, when the Royalist commanders heard psalms being sung in the Covenanter ranks, it may be that they believed an attack to be very unlikely and, in any case, it was too late in the day. Leslie thought otherwise. From Marston Hill he could see Prince Rupert's troops breaking ranks to cook some supper and, as a summer thunderstorm boomed over the battlefield, he ordered an all-out attack. It was about 7.30 p.m. in the evening. Oliver Cromwell led a division of cavalry that distinguished itself in what became a disordered melee, thought to be the most extensive, sprawling battle ever fought on English soil. But in the centre of the Army of Both Kingdoms were 19 regiments of Covenanter infantry and they ground out a signal victory for the Parliament.

Defeat at Marston Moor meant that Charles I had lost the support of the largely Royalist north of England. Leslie led the Covenanters to besiege Newcastle (the city having once more fallen into Royalist hands) and Cromwell began to exert increasing influence over the Parliamentarians. But, for Charles I, there was more encouraging news from Scotland. Irish troops did not take part in the war in England. Instead, they made landfall in Scotland where they were led by the charismatic and tactically brilliant James Graham, Marquis of Montrose. By 1644, Graham had changed sides and been appointed Lord Lieutenant by the king.

ROUNDHEADS AND CAVALIERS

When Charles I left London and set up his headquarters at Christ Church, Oxford, his soldiers soon acquired the nickname of Cavaliers. It came from the Spanish word, caballero, *meaning a 'knight' or 'horseman'. The association was clear. All Cavaliers supported a Spanish-style absolute monarchy and quasi-Catholic religious practices. By contrast, Roundheads wore their hair close cropped like the Puritans and the association was equally clear. Their leaders were dominated by militant Puritans. In fact, neither stereotype was accurate. All social classes and all regions of England were divided although it was true to say that very few Catholics were Roundheads and very few Puritans were Cavaliers. But Oliver Cromwell did wear his hair long.*

Alasdair Mac Colla Chiotaich Mac Domhnuill is better known as Alasdair MacColla but his formal name says something about his origins. Born on Colonsay, the son of Colla, the Left-handed MacDonald, he was a warrior, a MacDonald, a Catholic and an implacable foe of Clan Campbell. Archibald Campbell, Earl of Argyll, had signed the National Covenant and he used more recent differences to augment the traditional enmity between his people and Catholic Clan Donald. Having captured Colla, Alasdair's father, better known as *Colkitto*, Earl Archibald drove MacColla to flee to Ulster. There, he joined the Irish MacDonalds in attacks on the planter settlements of Antrim and Down. In 1644, his prowess earned him the leadership of a force of 1,500 to 2,000 men, most of them experienced soldiers or mercenaries, to be sent to Scotland to aid the Royalist cause – and to seek vengeance on Clan Campbell in the process. At Blair Atholl, Alasdair MacColla met the Marquis of Montrose and together they embarked on a brilliant campaign.

The generals immediately resolved to march on Perth and, at Tippermuir, four miles west of the city, they met a much larger army of Covenanters under the command of Lord Elcho. Tactics were simple. Led by Highlanders and Irishmen, it was the first time the ferocious Celtic charge was seen in modern times. As was often the case, few were killed on impact. It was the ability of charging clansmen to turn an army and force it to flee in terror that brought casualties and perhaps as many as 2,000 were hacked down as they ran. Perth had been taken for the king and the first in a dramatic sequence of Royalist victories won. Montrose wanted to march south and draw Leslie's Covenanters north to protect the Lowland communities where most of their families lived. But MacColla would have none of it. He thirsted for Campbell blood.

In September 1644, the Highlander rode into the west to raise the Catholic clans. Two months later, he emerged with companies of men from Glengarry, Sleat, Glencoe, Keppoch, Clan Ranald, Camerons and the Stewarts of Appin. Even though winter was coming on, MacColla insisted that the combined army moved south-west though the passes to the country of the Campbells and the Earl's castle at Inverary.

Winter was deepening as bitter winds whipped across the mountains and heavy snowfalls made progress slow. In Inverary Castle, Archibald Campbell sat snug by his roaring fire, secure in the certain knowledge that no army could march or campaign in such weather. He had heard the news from Tippermuir but surely nothing would happen until the spring came. Only ten miles from where Campbell sat, at the head of Glen Shira, shepherds saw something that hollowed their bellies with fear. Over the plateau around the shores of Loch Sron Mor, through the deep snows, an army was marching towards them. The thousands of men, strung out in a long line, each following the steps of the man in front, were MacDonalds, Irish warriors and Stewarts and riding shaggy garron ponies were Montrose, MacColla and their captains. At the foot of Glen Shira, they could see the chill, grey waters of Loch Fyne. The town and castle of Inverary were less than a mile further to the south.

By the time Earl Archibald had been given the breathless news that an army was less than an hour from his walls, he had no time to organise defences. Instead, he bundled his family and what valuables they could quickly grab into a birlinn and, as the oarsmen pulled out into the loch, they probably saw Montrose and the MacDonalds marching along the shore road. Campbell knew what would happen next and, as the smoke billowed above Inverary, many died in an appalling massacre. The Principal of Glasgow University, Robert Baillie, had become a historian of the Wars of the Covenant and he was astonished at what happened: 'The world believed that Argyll could be maintained against the greatest army, as a country inaccessible, but we see that there is no strength or refuge against the Lord.'

Montrose was determined to maintain momentum. On 8 January, he led his men up the Great Glen towards Inverness but, at the southern end of Loch Ness, Iain Lom, the great MacDonald bard, was waiting with bad news. Two Covenanter armies had moved to block any retreat. At Inverness the Earl of Seaforth, Chief of the MacKenzies, has mustered a substantial force and, at the south-western end of the Great Glen, there was a Campbell army reinforced by 1,000 Lowlanders. More than that, they were led by Sir Duncan Campbell of Auchinbreck, an experienced, resourceful soldier. Knowing that Seaforth was not an enthusiastic Covenanter and that his force was the smaller, it made sense to continue north-eastwards. But instead, MacColla and Montrose decided to turn south to attack the Campbells. Hatred would spur an army of MacDonalds into the charge.

Sir Duncan had pitched camp by Inverlochy Castle, where there is open countryside and where his superior numbers would tell. He had mustered perhaps twice as many men as the Royalists. And Campbell knew which way the enemy would come. There was only one road down the Great Glen. Montrose knew that too and his intelligence appears to have been reliable, telling him where the Covenanters had camped, where they waited. And he knew that, in open field, the longer battle line of a larger force could quickly outflank his men, roll them up and slaughter them and vengeance for Inverary would surely follow. Another way down the glen had to be found.

This was Cameron country and they knew of a high pass to the south of the Great Glen that ran parallel. The Allt na Larach threaded its way between two mountains, Carn Dearg and Carn Leac, but it could only be used in good weather and, since it climbed to 2,000 feet, it could not be traversed in the winter. Men would disappear into snowdrifts, fall into unseen crevasses or simply die of cold and exhaustion, their legs drained and leaden, their plaids frozen stiff. It was impossible, the Cameron scouts were adamant.

Somehow Montrose and MacColla persuaded their men to march into the winter mountains. It was a huge risk. Blizzards could swirl at any moment, blinding men, disorienting them, cutting them off from their comrades, but, despite what they all knew, the men began to climb. Using sticks to probe the drifts, men took turns in the vanguard, carving out a safe path as the line of soldiers snaked up into the high pass. As darkness fell, they kept moving. Perhaps there was a moon reflecting a blue light off the snow. But, towards dawn, the men in the van, probably Camerons, passed the word back down the line that the ground was beginning to fall away. Soon they could make easier progress down a path from the head of Glen Roy and then along the banks of the River Spean. Montrose and MacColla had taken a tremendous risk but, in only 36 hours, they found themselves close to Inverlochy entirely undetected.

And then it almost all went wrong. Parts of the Royalist army made contact with the Campbells and there was skirmishing. But Sir Duncan Campbell was unperturbed. Probably a party of Camerons. Nothing to be concerned about. His scouts were still looking to the north-east, to the road down the Great Glen and there was no sign of Montrose and MacColla's men. In fact, the two generals were waiting until all of their men could muster and throughout 1 February, they lay concealed, recovering from the exhausting night march through the mountains.

When dawn broke on 2 February 1645, the Campbell captains were aston-ished to see the lines of the Royalist army drawn up opposite their flank and not emerging from the road down the Great Glen. MacColla's Irish warriors would attack the Lowland contingents, men unused to the ferocity of the Highland charge, and Montrose would engage with the Campbells with his MacDonald regiments at his back. It was less a battle fought between an army of the Covenant and supporters of Charles I than a vicious clan battle. The Lowlanders ran, the Campbells gave ground and, once again, there was greater slaughter in the flight than in the fighting. Many drowned in Loch Linnhe, Sir Duncan fell and perhaps 1,500 died.

Inverlochy badly damaged the power of Clan Campbell for a generation and it spurred on Montrose and his men to four more brilliant victories. But the old Highland enmities still simmered. By early September 1645, Alasdair MacColla, almost all of his clansmen and half the force of Irish warriors decided to turn west again and mount another raid on Campbell territory. With fewer than a thousand men, Montrose marched south to appeal for support from Borders Royalists. Only a handful responded but he made camp at Philiphaugh, a mile to the west of Selkirk. The morning of 13 September was misty and Montrose appears to have been entirely unaware that a large Covenanter army led by Sir David Leslie was fast closing in on his position by the Ettrick. The ensuing battle was scarcely a contest as Montrose's men were overwhelmed by a force ten times larger. What sealed defeat for the Royalists was the flanking manoeuvre of Leslie's cavalry along the Hartwood Burn and around the back of Howden Hill. 'Jesus and no quarter!' was the baleful, bloodlusting cry and, even though 100 Irishmen surrendered, they were killed at the insistence of the ministers, as were 300 camp followers, most of them women and children. The nearby place name of Slain Men's Lea remembers the slaughter. Montrose cut his way out of the melee and, with 30 men, fled into the Border hills and eventually into exile.

Following Parliamentary victories in 1645 at Naseby and Langport in the west of England, Charles I was, at last, forced to accept defeat. But, rather than negotiate with Oliver Cromwell and his fellow generals, the king rode to Newark near Nottingham in May 1646. There, the Army of the Covenant had built a fortress astride the Great North Road to house their headquarters and, at its gates, it became clear that Charles I wished to surrender. Surprised but quickly realising what a great prize had fallen into their hands, the Scots quickly took the king north to Newcastle. Negotiations began but Charles obstinately refused to sign the National Covenant and, as peace proposals were put forward by the Scots and English commissioners, he rejected them out of hand. Perhaps he hoped to set his enemies at each other's throats. But, by the end of 1646, the Scots had seen enough of their king, and their mercenary instincts prompted a resolution. In return for payment of arrears of pay, they would, in effect, sell Charles to the English. On 30 January 1647, £100,000 was handed over and, as the Army of the Covenant marched north out of the Newcastle, a further £100,000 was paid. Charles was left in the hands of English Presbyterian moderates but, in June 1647, he was kidnapped by a group of soldiers from the New Model Army. The creation of Cromwell and Thomas Fairfax, the men known as the Ironsides had become the focus and fount of political power in England.

Not everyone in Scotland approved of the sale of the king to the English and, in late 1647, John Maitland, the Earl of Lauderdale, made the long journey to visit Charles in Carisbrooke Castle on the Isle of Wight. In return for military support from Scotland, the king agreed that he would revive the central condition of the Solemn League and Covenant and impose Presbyterianism in England, for a trial period of three years. What was known as the 'Treaty of Engagement' was signed in December 1647. It divided opinion. Radicals refused to believe that Charles was sincere but noblemen like Lauderdale were enthusiastic. They were called the Engagers.

Their ascendancy was short-lived. Led by the Duke of Hamilton, the Engagers mustered an army of at least 11,000 to march south and support the king's cause. A rash of Royalist rebellions had broken out all over England in what used to be called the Second Civil War and Hamilton and his captains aimed to take advantage. But the refusal of the Kirk party in Scotland to support the Engagers meant that Sir David Leslie and thousands of experienced officers and men had declined to serve. They might have matched the discipline of the New Model Army but, when Cromwell attacked the Scots at Preston, around 2,000 were killed and 9,000 taken prisoner. The brief leadership of the Engagers was at an end but it was to be followed by a remarkable episode.

The Whigs entered history, in heavy disguise. Only weeks after news of the heavy defeat at Preston had filtered north, the Whiggamores marched on Edinburgh. A Scots word, *whigg* means 'whey' or 'sour milk' and it was supped by the poor but righteous. The Whiggamores originated in the radical south-west of Scotland. Covenanting had set down powerful roots in the Galloway Hills and the Solway towns. With the support of Cromwell and Archibald Campbell, Marquis of Argyll, and led by Alexander, Earl of Eglinton, a poorly armed, psalm-singing band of about 2,000 men descended on Edinburgh and, in what amounted to a coup d'état, their leaders dismissed the Committee of Estates and began a godly purge of government in Scotland. Parliament was convened in January 1649 and quickly voted through The Act of Classes. This removed all Engagers and Royalists from any public office and was rigorously applied in the burghs and the ranks of the army.

This government of the saints began a programme of social engineering. Kirk sessions were to take direct responsibility for poor relief as well as the morals of their congregations. And, for a brief moment, the nobility could be called out in the Kirk for the sin of adultery. The power to choose a new minister was returned to the Kirk sessions and the army was repeatedly purged. Radical they may have been but the Whigs were profoundly shocked at the events of 30 January 1649, in London. 'Charles Stuart, that Man of Blood' stepped through the middle window of the Banqueting House in

Whitehall and on to a scaffold. Wearing a plain white shirt, he conducted himself with great dignity. When his head rolled over the boards and was picked up by the hair by the masked executioner, Charles I immediately became a martyr.

In Scotland, the Whigs reacted with horror. They had supported a constitutional monarchy and quickly moved to contact the heir apparent, the man who would become Charles II. He was offered not only the crown of Scotland but also those of England and Ireland. But there were conditions. The government of the saints insisted that Charles sign the National Covenant and support the imposition of Presbyterianism in England, Wales and Ireland. Having sent Montrose back to Scotland to make war on the Covenanters, he delayed negotiations, waiting to hear if his famous general could repeat the stunning successes of five years before. But it was not to be. Montrose's small, badly equipped army had failed to attract recruits from the northern mainland clans. In fact, the Munros and Rosses joined a Covenanter cavalry force led by Archibald Strachan and, when they attacked Montrose at Carbisdale in Easter Ross, they routed the Royalists.

On board a ship lying at anchor in the Moray Firth, Charles II heard the news quickly and had no choice but to sign the National Covenant and the Solemn League and Covenant. Meanwhile, the captured Montrose was taken to Edinburgh to suffer a traitor's death. Those who saw him in the tumbril remembered that he resembled a bridegroom more than a condemned man. In a show of what seems like bravado or at least a sense of style in the face of death, the great general had dressed in a scarlet cloak fringed with lace, white gloves, silk stockings and ribboned shoes. Before he was pushed off the ladder propped against the gallows, the hangman hung a copy of *Memoirs of the Most Renowned James Graham, Marquis of Montrose*, the Rev. George Wishart's laudatory biography, around his neck.

Now that they at last had their Covenanted King, the government of the saints had to look to the south and contend with Oliver Cromwell and the crack troops of his New Model Army. Scotland had proclaimed Charles II not only King of Scotland but also of England and Ireland while, less than a month after the execution of his father, the English Parliament had abolished the monarchy. A collision was inevitable. In the summer of 1650 the New Model Army crossed the Tweed at Berwick but the reaction of the Scottish government swung the balance significantly in Cromwell's favour. The Purging Committee of the army reduced its fighting effectiveness dramatically by weeding out all those suspected of having low morals or of being Royalists rather than loyal to the Kirk. In all, 80 officers and around 3,000 experienced soldiers, some of them no doubt given to swearing and cursing, were dismissed. There existed a profound, fundamental belief that righteousness rather than military might was what mattered.

Like the pragmatic soldier he was, Sir David Leslie adapted his tactics. He sensibly avoided a direct confrontation in open field and instead adopted a scorched earth policy while barricading his weakened army behind strong fortifications around Edinburgh. In the absence of foraging or sourcing food locally, Cromwell was forced to supply his army through the harbour at Dunbar and, when they withdrew to be closer to the port, Leslie mistook this for a general retreat. He deployed the Covenanter army on Doon Hill, which lay to the south of Dunbar, overlooking the Great North Road, Cromwell's only feasible line of march. It was a strong position and the commander of the New Model Army despaired: 'We are upon an engagement very difficult. The enemy has blocked up our way at the pass of Copperspath [Cockburnspath], through which we cannot get without almost a miracle. He [Leslie] lies upon the hills that we know not how to come that way without great difficulty; and our lying here daily consumes our men, who fall sick beyond imagination.'

But righteousness once again prevailed over sound military sense when the radical ministers pressured Leslie to bring his men down off Doon Hill to attack Cromwell. Perhaps they could not wait for what seemed a certain victory for the invincible Army of the Covenant. Seeing that his enemy had inexplicably surrendered their great advantage, Cromwell ordered a general advance and his cavalry charged the Scots' flank. He is said to have exclaimed, 'The Lord has delivered them into our hands!' It was more true than he knew.

The victory at Dunbar did not immediately secure control of all of Scotland and on 1 January 1651 Charles II was crowned at Scone, a conscious harking back to centuries of tradition as well as a solution to the fact that a coronation in Edinburgh was not an option. Cromwell had occupied the city. Once he had been safely crowned, the Covenanted King must have been persuasive. Yet another army was raised – this time for an invasion of England and the complete restoration of the monarchy. At Worcester, having once again failed to attract English support, the Scots were cut to pieces by Cromwell's cavalry on 3 September 1651. Charles II ignominiously avoided capture by hiding in an oak tree before fleeing into exile in Holland. The Wars of the Covenant had finally concluded and the colonisation of Scotland began.

For thirteen years, the nation had been at war and its people had paid a heavy price. Uncountable numbers of women had been widowed, towns were sacked and an outbreak of the bubonic plague in 1645, said to be the worst for two centuries, killed many in the east of Scotland. Two thirds of the population of Brechin and many in Leith perished. And the invading Cromwellian army plundered not only material goods as Dundee was savagely attacked and looted in 1651 but many of Scotland's public records were also removed. Taxation increased to pay for the maintenance of the occupying army, a cost of £90,000 a year. And humiliation was heaped upon hardship as the English Parliament prepared legislation asserting 'the right of England to Scotland' and the Scottish monarchy and the Scottish Parliament were deemed redundant. In a moment of pantomime, the royal arms were taken down off the mercat cross in Edinburgh and symbolically hanged.

Cromwell's impatience with what was known as the Rump Parliament meant that the new 'Commonwealth of England, Scotland and Ireland' took time to be formally constituted but there was no doubt that a British Republic had been created. In what was essentially a colonial relationship Scotland was permitted to send 30 members to an enlarged Westminster Parliament but half of these were English army officers. General George Monck was made military governor of the new northern province and, in 1654, a union flag was devised as four quarters with the cross of St George in two, the Scottish lion in one and the Irish harp in the other. In a much shorter time, Cromwell had achieved more than Edward I and, while it may not have been perfect, the union dreamed of by James VI, I and I had come about.

The dream of a British republic became ever more clouded. Cromwell found it impossible to resolve the central contradiction that rendered it no republic at all but an autocracy – what increasingly resembled a dictatorship. On 23 April 1653, for reasons no one at the time understood, he became enraged at the actions of the Parliament and summarily dismissed it. Government was carried on by an Army Council, a military junta which quickly appointed Cromwell as Lord Protector.

In 1653, what might be reasonably termed the first Jacobite Rebellion broke out in the Highlands. Known as Glencairn's Rising, it was, in reality, a farrago of petty disputes and quarrels between different elements of its small army. When the exiled Charles II sent word that William Cunningham, Earl of Glencairn, was to be demoted and command given to John, Earl of Middleton, the former challenged Sir George Munro, one of Middleton's officers, to a duel. They then disagreed what weapons should be used, finally wounding each other with swords. At Dalnaspidal, near Loch Garry, one of General Monck's commanders, Thomas Morgan, led his cavalry in what quickly became a rout of the fractious Highland army. This insurrection and another in Wiltshire prompted Cromwell to tighten his grip on Britain and Ireland by creating eleven regions, each under the control of a major general. It was an effective measure, especially in raising taxation and keeping order.

Early in 1658, it seemed that anarchy might be loosed on the British Republic. A malignant fever known as 'the new disease' afflicted London and the Lord Protector was said to be ill. George Fox, one of the leaders of the Quakers, visited Cromwell and reported: 'I saw and felt a waft of death go forth against him, and when I came to him he looked like a dying man.'

Much affected by the early death of his beloved daughter, Elizabeth, Cromwell's health appeared to decline quickly and he died on 3 September, the anniversary of his victories at Dunbar and Worcester. The new Lord Protector was accepted without opposition but Richard Cromwell shared little more than his surname with his father and, after only a year, he retired to his estates. A yawning, dangerous political vacuum opened and wide-spread disorder beckoned. The army had not been paid, the navy mutinied at Portsmouth and blockaded the Thames, Londoners rioted and extreme religious groups threatened trouble. It seemed to many that the only powerful figure who might settle the building sense of crisis was the major general in Scotland, George Monck.

Paid for by punitive taxation in Scotland, the army in Scotland was loyal and their leader impatient with the turmoil and endless bickering in London. Monck resolved to intervene. Using his Scottish revenue as a war chest, he raised companies of foot guards in the Borders who would soon become known as the Coldstream Guards after the little town on the north bank of the Tweed. Having overawed opposition, Monck marched his well-paid and well-equipped recruits to London where a rapid series of epoch-changing events unfolded. Parliament met, formally appointed Monck as commander-in-chief, voted funds to pay off the arrears owed to the army in England, removed the ability of radical groups to associate themselves with local militias and then dissolved itself. It was clear to Monck and his comrades that a new parliament would be strongly Royalist; the return of the king was the only solution to the political vacuum created by the death of Cromwell most could envisage. He saw no option but to agree and, in the Declaration of Breda (the Dutch town where Charles II's exiled court had set up) on 1 May 1660, the king proclaimed an amnesty for all his former enemies and promised to follow the advice of parliament and allow religious toleration.

In Scotland, the Act of Rescissory of 28 March cancelled all legislation enacted by the Covenanter and Cromwellian governments. Not only were all the institutions of monarchy formally restored, bishops returned to govern the Kirk and scapegoats were soon sought. The Covenanting Marquis of Argyll had collaborated with the Cromwellian regime and he was executed. An example was made of the Rev. Dr James Guthrie, an elderly radical minister, and his severed head was spitted on a spike on the Netherbow Port. It was joined in 1663 by the head of Archibald Johnston of Warriston, one of the authors of the National Covenant.

John Maitland, Earl of Lauderdale, had visited Charles I in Carisbrooke Castle and, when he met the future Charles II in 1649, he persuaded him to come to Scotland. Taken prisoner at Worcester in 1650, Maitland spent ten long years in prison but, when the king was restored, he rewarded Lauderdale's loyalty and appointed him Secretary of State for Scotland – in effect, his viceroy. He ruled until 1680, when he suffered a stroke or heart attack and was forced out of office.

What dominated Lauderdale's Scotland was the toxic issue of religious dissent. Both the Church and the universities were purged of the more radical ministers and, more divisively, the National Covenant and the Solemn League and Covenant were declared to be treasonous documents. Those who persisted in subscribing to the principles enshrined in them could expect to be executed as traitors. About a third of all parish ministers were removed and, in the south-west, a centre of radicalism, 200 were turned out of their manses. But those congregations with strong Covenanting beliefs were not going anywhere and outdoor services known as field conventicles began to be held, often in remote, windswept places. Some of these are remembered and in the foothills of the central Cheviots, near Morebattle, there is a hillside known as the 'Singing Braes'.

Lauderdale's government attempted to disperse field conventicles by force and this approach soon produced an armed response. Echoing the successful march of the Whiggamores on Edinburgh, about a thousand men from the south-west made a very unsuccessful attempt to repeat it. At Rullion Green, on the eastern flanks of the Pentland Hills, they were intercepted and scattered by a government force led by General Tam Dalyell. About 50 men were killed, a further 21 executed and many were transported as convicts to Barbados in the West Indies. Anxious to avoid an escalation of protest, Lauderdale began to relax persecution and 132 radical ministers were allowed to return to their parishes. And to discourage the remaining dissidents, the Act of Supremacy not only established Charles II as Head of the Church of Scotland, it also made the attendance of field conventicles a capital offence.

West of Dumfries rise the pillowy hills of Galloway, their rounded summits allowing long vistas, their windbent, tussocky grass making walking difficult. On Skeoch Hill, the rough pasture is interrupted by a strange, regular feature – five rows of flattish stones have been laid out in straight lines. They are all that remain of a vast, open-air church. In the summer of 1678, more than 4,000 people climbed through the tussocks and sikes to reach a plateau close to the top of Skeoch Hill. Above where they gathered, armed men stood on the summit scanning the far horizons for troops of dragoons. Others with muskets and swords guarded the lower slopes as the long lines of worshippers made their way to where the stones had been laid out. These were communion tables, perhaps some of them seats for the old and the infirm exhausted by the climb. Four ministers waited to lead the services, all of them men who had been turned out of their parishes. The Rev. John Welsh was the great-grandson of John Knox and he was supported by the Rev. John Blackadder, formerly of Troqueer, the Rev. Samuel Arnot, formerly of Tongland, and the Rev. John Dickson, formerly of Rutherglen.

As the whaups wheeled and cried in the updrafts and the summer breeze ruffled the pages of bibles and hymnbooks, the huge congregation sang psalms, listened to sermons and took communion. Even though they had walked far and were risking their lives by attending a field conventicle, most of these people were not zealots and almost all were not anxious to be martyrs. In an age of profound belief, their Church and regular worship were vital, central parts of their lives. They needed to climb the hill to worship their God according to their creed, according to the precepts enshrined in the National Covenant. They needed to risk being shot or cut down by dragoons because it was their sacred duty to take communion, have a child baptised, be married, or hear a eulogy for their dead. Skeoch Hill was their only church.

When Lauderdale's government turned out ministers and introduced Episcopalian government to the Kirk, they were faced with a manpower shortage. Who would take the place of men like John Welsh and John Blackadder? The solution was far from satisfactory. Most Episcopalian ministers were either untrained, poor preachers or men who simply accepted the stipend without troubling to do much to earn it. Even though parishioners who refused to attend Episcopalian services were fined and one Dumfries merchant paid more than £1,000, they nevertheless walked into the hills in large numbers to worship at field conventicles.

There exists a fascinating record of a great conventicle that took place in the Borders, at East Nisbet on the banks of the River Teviot near Jedburgh. This was the birthplace of Samuel Rutherford, a Covenanting intellectual and theorist. As might be expected from these courageous, determined and deeply pious ministers, the language is sonorous, replete with scriptural parallels, but the description left by the Rev. John Blackadder does not fail to recognise the realities as he mentions the soldiers of the Covenant, the men who made worship possible for many thousands.

We entered on the administration of the holy ordinance, committing it and ourselves to the invisible protection of the Lord of Hosts, in Whose name we were met together. The place where we convene was every way commodious, and seemed to have been formed on purpose. It was a green and pleasant haugh, fast by the waterside. On either hand, there was a spacious brae, in form of a half round, covered with delightful pasture, and rising with a gentle slope to a goodly height. Above us was the clear blue sky, for it was a sweet and calm Sabbath morning, promising to be indeed one of the days of the Son of Man. The Communion tables were spread on the green by the water, and around them the people had arranged themselves in decent order. But the far greater multitude sat on the brae face, which was crowded from top to bottom.

Each day, at the congregation's dismissing, the ministers with their guards, and as many of the people as could, retired to their quarters in three several country towns, where they might be provided with necessaries. The horsemen drew up in a body, and then marched in goodly array behind the people, until all were safely lodged. In the morning, when they returned, the horsemen accompanied them. All the three parties met a mile from the spot, and marched in a full body to the consecrated ground. The congregation being fairly settled, the guardsmen took their stations as formerly. They secured the peace and quiet of the audience; for from Saturday morning, when the work began, until Monday afternoon, we suffered not the least affront or molestation from enemies: which appeared wonderful. The whole was closed in as orderly a way as it had been in the time of Scotland's brightest noon. And, truly, the spectacle of so many grave, composed, and devout faces must have struck the adversaries with awe, and been more formidable than any outward ability of fierce looks and warlike array. We desired not the countenance of earthly kings; there was a spiritual and divine Majesty shining on the work. Amidst the lonely mountains we remembered the words of our Lord, that true worship was not peculiar to Jerusalem or Samaria – that the beauty of holiness consisted not in material temples. We remembered the Ark of the Israelites, which had sojourned for years in the desert, with no dwelling but the tabernacle of the plain. We thought of Abraham and the ancient patriarchs, who laid their victims on the rocks for an altar, and burned sweet incense under the shade of the green tree.

In a quiet and green landscape, on warm summer days, these armed outdoor services must sometimes have shed their fearful context and seemed Edenic, an imagined memory of the simplicity of the early days of Christianity.

Small conventicles could be held in houses but, in hamlets, villages and towns, where there were prying eyes, it was much more dangerous. So many were gathering in the hills and in remote country places that Lauderdale's government felt compelled to act. In 1678, a force of about 8,000 clansmen and others was recruited and immediately became notorious as the 'Highland Host'. They plundered communities, stealing goods and money and attacking conventicles. This initiative sparked a rapid response. On 3 May 1679, nine armed men waited by the roadside on Magus Moor, two miles west of St Andrews. Led by John Balfour of Kinloch, they expected to intercept a coach carrying the Sheriff of Cupar and assassinate him in retaliation for his persecution of Covenanters. But news came to them that a far greater prize was on the road – the coach of Archbishop James Sharp of St Andrews. Appointed as the Primate of Scotland by Charles II, he had acquired a fearsome reputation. Eleven prisoners had surrendered at Rullion Green on a promise of mercy, but Sharp subsequently condemned them to death with the words: 'You were pardoned as soldiers, but you are not acquitted as subjects.' The Archbishop's own enmities may have been augmented by frustration. When the Rev. John Blackadder preached at a field conventicle on Kinkell Braes, the high ground on the coast road to the south of St Andrews, Sharp was incensed. Unless an offshore wind blew the sound in another direction, it will likely have been possible to hear the low rumble and cadences of the psalms in the streets of the town. The angry Archbishop called on the Provost to turn out the militia to disperse the large congregation but he responded that he could not – the militia had all joined the worshippers.

When the coach trundled into view on Magus Moor, the nine Covenanters who surrounded it discovered that Sharp was accompanied by his daughter, Isabella. They did not hesitate. Having dragged the Archbishop out of the coach, James Russell, one of the assassins, spoke the indictment, remembering the cruel injustices of Rullion Green. Russell 'declared before the Lord that it was no particular interest, nor yet for any wrong that he had done to him, but because he had betrayed the church as Judas, and had wrung his hands, these 18 or 19 years in the blood of the saints, but especially at Pentland [Rullion Green]'. And then they stabbed and slashed at Sharp until he was dead. This shocking incident immediately raised the stakes.

In the west of Scotland, rebellion flared. Four weeks after the assassination, a field conventicle gathered on the slopes of Loudon Hill, the place where Robert Bruce had defeated the English cavalry over 370 years before. Perhaps these martial memories inspired what happened next. John Graham of Claverhouse, later to become notorious as 'Bluidy Clavers', had been appointed to suppress conventicles in the south-west and his spies had told him that worshippers would gather on Sunday, 1 June. When news reached the presiding minister, the Rev. Thomas Douglas, that government dragoons were approaching Loudon Hill, he broke off his sermon with the words: 'Ye have got the theory, now for the practice.' As worshippers dispersed, about 200 armed Covenanters, 40 of them on horseback, moved east to meet Claverhouse's detachment at the moor near Drumclog farm. Led by William Cleland, the small group of cavalry charged the government force and scattered them, leaving 36 dead. The righteous had triumphed once more and, although its scale scarcely deserved the status of a battle, the propaganda value of the victory at Drumclog was immense, encouraging the persecuted to believe that the soldiers of the Covenant could defy the might of the State. But it was short-lived.

In the weeks following the events of 1 June, the Covenanters and Claverhouse mustered their forces. John Balfour of Kinloch and David Hackston of Rathillet had been part of the group who killed Archbishop Sharp and, with Robert Hamilton and William Cleland, they led the army that marched to Bothwell Bridge, north of Hamilton. About 3,000 in all, the Covenanters were outnumbered by Claverhouse's 5,000, bolstered by the arrival of James Scott, the Duke of Monmouth, the eldest of Charles II's illegitimate sons, and the men he brought with him. The narrow bridge across the Clyde was crucial and, for an hour, David Hackston's detachment held it. But the Covenanters had no artillery and, when forced to retreat and allow the superior numbers of the government army to cross, the battle in open field quickly turned into a rout. About 1,200 Covenanters were taken prisoner and marched to Edinburgh where they were held in Greyfriars kirkyard. Many were later transported to the colonies in the West Indies.

Sharp's assassination, Drumclog and Bothwell Bridge ratcheted up tension on both sides but, even at the time, it was clear to many what the eventual outcome would be. The remarkable story of Richard Cameron is illustrative. Later called the 'Lion of the Covenant', he was to become its most famous martyr, a role he appears to have embraced from the outset. When Cameron was ordained a Church of Scotland minister in exile in Rotterdam, the ceremony was led by the Rev. Robert MacWard and he addressed these chilling remarks to the young man:

> Richard, the publick standard of the Gospel is fallen in Scotland; and, if I know anything of the mind of the Lord, ye are called to undergo your trials before us, and go home and lift the fallen standard, and display it before the world. But, before you put your hand to it, ye shall go to as many of the field ministers as ye can find, and give them your hearty invitation to go with you; and if they will not go, go your lone, and the Lord will go with you. Behold, all ye beholders! Here is the head of a faithful minister and servant of Jesus Christ, who shall lose the same for his Master's interest; and it shall be set up before sun and moon in the public view of the world.

In late 1679, Cameron began his ministry, preaching to field conventicles, mainly in Ayrshire and the south-west. By 22 June 1680, he had met David Hackston and, with 20 others, they rode into Sanquhar in Nithsdale, the heartland of the Covenant. After singing a psalm at the mercat cross, Michael Cameron, Richard's brother, read out what became known as the 'Sanquhar Declaration'. It denounced Charles II as a tyrant, demanded that his openly Catholic brother, James, Duke of York, be excluded from the succession and, in effect, declared war on the king. A week later, the Privy Council put a huge price of 5,000 merks on Richard Cameron's head and, despite having an escort of 60 armed men, he was hunted down and killed three weeks later at Airds Moss in Ayrshire. His followers became known as Cameronians.

To root out what was seen as treasonous dissent, the Privy Council sanctioned summary execution without trial. When dragoons came across Covenanters, they simply shot them where they stood. All over Galloway there are stones and cairns, informal monuments often found in remote moorland, places where field conventicles could be held. These martyrs were often buried where they fell because interments in parish church graveyards were forbidden. But perhaps the most poignant memorial is one erected in the sea.

At low tide, Wigtown Bay appears like a vast, flat expanse of sand, broken only the course of the River Cree as it winds towards a distant sea. But in spring, the tides roll in rapidly, sometimes surging towards the shore. On 11 May 1685, the broad bay was the scene of a cruel, theatrical execution when two Covenanters were chained to wooden stakes at low tide to wait for the Solway to flow back across the sands and drown them.

Margaret Wilson was born on a farm near Newton Stewart, the daughter of parents who had accepted the Episcopalian Church. But their children did not. Margaret, Thomas and Agnes may have attended a field conventicle where the charismatic Cameronian leader, the Rev. James Renwick, preached. In February 1685, Thomas left home to live wild out on the hills with a band of Covenanters. Soon afterwards, his sisters secretly visited Wigtown where they met Margaret McLachlan, a much older women who had been widowed. Her husband may have been shot by dragoons.

Around the same time, news of great change travelled north. Charles II had died and been succeeded by his brother, James VII, II and II, a Catholic. In Wigtown, the centre of the county and a place where the news would have been announced publicly, Margaret Wilson, Agnes Wilson, only 12 years old, and Margaret McLachlan were arrested almost certainly for refusing to drink the new king's health. They were flung in the 'thieves' hole' in the tollbooth. A week later, they appeared before the Government Commission, a body charged with the extirpation of Covenanting dissent, where they were accused of attending field conventicles and refusing to repudiate the Sanquhar Declaration. All three were quickly pronounced guilty and, as their father, Gilbert Wilson, watched, the sisters and the old widow were sentenced to death by being 'tied to palisades fixed in the sand, within the floodmark of the sea, and there to stand till the flood overflowed them'.

Gilbert Wilson rode like the wind for Edinburgh. Before the Privy Council, he pleaded for his daughters' lives and claimed that Margaret McLachlan had recanted. Twelve year-old Agnes was bailed on a bond of £100 Scots on account of her youth and reprieves were granted for her sister and the old widow. But they were ignored. At low tide on 11 May, two stakes were rammed into the sands of Wigtown Bay, one much nearer the shore than the other. A large crowd had gathered. Margaret McLachlan was led out by dragoons and chained to the far stake. Margaret Wilson was chained to other but turned to face the sea and the incoming tide so that she could see the old lady. The commander of the execution party, Major Windram, believed that, when the young woman saw Margaret McLachlan struggle against the chains to avoid the agonies of drowning, she would recant.

As the Solway tide flowed in and the old woman strained to lift her chin to stay alive for a few more moments, Windram approached Margaret Wilson. She shook her head: 'I see Christ struggling there.' As the water rose ever higher, her resolve did not waver. When the soldiers lofted her chin to ask if she would swear an oath of allegiance to the king, Margaret replied, 'I will not. I am one of Christ's children – let me go.' Perhaps angry, the soldiers pushed her head under the water until her body was still.

Privately Catholic, publicly Anglican and Presbyterian, Charles II's brother, then styled James, Duke of Albany and York, had taken charge of the government of Scotland in the early 1680s and the ruthlessness behind the persecution of Covenanters stemmed from him. Scottish noblemen made hasty conversions to Catholicism and the likes of the Drummond brothers, the Earls of Perth and Melfort, were favoured with promotion. Despite James's relative openness about his beliefs and the likelihood that he would succeed his brother (whose many sons were all illegitimate), there was little appetite for opposition. When it did come in 1685, at James's accession, it was brief and feeble. James Scott, Duke of Monmouth and Charles II's eldest natural son, landed at Torbay with a small force, proclaimed himself king and led his men to battle at Sedgemoor in Somerset. They were cut to pieces by Royalist troops. At the other end of Britain, Archibald Campbell, Earl of Argyll, landed in Kintyre with a few men and proclaimed Monmouth king but, even before he could engage, he was arrested at Inchinnan in Renfrewshire. Both were beheaded as traitors.

When James II arrived in a gilded coach for his coronation at Westminster Abbey on 23 April, he believed that he had already been crowned king. In a private ceremony conducted by Catholic priests at Whitehall Palace, he had already undergone coronation. The same arrangement took place in Scotland where the Chapel Royal at Holyrood Abbey had been once again fitted out to celebrate Mass. There was no great fuss. James's queen, Mary of Modena, had endured the terrible experience of ten pregnancies which had resulted in five stillbirths and five babies who died soon after they were born. The heir apparent was Mary, a daughter by Anne Hyde, his first wife. And she was a committed Protestant. But, in June 1688, everything changed when Queen Mary gave birth to a healthy boy, James Edward Stewart – a child who would be raised in the Catholic faith.

By this time, members of the English Parliament had begun to arrange themselves into loose affiliations. Remembering the Whiggamore Raid, the Whigs stood for the principles of a constitutional monarchy accountable to parliament, while the Tories (the term derived from Irish Gaelic – *toraidhe* was an 'outlaw', a Royalist) supported James VII, II and II. When the birth of an heir made real the prospect of a Catholic, absolutist line of Stewart kings, the Whigs, with the support of some Tories, made contact with William of Orange, Mary's very Protestant Dutch husband. As the leader of Protestant northern Europe against the immensely powerful Louis XIV of France, he could see that the crowns of the three kingdoms could tip the strategic balance and he readily accepted what was being offered. On 11 November 1668, a Dutch fleet put in at Brixham in Devon and a Dutch army disembarked. Even though the sequence of events that unfolded became known as the Glorious Revolution, this was an invasion and William a usurper. When news of the landing reached London, King James prepared to fight, then panicked and fled to France.

It was a curious moment. For more than 300 years, Stewarts had reigned without interruption first in Scotland and then in England and Ireland. And yet James gave up his kingdoms without a fight. Conflict would come quickly as the history of Scotland was dominated by the ebb and flow of the Jacobite cause.

IO

Rebellious Scots

※

WHILE INTERNATIONAL politics played out in London, Paris and the Netherlands, as new kings came and old kings fled and the balance of power in Europe shifted, it seemed that little had changed for the local politics of the Highlands. Since the fall of the Lordship of the Isles at the end of the 15th century, disorder had flared, often beyond the Highland Line, as clans fought each other with undimmed spite. Coll MacDonald, the Chief of the MacDonalds of Keppoch, had studied at the University of St Andrews and, although he probably had a keen sense of history, he could not have known that he would lead his men in what would be the last clan battle in Scotland.

At issue, as always, was land and title. The Clan Chattan Confederacy claimed an ancient right to lands in Lochaber but, these being distant from their core territory on the southern shores of the Moray Firth, they had been unable to prevent MacDonalds from occupying their property. In 1688, Lachlan Mackintosh, Chief of Clan Chattan, sought a commission of fire and sword from the Scottish Parliament in Edinburgh – that is, the right to remove the MacDonalds by force. It was not only granted but a detachment of government soldiers, commanded by Captain Kenneth Mackenzie, was added to the forces of Clan Chattan. In July, they marched unopposed into Lochaber. Where Coll MacDonald was waiting for them.

Keppoch had been joined by contingents sent by his kinsmen of Glengarry and Glencoe and by the MacMartins, a sept of Clan Cameron who had probably taken possession of Mackintosh land. With about 800 men at his back, Coll MacDonald deployed on Maol Ruadh, a low hill at the mouth of the glen, not far from Spean Bridge. They were outnumbered two to one but the MacDonald captains would employ a simple tactic – one that would

1. The Ness of Brodgar, Orkney: the largest Neolithic building in Europe. With its inner and outer sanctums and huge roof, even today this would represent a spectacular sight. Copyright © Hugo Anderson-Whymark

2. Burnswark. Roman siege works and catapult platforms menace a native fort. Are these remnants of a real siege, or simply a training ground? © RCAHMS. Licensor www.scran.ac.uk

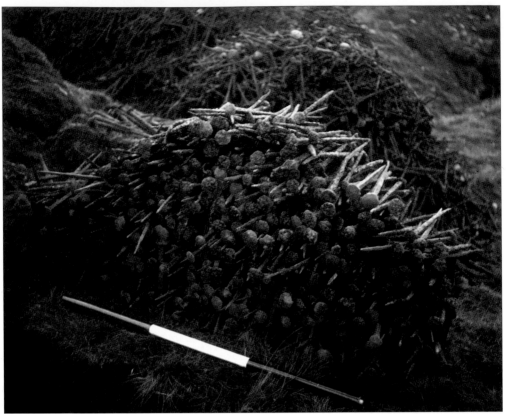

3. Nails, carefully stored for re-use, being excavated at the legionary fortress of Inchtuthil. But it wasn't the Romans who re-used them (see plate 10). © RCAHMS. Licensor www.scran.ac.uk

4. Athur's O'on, the probable dedicatory temple of the Antonine Wall, demolished in 1743 by the local landowner, Sir Michael Bruce. 'The Elegancy and Magnificence of this Work, appeareth in the agreeable Pulchritude of it, that the Stones were polished, and so artificially placed, that by being set in other [sic], they upheld the Structure, each of them keeping the other fast and firm; so that they have now lasted above Fifteen Hundred Years.'

5. St Columba's Shrine, Iona. Partly 7th century, this is the earliest upstanding building on the site and is reputed to be the burial place of the saint. 'If death in Iona be my fate, / merciful would be that taking. / I know not beneath blue heaven / a better spot for death.'
© Crown Copyright Historic Scotland. Licensor www.scran.ac.uk

6. Eileach an Naoimh, the Garvellachs, the best preserved early monastic site in Scotland and possible burial place of Eithne, mother of Columba. Although it now seems an isolated location (like many monasteries), it was actually built in the middle of the busy sea highway of the Firth of Lorne and Sound of Mull. © Crown Copyright Historic Scotland. Licensor www.scran.ac.uk

7. *Left.* The baptistery at Hoddom, Mungo's see while in exile from Strathclyde. Baptism was a crucial stage in the process of conversion to Christianity. © Crown copyright Historic Scotland

8. *Below.* The Aberlemno stone. Does this show the death of an Anglian King? Note the distinctive helmet of the horseman and his final end with a bird/raven standing over him in the bottom right to signify his defeat and death.

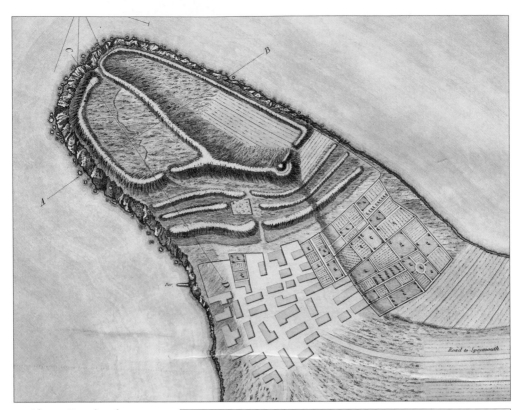

9. *Above*. Burghead, a
Pictish royal centre in the
north now sadly much
diminished by a modern
village. Even today, however,
the underground well and
massive ramparts still give
some sense of the power
of this great fortress.

10. *Right*. In AD 683 the
Annals of Ulster record
'the siege of Dunadd and the
siege of Dun Durn'. The
great Pictish fortress was
built with Roman nails,
possibly from Inchtuthil
(see plate 3). Built on a
major route across Scotland,
it still dominates St Fillans.
The laconic annal entry, like
so many, leaves the 'who',
the 'why' and the 'what
happened' of the siege a
mystery. © Crown Copy-
right Historic Scotland.
Licensor www.scran.ac.uk

11. Is this the face of a Pictish King? David from the St Andrews Sarcophagus, a masterpiece of Dark Age art. It was probably carved between 750 and 850 and is possibly the tomb of Onuist (Oengus) I, the dominant warrior of what became Scotland. © RCAHMS. Licensor www.scran.ac.uk

12. Dupplin Cross, commissioned by Constantine I. The lines of priests and warriors show the growing wealth and power of what was to become the heartland of Alba. © Crown Copyright Historic Scotland. Licensor www.scran.ac.uk

13. *Above*. The Runes of Maes Howe, carved in the presence of Earl Harald of Orkney as he and his retinue sheltered from a storm in the Neolithic burial chamber at Christmas 1153. As chapter 93 of *Orkneyinga Saga* relates: 'On the thirteenth day of Christmas they travelled on foot over the Firth. During a snowstorm they took shelter in Maes Howe and two of them went insane, which slowed them down badly so that by the time they reached Firth it was night time.'

14. *Left*. Temple Pyx. The Norman armoured knights who smashed the old order across Europe. Burrell Collections, Glasgow. © Culture and Sport, Glasgow

15. The great cathedral of Glasgow, one of the masterpiece of Scottish Gothic architecture and the only cathedral in Scotland not to be unroofed during the Reformation.

16. Alexander III (third from left), from the Wriothesley Garter Book. Royal Collection Trust. © HM Queen Elizabeth II, 2015/Bridgeman Images

17. Edward I receives the homage of Scotland as John de Balliol kneels before him (from the St Albans Chronicle). © Lambeth Palace Library, London, UK/Bridgeman Images

18. Doune Castle. A few miles from Stirling Castle, the Dukes of Albany, Regents of Scotland, built their own statement of power. © Nella

19. Bishop Elphinstone's tomb, outside King's College Chapel, Aberdeen.

20. Ardtornish Castle, site of the signing of the great Treaty of Westminster–Ardtornish, which doomed the Lordship of the Isles. © Crown Copyright Historic Scotland. Licensor www.scran.ac.uk

21. The possible Viking Age canal at Rubh an Dunain, Skye. The galley noosts of the Macaskill Wards of the Sea to the Macleods of Dunvegan lie beside it. © Richard Dorrell

22. A page from the Carver Choir book, one of the great sources for Renaissance music. Some have suggested the magnificent 10-part mass *Dum Sacrum Mysterium* was intended as a victory mass for the anticipated triumph of James IV at Flodden. Reproduced by permission of the National Library of Scotland

23. *Above and overleaf.* The Great Hall of Stirling Castle. James IV impresses his new Queen, Margaret Tudor. © Crown Copyright Historic Scotland. Licensor www.scran.ac.uk (interior) © TanArt (exterior)

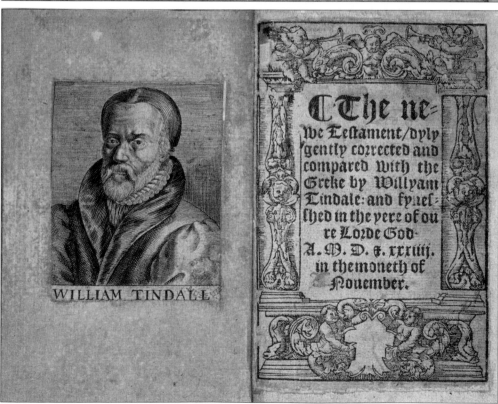

24. Tyndale's New Testament. The Word of God was at last revealed as the mysteries of Latin were replaced with the vernacular. © British Library Board. All rights reserved. Bridgeman Images

25. Woodcut of George Wishart being burned alive. As the wind whipped off the sea, it may have prolonged Wishart's terrible agonies since it blew away the smoke that might otherwise have asphyxiated him. Private Collection/The Stapleton Collection/Bridgeman Images

26. *Right*. John Knox.
'Resistance to tyranny is
obedience to God.'

27. *Below*. The North Berwick
Witch Trials of 1591. Between
three and four thousand
supposed witches might have
been killed in Scotland between
1560 and 1707. © Glasgow
University Special Collections.
Licensor www.scran.ac.uk

28. Culross Palace. A 17th-century merchant shows his wealth. Baltic pine, Dutch tiles and glass and English pottery all feature. © National Trust for Scotland. Licensor www.scran.ac.uk (interior) © Victor Denovan (exterior)

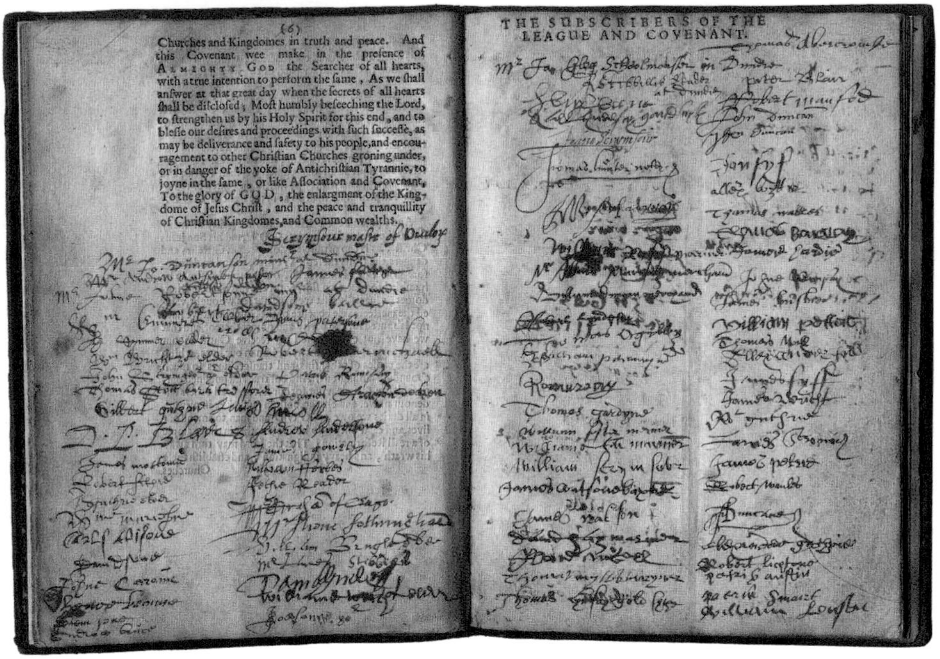

(6)

Churches and Kingdomes in truth and peace. And this Covenant wee make in the presence of ALMIGHTY GOD the Searcher of all hearts, with a true intention to perform the same, As we shall answer at that great day when the secrets of all hearts shall be disclosed; Most humbly beseeching the Lord, to strengthen us by his Holy Spirit for this end, and to blesse our desires and proceedings with such successe, as may be deliverance and safety to his people, and encouragement to other Christian Churches groning under, or in danger of the yoke of Antichristian Tyrannie, to joyne in the same, or like Association and Covenant, To the glory of GOD, the enlargment of the Kingdome of Jesus Christ, and the peace and tranquillity of Christian Kingdomes, and Common wealths.

THE SUBSCRIBERS OF THE LEAGUE AND COVENANT.

29. A Solemn League and Covenant. Scotland takes a fateful step on the path to war. Famously signed in Greyfriars churchyard, Edinburgh, copies were signed all over Scotland. This one is from Dundee. © Dundee Central Library. Licensor www.scran.ac.uk

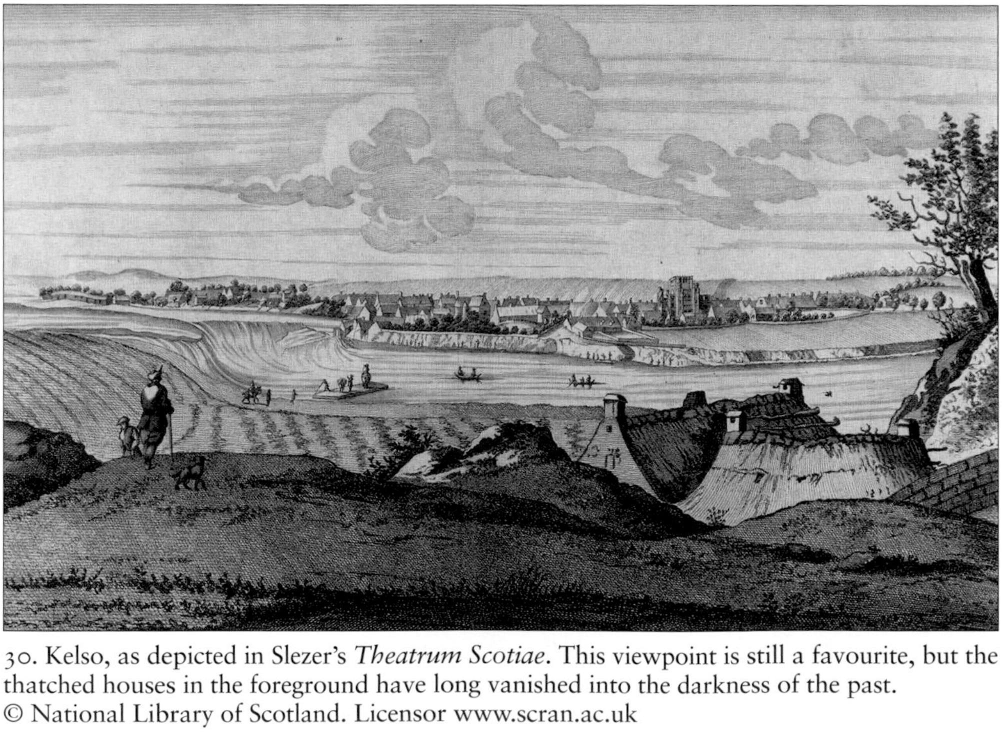

30. Kelso, as depicted in Slezer's *Theatrum Scotiae*. This viewpoint is still a favourite, but the thatched houses in the foreground have long vanished into the darkness of the past. © National Library of Scotland. Licensor www.scran.ac.uk

31. Bernera Barracks. This imposing building lay astride a meeting of several roads – on sea and land. © RCAHMS. Licensor www.scran.ac.uk

32. Culloden, painted by Paul Sandby. The fact that this battle, fought in the far north of Britain, was much better illustrated than any in the past shows an understanding of its significance.

33. *Above.* Surveying the Highlands. Not simply through roads but through maps were the Highlands to be tamed. This is part of William Roy's famous survey which produced The Great Map. 'The rise and progress of the rebellion ... convinced Government of what infinite importance it would be to the State, that a country so very inaccessible by nature, should be thoroughly explored and laid open.'

34. *Right.* Adam Smith, by Alexander Stoddart. 'A nation is not made wealthy by the childish accumulation of shiny metals, but it enriched by the economic prosperity of its people.'
© Rob van Esch

35. Mavisbank, possibly William Adam's greatest achievement, now a sad and neglected ruin. © University of Strathclyde Licensor www.scran.ac.uk

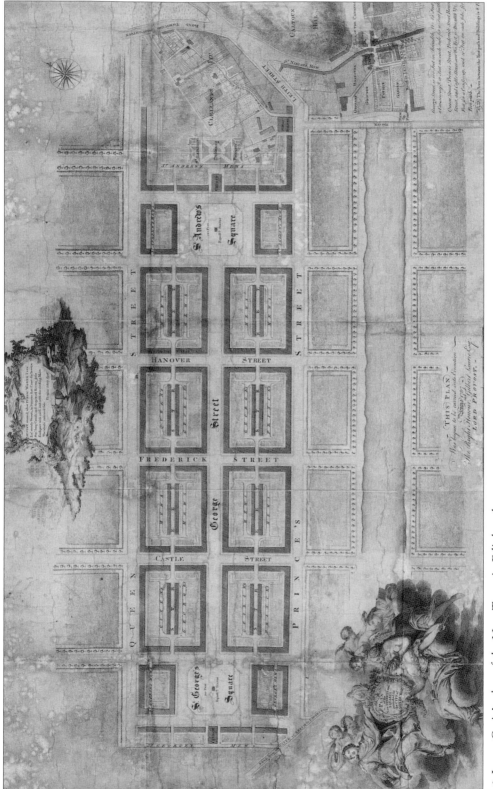

36. James Craig's plan of the New Town in Edinburgh.

37. *Left*. Henry Dundas' house at 36 St Andrew Square, Edinburgh. Licensor www.scran.ac.uk

38. *Below*. James Hogg in his shepherd's plaid. © Scottish National Portrait Gallery. Licensor www.scran.ac.uk

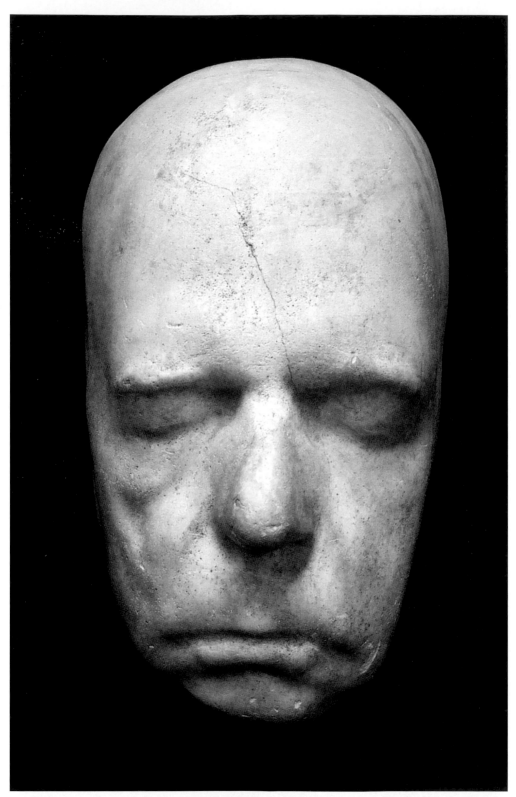

39. Walter Scott's death mask, showing the effect of the stroke that killed him.

40. Steaming into a new age: the *Comet* speeds past her competition on the Clyde.

41. David Octavius Hill's painting of the 1843 General Assembly, which led to the creation of the Free Church of Scotland. Reproduced by permission of the Free Church of Scotland.

42. 'Balmorality' – Queen Victoria's Highland residence at Balmoral Castle.
© Bildagentur Zoonar Gmbh

43. St Andrews fisherfolk, photographed by David Octavius Hill and Robert Adamson in 1849. © St Andrews University Library. Licensor www.scran.ac.uk

44. *Above*. The Forth Rail Bridge under construction.

45. *Left*. Keir Hardie. 'We are called upon at the beginning of the twentieth century to decide the question propounded in the Sermon on the Mount, as to whether we will worship God or Mammon. The present day is a Mammon-worshipping age. Socialism proposes to dethrone the brute-god Mammon and to lift humanity into its place.' Getty Images

46. Municipal pomp and pride – Glasgow City Chambers. © meunierd

47. Glasgow School of Art, Charles Rennie Mackintosh's masterpiece. © Claudio Divizia

48. The Glasgow Rent Strike, 1915. © CSG CIC Glasgow Museum and Library Collections

49. The end of the First World War. The German High Seas Fleet steams to surrender in the Forth.

50. Eric Liddell running in his characteristic style. © MacGregor/Topical Press Agency/ Getty Images

51. Hugh MacDiarmid. © The Scotsman Publications Ltd. Licensor www.scran.ac.uk

52. The independence referendum of 2014 polarised the country. Getty Images

help determine the course of British politics over the following 60 years. Lachlan Mackintosh should have known better when his men and Captain Mackenzie's government soldiers, probably believing that their numbers would prevail, made the cardinal mistake of advancing uphill against a force of Highlanders. One of Mackenzie's recruits was Donald MacBane. As a civilian, he had been a tobacco spinner in Inverness and he left a frank, funny and fascinating record of what happened next. It is a rare memoir of what it was like to face a Highland charge:

> The two clans were both on foot and our company was still with Mackintosh, who marched towards MacDonald and his clan, until we came in sight of them (which made me wish I had been spinning tobacco). Mackintosh sent one of his friends to MacDonald to treat with him, and see if he would come to reasonable terms. MacDonald directly denied, but would fight it by the event as it would [turn out]. Then both parties [the Mackintoshes and the government troops] ordered their men to march up the hill, a company being in the front, we drew up in line of battle as we could, our company being on the right. We were no sooner in order but there appears double our number of the MacDonalds, which made us then fear the worst, at least for my part. I repeated my former wish (I never having seen the like). The MacDonalds came down the hill without either shoe, stocking or bonnet on their head. They gave a shout and then the fire began on both sides, and continued a hot dispute for an hour. Then they broke in upon us with sword and targe, and Lochaber axes, which obliged us to give way. Seeing my captain sore wounded, and a great many more with heads lying cloven on every side, I was sadly affrighted, never having seen the like before. A Highlander attacked me with sword and targe and cut my wooden-handled bayonet out of the muzzle of my gun. I then clubbed my gun and gave him a stroke with it, which made the butt-end fly off. Seeing the Highland men come fast upon me, I took to my heels and ran thirty miles before I looked behind me. Every person I saw or met, I took for my enemy.

Mackintosh's commission of fire and sword had failed but its granting by Parliament was evidence of a victory of another sort. While the Scots may not have been consulted directly on the invitation to William of Orange to invade and seize the throne of England, they did have the power to decline to offer him the crown of Scotland. In the event, they did not but, when the Scottish Parliament formally accepted the new king, in legal terms a usurper who had deposed a legitimate sovereign of Scottish descent, a different relationship was understood by both parties. The divine rights of the Stewarts belonged in the past – or so many hoped – and a constitutional monarchy had replaced them. King William III and II was king by consent.

In 1690, the Edinburgh legislature again asserted itself. Bills to go before Parliament had been initiated and drafted by a committee known as the Lords of the Articles. In the past, these men had been appointed by the Privy Council and, through them, the king could exert control. Only two years after William's accession, the committee of the Lords of the Articles was disbanded and, at the same time, bishops were expelled from Parliament. Very quickly, it became more powerful, more independent.

Thanks to Walter Scott's gift for names and phrases, Bluidy Clavers, the scourge of the Covenant, has morphed into Bonnie Dundee, the romantic hero who first raised the standard of the exiled Stewarts in 1689. A year before, James VII and II had raised Claverhouse to a viscountcy and made him commander-in-chief of the army in Scotland, a promotion that sounded grander than the reality. When the Scottish Parliament met in Edinburgh to consider their reaction to the seismic political shifts in London, it was clear that the majority were hostile to the exiled Stewart king. Nevertheless, the city was divided. The castle was held for James VII by the Duke of Gordon but his resolve was said to be wavering. There is a barred postern gate in the western walls that is very difficult to reach because of the steepness of the castle rock but, nevertheless, Viscount Dundee was seen clambering up to it to confer with Gordon. The conversation must have come to nothing for, on 18 March 1689, Dundee left Edinburgh with fifty loyal dragoons. A few weeks later, he climbed another hill when he raised the royal standard on Dundee Law. Despite the dramatic setting, the citizens in the burgh below were unimpressed and the gates were locked against the viscount. Equally, the large government garrison made no attempt to attack or capture the rebel general and Dundee turned his horse northwards to seek support for the Stewart cause in the Highlands.

Sir Ewen Cameron of Lochiel was General George Monck's unlikely companion on his march to London to seek the restoration of the Stewarts in 1660. The role given to him as peacemaker amongst the Highland clans had only broken down when he was not in Lochaber. And it was during a visit to the court in London that some of his men joined Coll MacDonald to charge down the slopes of Maol Ruadh. With the coming of William of Orange, Cameron's thoughts turned to rebellion and he began to organise, creating an alliance of the mostly Episcopalian or Catholic clans of the western Highlands and Islands in support of James VII and II. It was more than ironic that these were the same clans and chiefs that James VI and I had worked so hard to suppress.

When Dundee rode north, he was pursued by a government army led by General Hugh MacKay of Scourie, a Highlander who had served the new king as a mercenary commander in Europe. Then, as now, geography dictates that the principal route into the central Highlands follows the banks of the Rivers Tay, Tummel and Garry, and Dundee knew that MacKay would have to come that way. Quickly linking up with small forces of clansmen and hoping that Ewen Cameron and his men and others would join them as they hurried south to meet the advancing government army, the Jacobite commander sent word that Blair Castle should be seized and fortified. It stood astride the north road. The seat of the Murrays, at that time government supporters, the castle was a strategically vital strongpoint. With a force loyal to William of Orange, Lord Murray immediately marched to Blair in order to lay siege to his own castle. Meanwhile Dundee was moving very quickly through the mountain passes and down into Glen Garry. Hugh MacKay's army marched out of Perth to support Murray's siege. Speed was becoming all-important.

Well used to the terrain and carrying little equipment, Dundee's Highlanders won the race to Blair and, by the time they reached the castle, their insurgent army had swollen to about 2,400 men. A mile or so to the south, the north road winds through the Pass of Killiecrankie, where the Garry dashes through a rocky defile. Dundee sent snipers to slow down MacKay's advance while he found good ground for his Highlanders to charge across. After a brief council of war with Ewen Cameron and the other chiefs, a ridge to the north of the Garry was chosen. It commanded the road below. When MacKay's larger force marched through the pass, he ordered them to form line but not engage. The Highlanders were too well positioned above them. Instead they loaded their muskets and began to fire volleys. It was late afternoon and the high, bright July sun was in the Highlanders' eyes. Dundee ordered them to sit on their plaids, make themselves as difficult a target as possible and wait.

Ewen Cameron's men had been set in the centre of the line but, to his right, the government line was longer and could have outflanked Dundee's army. To forestall that, an all-out charge was ordered. The war pipes sounded and the Highlanders stood to. If they had muskets, they fired them, threw down their heavy plaids, raised their broadswords, roared their war cries and raced down the slope to the government lines. The centre was 'swept away by the furious onset of the Camerons' and MacKay's army was smashed off the battlefield. The battle at Killiecrankie lasted only minutes before it became a rout. One of the fleeing government soldiers jumped across the gorge of the River Garry at a place now known as the Soldier's Leap. He had seen a Highland charge before at Maol Ruadh and his name was Donald MacBane.

Although it was brief, Killiecrankie was bloody. More than 2,000 government soldiers were cut down and killed, most of them as they fled, and 600 Highlanders died. But the most important casualty was the leader of the uprising. In one of the last actions of the battle, Viscount Dundee was shot out of the saddle and later died. And, despite a stunning victory, the Jacobite advance faltered.

On 14 May 1689, three months before the slaughter on the braes above Killiecrankie, William Cleland must have pondered the vicissitudes of history. The victor at Drumclog as he charged with the Covenanting cavalry and then one of the vanquished at Bothwell Bridge, his faith had not changed but events had and they delivered him to the banks of the Douglas Water in Lanarkshire. Anxious to raise troops to support the accession of William of Orange and to suppress any attempts by Royalists to restore the Stewarts, the Privy Council had encouraged the Marquis of Douglas to call on the Cameronians to form a regiment. Passionate, battle-hardened and constant, many soldiers of the Covenant gathered by the river and it was said that 1,200 enlisted on the first day without 'beat of drum', the need to recruit actively or pay a bounty. Douglas's son, the Earl of Angus, was named as their first colonel but it was Lt. Col. William Cleland who was given effective command of the regiment that came to be known as the Cameronians. They did not have to wait long to see action.

With the death of Dundee, Sir Ewen Cameron expected to become the leader of the victorious Jacobite army as they moved south through Strathtay. But, instead, command was assigned to Col. Alexander Cannon. He had brought 300 Irish soldiers to join Dundee at Blair Castle. Mortified at the insult, Cameron stalked off in the opposite direction with most of his clansmen, making his way back home to Lochaber and taking no further part in the uprising.

Meanwhile the Privy Council believed that the cathedral town of Dunkeld was both strategically and politically important. If it could be held against the Jacobites, it meant that they would fail to advance out of their Highland heartlands but, if it fell, then the uprising would gain momentum and perhaps attract Lowland support. Orders were sent to Lt Col. Cleland to lead his new regiment to defend Dunkeld.

When the Cameronians arrived, they quickly realised that they could not fortify the town. There was no wall around it and therefore no gates and its situation meant that it could be attacked from three sides, with the River Tay preventing an approach from the south. Cleland decided that, while the town itself could not be held against what he was sure would be a much larger force, the cathedral and its precinct could be defended as a redoubt. There was a dyke around the graveyard with a ditch below it except to the east where the High Street ran. But there was an iron gate which could be closed and secured. And the Marquis of Atholl's house bordered the precinct and it was defensible, the upper floor giving musketeers the advantage of height. Those townspeople who barricaded themselves in their houses along the High Street and in the wynds off it would regret rejecting Cleland's strong advice to leave. The Cameronians deepened the ditch around the precinct, repaired the crumbling walls, and sent lookouts up the cathedral tower.

On 21 August, the alarm was raised. The sharp-eyed soldiers in the tower could see clansmen moving in the woods on Stanley Hill, high ground immediately to the north-east of the cathedral, and they could hear the sound of horses and men approaching from the north. Cleland ordered his men to stand to and prime their muskets and those at the gates of the precinct formed three ranks so that a constant hail of musket fire could be directed down the High Street, the likely approach of the Highlanders. Col. Cannon wasted no time and quickly ordered the charge. But the narrow street and wynds were no place for the furious onset of men with bladed weapons and, time and again, the volleys of the Cameronian musketry threw them back. Cannon sent snipers to occupy the upper floors of the town's larger houses and it seems that one man found his mark. William Cleland was fatally wounded by musket balls in his chest and head but he died a hero's death. So that his men might not witness it and become disheartened at the loss of their commander, Cleland summoned all of his strength to drag himself out of the sight of his fellow Cameronians before the breath went out of him. He was only 28 years old.

For 16 hours, the battle raged around the walls of the old cathedral but the defences held. When the Cameronians ran out of musket balls, they stripped lead off the cathedral roof and cast new ones. In their frustration, the Highlanders fired the roofs of several houses in the High Street and those inside suffered terrible deaths. By 11 p.m., when gloaming had come and his men were exhausted and disheartened, Cannon called them back. Three hundred Highlanders lay dead in Dunkeld's streets and many Cameronians had been killed.

The first Jacobite rebellion had been stalled and a year later a remnant of those who had won at Killiecrankie were defeated at the Haughs of Cromdale on Speyside. In May 1690, General Hugh MacKay marched his men into Lochaber and, at the south-western end of the Great Glen, he built a fort named after the new king. The Gaelic place name for Fort William is a blunt recognition that battle lines had been drawn and rebel territory occupied. It is *An Gearasdan*, 'the Garrison'. Also in 1690, the Jacobite cause suffered a further setback when James VII and II's forces were defeated in Ireland at the Battle of the Boyne. The exiled Stewarts and their supporters would take a generation to regroup.

An unlikely Jacobite, John Slezer, was released from prison soon after the siege of Dunkeld. He was a Dutch engineer who had been appointed Surveyor of His Majesty's Stores and Magazines or, more precisely, he compiled detailed accounts and made drawings of Scotland's fortified places. But he is much more famous for his *Theatrum Scotiae*. Published in 1693, it is the first pictorial survey of Scotland and its seventy engravings of towns and buildings offer a fascinating snapshot of the last quarter of the 17th century, when the nation stood unknowingly on the brink of change. Slezer's drawing of Dunkeld from the southern bank of the Tay appears to predate the siege since most of the buildings are intact but the separate drawing of the cathedral does show damage.

Slezer's Scotland is surprising. The focus is firmly on towns and much that he notices makes the viewer pause – seagoing sailing ships moored in the Tay below the walls of Perth and the extent of the Nor Loch below Edinburgh Castle rock – but it is his depiction of the countryside beyond the towns which is most interesting. In the closing decades of the 17th century, Scotland was home to about a million people and 900,000 of them did not live in the towns Slezer drew. In a reversal of modern demographics, the vast majority were involved in farming or at least in the production of food. And while care must be taken with the *Theatrum Scotiae* – Slezer repeats stock drawings, especially in the rural foregrounds of the engravings – they show a landscape little changed since the time of the macMalcolm kings and even before.

The fields are open and cultivated by the long, sinuous strips of runrig ploughing. There are few trees except around the castles and the houses of the powerful and there is a good example in the drawing of Dundee. To the north of the Law where John Graham set up the royal standard, there is a tower house with characteristic crow-step gables (perhaps Claypotts Castle) which has had broadleaf trees planted in its policies and they also seem to form an avenue. In the view of the town of Hamilton, there is a stag hunt taking place in the foreground and the only cover for the terrified animal is a small copse to the left.

Farmsteads in this open landscape tended to be enclosed. South of the walls of the cathedral precinct at St Andrews stands a small steading that is entirely surrounded by what look like high stone walls. These were built to keep out animals and not only the domesticated sort. Divided into four sections, the steading comprises a stack yard where three conical haystacks can be made out. The farmhouse seems to look out over the yard and behind it is a long, low L-shaped barn with a curved thatched roof. Its unusual construction suggests that this is a drawing of a real building. To the south of that is a walled garden with rows of vegetables planted in plots and what appear to be berry bushes on the fringes. Across another wall are the much taller trees of an orchard. This would seem to be the substantial farmstead of a family of some means. But, in the prospect of Perth, the foreground is partly filled by a row of hinds' cottages. Most appear to have only one door and, where a wall has windows, they are tiny. It is possible that these are but-and-ben cottages which accommodated beasts overnight. On the southern bank of the Tweed at Kelso, Slezer included a large and detailed drawing of the thatched roofs of what seem to be two neighbouring houses tucked against the steep bank at Maxwellheugh, where the Tweed turns east towards the sea. On what are almost certainly stone gables, there are lantern chimneys with a cowl arrangement to create a draught and the farther house has long tree boughs slung from the ridge to prevent the wind from getting under the sheaves of thatch and lifting them.

At both Kelso and Perth, there are no bridges across their great rivers. Instead, ferries known as cobles are being punted across the Tweed and the Tay. In the Kelso drawing there is a man on horseback on the flat bed of the coble, surely a very confident rider and a horse that does not spook. Few animals are shown in the *Theatrum Scotiae* but, when they do appear, they seem to be drawn from the life. In the view of Ayr, there are a few sheep and close by is the figure of a man. And the sheep look small, no bigger than dogs, as indeed they were in the late 17th century. The Agricultural Revolution lay in the future.

Slezer's is a view of a nation that had survived the Wars of the Covenant, the occupation during the Commonwealth and sweeping political change but, if his townscapes and landscapes appear peaceful, even prosperous, the events of the 1690s would change that. In a pattern that was repeated through the centuries of the Little Ice Age, cycles of cold springs and summers could produce periods of devastating famine across northern Europe. It is estimated that, between 1694 and 1698, the average annual temperature dropped by 1.5°C. Ice formed on big rivers such as the Thames and France suffered the worst famine since the medieval period. Around the shores of the eastern Baltic, hundreds of thousands starved to death, especially in Estonia and Finland, and the weather was so cold for so long that the dead could not be buried in the frozen ground. In Scotland, a calamitous sequence of bad harvests beginning in 1693 led to the death of about 15 per cent of the population, about 150,000 people perishing between 1695 and 1699. Famine seems to have struck hardest in the north and perhaps a quarter of the people of Aberdeenshire died. For good, grim reasons these were known as 'the Seven Ill Years', the name given to a biblical famine in the Book of Genesis.

In 1698, Andrew Fletcher of Saltoun estimated that about 200,000 Scots, a fifth of the population, had been forced to leave their homes to beg for food. Parish poor relief simply could not cope and so many starving beggars arrived in Edinburgh that the town council set up what amounted to a refugee camp in the Greyfriars Kirkyard. One observer wrote: 'Some die by the wayside, some drop down in the streets, the poor sucking babs are starving for want of milk, which the empty breasts of their mothers cannot furnish them, everyone may see death in the face of the poor that abound everywhere.'

People were forced to eat grass, nettles or rotting meat and it was common to see dead bodies lie for a long time where they had fallen by the roadside. It was no better in the glens and on the islands. Patrick Walker was a chapman who sold small items as he walked around Highland communities. The price of oatmeal rocketed and the effects of the famine horrified the pedlar: 'Meal became so scarce . . . and many could not get it . . . I have seen . . . women clapping their hands, and tearing the cloths off their heads, crying, "How shall we go home and see our children die in hunger?" . . . deaths and burials were so many and common, that the living were wearied in the burying of the dead.'

Hunger was one of the few conditions shared by the Scots who lived on either side of the Highland Line. Culturally and now politically, the gulf between Lowland and Highland yawned ever wider. Dundee's uprising may have foundered against the dyke around Dunkeld Cathedral but King William continued to look north anxiously. His grand European strategy to defeat Louis XIV might be stabbed in the back by the return of a Catholic king to Scotland with French support. His anxieties were matched by Lowland prejudices and they found expression in a notorious incident.

Oaths still mattered to kings and their noble subjects, and William of Orange rightly believed that if the clan chiefs of the Highlands would swear allegiance to him it would be more than a gesture. After 1689, various attempts were made to gather the oaths of the chiefs but a despatch sent from King William's camp in Flanders on 17 August 1691 brought matters to a head. If the chiefs would swear an oath to him in front of a local magistrate before 1 January 1692, then they could expect to be pardoned for their part in Dundee's uprising. But there was an immediate difficulty. Most had already sworn allegiance to James VII and II and, torn between compromising their honour and risking their lives and those of their people, the chiefs sent urgent messages to the exiled Stewart court at St Germain-en-Laye, near Paris. After months of characteristic dithering, a messenger was sent with authority to release the chiefs from their previous oaths, but he only arrived in the Highlands in mid December. As the winter weather closed in around the mountains and the sea lochs, there was very little time left before the deadline expired.

Alasdair MacIain, 12th Chief of the MacDonalds of Glencoe, was known to his people as Alasdair Ruadh, a reference to his red hair. By 1691, it was probably white and this giant of a man was bent with age. His birth date is uncertain, probably some time in the 1620s, and he had led his clansmen for forty years since the death of his father. Even amongst Highlanders, the reputation of the MacDonalds of Glencoe was low for they had raided the cattle of their neighbours in the east and south-west for generations. When the messenger from St Germain-en-Laye arrived in the western Highlands, MacIain knew that time was pressing hard.

It was a deep and snowy December as the old man mounted his shaggy garron and set out for the garrison at Fort William. But Col. John Hill could not be of help, explaining to MacIain that he was not authorised to receive an oath of allegiance and telling him that he needed to make his way through the snow to Inverary, a very long way to the south-west. Hill gave the old chief a letter of protection and reassured him that no action would be taken without him being able to plead before the Privy Council. Delayed by blizzards and detained for a day by Captain Thomas Drummond of the Argyll Regiment in what seems to have been a deliberate attempt to make him even later, MacDonald finally reached Inverary. And then had to wait another three days for Sir Colin Campbell, the Sheriff of Argyll, to arrive. Apparently he had spent New Year with his family on the other side of Loch Fyne. Eventually and reluctantly, he accepted the old man's oath but, in the event, it would mean nothing.

The sense of a set-up is reinforced by the correspondence of John Dalrymple, the Master of Stair and William of Orange's Secretary of State for Scotland. In Stair's letters to the Earls of Argyll and Breadalbane, he wondered if the use of 'fire and sword and all manner of hostility' against the clans who had not yet sworn should not be put in hand. And he wrote to the Deputy Commander of Fort William, saying, 'Let me hear from you whether you think this is the proper season to maul them in the cold, long nights.' Stair also believed that the MacDonalds of Glencoe should be singled out since they were 'a popish clan'. In fact, they were Episcopalians.

As old MacIain pulled his plaid tight around his shoulders and his pony plodded against the blizzards that blew in off Loch Fyne, Stair had already given instructions that a detachment of soldiers from the Earl of Argyll's regiment should be assembled for an action in Glencoe. The choice of their commander appeared to be astute. Even though he was 60 years old, an inveterate drunk and a gambler, Captain Robert Campbell of Glenlyon was given the mission because he had a score to settle. On their way back home from the Siege of Dunkeld, the MacDonalds of Glencoe had burned and looted farms in his territory and thereby greatly impoverished him. Penury was part of the reason he was forced to accept a commission in Argyll's regiment. Revenge was another. As the snow fell, the pace of events began to quicken.

Here is the Master of Stair writing to William III: 'Glencoe has not taken the oath, at which I rejoice . . . It will be a proper vindication of the public justice to extirpate that sept of thieves . . . It must be done quietly, otherwise they will make shift for both men and cattle . . . Let it be secret and sudden.'

And, on 1 January 1692, the king signed a document ordering that the MacDonalds of Glencoe be massacred. Here is the full text of the orders eventually passed to Glenlyon:

You are hereby ordered to fall upon the rebels, the McDonalds of Glencoe, and put all to the sword under seventy. You are to have a special care that the old Fox and his sons do upon no account escape your hands, you are to secure all the avenues that no man escape. This you are to put in execution at five of the clock precisely; and by that time, or very shortly after it, I'll strive to be at you with a stronger party: if I do not come to you at five, you are not to tarry for me, but to fall on. This is by the Kings special command, for the good & safety of the Country, that these miscreants be cut off root and branch. See that this be put in execution without feud or favour, else you may expect to be dealt with as one not true to King nor Government, nor a man fit to carry Commission in the King's service. Expecting you will not fail in the full-filling hereof, as you love your self, I subscribe these with my hand at Ballachulish Feb: 12, 1692.

For their Majesties' service
[signed] Robert Duncanson
To Capt. Robert Campbell of Glenlyon

By the time these orders were signed, Campbell and about 120 men had been billeted in the settlement along the glen. The MacDonald families managed to accommodate the soldiers in their blackhouses, sharing warmth and food with them. Apparently, the two old men, the chief and the soldier, both of them between 60 and 70, played cards by the fire. On 12 February, the same Captain Drummond who had arrested MacIain on the road to Inverary arrived with the orders from his superior officer, Major Duncanson. At dawn on Saturday, 13 February, the soldiers suddenly attacked the unsuspecting MacDonalds. As he got out of his bed, a startled MacIain was shot in the back at close range and his wife was stripped naked before soldiers pulled the rings off her arthritic fingers with their teeth. At the townships of Invercoe, Inveriggan and Achnacon, men were shot or cut down. But the operation appears to have been both sabotaged and bungled. About 40 were killed but most escaped into the winter landscape, climbing the steep flanks of the glen to safety. Some may have perished in the bitter cold – perhaps another 40 – but others may have been better prepared for flight. It seems likely that Glenlyon's soldiers (who can have had little idea of what was intended when they first marched into Glencoe since the orders were delivered at the last moment) gave warnings. Two junior officers, Lt Farquhar and Lt Kennedy, broke their swords rather than do murder and they were arrested and imprisoned. MacIain's sons, Iain MacAlasdair and Alasdair Og, both escaped into the mountains.

There was outrage. The massacre was widely seen as an act of callous brutality even though it was by no means the worst or only example. Two years before MacDonald blood was spattered on the snows of Glencoe, a naval force under the command of an Ulsterman, Edward Pottinger, raided the Clanranald island of Eigg. An unknown number of men, women and children were killed and, in the absence of those clansmen who were with Dundee, many women were raped by the soldiers. But this atrocity was covered up and Pottinger altered his ship's log to conceal the truth of what happened. By comparison, Robert Campbell of Glenlyon showed his explicit orders in the inns of Edinburgh to anyone who was interested. And plenty were. Word of what happened to MacIain and his people spread quickly. There was clamour for an enquiry because, under Scots Law, there was a special abhorrence of what was known as 'murder under trust'. The conclusion of the Parliamentary enquiry was unequivocal: 'Though the command of superior officers be very absolute, yet no command against the laws of nature is binding; so that a soldier, retaining his commission, ought to refuse to execute any barbarity, as if a soldier should be commanded to shoot a man passing by inoffensively, upon the street, no such command would exempt him from the punishment of murder.'

Eventually, the Master of Stair was forced to resign but he did not fall out of royal favour for, in 1702, he was raised to an earldom. While the central role of King William was ignored, there was a general revulsion at the notion of the ministers of a constitutional monarch sanctioning the massacre of his subjects, who themselves had been guilty of no crime. The MacDonalds of Glencoe died because of who they were thought to be – savages, sub-humans who spoke a barbarous tongue and who lived in primitive conditions in a wild and uncultivated landscape. At the time, the massacre was also a propaganda gift to the Jacobite cause but the shame of what happened long outran 17th- and 18th-century politics, lasting until modern times. The close involvement of King William has only recently become clear.

The 1690s in Scotland seem to have been blood-soaked and bleak, the land scarred by famine and traversed by straggles of starving beggars. But there was hope and enterprise in the air – at least, in Edinburgh and in London.

The Battle of Beachy Head was the stimulus. A catastrophic defeat for William II and III in his long war with Louis XIV in 1690, it saw the loss of 11 ships and brought the navy to its knees. And, if England was to be a naval power, as befits part of an archipelago, money was urgently needed to rebuild. The royal treasury was empty but William Paterson, a wealthy Scots merchant from Tinwald in Dumfriesshire, came to the rescue with an innovative idea – the Bank of England. He had written a paper three years before, outlining how such a bank might work and his proposals were put into practice. William III needed to borrow £1,200,000 but his credit rating was so low that few were prepared to lend directly to him. Paterson had the idea of forming potential lenders into a limited liability company which could issue banknotes. This was possible because, when the lenders gave the government cash to rebuild the navy, they received bonds in return. With the backing of the bank, these immediately acquired value and the banknotes were issued against them. Paterson's enterprise was quickly rewarded when the vast sum of £1.2 million was raised in only 12 days. With an interest rate of 8 per cent and an annual fee of £4,000 for servicing the loan (an early idea which has sadly blossomed in modern banking), the Bank of England quickly began to prosper. And Paterson turned his mind to what might be achieved in his native Scotland.

Only a year after the foundation of the Bank of England, the Scottish Parliament enacted legislation to bring the Bank of Scotland into being. It was very different. Instead of funding government expenditure and moving down the path of becoming a central bank, the Bank of Scotland was expressly forbidden to lend to governments and encouraged to support Scottish business. Granted a monopoly for 21 years, it quickly raised £1.2 million in capital and was the first bank in Europe to print its own banknotes. The final clause in its founding act was fascinating. The first Governor was an Englishman, John Holland, and it seems that special provision was made to accommodate him: all foreign-born proprietors of the Bank of Scotland could become naturalised Scotsmen 'to all intents and purpose whatsoever'. The clause remained in force until 1920.

Meanwhile, William Paterson believed that he had conceived another brilliant idea. Having made his own fortune in the West Indies, he was well aware of both the geography of the area and the ebb and flow of international trade. Paterson knew that the Isthmus of Panama was narrow and, if a port could be established on the Caribbean shore and eventually another on the Pacific side, then the long, expensive and dangerous passage around Cape Horn could be avoided. The brilliance of the concept was that the success of any colony in that pivotal location did not depend on the discovery and exploitation of natural resources but simply on the operation of trade. And this first Scottish colony would make money from the beginning. It was to be named New Caledonia although the name of the Gulf of Darien would be what history remembered.

In 1695, the Company of Scotland was set up by the Scottish Parliament but it immediately ran into difficulty. Paterson aimed to raise funds for the Darien Scheme in London and in the markets of Europe but, fearing for its monopoly position, the powerful East India Company blocked investment. Very soon it was clear that Scotland would be the sole source of funding. But, even so, a staggering sum was raised – about £400,000, around 20 per cent of the disposable wealth of the entire nation. All manner of people, from earls to burgesses, invested. Scotland looked as though it was mortgaging its future on a single project.

From the outset, the Darien Scheme was beset by poor preparation and little or no sensible planning. When five ships set out from Leith in 1698 with 1,200 colonists on board, they had very little idea of what conditions waited for them on the other side of the Atlantic. When they reached the Gulf of Darien on 2 November, they immediately began the work of founding a colony. Under the direction of the same Captain Thomas Drummond who brought Glenlyon his orders in Glencoe, they dug a defensive ditch across a narrow peninsula and behind it built Fort St Andrew. It had no source of fresh water.

Such an elementary lack of foresight was only the beginning of the difficulties of the Darien colony. Supplies ran low, the settlers could grow very little food in the humid climate, they stored it badly and, by the following summer, malaria and fever had begun to thin their numbers dramatically. Worse, there was no help available. Anxious not to upset the Spanish who were needed as allies in the war against France and whose growing American empire surrounded the colony, William II and III instructed the English and Dutch merchants in the Caribbean not to supply the beleaguered Scots. When a desperate ship from Darien sailed to Port Royal in Jamaica, it was refused any assistance and turned away empty-handed. But messages sent home said little of this and gave a misleading impression that all was well and, in 1699, a second expedition set out from Leith. A year later, the Spanish decided that the Scots had no place in the midst of their possessions and they sailed to Darien and blockaded the settlement of New Edinburgh. Their commander offered terms – if the Scots surrendered, they would be spared. They agreed. Darien ended in disaster and, of the 2,500 who sailed with high hopes, only a few hundred returned. And the Scottish economy was left in ruins.

Having lost a catastrophic amount of money, many Scots – and not only the wealthy and titled – were close to bankruptcy. England and King William were blamed and with justification. How could the King of Scotland fail to act in Scotland's interest and favour England? Enmity was fuelled by what was seen as high-handed and deeply anti-Scottish behaviour and it simmered for years. In July 1704, the *Worcester*, a ship that had docked at Leith to wait out a storm, was declared to be an East India Company vessel and its crew were accused of piracy. Frustration boiled over when Thomas Green, the captain, and two of crew were tried and found guilty on trumped-up charges and hanged on Leith Sands. After the tragedy of Darien, the hundreds of thousands of deaths in the Ill Years and the parlous state of the economy, prospects at the outset of a new century cannot have looked bright for many Scots. But, within a few short years, everything would look different.

The Act of Union of 1707 was never inevitable and, at the time, it was very unpopular in Scotland. The momentum for union began with the difficulties and dynastic dead-ends of the regal union of 1603.

Widowed, asthmatic and childless, William of Orange died in 1702 and was succeeded by his sister-in-law who ruled as Queen Anne. After 17 pregnancies and the death of her 11-year-old son, the Duke of Gloucester, in 1700, it was clear that she could only be a temporary solution as the last available Protestant Stewart. Even before William's death, the English Parliament had legislated for the future with the Act of Settlement in 1701. It excluded Catholics from the royal succession. After some negotiation and casting around, it was decided that the throne should be offered to the enthusiastically Protestant Sophia, the Electress of Hanover. She was also the granddaughter of James VI and I and therefore could claim some, but not too much, descent from the Stewarts. And, even though she was not young, Sophia had a son, George Ludwig von Braunschweig-Luneburg, the Duke and Elector of Hanover. The facts that he was notoriously foul-tempered, had divorced his duchess and incarcerated her in a castle for life and was no longer on speaking terms with his son, George Augustus, were less important than his firmly Protestant faith.

The Act of Settlement settled something else. By setting aside the hereditary rights of the Stewarts (and no fewer than 57 legitimate claimants in that lineage), it underlined very emphatically that the monarchy was subservient to parliament. For once and for all, the Stewart notion of the divine right of kings was consigned to the past. And what made the Hanoverians even more attractive was that they were foreigners who did not speak a syllable of English (and continued to use German as a family language until the 19th century) and therefore would be heavily dependent on the advice of English ministers and the English Parliament. Finally, there were plenty of them. George had five brothers and many nephews. The only problem was Scotland.

The campaigns of Montrose and Dundee had shown how much more attached to the Stewarts the Scots were. There was also the Auld Alliance, an occasional but persistent factor in Scottish foreign relations since the medieval period. After the disaster at Darien, English politicians knew that their near-bankrupt neighbour in the north might easily succumb to French bribery as a welcome price for the return of the Stewarts. James VII and II had died on 17 September 1701 and Louis XIV had moved quickly to proclaim his son, James Francis Edward, as James VIII and III. From the use of 'pretend' to mean 'claim', he became known as the Pretender.

The Act of Settlement was not well managed. It appears that the Scottish Parliament was not consulted and its compliance assumed. In 1704, a game of legislative tit for tat began to be played across the border. That year the Scottish Parliament passed the Act of Security and this clearly set out the Scots' right to decide who should be their monarch irrespective of the views of the English Parliament and, after the death of Queen Anne, it also made it clear that England could not drag Scotland into war without consent. The European campaigns of William of Orange had been costly and particularly onerous for Scotland. Of the twenty British battalions who fought at the 1692 Battle of Steinkirk, not far from Brussels, eight were Scottish and two who were centrally involved in the 1689 uprising suffered terrible casualties. General Hugh MacKay had advised a strategic withdrawal but King William insisted that he advance at the head of his clansmen and attack the French. Mackay and many of his men were killed and the Cameronians were also badly depleted in the same action. Such heavy demands for manpower from a famine-stricken nation were the cause of much bitterness.

The Act of Security was buttressed by the Act Anent Peace and War passed in the same year and it asserted the Scots' right to an independent foreign policy after the queen's death. When taken alongside the Wine Act, a vital measure to allow the import of wine from France (whose ports were at that time blockaded by the English navy), these initiatives dropped heavy hints about the direction an independent Scottish foreign policy might take. It seemed that pressure was building. Queen Anne's health was fragile and it appeared to many in the English Parliament that the least-worst solution to any looming succession crisis would be a complete union with Scotland. When he suggested the same in the early 1690s, William of Orange had been rebuffed, just as James VI and I had been after 1603. Now the English Parliament forced the pace when it passed the Aliens Act in 1705. This measure gave the Scots a deadline. If, after ten months of negotiation, they could not agree to the succession of the Electress Sophia and also make progress on what the terms of union with England might be, then all exports from Scotland to England would be banned and all non-naturalised Scots living in England would be expelled. This was unvarnished blackmail since more than half of all Scottish exports went south and the naval blockade made it very difficult to find alternative markets in Europe. Negotiations began. And England set the terms.

A Bill of Union was drawn up for the English Parliament in 1706 and, in essence, the Scots could either accept it or reject it. There was only one realistic option and a party of negotiators travelled to London. Appropriately, both sides convened at the Cockpit, an old theatre at the back of where the Palace of Whitehall had stood (it had recently burned down). During the reign of Queen Anne it was where Treasury officials met. The two negotiating teams did not. Like old-fashioned disputes between trade unions and employers, the Scots sat in one room, the English in another and they communicated only in writing. Despite this, they had an outline agreement after only ten days and, after three months, 25 detailed articles of union. All that remained was for the articles to be approved by the Scottish Parliament.

Popular opposition to the proposals had not abated. When the Scottish Parliament met in Edinburgh to consider the articles, there was rioting and in Glasgow it flared sporadically for a month. The Provost was forced into hiding. The Queen's Commissioner, the Duke of Queensberry, needed a military escort so that he could reach Parliament Hall safely. Many burghs had sent petitions objecting to the union and the Convention of Royal Burghs, as a body, opposed it. Not one petition in favour was received. From their pulpits, Kirk ministers railed against union and such was their influence on ordinary people that widespread unrest was thought likely. Rioting broke out in Dumfries where the articles were burned at the mercat cross and the Covenanting south-west saw repeated outbreaks of vigorous dissent. There were even rumours of armed insurrection. These prompted Queensberry to order the small Scottish standing army to camp near Edinburgh and, in case they were insufficient to keep order, English troops massed on the border. All of this fed a popular belief that, unless Parliament passed the Act of Union, the English would invade and impose it.

In the event, a persuasive mixture of bribery, necessity and some statesmanlike vision ensured that there was a substantial majority in favour. On 16 January 1707, the Scottish Parliament voted itself out of existence, by 110 votes to 67.

The terms were mixed. On the one hand, Scots producers and merchants were given access not only to English markets but also to English colonies. After 1713, these were much expanded. When the Treaty of Utrecht concluded the war with France, Great Britain acquired new territory, from vast tracts of Canada to the Rock of Gibraltar. In addition, the English Parliament agreed the payment of a huge sum to the Scots, almost £400,000. Known as 'the Equivalent', it was seen as compensation for the losses incurred by the Darien Scheme.

On the other hand, Scottish representation in the new parliament at Westminster was disproportionately low. Even though democracy would not be a feature of political life until the 20th century, the Scottish population of one million was poorly represented compared to England's five million. There were to be only 45 Scottish members of the House of Commons out of a total of 513 and only 16 Scottish peers in the House of Lords. Also, Scotland was compelled to accept a proportion of the English National Debt and to pay higher taxes. Finally, it was agreed that the Church of Scotland and the legal system should remain distinct and independent.

The moment when Great Britain came into being was not 16 January 1707, when the Scottish Parliament dissolved itself, or even when the Scots delegation delivered its consent to London. The events of the afternoon of 6 March 1707 were what turned the direction of our history. Queen Anne had come to Parliament to sit on her throne in the House of Lords while Black Rod was despatched to the chamber of the House of Commons to bang three times on the great door with his staff. Once all were assembled in the royal presence, the Clerk of the Crown read out the titles of the eight bills to be passed into law that day. Four concerned public matters and they were:

1. An Act of Union of the two kingdoms of England and Scotland.
2. An Act for better preventing Escapes out of the Queen's Bench and Fleet prisons.
3. An Act for repairing the Highway between Hockliffe and Woodborne, in the County of Bedford.
4. An Act . . . for repairing the Highways in the County of Hereford.

To see an epoch-changing act of parliament given the same status as measures to prevent convicts escaping and another to enable the mending of a road between two villages lends some sort of perspective. Nevertheless, when the Clerk of Parliaments announced royal assent to the Act of Union in an old medieval formula, *La Reyne le veult*, 'the Queen wills it', it was the beginning, the moment when the British state, the United Kingdom of Great Britain, became a reality. And the moment when the history of Scotland changed utterly.

But still the union was fragile. There was no guarantee that it would continue and there were those who would repeatedly attempt to undo the articles of the act that was given royal assent in 1707. First amongst these was Louis XIV. As king of the wealthiest and most populous nation in Europe, he found himself in the uncomfortable position of not winning his war with the British and their allies. The brilliant John Churchill, Duke of Marlborough, had blazed his name in history with famous victories and would do more damage to French ambition at Oudenarde and Malplaquet. And, at a time when he needed cash for his war chests, Louis was paying for the considerable cost of the exiled Stewart court at St Germain-en-Laye. It was time to act decisively.

A French spy in England, Col. Nathaniel Hooke, sent encouraging reports and the remarkable George Lockhart reckoned that between 30,000 and 40,000 men would rally to the Stewart standard in Scotland. The MP for Edinburgh, Lockhart was a Jacobite spy at the centre of public life. He had been a negotiator at the Cockpit in London and sent regular reports of proceedings to St Germain-en-Laye. Sure that the time was right, seeing that popular resentment against the Union was powerful, Lockhart advised James VIII and III to compile a manifesto – a series of assurances to the Scottish people. In the subsequent Declaration, the exiled king made it clear that he claimed only the throne of Scotland, that he would dissolve the Union, be subservient to the will of parliament and uphold the independence of the Kirk. A Stewart less like his immediate ancestors is hard to imagine.

In February 1708, six French regiments and the Irish Brigade mustered at Dunkirk where they prepared to board five warships and twenty frigates. It was a credible invasion force of about 6,000 battle-hardened soldiers. And, in the holds of the frigates, they had stowed arms for a further 13,000 men, the Scots Jacobites who would flock to the royal standard. But there was a problem. James VIII and III had contracted measles. This delayed departure from Dunkirk and may have softened morale. The plan had been to sail north to the Firth of Forth and, at a prearranged signal from the shore, land the invasion force within striking distance of Edinburgh. With the focus on the wars in Europe, Lockhart believed that there were only 2,500 regular soldiers, at most, stationed in Scotland and the French would easily overrun so few.

When the fleet eventually sailed on the morning tide on 17 March, with a recovered king on board, it immediately ran into difficulty. The weather closed in and such a fierce storm blew up that the French admiral, Le Comte de Forbin, feared for the fleet's safety. But he was impressed with the composure of the 19-year-old James VIII and III: 'That very night a gale of wind put the whole fleet in peril. The king, young as he was, faced the danger with a courage and coolness beyond his years; but his suite [retinue] was thoroughly frightened.'

When the sea settled, de Forbin realised that he had missed the rendezvous point on the southern shore of the Forth and he instructed his captains to drop anchor off Crail in Fife. But worse, Admiral Byng arrived with a fleet of British warships. James begged de Forbin to put him and his soldiers ashore but the admiral preferred to weigh anchor quickly and attempt to outrun Byng. He will also have borne in mind Louis XIV's express instruction that, whatever happened, he had to keep James alive. De Forbin managed to shake off the British pursuit – in fact, Byng doubled back down the Angus coast believing that he may have missed the French. But all the while, they were sailing farther north, through the Pentland Firth, around Cape Wrath and running south for their home port of Dunkirk. King James was devastated.

Ignored as nothing more than a fiasco, the abortive invasion of 1708 in fact stood a reasonable chance of success. But bad luck, bad weather and a faltering resolve brought the soldiers back to France and these would be characteristics that would curse future attempts to restore the Stewarts. However, it was clear that, if either France or Spain was prepared to back the restoration with substantial resources, they might be able to roll back the tide of history.

Meanwhile, most Scots turned their minds to the everyday business of survival. The immediate economic impact of the Union was patchy. Some Scottish producers found it difficult to compete in the new, open market of Britain with their English equivalents but one aspect of Scottish agriculture certainly did thrive and even prosper. Between 1707 and 1750, the export of black cattle from the Highlands to England grew from 30,000 head to 80,000. This was the beginning of the great age of cattle droving, a business that left its mark on the landscape. Part of the reason for the expanding market was the demand for salt beef from the army and the navy as Britain sought to be Great and embarked on a series of imperial wars, both in Europe and North America. Not only did the glens and the islands supply many of the soldiers who fought and died to create the Empire, those they left at home also reared the beef the armies marched on.

Droving left few accounting records but historians have pieced together some colourful sources that show that the organisation of the trade was simple yet impressive in its scale. Highland chiefs and landowners were generally paid rents in kind rather than cash and cattle was the main currency. Landowners also acted as agents for tenant farmers who had surplus to sell or they bought from them directly. Many crofter-farmers had to sell their beasts before the winter in any case since they did not have easy access to the new sources of fodder being grown in the Lowlands. And cattle supplied their own transport. They walked to market.

After the first herds were collected in localities, the cattle were driven to a larger, more central market. Aikey Fair at Old Deer in the Buchan was one such, the largest in the north of Scotland and very busy at the end of July. After one fair day in 1839, a drove of 6,000 beasts moved south through Tarves in a continuous line, a mile long.

Lairds and their tacksmen, the men who drove their herds to Lowland markets or trysts but most men walked and had dogs with them to keep the herds together. It was thought that one man and a good dog could manage fifty to sixty head. And when drovers stopped for the night, the first thing they did was to find food for their faithful dogs. Often these men were farmers who could afford to be away between sowing time and harvest time. All were armed. Moving large herds of valuable animals through countryside that was not necessarily friendly could be problematic and men carried dirks, pistols, swords and even muskets. In the Disarming Acts after the Jacobite Rebellions of 1715 and 1745, drovers were exempted. The trade was so important to England that it could not be jeopardised and, in the Highlands, cattle stealing was almost an honourable tradition and very widespread.

At the likes of Aikey Fair in the Buchan and St Lawrence Fair in the Garioch, cattlemen who assembled droves as large as that of 1839 may have done so for security but such scale did present problems. As thousands of beasts moved through the countryside, especially in late July, they could be a danger to crops and stampeding or panicked animals would break down fences in moments. Eventually droving paths were made, corridors 50–100 feet wide enclosed by dykes or turf banks on either side. Some are still visible in the Border hills. However many there were in a drove, the beasts were not to be hurried. So that they kept their condition and could graze and drink along the way, dogs did not snap at their heels and men tried only to keep the herd moving forward as one. If a drove covered ten or twelve miles a day, it was a good day.

In the late summer of 1723, a large drove was collected at Broadford on the Isle of Skye and then moved eastwards to the shore at Kylerhea, where there is a narrow strait. An account of 1813 tells what happened next:

All the cattle reared in the Isle of Skye which are sent to the southern markets pass from that island to the mainland by the ferry of Kylerhea. Their numbers are very considerable, by some supposed to be 5,000 but by others 8,000 annually, and the method of ferrying them is not in boats . . . but they are forced to swim over Kylerhea. For this purpose the drovers purchase ropes which are cut at the length of three feet having a noose at one end. This noose is put round the under-jaw of every cow, taking care to have the tongue free. The reason given for leaving the tongue loose that the animal may be able to keep the salt water from going down its throat in such a quantity as to fill all the cavities in the body which would prevent the action of the lungs; for every beast is found dead and said to be drowned at the landing place to which this mark of attention has not been paid. Whenever the noose is put under the jaw, all the beasts destined to ferried together are led by the ferryman into the water until they are afloat, which puts an end to their resistance. Then every cow is tied to the tail of the cow before [in front] until a string of six or eight be joined. A man in the stern of the boat holds the rope of the foremost cow. The rowers then play their oars immediately. During the time of high water or soon before or after full tide is the most favourable passage because the current is then least violent. The ferrymen are so dextrous that very few beasts are lost.

Once the cattle had shaken off the seawater and been untied, the drovers moved them inland from Glenelg to Glen Shiel before reaching the Great Glen at Fort Augustus. From there, they pushed on into the mountains and over the difficult Pass of Corrieyairack and thence to Dalwhinnie. There, in the late summer of 1723, they met a travelling clergyman, Bishop Forbes, and he was also impressed at the drovers' skill, organisation and resourcefulness:

They had four or five horses with provisions for themselves by the way, particularly blankets to wrap themselves in when sleeping in the open air, as they rest on the bleak mountains, the heathy moors, or the verdant glens, just as it happens, towards the evening. They tend their flocks [he means herds] by night and never move till about eight in the morning and then march the cattle at leisure that they may feed a little as they go along. They rest awhile at midday to take some dinner and so let the cattle feed and rest as they please. The proprietor does not travel with the cattle but has one [man] for his deputy to command the whole and he goes to the place appointed against the day fixed for the fair. When the flock is very large, as the present, they divide it, though belonging to one, into several droves that they may not hurt one another in narrow passes, particularly on bridges many of which they go along. Each drove has a particular number of men with some boys to look after the cattle.

What kept the herds together was mostly instinct. Compared with modern bullocks that spend winters in huge cattle courts and are fed on silage, Highland cattle of the 18th century were wild and often difficult to manage. Having spent all their lives, winter and summer, out in unfenced, open pasture, conforming to their own hierarchies, deferring to king bulls, they could be a handful for the herd laddies and their dogs. Not shaggy like the familiar picture-postcard Highland cattle, they were in reality small and most of them black. But they did have horns and in the narrow places mentioned by Bishop Forbes or in potentially panicky situations like river crossings where they might at best spook or at worst stampede, they could be difficult and dangerous.

Armed, kilted, weather-beaten and used to living outside, Highlanders also presented a vivid spectacle as the herds moved through the Lowlands at the end of their journeys. Observers thought them bear-like, swathed in thick plaids that smelled of heather and peat smoke, and some believed the drovers to be wild, shaggy like their ponies and uncultured. What helped convert the unfamiliar into a threat was, of course, language. The herdsmen shouted at their cattle and their dogs in Gaelic and many will not have had much English.

But the drovers were much respected for their skill and hardihood. Here is Edward Burt, writing in the 1720s, watching a difficult moment in a drove: 'It was a time of rain by a wide river where there was a boat to ferry over the drovers. The cows were about 50 in number and took the water like spaniels, and when they were in, their drivers made a hideous cry to urge them forwards: this, they told me, they did to keep the foremost of them from turning about, for in that case, the rest would do the like and then they would be in danger, especially the weakest of them, to be swept away and drowned by the torrent.'

Even now, long after the end of droving, their routes can still be made out, especially in the more remote glens. At their habitual overnight stopping places, what were known as stances, the beasts' droppings mucked the ground over many summers. Consequently, the grass in those places still looks significantly greener in the springtime and the ewes and their lambs graze there because it is the most succulent. It is a surprising but appropriate elegy for a remarkable age – a period when many peaceful journeys were made across the Highland Line.

There was rather less economic activity in the Lowlands – or at least less than anticipated. Because the idea of the Union had been so unpopular before 1707, the commercial benefits of an open border and the beginning of free trade with England and her burgeoning empire were overstated. After 1707, the Scottish economy grew only very slowly, and in some sectors, contracted, as industries, such as paper-making, salt-making, woollen manufacture and candle-making, seemed particularly to suffer from stronger English competition. The author of *Robinson Crusoe*, Daniel Defoe, had been an English spy in Edinburgh in 1707 and, in *A Tour Thro' the Whole Island of Great Britain*, published in 1726, he admitted that the predicted increase in trade was 'not the case, but rather the contrary'.

Grumbles grew louder. The £400,000 of The Equivalent had been promised in coin but, in fact, not only was it three months late, three-quarters of it was in Exchequer bills. Paper money was still new – as, indeed, was the notion of English notes having value north of the Tweed. This disappointment had little impact with the mass of the people but, when English MPs insisted that a tax on malt be imposed, there was uproar. In an age before reliable water supplies, beer was drunk by many – often for its calorific value as well as for the effect of the alcohol. Scots MPs boycotted Westminster in protest although the tax was not levied until much later.

The Act of Union had guaranteed the independence of the Church of Scotland but in 1712 two acts of the British Parliament threatened its status and governance profoundly. Kirk sessions had enjoyed the right to choose their parish ministers and reckoned, probably rightly, that their selection would reflect the preferences of the congregation. But, when the Westminster parliament passed the Patronage Act of 1712, this power was transferred to local landowners, the nobility and the Crown. It was a divisive measure – one which led to a bewildering sequence of splits and secessions which splintered the Church of Scotland again and again until the great Disruption of 1842. A month before the Patronage Act, the Toleration Act had soured relations between the Kirk and Westminster on another front when it allowed Episcopalians the right to use the Anglican liturgy. From then on their churches were known as the English kirks. The Union was growing ever more unpopular. In 1713, Viscount Seafield, one of the most active campaigners in favour of the Union, brought a motion to the House of Lords. He proposed nothing less than the dissolution of the Union of 1707 and his motion was defeated by only four votes.

What brought matters to a head was the death of Queen Anne, the last Stewart monarch, in 1714, and the accession of George I, the first Hanoverian. When the new king arrived in London in September, one of his first executive actions was to sack John Erskine, the Earl of Mar. He had been Third Secretary, the government minister in charge of Scottish affairs. In the election of January 1715, the leading Whig noblemen, the Marquis of Montrose and the Duke of Argyll, managed the very restricted poll so adroitly that they secured the election of 40 of the 45 Scottish seats in the House of Commons for pro-Hanoverian Whigs. And, all over Britain, Tories who might have favoured the restoration of James VIII and III were ejected from office. This overwhelming victory in Scotland obscured a very different picture of popular opinion – one of widespread sympathy for the Jacobite cause. When George I was proclaimed at the mercat cross in Inverness, the ritual cheers of 'God save the King' were swamped by crowds shouting 'God damn them and their king'. Disaffection was not confined to Scotland and there were disturbances all over England at the coming of the German king. Rebellion was more than in the air, it was expected imminently.

The Fifteen began and ended in disappointment. Sacked by George I and deeply embittered, John Erskine, Earl of Mar, sailed north to Scotland on board a collier, a coal ship, so anxious was he to be away. Eventually reaching Braemar, he summoned sympathetic lairds and noblemen to a deer hunt. There, plans were laid to raise the standard of James VIII and III on the Braes of Mar on 6 September. Thousands came. Most were led by the noble families of the north-east Lowlands and the Highland chiefs of the eastern Grampians. Mar had also contacted western chiefs and, avoiding the garrison at Fort William, they marched south with a force of 3,000 to the Duke of Argyll's town of Inverary. They failed to take it.

In the east, Mar had more immediate success and both Perth and Inverness fell to the Jacobites on the same day, 14 September, while King James was proclaimed at the mercat cross of Aberdeen a week later. Meanwhile, in the north of England and the south of Scotland, troops rallied to the cause under the command of Viscount Kenmure and William MacKintosh of Borlum. There was a plan for King James to land in the south-west of England. But, five days before the standard was planted on the Braes of Mar, the rebellion began to unravel. Louis XIV died and the Regent, the Duke of Orleans, was much less enthusiastic. The Spanish gave money but no soldiers or ships. Mar seemed to freeze, waiting for more than six weeks in Perth for reinforcements that never came.

When the Duke of Argyll marched east to challenge him with a much smaller force, it seemed that the Jacobites might be provoked into action and a decisive victory won. But the Battle of Sheriffmuir near Dunblane was indecisive, even baffling. On ground good enough for an all-out Highland charge to succeed and with three times as many men as Argyll, Mar should have won easily. The left wing of the government army was much shorter than the Jacobites' and it should have been quickly outflanked, rolled up and defeated but orders were unclear. Mar seemed reluctant to commit all of his forces and Argyll seized the initiative. He attacked the Jacobite left wing and drove them back before turning back to supplement his outnumbered left wing. Mar continued to hesitate and Argyll was able to get his army off the field and claim victory. A traditional song captured the confusion:

> There's some say that we wan and some say that they wan
> And some say that nane wan at a', man,
> But one thing is sure that at Sheriff Muir
> A battle was fought on that day, man,
> And we ran and they ran and they ran and we ran,
> And we ran and they ran awa' man.

Mar was no Montrose or Dundee, commanders used to fighting against the odds, inventive and brave, and the indecisiveness of Sheriffmuir did decide one vital strategic imperative. Argyll and his army placed themselves astride the road south past Stirling Castle rock. Mar could not easily combine with the southern Jacobites but, in any case, they were defeated at Preston the day after the fiasco at Sheriffmuir. There then followed a sorry but characteristic postscript.

ROBINSON SELKIRK

Born in Lower Largo in Fife, an unruly youth with a taste for buccaneering, Alexander Selkirk joined an expedition to the South Seas in 1704. And then he made a terrible decision. As his ship dropped anchor off the uninhabited Juan Fernandez archipelago, about 400 miles west of Chile, Selkirk told the captain that he thought the ship was so leaky and unseaworthy that he would rather be left on Juan Fernandez than sail on. OK, said Captain Stradling, and he landed Selkirk on the islands with all his gear. Almost immediately, the Scot changed his mind but the captain did not and sailed away. Selkirk spent more than four years as a castaway, entirely alone. He survived by hunting and gathering wild fruits and roots. One of his worst problems was attacks by aggressive rats as he slept but the resourceful castaway domesticated feral cats and they protected him. When he visited Lower Largo after his rescue, the locals called him 'the Man Who Taught the Cats to Dance'. Selkirk was of course the inspiration for Daniel Defoe's Robinson Crusoe. *First published in 1719, it is believed by many to be the first genuine novel to be written in English.*

Long after matters had effectively been decided, James VIII and III disembarked at Peterhead, well inside territory loyal to him. It was a few days before Christmas 1715 and the Stewart court had planned what they were sure would be a triumphal progress through the regained kingdom of Scotland. Scone Palace would become a royal palace, a grand proclamation would be issue to his subjects and James would be inaugurated on the Hill of Faith, just as kings of Scots had been since the ancient days of Kenneth macAlpin. It never happened. Although he was 27 years old and had showed eagerness to fight in 1708, the Pretender seemed out of his depth now that he had actually landed in Scotland. Raised in the febrile, frustrated neverland of St Germain-en-Laye, the king seemed distant, cold and aloof, surrounded by clan chiefs and loyal noblemen he had never met and could barely under-stand, making a winter journey through a country he had never visited. James appeared devoid of charisma and could inspire no one around him and the plans for the inauguration and coronation at Scone were set aside. By the end of January, government troops were massing and the garrison at Stirling Castle was strengthened. As the days passed and nothing happened, more and more clansmen slipped away, going home to their winter hearths.

It was indeed time to go. On 4 February, King James boarded a ship at Montrose, shrouded in failure, bound for France and exile.

With better and more resolute leadership, the 1715 Rising might well have succeeded. It had significant Lowland and English support and there was an unpopular German on the throne but, crucially, no French soldiers crossed the Channel to invade the south coast of England.

Recriminations were sensibly muted. Mar fled to Europe with his king while Viscount Kenmure and other leaders lost their heads. A Disarming Act banned those clans considered hostile from carrying arms (but not from owning them) and, in 1717, an Act of Grace and Pardon allowed those Jacobites in prison to go free. There would be more rebellions but prospects of success dimmed as the 18th century wore on and Scotland slowly began to embrace the opportunities offered by the Union.

Place names offer memories of one of the initiatives taken by the Board of Trustees for Manufacture. It was set up in 1727 with an annual budget of £6,000 to improve woollen production, the Scottish fisheries and the manufacture of linen. Lint is the Scots word for flax, the plant from which linen yarn is made and, all over the Lowlands, there are places such as Lintmill, Linthill, Lintalee and many others. Now entirely absent from the landscape, lint was grown by many farmers. Seen as a hungry crop that drained the ground of nutrients, it was also difficult to harvest. Because the whole plant was needed to make yarn, it could not be cut like cereals with sickles or scythes. It had to be pulled up by the roots. Once harvested, the lint was tied in bunches and then soaked in water for weeks to soften it. Often mistaken for quaint duck ponds, on many farms there are old flax stanks or lint holes. After being beaten to begin the process of separating the fibres, it was pulled through a heckle – a board studded with thin iron spikes, like a bed of nails. This tiring work was often done in heckling sheds by men who could afford to relieve the long days by paying someone to read to them. Newspapers and pamphlets were their staples and these meant that the men in the heckle sheds were uncommonly well informed. So much so that hecklers were not usually a welcome sight at political meetings. They were liable to ask pointed and pertinent questions. The modern sense of the word does its history a disservice.

Many Scots could afford to wear linen sarks or shifts under their outer clothing (underpants and knickers being a thing of the future) in the 18th century and there was a ready and regular market for good quality linen at the right price. The soldiers and sailors who were carving out Britain's empire valued the cool and light nature of linen sarks and the government could be an important customer. In Scotland's towns and villages linen looms began to clack and output rose. Linen manufacture went from 3,488,232 yards in the period 1728–31 to 30,700,200 yards in the period 1818–22. It employed around 20,000 weavers (to say nothing of hecklers and spinners) and grew into Scotland's most important industry. Towns as well as farms remember it in street and place names. Linen was whitened in the sunshine by being pegged out on bleach fields.

The Union altered the look of the Scottish countryside in a more enduring manner. Those few who profited not only from the proceeds of the Equivalent but also rose to lucrative positions of power in the new British state began to spend their money on big houses and lay out large estates. An account of how one family achieved this was compiled, very unusually, by a woman. Lady Grizel Baillie's household accounts ran to more than a thousand pages of great detail from 1692, the date of her marriage to George Baillie, until her death in 1746.

Both she and her husband had experienced the brutality of political life in Scotland at first hand. George made a memorable, grim prison visit to his father, Robert Baillie of Jerviswood, who was being held on a charge of high treason in Edinburgh's tollbooth. He had been a supporter of the Duke of Monmouth and a committed Presbyterian. When George saw his father, he learned that the old man was to suffer the agonies of being hanged, drawn and quartered the following day at the mercat cross. A remarkable man, Robert Baillie consoled his son, by saying, 'If you have a strong heart, you may go and see me nagled. But if you have not the heart for it, you may stay away.'

THUMBIKINS

They sound like a toy but, in fact, thumbikins were an instrument of torture, widely used in the 17th century. They worked like a nutcracker. A victim's thumbs or fingers were sandwiched between two small iron bars that were screwed tight with a key to inflict excruciating pain. Thumbikins could be carried in the pocket and produced in a courtroom to extract whatever a judge wished to hear. William Carstares was tortured with this instrument. When he later became Principal of Glasgow University, Carstares had occasion to meet King William of Orange, who asked him about the thumbikins. At a subsequent meeting, the Principal produced a set and a curious king inserted his thumbs between the bars. Carstares offered to turn the key.

When news of the execution reached Grizel's father, Sir Patrick Hume, at Redbraes Castle in Berwickshire, he fled into hiding as soldiers occupied his house. Under cover of the winter dark, Grizel took food to her father as he shivered in the crypt of Polwarth Church. She had also taken letters to his friend, Robert Baillie, when he was imprisoned in the tollbooth. Eventually the Humes and George Baillie secretly made their way to Utrecht in Holland to wait for better times.

They came with the accession of William of Orange. George had enlisted in the prince's horse guards and sailed with the invasion fleet that landed at Torbay in 1688. Elected MP for Berwickshire, George married Grizel four years later and she began to write her household accounts. Although badly stung by the Darien Scheme, the couple's fortunes swung upwards with the Union of 1707, for George was one of the 45 Scots MPs at Westminster. Appointed Commissioner for Trade, he began to make money. And he planned to hang on to it, come what may.

When rebellion loomed in 1715, there were significant numbers of Jacobite supporters in the Borders and the household accounts record the purchase of 30 swords, 30 guns and bayonets and a barrel of gunpowder weighing seven and a half stones. Sadly for the Baillies, their tower house at Whiteside was looted by the Jacobite army on its way to Kelso to proclaim James VIII and III and they almost certainly helped themselves to the cache of weapons. But the Baillies managed to evade capture or personal harm.

After the crisis had passed, Grizel often found herself in London because George I appointed her husband to high office, making him a Lord of the Admiralty and a Lord of the Treasury. As befitted their new status, they needed a new house in Scotland and, in 1724, William Adam, the most pre-eminent architect available, was engaged to design Mellerstain House. It is splendid, with long southerly vistas to the distant Cheviots, and, around it, the Baillies had the landscape remade to suit. Long, straight avenues led to the house. The River Eden was canalised and dammed to form a lake in the foreground of the magnificent view. And to finish the vistas to the nearer horizon, a fashionable Gothic folly called the Hundy Mundy was built.

Houses like this were a spectacular break with the past. Undefended, built to impress and often on a grand scale, many of them rose in the 18th-century landscape, shaping it in a new way. These were the centrepieces of estates and policies were laid out to please the eye of powerful and wealthy families rather than be useful or productive. Everything in these estates revolved around their wishes and needs. The big hooses employed servants who lived either below stairs or in attic rooms. And, perhaps most strikingly, airs and graces began to arrive and deference became more pronounced. Even though they continued to speak Scots (at least in Scotland), Grizel and George Baillie began to see themselves as very different from the ordinary people who served them or who lived and farmed around them. The household accounts record a letter of 1726 from William Adam to George about the design of Mellerstain House. He proposed to lower the level of the floor of the kitchen in the servants' wing to five feet below the windowsills – this would be 'so much better in that it prevents those in the kitchen and scullery from looking into the gardens'. Probably much influenced by her visits to London, Grizel set down 37 different directions for her butler ('You must keep yourself very clean.') as well as detailing a system of signs to let him know when to clear away one course of a meal and bring in another and so on. Scotland was beginning to break up into more sharply defined social classes.

Rebellion continued to flicker on the edges of Scotland. And bad luck and bad weather continued to dog the grander schemes of the Pretender. James VIII and III was now 29 and had been a claimant for a generation. France had entered a period of relative peace with Britain and James had successfully sought to persuade another sponsor to back him. On 19 March 1719, a substantial fleet of 29 Spanish ships carrying 5,000 soldiers, with arms for another 30,000 men to be distributed to British Jacobites, set sail from Cadiz. Its captains intended to make landfall on the south-west coast of England where it was thought support might be enthusiastic. Another, much smaller, force of 307 men led by George Keith, the Earl Marischal, sailed much further north to the Isle of Lewis where they made camp at Stornoway. A pincer movement was planned, with simultaneous moves on London from the north and west. But yet another disaster struck as storms off Cape Finisterre dispersed the larger Spanish invasion fleet and their ships ran for their home ports and stayed there.

Unaware that there would be no landing and no action in the south, Keith sailed to the mainland and occupied the picturesque sea castle on Eilean Donan on the north shore of Loch Duich. Few clansmen rallied to the standard – perhaps 400 from Clan Mackenzie, 150 from the Camerons; Rob Roy MacGregor came with 40 men. Lord George Murray was also with Keith's small force of about 1,000 men as they moved inland.

PROFESSORS MACGREGOR

Walter Scott's eponymous novel about Rob Roy told a tale of a cattle-rustling Highland chancer and the films made subsequently carry on the image. But MacGregor was much more than that. Probably a graduate of Glasgow University, he owned books and several of his letters survive. When the men of Clan Gregor were dis-named – it became a crime to carry the surname in the 17th century and later – they changed it and the bearers of one of the variants carried on the intellectual traditions of the family with great distinction. David Gregory (c. 1569–1708) was a professor of mathematics and astronomy at the Universities of Edinburgh and Oxford, while his uncle James Gregory (1638–75), a professor of mathematics at St Andrews and Edinburgh, discovered calculus. They were part of a remarkable dynasty of academics and 14 Gregorys became professors of medicine, history, mathematics, chemistry and philosophy in Scotland's universities.

From Inverness, General Joseph Wightman had marched to meet them with roughly equivalent numbers at his back and, on 9 June, they clashed in Glen Shiel, where it narrows at the foot of the range known as the Five Sisters of Kintail. The Spanish stood their ground but the clansmen suffered a mortar bombardment before being pushed back and then scattered. The fighting is commemorated by the name given to the southern end of the line of the Five Sisters peaks. One of the smaller is called Sgurr nan Spainteach because the Spanish soldiers fought a stubborn rearguard action on its lower slopes. The defeat at Glen Shiel was enough to snuff out the 1719 Rising. Many must have hoped that James VIII and III's ambitions had become very forlorn indeed.

Wightman's march from Inverness had contained the Jacobite incursion quickly, preventing Keith, Murray and the others from moving deeper inland and recruiting more support from the mainland clans. Ease of movement through difficult terrain was the key to any successful strategy to deal with rebellion in the Highlands, and when Field Marshal George Wade was appointed Commander-in-Chief of His Majesty's forces, castles, forts and barracks in North Britain, he wasted no time. Roads were required. Between 1728 and 1730 a major route was driven through the heart of the Highlands as a spectacular road was laid down between Perth and Inverness. The modern A9 follows Wade's route and relics of its original military purpose can still be seen by the roadside. Perched on a regular, man-made mound near Kingussie stands the shell of Ruthven Barracks. It could accommodate 120 soldiers and stable 28 horses for dragoons.

By 1740, all of the garrisons in the Highlands were linked by good roads that not only allowed marching soldiers to move quickly but also meant limbers of horse-drawn artillery could accompany them. Carts were also able to supply Fort William, Fort Augustus (built between 1729 and 1742 and intended to have a planned village around it called Wadesburgh), Ruthven, Inverness and the other barracks. Wade never won a set-piece battle against Highlanders but the military importance of his work is recognised in the sixth verse of the British national anthem. It is not often sung in Scotland – or, indeed, anywhere.

> Lord, grant that Marshal Wade
> May, by thy mighty aid,
> Victory bring.
> May he sedition hush
> And, like a torrent rush,
> Rebellious Scots to crush.
> God save the King.

While the process of laying down metalled roads was labour intensive, the building of essential bridges was very expensive. Known as Wade bridges, 40 were constructed in this period and perhaps the most famous and the most elegant crossed the Tay at Aberfeldy. Completed in 1734, it cost £4,000 – a large outlay. Beside the bridge stands a commemorative stone that recalls another of Wade's initiatives. In 1724, he attempted to drain some of the clans' military capability by raising a militia known as the Highland Watches – men who would be paid by the government for policing the glens and monitoring activity. The Aberfeldy stone marks the founding of the Black Watch. At first, it comprised three companies of men from loyal Clan Campbell and later more were recruited from the Frasers, Grants and Munros. By 1739, the regiment had been give the name of *Am Freiceadan Dubh*, 'the Black Guards' or 'the Black Watch'. Having fought with great distinction in the ranks of the British army at Fontenoy in 1745 under the command of the Duke of Cumberland as he attacked the French at Tournai, it was described as 'the Black Watch of Battles, first to come and last to go'. In what was to become a rehearsal of events yet to come, the Highlanders were repulsed by the Irish Jacobite Brigade who fought for the French king.

Over three centuries of service, the Black Watch won 172 battle honours, a unique achievement in the annals of British military glory and more than any other regiment of foot. They began a tradition of Highlanders fighting in the British army, a deliberate policy of emptying the glens of young men who might, in other circumstances, have fought against the British state. In the Seven Years War of 1756–63 against France and her allies, it is estimated that 12,000 clansmen marched with the army. Between 1756 and 1815, a total of at least 40,000 men and perhaps as many as 75,000 were recruited in the great drive for empire.

In 1757, the young prime minister, William Pitt, defended his policy with these fine words to the king: 'I sought for merit wherever it was to be found. It is my boast that I was the first minister who looked for it and found it in the mountains of the north. I called it forth and drew into your service a hardy and intrepid race of men . . . [T]hey served with fidelity as they fought with valour and conquered for you in every part of the world.' In his operations in French Canada, General James Wolfe was more candid: 'The Highlanders are hardy, intrepid, accustomed to rough country, and it is no great mischief if they fall. How can you better employ a secret enemy than by making his end conducive to the common good?' And in London, William Pitt was more honest when he reckoned that 'not many of them will return'.

The Black Watch retained the right to wear the kilt when it was later banned and their tartan was very distinctive, probably the oldest sett in existence. It may have been what gave the regiment its name. Also known as the Government Tartan, it is a very dark blue, green and black and it was later adopted by Clan Campbell. An illustration made in 1744 of soldiers who may have been in the Black Watch shows them wearing the *feileadh mor*, the 'great plaid', the original form of the kilt. It was a large piece of thick cloth worn belted around the waist and often folded in pleats. The upper part could be worn around the shoulders or even as a hood and one of the soldiers is shown keeping the flintlock mechanism of his musket dry with his plaid. Before they charged into battle, clansmen often threw off the heavy *feileadh mor* and charged in a *leine*, the Gaelic word for a 'shirt' that is simply a version of linen.

A letter written by Ivan Baillie in 1768 and published in the *Edinburgh Magazine* in 1785 purports to tell the tale of the invention of *feileadh beag*, the 'small kilt' – what most men wear now. According to Baillie, it was invented by an Englishman in the 1720s. Thomas Rawlinson was a Quaker from Lancashire who had negotiated with the chief of the MacDonnells of Glengarry to cut down his oak woods and make charcoal so that he could smelt local iron ore. Noticing that the big kilt encumbered his foresters and his foundrymen as they smelted ore, he promoted the wearing of the small kilt. He may have contacted a tailor in Inverness who made one that belted round the waist and was more heavily pleated but did not have the upper part. It was more likely a development encouraged by the Englishman for there exist illustrations of men wearing something like the *feileadh beag* before the 1720s.

Other elements of Scotland's distinct national iconography were finding their way into recorded history in the early years of the 18th century. Games involving hitting a small ball with a long stick were apparently played in medieval Holland but no serious historian believes that golf was not invented in Scotland. However, the name itself appears to derive from a Scots version of the Dutch word *colf* or *colve*, meaning a 'stick'. Perhaps it does. In any event, it was first noted in Scotland with disapproval. In a 1457 act of the Scottish Parliament, the playing of 'gowf' (and football) was forbidden since it interfered with archery practice. The earliest known lady player may have been Mary, Queen of Scots, who was said to have played a round of golf after the murder of her husband, Henry Darnley. She may have played on 'links-land', coastal areas of sandy soil which could not be cultivated and where beasts were often pastured on the tough grasses. From the Old English word *hlinc* meaning 'ridges' or 'rising ground', links in Scotland referred to sand dunes and the undulating grassland behind them.

The earliest courses on record are to be found around Edinburgh. Bruntsfield Links is some distance from the sea but the soil is sandy and the ground undulating. Golf is still played there, a pitch and putt version, and on summer evenings players can be seen on the ancient course on the rising ground to the south-west of The Meadows and the centre of the Old Town. The earliest coaching advice has been found in the diary of Thomas Kincaid for 1697. He liked to play at Bruntsfield and Leith Links in the evenings after his supper: 'I found that the only way of playing at the Golf is to stand as you do at fencing with the small sword bending your legs a little and holding the muscles of your legs and back and arms exceeding bent or fixed or stiff and not at all slackening them in the time you are bringing down the stroke (which you readily do).'

Leith Links was the course used by what is generally accepted to be the oldest golf club on record. It was a five-hole course usually played twice and the club gave itself the sonorous title of the Honourable Company of Edinburgh Golfers. The oldest surviving set of rules was codified at Leith and all subsequent versions are based on it. In 1744, the club trophy, a silver golf club, was won by an Edinburgh surgeon, John Rattray. A year later, he enlisted in Prince Charles's rebel army and, after the defeat at Culloden, found himself in Inverness jail. His sentence of death by hanging was commuted after the impassioned pleas of Duncan Forbes of Culloden, the Lord President of the Court of Session. He was a fellow golfer. After his release in 1747, Rattray resumed his membership at Leith Links and won the silver club on two occasions, his political beliefs not a handicap.

In the aftermath of the failure of the Fifteen and the death of their great supporter, Louis XIV, the exiled Stewart court was exiled once more. With a monthly subsidy of 50,000 livres, James VIII and III and his retinue had lived in some splendour at St Germain-en-Laye and they, in turn, supported between 750 and 1,000 exiled pensioners. With his claim to be the rightful Catholic king of England, Scotland and Ireland, James could expect the support of the papacy and he was not to be disappointed. After a colourful interlude in the famous renaissance Palazzo Ducale at Urbino, the Stewarts were made welcome in Rome by Clement XI who gave them the use of the Palazzo de Re, appropriately, the Royal Palace, and also the use of his country house at Albano when the heat of the summer made the city uncomfortable. To pay for his retinue and sustain a large circle of exiles, James had intermittent pensions from Spain and France as well as life annuity of 8,000 scudi from the papacy.

On 3 September 1719, the Pretender married Maria Clementina Sobieska, the granddaughter of the king of Poland, and, a year later, their first son, Charles Edward Stewart, was born and the succession assured. To pass the long Roman days and nights, the king became interested in opera and maintained a royal box at the main theatres. He even sponsored singers. But what animated the court was intrigue, intelligence from Britain and the making of alliances and understandings with supporters. As whispers threatened to become realities, many plots were unravelled and disabled by British spies. The Stewart court in Rome had been thoroughly infiltrated and security was laughably lax as letters not written in code were sent to Jacobites in Britain through the normal postal service. Paranoia produced some preposterous episodes. The Earl of Middleton helped plan the abortive invasion of 1708 and sailed to Scotland with the fleet. But he was accused of betraying the plans to the London government. Fevered faction fighting also absorbed the court's energies and, in 1726, a British spy noted: 'The Irish, Scotch and English seem to have quite different views and ways of thinking, and there are two parties of each nation, so that I may justly say there are six parties.'

Paranoia extended to Scotland. It was widely believed that the Bank of Scotland had Jacobite sympathies and, when a company of wealthy individuals (who had been recompensed by the Equivalent) proposed the foundation of a rival bank, their request was readily granted. The Royal Bank of Scotland was incorporated in 1727 and immediately began to innovate. A year later, it invented the overdraft and William Hogg, a merchant in Edinburgh's High Street, was one of the first businessmen to make use of one. Since its foundation, Royal Bank notes have carried a portrait of their first Governor, Archibald Campbell, Lord Ilay, who had by that time become the most powerful man in Scotland. George II called him his 'Vice Roy' and he was an early example of a continuing type in Scottish public life, a Scottish aristocrat educated in England (at Eton College), who mostly lived in London but exercised power and influence north of the Tweed.

After 1707, many Scots on the make had arrived in the capital and caused considerable resentment but Ilay's upbringing helped him avoid being seen as one. After 1715, he did not visit the Campbell seat at Inverary for 30 years, preferring to operate from London and occasionally Edinburgh. Through a well-oiled network of bribery and preferment, Ilay managed Scotland for the crown and the Westminster parliament, and his brother, John Campbell, Duke of Argyll, supported him – even though they were barely on speaking terms. A career soldier, Argyll was appointed to many military roles, including the colonelcy of the Royal Horse Guards. Both had old Scottish names and titles but they were thoroughly anglicised. And both were thoroughly anti-Jacobite. Their grandfather, Archibald Campbell, Earl of Argyll, had supported the Duke of Monmouth's rebellion in 1685. After his capture, Argyll was condemned to death and James VII and II insisted that his grandsons be present to witness his execution. The Maiden, a version of the guillotine, was used and as the old man's head was placed under the blade, the two boys were forced to watch it fall. Archibald was three years old and John was five.

To the extent that the country was peaceful in the decades after 1715, Ilay's management of Scotland worked but, as a form of government, it allowed little or no expression of wider Scottish interests or issues. Westminster paid little attention. Between 1727 and 1745, only nine acts concerning Scotland were passed as the British parliament and its leaders directed their attention elsewhere, especially overseas as they began to build an empire.

When Frederick the Great of Prussia invaded the Austrian province of Silesia in December 1740, Europe was plunged into war once more. Alliances formed and soldiers marched. What became known as the War of the Austrian Succession killed more than half a million people over the following eight years as armies clashed across the Low Countries, central Europe and in Italy. Two years before the Black Watch took the field at Fontenoy, George II fought at Dettingen, the last British monarch to lead his troops into battle – or at least that is one interpretation. In 1745, another man with a claim to be King of Britain would lead his men into battle. The eldest son of the Old Pretender, Charles Edward Stewart, was much encouraged by what he saw at Fontenoy, when the Irish Jacobites fought so fiercely and drove back the Black Watch.

As war raged between the French and Spanish on one side and the British, Austrian and Dutch troops, usually, on the other, the Jacobite cause came once more into focus. For the Catholic combatants, a diversion in Scotland might prove very helpful and, in 1744, Prince Charles travelled to France. Plans had been made and a fleet assembled at Dunkirk to transport between 12,000 and 15,000 men across the Channel. Much of the regular British army was campaigning in Europe and the invasion stood a good chance of success against a depleted home front. But British spies had informed London who the waiting supporters were in Britain and then, as usual, the weather obliged. On 24 February, a storm blew up the Channel, scattered the French fleet and the plan was abandoned.

Showing remarkable resolve, Prince Charles decided that he would not be diverted. Using Queen Clementina's jewellery as security, the Jacobite banker, Aeneas MacDonald borrowed 40,000 livres in Paris to procure weapons and part of the Irish Brigade volunteered. An Irish slave trader based in Nantes, Antoine Walsh, supplied an armed frigate, the *Doutelle*, and Sir Walter Ruttlidge gave the *Elizabeth*, a captured British warship. On 5 July 1745, this pathetically inadequate force sailed north from Brittany on an impossible mission. Which almost succeeded.

The two ships were attacked by a British warship off the Lizard and the *Elizabeth* was so badly damaged that it was forced to limp back to port. But Prince Charles pressed on and, on 23 July, the *Doutelle* dropped anchor off the tiny island of Eriskay in the Outer Hebrides. Rumours began to circulate but no one could believe them. Norman MacDonald of Skye wrote to Duncan Forbes of Culloden: 'As I've heard nothing further from any of these places, but peace and quiet, I think you may entirely depend on it, that either there never was such a thing intended, or if there was, that the project is entirely defeated and blown into the air.'

The clan chiefs were not encouraging. Several would not even meet the

Prince. MacDonald of Clanranald and MacDonald of Kinlochmoidart tried to persuade him to return to Rome but, in an emotional exchange, Prince Charles's charisma swayed them and they agreed to support the uprising. The *Doutelle* sailed to the mainland and, near Arisaig, the Young Pretender began a remarkable journey.

It had been decided that the royal standard would be raised at Glenfinnan, a place accessible to the western clans and astride the road to Fort William and the Great Glen. On the morning of 19 August, Col. John O'Sullivan of the Irish Brigade sat in a rowing boat making its way up Loch Shiel, heading for the foot of Glenfinnan. The time of the rendezvous had been set for the hour after midday but the Irishman could see few men and no banners fluttering in the summer air. Beside him sat Prince Charles and both men must have been anxious. Where were the Highlanders? Soon after they splashed ashore, Alan MacDonald of Morar arrived with about 150 men but this was little more than an escort and very far from an army. The ignominy of an immediate return to Rome beckoned.

Around the middle of the afternoon, from somewhere to the north, came the sound that changed everything. The skirl of the war pipes floated down on the breeze. Men recognised the music and all turned to look. Down the flanks of the ridge of Sgurr Thuilm, a long line of armed clansmen wound its way down the sheep paths. Clan Cameron had come.

Led by Sir Donald Cameron of Lochiel, about 700 of his clansmen and another 300 MacDonalds of Keppoch had come to the muster. It was the beginnings of an army, and if the brave Camerons had come, others would follow. The Prince greeted Sir Donald with great warmth and, as his equerries unfurled the scarlet and silk standard of the Stewarts, the Marquis of Tullibardine proclaimed James VIII and III as the rightful king. Soon afterwards, 300 MacDonells of Glengarry arrived at Glenfinnan and they had prisoners with them. Having ambushed a company of redcoats, they had taken a Captain Swettenham captive and he turned out to be a tremendous asset. Having given a chivalric promise that he would not fight the Prince's soldiers for a year and a day, he was released. Col. O'Sullivan, an Irish officer, later wrote:

> The officer behaved very gallantly, he frightened the governors of those garrisons he passed by, and even [General] Cope. For he told them all that the Prince had 6,000 men, and that neither arms nor money was wanting to them: he gave everywhere the most favourable account that could be given of the Prince's activity and person. It is said the Elector [George II] sent for him

when he arrived in London, and asked him what kind of a man the Prince was, [and] he answered that he was as fine a figure, as clever a Prince as a man could set eyes on, upon which George turned his back and left him there.

Swettenham was a propaganda gift to the Jacobites. His testimony was widely believed and, from the outset, the 1745 Rebellion acquired an air of glamour and a hint of possibility.

Having recruited on their progress south, the Jacobites took Perth without a fight and they were joined by a key figure. Lord George Murray was the young brother of the Duke of Perth and had fought at Glen Shiel in 1719. A gifted commander, brave and ingenious, he had the military ability to lead the insurgents to glory. And, crucially, he understood how the clansmen fought, what sort of ground suited the charge and where to direct its power and fury. But, from the first, the Jacobite appetite for faction meant that he and Col. O'Sullivan did not often agree and what was more damaging was that Murray's relationship with Prince Charles was said to have been cold and sometimes abrasive. James Johnstone had returned from exile to fight for the cause and, in a memoir, he wrote: 'Had Prince Charles slept during the whole of the expedition, and allowed Lord George to act for him, according to his own judgement, there is every reason for supposing he would have found the crown of Great Britain on his head when he awoke.'

Government forces were caught out by the speed and direction of the Jacobite advance and General Sir John Cope was forced to march his men north to Aberdeen and ship them quickly south in an attempt to contain the rebellion to Scotland. But they were too late to defend Edinburgh. At the news of the Jacobite advance, the city's 400-strong Defence Volunteers mustered on the morning of 15 September but, when they were ordered to march out and confront the Highlanders, 358 of them found reasons not to fall in. Standing amongst the brave and hopeless remnant was a young David Hume. The philosopher and historian seemed willing to risk his life for his convictions – to make history as well as write it – and, in the ensuing decades, his courage seemed never to fail him.

In the event, Edinburgh fell without a shot being fired. When Provost Coutts attempted to see the Prince at his camp, he was turned away but, as his coach left the city by the Netherbow Port, Cameron of Lochiel and his men rushed in and made all the guards prisoner. The castle held out but Prince Charles set up court at the Palace of Holyroodhouse.

Meanwhile, General Cope's forces disembarked at Dunbar on 17

September and marched along the coast road to Edinburgh. At Prestonpans, they formed up in battle order, expecting the Highlanders to attack from the west. Cope had chosen good ground with an impassable bog on one flank and a dyke on the other. To the west of his battle line, directly in front, there was a ditch which would greatly slow down the Highland charge, reducing its impact and presenting easy targets for musket volleys.

Lord George Murray learned from an East Lothian sympathiser, Robert Anderson, that there was, in fact, a path through the bog to the south of the government army's position. And, at dead of night and in complete silence, Anderson led the Highlanders through it so that they could attack Cope's army in the rear. The ground was better there and the charge had a much higher chance of success. When dawn broke on 21 September, the government soldiers were horrified to see an entire army behind them 'looking like a black hedge moving towards [them]'. The Battle of Prestonpans lasted only about 15 minutes as the Highlanders tore into the ranks of redcoats, slashing with their broadswords and swinging their Lochaber axes. As the government soldiers fled, there was carnage and about 500 were killed. Prince Charles rode around frantically trying to prevent what was developing into a massacre. But Prestonpans simply added to the sense of the rebellion as a force of nature, a juggernaut of screaming savages who would cut any army that stood in its way to pieces. London gasped at the news and George II's generals began to mobilise.

After waiting too long in Edinburgh for more recruits and money and reinforcements from the French, the Prince's army marched south. By 4 December, virtually unopposed, they had reached Derby, only 127 miles from London, but dissent was simmering. At a council of war the following morning, Lord George Murray advocated turning back. Government armies were circling and many of the Highlanders wished to return home. The chiefs would go no further. But what sealed the argument was the intervention of Dudley Bradstreet. Posing as a fervent Jacobite, Captain Oliver Williams, he was, in fact, a government spy and had somehow gained access to the council. Bradstreet informed the Prince, Murray, O'Sullivan and the other leaders that there was a large army, about 9,000 strong, waiting to intercept the Jacobites at Northampton. It was a complete fiction and the truth was that the road to London lay open. But the Highlanders turned back north.

Having conducted a brilliant fighting retreat, Lord Murray led the Highlanders to yet another victory. At Falkirk on 15 January 1746, they charged a government army led by General Henry Hawley and routed them. Instead of pressing home any advantage, the clansmen marched north, back home to families they had not seen for six months.

In April, the clans mustered once more at Inverness. It may be that the Prince and Murray thought a successful spring and summer campaign in the Highlands would attract more support from the French, perhaps even a move against the south coast of England. But they had been pursued. The King's brother, William Augustus, the Duke of Cumberland, had taken command and his army was camped at Nairn. Meanwhile the clans marched to Drummossie Moor, not far from Culloden House. Murray believed that Cumberland's camp could be surprised and he led the army on a night march to Nairn. It was raining but, through the mirk, government pickets saw the Highlanders advance and raised the alarm. Murray ordered a retreat to the moor. And so, on the morning of 16 April, the clansmen stood in their regiments, exhausted, soaked and hungry, looking at the ground in front of them. It was wet, boggy in places, not good for the charge.

At about 11 a.m., the government army advanced to the moor, their silk banners flying and their drummers rattling a steady beat. The rain and sleet blew in from the east, into the faces of the Highlanders watching the enemy approach. Once the redcoats had formed up and their sergeants had dressed the line, roaring at them to look to their fronts and stand fast, something happened that was emblematic of the centuries of difference between Highland and Lowland, of incomprehension and, ultimately, animosity.

At first it seemed to the government soldiers that the clansmen opposite were singing but the many Scots and Highlanders loyal to the Hanoverians realised that they were not hearing psalms but something much more ancient, an echo of the long Celtic past. The clansmen were summoning the army of the dead. Each man recited his genealogy, the *sloinneadh*, the naming of the names of memory. Some could go back twenty generations as they chanted, '*Is mise macIain, 'ic Sheumais, 'ic Iain Ruadh.*' – 'I am the son of John, the son of James, the son of Red John.' The clansmen stood in family groups, fathers with sons, nephews with uncles, brothers, and it was their habit to set the older men in front to lead the charge. Courage was thought to flow down the generations.

Murdoch MacLeod of Inverness was determined to fight, to stand with the names of his blood, and, on the morning of 16 April, he made his way through the wind and rain to Drummossie Moor. Somehow he acquired a broadsword, a targe and a dirk, perhaps quietly lifting them from a bivouac of sleeping clansmen as he walked up to the high moorland. But he should not have been there – he should have been at school. Murdoch was 15 years old.

Never having seen anything remotely like it, the boy must have looked open mouthed at two armies drawn up 500 yards apart, 15,000 men ready to kill each other. On one side were the red, regimented rows of government soldiers keeping their muskets' firing plates dry and preparing their artillery. On the other were the clans, men who had come to the moor not for pay and rations but because of the bonds of blood and obligation. At the head of each group, the war pipes skirled the battle rants, each of them remembering a different history of long-gone skirmishes and campaigns. On the right of the Jacobite line, under the command of Lord George Murray, was the Atholl Brigade – Robertsons, Menzies, Murrays and a few MacGregors. To their left stood Lochiel with 700 Camerons at his back, waiting for, itching for, the *claidheamh mor*, the order to charge. With them were the Appin Stewarts and their famous swordsman, Charles Stewart of Ardshiel. The centre of the line was commanded by Lord John Drummond at the head of the Fraser regiment with Clan Chattan next to them. There were MacLeans and Chisholms and then, on the left wing, insulted to have been set there, stood the MacDonald regiments – Glengarry, Keppoch and Clan Ranald. Because of the poor ground, they had been forced to form up 700 yards away from the government lines. Too far away.

For some reason, Prince Charles had insisted that he take personal command of the army and, with his lifeguards by his side, he sat on horseback behind the centre. At about 1 p.m. the war pipes stilled and the first volley of cannon fire boomed over Drummossie Moor as the government guns recoiled, sending up puffs of smoke. Ricocheting off the ground, round shot skimmed across the heather and plunged into the Highlanders' ranks, causing carnage. Canister shot, like shrapnel, was fired in the air and there were many casualties. Men roared over their shoulders at their captains, begging for the *claidheamh mor*, the charge. Prince Charles seemed paralysed by indecision and, as the cannon continued to cut down the clansmen, no order came.

Unable to bear the bombardment any longer, Clan Chattan finally broke away into the charge, screaming their war cries as they raced across the heather. When he saw that the Mackintoshes were away, Cameron of Lochiel raised his broadsword with the shout, *'Is sinne clan Thearlaich!'*, 'We are the children of Charles!', and, with his men, the Appin Stewarts and the Atholl Brigade, he roared away and smashed into the left wing of Cumberland's army. Gillies MacBean, a captain of Clan Chattan, broke through the front rank, killing several redcoats. With him was another officer, John McGillivray, who killed 12 men before the second rank cut him down. James Wolfe, later to lead a

British army on the Heights of Abraham in Canada, recorded that, when the Camerons clashed with Barrell's Regiment, they did not turn and run as they had at Prestonpans and Falkirk. A new drill where a redcoat aimed to bayonet not the Highlander directly in front of him but the man to his right as he raised his sword arm seemed to be working well. Here is what Wolfe later remembered:

> They were attacked by the Camerons (the bravest clan among them), and it was for some time a dispute between the swords and bayonets; but the latter was found by far the most destructible weapon. The regiment behaved with uncommon resolution, killing, some say, almost their own number, whereas forty of them were only wounded, and those not mortally and not above ten killed. They were, however, surrounded by superiority, and would have been all destroyed had not Col. Martin with his regiment (the left of the second line of foot) moved forward to their assistance, prevented mischief, and by a well timed fire destroyed a great number of them and obliged them to run off.

On the Jacobite left the MacDonald regiments never engaged properly and, after the smoke of the cannon fire lifted, it was clear that the charge had failed. Having lost his wig and abandoned his horse, Lord George Murray ran about the moor, trying to rally the retreating clansmen but defeat turned into disaster as Prince Charles gave the order, *'Sauve qui peut!'*, 'Run for your lives!', and his lifeguards led him away.

JACOBITES NO MORE

In 1745/6 more Scots fought against the Jacobites than for them. This represented a seismic shift from the position in 1715, when the Hanoverian dynasty was much less well established. But allegiances could be very divisive, and it was said that many families had a Hanoverian at home and a Jacobite in exile. But these exiles created a Scottish network around the world which supplied information and facilitated contacts for trade. The increased loyalty to the Hanoverians in the Highlands was much aided by the efforts of Duncan Forbes of Culloden, who exerted himself greatly to persuade clan chiefs inclined to Jacobitism to stay at home and not join the Pretender. Forbes' tireless work appears to have exhausted him, and he died in 1747.

When the Earl of Kilmarnock found himself surrounded by government cavalry, he had no option but to surrender. As his horse was led through the lines of the Royal Scots Fusiliers, tears streamed down the old man's face and a young officer came forward to hold a hat in front so that his distress might not be seen. It was Kilmarnock's son, Lord James Boyd.

Culloden not only divided families, on a much wider scale it was a catastrophe for the clans and for the Gaelic language. In the decades that followed, the lands north of the Highland Line would empty. A working landscape would degenerate into scenery and a Celtic culture safely descend into cliché and romance. After 16 April 1746, the focus of Scotland's history shifted decisively south to the Lowlands.

North Britain

✦

IN 1713 SIR FRANCIS GRANT bought the estate of Monymusk in Aberdeenshire without ever having seen it. Perhaps it was just as well. Here is a description of Monymusk from his son, Archibald:

The House was an old castle with battlements and six different roofs of varying heights and directions, confusedly and inconveniently combined, and all rotten, with two wings more modern, of two storeys only, the half of windows of the higher rising above the roofs, with granaries, stables and houses for all cattle, and of the vermin attending them, close adjoining, and with the heath or muir reaching in angles or gushets to the gate, and much heath near, and what land near the farms was in cultivation, by which their cattle and dung were always at the door. The whole land raised and uneven, and full of stones, many of them very large, of a hard iron quality, and all the rigs crooked in the shape of an S, and very high and full of noxious weeds and poor, being worn out by cultivation, without proper manure or tillage. Much of the land and muir near the house, poor and boggy; the rivulet that runs before the house in pits and shallow streams, often varying channel with banks, always ragged and broken. The people poor, ignorant and slothful: and ingrained enemies to planting, enclosing or any improvements or cleanness; no keeping of sheep or cattle or roads but four months when oats and barley, which was the only sorts of their grain, was on the ground. The farm houses, and even corn mills and mains and school, all poor dirty huts, pulled in pieces for manure, or fell of themselves each alternate year.

Clearly a place with potential! What Grant described was the medieval landscape depicted in John Slezer's *Theatrum Scotiae* of twenty years before, a landscape that had not yet recovered from the famine of the 1690s. Archibald resolved to improve Monymusk and, as all improving landowners must, he took a long view. In 1716, he enclosed and planted tree nurseries, bringing on thousands of saplings each year before replanting them on the estate to create shelter belts and woods to supply timber for all sorts of uses. This would be a major improvement, for all that Grant found when he first came were a few old trees around the castle, a small copse browsed by beasts and a some trees at the farmyards. Over a long life, he had millions of trees planted on what had been a bare, ill-kept, windswept place.

At the same time, Grant began to have the open runrig enclosed and, to make dykes, stones were cleared so that ploughing could be more efficient. He reckoned to have doubled the acreage of cultivable land by this initiative alone. The boggy ground he noted was much improved by runs of stane drains and these were later augmented or replaced by tiled conduits made from fired clay. And the rivulet near the castle was dug out and the upcast piled along its banks to prevent flooding.

What accelerated the laborious, slow process of improvement at Monymusk was an election. In 1722, Grant was sent to Westminster by the electors of Aberdeenshire and there he came into contact with a notable English agricultural pioneer who was also a government minister. Viscount 'Turnip' Townshend was appointed Secretary of State and Lord President of the Council by George I's Privy Council and he occasionally accompanied the king to Hanover. On his way, he passed through the Waasland region of Belgium and, as an enthusiastic Norfolk farmer, he was much taken with their new agricultural methods. Instead of the wasteful tradition of allowing fields to recover their fertility by lying fallow, the Belgians had developed a four-field rotation of crops. These included wheat, barley, clover and turnips. There was no need to leave any fields fallow because clover replaced the nitrates in the soil which had been taken out by the cereal crops and, as a root crop, turnips needed different nutrients. And the value of the latter was that they could be used as winter feed for beasts, thus avoiding the annual autumn cull. Charles Townshend did not deserve to be demeaned by the nickname of Turnip. They had been grown in Norfolk since the 1660s but the alliteration ensured that the name stuck.

Turnips are sometimes called swedes because a popular variety was produced in Sweden and it was, in fact, a cross between a turnip and a cabbage. Farmers preferred these yellow swedes to the fatter and larger turnip because cattle could eat the green shaws as well as the nourishing roots and they could browse the fields without the need for the crop to be harvested. The Swedish word is *rutabaga* and, in Scots, they became known as 'baigies'. They were first grown in Scotland at Monymusk after Townshend had recommended the four-field rotation to Grant. This innovation immediately improved the diet of his Aberdeenshire tenants. Because beasts could live on baigies through the winter, many more were able to grow to maturity and more milker cows could produce more and better quality dairy products. The so-called 'Agricultural Revolution' was more of an evolution but, when Grant's neighbours saw the effects of using four-field rotation and, especially, the use of baigies, they imitated it and the four-field system spread.

However gradual, these changes were important because they changed lives, usually for the better. In 1750 only one Scot in eight lived in a town or city. The overwhelming majority were involved in agriculture to a greater or lesser degree, and the gathering of a good harvest each autumn was everyone's hope. Writing in the 1750s, the Scottish novelist Tobias Smollett described the simple, even tedious diet of ordinary people: 'Their breakfast is a kind of hasty pudding of oatmeal, or peasemeal eaten with milk. They have commonly potage to dinner composed of cale or cole, leeks, barley or bigg [four rowed barley] and this is reinforced with bread and cheese made of skimmed milk. At night they sup on sowens [a kind of porridge] flummery of oatmeal.'

For Townshend's four-field rotation to work, there had to be fields. At Monymusk, Grant began to enclose the S-shaped open rigs earlier than most but, over much of Lowland Scotland progress was very slow. But one dramatic change that accelerated enclosure and affected many was the long land grab of 'commonties' – tracts of common land used by towns, villages and farms. Around 1500, about half of the total land area of Scotland was used as common land – places where farmers, villagers and townspeople could graze their beasts, especially milker cows, where they could cut peat, bracken for flooring or turf for walling and gather firewood. The commons were an enormously important resource but, by the middle of the 19th century, virtually all of Scotland's common land had disappeared into private ownership. An act of the Scottish Parliament of 1695 allowed adjoining landlords to divide the commons between them and, throughout the 18th century, this process accelerated. Only in three towns in the Borders – Lauder, Selkirk and Hawick – have substantial commons survived and, each summer, large cavalcades of riders patrol the boundaries in ceremonial checks to ensure that the markers have not been moved. In Hawick, the Cornet carries the town flag and he and his supporters shout, 'Aye defend your rights and common!' Perth still owns the North and South Inch and Dornoch owns the Links but these are small parcels of land.

Smaller-scale enclosure crept over the landscape more slowly and it was not until the 1790s that the majority of the best cultivable farmland in the Lowlands had been hedged about or had dykes built. As landowners began to bring more and more land under the plough, they often rationalised their holdings, sometimes brutally. For centuries many cottars had rented small patches of land, many of them little more than large gardens, in return for cash and services at ploughing, sowing and harvest times. In addition, some had learned other skills that depended on the produce of farms, such as weaving, spinning, shoemaking, horn-working and other useful trades which could supply a modest cash income. But, with the disappearance of the commons, enclosure and the introduction of the four-field rotation system, the Lowland Clearances began.

At Longnewton in Roxburghshire, not far south of St Boswells, there is an old graveyard by the side of the road, close to the Ale Water. Guarded by a stag-headed old oak and a yew, some tumbled-down headstones can still be seen amongst the grassy hummocks but there is no kirk or village nearby. Longnewton was swept away by the Lowland Clearances. The Earl of Lothian wanted to combine several small tenancies into one substantial farm. Some time after 1785, John Younger recorded what happened. His father had a smallholding of 14 acres with a house but all of the land was to be absorbed into the big new farm. Younger was only allowed to stay on in the house because he was a cordwainer – a craftsman who could make shoes and boots – and this was thought to be a trade worth keeping on. But all of the dykes were thrown down and cleared away to make larger fields and, when they were cultivated, the plough teams worked right up to the walls of the house. Even Younger's hens were shot. And, over a very short time, the twenty or so houses of the village of Longnewton disappeared, its people forced to seek work and housing in the towns and larger villages. All that remains is the old graveyard. And this was a pattern repeated all over Lowland Scotland in the 18th century.

With the reallocation of land and its ownership, precision mattered and, in Scotland and, eventually, in the whole of Britain, this was greatly facilitated by the Ordnance Survey. An unexpected legacy of the Jacobite Rebellions, this uniquely detailed sequence of maps is a national adornment, unparalleled anywhere else in the world. The name betrays its military origins. The fast-moving Jacobite armies, unencumbered by much equipment or artillery, managed to penetrate deep into England and evade engagement in Scotland because of a lack of good roads and good maps. The more lumbering government armies quite simply could not keep up or get at them quickly. In 1747, Lt Col. David Watson proposed that reliable and detailed maps of the Highlands be made so that rebels could not simply disappear into the trackless and unknown wastes of the more remote glens and mountains. A Scot born in Lanarkshire, William Roy, undertook much of the responsibility for surveying and drawing and the result was his 'Military Survey of Scotland, 1747–1755'. His interest in Roman antiquities meant that the earliest graphic evidence for the location and shape of forts and especially those along the Antonine Wall are included. Roy also shows a great deal of runrig still being ploughed in the landscape. Change was happening but very slowly.

SICCAR POINT

In the spring of 1788, the great Enlightenment scientist James Hutton clambered into a boat with his friends, James Hall and John Playfair. They wanted to look at the rock formations at Siccar Point, on the North Sea coast of Berwickshire, but from the seaward side. In his enormously influential Theory of the Earth, *Hutton argued that the rock formations he could see at exposed sites proved his belief that the landscape was formed by a series of convulsions and the altogether less dramatic process of sedimentation. At Siccar Point it was possible to see gently sloping horizontal strata of 345-million-year-old Red Sandstone overlying near-vertical layers of 425-million-year-old strata of greywacke rock. Hutton was also an improving farmer in Berwickshire with a direct interest in the properties of the landscape.*

The Union of 1707 and the trade winds brought prosperity to Glasgow. Incorporation into Britain allowed Scots merchants to trade with the former English colonies along the Atlantic seaboard of North America and the pattern and direction of the world's winds brought sailing ships to Glasgow two to three weeks earlier than to ports further south. The winds encouraged trade but their name in fact derives from an Old English term meaning a 'track' or 'course'. They first blew smoke into British culture because the principal cargo to cross the ocean between c. 1710 and c. 1760 was tobacco, especially from the colony of Virginia.

Glasgow flourished and the trade made some men fabulously wealthy. They were known as the Tobacco Lords. Perhaps the greatest of them was John Glassford. Born in Paisley, the third son of a merchant, he was ambitious and enterprising. While he built his business, he also climbed the social scale, marrying first a merchant's daughter and, when she died, a baronet's daughter and, when she died, the daughter of an earl. Glassford fathered 14 children and his family portrait in the People's Palace features a black servant, human cargo from the plantations in Virginia and the Carolinas. Tobias Smollett was deeply impressed: 'I conversed with Mr Glassford, whom I take to be one of the greatest merchants in Europe. In the last war, he is said to have had at one time five and twenty ships with their cargoes – his own property – and to have traded for above half a million sterling a year.'

Sometimes also known as the Virginia Dons, these merchants built huge mansions that eventually gave their names to some of Glasgow's streets – the likes of Thomas Buchanan and Archibald Ingram. But trade with the American colonies was fatally interrupted when they fought to break free in the War of Independence that began in 1776. Ingram, Buchanan and the other Tobacco Lords had prudently invested in other manufactures, notably cotton. But Glassford did not diversify and died in 1783 with debts of £93,000.

Tobacco had transformed Glasgow and the Scottish economy. By 1771, around 47 million pounds of tobacco was landed on the Clyde quays, most of it for re-export to European markets. Not only was this huge volume a very substantial proportion of total British trade at the time, about 40 per cent, it also helped reopen Scotland's old European connections to Holland, Germany, France and the Baltic. Linen manufacture boomed – much stimulated by the British Linen Company. Founded in 1746 and later to become the British Linen Bank, it was the only British bank whose articles expressly encouraged investment in industry. In addition, the tobacco trade created a pool of private capital held in Scotland. On the banks of the River Carron, near Falkirk, the Carron Ironworks was set up in 1759 – a crucial initiative and the earliest example of the heavy industry that was to become so characteristic of 19th- and 20th-century Scotland.

Using the methods pioneered by Abraham Darby of Coalbrookdale, the smelters used coke made from coal rather than the traditional charcoal made from hardwood to convert iron ore from Bo'ness into workable iron. Carron's first large contract was from the government's Board of Ordnance in 1762 to make cannon for the armed forces. Engineers later developed a new, more easily manoeuvrable design and it was called the carronade. These cannon remained in production until the 1850s. The ironworks expanded to become the largest in Europe, employing more than 2,000 people by the early 19th century. And its output would be a key element in the growth of the Scottish industrial economy.

THE DUMBIEDYKES

Thomas Braidwood founded the first school in Britain designed to teach deaf and dumb children. It was set up in a house in the Canongate in Edinburgh. Developing out of what he called the 'combined system', Braidwood codified the earliest version of British Sign Language. It was based on the use of the hands, the shapes they made and how they were turned, placed and moved. C is made by curving the thumb and index finger into a semicircle and D by adding the straight index finger of the other hand to the semicircle. Deaf and dumb people talk in a mesmerising flurry of hand movements and British Sign Language has developed regional dialects. Some Scottish signs are not understood in the south of England. By 1783, Braidwood himself had moved to London to found a new school and his grandson set up a school in Virginia in the USA. Scots pioneered this field of education and Thomas Braidwood would have smiled to see British Sign Language recognised alongside English, Welsh, Gaelic and others as one of Britain's official languages. And also to see that his original school in the Canongate is remembered in the nearby district of Edinburgh, the Dumbiedykes.

Textiles drove initial industrial growth but politics and the Scottish weather intervened to determine what sort of cloth was made north of the Tweed. Cotton had come to the Clyde from plantations in the British colonies in the West Indies but in relatively small amounts – only 137,000 pounds in 1775. But 'cotton wool' was an attractive raw material. It was easier to spin because it was more elastic than flax and dampness and humidity also helped keep the yarn supple. By 1812, ships were unloading 11 million pounds of cotton at the quaysides of Glasgow and cotton manufacture had become Scotland's greatest industry.

Other factors were at play. The Union had allowed technological break-throughs in England to be quickly adopted in Scotland and the work of men like Richard Arkwright in mechanising spinning methods was central. He briefly became a partner of David Dale as the cotton mill complex was built at New Lanark, near the Clyde's only waterfall. But what stimulated the production of cotton most immediately was not technological improvement but a sharp fall in the price of West Indian cotton in the late 1770s and a rise in the price of raw flax. Linen spinners and weavers could quickly adapt to working with the new cotton wool and many of them did.

BARBARA GILMOUR'S CHEESE

At the turn of the 18th century in the parish of Dunlop in East Ayrshire, Barbara Gilmour pioneered the manufacture of a new cheese made from sweet milk from her Ayrshire cows. Much cheese was made from skimmed milk because it kept longer and better but Barbara perfected a method of storage that allowed Dunlop cheese to become very popular and widely copied. Using salt from the saltpans at Saltcoats, she gave the cheese a distinctive flavour as well adding vitamins and preserving it. Because its richness means that a process of fermentation continued, the cheeses had to be turned. And they needed to be kept in a very dry environment. Dunlop's closest competitor was Cheddar cheese and it eventually came out on top because Barbara's cheese lost weight as it matured while Cheddar did not. The making of Dunlop gradually died out but now, mercifully, it is made again in Ayrshire at West Clerkland Farm and on Arran and Islay.

New Lanark and its determined decision to foster a healthy and happy workforce is perhaps the most famous monument to cotton production in Scotland. But Stanley Mills on the River Tay, six miles north of Perth, is one of the most intriguing. Many of the factory buildings are now converted into attractive flats but there is a superb series of exhibitions which recreates the busy life of the mills and the planned village of Stanley that sits at the top of the mill brae. To the east is a long tongue of land, a river peninsula where the Tay almost turns through 360 degrees before flowing south to Perth. The land belonged to John, Duke of Atholl, the older brother of Lord George Murray, and he and his factor conceived a clever notion. The Tay flows fast past Stanley because the top bend to the north of the peninsula is 21 feet higher than the bottom bend. In 1729, a tunnel was dug through the peninsula and the water rushed directly down it to power a corn mill. Atholl was persuaded by George Dempster, the local MP, to invite Richard Arkwright to come to Stanley. He had not only patented a much more efficient cotton spinning frame, known as the water frame, but also a rotary carding engine that greatly speeded up the making of cotton lap, an important stage in the spinning of cotton fibre and thread. New machines were installed but the commercial history of Stanley Mills was chequered, alternating between boom and bust, but before its closure in 1989, it was still making cotton tape for cigarettes. The Tobacco Lords would have approved.

Invention was not confined to industry. In the 1760s, a little-known Berwickshire blacksmith redesigned the old Scots plough and changed the world. James Small worked in a large smiddy at Blackadder Mount, a farm a few miles east of Duns, and his single-minded mission was to improve the performance of the auld ploo. Once described as a heavy wooden wedge dragged through the ground by the brute force of at least four beasts, usually oxen, it was very inefficient. The mouldboard did not turn the furrow-slice completely and so weeds had to be pulled out by plough followers who also bashed down big clods with a mel or mallet. The oxen or horses had to be led by a goadman and often the ploughshare jumped out of the ground because it was too large to delve deep. That meant another man was sometimes needed to put his weight on the beam. And the ploo often broke down when it hit big stones. All very labour intensive and slow.

Small's new design was brilliant. After making so many prototypes that he bankrupted himself, he came up with a revolutionary screwed shape for the ploughshare, essentially the same shape as modern ploughs. And crucially he had the ploughshare cast in one piece in iron at the Carron Ironworks. The result was revolutionary. Because it encountered less friction, Small's swing plough could be pulled through the ground by only two strong horses guided by one man and because the screwed shape turned the furrow slice completely, no plough-followers were needed. What had been slow work for an entire family became something one skilled man could do more quickly and better.

The effects of this brilliant invention were not seen quickly. Probably because they feared the loss of their jobs, there was resistance from farm-workers. John Sinclair recorded this: 'The late Mr Lumsdaine of Blanerne was one of the first who ordered the new improved plough, but his servants did all they could to prejudice their master against it, pretending it did not go well, etc. Small was then obliged to appear in the field himself, and taking the plough into his own hand, he proved to Mr Lumsdaine and all his ploughmen how well it could work. Had he not been a good ploughman, as well as an able mechanic, he could not thus have triumphed over those who opposed the introduction of his improvements.'

Once the plough had been widely adopted, more land came into cultivation since deeper ploughing improved drainage and the much smaller plough team could reach awkward corners and turn more easily than the lumbering oxen. The net effect was a gradual drift of more labour from the countryside to the towns and villages, places where manufacturing was beginning to recruit. James Small died in 1793, penniless and exhausted. He had not patented the design of his swing plough and, for that reason, it was widely adopted. Lord Kames, a neighbour in Berwickshire, summed up Small's achievement in his book, *The Gentleman Farmer*: 'Of all the ploughs fitted for a cultivated soil free of stones I boldly recommend a plough introduced into Scotland about twelve years ago by James Small in Blackadder Mount, Berwickshire, which is now in great request; and with great reason, as it avoids all the defects of the Scotch plough.'

Henry Home was a remarkable man. A Scottish judge, he took his judicial title from his birthplace, Kames House, not far from Blackadder Mount. Despite having had no formal schooling, he attended Edinburgh University and, in 1724, was called to the bar as an advocate. *The Gentleman Farmer* was published in 1776 but it was a late work – Kames was 80. But his long life was immensely influential and his fascination with improved farming emblematic. He was one of the leaders of what became known as 'the Scottish Enlightenment', perhaps the most glittering period in our history.

John Amyatt was an English chemist who believed that Edinburgh was unique. On a visit to the city probably some time in the 1770s, he remarked to his friend, William Smellie, editor of the first edition of the *Encyclopaedia Britannia* that 'Edinburgh enjoyed a noble privilege not possessed by any other city in Europe'. He was not referring to its spectacular location and long aspects in all directions but to the intellectual excitement of the Enlightenment at its zenith. When Smellie asked Amyatt what he meant, the Englishman replied, 'Here I stand at what is called the Cross of Edinburgh, and can in a few minutes, take 50 men of genius by the hand.'

And it was true. Scholars, lawyers, academics, doctors, writers, artists, poets and architects in Edinburgh, Glasgow, Aberdeen and indeed across Scotland had begun to produce ideas which would change the way in which the world was understood. Without exaggeration, the men met by John Amyatt, and many others, laid the foundations of modern society.

The seeds of the Scottish Enlightenment were planted in the Reformation of the mid 16th century, when the doctrine of the priesthood of all believers demanded mass literacy, a school in every parish. It was an ideal that took a long time to realise but, by the early 18th century, most Scottish children had access to some degree of education. The reformers had also demanded that ministers be trained and, in contrast to England, with only two universities at Oxford and Cambridge, Scotland met that need with five universities, two of them in Aberdeen. History abounds with irony and what John Knox or Andrew Melville would have made of the fundamental belief of Enlightenment thinkers in the paramount importance of human reason and the rejection of any authority that could not be justified by reason need not be guessed at.

The Union also had a determinant impact on intellectual life. With the departure of parliament, politicians, placemen and aristocrats to London, Scotland's remaining independent institutions flourished – the law, universities and the Church of Scotland. Especially in Edinburgh but also in the universities, a talented middle class formed, sometimes energised and refreshed by men from humble backgrounds who had seized the opportunities offered by parish schooling. And these were people who knew each other and met often. Lawyers, academics, doctors, artists and ministers developed a loose, unstated sense of common purpose as they debated, competed and published new ideas. Just as the hothouse intensity of city life had allowed intellectual and artistic achievement to blossom in Athens, Rome and Florence, new thinking began to pour out of Edinburgh in particular.

These were often ideas with clear practical applications rather than intellectual activity for its own sake. It was this that made Lord Kames an emblematic figure. Not only did he publish *Elements of Criticism* in 1762, which was quickly recognised as the standard textbook on literary style and rhetoric, he was also fascinated by the possibilities of agricultural improvement and a powerful supporter of the brilliant blacksmith, James Small. And he almost certainly knew him. The family home of David Hume (who anglicised the spelling of his original surname of Home), reckoned by many to have been the greatest philosopher ever to write in the English language, was at Ninewells, near Chirnside in Berwickshire. He may have been distantly related to Henry Home of the Kames and Ninewells is only two miles north of Blackadder Mount. These three men must have met.

Early flickers of progressive thinking and new ideas could be seen in Scotland's universities. After the convulsions of the Wars of the Covenant and the restoration and then removal of the Stewarts, they began to recover and develop a lecture-based curriculum that embraced not only the needs of the Kirk and the traditional liberal arts but also taught economics and science. In all five universities, chairs of mathematics were established. At both Marischal and King's College in Aberdeen and at St Andrews, observatories were built and the principles of astronomy began to be studied. At Edinburgh, Robert Sibbald was appointed the first professor of medicine in 1685, the beginning of a long and very distinguished history. A fascinating polymath, he was also instrumental in the founding of the Royal College of Physicians of Edinburgh but, like many of his successors, his interests were much wider. In 1682, Sibbald was appointed Geographer Royal and his fascination with antiquities prompted much scholarship. In his *Description of the Isles of Orkney and Shetland*, published in 1711, he set down the first scientific description of the blue whale, which used to be known as Sibbald's rorqual. By the time this remarkable man died in 1722, access to universities in Scotland was more open to the products of the parish schools, boys commonly known as 'lads o' pairts', and crucially it was much less expensive to study there than in England or in Europe. This wider access was one vital reason the candles of the Enlightenment burned so brightly in Scotland.

Clubs and publishing also brightened the intellectual climate. In 1763, there were six printer-publishers and three paper mills in Edinburgh, but only twenty years later, sixteen printer-publishers were in business, buying paper from twelve mills. Clubs began to form in the taverns and meeting places of the warren-like Old Town. One of the first was the Easy Club, founded in 1712 by Thomas Ruddiman. He was a printer-publisher, the owner of a newspaper, the *Caledonian Mercury*, a Jacobite sympathiser and a controversialist. The clubs were, no doubt, cauldrons of gossip and certainly cockpits of debate. When Ruddiman attacked the liberal views of George Buchanan, the historian and tutor of James VI, a society of scholars was formed in Edinburgh to 'vindicate that incomparably learned and pious author from the calumnies of Mr Thomas Ruddiman'. The Select Society lived up to its name with the first fifteen members, who included Lord Kames, David Hume, Adam Smith, William Robertson and its founder, the painter Allan Ramsay. The Poker Club had nothing to with card games and everything to do with 'poking things up a bit', as Adam Ferguson remarked. It met in the evenings and David Hume found it a welcome break from his work and what might have been occasional bouts of depression. 'Most fortunately it happens that since reason is incapable of dispelling these clouds, nature herself suffices to that purpose . . . I dine, I play a game of backgammon, I converse, and am merry with my friends; and when after three or four hours amusement, I return to these speculations, they appear so cold, and strained, and ridiculous, that I cannot find it in my heart to enter into them any farther.'

Hume was one of the towering figures of the Scottish Enlightenment. Perhaps in part motivated by his own inner struggles (although one of his therapies for what sounds like depression was the daily consumption of a pint of claret), he began to consider what he called the science of man. With *A Treatise of Human Nature*, published in 1739, Hume set out his reasons for believing that desire rather than reason was what governed the behaviour of human beings. Ideas, he argued, were not innate and people only had real knowledge of things they directly experienced. Hume's conclusion was that humans have no actual concept of self but, rather, are aware only of a bundle of sensations associated with the self. More, he believed that ethics are based on feelings rather than a set of moral principles. Hume's work was enormously influential on figures as diverse as Albert Einstein and Immanuel Kant, and the great German philosopher Arthur Schopenhauer wrote that 'there is more to be learned from each page of David Hume than from the collected philosophical works of Hegel, Herbart and Schleiermacher taken together'.

Despite the fact that his brilliance was also obvious to contemporaries, David Hume failed to gain appointment to a chair at both Edinburgh and Glasgow universities. He was thought to be an atheist and did little to dispel that impression. A story he liked to tell probably also supported prejudice against him in the universities. 'The best theologian he ever met, he used to say, was the old Edinburgh fishwife who, having recognised him as Hume the atheist, refused to pull him out of the bog into which he had fallen until he declared he was a Christian and repeated the Lord's prayer.'

Instead, Hume turned to writing history to support himself. His Berwickshire family survived on slender means and he could not hope for income from their farm. He also worked as a tutor and a secretary to make money. In 1752, the Faculty of Advocates appointed Hume as their librarian and, although he received little or no salary, he enjoyed 'the command of a large library'. It was there he researched and wrote his six-volume *The History of England*, from the invasion of Julius Caesar to the revolution of 1688. It was a bestseller and it made Hume famous.

When John Amyatt met William Smellie, he was talking to a man who had undertaken a great enterprise. Between 1768 and 1771, *Encyclopaedia*

Britannica was edited by Smellie in premises in Anchor Close, just off the High Street. Work began on setting down all human knowledge. This was an age when such a feat was thought possible – the listing of all there is to know. The great *Encyclopaedia* appeared in 100 weekly instalments and its entries could be pithy. 'Woman' was four words long – 'the female of man'. But it proved very popular and a second edition was put in train.

David Hume wrote on economics, coining the phrase 'the balance of trade' but the impact made by the work of his fellow member of the Select Society, Adam Smith, was much more profound. A son of Kirkcaldy, educated in the burgh school, he matriculated at Glasgow University when he was 14 years old. His mother had been widowed only two months after Smith's birth and a 19th-century biography related that, at the age of three, he was abducted by gypsies. But, undeterred, he went on to gain a scholarship and completed his studies at Glasgow before going to Oxford, which, by comparison, he found intellectually stifling: 'In the University of Oxford, the greater part of the public professors have, for these many years, given up altogether even the pretence of teaching.'

Hugely influenced by the brilliant professor of philosophy at Glasgow, Francis Hutcheson, Smith returned to Scotland and began to lecture at Edinburgh University with sponsorship from Lord Kames. In 1750, he met David Hume and they became close. A year later Smith was appointed to a chair of logic and worked in universities for the following 13 years – 'by far the most useful and therefore by far the happiest and most honourable period' of his life. Some of his lectures formed part of *The Theory of Moral Sentiments* published in 1759. Its central thesis was that human morality depended on sympathy – or what might known now as empathy – between individuals, an ability to recognise the feelings experienced by another person. The book made Smith famous and students flocked to Glasgow to listen to his lectures. In 1763, Charles Townshend, the grandson of Turnip Townshend, made Smith a lucrative offer to tutor his nephew, Henry Scott, the young Duke of Buccleuch. Smith accepted. The new job allowed him to tour Europe with his young charge and, in Paris, he met the group of great intellectuals led by François Quesnay. Benjamin Franklin was another acquaintance.

In 1766, Smith returned to Kirkcaldy to spend ten years working on *An Inquiry into the Nature and Causes of the Wealth of Nations*. It laid the foundations of the study of economics and his exposition of how mutual self-interest and competition can lead to prosperity. It has been interpreted as a manifesto by politicians on both the right and left wings of the spectrum. It is better to allow Smith to speak for himself and here is a key passage:

> As every individual, therefore, endeavours as much as he can both to employ his capital in the support of domestic industry, and so to direct that industry that its produce may be of the greatest value; every individual necessarily labours to render the annual revenue of the society as great as he can. He generally, indeed, neither intends to promote the public interest, nor knows how much he is promoting it. By preferring the support of domestic to that of foreign industry, he intends only his own security; and by directing that industry in such a manner as its produce may be of the greatest value, he intends only his own gain, and he is in this, as in many other cases, led by an invisible hand to promote an end which was no part of his intention. Nor is it always the worse for the society that it was no part of it. By pursuing his own interest he frequently promotes that of the society more effectually than when he really intends to promote it. I have never known much good done by those who affected to trade for the public good. It is an affectation, indeed, not very common among merchants, and very few words need be employed in dissuading them from it.

And, expressing his core ideas in a more concrete, succinct form, here is Smith's famous dictum: 'It is not from the benevolence of the butcher, the brewer, or the baker, that we expect our dinner, but from their regard to their own interest. We address ourselves, not to their humanity but to their self-love, and never talk to them of our own necessities but of their advantages.'

While David Hume and Adam Smith were fundamentally changing the ways in which people thought, the Lord Provost of Edinburgh was considering changing the way in which the citizens of the capital lived. The tottering tenements of the Old Town were dangerous and the Town Council had long been anxious to break out of the confines of the Flodden Wall and expand Edinburgh. Continuing upward growth was neither feasible nor safe. After the devastating fire of 1676, Robertson's Land had been built, rising to a dizzying fourteen storeys between the Cowgate and Parliament Square. It was completed in 1684 but only stood for 16 years until fire ripped through the rookeries of the Old Town once more. Other buildings sometimes suffered partial collapse, losing a gable end, roofs caving in, and the city seemed almost organic, like an ant heap. A map of 1724 shows an astonishing 337 closes leading off the spinal streets of Castlehill, the Lawnmarket, the High

Street and the Canongate. By 1984, there were only 110 and 18 of these are closed to public access.

The legal and mercantile classes of the Old Town had long lived a dense, intense version of urban life, full of stark contrasts. While they dined in elegant rooms in the vast tenements, people far down the social scale could live in tiny, filthy hovels reached by the same stair. It was in this atmosphere that the Enlightenment was born and flourished, often fuelled by the consumption of copious quantities of claret, medicinal or otherwise. According to the Edinburgh chronicler, Robert Chambers: 'Nothing was so common in the morning as to meet men of high rank and dignity reeling home from a close in the High Street where they had spent the night in drinking.' Drunks who could afford it were sometimes escorted through the streets and closes by caddies. Not only could they interpret the vague directions waved at them by a wealthy inebriate, they could also fend off any who wished to relieve their charge of his cash and valuables. These men and boys were themselves described as a ragged, half-blackguard-looking set but they had a sound reputation for honesty. Holding up a storm lantern in the darkened streets, the caddies not only led drunks back up their closes and stairs to their front doors and what was waiting behind them, they also acted as an informal and effective police force. The impression is of native guides in an urban jungle.

Indoors, similarly primitive social practices might have raised a modern eyebrow. Even in the grand flats of the Old Town, sanitary arrangements were often somewhat sketchy. Under the sideboard in many dining rooms sat a chamber pot and one of the persuasive reasons why the ladies were in the habit of withdrawing to the drawing room was to allow the gentlemen to use it – without a break in the conversation. Life in the tenements had its attractions but, in the middle of the 18th century, the Old Town was decaying and change was in the air.

In 1716, the Town Council bought land to the north, the fields beyond the Nor Loch known as Bearford's Parks and, in 1752, Lord Provost George Drummond announced a competition to find the best layout for a New Town to be built on that site. By 1767, a winner had been chosen, the 28-year-old James Craig, and his simple three-street grid connecting two squares was adopted. It used the ridge which ran from east to west across Bearford's Parks and the gentle inclines on the southern and northern flanks. Work began immediately and the foundations for the first houses were dug at what is now Thistle Court in Thistle Street, just off St Andrew Square.

Craig's plan resembled a political diagram. The street names were a self-conscious affirmation of the Hanoverian succession and the Act of Union as well as a rejection of the Stewart dynasty and the rebellion of 1745–46. George Street was named after George III and it was to run along the central ridge to connect St Andrew Square with St George's Square but an immediate difficulty arose. Only a year or two earlier, Edinburgh's first major development was another George Square on the south side of the city. It was not named after the mad king or the saint but after George Brown, the elder brother of the square's architect, James Brown. A compromise was reached and St George's Square was named after Queen Charlotte. And, when the one-sided street running parallel to George Street to the south was named St Giles Street, the king would have none of it so it was called Princes Street after his sons. The street parallel to George Street to the north was named Queen Street and the most westerly street linking Queen Street to Princes Street to the east of Charlotte Square was called Castle Street. And, when the other two streets joining Queen Street and Princes Street were named Hanover Street and Frederick Street, the dynastic picture was complete.

Edinburgh's New Town was the largest and most ambitious example of urban planning in 18th-century Britain – but Craig's layout did not quite work, especially at its east and west ends. Designed as a direct link between the Old Town and the New Town, the building of North Bridge began in 1765. It should have connected with St Andrew Square, which, in turn, should have been built a little further to the east. But the Town Council had not been able to purchase the land. The owner, Sir Laurence Dundas, planned to build a grand house on the site and this caused all sort of problems. Not only did it block the connection with North Bridge, it also forced Craig to locate St Andrew's and St George's Church on George Street and not in the square where it was intended to finish the vista. Dundas's house survives – the only detached house in the New Town. Once the headquarters of the Royal Bank of Scotland, it is still used as one of its branches.

Halfway along Princes Street The Mound was slowly rising. After the Nor Loch had been drained, the Town Council ordered that all the earth dug out of the founds of the buildings of the New Town should be piled up to make a land bridge between the foot of the Lawnmarket and the new development. But once again there were difficulties. The roads did not quite connect, there being an awkward wiggle between the foot of The Mound and Hanover Street.

Further west, Craig's rectilinear layout hit yet another snag. The line of the old road to South Queensferry (now Queensferry Street) ran north-west at an awkward angle. When Hope Street attempted to link Charlotte Square with Princes Street, an unfortunate hairpin turn had to be allowed for as well as the junction with the bottom of Lothian Road. It was a mess only recently sorted out by continuing the pavement from Princes Street to Shandwick Place and separating the competing traffic flows.

ROBERT ADAM AND THE EMPEROR

The son of Scotland's most successful architect of the early 18th century, William Adam, Robert Adam learned all he could in the family firm and at Edinburgh University (where his studies were briefly interrupted in 1745 by the arrival of Prince Charles and his Highland army) before going to Europe on the Grand Tour. In Rome he was tutored by the French architect Charles-Louis Clerisseau and the Italian artist Giovanni Batista Piranesi. On his way home, Adam made a diversion to go to Split in Croatia because he wished to study the ruins of the palace of the great reforming Roman Emperor, Diocletian. They are vast, essentially forming the centre of the city. More like a fortress, the palace was intended for the emperor's retirement. It was designed to house 9,000 people. Robert Adam was fascinated and spent months making measured drawings which he later published. The palace was the inspiration for his new style, known as neo-classical architecture. Adam wanted to move away from what he saw as the plodding sterility of the Palladian style, introducing a sense of movement or fluidity in his designs. He also insisted that he designed every last detail, including furniture. Although they maintained strong links with Scotland, Robert and his brother, James, set up in business in London, and the plans of many famous buildings flowed from their drawing office. One of the most striking is the Pulteney Bridge in Bath. With shops on both sides, it was a reminder of Robert's visit to Florence and the Ponte Vecchio. The brothers published two volumes of their designs and they were very influential, especially in the USA.

But, despite these kinks, Edinburgh's New Town is very beautiful – the most complete and coherent scheme of Georgian architecture to survive – and, in some ways, a monument to the rationalism of the Enlightenment. Most of the time.

As the rectilinear streets were laid out on the other side of the Nor Loch and the fields beyond them were enclosed with dykes and hedges, Scotland began to build roads to link her cities, towns and ports. Until Field Marshal Wade had metalled surfaces put down in the Highlands, most roads were tracks and the medieval pattern of slow movement, mostly on foot or on horseback and the use of carts much affected by the winter, had changed little. Even stretches of the ancient Roman roads were still in use in places. But between 1790 and 1815 turnpike trusts spent between £2 and £3 million on building new roads and bridges.

These bodies took their name from the gates at each end of a turnpike road. They had sharpened pikes attached to a horizontal bar, rather like the weapons used by Bruce's schiltrons to repel charging cavalry. And because the pikes were turned or lifted to allow access to those who had paid the toll, the gates became known as turnpikes. The trusts were in business to make money and hoped to recoup the costs of making the roads and bridges by charging for their use. Many tollhouses at the ends of bridges survive in Scotland. At the same time, wealthy landowners and even parishes were paying for roads to be made. This development was driven by increasing economic activity – the need to move goods in bulk by wheeled cart rather than packhorse. And, incidentally, this surge in road building provided welcome work for cottars who had been driven off the land in the Lowlands.

Carts were the goods vehicles of both the new agriculture and of industry. As the New Town rose, many carters brought loads of building materials for the houses on the streets and the squares. The techniques and materials of masonry had changed little since the great medieval abbeys were built but one new product came in bulk in the carts rattling along George Street. This was straight-sawn timber. The development of mechanical saws had largely replaced the laborious work of the saw pits and the techniques of splitting tree trunks with wedges and mels. One of the great risks of building the soaring tenements of the Old Town was the irregularity and variable load-bearing qualities of timber cut in the old ways. The fourteen storeys of Robertson's Land may have been faced and partitioned in stone but the floors, ceilings and roofs were sometimes very unstable. In the later 18th century, building methods immediately improved with the availability of quantities of squared-off joisting all cut to the same length and width.

In the countryside, many two-storey farmhouses date from the 1770s and slates began to replace thatch as straight purlins were fitted to the ridge and wall heads to support the sarking needed to accommodate them. The new need (and fashion) for courtyard steadings in the large farm units created out of the consolidation of cottars' smallholdings also benefitted as barns and cart sheds and loose boxes went up quickly. Place names sometimes remember these developments – New Mains or Newbiggin. Further down the social scale, farm workers (usually known as hinds in the Lowlands) also saw their domestic lives change. As the likes of the Carron Ironworks turned out affordable nails, hinges and latches, ordinary people began to acquire what we might recognise as furniture. Chests or kists kept clothes dry, stored food and kept it free from vermin and could be sat on. Carpenters began to make box beds and these could be moved around to create small, partitioned spaces where a degree of privacy was possible, and they also were a barrier to a leaky roof. Box beds signalled the end of communal sleeping around the hearth, a habit that had endured for millennia, since the roundhouses of the 3rd millennium BC and probably even as far back as the tipi houses at East Barns and Echline. Tables, benches, cupboards and shelving all gradually became available to make everyday life easier.

For the people of the glens north of the Highland Line, life could not have been more different. In high contrast with the developing elegance of the Georgian New Town in Edinburgh and the elevated thoughts of the great Enlightenment intellectuals, the aftermath of Culloden saw a systematic programme of savagery meted out to Highlanders, men and women and children, whether they had been involved in the Jacobite Rebellion or not. A blood price was to be paid. As Prince Charles fled into hiding and into history and romance began to swirl around a series of escapades in the islands and the mountains, the Duke of Cumberland set in train a campaign of mass punishment, plunder, rape and killing. It was a sadistic mixture of genocide and clinical ethnic cleansing. And much of it was carried out by Lowland Scots.

The killing began in earnest immediately after the Prince had been led off Drummossie Moor by his lifeguards. In an age before automatic weapons and bombs made slaughter faster and more efficient, battles that involved hand-to-hand fighting left many more men wounded than dead. Bayonets and broadswords rarely killed outright and cannon fire maimed many, shattering limbs. Government burial parties reported that, on the evening of the battle, many wounded Highlanders lay in the heather, still alive, passing in and out of consciousness, slowly bleeding to death. And this was despite the efforts of General Henry Hawley, the commander humiliated at Falkirk, who had led execution squads around the field, ordering them to bayonet the wounded rather than incur the expense of musket balls and powder.

It was carnage and an officer reported what sounded like unbridled blood lust: 'The moor was covered with blood and our men, what with killing the enemy, dabbling their feet in the blood, and splashing it about one another, looked like so many butchers rather than Christian soldiers.'

In the summer months after Culloden, the commanders of the forts down the Great Glen sent raiding parties into the mountains to reive all the livestock they could find. One raid brought back 8,000 head of black cattle and the pasture around Fort Augustus was grazed to the roots. Chiefs who had papers of indemnity verifying that they had not been out with the Prince in what was known in Gaelic as *Bliadhna Thearlaich*, 'The Year of Charles', were ignored. The herds were sold on to Lowland Scots and Northern English dealers at knock-down prices. The Duke of Cumberland did not care – his purpose was to destroy the pastoral economy of the clans, not make money. And the king's brother advocated even more drastic measures, nothing less than the wholesale removal of people as well as their livestock. He was determined to empty the glens. Here is part of a letter from Cumberland to the Prime Minister, the Duke of Newcastle: 'I mean the transporting of particular clans, such as the entire Clan of the Camerons and almost all of the tribes of the MacDonalds (excepting some of those of the Isles) and several other lesser Clans, of which an exact list may easily be made.'

Throughout the fatal summer of 1746, atrocities were committed across the Highlands and, as with many acts of this nature, it is likely that few were recorded or reported. But many of those that did find their way into the historical record (usually through the testimony of survivors) were overseen and ordered by officers who were Lowland Scots. The excesses of three men in particular show how wide was the gulf between those who lived on either side of the Highland Line. What many Lowlanders understood of Gaelic-speaking culture was that it came racing across the heather, roaring for blood and death, a swarm of half-naked primitives fighting in their sarks, nothing but savages, tribesmen. The clansmen who had hacked each other to death on the North Inch in Perth in 1396 were the ancestors of the rabble at Culloden, all of them babbling, barbarian sub-humans. Easy to kill.

Cholmondley's Regiment, which fought at Culloden, despite its English origins, recruited Scots and Major I. Lockhart led a detachment out of Fort Augustus in the summer of 1746. They marched into the territory of the Grants of Glenmoriston and met three clansmen on the road. Without hesitation, the soldiers shot them before beginning to round up grazing cows that belonged to Grant of Dundreggan. When the old man appeared with a letter of indemnity, Lockhart ignored it. And when Grant persisted, he had his soldiers seize the old man and strip him naked. And, when his wife joined the protest, she was stripped and humiliated as soldiers tried to cut her rings off her fingers. When they took Grant to the tree where they had strung up the three men who had been shot and threatened to hang Grant, it was all too much for a young officer. Also by the name of Grant, he had fought at Culloden. He threatened to draw his sword to protect the old couple who were clearly not Jacobites. Surprisingly, Lockhart backed down and he ordered his men to fall in and march further up Glenmoriston.

Perhaps young Grant had been dismissed or had left the detachment on other duties for in his absence further outrages took place. At a township, the clachans were fired, the children scattered and women were raped outside their front doors. As her husband watched, hidden in the heather, Isobel MacDonald was repeatedly raped by five soldiers. When the detachment departed, these brutalised families were left with nothing but their unimaginable pain as their cattle were rounded up and driven south to be sold to the dealers.

When the royal standard was raised at Glenfinnan and the Prince's army marched east, they failed to take Fort William, not having the artillery needed to reduce it. The garrison commander was Captain Caroline Scott (in the 18th century, the name was given to men and ironically it came from Kings Charles I and II and meant 'manly') and he was an officer in Guise's Regiment at Culloden. After the battle, he led soldiers on a series of expeditions in the glens that exacted a terrible vengeance, hanging, raping and burning houses indiscriminately. But, as is often the case, it is the random, petty acts of malice that lodge themselves in memory. On the Wade road near Fort William, Scott's men took hold of an old woman and cut off all her hair, joking that it would make a good wig for a gentleman. Humiliated, the old lady had the effrontery to ask the soldiers for the return of her handkerchief so that she might cover her bleeding and scalped head. Calling her an old bitch, the soldiers threw her to the ground and kicked her.

HMS *Furnace* sailed through the Hebrides on a mission to mete out punishment in the smaller islands. Under the command of Captain John Fergusson of Aberdeen, the sailors raped a blind woman on the island of Rona, off Skye, and continued to kill and burn wherever they dropped anchor. When Fergusson ordered the flogging of a captured French officer, technically a prisoner of war and not a rebel, a lieutenant in the Royal Scots Fusiliers stopped this particular minor act of cruelty, but much else went on uninhibited and unrecorded.

The Duke of Cumberland ordered that a campaign medal be struck for Culloden, one of the very earliest to be assigned to a specific battle. One side carried the portly duke's profile and on the other is the figure of the Greek god, Apollo, pointing at a wounded dragon. The inscription reads ACTUM EST ILICET PERIIT and the date AP XVI MDCCXLVI. It translates as 'The deed is done. It is all over. He has perished. April 16 1746'. And it was all over. By the end of that appalling summer of terror, thousands of Highlanders had been killed, their property burned, their cattle stolen, the economy left in ruins and their Gaelic-speaking culture fatally wounded. Before long, the time of the great emigrations would begin.

Many Highlanders fled south, most to the growing cities to find work. By 1775, Aberdeen, Glasgow and Dundee had seen their populations rise by more than 25 per cent in only 20 years as a result of immigration from the countryside and from beyond the Highland Line. Edinburgh was the largest with about 70,000 inhabitants and the maintenance of public order, especially in the warrens of the Old Town, meant that more men were needed for the police force. Known as the City Guard (or 'black banditti' to those they arrested), their officers began the long and colourful tradition of recruiting Highlanders, 'big, steady lads'. One such was Duncan Ban MacIntyre. Born in Glen Orchy in 1724, he fought at the battle of Falkirk as a young man before coming to the city to join the City Guard in 1767. Completely illiterate, Duncan was one of the greatest poets of the age. He composed his beautiful Gaelic lyrics entirely in his imagination and then dictated them to an amanuensis – one of whom was certainly James Stewart of Killin. He arranged for the poems to be published in 1768 with the help of John Campbell, the Principal Cashier of the Royal Bank of Scotland. These men must have recognised the significance of Duncan Ban's work for they too hailed from the same Highland districts. It was an elegiac farewell to a life that was passing, the experience of men and women who lived in glens and straths now slowly emptying, people who had lived their lives as part of the natural world, a world never better captured than by the music of MacIntyre's Gaelic.

When he remembered Ben Dorain, a singular mountain north-east of Glen Orchy, he also remembered the deer he loved so much and they are at the centre of perhaps his greatest poem, their description precise and time-less. This is from a beautiful translation of '*Moladh Beinn Dobhrain*' ('In Praise of Ben Dorain') by Iain Crichton Smith:

Pleasant to me rising
At morning
To see them the horizon
Adorning.
Seeing them so clear
My simple-headed deer
Modestly appear
In their joyousness
They freely exercise
Their sweet and level cries.
From bodies trim and terse,
Hear their bellowing.

Publishing reached across the spectrum from poetry like Duncan Ban's to the works of Hume, Smith and their contemporaries. But the presses also produced much more popular, much less timeless material in the shape of newspapers, journals and pamphlets. Appearing first in 1739, *The Scots Magazine* is still published once a month and one of the earliest newspapers was owned by Thomas Ruddiman. From 1720 onwards, the *Caledonian Mercury* was sold in booths and on the streets, usually publishing weekly, and, before 1739, it had a virtual monopoly of the news. A year after Culloden, *Aberdeen's Journal* first came out and, since it was renamed the *Aberdeen Press and Journal*, it can claim to be the oldest title still circulating in Scotland. The *Glasgow Herald* was launched with a scoop supplied by the Lord Provost. He had information on the Treaties of Versailles, concluded in 1783 at the end of the American War of Independence but the story came so late that the editor, John Mennons, could only run it on the back page. The *Dundee Courier* followed in 1801 and the youngest of Scotland's major newspapers is *The Scotsman*, first published in 1817. Known as the *Tenpenny Thunderclap*, it was produced at 347 High Street in Edinburgh's Old Town and, until the 21st century, did not stray far. When newspaper stamp tax was abolished in 1850, *The Scotsman* became a daily paper and, in 1902 it moved to the grand offices at the southern end of North Bridge whose facade still carries the splendid masthead. With Waverley Station only a few storeys below, the whole newspaper operation became wonderfully well streamlined. Copy was written and edited in the Olympian new offices while newsprint was delivered several floors below to the printing works on Market Street (where the City Art Centre is now) and the printed papers barrowed across the cobbles to the station for distribution by train all over Scotland and down to London.

The trains that carried the news across the nation were powered by steam engines and, in that form, they were the invention of a great Scotsman, probably the most influential scientist of the Enlightenment. Born in Greenock in 1736 to parents who were staunch Covenanters, James Watt did not go on to invent the steam engine as such but he made crucial modifications to the steam-driven pump built by Devon-born Thomas Newcomen, to clear water out of the tin mines.

Watt was employed as an instrument maker and repairer by Glasgow University and, in 1763, a Newcomen engine was brought to him to be mended. He saw that its notorious inefficiency was in large measure the consequence of the use of cold water to condense the steam in the piston in order to reduce pressure. After much experimentation, Watt came up with a revolutionary modification. He fitted a separate chamber to act as a condenser instead of the piston and, by building what was called a steam jacket around it, he also maintained the piston's heat so as not to waste energy.

Watt needed money. To make his design and model practical, he needed to build a new full-scale engine that would work. The founder of the Carron Ironworks, John Roebuck, supplied the capital needed to do that but, soon afterwards, he went bankrupt. When Matthew Boulton, a Birmingham ironmaster, became James Watt's partner, the theory took a great stride towards becoming a reality. A central difficulty had been the manufacture of a sufficiently tight-fitting piston and Boulton brought in John Wilkinson, a cannon maker. Used to making smooth-bored barrels for artillery, Wilkinson developed a reliable technique for engineering efficient pistons. Boulton and Watt were in business.

The partners did not accept contracts to build their engines at the pitheads of coalmines and tin mines. Instead, they took out patents and, from 1776 onward, they allowed local engineers to build for clients. In recompense, they took one third of the value of the coal that was saved by replacing the old Newcomen pump with a Boulton and Watt engine.

The action of the new engines was the same as the old in one sense – the pistons drove the arms of the pumps up and down. But, when Watt devised a means to convert this into rotary motion, essentially using a steam engine to turn a wheel, he supplied the process of industrialisation with momentum in every sense. Perhaps the best illustration of this, for those who can remember them, were the old steam trains that puffed their way around Britain's rail network, some of them early in the morning, throwing bundles of newspapers off as they slowed at country stations. On the outside of the older engines, a development of the crankshaft pioneered by James Watt could be seen working like a mechanical elbow, turning the clanking iron wheels. His great friend, Adam Smith, did not live to see the influence of the steam engine but it was very profound as it laid the foundations of the wealth of the nation.

But only for a very few. As Scotland industrialised, factories sprang up and, as steam power began to replace the water power used at places like New Lanark and Stanley, more and more coal was needed. While the new pumps could greatly mitigate the effects of flooding and allow more coal to be mined, the working conditions in the second half of the 18th century and on into the 19th were appalling. Because the coal seams were often narrow, men could not work them. Instead, women and children had to pull cartloads of coal in almost pitch-black conditions. Here is a chilling extract from a government commission on the mining industry: 'In the east of Scotland, where the side roads [shafts following narrow seams] do not exceed from twenty-two to twenty-eight inches in height, the working places are sometimes 100 and 200 yards distant from the main road; so that females have to crawl backwards and forwards with their small carts in seams in many cases not exceeding twenty-two to twenty-eight inches in height. The whole of these places, it appears, are in a most deplorable state as to ventilation. The evidence of their sufferings, as given by the young people and the old colliers themselves, is absolutely hideous.' Some of the observations of the commissioners are almost beyond belief. In one mine, they found a six-year-old girl who carried half a hundredweight of coal (56 pounds or 25 kilos) on her back for 14 journeys up the main shaft to the pithead every working day. Each journey was the equivalent of climbing to the top of St Paul's Cathedral.

Men resisted employment in the early factories of Scotland, perhaps a legacy from the traditional division of labour on the land where men were horse workers or in charge of livestock and women and children did the more menial tasks, like weeding and hoeing. In the first cotton factories, women and children worked very long hours, sometimes 14 hours a day for 6 days a week. The factories were dangerous places and the children were sent to crawl under the rattling looms to pick up bunches of cotton or retie threads – while the machines were still working. Mill owners did not wish to waste production time by stopping the looms during the working day for any reason, least of all safety. Fingers and limbs were routinely lost and sometimes children were decapitated or crushed. These dreadful conditions in the mines and factories did not improve until well into the 19th century.

The process of industrialisation in Scotland was halting, patchy and slow. The great age of heavy industry lay in the future, in the second half of the 19th century when Scotland would supply an empire with locomotives, boilers, ships and iron and steel goods of all sorts. Although the number of cotton spinning mills increased dramatically after the introduction of the flying shuttle in the 1770s (by 1795, there were 95 mills and, by 1839, 192), the majority of the population continued to work in agriculture and in domestic service. This pattern continued until the 1830s. But the total population was rising.

The first census in Scotland was compiled in 1755 by the Rev. Alexander Webster, a parish minister in Edinburgh, and he reckoned that there were 1,265,400 Scots. Twenty years later, the population had risen by about 10 per cent to 1,398,250. The most rapid growth rates were seen in the towns with Aberdeen, Dundee and Glasgow all increasing by a third, and in Paisley, the need for workers in the yarn spinning mills doubled the population. Cheap labour for the mills and other growing industries arrived in the towns and cities in a steady flow as the Lowland and Highland Clearances gathered pace.

After Culloden, the government had enacted repressive legislation. A dress act banned the wearing of kilts (except for the soldiers of the Black Watch and the other Highland regiments), the playing of the pipes was not permitted since they were seen as part of the clans' way of warfare and a series of disarming acts effectively demilitarised the Highlands. More insidious was the work of the Scottish Society for Promoting Christian Knowledge. It was a branch of an Anglican body formed in 1698 by Thomas Bray. His principal mission was the opening of schools for children aged from 7 to 11 (an incidental legacy was the modern notion of primary and secondary education). In the Highlands, the mission of the Scottish branch was more political – the schools were to act as a bulwark against Roman Catholicism and Jacobite sedition. By 1758, there were 176 schools in Scotland, many of them in the Highlands. At first, the SSPCK attempted to teach in English but soon it became clear that the children were learning the words by rote without much idea of what they meant. In 1767, they introduced a New Testament with Gaelic and English versions on facing pages and also changed the language of instruction to Gaelic. But there was a general hostility towards native speakers and some historians have seen the SSPCK as little more than a means to use religion to spread the use of English in an otherwise monoglot society – a means to deprive Highlanders of their identity.

PAISLEY PATTERN

In the late 18th century, soldiers returning from the wars in India brought back silk and woollen Kashmir shawls decorated with the boteh, a droplet-shaped vegetable motif of Persian or Indian origin. From c. 1800 onwards, weavers in Paisley began to produce shawls with this design. Their looms were sufficiently sophisticated to allow them to weave with five colours of yarn. The boteh quickly became known as the 'Paisley pattern' and, in the 19th century, as well as being woven, it was printed on cotton and woollen shawls and headsquares. The printed Paisley pattern was much cheaper than woven and almost as fashionable.

On a summer afternoon in the 1890s, Donald MacIver drove his pony and trap along a track by Loch Roag on the Atlantic coast of the Isle of Lewis. Beside him sat an old man, his uncle, Domhnall Ban Crosd, and, as they breasted the rise at Miabhig and gazed as the endless horizon of the ocean opened before them, both knew that they were completing a long journey into the past. Domhnall Ban had sailed to Lewis from Canada so that, before he died, he could return home to the place where he was born, the place that had made him.

As a boy, Domhnall Ban, his family and their neighbours had been cleared off their crofts in the township of Carnais. Like many, his parents had paid for a passage to Canada to make a new life but it was never their home place, always a destiny forced on them. For 50 years, the old man had seen Carnais only in his dreams as he suffered the pain of *ionndrainn*. More than 'homesickness', it means 'something missing' or 'emptiness'. And, when Donald MacIver braked the trap at the place where his uncle had lived, Domhnall Ban's face at last crumpled and the old man wept for all that experience in one place. For the place had gone, been obliterated. '*Chaneil nith an seo mar a bha e, ach an ataireachd na mara.*' There was nothing to see. The old croft houses of the township had tumbled down and their fences and fields opened to sheep pasture. All that was still familiar to Domhnall

Ban was '*an ataireachd na mara*', 'the high surge of the ocean', the sound of his childhood, as the breakers crashed on the sands below Carnais.

Much moved by his uncle's tears, Donald MacIver wrote his great lyric, '*An Ataireachd Ard*', 'The Ceaseless Surge of the Sea'. In memory of loss and change as the tides of history washed over the Highlands and Islands, it begins:

> *An ataireachd bhuan*
> *Cluinn fuaim na h'ataireachd ard*
> *Tha torun a' chuain*
> *Mar chualas leums' e 'nam phaisd*
> *Gun mhuthadh, gun truas*
> *A' sluaisreadh gainneimh na tragh 'd*
> *An ataireachd bhuan*
> *Cluinn fuaim na h' ataireachd ard*
>
> The ceaseless surge
> Listen to the surge of the sea
> The thunder of the ocean
> As I heard it when I was a child
> Without change, without pity
> Breaking on the sands of the strand
> The ceaseless surge
> Listen to the surge of the sea.

Domhnall Ban Crosd's visit to Carnais and his nephew's elegiac lyric marked the end of a long departure that was under way even before the clans charged across the heather at Culloden. In the 1730s, some Highland chiefs began to raise rents and those who did not have the means to pay were evicted and forced to emigrate, many to the Carolinas and Georgia in what were still the American colonies. In particular, the Duke of Argyll had not hesitated to begin the exploitation of the great Campbell patrimony, extracting as much revenue as possible from an area almost as large as the county of Argyll. On Skye, two chiefs who had attempted to discourage Prince Charles in 1745 were guilty of disreputable practices. Norman MacLeod of Dunvegan and Sir Alexander MacDonald of Sleat had tried to sell some of their clansmen and their families into what amounted to slavery, sending them to the Americas to work in the plantations as indentured servants. This was seen as scandalous behaviour but it marked the beginning of a process. The ancient bonds of *duthchas* were loosening, and quickly.

SCOTTICISMS

In 1763, less than ten years after Dr Samuel Johnson's definitive English dictionary was published, Alexander Donaldson, the bookseller and printer who also founded the Edinburgh Advertiser, *published another one in Edinburgh. It was a perfectly serviceable dictionary but it contained a curious preface. This dealt with Scotticisms, translating what it termed 'Scotch' words into 'proper English'. This may have been thought very handy at the time. Even men as self-possessed as David Hume were anxious to expunge Scotticisms from their writing and speech. It is often forgotten that in the 18th century accent was much less of an identifier of social class. Judges spoke in Scots but, after the Union of 1707, there was a tendency amongst intellectuals to prefer standard English English. The Donaldson family fortune was later used to set up Donaldson's Hospital, Scotland's national school for the deaf.*

After Culloden, chiefs began to exert more pressure on their tenants and the clan gentry, *na daoine uaisle* – men who were often relatives of the chiefly family who had collected rents and acted as an officer class in time of war – were increasingly dispensed with in an attempt to cut out middlemen. Often led by *na daoine uaisle*, more than 20,000 clanspeople, men, women and children, left the Highlands between 1763 and 1775. Many boarded ships bound for the Americas, others walked to the Lowlands to find work as Scotland industrialised and Glasgow became home to a large Gaelic-speaking community. By 1836, there were perhaps 22,000 Gaels living in the city's tenements and districts like Partick, or Partaig, still retain residual links with the Highlands.

In 1773, Dr Samuel Johnson and James Boswell were touring the north and, in an interval between complaints, the great lexicographer left this acute observation: 'There was perhaps never any change of national manners so quick, so great and so general as that which has operated in the Highlands by the late conquest and subsequent laws . . . The clans retain little now of their original character. Their ferocity of temper is softened, their military ardour is extinguished, their contempt for government subdued and their reverence for their chiefs abated.'

Even more than the law or the Cumberland atrocities, the dynamic and expanding economy of Britain and her growing empire forced the pace of transformation. As imperial wars were fought and won, especially in India and Africa, the demand for beef cattle and mutton (both salted to supply the armed forces), wool, timber, slate and kelp products rose markedly and this meant that there were handsome profits to be made. Rents rocketed and, between 1750 and 1775, they trebled on Skye, increased by 56 per cent on Cameron of Lochiel's estates in Lochaber and MacDonell of Glengarry lifted his rental income from £732 in 1768 to £4,184 in 1803 – a staggering 472 per cent increase in 35 years. Clansmen could not compete and, as tenancies were sold to those who could afford them, more and more families left.

HADDIES AND SMOKIES

In the late 18th century, James Boswell gained a literary reputation as the biographer and companion of Dr Samuel Johnson. But he also had something to say about Finnan haddies. Being very partial to the lightly smoked haddock from the village of Findon, near Aberdeen, Boswell was pleased to see them available in London. But less happy when he tasted them. So that they made the sea journey unspoiled, the Finnan haddies had been much more heavily smoked and were, frankly, a bit tough. Arbroath Smokies are the other famous product of the east coast. Also haddock, they are first salted overnight and then tied in pairs with hemp twine. Left to dry, they are hung over a triangular piece of wood and set over a fire of hardwood in a barrel. This is then sealed with a wet jute sack (so that it won't catch fire) and within only an hour, the haddocks are cooked. A beautiful rich brown, Arbroath Smokies are a genuine delicacy – although not delicate but strong tasting.

The year 1792 was a seminal one – a date still remembered by modern Highlanders. Known as *Am Bliadhna nan Caoraich Mora*, 'the Year of the Big Sheep', which was a reference to the introduction of Cheviots, a breed developed in the Borders. Bigger and better wool and mutton producers, these animals could realise a rise in profits quickly but they were not as hardy as the smaller Highland sheep. Cheviots needed to winter in the glens and the low-lying straths. When large herds arrived in Sutherland in 1792, driven north by Border shepherds and their dogs, they began to disrupt the traditional pattern of land use immediately. Not only did the big sheep graze where crofters had been used to cultivating, they also cut down the pasture available to black cattle. In two Sutherland parishes, the figures are eloquent. Between 1790 and 1803 in Assynt and Creich, the number of cows fell from 5,140 head to 2,906 and the flocks of sheep multiplied dramatically from 7,840 head to approximately 21,000.

To the landlords, at least, it was clear that people had to move. The *bailtean*, the traditional townships such as Carnais where crofting families had lived in strung-out communities, usually along a track, began to wither. The *bailtean* were the heart of Highland life – communities who wrung a living from the ground, cooperating in communal, seasonal tasks, such as the movement of stock up to the summer pasture or the digging of peats, because they had to and cohering in that way maintained a working, productive landscape. When they emptied, the glens and the mountains became mere scenery.

Landlords and clan chiefs did not at first want to see their people leave. Their presence on the land added value but only if it was the right sort of land. As the big sheep took over the glens, many families were turned out of their crofts and forced to move from the *bailtean* to the coast. What waited for them was a forgotten industry. Kelping was profitable but harsh, wet and windswept. Seaweed contains valuable chemicals such as potassium, sodium and magnesium and these were essential ingredients in the manufacture of glass, candles, soap and other products. When the Napoleonic wars cut off European supplies, the price of kelp rose steeply to around £22 a ton and the pace of clearance to the coasts accelerated.

It was grim work. Kelp was best collected in winter when it was likely that storms would have loosened large quantities and driven it onshore to mark the tideline. Gathering it from beaches was not difficult but, if kelp had to be cut from its holdfasts on the rocks with saw-toothed sickles held by hands under the chill seawater for long periods, it was a miserable task. Once the kelp had been harvested, it was dried on raised wooden steethes before being burned. Coffin-shaped and about five feet long by three feet wide, kelp kilns were dug in the sandy soil of the machair. The fires had to be stoked regularly and left smouldering for a long time before the ash cooled and the chemical-rich lumps lifted out. In peak years, between 15,000 and 20,000 tons of kelp left Highland shores for the factories of the south. At that time, the industry was worth around £400,000 a year, a huge sum. But, of course, the kelpers themselves saw nothing of such riches.

Crofting in those conditions could be a desperately difficult life. The coastal settlements were often on poor, marginal land and earth usually had to be brought in baskets to make beds where potatoes might grow. Many probably wanted to emigrate, and some did, but the chiefs needed their people to be tied to their land to make it profitable. In 1803, they lobbied the government to pass the Passenger Vessel Act, which insisted on improvements in transatlantic travel because they knew it would make passage on a ship much more expensive and extend it far beyond the reach of most of their tenants.

Amongst the most ruthless landlords were the Marquess of Stafford and his wife, Elizabeth, Countess of Sutherland. They owned a vast area of northern Scotland between Cape Wrath and the Dornoch Firth and, as she brusquely remarked of her husband, 'He is seized as much as I am with the rage of improvements, and we both turn our attention with the greatest of energy to turnips.' To the business-like Elizabeth, her tenants, the people of Strathnaver, Strathbrora, Kildonan or Halladale, should not be compared to vegetables – they were more like the native breeds of cattle or sheep: 'Scotch people are of happier constitution and do not fatten like the larger breed of animals.'

The first great clearances of the Sutherland estates began in 1814 – *Am Bliadhna an Losgaidh*, 'the Year of the Burning'. The brusque Elizabeth and her fabulously wealthy husband had appointed James Loch of Drylaw as their Commissioner of Estates and he was an utterly ruthless man. Most of Strathnaver was cleared, its families evicted and driven north to the jagged coastline to gather kelp around Torrisdale Bay and to fish, a skill few had. People were brutally bundled out of their homes, places they had lived for many generations, with those of their possessions they could carry or load on a handcart. 'The idle and lazy,' said Loch, 'alone think of emigration.' Roofs and their timbers were fired so that there could be no return. Bands of thugs were led by Patrick Sellar, the factor responsible to James Loch, and it appears that there were two or perhaps three deaths as old people succumbed to shock and exposure. Even the Countess was unhappy: 'He [Sellar] is so exceedingly greedy and harsh with the people, there are heavy complaints against him from Strathnaver.' At the Circuit Court in Inverness, Sellar was charged with murder but quickly acquitted and the Sheriff-Substitute who brought him to trial felt it necessary to write a letter of apology.

Clearances continued on the Sutherland estates for a further five years as people were evicted from Kildonan, Rogart, Lairg and the rest of the Strathnaver but the melancholy march of crofting families no longer halted at the ocean's edge. Waterloo and the final fall of Napoleon opened up European trade for the first time in a generation and the chemicals derived from kelp could be sourced elsewhere more cheaply. Now there was no compelling economic argument for having tenants at all. They may as well be gone. What was known as *Fuadach nan Gaidheal*, the 'Driving Out of the Gael', began in earnest and a MacKenzie bard wept as he wrote:

> I see the hills, the valleys and the slopes,
> But they do not lighten my sorrow.
> I see the bands departing
> On the white-sailed ships.
> I see the Gael rising from his door.
> I see the people going,
> And there is no love for them in the north.

Many of the 'white-sailed ships' slipped over the Atlantic horizon, bound for Canada and the sadness they carried with them endured for many years. Communities of Gaelic-speakers settled on Cape Breton Island, off the north-east coast of the Nova Scotia peninsula and the great Canadian writer, Alistair MacLeod, was a descendant. He remembered an old lady remembering: 'My grandmother gets up and goes for her violin which hangs on a peg inside her bedroom door. It is a very old violin and came from the Scotland of her ancestors, from the crumbled foundations that now dot and haunt Lochaber's shores. She plays two Gaelic airs – '*Gun Bhris Mo Chridh' On Dh'Fhalbh Thu*' ('My Heart Is Broken since thy Departure') and '*Cha Till Mi Tuille*' ('Never More Shall I Return'). Her hands have suffered stiffness and the lonely laments waver and hesitate as do the trembling fingers on the four taut strings. She is very moved by the ancient music and there are tears within her eyes.'

The eastern vista along Edinburgh's George Street may not have been finished by the grand church James Craig intended for St Andrew Square. Instead, the eye is drawn to a towering fluted column topped by a statue of a man whose extraordinary power and influence in Scotland has largely been forgotten. Henry Dundas took such total control of Scottish politics between 1775 and 1805 that his hapless detractors dubbed him King Harry the Ninth. The fourth son of Robert Dundas of Arniston in Midlothian, Henry attended the Royal High School and Edinburgh University before becoming a member of the Faculty of Advocates. At the age of only 24, he was quickly appointed Solicitor General for Scotland. His early success was, in part, due to the influence of his half-brother, Robert Dundas, who was Lord President of the Court of Session and it was a transaction Henry never forgot.

Family links still operate in the upper echelons of the Scottish legal hierarchy.

In 1774, the young man became MP for Midlothian and, at Westminster, speaking in Scots, he made forceful speeches and joined the Tory Party of Lord North. A year later, Henry Dundas became Lord Advocate – in effect, Secretary of State for Scotland (the office had been abolished in the wake of the 1745 rebellion) – and the long reign Harry the Ninth began.

His control tightened very quickly as he built a power-base of patronage, friendship and obligation. The franchise was very restricted and, in the main, controlled by a handful of landowners, men whom Dundas could influence. In the election of 1780, 41 of the 45 Scottish MPs were men who would support the Tory government and 12 of these were directly managed by Dundas. Spreading his web wider than politics, he controlled patronage over the universities and the Church of Scotland, deciding who would get what position and extracting undertakings in return.

Dundas was also powerful in the British government as Treasurer of the Navy and President of the Board of Control after 1784. This last made him de facto Secretary of State for the vast new Colony of India. Once he had forced the transfer of the oversight of the government of the subcontinent from the East India Company to Westminster, he used patronage to widen his network to reach halfway round the world. Vigorously and shamelessly promoting his countrymen, Dundas's influence resulted in about 12 per cent of all the East India Company employees, one in three officers in the Indian army and the first three Governors General all being Scots. So many lived in Calcutta that an entire regiment known as the Calcutta Scots could be raised. Through the links established by Dundas, Scots began to invest so heavily in the Indian tea trade that production quickly outstripped that of China. Dundee became a centre for the processing of Indian jute, a vegetable fibre that was used for making sacking, carpet backing and eventually linoleum as well as a host of other products. And India itself became a market for Scottish manufactures such as cotton fabric.

Dundas ran the country for long enough to effect a profound change. After the upheavals of the Jacobite rebellions and the disappointments following 1707, he integrated Scotland into the Union by making it possible for Scots to share in the abundant fruits of the growing empire. In 1821, Walter Scott wrote, 'India is the corn chest for Scotland, where we poor gentry must send our younger sons as we send our black cattle to the south.' He was right but there was perhaps no need to bemoan the departure of young men – many of them came back having made fortunes.

UBIQUITOUS SCOTS

As the British Empire grew, Scots found themselves scattered to the corners of the Earth – an experience which often profoundly changed them. Few changed as much as Thomas Keith. Born in Edinburgh, he enlisted in the 78th (Highlanders) Regiment of Foot and was sent to Egypt as part of the Alexandria expedition of 1807. Captured near Rosetta, he was bought as a slave by Ahmad Aga, and he and his compatriot, William Thompson, decided to convert to Islam. Thomas became Ibrahim Aga and William, Osman. After fighting a duel with an Egyptian soldier, Thomas sought the protection of the wife of a powerful figure, Muhammad Ali Pasha, and she sent him into the service of her son, Tusun Pasha. In 1811 he joined an expedition to fight the Wahhabis of what is now Saudi Arabia, and four years later he was appointed Acting Governor of the holy city of Medina, the burial place of the Prophet Mohammed.

If Dundas succeeded in creating a form of political stability fuelled by self-interest in Scotland, his achievements were tested by world-shaking events in Paris. Beginning in May 1789, the French Revolution developed an unstoppable momentum as its leaders became ever more radical, sweeping away almost all traditional institutions, executing the king and queen, purging themselves repeatedly, engaging in foreign wars and eventually finding a form of stability with the return of monarchy in the shape of the brilliant Napoleon Bonaparte.

Along with the rest of Europe, Scotland looked on in amazement and events in France were very influential. Writing some years later of the 1790s, the famous Edinburgh lawyer Henry Cockburn believed that 'everything rung and was connected with the revolution in France, which for above twenty years, was, or was made, the all in all, everything; not this thing or that thing, but literally everything was soaked in this one event'.

At first, there was support for the overthrow of what had been seen as an absolute monarchy and a sense that the French were engaged in a struggle similar to that which had engulfed Britain in the mid 17th century. William Wordsworth happened to be in Paris as momentous events unfolded and he was exultant, hailing a time when Europe rejoiced with 'France standing on the top of golden hours, / And human nature seeming born again.'

After the execution of Louis XVI and Queen Marie Antoinette in 1793 and the raging bloodlust of the Terror, enthusiasm cooled and some of those who supported the revolutionaries began to be seen as dangerous subversives. What fed the flame of dissent was the huge popularity of *The Rights of Man* by the English-American political theorist, Thomas Paine. It seems that more than 200,000 copies of his book were circulating all over Britain.

In Scotland, 10,000 joined the Scottish Association of the Friends of the People and one of its leaders, Thomas Muir, was arrested for preaching sedition in August 1793. At his trial, it was said that the Lord Justice Clerk, Lord Braxfield, was less than impartial when he was overheard saying to one of the jury, 'Come awa', Mr Horner, come awa', help us hang ane of them damned scoondrels.' Muir was given a savage sentence of 14 years' transportation to the new colony of Botany Bay in Australia but he was rescued by American sympathisers before he reached that fatal shore.

If revolution was not imminent in Scotland in the 1790s, there was certainly significant popular discontent. The increasing concentration of population in towns and cities brought comparatively large numbers of people together for the first time and, as a consequence of the long working week, they were together for long periods. And they began to act together. There were riots when food prices rose or when merchants engaged in sharp practices such as hoarding to drive up prices. One of the most serious was the Tranent Militia Riot of 1797. To counter the possibility of attack by the armies of the French Revolution, an act of parliament insisted on creating a form of conscription for a militia, a local defence force. Men between the ages of 19 and 23 could be chosen by lot to serve but peers and other wealthy men were permitted to buy themselves out by paying for a substitute. It was this latter exemption that angered ordinary people and there was widespread rioting. Between 12 and 20 people were killed by troops in Tranent. Protest was sporadic, ill organised and largely unsuccessful but it did signal something simple – a popular will for change.

> Is there for honest poverty
> That hings his head, an' a' that?
> The coward slave – we pass him by,
> We dare be poor for a' that,
> For a' that and a' that,
> Our toils obscure and a' that,
> The rank is but the guinea stamp,
> The Man's the gowd for a' that.

What though on hamely fare we dine,
Wear hodden grey and a' that;
Gie fools their silks and knaves their wine,
A Man's a Man for a' that;
For a' that and a' that,
Their tinsel show and a' that,
The honest man, though e'er sae poor,
Is king o' men for a' that.

Ye see yon birkie ca'd a lord,
Wha struts and stares and a' that?
Though hundreds worship at his word,
He's but a coof for a' that;
For a' that and a' that,
His riband, star and a' that,
The man o' independent mind
He looks and laughs at a' that.

A prince can mak a belted knight,
A marquis, duke and a' that;
But an honest man's aboon his might,
Gude faith he mauna fa' that!
For a' that and a' that,
Their dignities and a' that,
The pith o' sense and pride o' worth,
Are higher rank than a' that.

Then let us pray that come it may,
(As come it will for a' that)
That Sense and Worth, o'er a' the earth
Shall bear the gree and a' that.
For a' that and a' that,
It's comin' yet for a' that,
That Man to Man the warld o'er,
Shall brothers be for a' that.

Written in 1793, Robert Burns's great hymn to democratic principles and the common man has been defining. Set to music, it is perhaps the most fitting anthem for a nation without one and it was sung with palpable emotion by Sheena Wellington and the members of the new Scottish Parliament at its opening in 1999. Burns sent guns to the revolutionaries in Paris in the same year as he composed 'Is There for Honest Poverty' and his passion reaches across two centuries to touch what seems a timeless sense of egalitarianism, fraternity and liberty. But its expression was new and the 1790s and the early decades of the 19th century saw sporadic outbursts of political agitation and an abortive armed rebellion.

In a brief but dazzlingly productive life, Burns saw all this too and gave it its greatest lyrical expression. Born in 1759 in humble circumstances, the son of a gardener and an unsuccessful tenant farmer, he was nevertheless well educated and well read. In the preface to his *Poems, Chiefly in the Scottish Dialect*, Burns wrote that poetry was an escape from the grinding routine of day-in, day-out toil on the land – it supplied 'some kind of counterpoise'. He also planned a more permanent escape, making arrangements to emigrate to the West Indies and a better, sunnier life than trudging through the rain-soaked, mud-clogged rigs of Ayrshire. Burns may also have been prompted to leave Scotland because of a broken love affair.

But good luck intervened. In the summer of 1786, his poems were printed and published by John Wilson in Kilmarnock. The collection was a sensation, an immediate success, and, instead of taking ship across the Atlantic, Burns travelled to Edinburgh. Although he was unquestionably a child of the Enlightenment, educated in a parish school in Ayrshire, with ready access to books, and a supremely gifted poet and song collector, Burns met with some condescension in the salons of the Old Town and the New Town. Henry Mackenzie, the author of the sentimental novel, *The Man of Feeling*, saw 'the power of genius' in the young man and conferred the famous phrase 'this Heaven-taught ploughman'. His undoubted good looks made an impression on the ladies of Edinburgh society and a leading light, Mrs Alison Cockburn, wrote to a friend in December 1786: 'The town is at present agog with the ploughman poet, who receives adulation with native dignity, and is the very figure of his profession, strong and coarse, but he has a most enthusiastic heart of LOVE.' This description chimed with fashionable theories about primitive genius expressing itself unbidden, appearing, as it were, out of nowhere. In reality the observations of Mrs Cockburn and others are more eloquent about the hardening of class division in late 18th-century Scotland.

Once he had been paid part of the royalties for the Kilmarnock edition, Burns embarked on a tour of Scotland, visiting the Highlands and the

Borders. In addition to educating himself, his purpose was to collect songs and, near Dunkeld, he felt himself privileged to hear the great fiddler Neil Gow play traditional airs. Although James Johnson is named as editor of the *Scots Musical Museum*, whose six volumes were published between 1787 and 1803, Burns was centrally involved in the project, contributing more than 200 songs. He also sent songs for inclusion in George Thomson's *A Select Collection of Original Scottish Airs for the Voice*, a five-volume work published between 1798 and 1818.

Reluctantly, Burns returned to farming and took a tenancy near Dumfries at Ellisland but soon also found work as a part-time excise man or customs officer. In 1790, he wrote what is probably his most famous poem, the rollicking 'Tam o' Shanter', and worked hard at both his jobs and his passion for collecting and reworking traditional songs. By 1794, when he was promoted to acting supervisor in Dumfries, there were clear concerns about Burns's health. It appears he was suffering from a degenerative heart condition, something that might turn out to be fatal. And he knew it. Here is an extract from a letter to James Johnson: 'This protracting, slow consuming illness which hangs over me, will, I doubt much, my ever dear friend, arrest my sun before he has well reached his middle career, & will turn over the Poet to far other and more important concerns than studying the brilliancy of Wit or the pathos of Sentiment.'

In July 1796, Burns took to sea bathing in an attempt to alleviate his symptoms. At the Brow Well on the Solway coast, he met an old acquaintance, Maria Riddell, and, perhaps only half-joking, asked her, 'Well, Madam, have you any commands for the other world?' On 21 July, the poet died in Dumfries.

Robert Burns is venerated, even loved, in a way no other figure in Scotland's history is. Across all social, political and religious divides, his poetry and personality, the one bound up with the other, are celebrated in the unique institution of the Burns Suppers held on or around his birthday on 25 January and in the activities of Burns Clubs. These did not develop until long after his early death, proliferating in the last decade of the 19th century. In 1885, there were only 8 Burns Clubs but by 1911 there were 200 in Scotland. And, all over the world, wherever the Scots diaspora settled, his work is enthusiastically read and performed. Reaching far beyond Scotland, perhaps the most famous song in the world, sung by almost every culture, is 'Auld Lang Syne'. The nature of this undimmed and widespread love for Robert Burns, Rabbie Burns, and his work is perhaps to be found in his fundamental humanity, his hamely warmth and an ability brilliantly to express widely held sentiments and passions. He spoke and continues to speak eloquently for the lives of ordinary people in a way no other poet has done before or since. There are no Shakespeare Suppers or Eliot Evenings.

The revolutionary movement that inspired Burns had become a warlike autocracy built around the charismatic figure of Napoleon Bonaparte. He longed to add Britain to the French Empire and, in the winter of 1803–04, an invasion force mustered at Boulogne. Even though the weather was against a crossing of the Channel or a landing further up the North Sea coast, the threat was taken very seriously. Despite the Militia Riots, forces of local volunteers had been organised and a system of early warning of a landing put in place. This was a relay of balefires on hilltops with inter-visibility. In the Borders on 31 January 1804, the warning system went into spectacular action. A volunteer sergeant who was new to the area was on lookout duty at Hume Castle, a Berwickshire landmark and the site of a balefire. Peering into the winter darkness, he believed he could see the yellow flames of a lit beacon to the east, somewhere that seemed to be near the coast. The French had landed! He immediately lit the balefire at Hume Castle and the alarm crackled through Tweeddale and Teviotdale as beacons flared on Peniel Heugh, the Dunion near Jedburgh and Crumhaugh Hill at Hawick and across the Mosspaul watershed and down into Dumfriesshire and Cumberland. When volunteers saw the flames, they tumbled out of their beds, adrenalin pumping, pulled on their boots and grabbed for weapons. Horses were saddled, messages sent and near pandemonium reigned. There was no time to be lost! Walter Scott was in Cumberland when the flames were seen on Hume Castle and he rode 100 miles to join his regiment in Dalkeith. Southern Scotland was in uproar as wild rumours ricocheted from village to town. As volunteers blundered about in the darkness, breathlessly asking each other what was happening, regiments of Napoleon's feared cuirassiers, their harnesses jingling and breastplates gleaming, were expected to be seen clattering along the Berwick road at any moment. But they were not. No landing took place. What the unfortunate sergeant saw from Hume Castle was not a warning beacon but the fires of Northumberland charcoal burners. Glory there was none, only farce. Walter Scott must have been deeply disappointed.

If he could not himself be a part of military history, the great poet and novelist would go on to establish himself as an absolutely central figure in Scotland's cultural history. Walter Scott's achievement was simply immense and difficult to comprehend fully at 200 years' distance. Not only was he the first truly bestselling writer whose work sold in many tens of thousands, print runs drying up in a matter of days, he was also an international best-seller, very popular in the Americas and in Europe. More, he is commonly accepted as the inventor of the historical novel. His device of inserting a fictional character and plot into a narrative framework of real events has been widely used and developed ever since the publication of *Waverley* in 1814. Sub-titled *'Tis Sixty Years Since*, the novel takes the Jacobite Rebellion of 1745–46 as the setting for the tale of Edward Waverley, a young Englishman who became embroiled in the conflict. Success was immediate and lasting – long enough for the title of the novel to be conferred on what was at the time Scotland's largest building, Waverley Station. It stands about 100 metres from the tallest and grandest memorial to a writer ever raised in Britain, the Scott Monument in Princes Street.

The real history of how this remarkable achievement developed is worthy of the master's imagination. It began with a debilitating illness. Born in Edinburgh in 1771, Walter Scott contracted what was probably poliomyelitis. Affecting his left leg when he was barely a toddler, it left him lame all his life. At first, his father, also Walter Scott, believed that the bracing country air of the Borders would help to cure him and the 'wee, sick laddie' was sent to Sandyknowe Farm near Kelso. It was his grandfather's home and the boy's time there was formative. Forced to spend much time indoors, in the warmth of the farm kitchen, happed in a blanket, young Walter listened to tales from his grandfather. His Auntie Jenny also sang to him and the old cow bailie, Sandy Ormistoun, regaled the rapt and open-mouthed child with stories of Border reivers and the clash of war as armies crossed the Cheviots, the hills clearly visible from the windows of Sandyknowe. In the third Canto of his great poem of the Battle of Flodden, *Marmion*, Walter Scott remembered the stories and the ballads in the farm kitchen in the house that lay in the shadow of Smailholm Tower, the ruined reiver fortress on the crag behind.

> And still I thought that shatter'd tower
> The mightiest work of human power;
> And marvell'd as the aged hind
> With some strange tale bewitched my mind,
> Of forayers, who, with headlong force,
> Down from that strength had spurr'd their horse,
> Their southern rapine to renew
> Far in the distant Cheviot blue,

And, home returning, fill'd the hall
With revel, wassail-rout and brawl.
Methought that still with trump and clang,
The gateway's broken arches rang;
Methought grim features, seam'd with scars,
Glared through the window's rusty bars,
And ever, by the winter hearth,
Old tales I heard of woe and mirth,
Of lovers' slights, of ladies' charms,
Of witches' spells, or warriors' arms;
Of patriot battles, won of old
By Wallace wight and Bruce the bold;
Of later fields of feud and fight,
When, pouring from their Highland height,
The Scottish clans, in headlong sway,
Had swept the scarlet ranks away . . .
Still, with vain fondness could I trace
Anew, each kind familiar face,
That brighten'd at our evening fire!
From the thatch'd mansion's grey-hair'd Sire,
Wise without learning, plain and good,
And sprung of Scotland's gentler blood . . .

Scott's long poems, *The Lay of the Last Minstrel*, *Marmion* and *The Lady of the Lake*, were enormously popular but it was a collection of traditional songs and ballads that first inspired the young man. Just as Robert Burns had toured Scotland listening to ancient music, Scott first went to Liddesdale, the quintessential reiver valley, to write down an oral tradition, the words of the ballads still sung by the fireside. Although he had qualified as a lawyer, like his father, and practised all his life, Scott found himself fascinated by what he heard in his first 'raid' or expedition in 1792. Eventually, after another six raids, he compiled and 'improved' all he had recorded in his *Minstrelsy of the Scottish Border* of 1802–03. With its erudite and sometimes amusing notes, it made Walter Scott's reputation, establishing him as a substantial literary figure. His friend, Robert Shortreed, accompanied him on his raid to Liddesdale and made this astute observation when he spoke to Scott's biographer, J. G. Lockhart: 'He was makkin himsell a' the time, but he didnae ken maybe what he was about till years had passed. At first he thought o' little, I dare say, but the queerness and the fun.'

By 1821, Scott had enjoyed unparalleled success with the publication of *Waverley, Guy Mannering, The Antiquary, Heart of Midlothian, The Bride of Lammermoor, Ivanhoe, Kenilworth* and several other novels. He had reached a pinnacle, the most famous Scotsman in history, a man feted wherever he went. When he visited Paris, people stood on chairs as he passed by to catch a glimpse of him. With his reworking of Scotland's history, he had achieved a stated aim. In the preface of the *Minstrelsy*, he wrote: 'By such efforts, feeble as they are, I may contribute somewhat to the history of my native country; the peculiar features of whose manners and character are daily melting and dissolving into those of our sister and ally.'

The opportunity to set a seal on his efforts to assert a Scotland distinct from England presented itself in 1822. It was proposed that King George IV should make a state visit to his kingdom of Scotland. Old, ill and daft, George III had died in 1820 and his son at last ascended the throne after nine years of regency. A royal progress to Scotland was long overdue. The last reigning monarch to come north was Charles II, who was crowned at Scone in 1651, nearly a decade before England restored its monarchy. If the United Kingdom of Great Britain and Ireland was to become stronger, then its king should come to Edinburgh – and arrive in some style.

The man chosen to be master of ceremonies was of course the most famous Scotsman who had ever lived and Walter Scott grasped the opportunity with gusto. And what he chose to do turned out to be immensely influential, altering the character and look of Scotland's sense of itself at a stroke. In one of the greatest publicity stunts in British history, Scott conceived the state visit as a tartan-wrapped celebration of all things Highland – except armed insurrection. What could be more different, more un-English, more mistily romantic than the Celtic culture of the north? It appeared to matter little that only 76 years after Jacobites were being hanged at Carlisle, after the brutal genocide perpetrated by Cumberland's soldiers and after the Disarming Acts after 1746, that Scott had persuaded the king to put on the clothes of his family's enemies. The portly George IV arrived in Edinburgh dressed in a Royal Stewart kilt. It was apparently worn some distance above the royal knee over flesh-coloured tights designed to hide varicose veins. When she beheld this remarkable vision, an Edinburgh lady is said to have remarked, 'Since the king is here for such a short time, it is as well that we see so much of him.'

In the early 19th century, what royalty did and what royalty wore were immediately aped by the upper echelons of society. The sales of previously proscribed kilts and tartan rocketed (no indication of a rise in the sales of flesh-coloured tights is detectable) and the Borders mills thrummed and clacked as production intensified to meet demand. And, as the gentry reeled, strathspeyed and sweated, swathed in all that cloth, at balls at the Palace of Holyroodhouse, some took a more cynical view. Walter Scott's son-in-law and biographer, J. G. Lockhart, muttered that the whole affair was a 'hallucination' and complained that the Scots were being portrayed as 'a nation of Highlanders'. And it was true. But such was Scott's sureness of touch and judgement of the public mood that the hallucination hardened into a reality. Now, two centuries after George IV appeared resembling a tartan dumpling, few formal occasions are kilt-free. Lowland bridegrooms and their male guests routinely put on the dress of men who were believed by their ancestors to be sub-human savages. By contrast, few Highlanders or Islesmen are ever seen wearing kilts. Lowlanders have adopted and adapted much of the iconography of the Gael but with little or no understanding of the culture. As the wearing of tartan becomes ever more popular, the Gaelic language that first described it withers into a lexical curiosity.

Walter Scott created his own personal fantasy in the shape of Abbotsford, the name he gave to the house he had built on the banks of the Tweed near Melrose. Perhaps the abbots did use the ford there but, in any case, the new name was better than the old. The original farm of Cartleyhole was nicknamed Clarty Hole. The new house and the land bought around it cost a fortune and it turned out to be a fortune Scott did not have. He had become a partner in his publisher's company, Archibald Constable & Co. of Edinburgh, and it became dramatically clear that they were severely under-capitalised, relying on bank borrowings to run their business. Which was not necessarily a difficulty as long as Scott's work continued to sell in quantity and the banks were willing to lend. But, in the financial crash of 1826, when too much speculative investment and insufficient security to back it caused a run on the banks and persuaded them to cease lending, there was immediate trouble. The ensuing panic was disastrous for Constable and for Scott. For years, the author had been paid his advances with promissory notes which he then discounted for cash. These were redeemed over time as book sales continued to flourish. But, when the notes became worthless, bankruptcy loomed.

In 1826, there was no such thing as limited liability for companies and, instead of declaring himself bankrupt and offering to pay a small percentage

North Britain

of what was owed to creditors, Scott took on the whole debt – a staggering sum of £116,858, 11s and 3d. To him it was the only honourable course of action and, when his supporters offered help, he declined. 'My own right hand will do it,' he declared and, between 1826 and 1832, he killed himself with hard, unremitting work, turning out six novels, a vast biography of Napoleon and a history of Scotland amongst much else. By 1834, £90,000 had been paid off and, as Scott's work continued to sell well, the entire debt was discharged by 1848.

Although his work is, sadly, little read now, Walter Scott's influence is everywhere in Scotland. By fashioning stories around episodes in Scotland's history, by putting the Scots language into the mouths of many of his characters and by examining national institutions, he fostered a much sharper consciousness of Scotland and helped create a national identity for a people who had never taken to the notion of being North British. However confected, romantic and Highland-ised Scotland had become, the country was given a distinct sense of itself by Scott, something that marked out the Scots as unmistakably themselves.

Politically, Walter Scott saw himself as a Tory and, despite his fame, his views did not always make him popular. Only two years before the theatre of George IV's visit, Scotland simmered with discontent amongst people who held very different opinions. With the defeat of Napoleon at Waterloo in 1815, the war economy in Britain quickly contracted and returning soldiers swelled the ranks of the unemployed. Adding to widespread hardship was the growing sense that the mass of people should no longer be excluded from representative politics. The number of eligible voters in Scotland remained tiny.

In England, the movement for reform was led by the Hampden Clubs which were named after John Hampden, the English parliamentarian who was one of the earliest challengers of the authority of Charles I. Their leader, Major John Cartwright, came to Glasgow in 1816. Forty thousand came to hear him speak. In early 1820, weavers in the west of Scotland planned a general strike for 1 April to highlight their economic plight. All of the textile weavers in Glasgow were to be involved, around 60,000 in all. There were armed parades of men with pikes and muskets and, on 5 April, things escalated into the beginnings of armed insurrection. Believing that Glasgow had been seized by insurgents, James Wilson, a former weaver from Strathaven, led a tiny force of twenty armed men to the city. When it became quickly clear that no such thing had happened, they fled but Wilson was arrested.

361

Another group attempted to occupy the Carron Ironworks, where the army's cannon were manufactured. They were scattered by soldiers at Bonnymuir and their leader, Andrew Hardie, was taken and imprisoned. In front of a huge crowd of 20,000 in Glasgow, James Wilson was led out on to a scaffold to suffer a version of the horrific rituals of the traitor's death. His hanging and beheading were designed to shock the assembled multitude into inaction.

The weavers were not radicals in that they did not seek political reform – their protest was against the decline of their wages and status. But these sparks of dissent in Scotland and the drama of the slaughter at what became known as the Peterloo Massacre in Manchester in 1819, when 11 people were killed and 160 were injured as hussars charged into a peaceful crowd, did ignite a process of political change. Rotten boroughs were abolished in England, the anti-trade union legislation of the Combination Acts was repealed and the Catholic Emancipation Act of 1829 allowed Catholics full participation in public life. The death of George IV in 1830 prompted a general election and the extension of the franchise became a major issue. Under Lord Grey, the new Whig government drafted legislation which was eventually piloted through both houses of parliament and received reluctant royal assent from William IV.

The Great Reform Act of 1832 led to the allocation of additional MPs for Glasgow and Edinburgh and dispensed with the need for a town to be a royal burgh before it could have representation in parliament. Growing towns like Greenock and Paisley were to elect their own MPs and six other new burgh seats were created. Scotland's ancient universities were represented. Glasgow and Aberdeen each sent an MP to the House of Commons and, in a unique co-operation, the universities of St Andrews and Edinburgh shared one. The most dramatic effect was the extension of the franchise. In 1820, only 4,250 Scotsmen had a vote but, after the Reform Act, the electorate expanded enormously to approximately 65,000. Men of property still controlled elections and there was little immediate sign of political change but a process had begun.

12

Imperial Scotland

✻

COAL MINERS IN early modern Scotland were in effect slaves. An act of the Scottish Parliament of 1606 bound miners, many of them dependent women and children, to the pits owned by aristocrats such as the Duke of Hamilton and the Marquis of Lothian. Runaways were rigorously pursued and prosecuted. The act was designed to prevent the poaching of miners by those opening up new workings. Another act of 1672 authorised more powers for 'coal-masters, salt-masters, and others, who have manufactories in this kingdom, to seize upon any vagabonds or beggars wherever they can find them, and put them to work in the coal-heughs or other manufactories, who are to have the same power of correcting them and the benefit of their work as the masters of the correction-houses.'

After 1760 and the gradual expansion of mining in the wake of James Watt and Mathew Boulton's installation of more efficient pumps, the serfdom of miners was increasingly seen as a hindrance to recruitment. Two acts of parliament, in 1775 and 1799, swept away this punitive, antiquated legislation. Nevertheless, it was difficult to persuade people to work in the appalling conditions of the pits. Few did it willingly. In a report on the employment of children compiled in 1842 by R. H. Franks, authentic voices are at last heard. Here is the testimony of three young girls. The first, Janet Cumming, was 11 years old:

I gang with the women at five and come up at five at night; work all night on Fridays and come away at twelve in the day. I carry the large bits of coal from the wall-face to the pit-bottom, and the small pieces called chows in a creel. The weight is usually a hundredweight; do not know how many pounds there are in a hundredweight, but it is some weight to carry; it takes three journeys to fill a tub of 4cwt. The distance varies, as the work is not always on the same wall; sometimes 150 fathoms, whiles 250 fathoms. The roof is very low; I have to bend my back and legs, and water comes frequently up to the calves of my legs. Have no liking for the work; father makes me like it. Never got hurt, but often obliged to scramble out of the pit when bad air was in.

A fathom is about two metres and when Janet talked of bad air, she was probably referring to methane or other noxious gases released by hacking the coal from a seam.

This is the testimony of Isabella Read who was also 11 years old:

I am wrought with sister and brother; it is very sore work. Cannot say how many rakes or journeys I make from pit-bottom to wall-face and back, thinks about 30 or 25 on the average; distance varies from 100 to 250 fathoms. I carry a hundredweight and a quarter on my back, and am frequently in water up to the calves of my legs. When first down, fell frequently asleep while waiting for coal from heat and fatigue. I do not like the work, nor do the lassies, but they are made to like it. When the weather is warm there is difficulty in breathing, and frequently the light go out.

At 17 years old, Agnes Moffat was a relative veteran:

Began working at ten years of age. Work 12 and 14 hours daily. Can earn 12s in a fortnight, if work be not stopped by bad air or otherwise. Father took sister and I down; he gets our wages. I fill five baskets; the weight is more than 22cwt; it takes me five journeys. The work is o'er sair for females. Had my shoulder knocked out a short time ago, and laid idle some time. (It is no uncommon thing for women to lose their burthen (load) and drop off the ladder down the dyke below.) Margaret McNeil did a few weeks since, and injured both her legs. When the tugs [ropes or chains] that pass over the forehead break, which they frequently do, it is very dangerous to be under a load. The lassies hate the work altogether, but they canna run away from it.

Coal production in Scotland soared from approximately 16 million tons in 1815 to 30 million in 1830, much aided by the invention of a miners' safety lamp by Sir Humphry Davy. One of the greatest logistical difficulties for mine owners was distribution once coal had been carried to the surface in baskets and creels. Bulky and heavy, its value could only be maximised if it could be delivered cheaply to the point of use. One of the earliest initiatives was the creation of the Clydesdale breed of heavy horses. The Dukes of Hamilton owned much of Scotland's largest coalfield in North Lanarkshire and their small pack horses with panniers slung either side of a wooden pack saddle could not satisfy growing demand. They needed big and powerful animals capable of pulling 3-ton carts, so they had larger and more muscular stallions brought over from Flanders to cover local mares and a breeding programme began. By the 1790s, the largest Clydesdales could weigh a ton and a well-trained pair could pull very large cartloads of coal.

DUNURE FOOTPRINT

As both agriculture and industrial haulage came to depend on the heavy horse's muscles, the possession of a good Clydesdale stallion became very lucrative. Before the arid processes of artificial insemination became universal, natural covering was the means by which a farmer's brood mare became pregnant. That meant the owners of stallions had to walk them around the countryside in the early spring. The gestation period of horses is about 11 months and it is best for foals to be born in the spring following a cover, just as the new grass is flushing to make rich milk. Born in 1908, the greatest sire in Clydesdale breeding history was Dunure Footprint, who fathered more than 5,000 foals in his long career. His owner, William Dunlop, fed Footprint on a diet of milk and beaten raw eggs and, at the height of his powers, he could cover a mare every two hours. Towards the end of each spring season, he grew tired and, while he could still serve a mare presented to him, the exhausted stallion fell off her as soon as the deed was done. At a stud fee of £60, Dunure Footprint made a lot of money for Dunlop.

Eventually mine owners had wagon ways built. These were essentially railways laid down with wooden and, later, iron rails to allow heavy horses to pull coal wagons in all seasons to a canal where they could be loaded on to barges. The largest network was the Monklands system and it linked with the Monklands Canal which was dug in 1792–93 and intended for the transport of coal into Glasgow. The Forth and Clyde Canal had been opened to traffic three years earlier and its barges also facilitated the delivery of coal in bulk. But gradually wagon ways were transformed into railways able to function as a complete system. The first was the Kilmarnock and Troon line.

Opening in 1812, it carried passengers and experimented with steam power in 1816 or 1817, using a primitive locomotive. When George Stephenson's railway connecting collieries around Shildon with Stockton and Darlington opened in 1825 and was an instant success, the future was glimpsed and new track was quickly laid in Scotland.

By 1831, three short lines opened between Dalkeith and Edinburgh, Garnturk and Glasgow and at Newtyle. What encouraged investment in new rail links was the invention of hot blast iron smelting in 1828. Born in Shettleston, at that time a village outside Glasgow, James Neilson devised a method of improving the production of iron by using hot air in the process. And because of a happy accident of geology, foundries quickly grew up in Glasgow and North Lanarkshire. Not only were there plentiful reserves of coal nearby (and it was hard, bituminous coal known as splint which burned at very high temperatures), there were also substantial deposits of black band ironstone in Lanarkshire. The Monklands and Garnturk railways began to haul ore as well as coal and this traffic, in turn, fuelled the rapid expansion of the rail network.

BURKE, HARE AND THE CANAL

In the early 19th century, work began on digging a canal between Fountainbridge in Edinburgh and Port Dundas in Glasgow. Many of the workforce were Irish, including the notorious William Burke and William Hare. They committed a series of murders in 1828 which was unusual and whose details were very memorable. They sold the corpses of their 16 victims to Dr Robert Knox. He was an anatomist at Edinburgh University and needed fresh bodies for dissection. He charged fees for his lectures and, although he was never arrested or brought to trial, the Edinburgh mob and the press believed that Knox was complicit in the murders. Burke and Hare were convicted of the murders although only Burke was sentenced to death, Hare having turned King's evidence. The judge specified that Burke's body be publicly dissected. This famous case did not spark any anti-Irish rioting but it did spawn many films, TV programmes, plays, novels and songs.

Canals were comparatively slow, needed locks to deal with gradients and could freeze over in winter. Bulk quantities of ore and coal could be moved cheaply and reliably by rail and, as the gangs of navvies (navigators) laid track, industry grew and prospered. Scottish wages were, at first, lower than in England and substantial profits were generated and a proportion was ploughed back into the creation of more infrastructure. By 1842, a passenger and goods line linked Edinburgh with Glasgow. Railway mania grew and all sorts of impractical schemes were considered but, eventually, a government commission introduced some regulation. In 1850, Scotland's fledgling network was connected with England's at Berwick-upon-Tweed when the spectacular Royal Border Bridge was opened by Queen Victoria. It was a turning point. Goods and people could travel between Edinburgh and London in a day and Scotland became part of a vast imperial network.

As railways quickened the pace of industrialisation, Scotland began to change radically. In the same year that Queen Victoria cut the ribbon at Berwick, one Scot in every five lived in the largest four cities – Glasgow, Edinburgh, Dundee and Aberdeen, which were growing at a remarkable rate. Early estimates showed that Glasgow had 147,000 inhabitants in 1820; by the time of the first formal census in 1841 there were 255,000, with 396,000 in 1861, 511,000 in 1881 and, by 1901, there were 762,000.

Living conditions were primitive, very overcrowded and dangerous. Sanitation was often non-existent and water-borne diseases like typhus and cholera claimed many thousands of lives. When fresh water reached the city from Loch Katrine in the Trossachs in 1859, the incidence of epidemics declined markedly and the town council began to grapple with the continuing problem of housing as more and more people flooded into Glasgow. The situation was most acute in the East End, in the closes and wynds of the High Street, the Saltmarket and the Gallowgate. In 1840, the Chief Constable, Captain Miller, made a speech in which he observed that 'in the very centre of the city there is an accumulated mass of squalid wretchedness which is probably unequalled in any other town of the British dominions'. The census of 1861, when Glasgow's population had rocketed to 396,000, showed that 34 per cent lived in one room, a single end, and that a further 37 per cent lived in only two rooms.

The living conditions for the mass of the people of Edinburgh were little better. At 14 feet by 11.5 feet, the average size of a single room was small and a survey carried out in the tenements of the Old Town, in the Grassmarket, St Giles, the Tron and the Canongate areas found that 1,530 single-room homes had between 6 and 15 people living in them. And, incredibly, one in ten of these had lodgers. They must have taken it in turns to sleep.

The same census of 1861 produced a remarkable statistic for Dundee. The population of the city had mushroomed to 91,664 but there were only five

WCs and three were in hotels. All drinking water was drawn from wells and the most used, the Lady Well, was badly fouled by the nearby slaughterhouse. In 1866, John Symington wrote of Edinburgh, 'Sanitary arrangements are of the most defective description. The absence of conveniences . . . is a great preventive of that thorough cleanliness and purity . . . as a consequence, the atmosphere is foully tainted, and rendered almost unendurable by its loathsomeness at those periods when offal and nuisance require to be deposited on the streets.'

Poverty in the growing cities and towns could be utterly abject. In a submission for the Chadwick Report of 1842, which looked at living conditions amongst the poorest, Dr W. L. Lawrie wrote about the lack of sanitation in the tenements of Greenock and its appalling impact. Because drainage did not exist or was constantly clogged, families were in the habit of tipping human waste out of their windows into the narrow closes or emptying buckets on the nearest dunghill. There was one behind Dr Lawrie's surgery and the smell was so bad that he could not open his window. A decent and caring man, he must also have had a strong constitution. In his submission to the Chadwick Report, Lawrie described a pitiful, medieval scene:

As I was passing one of the poorest districts not long ago, a little girl ran after me and requested me to come and see her mother as she could not keep her in bed; I found the mother lying in a miserable straw bed with a piece of carpet for a covering, delirious from fever; the husband, who was a drunkard, had died in the hospital of the same disease. There was no fire in the grate; some of the children were out begging, and the two youngest were crawling on the wet floor; it was actually a puddle in the centre, as the sewer before the house was obstructed, and the moisture made its way to the middle of the floor by passing under the door. Every saleable piece of furniture had been pawned during the father's illness for the support of the family. None of the neighbours would enter the house; the children were actually starving, and the mother was dying without any attendance whatever.

In the early 19th century Scotland was clearly a society of very stark contrasts. While children starved in Greenock, those with time and money began to find new ways to enjoy themselves.

Loch Katrine not only supplied Glasgow with clean water, it was also a very early tourist destination. The fictional setting of Walter Scott's *The Lady of the Lake*, it began to attract visitors in the decades following publication

in 1810. An important part of the attraction of the Trossachs was conveni-
ence – it lies just across the Highland boundary fault and its scenery is
unmistakably different, and it is also not far from the major cities of central
Scotland. At the same time, the Scottish Highlands were increasingly seen
as romantic, mysterious, even beautiful, rather than the remote resort of a
warlike Jacobite rabble. These notions began to circulate only 15 years after
the last rebellion.

In 1761, James MacPherson claimed that he had rediscovered a lost
epic poem by a bard he called Ossian. Complete and pristine, it told the
heroic story of Fingal and its finder announced that he had translated it
into English. A British epic poet to rival Homer and Virgil, Ossian's great
work was a sensation when it was revealed to the world. And it immediately became wildly and enduringly popular. More poems allegedly came
to light and were translated and, in 1765, a collected edition, *The Poems of
Ossian*, was published. Thousands of copies were soon in circulation. Goethe
translated parts of it into German, Napoleon carried a copy as he led the
Grande Armée into Russia and great writers such as Blake, Thoreau, Byron,
Scott and Arnold either praised or imitated Ossian – or both. Mendelssohn,
Schubert and Brahms were inspired to compose music and the name Oscar
(it appeared first in Ossian) was widely bestowed. In the USA, the city of
Selma, Alabama, was named after Fingal's palace. And, of course, his remark-
able cave is seen on the island of Staffa by many thousands each year.

There were other reactions. Some literary figures were very suspicious. Dr
Samuel Johnson called MacPherson 'a mountebank, a liar and a fraud'. When
calls for the ancient manuscripts of Ossian to be produced for examination
were ignored, doubts about authenticity intensified. The problem was that
there was almost certainly no single manuscript and that MacPherson had
inflated and conflated what he had discovered as a sales ploy. David Hume
remarked that 'fifty bare-arsed Highlanders' could not convince him. But
Hugh Blair, Professor of Rhetoric at Edinburgh University, stood by the
young author and wrote an introduction to the poems that supported their
authenticity.

Somewhat embarrassed, the Committee of the Highland Society began
an enquiry. What became known as the Glenmasan manuscript eventually
came to light. It was certainly old and it contained material resembling some
of what was to be found in Ossian. And crucially, the respected figure of
Adam Ferguson, Professor of Natural Philosophy at Edinburgh University,
realised that the poems were not a fabrication. As a Gaelic speaker whose ear

was tuned to the oral tradition of the Highlands, he could discern genuine elements. Modern Gaelic scholars have agreed with Ferguson's general assessment. The problem was that MacPherson over-claimed – there never was a manuscript but the work was full of genuine references. Many of the names had been anglicised or slightly changed. Fingal is from Fionn mac Cumhaill, Temora is Tara, Dar-Thula is Deirdre of the Sorrows and so on. It seems clear that, in pursuit of a Homeric creator, MacPherson did a great deal of reorganisation and invention to create a coherent narrative. But, then, Walter Scott would later alter Border ballads as he 'improved' them.

Leaving aside the controversy, perhaps the most profound effect of the Ossian poems was to change perceptions radically. From the redoubt of wild savagery and sedition, the Highlands very quickly became the fount of romance. Instead of the rain-swept home of a rabble of cattle-stealing, Gaelic-speaking primitives, the mountains and glens had once seen noble kings, beautiful princesses and great and brave warriors and picturesque palaces. And, from the 1760s onwards, the Highlands began to fit the romance of its imagined past as the emigrations emptied the glens and straths and a working landscape slowly decayed into scenery, a vacant stage set for epic tales.

JARDINE MATHESON

Now known as Jardine Matheson Holdings, listed on the London Stock Exchange and incorporated in Bermuda, this company was once one of the most active drug dealers in the world. Founded in Canton in 1832 by two graduates of Edinburgh University, William Jardine and James Matheson, it initially traded in smuggled opium, tea and cotton. The company is now controlled by the Keswick family, descendants of William Jardine's sister, Jean, and it has wide interests in the hotel business and much else, though not in drugs. It is said that a portrait of James Matheson, founder of the firm and opium dealer, hung above the Sheriff's bench in Dingwall Sheriff Court until a local councillor pointed out that it might not be appropriate.

Perhaps inspired or intrigued by the Ossian poems, William Wordsworth, his sister, Dorothy and the poet Samuel Taylor Coleridge, visited the Trossachs in 1803. Painfully patronising even for the times, Dorothy's journal did awaken even more interest in the Highlands but the first real surge in tourism came with the publication of *The Lady of the Lake*. Robert Cadell, the son-in-law of Scott's publisher, recorded the reaction: 'The whole country rang with the praises of the poet – crowds set off to view the scenery of Loch Katrine, till then comparatively unknown; and as the book came out just before the season for excursions, every house and inn in that neighbourhood was crammed with a constant succession of visitors. It is a well-ascertained fact that, from the date of the publication of *The Lady of the Lake*, the post-horse duty in Scotland rose in an extraordinary degree.'

When railways began to replace post horses and reached northwards, even more visitors came as the Highlands acquired a second, highly influential patron. After the success of the royal visit in 1822, George IV's niece, Victoria, first visited Scotland in 1842 with Prince Albert, having first read Scott's famous poem. They toured Perthshire and summer in Scotland quickly became a staple of the palace diary. By 1848, they had ventured further north and bought the Balmoral Estate from the 4th Earl of Aberdeen, George Hamilton Gordon. Balmoral's previous owners, Clan Farquharson had been enthusiastic Jacobites who had fought against the queen's ancestors in all the major rebellions of the 18th century and forfeited the estate after the 1745 Rebellion. When Victoria declared that, at heart, she was herself a Jacobite and that Stewart blood coursed through her veins, few heads were scratched at such nonsense. The Highlands had become safe – culturally neutered, their history was a mere backdrop, more colourful than threatening. But Victoria's near-obsession with Scotland had what was probably an unintended beneficial consequence. Balmoral, its tartan wallpaper and the bogus genealogy made the monarchy appear, for the first time, to embrace Scotland and so seem truly British. Unlike her predecessors, the little queen was popular.

Just as the gentry had swathed themselves in tartan in Edinburgh in 1822, so Victoria and Albert's purchase of Balmoral prompted more imitation and, by the end of the 19th century, hundreds of shooting lodges and grand residencies of various sorts had been built in the Highlands. After Prince Albert's death, the black-clad queen spent long periods, up to four months each year, at Balmoral. It was where her husband had been happiest and where she found some consolation in her friendship with John Brown, a Gaelic-speaking ghillie who had become Victoria's close companion. This annual absence was not popular with government ministers who had to make the long journey several times each summer, no doubt besieged by midges, to attend Privy Council meetings on Deeside.

In 1867, Victoria allowed her diaries to be published as *Leaves from the*

Journal of our Life in the Highlands, following it up with *More Leaves* in 1883. They sold many thousands of copies and, with her endless descriptions of scenery, mostly empty, the journals ensured that the tourist trade flourished. By the time they were published, the rail network had reached Aberdeen, Inverness and beyond. The trains carried more than tourists – they brought Scottish products to much wider markets and made them world-famous.

In 1832, Aeneas Coffey had patented a new type of still that could function continuously to produce vast quantities of whisky made from grain of any kind. Twenty years later in Edinburgh, Andrew Usher began to blend these new grain whiskies with the malts produced in the Highlands and elsewhere. These blends gave the cheaper spirit character and colour and made Scotch whisky more plentiful and affordable. But it might never have become popular outside of Scotland but for a calamity.

Hoping to rejuvenate the rootstock of their vines, French winemakers imported grafts from California but they soon discovered that more than roots had crossed the Atlantic. Between 1858 and 1865, French vineyards were all but destroyed by a plague of Californian insects know as *Phylloxera vastatrix*. All over Bordeaux and other famous regions ranks of vines rotted and died. Production ground to a standstill as many realised that they would have to replant. And this disaster delivered an opportunity to the makers of Scotch whisky.

For those who could afford it, the drink of choice was not only wine but brandy and soda. It was soon replaced by whisky and soda and many independent blends became famous – John Haig, Johnnie Walker, Whyte & Mackay and James Buchanan. Demand rose steeply and what had been a modest domestic industry became big business. Even Queen Victoria was known to take a dram and, in her journal, she recounted a day out in the mountains when she 'had a little whisky and water as the people declared pure water would be too chilling'. Absolutely.

George IV had drunk illicit whisky during his visit of 1822 for he demanded to be served only Glenlivet, well known as being of the best quality. Highlanders who lived in the glens that ran off the Grampian massif had been in the habit of making their own for many years and the trade was carried on in open defiance of the law and the best efforts of the excise men. Thomas Guthrie became a famous kirk minister and was one of the founders of the Ragged School network and, in his memoirs, he remembered the sales trips made by illicit distillers:

When a boy in Brechin, I was quite familiar with the appearance and on-goings of the Highland smugglers. They rode on Highland ponies, carrying on each side of their small, shaggy, but brave and hardy steeds, a small cask or 'keg' as it was called, of illicit whisky, manufactured amid the wilds of Aberdeenshire or the glens of the Grampians. They took up a position on some commanding eminence during the day, where they could, as from a watchtower, descry the distant approach of the enemy, the exciseman or gauger: then, when night fell, every man to horse, descending the mountains only six miles from Brechin, they scoured the plains, rattled into the villages and towns, disposing of their whisky to agents they had everywhere; and, now safe, returned at their leisure, or often in a triumphal procession. They were often caught, no doubt, with the contraband whisky in their possession. Then they were subjected to heavy fines besides the loss of their goods. But – daring, stout, active fellows – they often broke through the nets, and were not slack, if it offered them a chance of escape, to break the heads of the gaugers. I have seen a troop of thirty of them riding in Indian file, and in broad day, through the streets of Brechin, after they had succeeded in disposing of their whisky, and, as they rode leisurely along, beating time with their formidable codgels on the empty barrels to the great amusement of the public and mortification of the excisemen, who had nothing for it but to bite their nails and stand, as best they could, the raillery of the smugglers and the laughter of the people . . . Everybody, with a few exceptions, drank what was in reality illicit whisky – far superior to that made under the eye of the Excise – lords and lairds, members of Parliament and ministers of the Gospel, and everybody else.

Such widespread disdain for the law and the payment of duty were understandable. The costs of licensing a legal still and the rates of duty on its products were far too high, out of kilter with such small-scale production. Alexander Gordon, the 4th Duke of Gordon, owned vast tracts of Invernessshire, Moray and Banff, the heartland of malt whisky, and he understood that the law had to change. When it was, Gordon loaned cash to George Smith, the supplier of Glenlivet to George IV, to enable him to go into legitimate business in 1824. Smith was not popular with his illegal neighbours and, for years, he never rode out of his farm without a pair of pistols tucked into his belt. In 1827, a troop of cavalry was stationed at Corgarff Castle, not far from Glenlivet, and, by 1834, George Smith was the only distiller in Scotland's most famous whisky glen.

It was a pleasingly simple business whose ingredients were all at hand. According to the academic and writer, David Daiches, whose book, *Scotch Whisky: Past and Present* (1995), remains definitive, water matters. It must be 'soft water flowing through peat over granite' and, with Glenlivet's Josie's Well producing 3,500 gallons an hour, George Smith had a plentiful supply. Down in the Laigh of Moray, the fields of barley needed to make the malt waved in the summer breezes off the firth and above the distillery were the high moorlands where peat could be cut to heat the stills. Once Glenlivet had aged in oak barrels, they could be trundled down to Burghhead, where a new harbour had been cut out of the ancient Pictish fortress, and loaded aboard ship to slake thirsts around the world. Not that Glenlivet or, indeed, any of the other great malts should be drunk by thirsty men or women. As David Daiches memorably wrote: 'The proper drinking of Scotch whisky is more than indulgence: it is a toast to civilisation, a manifesto of man's determination to use the resources of nature to refresh mind and body and enjoy to the full the senses with which he has been endowed.'

Walter Scott's friend, James Hogg, certainly enjoyed a dram. He perhaps enjoyed them best at Tibbie Shiel's famous inn at the head of St Mary's Loch in the Yarrow Valley. The formidable hostess knew Hogg well and made a characteristic comment on her friend's literary output. She thought he 'was a gey sensible man for a' the nonsense he wrat'. The author of *The Private Memoirs and Confessions of a Justified Sinner* (1824) was a farmer and shepherd. The son of Meg Laidlaw who knew many of the Border ballads by heart – and disapproved on Walter Scott writing them down – Hogg was a man who loved the Borders with a native passion and he also played a key and conscious role in establishing another Scottish product that was to become famous.

Both Hogg and Scott made it a habit to wear the shepherd's plaid, also known as the shepherd's check or shepherd's maud. These were cloaks woven from undyed white and brown or black wool in a checked pattern. As the two authors were often shown wearing them in engravings and indeed they wrapped them around some of their characters, this weave became popular in the 1820. In fact, the Borders mills became so busy with its production that the owners invited Hogg and Scott to a dinner in 1822 to celebrate. As the drams flowed, Sir Walter favoured the company with a passable rendition of 'Tarry Oo' – shepherds applied tar to their sheep's fleeces to keep them free from pests and 'oo' is the local pronunciation of 'wool'.

Tarry Oo, Tarry Oo,
Tarry Oo is ill to spin,
Caird it weel, caird it weel,
Caird it weel ere ye begin.
When 'tis cairded, row'd and spun,
Then the work is halflins done,
But when woven, drest and clean,
It may be cleadin for a queen.

The queen may have preferred tartan but it made no difference to the Galashiels manufacturers. After the royal visit of 1822 and the publication of the journals of Queen Victoria, they made many thousands of yards of that too.

In 1829, a Galashiels cloth merchant, Archibald Craig, was in Glasgow and he noticed 'a man dressed in a pair of black and white large checked trousers'. At a time when men wore only plain colours, greys and blacks, what were sometimes called 'drabs', this was very unusual and Craig was certain that the trousers had been made from a shepherd's plaid. He saw more in Edinburgh and was soon receiving orders from London for the famous checks. Some of these came from James Locke, an expatriate Scot who owned a fashionable tailor's shop in Regent Street. Something of a dandy, he and his friends began to wear jackets and trousers made up from the same bolts of Borders cloth and no doubt they enjoyed the attention as they walked London's streets on a Sunday morning. Business boomed and Locke cleverly branded his cloth as tweed – that is, woven in the Tweed Valley and therefore closely associated with the most famous Scotsman in history, Walter Scott. Tweed suits were invented and business surged once more. But not without a further prompt from Locke, who had taken to using the royal 'we':

When gentlemen of the rod and gun began to enquire for that which would resemble the shooting ground, we had nothing of the kind, neither was there any in the market. We wrote to a Galashiels house for a range but they replied that they had never heard of such an article. By the following post we advised them just to imitate Buckholm Hill which overshadowed them, at this time in beautiful bloom. A boy was despatched to bring some heather. Now, when a handful of this was squashed together it had different shades, varying with the seasons. This proved to be the very thing we wanted, and led to the introduction of a variety of colourings before unknown. This was the origin of heather mixtures.

And the jaggy tweed suit.

While the mills in Galashiels worked out how to cope with changing fashion, much more fundamental change was simmering across the whole of Scotland. After 1707, the Kirk had been the most influential institution after the parliament ceased to meet in Edinburgh. It had maintained what some historians have called 'the parish state', administering poor relief, controlling education and wagging its finger at issues of personal morality. But, in 1843, the Kirk broke apart and gradually began a long retreat from its position as a dominant national institution.

The seeds of the Disruption were sown with the passing of the Patronage Act of 1712 which handed landowners the power to appoint ministers without reference to the Kirk Session. It was a fundamental break with one of the freedoms so dearly won in the Wars of the Covenant. A number of congregations refused to accept this and they formed the Secession Kirk. It was the first of many fractures. After the Jacobite Rebellion of 1745, congregations were asked to swear the Burgess Oath as a mark of loyalty but this was seen as implicitly recognising the legitimacy of the Church of Scotland. This caused further splits and the Burgher Secession Kirk was set up alongside the Anti-Burghers. Further disagreement led to yet another split over the state's support for the Church of Scotland and the Auld Licht Anti-Burghers and the Auld Licht Burghers were formed – as were the New Licht Anti-Burgher and the New Licht Burghers. The Auld Lichts cleaved to the traditions and beliefs of the Covenanters while the New Lichts were more concerned with personal salvation. Ultimately both sects of the New Lichts decided to forget the second disagreement and they merged into the United Secession Church (New Licht).

The longstanding resentments over patronage came to a head at the General Assembly of 1843, held at St Andrew's and St George's Church in Edinburgh's New Town. It was the culmination of a bitter conflict. On one side stood the Moderates who sought to avoid confrontation with the state and on the other were the Evangelicals who asserted the rights of kirk sessions to choose a new parish minister when vacancies appeared. In 1834, what had been a simmering crisis began to boil over. For the first time, the Evangelicals, under the leadership of the charismatic Thomas Chalmers, were in the majority in the General Assembly. In Auchterarder, a dispute arose immediately when the kirk session unanimously rejected the intrusion of Robert Young as their minister by the parish's patron, a local landowner. This followed the passing of the Veto Act by the General Assembly, a measure that allowed parishes to decline acceptance of new ministers. Robert Young appealed to the Court of Session and the judges supported him and ruled that the Veto Act illegally infringed the rights of patrons. This judgement was not unexpected but what needlessly inflamed the dispute was the Court of Session's declaration that the Church of Scotland was the creation of the Act of Union and was therefore entirely subject to secular law. To a Kirk that still held dear the ideals of the Covenant, the Godly Commonwealth and Christ's Kingdom of Scotland, this was an affront and resentment burned ever more fiercely.

In 1842, the Evangelicals formulated a Claim, Declaration and Protest anent the Encroachments of the Court of Session. It recognised that the state had jurisdiction over the endowments made to the Kirk but resolved to give these up since they compromised the Kirk's own right to allow parishes to nominate new ministers. This claim was rejected in January 1843. The stage was then set for a drama which played out at the General Assembly in May of that year. The Moderates and Evangelicals began to canvas support.

The moment of schism came when the outgoing Moderator, Dr David Welsh, read out a statement of protest on 18 May. He then walked out of St Andrew's and St George's followed by 121 ministers and 73 elders who rose from their seats to join him and, watched by large crowds, the seceders made their way down Dundas Street to the Tanfield Hall in Canonmills. There, the first Disruption General Assembly was held with Thomas Chalmers as Moderator. In all, 474 ministers out of a total of 1200 walked out to form the Free Church of Scotland, fewer than Chalmers hoped for and more than the established Kirk feared. About 40 per cent of the Church of Scotland's congregations preferred independence to conformity. It was a courageous act for the seceders and their families were left with nothing, losing their stipends, their manses and their kirks. The great majority of Highland and Gaelic-speaking ministers joined the Free Kirk, as did almost all of the missionaries. And yet, within a decade, they had raised huge sums from their supporters, built hundreds of new kirks and manses and established a network of parish schools. This burst of energy is the reason Scotland looks more pious than it really was and Scotland's towns and cities appear to have kirks and kirk halls on every corner. Perhaps the most famous concentration is Edinburgh's Holy Corner, in Morningside, where three kirks stand at the crossroads with a fourth nearby.

The intellectual focus of all this activity was Thomas Chalmers and, in a fast-changing Scotland, his ideas were attractive. The Free Kirk aimed to preserve the old sense of a Godly Commonwealth where communal, egalitarian traditions of self-help animated a society that cared about its poor and needy and continued to cleave to deep but simple beliefs. The background was the spectacular growth of the cities, their awful poverty and the dizzying speed of industrialisation. Memorably described as 'the Rebellion of the Pious', the Disruption was not so much a revolution as a harking back to old values. But, in reality, it had the effect of diminishing the national role of the Kirk.

After 1843, it was no longer possible for the Church of Scotland to claim that it represented even a majority of Scots and its powers were quickly stripped away as the parish state was dismantled and Scotland began to head down the road to secularism. Two years after the schism, the responsibility of administering poor relief was transferred to parish boards elected by ratepayers. In 1872, education was taken out of the hands of the Kirk with the establishment of parochial school boards set up by the new Scottish Education Department. And the traditional overseeing of personal morality was dented since so many of the Kirk's members had seceded in 1843 to add to the already substantial number of dissident congregations. The Free Kirk was strengthened in 1852 when the Original Secession Church joined it.

One of the rapt spectators at the unfolding drama of 18 May 1843 was David Octavius Hill and he and his business partner, Robert Adamson, decided to record the momentous events in a completely new way. Photography had been pioneered in England by William Henry Fox Talbot who had developed the calotype process, a new way of making photographic paper by coating it with silver iodide. Very sensitive to light, it was inserted in a camera and then, once a subject had been posed, it was exposed for one or two minutes if there was bright sunlight. Hill was a painter and his project was to create a vast group portrait of the General Assembly of 1843. The problem was that drawing the necessary likenesses of each minister and elder was logistically impossible. So he and Adamson shot calotypes of almost all who had been present and the vast, panoramic painting, measuring 11 feet by 5 feet, was ultimately completed by 1866. It was one of the largest group portraits ever made.

Perhaps more importantly, Hill and Adamson also made calotypes of everyday scenes and everyday people and these are the first photographic records of the appearance of ordinary Scots. Most attractive are the images of the Newhaven fishing community made in the 1840s. Both individual portraits and group shots, they have a quiet dignity, even confidence, as the men, women and children turn to the light so that the camera can capture their likeness. One study of a barefoot boy leaning on a creel dressed in an oversize pair of trousers (his faither's old breeks?) transcends charm, even though the pose has clearly been arranged by the photographers. It is an early documentary image that showed how people really looked when they were not dressed up or decorated but as they went about their everyday work. A much wider shot of 20 or so fishwives baiting hooks in the sunshine of old Fisherrow at the north end of North Street in St Andrews seems a little more natural. Most wear white bonnets and appear to be doing actual work while eight children and two babies sit around the group. Most remarkable is the figure of a woman, carrying one of the babies and a basket, walking across the street towards her friends, with her back turned to the camera. It takes only a little leap of the imagination for the woman to take another step and for the whole scene to come to life, people talking, seagulls squawking and the usual breeze blowing down North Street. The sense of a traditional community working together was probably what attracted Hill and Adamson to the Newhaven fisherfolk. Honest, wholesome toil, cooperation and a life lived out of doors for much of the time and not in the teeming, noisy factories and foundries of Central Scotland seem to have been persistent themes. Not many of their subjects were photographed smiling but, when the partners showed their prints to the people of Newhaven, it is not hard to imagine the shrieks, giggles and general hilarity.

Each day, the fisherfolk were used to walking three miles carrying their creels into Edinburgh, calling out, 'Caller herrin' [fresh herring] for sale.' It was a journey that had been made since a time out of mind but, far to the north, another traditional journey that aimed to feed hungry mouths was coming to an end. The arrival of the railways gradually put the Highland drovers out of business because cattle wagons could transport prime Scottish beef to Scottish and English markets far more rapidly. Trains also changed breeding and, when the railway reached Aberdeen and Aberdeenshire in the 1850s and 60s, the small black cattle of the glens were replaced by a breed that became world famous.

William McCombie farmed Tillyfour near Alford and he was a marketing genius. He realised that beef cattle could be bred much larger because they did not have to walk to market and be fit enough to make a long journey of 200 or so miles. If they travelled in cattle wagons, taking less than a day to reach the great market of Smithfield in London and only half a day to reach Scottish markets, they also kept their glossy condition and weight. McCombie began to cross his polled stock (hornless cattle were essential because of how close they were packed into the wagons and it also made covering cows safer) with the progeny of prime Angus cows, particularly those bred by Hugh Watson of Keillor. And of course, he called the result Aberdeen Angus.

Wishing to enlist royal approval as well as ride the wave of 19th-century interest in many things Scottish, McCombie sent his prime bullock, Black Prince, to the Birmingham and Smithfield shows in 1867, where it took the top rosettes. But then came his masterstroke. He arranged for Black Prince to be taken to Windsor Castle where the great beast was led around the Middle Ward in the presence of Queen Victoria. And, at Christmas, McCombie had the bullock slaughtered and he sent generous cuts of beef, by train, to the palace. When in 1869, the Queen visited Tillyfour, not far from Balmoral, the royal seal of approval was complete. The canny Aberdeenshire farmer may have risked putting a foot wrong when he christened a prime heifer The Queen Mother but it did not matter. In an age when royalty set trends, the sales of Aberdeen Angus soared and no self-respecting London restaurant could fail to serve it.

Many miles to the west of the lush pastures of Tillyfour, there was famine. In 1846 a fungal potato blight, *Phytophthora infestans*, had caused the crop to fail in three-quarters of the crofting parishes of the Highlands. The reported death rates for the old and the young rose dramatically and this suggested serious food shortages. It seemed that a biblical famine was about to happen and *The Witness*, the Free Kirk newspaper, sermonised that 'the Hand of the Lord has indeed touched us'. But relief came relatively quickly and, in any case, Highland communities were not overwhelmingly dependent on potatoes. In Ireland, the consequences of crop failure were disastrously different. There, *an Gorta Mor*, 'the Great Hunger', was a catastrophe. In a very short period, more than a million people died of starvation or diseases related to malnutrition. It was a tragedy unparalleled in Western Europe in the 19th century. Two million more were forced to emigrate and many made the relatively short passage to Scotland. At its peak in 1848, it is reckoned that immigration from Ireland saw a thousand people disembark each week on the Glasgow quays. Between January and April of that year, 42,860 crossed the North Channel and the impact on Glasgow and the surrounding area was profound, even in an era when the city was expanding rapidly.

This demographic phenomenon was probably the largest and most rapid influx of new people in Scotland's history. By 1851, the number of Irish-born had risen by 90 per cent to more than 200,000 and the largest initial concentration of immigrants, most of them women, was in Dundee. The jute industry was growing and the majority of its workforce was female. Around 19 per cent of the city's population was Irish – a community of about 20,000 folk – and they were vigorous. In the early 1860s, Dundee had only two Catholic churches and three Catholic schools (and one was said to have been little more than a cellar under the chapel). But, within a decade, this community of mostly low-paid workers had scraped together sufficient funds to have two more churches and three more schools built.

There was considerable resentment. For those who had fled in the baleful shadow of the famine, running from Ireland in droves, any work at almost any rate of pay was welcome if it put bread on the table. Irish immigrants sometimes priced native Scots out of jobs by accepting wages lower than the pre-existing market rate and, as the region closest to Ireland, Dumfries and Galloway saw a significant influx between 1845 and 1851. Here is a quote from the *Dumfries Courier* of 1851: 'In Dumfriesshire and Galloway there are plenty of Irishmen ready to take the bread out of the mouths of our own poor. An Irishman who lives in a hovel, feeds on potatoes and neither clothes or educates his children, can always work for less than a Scot. There are too many people who employ only the cheapest workers and do not think of the consequences.'

And this from a report from the 1871 census: 'The immigration of such a number of people from the lowest class and with no education will have a bad effect on the population. So far, living among the Scots does not seem to have improved the Irish, but the native Scots who live among the Irish have got worse. It is difficult to imagine the effect the Irish immigrants will have upon the morals and habits of the Scottish people.'

Travel in another direction was not uncommon and a steady flow of emigrants from Scotland crossed the border to settle and work in England. The Gledstanes family moved from farming near Biggar to Leith where they became successful corn merchants and changed their name to Gladstones. In 1787, John Gladstones moved to Liverpool, dropped the 's' from the end of the family surname and became a partner in the prosperous grain-dealing business of Corrie, Gladstone and Bradshaw. With his second wife, Anne Robertson from Dingwall, he had six children who survived into adulthood. They christened their fourth son William Ewart Gladstone and, born in

1809, he went on to be elected Prime Minister of Great Britain and Ireland four times – more times than any other. He reshaped the politics of the nation profoundly, over a long career that paralleled the development of modern political parties and the gradual extension of the franchise. But his own political development took an unusual course.

After taking full advantage of the best education his father could buy, at Eton and Oxford, Gladstone was first elected to parliament in 1832 for Newark as a Tory under the patronage of the Duke of Newcastle. He opposed the abolition of slavery, parliamentary reform and the introduction of legislation to improve the conditions of those working in factories. But, when he was appointed to Sir Robert Peel's first government as a junior minister, his thinking began to change, possibly for surprising reasons. In 1840, the young MP began to walk the streets of London seeking out prostitutes so that he could attempt to rescue and rehabilitate them. Sometimes he took them home and apparently recorded their names in a private notebook. In 1848, he founded the Church Penitentiary Association for the Reclamation of Fallen Women. This was a cause Gladstone supported all his life and, despite persistent rumour, it appears to have been a genuine attempt to improve lives. It has been suggested that his night-time walks around London's red light districts revealed a world of squalor and hopelessness and softened his political views.

In any event, Gladstone's powerful sense of morality and improving instincts chimed with the times. In Scotland, the new Poor Law of 1845 appointed parish boards whose criteria for distinguishing the deserving from the undeserving poor were strict and especially severe on women. Deserted wives were often suspected of collusion with husbands who had not in fact gone but were seeking to exploit the poor laws. Women with illegitimate children were disqualified because 'they have transgressed the moral law' but orphans and children in general were more sympathetically treated. Gladstone's attitudes were a similar mixture of Christian charity and absolute judgement.

By the 1840s, the Tories had become known as the Conservative Party but, when Sir Robert Peel forced a vote on the repeal of the Corn Laws to bring down prices so that food could be sent to Ireland more cheaply, his party split on the issue. Gladstone became one of the leaders of the Peelites after Sir Robert's death in 1850. Two years later, Lord Aberdeen led a coalition of Whigs and Peelites into government and he appointed Gladstone as Chancellor of the Exchequer. Well organised and clear-thinking, he used his first budget to modernise the tax system and immediately became a powerful player.

In 1859, Lord Palmerston formed a new government out of a coalition of Whigs, Peelites and the more radical MPs such as Richard Cobden. They became known as the Liberal Party and power swung between them and the Conservatives for the following 60 years. Gladstone was again appointed Chancellor and immediately began to advocate the further extension of the franchise, particularly to the working householders of the expanding towns and cities. Lord Palmerston opposed this by the simple expedient of ignoring his Chancellor. It was said that at each meeting of the cabinet, Gladstone would launch into a speech encouraging his colleagues to support him while the Prime Minister stared fixedly at the papers in front of him. When the Chancellor finally drew breath, Palmerston would rap his knuckles on the table and say, 'Now, my Lords and gentlemen, let us go to business.'

The two men loathed each other. And it was only with Palmerston's death that an opportunity at last presented itself and Gladstone and Lord John Russell attempted to push a second reform bill through parliament. When they were defeated and the Conservatives came to power under Benjamin Disraeli, they proposed a reform bill which, after debate and amendment, became more radical and it was voted through in 1867. The new prime minister argued successfully that if reform was inevitable, it was better that his party should control its nature and extent.

The Second Reform Act gave the vote to one in three adult males and it was based on household suffrage, qualification by property. Scotland had voted overwhelmingly for the Liberal Party and Disraeli manipulated the boundary changes made necessary by the industrialising of the nation in order to minimise any advantage to the opposition. The relative rise and distribution of Scotland's population should have meant an increase in the number of seats from 53 to 68 but the act added only a further 7. But the extension of the franchise did create something completely new – a mass electorate. In the 1865 election, 47,785 votes were cast but the turnout tripled in 1868 when 149,341 people voted in Scotland. Disraeli's machinations were not sufficiently effective to keep him in office as William Gladstone led the Liberals to victory and won him his first term as prime minister.

It was a time of reform in several directions. The army was modernised as the sale of commissions ceased and punishment by flogging was greatly reduced. Gladstone also advocated a foreign policy that promoted the peaceful settlement of international disputes. He introduced the secret ballot and abolished the Test Acts that excluded Catholics from the universities. But, in January 1874, he unexpectedly asked the Queen to dissolve parliament and a general election was held only three weeks later. Mainly because of poor organisation and campaigning, the Liberals lost power. It was a lesson Gladstone took to heart.

In 1873, 1874 and 1876, Archibald Primrose, Earl of Rosebery, toured the USA. On his first and third visits, he witnessed first hand the campaign of Ulysses S. Grant to win a second term as president and also Rutherford B. Hayes's successful bid. Rosebery saw a different approach to politics, one that used modern technology to reach a mass electorate. He persuaded Gladstone to stand for election in Midlothian, a seat close to his family's house at Dalmeny, and, between 1878 and 1880, he ran the first modern political campaign in Britain. Exploiting his impeccable Scottish ancestry on both sides, Gladstone took time to make himself known to the electorate and made the long and impassioned speeches that were usual at the time. Most focussed on Disraeli's unpopular foreign policy but what was different was Rosebery's efforts to make sure his candidate was heard by as many of the newly enlarged electorate as possible. Whistle-stop tours were organised and Gladstone spoke to huge crowds from open-decked trains. His speeches were therefore widely heard, widely discussed and widely reported. Such was the fire and energy of the 71-year-old's oratory that the Conservatives were heavily defeated and, although Lord Hartington was nominally leader of the Liberal Party, he stood aside to allow the new MP for Midlothian to become Prime Minister for a second time. It was the first time that an incumbent had represented a Scottish constituency. It may be that Queen Victoria was less than amused at the news. She is said to have complained that Mr Gladstone spoke to her as though he was addressing a public meeting.

Some of the locomotives that pulled the open-decked trains around Midlothian and elsewhere were almost certainly made in Glasgow. In 1861, Neilson & Co. moved to bigger premises at Springburn and these expanded to become the largest locomotive works in Britain. Business boomed as orders came in from Europe and the burgeoning British Empire but, at the same time, tempers frayed. Walter Neilson appears to have been an irascible man and he and his chief designer and works manager, Henry Dübs, found themselves increasingly in disagreement and, in 1863, they parted company. A year later, Dübs & Co. set up the Glasgow Locomotive Works across the city at Queen's Park and began to compete fiercely with Neilson. There appears to have been high demand and they won orders in Britain,

Russia, India, New Zealand and China and the new company prospered. In 1876, Walter Neilson fell out with his managing partner, James Reid, who had replaced Henry Dübs. It must have been acrimonious for Neilson left the company that carried his name to establish the Clyde Locomotive Company, also in Springburn. Despite all the bickering, thousands of jobs were created and money was made. Such was the reach and output of the Glasgow companies that, of the 7,024 locomotives running on the vast rail network of India, more than half had been built in Scotland.

Along the banks of the Clyde more heavy industry grew up very quickly in the 19th century – one that became a byword for engineering excellence. The first purpose-built iron shipbuilding yard was established in 1834 by Tod & MacGregor but the industry began to expand rapidly when Robert Napier opened his yard at Govan in 1841. All of the necessary skills and raw materials were close at hand and expansion was rapid as the riverbank saw more and more yards open. By the 1880s shipbuilding was the dominant industry in Glasgow. Its cranes punctuated the horizon and the rattle of riveting could be heard across the city. At Clydebank, what was virtually a new town was laid out to house shipyard workers. The term 'Clydebuilt' soon entered the language and a poem by Alexander Smith published in 1857 captured the atmosphere:

> The steamer left the black and oozy wharves,
> And floated down between dark ranks of masts.
> We heard the swarming streets, the noisy mills;
> Saw sooty foundries full of glare and gloom,
> Great bellied chimneys tipped by tongues of flame,
> Quiver in smoky heat. We slowly passed
> Loud ship-building yards, where every slip contained
> A mighty vessel with a hundred men
> Battering its iron sides.

By 1913, the Clyde's output was a staggering 756,000 tons of shipping, more than the entire production of the USA or Germany.

The monsoon climate of Bengal, now Bangladesh, suited the cultivation of jute. Fed by the rains and thriving in humid conditions, this fibrous-stemmed plant grew very tall, like a giant version of flax. The agents of the East India Company who worked out of Kolkata (Calcutta) noticed how versatile the fibre was as the native people made garments, floor coverings and rope from it. Like flax, jute needed to be softened by retting – the process of soaking it in water – but it was much tougher, bulkier and harder to work than flax. But two unlikely factors, the products of two very different climates, came together to change that and create a famous industry in Scotland.

Since the 1750s, the Dundee whaling fleet had been hunting in the Arctic and bringing back the huge carcasses to the city's wharves for processing. One of the industry's by-products was oil. When twenty bales of jute were unloaded at Dundee in 1820, it was quickly realised that that whale oil might make the hard, wood-like fibre workable. In addition, the city had a long tradition of linen heckling, carding, spinning and weaving and expertise was to hand. The production of jute expanded rapidly. Because it was such a versatile product, useful in making sacking, ropes, carpet backing, roofing felt, tents, linoleum backing and much else, there was a range of ready markets. And it was cheap. By 1883, one million bales of raw jute were being landed at the Dundee quays to be processed in more than a hundred mills. The statistics are very striking. Between 1841 and 1901, the population of Dundee tripled from 45,000 to 161,000 and the jute industry employed about 50,000 people at its peak.

Wages were kept low because three-quarters of the workers in the dust-filled din of the mills were women and children. Before the term was invented, many men were househusbands and Dundonians knew them as 'kettle-bilers'. Hard work meant hard play and Dundee women were famously independent, 'loud, bold-eyed girls' and, on a Saturday night, they often got roaring drunk. Malnutrition was rife in the city with most existing on a diet of bread and potatoes and a frequently foul water supply. In 1863, the average life expectancy for a man was only 33 years. Health improved little in the second half of the 19th century for, in 1904, half of all the Dundonian men who volunteered for the army were deemed unfit for service. At the opposite end of the social scale, successful jute barons built vast mansions in and around the growing city, many of them along the banks of the Tay at Broughty Ferry. And shipbuilding expanded as big merchant ships were needed to bring the bulky bales of raw jute from Bengal and then carry the finished products to all the corners of the world.

Release from the dangerous, grinding toil of the mills, foundries, factories and shipyards of late Victorian Scotland was precious, necessary and government legislation began to recognise that. In 1850, the Factory Act stipulated that there should be a five-and-a-half-day week with all work to stop at 2 p.m. on a Saturday. In part, this was a trade-off. The relentlessness of the six-day week meant that all recreation, including a drink or two, had to be crammed into a Sunday and this led to a great deal of absenteeism on Mondays. The legislation of 1850 aimed to mitigate that. It also had the effect of creating a new facet to British and Scottish culture, a mass interest in, even obsession with, sport both as spectators and participants.

MARVELLOUS MERCHISTON

John Napier of Merchiston in Edinburgh counted differently. Born in 1550 into a landed family, he travelled in Europe as a young man and managed to acquire an education. In 1614, he published Mirifici Logarithmorum Canonis Descriptio, *essentially a guide, with 90 pages of tables, on how to count in a much more sophisticated manner. The logarithm of a number is the exponent to which another fixed value or number must be paired to produce that number. The logarithm of 1000, for example, to base 10 is 3, because 10 to the power of 3 is 1000. Napier's logarithms may have been the bane of many schoolboy's or -girl's life but they helped scientists make difficult calculations and even helped bankers work out compound interest. Merchiston Castle is hidden behind the modern buildings of what used to be Napier College in Edinburgh's Colinton Road. It has expanded to become Napier University, joining two other universities named after distinguished Scots – Queen Margaret and Heriot-Watt.*

In the past, hard agricultural work had left little energy or time to take part in any organised games. Several Scottish towns played 'handba" or the 'ba' game' at particular festivals. A mixture of rugby and football, a vigorous version is played twice a year by the townsmen of Jedburgh and also in Kirkwall. But it was clubs formed by middle-class men that first developed the game that would later divide into football and rugby. The second oldest in the world (after Dublin University) is the Edinburgh Academical Football Club and it was in existence by 1857. They played their first organised match against Merchiston Castle School in Edinburgh and it is the longest continuous sporting fixture in the world. At a series of meetings in 1863 in the Freemasons' Tavern in London, the games of football and rugby were more sharply defined. Ebenezer Morley drafted a set of rules to be universally adopted by all the clubs in England – except they were not. When it was decided to ban handling the ball and hacking (tackling by kicking an opponent in the shins), Blackheath Football Club withdrew. Other English clubs joined them and, in 1871, the Rugby Football Union was eventually formed. The Football Association went its own way and gave the world the word soccer.

In Scotland there was confusion. Edinburgh Academy and Merchiston schools and their former pupils clubs decided that they would play rugby, the 'carrying game', but the rules were vague, often a subject for negotiation. In 1871, three young men in Langholm decided to organise a rugby match on 31 December. William Scott, Alfred Moses and William Lightbody had all learned a version of the game at English public schools. When a large crowd turned up to play, they briskly divided them into two teams and got stuck in. Langholm Rugby Club was constituted and two years later Hawick and Wilton Cricket Club (founded by textile workers from Nottinghamshire and Yorkshire) decided to field a rugby team. In 1873, the two played their first fixture. But not before the teams of 20 a side had agreed on the rules. The main issue was the definition of a goal. Was one scored when the ball was kicked over or under the crossbar? On a previous Saturday afternoon, the millworkers of Langholm had triumphed over the men of Carlisle and they had settled on under rather than over. The Hawick players agreed but irony abounded when Langholm were forced to accept a draw because their kicker made a mistake and sent his final effort over the bar. In the same year, the Scottish Rugby Union was founded and was immediately dominated by the former pupils clubs from Edinburgh and Glasgow's private schools and the ancient universities.

Perhaps the most historically significant event took place two years earlier at Raeburn Place in Edinburgh when Scotland played England in the first-ever international rugby match. It was a response to a challenge issued by the captains of five Scottish clubs in a sports newspaper called *Bell's Weekly*. On 27 March 1871, an undying rivalry kicked off. Here is a report from the *Glasgow Herald* with a familiar ring to it and an all-too unfamiliar result:

This great football match was played yesterday, on the Academy Cricket Ground, Edinburgh, with a result most gratifying for Scotland. The weather was fine, and there was a very large turnout of spectators. The competitors were dressed in appropriate costume, the English wearing a white jersey, ornamented by a red rose, and the Scotch a brown jersey, with a thistle. Although the good wishes of the spectators went with the Scotch team, yet it was considered that their chances were poor. The difference between the two teams was very marked, the English being of a much heavier and stronger build compared to their opponents. The game commenced shortly after three o'clock, the Scotch getting the kick off, and for some time neither side had any advantage. The Scotch, however, succeeded in driving the ball close to the English goal, and, pushing splendidly forward, eventually put it into their opponents' quarters, who, however, prevented any harm accruing by smartly 'touching down'. This result warmed the Englishmen up to their work, and in spite of tremendous opposition they got near the Scotch goal, and kicked the ball past it, but it was cleverly 'touched down' and they got no advantage. This finished the first 50 minutes, and the teams changed sides.

For a considerable time after the change the ball was sent from side to side, and the 'backs' got more work to do. By some lucky runs, however, the Scotch got on to the borders of the English land, and tried to force the ball past the goal. The English strenuously opposed this attempt, and for a time the struggle was terrible, ending in the Scotch 'touching down' in their opponents' ground and becoming entitled to a 'try'. This result was received with cheers, which were more heartily renewed when Cross, to whom the 'kick off' was entrusted, made a beautiful goal. This defeat only stirred up the English to fresh efforts, and driving the ball across the field, they managed also to secure a 'try', but unfortunately the man who got the 'kick off' did not allow sufficient windage, and the ball fell short. After this the Scotch became more cautious, and playing well together secured after several attempts a second 'try', but good luck did not attend the 'kick off' and the goal was lost. Time being then declared up the game ceased, the Scotch winning by a goal and a 'try'.

Queen's Park, founded in 1867, is the oldest football club in Scotland. Taking its name from the district of Glasgow where it played, its players and officials dominated the game for much of the later 19th century. The team even lost finals of the FA Cup in England – twice. Queen's Park brought eight other clubs together in the Scottish Football Association in 1873. The year before, the Secretary of the Football Association, Charles Alcock, had issued a challenge that invited a Scotland team to play against England. Since it was not clear who he was challenging, there being no Scottish Football Association at that time, Queen's Park stepped in and responded. On St Andrew's Day 1872, at the West of Scotland cricket ground in Glasgow, the two sides met in the first football international. The entire Scotland team was made up of Queen's Park players and they wore dark blue because that was the colour of the club jerseys at that time. It had rained for three days before the match and the result was a 1–1 draw. Queen's Park's innovative passing game (dribbling was the thing in the 1870s) may have been inhibited by the heavy pitch and also the fact that the English played with eight forwards enabled them to operate an effective offside trap. At one point, the England goalkeeper, Robert Barker of Hertfordshire Rangers, switched places with a forward, William Maynard. Perhaps he was bored.

Football became much more popular than rugby, except in the Borders. It was a game that needed no more than a ball of some kind and no other kit or equipment was required. Jackets could be goalposts and it could be played on any surface by small or large groups. By contrast, rugby needed a grass pitch, somewhere more forgiving to fall on than cobbles or paving and, in the cities, it became a middle-class game, fostered by the private schools. It was exclusive and, even though Borders teams regularly defeated Edinburgh and Glasgow opposition, their players were rarely selected to play for Scotland. Between 1871 and 1914, 118 international matches were played between Scotland and other countries and yet only 11 Borderers were selected in all that time.

A crowd of 4,000 watched the first international football and rugby matches, but soon large stadia were built to accommodate huge crowds. Named after John Hampden, the English Parliamentarian of the 17th century, Hampden Park was and remains the home of Queen's Park and most spectators at first stood on ridges banked up around the pitch to form terracing. Grandstands were added later. But the significance of these early international matches was straightforward. For the first time, there were vigorous contests between two national sides whose passionate supporters could express a version of patriotism that was not overtly political. Scotland could safely defeat England (although not often enough) and, for an afternoon, escape the role of junior partner in the Union. It is no cultural accident that the Scottish rugby anthem is a song about the Battle of Bannockburn. International matches were and remain moments of sharp definition that could absorb tensions as well as be sources of pride and, occasionally, pleasure. And paradoxically, the promotion of sporting rivalry between Scotland and England helped hold the Union together.

However, football clubs and the massed ranks of their fans began to channel a degree of sectarianism in Scotland from the outset. Hibernian Football Club was founded in 1875 by Irish immigrants who lived along Edinburgh's Cowgate which was known as Little Ireland. The club was an initiative of Canon Edward Hannon of St Patrick's Church and, at first, all players had to be members of the Catholic Young Men's Society. The date of foundation was fixed to coincide with the centenary of the birth of Daniel O'Connell, the Irish Nationalist leader. Canon Hannon hoped that football would encourage a regime of temperance, discipline and religious adherence. He was Hibernian's first manager and they played matches on the Meadows in south Edinburgh. The proceeds for ticket sales went to charities. But the club's clear link to Irish Catholicism and nationalism sparked resentments and the members of the Scottish Football Association were discouraged from playing against them. Meanwhile, Heart of Midlothian Football Club had been set up by members of the dancing club of the same name. That came from the old jail at the tollbooth commemorated by the cobble mosaic in Edinburgh's High Street and Walter Scott's great novel, and they too played at the Meadows. On Christmas Day, 1875, Hearts ignored the SFA ban when they played against Hibs and they won the first Edinburgh derby 1–0.

In Glasgow, Celtic Football Club was also instigated by a Catholic clergyman, Brother Walfrid, and it enjoyed early success as it too raised cash for charity, especially the feeding of starving children in the east end of the city. A rivalry with Rangers soon developed and the Old Firm matches between the two clubs have been traditionally hard fought, sometimes between the fans as well as the players. At Celtic Park, the Irish tricolour used to be much in evidence as was the Union Jack and the Red Hand of Ulster flag at Ibrox. It was no more than a reflection of sectarian tensions generally in Scottish society.

Tension was not limited to the growing populations of the industrial midland valley. Elsewhere populations were shrinking. In the aftermath of the famine, Highland landlords resumed the process of clearance and it was as brutal as before. On 15 May 1851, the *Barlow* sailed into Loch Roag on the Atlantic coast of Lewis. The factor, Munro Mackenzie, complained that the 400 emigrants boarded too slowly, almost certainly looking over their shoulders, reluctant to leave their home places for a voyage into the unknown. Among them was Domhnall Ban Crosd and his family from Carnais. And so Mackenzie sent word ahead to the next port of call on Lewis to 'push them on without their luggage' and the extra room could accommodate more people.

In November 1852, 830 people were cleared off their crofts in Strath in Skye, Sollas in North Uist and Borve in Harris and herded on to the *Hercules*, bound for Adelaide. One of the emigrants remembered the pain of the first part of the voyage: 'The Cuillin mountains were in sight for several hours of our passage; but when we rounded Ardnamurchan Point, the emigrants saw the sun for the last time glitter upon their splintered peaks, and one prolonged and dismal wail rose from all parts of the vessel; the fathers and mothers held up their infant children to take a last view of the mountains of their Fatherland which in a few minutes faded from their view forever.'

'GREEK' THOMSON

If it were not for the 1960s high-rise flats behind it, the Caledonia Road Church in Glasgow might look like something the designer of the sets for the Hollywood epic Anthony and Cleopatra *had run up from pasteboard scenery with a few struts to hold up the fake façades. The pillared portico of a Greek temple sits behind what looks like an Egyptian take on an Italian Renaissance campanile. In fact it is the work of the remarkable Alexander Thomson, known as 'Greek' Thomson. The St Vincent Free Church is another arrangement that includes the classical elements that gave the architect his nickname. His Egyptian Halls on Union Street carry on an epic theme. Thomson was a devout Christian with a deep interest in 'sustainable building', a term he coined. His designs for public housing were revolutionary but never realized. It is his flamboyant churches which remind those who see them of the Victorian confidence, almost American in its scale, that informed the building of Glasgow.*

By 1881, after a series of poor summers and meagre harvests, there was growing unrest across the Highlands and Islands amongst the crofters who had been left on the land. Influenced by events in Ireland, there were rent strikes at Valtos and Kilmuir on Skye and matters quickly came to a head in what became known as the Battle of the Braes. The landlords' reaction was unhesitating and, on 7 April 1882, a sheriff officer was sent from Portree to serve eviction orders on several of Lord MacDonald's tenants in the district of Braes, on the narrows between Skye and Raasay. He left an account of what happened: 'and at that Mairi Nic Fuilaidh suddenly cried, "Men, make them burn the summonses." At that, they yelled, "Put them down on the road." I put them down on the road. And with stones in their hands ready to kill me if I disobeyed, they compelled me to make a heap of the summonses . . . a boy came running with a burning peat . . . never was an officer of the law so disgraced to come so far as to have burned them myself . . . that hurts me more than the stones and the clod.'

Ten days later, reinforcements arrived on Skye and two sheriffs, two procurators fiscal, a captain of police with 47 constables brought north from Glasgow and some local policemen made several arrests despite a barrage of stones and clods. This incident was widely reported in the national press as 'the Battle of the Braes' and it made a deep impression. More rent strikes, more seizures of land and more resistance to police action ensued and it seemed that, at last, the Highlanders were fighting back. The Sheriff Principal of Invernesshire and Harris, William Ivory, appeared to panic and wrote to the Lord Advocate calling for the immediate dispatch of a gunboat and marines 'to protect the police and assist them in protecting the property and persons of the lieges of that island [Skye]'. The police requisitioned the steamship *Lochiel* from David MacBrayne of Glasgow but the Highland captain and crew refused to sail and replacements had to be found. Eventually a force of more than 500 soldiers and many police constables were landed on Skye. Knowing they could not take any action, the crofters resisted passively and the rent strikes continued.

William Gladstone was Prime Minister and his government reacted to the widespread support for the crofters by setting up the Napier Commission. Pressure intensified as the 1884 Reform Act extended the franchise to agricultural labourers and, in the general election of 1885, Gladstone's Liberals were defeated and five crofter MPs were returned to Westminster for Highland and Island constituencies. Events moved quickly and, after the Napier Commission had reported, the Crofting Act was passed into law in 1886. It guaranteed security of tenure in perpetuity, a great advance, and it established the Crofters' Commission to fix fair rents. But other grievances were not addressed and agitation continued with land raids. The *Oban Times* described the act as 'an instalment of justice'.

In the same year that legislation recognised the realities of life in the Highlands, a great novel was published that reflected the romance of an imagined life amongst the mountains and the glens. Robert Louis Stevenson almost gave away the entire plot of *Kidnapped* with its tremendously long subtitle: *Kidnapped: Being Memoirs of the Adventures of David Balfour in the Year 1751: How he was Kidnapped and Cast away; his Sufferings in a Desert Isle; his Journey in the Wild Highlands; his acquaintance with Alan Breck Stewart and other notorious Highland Jacobites; with all that he Suffered at the hands of his Uncle, Ebenezer Balfour of Shaws, falsely so-called: Written by Himself and now set forth by Robert Louis Stevenson.*

He advertised it as a 'boys' novel' but, in fact, it is arguably the greatest work of historical fiction to be published since Walter Scott laid down his pen. *Kidnapped* opens unforgettably with the hero's encounter with his uncle, or possibly not his uncle, Ebenezer Balfour and his blunderbuss at the spooky House of Shaws. There then follows a glorious chase, much of through the Highland landscape with the fictional version of a real Jacobite, Alan Breck Stewart. Stevenson published the novel in serial form in the magazine *Young Folks* in 1886 but its appeal was, in truth, to young folks of any age. In the same year, he published an altogether entirely different book, *The Strange Case of Dr Jekyll and Mr Hyde*, and, three years before, *Treasure Island* had appeared. The 1880s were a very fertile decade for one of Scotland's very greatest novelists. Suffering from chronic ill health, Stevenson often moved, in search of a climate that would ease his respiratory problems, and *Kidnapped* and *Jekyll and Hyde* were written in Bournemouth in Dorset. *The Black Arrow*, *The Master of Ballantrae*, *The Wrong Box* and his wonderful *A Child's Garden of Verses* were all the products of this golden period.

Eventually Stevenson settled on the Pacific island of Samoa where he took the native name of *Tusitala*, 'Teller of Tales'. After completing *Catriona*, a sequel to *Kidnapped* and two other novels, he became depressed, fearing that his powers were fading and that he might decline into permanent ill health. 'I wish to die in my boots; no more Land of Counterpane for me. To be drowned, to be shot, to be thrown from a horse — ay, to be hanged, rather than pass again through that slow dissolution.'

But then he revived and his optimism and energy flooded back as he began work on a novel he would not complete, *Weir of Hermiston*. 'It's so good that it frightens me.' All appeared to be well but, when attempting to open a bottle of wine, Stevenson felt something happen. It was a stroke, a cerebral haemorrhage, and, within hours, he was dead. His Samoan friends buried him on a ridge of Mount Vaea that overlooks the ocean and a requiem he had written for the purpose was inscribed on his headstone. It is simple, timelessly beautiful.

> Under the wide and starry sky,
> Dig the grave and let me lie.
> Glad did I live and gladly die,
> And I laid me down with a will.
> This be the verse you grave for me:
> Here he lies where he longed to be;
> Home is the sailor, home from sea,
> And the hunter home from the hill.

Novelists in particular go in and out of fashion but the dismissal of Robert Louis Stevenson as an author for children for much of the 20th century is inexplicable. His spare, unfussy style and his simplicity are entirely at the service of brilliant story-telling. He wrote several great and memorable novels and, because they are all so accessible, he has been simultaneously introducing children to both reading and literature of the first rank for generations.

At the same time as the young Stevenson was avoiding attending lectures on engineering at Edinburgh University (he came from a famous family of lighthouse builders), several other students were having difficulty in being admitted. In 1869, Sophia Jex-Blake overcame great opposition and was allowed to matriculate at the Edinburgh Medical School, the first woman to achieve that. Amongst many others, the central difficulty was that the medical faculty would not allow her to attend lectures with male students. Bodies were being discussed. And, since it was unlikely that lectures would be scheduled 'in the interest of one lady', Jex-Blake took matters into her own hands and advertised for other women with medical ambitions to join her. Six women joined her and they became 'the Edinburgh Seven'. But trouble continued to simmer, particularly amongst male students, and, when the women attempted to take an anatomy examination at Surgeons' Hall, Jex-Blake recorded what happened. 'On the afternoon of Friday 18th November 1870, we walked to the Surgeon's [sic] Hall, where the anatomy examination was to be held. As soon as we reached the Surgeon's Hall we saw a dense mob filling up the road . . . The crowd was sufficient to stop all the traffic for an hour. We walked up to the gates, which remained open until we came within a yard of them, when they were slammed in our faces by a number of young men.'

But the women had support and a sympathetic group of students managed to get them into the examination hall and all passed. Here is the comment from *The Scotsman*. 'A certain class of medical students are doing their utmost to make sure that the name of medical student [is] synonymous with all that is cowardly and degrading, it is imperative upon all . . . men . . . to come forward and express . . . their detestation of the proceedings which have characterised and dishonoured the opposition to ladies pursuing the study of medicine in Edinburgh.'

The Surgeons' Hall Riot had been the most dramatic incident in a sustained campaign of abuse. Jex-Blake and her comrades had suffered obscenities hurled at them in the streets, foul letters and doors slammed in their faces in faculty buildings. But, despite growing support, the Edinburgh Seven were not awarded degrees. The decision of the Edinburgh University Senate was upheld in the Court of Session who also ruled that the women should not have been allowed to matriculate in the first place. Undaunted, Sophia Jex-Blake and five of the Edinburgh Seven set up the London School of Medicine for Women. It opened in 1874 and, by 1892, the Universities Act (Scotland) Act was passed to allow women to matriculate and attend mixed lectures, except for anatomy. They were also excluded from the law and divinity.

Perhaps encouraged by the dogged courage of Jex-Blake and her comrades, women began to radicalise, forming suffrage societies that demanded votes for women. The Third Reform Act had doubled the size of the electorate in Scotland but 40 per cent of men and all women were still excluded. These groups merged into the National Union of Women's Suffrage Societies and one of its leaders was Lady Frances Balfour, a daughter of the Duke of Argyll. Their policy was peaceful protest – the gathering of signatures for petitions, marches and lobbying. But not everyone shared this approach and the Women's Social and Political Union was founded by Emmeline Pankhurst and her daughters. They advocated – and carried out – attacks on property such as arson and smashing windows and, when members were arrested, they embarked on hunger strikes. These resulted in brutal methods to bring them to an end.

Scottish suffragettes did break the law – Arabella Scott tried to set fire to the stands at Kelso Race Course before enduring five weeks of force-feeding in Perth Prison – but their approach was generally less violent than in England. Frances Balfour believed that acts of terrorism only stiffened government opposition. In this view she was supported by the remarkable Dr Elsie Inglis. Having gained qualifications at both Edinburgh and Glasgow Universities, she set up a maternity hospital and midwifery service in Edinburgh for those unable to afford medical care. Inglis worked tirelessly with women and children and it was the lack of provision for them that radicalised her. She was honorary secretary of the Scottish Federation of Women's Suffrage Societies from 1904 to 1914.

Once the Great War broke out, Dr Inglis set about organising field hospitals and finding nurses to staff them and she herself went to Serbia to care for wounded soldiers. As with many others, it was her war service that helped persuade government that women should at last be given the vote.

As the franchise included more and more people, it was perhaps inevitable that the political landscape of Scotland would be changed. In fact, it turned out that Scotsmen were instrumental in changing the political shape of Britain. From the outset, James Keir Hardie learned harsh life lessons in the industrial ferment of the North Lanarkshire coalfield. Born in 1856 in a one-room cottage in Holytown, he went to work at the age of seven and, by ten, he was in the mines, first as a trapper who opened and closed doors to ventilate the shafts and finally at the coalface as a hewer. Hardie spent ten hard years in the mines, an experience that formed him. With little opportunity for formal schooling, he learned to read and write in the evenings and also picked up the rudiments of shorthand. His profound Christian belief took him into the United Reform Church and the Temperance movement. Soon his skills as a preacher were recognised and these transferred easily to public speaking. His fellow miners began to look to Hardie to speak for them and negotiate with the hard-nosed mine owners. He was quickly labelled an agitator and, with his two brothers, was blacklisted.

Instead of forcing the young man to seek other work, the ban motivated Hardie to organise miners into trade unions. In 1879, he was appointed Corresponding Secretary in Lanarkshire and was in contact with groups of miners across Scotland. At that time, unions were local organisations but, in the same year, Keir Hardie attended a national conference in Glasgow. As trade unions consolidated, it became clear to others that the Liberal Party could not represent working men fully and would always compromise to maintain a wider appeal. In 1886, R. B. Cunninghame Graham, MP for North West Lanarkshire, defected from the Liberals and sat at Westminster as the first socialist. In a by-election in April 1888, Hardie stood unsuccessfully as an independent in Mid Lanarkshire but he was not discouraged when he came bottom of the poll. In August of that year, he and Cunninghame Graham formed the Scottish Labour Party at a meeting in Glasgow.

In 1892, Keir Hardie was invited to stand as an Independent Labour candidate for the East London seat of West Ham South. The Liberals did not field a candidate and he defeated the Conservative by 1,200 votes. But immediately Hardie became caught up in gesture politics. Instead of donning the Westminster uniform of a black frock coat, he took his seat wearing a tweed suit and a deerstalker hat and was ridiculed before he could open his mouth. When he did, Hardie advocated a progressive series of policies such as a graduated income tax, state pensions, free education, votes for women and the abolition of the House of Lords. In 1894, there was appalling loss of life in a mining disaster at Pontypridd in South Wales when 251 men were killed as a result of an explosion. When the heir to the throne was born, the future Edward VIII, Hardie asked that a message of condolence to the victims' families be attached to the House of Commons' address of congratulations. When this was refused, the angry MP for West Ham South made a speech critical of the institution of monarchy. It was electorally fatal, and a year later, he lost his seat to the Conservatives.

At the top of the central part of the facade of Glasgow's City Chambers there is an architectural statement, not something conceptual but a clear concrete statement about what enabled the building of this astonishing civic monument of such eye-watering opulence. In the middle of the tympanum, the triangular part of the neo-classical pediment, sits Queen Victoria. Enthroned, she is attended by figures symbolising Scotland, England, Wales and Ireland and the vast territories of the British Empire whose raw materials arrived on British quays to fuel what has been called the 'Victorian economic miracle'. Originally, the centrepiece was to have been an allegorical figure representing Glasgow with the Clyde at her feet, the highway that first carried her manufactures to the rest of the world. But, with the completion of the building coinciding with the Queen's golden jubilee, the 50th anniversary of her accession in 1887, it was decided that she should replace the allegory. Perhaps it was indeed more fitting that the Queen Empress should be the dominating figure.

MR SMITH'S BOYS

Founded in Glasgow by William Smith in 1883, the Boys' Brigade became very popular. Its formula of combining drill, games and Christian values spread quickly, and by the 1890s it had become a worldwide organisation. It predates the Boy Scout movement (in fact Robert Baden Powell became the vice-president of the Boys' Brigade in 1903) and camping became a central activity. The BBs were very military with several ranks. The highest is the Captain of a company, then there is an Adjutant and most officers are known as Lieutenants. Boys can attain non-commissioned ranks, as Lance Corporal, Corporal, Sergeant and Staff Sergeant. By passing tests, boys can also be awarded badges and these have been updated over the years. The BBs remain popular and across the world, in 60 countries, more than half a million boys are members. Mr Smith would have been proud.

The factories, foundries and shipyards of Glasgow flourished because its skilled workers and risk-taking entrepreneurs were at the centre of an imperial trading network that operated simultaneously as a market for finished goods and the source of the cotton, jute, rubber and a host of other primary products that were shipped to Britain. It was an economic engine of hitherto unparalleled power. There was little exaggeration in Glasgow's claim to be the Second City of the Empire and, in the second half of the 19th century, Glasgow began to look the part.

As profits began to flow from all that activity and the personal tax burden remained light, cash piled up. Some of it went into private housing projects that matched the scale and reach of successful ventures. Long boulevards such as Great Western Road were lined with magnificent villas and terraces built in a variety of styles, from Scottish Baronial to Palladian. In the centre of the city, grandiose office buildings rose and, in the 1860s, Gilbert Scott's Neo-Gothic Glasgow University on Gilmorehill dominated the skyline. After the Disruption of 1843, church building surged but perhaps the most compelling monument to the status of the Second City stands in George Square. City Chambers is a glorious celebration of all that Glasgow had become. Materials came from all over the world to decorate the interior, its halls and the splendid central staircase – marble from Italy, satinwood from Australia, mahogany from Spain. Murals depict the city's history, actual and mythic, and on the floor at the entrance is a mosaic of the coat of arms and the iconography of the patron saint, Mungo, is remembered in a famous rhyme:

> Here's the Bird that never flew
> Here's the Tree that never grew
> Here's the Bell that never rang
> Here's the Fish that never swam.

Wealthy Glaswegians competed to commission grand houses and, to decorate the interiors, painters and other artists were employed. Some also began to collect the best art from around the world. Most famous was William Burrell. A shipping merchant, he made several fortunes by riding the regular boom and bust cycle of the Victorian economy. When downturns occurred, Burrell waited until he could order ships from the Glasgow yards and elsewhere at rock-bottom prices. By the time they were built and fitted out and trade had begun to pick up again, he then used the new ships to carry at maximum capacity or sold them on at a hefty profit. Flushed with cash, Burrell began to buy objets d'art, ceramics, carpets, tapestries, paintings and much else. Soon outgrowing his Palladian terraced house in Great Western Road, he eventually purchased and extended Hutton Castle in Berwickshire. His passion for collecting bordered on the irrational and Burrell bought far more than he could ever display. The castle garages had no cars in them – instead, they were piled high with Persian and Chinese carpets. But Burrell had an excellent eye for high quality and he rarely made misjudgements. Burrell bequeathed his vast collection to the city of Glasgow and, in 1983, a superb building to house it was opened in Pollok Park.

Much of the architecture of late Victorian Glasgow and the other growing cities of Scotland was derivative, off-the-shelf borrowings from the great European traditions of the Renaissance, the Gothic and Romanesque periods. But the city did produce a native architect of genius, a man whose ambitions and talent reached across almost all of the visual art forms, almost certainly the greatest Scottish artist who ever lived. Charles Rennie Mackintosh was born in 1868, the son of a police inspector, one of 6 surviving children, a boy with few obvious advantages. Because of a severe chill, he had a drooping eyelid and a contracted sinew in his left leg caused him to limp. But from an early stage, it was clear that Charles was gifted.

At the age of 16, Mackintosh was apprenticed to John Hutchinson, a firm of architects, and he also enrolled for evening classes at the Glasgow School of Art. It was to be an enduring link. After he joined another Glasgow architectural practice, Honeyman and Keppie, in 1889, the young man's career began to burgeon. Glasgow's companies, institutions and successful businessmen were commissioning buildings and, in quick succession, Mackintosh had a central role in the design of the tower for the old *Glasgow Herald* building, Queen Margaret Medical College off Great Western Road, the Martyrs' Public School and, most triumphantly, the new Glasgow School of Art.

A native of Devon and Dorset and a very gifted painter, Fra Newbery had been appointed Headmaster or Director of the School of Art in 1885. He noticed Mackintosh immediately and, when limited funding became available for a purpose-built new school, Newbery encouraged the young man to enter the competition to design it. He won and work began in 1897. Because of a lack of funds (only £14,000 was allowed for the construction, decoration and equipment), the building was planned in two stages. While one part rose, the founds were laid for the other. The site at 167 Renfrew Street was very awkward – long, narrow and on a steep slope up from Sauchiehall Street. And the brief set by Newbery and his governors was very exacting. It had to be 'a plain building' using only inexpensive materials – brick, stone, steel and timber. Mackintosh combined these brilliantly to create one of the greatest examples of modern architecture in Europe.

The daughter of Fra Newbery, Mary Newbery Sturrock, knew Mackintosh well and, in 1985, she recalled the impact of the new building:

When they saw the School of Art, it was too much – forty years ahead of its time. But that was the appearance of the Glasgow School of Art, inside it worked so well. It was a splendid working building, the people who objected or couldn't swallow it didn't go inside to see what it was like. They just saw this curious castle-like place from Sauchiehall Street. It's still rather an odd building. Maybe a businessman wouldn't order a building like that. Even today when people look at the furniture, and say how modern it is – not only that but the carpets, the lights – all look very suitable for today, they could have been designed yesterday.

And yet it is very much his building, designed in the 1890s. Someone once said to me that since Mackintosh was a junior partner in the firm, there must have been other people working on the designs for the School. I said, but you didn't know Mackintosh. If anyone else touched his work, he'd have literally torn them apart. While he was away once while the School was being built, Keppie, who was the head of the firm, arranged for a cornice to be put at the top, just above the stairs. Mackintosh didn't like cornices, he liked the walls to reach the ceiling, and when he came back he bounced with anger and fury and passion and he had it all cut out, put the workmen on to cutting it out. And there is still no cornice.

Thinking back now I can see that the Glasgow School of Art alarmed people and after the second phase, he never really got work. Le Corbusier did some very odd things in France but went on doing them. But Mackintosh didn't get the chance. He might have got more orthodox, you can't really tell. The Glasgow School of Art was so ahead of its time, he just had to wait for people to assimilate his ideas.

Despite the design of two consummately elegant houses in Kilmacolm and Helensburgh, Mackintosh was never again commissioned to create substantial projects after the completion of his masterwork in 1906. Instead he began to paint watercolours, many of them flower and plant studies, and he also carried on designing interiors and furniture for tearooms in Glasgow. But, by 1913, he had resigned his partnership in Honeyman and Keppie and, a year later, Mackintosh moved with his wife to Walberswick on the Suffolk coast and then to London. His architectural career was effectively over and in 1923 the couple moved to Port-Vendres on the south-eastern Mediterranean coast of France where their very limited funds would go further. The watercolours he painted in the crisp French light began to sell but for modest prices. In 1928, Charles Rennie Mackintosh died of cancer and Mary Newbery Sturrock mourned:

> Looking back now I feel terribly, terribly sad at the waste. Here we have this brilliant man whom it would pay you to use. And he wasn't given any real use at all, apart from the Glasgow School of Art and the odd jobs he got in Glasgow. Of course if he'd got Liverpool Cathedral [the competition was won by Giles Gilbert Scott], if he'd got these studios in London, he could have gone ahead from that . . .
>
> Mackintosh could have designed anything, but he just didn't get a chance. Perhaps he did all he was going to do, but I'd like to have seen his fiftieth house. I don't know how many houses Robert Adam did but his fiftieth house mustn't have been a bit like his first. I would like to have seen Mackintosh's fiftieth house, with all the edges rubbed off and all his experience and development brought into play. We could have had somebody as good as Corbusier but we weren't able to do it.
>
> Thinking back now, the tears come to my eyes and I feel so sad that the genius was wasted. I feel great sadness. When I hear of these high prices, I think if the Mackintoshes could have got a hundredth part of the money, how happy they would have been, and I would now. I've got a lot of pleasant, friendly memories but I must say that I could weep at the waste of his genius.

In May 2014 the interior of Glasgow School of Art was destroyed by a work of art. Flammable gases from a foam canister used in a student project were ignited by the heat from a projector and the building was quickly engulfed. The library, one of Mackintosh's greatest interiors, was gutted and many rare archival materials lost. As flames roared out of the windows and black smoke billowed over the city, many of the hundreds who watched in the street below wept. Restoration should be complete by 2018.

At the same time as Mackintosh was working in Glasgow, many were leaving the city's quays in search of a better life. The number of emigrants from 19th- and early 20th-century Scotland is very striking. Between 1825 and 1938, more than 2.3 million sailed from home ports and, in the 80 years from 1834 to 1914, more than half of the natural increase in the population left. Most arrived on the shores of the Americas, Canada and the USA, others made the long voyage to Australia and New Zealand, and significant numbers also settled in Argentina and Uruguay.

Even after the dissolution of the East India Company in 1857 and the introduction of competition for jobs, many Scots continued to go to India to seek fortunes. Seven of the twelve viceroys who governed the subcontinent were Scots and many served as district commissioners and judges. In fact, the role of Scots in the government and the exploitation of the vast British Empire prompted a famous quote from the Liberal MP, Sir Charles Dilke, in 1888: 'In British settlements, from Canada to Ceylon, from Dunedin to Bombay, for every Englishman that you meet who has worked himself up to wealth from small beginnings without external aid, you find ten Scotchmen.'

In the USA, Scots enjoyed spectacular success in business. David Dunbar Buick from Arbroath founded a famous car manufacturing company in Detroit and it eventually formed the basis of the mighty General Motors corporation. To date, 35 million cars have carried his name. Andrew Carnegie left a widely recognised legacy of a different sort. Having made fortunes in the iron and steel businesses, he gave away almost all he had accumulated, much of it to pay for the building of thousands of libraries. Generations of Scots have benefitted directly from Carnegie's sustained generosity, gaining free access to books in almost every town and city. Born on Ulva, a small island off the west coast of the Isle of Mull, Lachlan Macquarie emigrated to Australia where he became the first and a highly influential governor of New South Wales. Catherine Spence's family arrived in South Australia in 1839 and, through her work with women and children, she had a profound impact. Spence worked to rehome destitute children from institutions and place them with approved families. At the same time, she campaigned for female suffrage and also proportional representation in elections. Her achievements are remembered in Scotland with a modest plaque on the facade of the house where she was born in Melrose and, in Australia, her likeness is on a five-dollar note.

Relatively few Scots migrated to Africa to settle but some of those who went to explore and proselytise became famous and much admired. Born in Blantyre in Lanarkshire in 1813, David Livingstone began his working life at the age of 10 as a piecer in the local cotton mill. Dangerous, dirty and dusty work, this involved retying the broken threads of the spinning machines over a 14-hour day, from 6 a.m. to 8 p.m. Despite this, Livingstone gained an education and also became a devout Congregationalist. He scraped together sufficient funds to study medicine at Anderson's College in Glasgow with the intention of becoming a medical missionary in China. When the outbreak of the Opium Wars in 1839 closed down that option, Livingstone happened to meet Robert Moffat in London. He was home on leave from missionary work in southern Africa and encouraged the young man to go there to explore and take Christianity to the native peoples.

On his first expedition to what was Bechuanaland, now Botswana, he was badly mauled by a lion in an attempt to protect villagers' sheep. Livingstone's wounds left his left arm permanently damaged. His habit of travelling light, without an armed escort and with only a few porters to carry essential supplies allowed the young Scot to negotiate safe passage through tribal territories. He was the first European to see *Mosi-oa-Tunya*, 'The Smoke that Thunders', a vast waterfall on the Zambezi River that he named Victoria Falls. Much of Livingstone's enduring fame rested on his writings, especially his journals, and he described the spectacular waterfall with a memorable phrase: 'scenes so lovely must have been gazed upon by angels in their flight'.

Believing exploration to be more immediately beneficial to native Africans than any attempts at conversion, Livingstone resigned from the London Missionary Society. Commerce and its civilising effects would, he hoped, help eradicate the appalling cruelties of the slave trade. But his expedition to open up the Zambezi as an artery leading into the interior of Africa was a failure and, on his return to Britain, Livingstone had great difficulty in raising funds for further exploration. But eventually he was able to mount a new expedition to discover the source of the River Nile. It too turned out to be a failure but it was a heroic failure. Livingstone lost all contact with the outside world for six years. Speculation was rife and, in 1869, the *New York Herald* sent Henry Morton Stanley to Africa to find him. There followed a famous encounter – and some fictional dialogue. When, on 10 November 1871, Stanley at last encountered Livingstone, he said he said, 'Dr Livingstone, I presume?' Since the Scot's own account does not mention this amusing moment of irony and Stanley later tore out the relevant pages of his journal, the phrase is likely to have been a journalistic fabrication. Livingstone was said to have replied, 'Yes, and I feel thankful that I can be here to welcome you.'

Stanley's book, *How I Found Livingstone*, was a bestseller and other widespread coverage began to build an aura around his heroic efforts. When Livingstone died of malaria and dysentery two years after meeting Stanley, his two faithful followers, Susi and Chuma, carried his body eastwards for a thousand miles to the port of Bagamoyo on the Indian Ocean coast. He was buried in Westminster Abbey, a national hero whose popularity has faded only a little.

Bagamoyo lay in what became German East Africa. This was a vast territory that encompassed modern Tanzania (except Zanzibar) and Rwanda and Burundi. It was part of the spoils of the scramble for Africa, an intense, even frantic, period of colonisation that took place at the end of the 19th century and the beginning of the 20th. In 1881, only 10 per cent of Africa was under European control but, by 1914, this had mushroomed to 90 per cent. The only independent states were Liberia on the Atlantic coast and Ethiopia (Abyssinia) in the east. Having unified in 1871, Germany was late into the game but nevertheless managed to grab Togoland, South-West Africa (now Namibia), Cameroon and East Africa, about 9 per cent of the continental population. Meanwhile Britain ruled over 30 per cent of all Africans. Colonial and commercial rivalry was one of several factors that led to the outbreak of the Great War in 1914.

THE DEVIL'S PORRIDGE

A huge munitions factory, HM Factory Gretna, stretching for 12 miles over 4 sites across the English/Scottish border was built in 1915 to supply the British army. It produced 800 tons of cordite a week. When Sir Arthur Conan Doyle visited, he recorded, 'The nitroglycerine on the one side and the gun cotton on the other are kneaded into a sort of devil's porridge.' The name stuck. Two townships were built to house the workers – 11,576 women and 5,066 men. The government was so anxious about drunkenness that they instituted the State Management Scheme and took control of all the pubs in the area, including Carlisle and Gretna. It attempted to minimise drunkenness with a 'no treating' policy that forbade the buying of rounds of drinks. It lasted in Carlisle until 1973.

In the early 1900s, an arms race gathered pace and added to the tension as Germany launched an intensive ship- and U-boat-building programme in an effort to match the might of the Royal Navy. The shipyards on the Clyde were swamped with work and John Brown & Company doubled their capacity. What particularly impressed the Admiralty was the development of the Brown-Curtis turbine engine and many Royal Navy warships were launched down Clyde slipways in the 1900s. By the end of the Great War, John Brown's had built more destroyers than any other British shipyard and broken all sorts of production records. The destroyer, HMS *Scotsman*, took only 22 weeks to build, from the laying of the keel to departure. War and the developing threat of war were good for business.

Across Europe the major powers stockpiled arms and increased the fighting strengths of their armed forces after 1900. Conscription created large reserves who often undertook military training each summer. The French had a staggering 3.4 million reservists, Austria-Hungary 2.6 million and Russia 4 million. High commands constantly revised their war plans and, as developing technological skills devised ever more sophisticated weapons, from efficient machine guns that did not jam to the Dreadnought class of warships, both tension and expectation ratcheted upwards. It seemed to many that war was coming but none imagined the horror of what eventually took place. Military strategists anticipated a short war, when it came, and the swift victories and dramatic advances of the Franco-Prussian War of 1870 were what was planned for. In this febrile, shifting atmosphere, all that was needed to ignite the gunpowder was a spark. It came on 28 June 1914.

As his open car was driven through the streets on a state visit to Sarajevo, the heir to the Austro-Hungarian imperial throne, Archduke Franz Ferdinand, and his wife, Sophia, were assassinated. Serbian nationalists were responsible and a dangerous chain of events began to flicker across Europe as diplomatic telegrams delivered demands, ultimata and reinforced alliances and under-standings. Austria-Hungary made humiliating and near-impossible demands on Serbia, Germany supported the Austrian Emperor, both nations began to mobilise their armed forces and, a month after the assassination, war was declared. On 29 July, Germany informed the British ambassador in Berlin that war against France was being planned and enquired whether or not Britain would remain neutral. The wires crackled as the pace of diplomatic traffic quickened. French and German forces mobilised and, on 3 August, Germany declared war on France. A day later, Britain declared war on Germany.

In Scotland there was an overwhelming patriotic reaction – what the trade unionist, Harry McShane, called 'war fever'. So many men volunteered that there were not enough uniforms for them all and, by the end of August, more than 20,000 men had enlisted through the recruiting office in Glasgow's Gallowgate. By the end of 1915, 320,589 Scotsmen between the ages of 15 and 49 were serving in the British armed forces. By the end of the war, a huge proportion of the Scottish male population, 688,416, had been in uniform.

They were supported by virtually all parts of civic society. All denominations preached war from their pulpits and the Church of Scotland minister in Paisley, Walter Mursell, reflected popular outrage at German aggression with his outburst that 'Belgium is Christ for us today!' as the armies of the Kaiser advanced across its borders. Few dissented and women handed out the white feathers of cowardice to men of enlistment age who still walked the streets in civilian clothes. Conscientious objectors were tolerated but harshly treated and politicians who spoke against the war were shouted down. As armies were mobilising in August 1914, Keir Hardie called for 'no alliances, no increased armaments, no intervention in the Balkans [and] fraternity with the workers of the world'. Patriotism trumped all of these principles and, a year later, Hardie died, unheeded and disillusioned.

THE QUINTINSHILL RAIL DISASTER

On 22 May 1915, a troop train was carrying men from the Royal Scots and the Leith Battalion of the Territorial Army to Liverpool to embark for the Gallipoli campaign. They never reached their destination. Due to the incompetence of two signalmen, a passenger train had been shunted on to the main line and the troop train hit it. A minute later an express train from Glasgow smashed into the wreckage on the line and, because gas from the lighting system of the old wooden carriages of the troop train ignited, the triple crash became a huge inferno. Trapped under the burning wreckage, soldiers were forced to undergo agonising emergency amputations to free them, and for those who could not be pulled free, a horrific death by incineration waited. It is said that officers carried out several mercy killings, shooting their doomed comrades with their pistols. About 226 men were killed and 246 injured, the worst loss of life in a rail crash in Britain. Numbers are approximate because the ferocity of the blaze entirely consumed some bodies and some were never recovered. The signalmen were sent to prison for culpable homicide.

As thousands of Scotsmen sailed for the Western Front, industry was badly hit by a loss of manpower while itching to fulfil lucrative new government contracts for war materials of all kinds. The jute workers of Dundee were mostly women and their ability to turn out vastly increased quantities of fibres for sacking and uniforms remained largely unimpaired as the mill owners made fortunes. But elsewhere the only alternative was to recruit women. After so many of the employees of the Glasgow Corporation's tramways enlisted that they formed an entire battalion, women were taken on as 'clippies' and were dressed in their distinctive Black Watch tartan uniforms. By 1918, 31,500 women worked in the munitions industry alone and, to staunch the flow of recruits from industries vital to the war effort, key occupations such as mining and shipbuilding were reserved.

No part of the British Empire responded more enthusiastically than Scotland, whose soldiers were easily the highest proportion of the male population, outstripping the other home nations, the dominions and the colonies. But mixed with all that patriotism was exploitation. Most of the housing in the cities and towns of Central Scotland was rented from private landlords and, when it became clear that workers in reserved occupations were earning more from the accelerated pace of production and that women were also being paid higher wages, rents were raised. Such naked profiteering was greeted with outrage because many households had no male breadwinner. He was either fighting on the front or had been too badly wounded to find work. When many families failed to meet the raised rents – some of which had risen by as much as 23 per cent – their evictions were resisted and, in Glasgow, a rent strike was organised and based in Govan and other districts that were home to workers' families. By the end of 1915, 25,000 households were withholding their rents. Women took a leading role as landlords' factors were attacked and pelted with rubbish. When tenants were summoned to court, there were mass demonstrations with placards carrying the words 'We Are Not Removing'. In November 1915, workers at the Govan shipyards walked out to join the demonstrators and the slogan 'We Are Fighting Landlord Huns' marked this out as a potentially incendiary escalation that could gather patriotic support. The government was forced to act and the Rent and Mortgages Restriction Act set rents back to pre-war levels. This was a significant political moment – the first time the state had legislated in the private housing market. It showed that popular protest could be effective if well organised and in sympathy with the public mood. Working class politicians and trade unionists took note.

As the scale of the slaughter on the Western Front became clear and the likelihood loomed that hostilities would drag on as armies dug in for a static process of attrition neither side had expected, Scots began to turn against the war. Conscription was reckoned to be necessary by 1916. Until then, opponents had been isolated figures. The Marxist political activist John MacLean was fiercely opposed to the war. He could attract crowds of thousands with his powerful oratory but he inspired no mass movement and radicals like James Maxwell were imprisoned and neutralised. But, in 1917, the Scottish Trades Union Congress believed that 'the War Party is a discredited minority in nearly all Trades and Labour Councils north of the Tweed'. And on 1 May 1918, almost 100,000 Glaswegians went on a one-day strike to demonstrate in favour of a peaceful settlement. Scotland was exhausted – so many had died in the mud of the trenches and resistance to continuing the carnage was building. But, by 1918, Germany and her allies had fought themselves to a standstill. The Americans had entered the war and what became known as 'the Hundred Days Offensive' began in August. The allies pushed the Germans back and began to take many prisoners. One by one, Germany's allies began to seek peace terms and morale slowly crumbled before a rapid collapse at the beginning of winter. Revolutionaries declared a German Republic on 9 November and, two days later, an armistice was agreed. And the guns at last fell silent.

No family in Scotland was unaffected. For all combatants, the overall British death rate was 11 per cent, a huge proportion of the population. But, in Scotland, the death rate was more than double at 26 per cent – a quarter of those Scotsmen who had enlisted and a total of 142,218. The detail is very graphic. The Black Watch and the Highland Light Infantry each lost 10,000 men. Of the 13,568 who left their studies at the Scottish universities to join up, 2,026 were killed and more than 2,000 badly wounded. The toll was heaviest amongst the youngest cohort, the 16–34 age group, which lost 45,000 men. And more than 150,000 men were maimed or seriously injured. Others, especially those who had been gassed, never recovered their health and often died young. Half a generation was lost and damaged.

The memorials to the dead are to be found all over Scotland. In hamlets of only a dozen or so houses, the lists of names carved in stone seem impossibly long but they are witness to the number of farm workers who never returned to their native fields. Many were quickly called up because they had joined the Territorial Army which was disproportionately popular in country districts. For the businesses and industries of the towns and cities, the impact of the losses may have been more subtle but was equally telling. The poor performance of the Scottish economy in the 1920s and 1930s has been attributed to poor leadership and perhaps the loss of all those students and graduates who died on the Western Front contributed to that. In any event, a different Scotland emerged from the carnage of Flanders – a nation that would turn in new political and social directions.

13

Scotlands

✹

AT KYLE OF LOCHALSH, the railway line runs right to the water's edge as though someone had forgotten to build a bridge. Before the nearby road bridge to Skye was built, it used to connect with the ferry to the island and with other services to the Hebrides. On the evening of 31 December 1918, almost two months after the armistice had been agreed, hundreds of demobbed servicemen were milling around the crowded station, anxious to get home. An Admiralty yacht was tied up at the quayside, ready to take men to Lewis and Harris. Many had served in the Royal Navy, surviving the brutal sea battles of the North Sea, and, with their kitbags on their shoulders and gifts for families many had not seen for a long time, they crowded aboard the yacht. Reunions, New Year celebrations and the twinkling lights of home were waiting on the other side of the Minch, the last leg of a long journey.

The captain was said to have been unhappy. His Majesty's Yacht *Iolaire* (Gaelic for '*Eagle*') had lifejackets for only 80 passengers and two lifeboats but 284 men pushed on to her decks. There was little room for them below. It was a black-dark midwinter night and, as the yacht nosed out into the Inner Sound between Raasay and Applecross, the sea seemed unsettled. When the *Iolaire* set a course north-west into the open water of the Minch, high winds whipped up the waves and spindrift spattered over the decks of overloaded yacht. But many of the returning sailors had on their waterproofs and their sea boots.

By midnight the crew reckoned themselves to be within 12 miles of Stornoway harbour but they could not make contact with the drifter, *Budding Rose*, that had been sent out to guide the *Iolaire* home. The captain had never docked at Stornoway and needed to be led into the narrow entrance. An hour later, the crew of a local fishing boat saw the lights of the *Iolaire* to the north of them and realised that she was set on the wrong course. In what had blown up into a gale, the yacht was moving quickly, full steam ahead, making straight for the Beasts of Holm. The rocky outcrop at the mouth of the harbour had a warning light set on it but no one saw it – at least, not in time to pull the wheel hard round. At 2 a.m. the *Iolaire* smashed into the Beasts and quickly foundered as her timbers splintered. Men scrambled into the lifeboats but both capsized in the roiling darkness.

One man made it to the shore and using his immense strength, pulled with him a line wrapped around his body. John F. MacLeod of Ness fought his way through the undertow to claw his way onshore. He dragged a hawser behind him and secured it to a rock. With the help of others, he pulled 40 men along the line to safety. Thirty-nine others somehow survived but 205 men were drowned only 30 yards from the shore, within sight of the harbour lights of Stornoway. It was the worst peacetime disaster since the *Titanic*.

The sinking of the *Iolaire* was a sickening blow. Six thousand Lewismen and Harrismen had served in the Great War and a thousand never sailed home again. When the yacht ploughed into the Beasts of Holm, a further 205 island families lost a father, a son or a brother. Prime Minister since 1916, Lloyd George had promised a 'land fit for heroes' but, in the cold reality of the decades that followed, it turned out to be a land many wanted to leave. Between 1918 and 1950, the population of the Western Isles declined by a quarter and the number of men who worked in agriculture in the Highlands and Islands fell by 50 per cent. On Saturday, 21 April 1923, the steamship *Metagama* sailed out of Stornoway harbour, past the Beasts of Holm and the wreck site of the *Iolaire*. Bound for Canada, it carried 300 emigrants from Lewis, all but 20 of them young men whose average age was 22. Not only can this departure and the tragedy of 1 January 1919 be seen as a grim end to the years of slaughter, they were also emblematic of the unhappy 1920s and 1930s.

For many ordinary Scots, there was a moment of hope – an anticipation that the future might be different, perhaps better. They were given the vote. The Representation of the People Act of 1918 abolished almost all property qualifications and enfranchised men over the age of 21. And, in recognition of their war work, women were at last given the right to vote but not until the age of 30. This was a calculation made to avoid immediately installing women as the majority of the electorate. So many men had died in the Great War that women over 21 would have comprised about 54 per cent

SCAPA FLOW

It was Scotland's geography that was to play a part in perhaps the single most crucial mistake that Imperial Germany made in the First World War. Having proceeded on the assumption that the British fleet would be forced into a close blockade of the German coast and thus could be slowly worn down by mines, torpedoes and hit-and-run attacks, the Germans were stunned when the Grand Fleet chose instead to base itself in the great Orkney anchorage of Scapa Flow and operate a distant blockade well away from the German coast. German naval operations were characterised by increasingly desperate attempts to lure the Grand Fleet to destruction as slow starvation and the denial of raw materials for industry steadily crippled the German and Austrian war economies. Scapa meant that the British navy did not need to win; it simply had to avoid losing.

On 22 November 1918 the German Navy formally surrendered in the Firth of Forth. An eye witness records: 'So at dusk as the sky reddened over the Scottish hills, the buglers of the British fleet sounded the call "Sunset", the ensigns of the Imperial German Navy fluttered slowly down for the last time. And darkness closed like a curtain on the final act of this mighty drama at sea.'

It is somehow fitting that it was in Scapa on 21 June 1919 that the Kaiser's Navy, humiliated by the protracted Versailles negotiations, simply scuttled itself in one of the greatest acts of self immolation in history. A recently discovered letter paints the following picture of the incredible scene as the British fleet raced back to its moorings in Scapa Flow:

A good half of the German fleet had already disappeared, the water was one mass of wreckage of every description, boats, carley floats [life rafts], chairs, tables and human beings, and the 'Bayern' the largest German battleship, her bow reared vertically out of the water was in the act of crashing finally bottomwards, which she did a few seconds later, in a cloud of smoke bursting her boilers as she went.

The last surviving ship of the German High Seas Fleet, the pinnace of the battlecruiser Hindeburg, *played a part in the Dunkirk evacuation before serving as a ferry in Shetland and now rests in Shetland Museum under the more homely name of the* Brenda.

of the electorate rather than 43 per cent. In Scotland, the Act enfranchised 2,205 million voters and a predominantly working-class electorate came into being. And, for the first time, any general election was to be held on one day.

Before the Great War the Liberal Party had dominated Scottish politics but a feud between successive prime ministers, H. H. Asquith and David Lloyd George, had split the party. The National Liberals allied themselves with the Conservatives, known as the 'Unionists' in Scotland, and were in government at the end of the war under Lloyd George while Asquith led the Liberal Party. In the election of 1918, called very soon after the armistice was signed, the coalition of Conservatives and National Liberals gained a huge majority and Asquith lost his seat of East Fife. Led by Willie Adamson of neighbouring West Fife, Labour won 57 seats across Great Britain and Ireland, but only captured 6 in Scotland. Nevertheless, in a crowded field with a split Liberal vote, they gained the support of 265,744 Scots, ten times more than in 1910, when Labour won 3 seats.

After the execution of the leaders of the Easter Rising, including James Connolly from Edinburgh, in Dublin in 1916, Irish-born voters and those of Irish descent in Scotland deserted the Liberals whose government had sanctioned the death sentences and they began to support Labour. Part of the historic bargain was to be the maintenance of Catholic schooling. Trade union membership had doubled between 1914 and 1920 in Britain and many unions were disposed to affiliate with the Labour Party. In addition the Co-operative Movement became significant in Scotland, more so than in England.

The first glimmers of what became the Co-op were seen in Ayrshire in 1769 when a group of weavers bought a sack of oatmeal and sold its contents to fellow weavers at a discount, thereby forming the Fenwick Weavers' Society. Some time before 1839, the Galashiels and Hawick Co-operative Societies set up retail outlets (which still trade) and, in Edinburgh, the St Cuthbert's Co-operative was founded in 1859. The 'divi' was invented and profits from trading were divided up amongst members in proportion to the amount of goods they had purchased. Some co-ops built houses for renting to members. In 1868, the Scottish Cooperative Wholesale Society (SCWS) was formed to bulk-buy on behalf of local societies and a process of consolidation began. Known in parts of Scotland as 'the Store', the Co-op became a feature of life for many Scots as shops opened in all the cities and many towns. Country districts were served by a network of mobile shops and gradually every facet of life was catered for, from baby wear to funerals. The Co-op developed strong links with the Labour Party and, through its own political wing, it began supporting Labour candidates. Before the general election of 2015, there were 31 Labour and Cooperative MPs. There was also a close affiliation with the Temperance Movement and no local society that sold alcohol could be admitted to the SCWS. This ban remained in place until 1958.

Across war-scarred Europe economies stuttered and stumbled in the years following the Treaty of Versailles. Millions of demobbed men flooded the labour market and unemployment spiralled. In 1920, it stood at 16 per cent in Scotland and, within a year, had rocketed to 25 per cent. Markets for the products of Scotland's heavy industries had shrivelled as nations retreated behind tariff barriers and Germany's economy was crippled by very heavy war reparations. Employers either laid men off or cut their pay or both. In the 1922 general election, Labour doubled their popular vote in Scotland to return 29 MPs to Westminster. Nationally, Labour's total of 142 seats was, for the first time, greater than both factions of the Liberal Party but the Conservatives took power under Andrew Bonar Law. In Glasgow, a long tradition began as 10 out of 15 seats went to the Independent Labour Party.

WINSTON UNSEATED

Having lost his seat in Manchester, Winston Churchill stood as a Liberal candidate in a by-election in Dundee in 1908 and won. But, by 1922, the Liberal Party looked in difficulties and the noted lover of alcohol found himself opposed in the general election of that year by Mr Edwin Scrymgeour, a teetotaller and a Prohibition candidate. Sensing defeat, Churchill made a speech in Broughty Ferry on the eve of the poll and, not mincing his words, he attacked Mr D. C. Thomson, the local newspaper proprietor, as 'a narrow, bitter, unreasonable being eaten up by his own conceit, consumed with his own petty arrogance, and pursued from day to day and from year to year by an unrelenting bee in his bonnet'. As a sage once remarked, it is not a wise idea to pick quarrels with men who buy ink in barrels. There were two seats in Dundee and Churchill came fourth – some distance behind the sober Mr Scrymgeour.

After the election, a huge, euphoric crowd of about 250,000 gathered in the centre of Glasgow to give a rousing send-off to the new MPs as they boarded trains for London at St Enoch Station. Hymns were sung and speeches made as James Maxton, David Kirkwood, Emanuel Shinwell and John Wheatley left with their comrades. But they had little time to settle, for another election was called in 1923 and a historic moment followed. Although in a minority, Ramsay MacDonald's Labour Party was called upon to form a government. It lasted only 10 months but, in that time, a bill was enacted that changed lives in Scotland profoundly. John Wheatley was appointed Minister of Health and he drafted the Housing (Financial Provisions) Act of 1924. It increased government subsidies to local authorities by 50 per cent and extended the term over which they could be paid from 20 to 40 years. By 1933, more than half a million council houses had been built in Britain, 20 per cent of them in Scotland. This was achieved by careful planning as Wheatley approached employers in the building trades to seek assurances that there would be an expansion of the apprentice system so that skill levels could be maintained. Suppliers of building materials were also drawn into discussions so that profiteering could be avoided. Success was partial since rents were often beyond the means of the poorest but Wheatley's vision and his formula for implementing it transformed lives in Scotland for generations afterwards.

STOOKY BILL

From his teens, John Logie Baird had shown a precocious interest in invention. When he attempted to make diamonds from graphite, he shorted out the entire electricity supply to Glasgow. Suffering from cold feet, Baird decided to concentrate on inventing a warm pair of socks and he was moderately successful with the Baird undersock (a cotton lining inside wool). But, when he managed to transmit the first television picture, using a ventriloquist's dummy known as Stooky Bill, in 1924, he made a real breakthrough. Having transmitted the first long-distance image, from Glasgow to London, Baird's invention really took off. The Baird Television Company shot pictures of the Epsom Derby and sent images across the Atlantic. But others were developing TV systems at the same time and Baird never really benefited from his inventions as much as he perhaps should have.

Public works programmes such as council house building had a negligible impact on unemployment. In the 1920s, almost 8 per cent of the population, around 500,000 Scots, left to find work and a better life in North

America, Australia, New Zealand and elsewhere. Those who stayed were forced to endure indignities if they were unemployed. The 'not genuinely seeking work test' demanded that men prove to the authorities that each day they had been looking for jobs that, in reality, did not exist. If they could not, benefits were withdrawn.

There was some escape. Millions of Scots regularly went to the pictures, most of them once a week. Admission was not expensive and even the smallest towns and villages had cinemas. At the foot of Bowling Green Lane in the beautiful Fife fishing village of Crail a small picture house was built. It now supplies draughty accommodation for students. But, if locals did not like what was showing, there were also cinemas in nearby Earlsferry and Pittenweem. Kelso had two but, by contrast Glasgow had a staggering 114 picture houses. Only in Chicago were there higher audience figures. Even those with no job could afford a ticket and 80 per cent of the unemployed went to watch silent films every week.

Newsreels were very popular, even in the silent era when captions supplied information. For many, these moving images of everything from coronations to football cup finals were a new and fascinating window on a world far beyond their lives, long before the age of mass transport. In 1920, British Pathé began production of 'cinemazines' which were much longer and more comprehensive than the five- or ten-minute packages that were usually shown. Footage from the 1924 Olympics in Paris was of particular patriotic interest to Scots.

Outside the Olympic Stadium on 11 July, the pipe band of the 51st Highland Brigade were playing and, inside, the runners in the 400 metres final were lined up on the stagger around the first bend of the cinder track. In the outside lane was Eric Liddell, a unique sort of Scottish sporting hero. While a student at Edinburgh University, Liddell's speed and grit had propelled him into the Scotland rugby team, and, in only two seasons, he scored four tries, leaving tacklers floundering in his wake. Scotland won all but one of the matches he played in.

Liddell's devout Christianity had disqualified him from his best Olympic event, the 100 metres sprint, because the heats were to be held on a Sunday, the Sabbath Day. Instead, he entered for the 400 metres even though his times for the 440 yards were no better than modest. As he set himself on the starting line and the pipes played over the crowds, the American team masseur slipped a scrap of paper into Liddell's hand. It was a quotation from the Old Testament: 'Those who honour me, I will honour.'

The starting gun fired and a reporter from the *Edinburgh Evening News* was watching:

It was Liddell who first caught the eye as they came round the first bend. The Scot set up a terrific pace. He ran as if he were wild with inspiration, like some demon. And as he flew along to the accompaniment of a roar, the experts wondered whether Liddell would crack, such was the pace he set out to travel . . . Liddell, yards ahead, came round the bend for the straight, and as he did so he pulled harder at himself, for Fitch was getting nearer. There was Butler too, and Imbach to be reckoned with. It was the last fifty metres that meant the making or breaking of Liddell. Just for a second it was feared that he would kill himself with the terrible speed he had got up, but to the joy of the British camp, he remained chock full of fight. Imbach, perhaps fifty yards from the tape, fell. It was then Liddell or Fitch. The Scotsman had so surely got his teeth into the race that the American could not hold, and Liddell got home first by what, considering the formidable opposition, was almost a remarkable finish.

With his tongue firmly planted in his cheek, Liddell later revealed the tactics behind his famous win. 'The secret of my success over the 400 metres is that I run the first 200 metres as hard as I can. Then, for the second 200 metres, with God's help, I run harder.' He won his gold medal in a world record time of 47.6 seconds. It stood for 12 years.

A year after the Olympic Games, Eric Liddell sailed to China to work as a missionary. In 1943, Japanese invaders interned him and other foreign nationals in a prison camp. Only a few weeks before the war ended, he died of a brain tumour. When the Scots sprinter, Allan Wells, won Olympic gold in the 100 metres in Moscow in 1980, he dedicated his medal to Eric Liddell. The newsreel of the 1924 400 metres final has survived and it shows a unique running style, with the head back, mouth open and arms flailing. It was ugly but effective and, when in a race at Glasgow University, Liddell was far behind the leaders, a visitor remarked that he could not possibly win. 'Aye,' said someone who had seen this remarkable athlete before, 'but his heid's no' back yet.'

Scots gloried in the successes of their sporting heroes and, in the 1920s, there were many. It was a golden decade. Only recently completed, Murrayfield saw the Scotland rugby XV win their first Grand Slam, defeating Ireland, France, Wales and finally England in the new stadium in early 1925. A year later, they achieved a rare feat and beat England at home at Twickenham. But most Scots were football fans and their greatest day was 31 March 1928. The team known as 'the Wembley Wizards' trounced England by five goals to one and it was a game few expected them to win. When the team was announced and it included eight Scots who played for English clubs, the *Daily Record* reckoned, 'It's not a great side.' The tallest of the Scottish forwards was Alex Jackson at 5 foot 7 inches and, when the team captain, Jimmy McMullan, spoke to the players the night before the match, the lack of height was much on his mind. 'All I've got to say is, go to your beds, put your head on the pillow and pray for rain.' It poured on the Saturday morning and, in the afternoon, the small Scottish forwards skipped over the slippery pitch and the goals poured in.

Eleven football special trains travelled to London from Glasgow, crammed with supporters. Great sporting occasions were mass events, regularly attracting many tens of thousands. It was a form of escape, two hours when men could put their everyday cares to the back of their minds. And they were many. As unemployment levels climbed, hunger marches began, the first in 1922. Jobs and rates of pay were repeatedly cut and workers began to organise strikes. Because coal was central to British industry and the mineworkers' trade unions were well organised, many days were lost to strikes and workers in related industries were directly affected. Pressure built until, in May 1926, a General Strike was called throughout Britain as millions came out in solidarity with the miners. When middle-class students and others began to man essential services, it looked like a society dividing against itself – a class war simmering. But the General Strike lasted only nine days and, after some negotiation with employers and the government, the Trades Union Congress advised a return to work. Only the miners carried on, starving through the winter of 1926–27 until hunger forced them back, having gained nothing and lost a great deal.

> I amna fou sae muckle as tired – deid dune.
> It's gey and hard wark coupin' gless for gless
> Wi' Cruivie and Gilsanquhar and the like,
> And I'm no' juist as bauld as aince I was.

These are the opening lines of *A Drunk Man Looks at the Thistle*, Hugh MacDiarmid's masterpiece. Published in 1926, it incorporates a passage on the General Strike, a pessimistic reflection on its failure. As a communist,

MacDiarmid saw the strike as a first stage in a revolutionary process. Born Christopher Murray Grieve in Langholm, he wrote widely in Border Scots, adapting and augmenting it with inventions so that what had been seen as the language of ordinary people could deal with any and all concepts. *A Drunk Man Looks at the Thistle* has tremendous drive and a wonderful comic tone but it is written in an authentic language, with all its rhythms and cadences. It was published in what was probably MacDiarmid's most fertile period. Two other collections, *Sangschaw* and *Penny Wheep*, are full of superb lyrics in Scots.

In 1929, the Wall Street Crash saw the world economy plunge into deep depression. Confidence evaporated, shares became worthless overnight and banks failed. Many Scots who had emigrated to North America in the 1920s returned home to find work. But what they found was male unemployment in Scotland standing at over 30 per cent and at even higher levels in the heavy industries of Central Scotland. Elected in 1929, the second Labour government under Ramsay MacDonald was bewildered by events in America and met new circumstances with outdated measures. They rejected reflation as a policy, introduced drastic cuts in public expenditure and thereby deepened the crisis even further. By the end of 1930, unemployment in Britain had doubled to more than 2.5 million. More swingeing cuts were proposed and most of MacDonald's Labour Party colleagues would not support them. With the encouragement of King George V, MacDonald formed a National Government with the Conservatives and the Liberals. He was expelled from the Labour Party as a traitor and immediately called a general election. The Conservatives won a landslide with 473 seats, MacDonald's National Labour picked up 13 and the Liberals 68. It was a disaster for Labour who were reduced to a rump of only 52 seats. Isolated and ill, MacDonald gradually lost his grasp on power and, as Lord President of the Council, Stanley Baldwin ran the administration with the help of Neville Chamberlain as Chancellor of the Exchequer. In 1935, MacDonald resigned in favour of Baldwin and, in the subsequent general election, the new Prime Minister won with a reduced majority for the National Government. There were enormous economic difficulties to confront at home, also the looming possibility of an old enemy to confront in Europe. War clouds were gathering, Britain began to rearm and, under Adolf Hitler, the Germans reoccupied the Rhineland.

By the time the Nazis came to power in 1933, they had identified scapegoats for many of Germany's ills after defeat in the Great War. Amongst others, the Jews were persecuted as an enemy within. In Scotland, a similar way of thinking – although with very much less savage consequences – wormed its way into politics. In 1929, the Church of Scotland healed the rifts of the Disruption and reunited with the United Free Church and brought together 90 per cent of Scotland's Presbyterians. But it tended to be reactionary in its views, angry at the provisions made for Catholic schooling in the 1918 Education Act, suspicious of the Labour Party's representation of Irish Catholics and vehemently opposed to more immigration. Baleful language issued from pulpits and pamphlets as the Kirk talked of 'inferior' people and 'an alien race'. And, in 1923, a pamphlet entitled 'The Menace of the Irish Race to our Scottish Nationality' was circulated. Demonised as drunken, promiscuous, uncivilised and the carriers of deadly disease (typhus was popularly known as Irish fever), the Catholic Irish living in Scotland became the focus of political spite. In 1933, John Cormack founded the Protestant Action Society in Edinburgh and won 11 seats on the corporation with 31 per cent of the vote. Advocating the expulsion of Catholics, Cormack's followers sparked several bouts of sectarian violence and more than one rowdy demonstration took place in the douce, leafy suburb of Morningside, the location of the Catholic Archbishop of Edinburgh's residence and chapel. In Glasgow, the Scottish Protestant League won six seats on the corporation, polling more votes than Labour. But mainstream political parties distanced themselves and, amongst the Scottish press, the *Glasgow Herald* in particular undermined these groups and the Church of Scotland's scaremongering by good journalism and careful research showing that immigration had slowed to a trickle.

In 1934, another political party was founded. Six years before, R. B. Cunninghame Graham, Hugh MacDiarmid and others had formed the National Party of Scotland. The poet wrote a famous couplet:

> I'll hae nae halfway hoose
> But aye be whaur extremes meet

He was later expelled. The NPS at first struggled to be heard and, in 1933, the novelist Eric Linklater stood in a by-election in East Fife and came bottom of the poll. A brilliant by-product was his novel, *Magnus Merriman*, where the eponymous hero stands for parliament because he believes that 'small nations are safer to live in than big ones'. After the Scottish Party came into being in 1932, with the Duke of Montrose as one of its leading figures, a merger was proposed and the Scottish National Party came into being in April 1934.

The world economy was very slowly recovering, partly as a consequence of the vast schemes of public works undertaken in the USA and a policy of injecting demand into the economy but the living conditions of people in Scotland improved very little in the 1930s. The Gorbals district of Glasgow was one of the worst slums in Europe and perhaps the most eloquent chronicler of life amongst the decaying tenements was Ralph Glasser. He grew up in the Jewish quarter but eventually escaped by studying hard and gaining a scholarship to Oxford University. He became a noted psychologist and economist but his upbringing never left him and he felt 'the Gorbals at [his] shoulder always'. In 1986, he published a vivid, even painfully honest autobiography, *Growing Up in the Gorbals*, and it is so powerful and evocative that it demands to be quoted at length. From the age of 14, Glasser worked in a garment factory and here is an atmospheric, shockingly authentic account of what he heard one night as he walked through the Saltmarket, a district where prostitutes patrolled the streets.

We were walking home late from the factory late one night, about ten o' clock, the streets stilled. Something in his [Alec's] mood suggested he wanted a cue to talk.

I said: 'Have you ever had one of them?'

'Aye, a few times,' he replied in assumed indifference, 'when ah've been hard up for ma hole. That was where ah had ma first hoor, when ah was aboo' fifteen. Ah wis jist this minute thinkin' aboo' 'er! In fact she comes tae mind many a time. She wis ma first proper fuck!' He fell silent. 'But that's no' the reason. She wis, ah don't know how tae put i'. She wis warm an' understandin' an', well, she was genuine. She wanted me tae be happy! She made me feel ah wisnae jist anybody. Ah'll never ferrget it. Never. A wee thin-faced lassie wi' red hair, verry pale, shiverin' in the cauld wi' a thin coat an' skirt on. A guid bi' aulder than me she was, aboo' twenty-five. An' wi' a weddin' ring on'.

He pushed his lips out: 'It wis one payday, an' it was snowin' an' cauld, an' ah wis comin' away frae the workshop late at night dog tired an' for some reason ah don't remember ah wis gaun hame through the Saltmarket an' no' thinkin' aboo' anythin'. An' suddenly there was this lassie beside me an' caught a haud o' ma hand sayin': "C'mon ah'll show ye somethin' wonderful!" An' she pulled me intae a big dark archway an' before ah knew anythin' she'd put ma haun up 'er skirt – Jesus ah can feel it this minute – an' she got a haud o' me an' ah couldnae stop masel'! Christ wis ashamed! Bu' she said, quiet an' soft: "Never yew mind. Ah'll wait. An' ye'll be fine wi' me in a wee while." And she held me tight, an' kissed me as if she really meant i'. An' efter a minute she shivered and said: "Ah'm sae cauld! Ah'm tha' hungry. Will ye gie me a sixpenny piece an' ah'll go and ge' a bag o' fish an' chips?"

An' ah wis laft standin' there all flustered an' lonely an' wonderin' whit was happenin' tae me. Ah felt ah wis seein' this wurrld fer the verry fursst time. Aye, seein' a lot o' things fer the fursst time. Ah thought of 'er walkin' aboo' hungry in tha' God forsaken place, through piles o' rubbish an' horse shit dirty white wi' the snow left lyin'. A' the emptiness an' loneliness. An' the bitter cauld that had driven a' the ither hoors hame. An' her sae desperate. Grabbin' hold of a boy tae ge' a shillin' aff of, for a bag o' fish an' chips an' pennies fer the gas an' the price o' a pint o' milk! An' her bein' nothin' tae me, an' me bein' nothin' tae her. An' the next minute ah thought: "No. That's wrong! I' is somethin'! If it wis nothin' ah wouldnae be carin' at a'! It's got tae mean somethin'!" Ah started shiverin', standin' there under the arch, the freezin' cauld creepin' up ma legs frae the pavement. Ah wanted tae feel 'er warm body pressin' against me again, an' 'er gentleness, sayin' nothin', jist bein' there wi' me. An' then ah started wonderin' if it wid be different fuckin' her than blockin' ma sister'.

I should not have been shocked but I was, and I must have shown it, or at least that I was surprised, perhaps by the slightest shift in my step or a questioning turn of the head, for he looked at me in astonishment. 'Yours've done it wi' yew surely?'

Slums such as the Gorbals were often the only realistic, affordable option for those who were unemployed or poorly paid, and some women were forced on to the streets simply to feed their families. It was an appalling life. When Ralph Glasser's friend saw the red-headed woman again, she had been badly beaten by her husband, both eyes blackened. Two thirds of all house building between 1918 and 1939 was undertaken by local councils but rents were often high. In Dundee, they accounted for half of the average wages of textile workers, most of them employed in the jute mills. It was to be the steep escalation of international tension that would finally animate the bleak landscape of Scotland's heavy industry. As the government began to re-arm the navy, the air force and the army, warships, vehicles, tanks, uniforms and much else were made once more made on the Clyde, in North Lanarkshire and Dundee and agricultural production across Scotland was intensified.

Under the Conservative Secretary of State for Scotland, Walter Elliot, political power began to move north. The Scottish Office had been based in London but, over a short period of transition, it relocated to Edinburgh. Elliot had formulated the Local Government Act of 1929 that removed social responsibilities from parish councils and transferred them to local authorities, mostly based on the old Scottish county boundaries. In 1937, he also founded the Scottish Special Housing Association and it offered subsidies to local authorities where slum clearance was most urgent. In 1936, plans were put in place to rationalise devolved government by creating four new departments in the Scottish Office – Agriculture and Fisheries; Education; Health; and Home. And, a year later, the Scottish Office moved into new premises built on the site of the old Calton Jail in Edinburgh. St Andrew's House was a blunt architectural and political statement, a monument to the efforts of Walter Elliot and others to return a degree of self-government to Scotland, the beginning of a continuing journey.

As Hitler reasserted German power in Europe, it became clear to many Scots what was happening and what might be about to happen, again. A Borders dairy farmer, David Welsh, remembered:

> What influenced me was the newsreels. They were American and very good, especially about the rise of Hitler. And when you saw these people, well . . .
>
> And we had a chappie who was sort of stationmaster up at Sprouston [near Kelso] and he was an ex-soldier – with the Northumberland Fusiliers . . . and he would regale us with tales of the First World War. And your hair would be standing on end. I mean it would be pretty dreadful – because that would [have been] only 7 or 8 years after the First World War had finished. That impressed me more than anything. That and these March of Time newsreels.
>
> If anybody went to the pictures and read a newspaper then you realised that there was something going on in Europe that was decidedly unhealthy. And when Hitler marched into Czechoslovakia and Chamberlain said, 'Oh, it's a little country we don't know very much about.', you began to realise that there was some treachery going on here.
>
> You saw these men goose-stepping over Europe and you thought, my God, it's coming, it's coming.

By 1939 unemployment had fallen in Scotland to 15 per cent and many men without work would soon find themselves in the armed forces or taking over the jobs of others who had joined up. When it came, relayed to the nation in Neville Chamberlain's much replayed radio broadcast, the declaration of war against Germany in September 1939 moved many Scots, some to tears. The reaction was very different from the patriotic fervour, the 'war fever' described by Harry McShane in 1914. Within a generation, Britain was at war once more with the same enemy and many feared a repeat of the wholesale slaughter of the trenches. However, Hitler and his audacious generals ensured that did not happen when the panzer divisions dashed into France in 1940, forcing the French into abject capitulation within a week. But the new war would bring very different dangers.

On 16 October 1939, the declared hostilities suddenly became more than a radio broadcast for the towns along the Fife coast and the people of Edinburgh. Nine German bombers were seen droning up the Firth of Forth heading for the naval dockyard at Rosyth. The daylight raid was a complete surprise. No alarm was sounded and anti-air-raid gunners on the shores of the Forth were conducting an exercise with blank shells when the enemy aircraft flew over them. Passengers on a train crossing on the Forth Bridge stared, terrified, at the low-flying raiders, believing the bridge to be their target. Three warships were damaged by bombs but the German air crews realised that the Firth of Forth was at the extreme end of their range. When they wheeled around to return to base, two Spitfire squadrons from Turnhouse and Drem in East Lothian had been scrambled. As people stood in the streets on North Edinburgh and the Fife towns to watch, two Heinkels were shot down and another bomber plunged into the water off the Isle of May.

More raiders came and they penetrated ever deeper into Scotland. On the nights of 13 and 14 March 1941, the Luftwaffe attacked Clydebank and destroyed the town, killing 528 people and seriously injuring a further 617. Only seven houses were left undamaged. But the raid was a military failure. The strategic targets of John Brown's shipyard, Beardmore's Diesel Works, the Singer Corporation factory and a Royal Ordnance factory were all left largely untouched. More than 500 air raids crossed Scotland during the Second World War and the largest number were directed at Aberdeen with German aircraft operating out of Norwegian airfields. One raid was low level and especially terrifying as German machine gunners strafed pedestrians in the city-centre streets.

During the Great War, there had been significant unrest because of rent strikes and workers' pay and conditions and, once he had been appointed Prime Minister, Winston Churchill wisely gave Labour politicians those ministries that ran the home front. Their contacts with the trade unions might help to avoid problems. Herbert Morrison was Home Secretary, Ernest Bevin Minister of Labour and National Service and Tom Johnston Secretary of State for Scotland. This last appointment would lead to far-reaching changes – the beginnings of a new Scotland and a new Britain.

An intellectual and a pragmatist, a rare combination, Johnston was given substantial powers by Churchill. And he used them. He created the Scottish Council of Industry and it incentivised 700 businesses, employing 90,000 people, to relocate from industrial England to Scotland. He set up a series of committees with the executive ability to deal with social issues like juvenile delinquency and also agricultural and industrial problems. It is often reckoned that his most successful initiative was the setting-up of the North of Scotland Hydro-Electric Board. It harnessed water power in a series of spectacular schemes to supply remote areas with power and Johnston also saw it as a means of reviving the Highland economy. But perhaps more influential in the longer term was his creation of the Emergency Hospital Service. If there were to be more raids as devastating as Clydebank, then hospitals capable of coping with thousands of casualties would be needed. New hospitals were quickly built at Raigmore in Inverness, Stracathro near Brechin, Bridge of Earn in Perthshire, Killearn in Stirlingshire, Law in North Lanarkshire, Ballochmyle in Ayrshire and Peel in the Borders. New annexes were added to existing hospitals and some of Scotland's most luxurious hotels were commandeered as convalescent facilities.

When the anticipated raids failed to fly, Johnston decided that civilians waiting for scarce medical care should be treated free of charge. A new range of specialisms was developed and a blood transfusion service was set up. Waiting lists disappeared and, by the end of the war, about 33,000 civilian patients had been treated. With the Clyde Basin Scheme, Johnston launched an experiment in preventative medicine and it was later extended across Scotland. It total, this building programme supplied an additional 20,500 hospital beds and 30 per cent more nurses than in England as well as more GPs. Johnston had laid the foundations of what became the National Health Service.

The war cabinet was confronted with a crucial question in the early and most dangerous phase of the war. A citizen army would never again submit to the wholesale slaughter endured on the Western Front and, more than that, men had to know what they were fighting for – certainly not a return to the miseries of the 1920s and 1930s. William Beveridge was commissioned to write a report. Published in 1942 and entitled a 'Report to Parliament on Social Insurance and Allied Services', it was to change Scotland and Britain forever. It identified what Beveridge called the five 'Giant Evils' in society: squalor, ignorance, want, idleness (or unemployment) and disease. The hopelessness of Ralph Glasser's Gorbals was to be forever banished in a new Britain and citizens would have fundamental rights in what became known as a 'welfare state'. The weakest would be supported, decent housing would be provided, education made available to all, hunger would become a thing of the past, there would be full employment and a health service would be provided free to all at the point of need. It was universally welcomed. With Ernest Brown, the Minister of Health in the war cabinet, Tom Johnston was largely responsible for the original White Paper that described what a National Health Service would look like. What he had achieved in Scotland and its great success and popularity (as well as what had been done over the rest of Britain) informed what was approved by the cabinet on 9 February 1944. It was a turning moment in our history.

In May 1945, when the Second World War had at last ended in Europe, Prime Minister Winston Churchill's approval ratings stood at a staggering 83 per cent. And yet, in the general election held in July, Labour won a by landslide with an overall majority of 145, gaining 393 seats, compared to the Conservatives' 197. It was the first election for ten years and, because so many voters were still serving in the armed forces, the results of the vote on 5 July were not declared until 26 July. It was clear that servicemen had overwhelmingly supported Labour.

During the campaign, the Beveridge Report had remained centre stage. Clement Attlee, the Labour leader, promised its adoption under a Labour government and he guaranteed that there would be no repeat of the aftermath of the Great War. By contrast, the Conservatives accepted the principles of the report but publically worried about whether or not it was affordable. This wavering rang alarm bells with voters. Between 1918 and 1939, Britain had been run by Conservatives or Conservative-dominated coalitions with only two brief periods of Labour government and they still bore the stigma of economic failure as well as responsibility for the catastrophically mistaken policy of attempting to appease Hitler. They failed completely to deliver a land fit for heroes after 1918. Particularly amongst returning servicemen, there was a powerful sense that the ruling classes had led Britain into two wars and they could no longer be trusted with leadership. It was time for radical change.

Churchill also made a bad tactical mistake in the election campaign, one that cost his party dear. In a radio broadcast of 4 June 1945, he attacked Labour by saying that they 'would have to fall back on some sort of a Gestapo' in order to impose socialist measures. A day later, Clement Attlee elegantly rebutted the smear by thanking the prime minister for making clear the difference between Churchill the great wartime leader and Churchill the peacetime politician. There was also a gulf between the views of ordinary servicemen and those who had stayed at home. Many soldiers in particular believed that Churchill had prolonged the war unnecessarily and they voted to remove him from office.

DESTINY DIVIDED

In the week before Christmas, 1950, conspirators were making their way south to London. Led by Ian Hamilton, a student at Glasgow University, a group of young people, fervent nationalists all, were driving in freezing conditions with little idea of how they would achieve their objective. They planned to steal The Stone of Destiny from Westminster Abbey – and despite a farcical sequence of events, they succeeded. Hamilton's plan was to hide in the abbey as it closed for the day and then open the doors to his compatriots, but cowering under a cleaner's trolley with his overcoat over his head, he was discovered and ejected. When the conspirators finally broke into the abbey, they found the ancient stone in its traditional place under the throne of Edward the Confessor. But when they levered it out, the stone fell into two pieces. And it was much heavier than anyone imagined. One of the group, Kay Matheson, drove away with the smaller fragment in the boot of her car, but when she stopped at traffic lights in Knightsbridge, the catch opened and the stone fell out onto the road. Somehow she managed to lift it back. Meanwhile Ian Hamilton had lost his car keys. After much whispered searching in the pitch dark and many lit matches, he found them and then drove off with the other fragment. And got lost. Eventually, the group managed to get both bits of the stone back to Scotland.

Despite the enforced austerity, the dreary continuation of rationing and widespread war damage, there was optimism as Attlee's government began to put its programme in place. Scotland had suffered far fewer casualties than in the Great War, with 40,000 losing their lives (including 6,000 civilians) compared with 142,218 dead between 1914 and 1918. For those who came back, there were jobs and there were houses. From 1945 to 1951, more than 1.2 million new houses were built in Britain and some of the first to become homes were prefabricated. Estates of these remarkable little structures sprang up all over Scotland, many on greenfield sites, some even built in public parks. To the families who moved in, they were miniature palaces. Detached, with a garden to encourage vegetable growing (and a standard garden shed that resembled an Anderson air-raid shelter) and only one storey in height, the prefabs were a light and airy alternative to the crowded canyons of the city slums. Always pre-painted magnolia with light green door facings and skirting boards, these houses arrived on flat-bed lorries and were assembled and erected very quickly. Inside, there was a coal fire fitted in front of a back boiler which heated water that circulated around central heating pipes and supplied constant hot water. A specially insulated version was made for erection in the Hebrides. There was a fitted bath, a flush toilet located indoors and not shared with any other families, as many were in the tene-ments. In the prefab kitchen there was undreamt-of luxury with a built-in oven, a Baxi water heater and a fridge which could make ice lollies out of diluted orange squash. When prefabbers later moved into bricks-and-mortar council housing, it would be years before many of them could afford a fridge. Although they were designed to last only ten years, prefabs still stand in a few of Scotland's towns and cities and are much loved.

After 1945, the Attlee government began to nationalise key industries such as coal mining, the railways, road transport, civil aviation, electricity and gas. Some servicemen believed that they do not go far enough. With such a huge mandate for change, they could have nationalised the land, some argued, and, while the Bank of England was taken under government control, there was support for nationalising the entire banking sector.

The Family Allowances Act of 1945 encouraged a return to domestic life and the first baby boom started. The statistics are striking. The number of live births in Scotland jumped from 86,924 in 1945 to 104,413 in 1946 and then to 113,147 in 1947. Building on Tom Johnston's White Paper, the National Health Service Act of 1946 provided free medical care for all these new mothers and babies (as well as bottles of disgusting orange juice and cod liver oil) and the National Insurance Act of the same year provided sickness and unem-ployment benefits and also retirement pensions. A social safety net to catch anyone whose circumstances were not already catered for was enshrined in the

National Assistance Act of 1948. All of the building blocks of the welfare state had been doggedly put in place but they could do nothing about acts of God.

The winter of 1946–47 was a natural disaster. Unprecedentedly bitter, it was very cold indeed in December and snow began to fall on 21 January and it kept falling. February 1947 was the coldest month of the century and between 2 and 22 February no sunshine was recorded anywhere in Scotland. In the Highlands, snowdrifts up to 28 feet were measured. All of Britain was paralysed. Low coal stocks, power failures and shortages and general hardship were all blamed on Emanuel Shinwell, the former Red Clydesider, who was Minister of Energy and he needed police protection. The optimism of the 1945 general election was fading and life in Scotland seemed grey and unrelenting as rationing ground on.

In country districts, grey meant something else. It signalled progress. Harry Ferguson was an Ulster Scot who invented an affordable small tractor which revolutionised farming. They were grey and known affectionately as 'Wee Grey Fergies'. What was new was the three-point hydraulic linkage at the back end. This allowed the tractor's power to be transferred to whatever implement was attached. Before Ferguson's brilliantly simple invention, tractors had simply pulled implements with more power than heavy horses. And the new linkage meant that one man could do a range of jobs more efficiently, more quickly and without help. The Standard Motor Company turned out half a million Wee Grey Fergies and they were not expensive, as well as being much safer to operate.

The Attlee government recognised that efficient farming was vital in the immediate post-war years and the men from the ministry began to become involved. In order to make Britain less dependent on imports, where they were available, a new policy of subsidy was developed, essentially taking farming out of the market. Food prices were kept low and farmers were encouraged to put as much land under cultivation as possible, even more than during the war. In 1947, an annual price review system was set up and it maintained price floors that gave farmers a degree of stability and an ability to plan. With government help available, mechanisation began to gather pace and fewer hands were needed. By the end of the 1950s, horse working had all but disappeared from Scotland's fields and an entire equine culture began to fade.

Perhaps the least controversial piece of new legislation was the 1944 Education Act, adapted a year later for Scotland. It raised the school leaving age to 15 (although this was never properly ratified), made secondary education free for all and introduced an examination for 11-year-olds to determine what sort of secondary school they should go to. In Scotland, this was known as 'the Control' or 'the Qually' and it had three elements: English, arithmetic and a version of an IQ test. A daunting experience, it divided children early into two groups. Those who passed the Control were deemed to be academic and destined for higher education of some sort, while those who failed might be offered an apprenticeship or manual work. Across Britain secondary schools were allocated accordingly, but in Scotland the picture was patchy. Junior and Senior Secondary Schools did exist, mainly in the cities, but most towns had only the high school, some them called academies. The solution was to carry on streaming children according to academic ability into A, B, C and D classes. The 1945 Act saw many more girls stay on at school since more of them passed the Control than the generally less mature boys. But there was a difficulty. In the first half of the 20th century, Scotland's universities had fallen far behind through lack of investment and the continuing habit of giving job security or tenure to under-performing academics. While numbers rose in England, university entrance in Scotland was declining, particularly amongst women. But, as more Scots teenagers passed the entrance exams, numbers began slowly to revive in the 1950s. School qualifications were rationalised into the O-Grade exams, usually taken in 4th year, and the Highers sat in both 5th and 6th years. Both were generally and probably correctly seen as inferior to English O-Levels and A-Levels.

The baby boom of the late 1940s made for big infant and primary school classes of 30 and even 40 children. With such unmanageable numbers, discipline was often maintained by corporal punishment as teachers smacked children on the arm or leg with rulers or threw chalk and dusters across the classroom. Some as young as seven were belted on the hands with a forked leather strap known as 'the tawse', many of which were made in Lochgelly in Fife.

What complicated the Scottish educational landscape were the merchant company schools, most of them in Edinburgh and Glasgow. There was a sprinkling of public schools on the English model, such as Fettes, Glenalmond, Gordonstoun and Merchiston, but schools like George Heriot's or George Watson's in Edinburgh and Allan Glen's and Kelvinside Academy in Glasgow were something of a halfway house. Most were day schools, with very few boarders, and fees were not astronomically high. In addition, the founders had often stipulated that there should be generous provision for scholarships. But what did buttress the dividing line between these schools and the state sector was sport. The public schools and the merchant company schools played rugby and the rest played what they called football. Only in the Borders did the high schools ignore the round ball.

Labour was re-elected in 1950 with a very small majority of only five seats and, a year later, they lost as Winston Churchill stepped back into Downing Street. In Scotland, the Conservatives polled 1,349,298 votes and Labour 1,330,244, although each party gained 35 seats, with the Liberals taking only 1. Most people heard the results on their wirelesses, as they then called their radios. An announcer would simply read out the figures. On 22 February 1950, polling day, BBC Television mounted its first-ever results programme. It was a brave experiment because the 14-Day Rule banned coverage of issues debated in parliament until two weeks after they had taken place and had been reported in the newspapers. And no coverage of election campaigns was allowed. Nevertheless, the programme was a success and, by 1955, the reporting of the results had become much more sophisticated.

After the end of the Second World War, the Scottish Home Service was demerged from the BBC Home Service and normal service was resumed. But it was only an opt-out from national UK services and networked shows like the *Billy Cotton Band Show* and *The Goon Show* were very popular. On Saturday mornings, *Children's Favourites* was presented by Uncle Mac and the distinctive, comforting voice belonged to Derek McCullough, Head of BBC Children's Programmes. He was born in Plymouth of Scottish parents.

What did shift the cultural focus of Britain decisively northwards was the first Edinburgh Festival. Founded in 1947 by Rudolf Bing, General Manager of the Glyndebourne Opera Festival, and Harvey Wood, Head of the British Council in Scotland, it was a bold initiative. They wanted to do something to lighten the gloom of the immediate post-war years. Henry Wood left a record of why he and Bing opted for Edinburgh:

The Edinburgh International Music of Festival and Drama was first discussed over a lunch table in a restaurant in London, towards the end of 1944. Rudolf Bing, convinced that musical and operatic festivals on anything like the pre-war scale were unlikely to be held in any of the shattered and impoverished centres for many years to come, was anxious to consider and investigate the possibility of staging such a Festival somewhere in the United Kingdom in the summer of 1946. He was convinced and he convinced my colleagues and myself that such an enterprise, successfully conducted, might at this moment of European time, be of more than temporary significance and might establish in Britain a centre of world resort for lovers of music, drama, opera, ballet and the graphic arts.

Certain preconditions were obviously required of such a centre. It should be a town of reasonable size, capable of absorbing and entertaining anything between 50,000 and 150,000 visitors over a period of three weeks to a month. It should, like Salzburg, have considerable scenic and picturesque appeal and it should be set in a country likely to be attractive to tourists and foreign visitors. It should have sufficient number of theatres, concert halls and open spaces for the adequate staging of a programme of an ambitious and varied character. Above all it should be a city likely to embrace the opportunity and willing to make the festival a major preoccupation not only in the City Chambers but in the heart and home of every citizen, however modest. Greatly daring but not without confidence I recommended Edinburgh as the centre and promised to make preliminary investigations.

What neither man anticipated was that the Festival would quickly acquire a Fringe. At the inaugural festival in 1947, eight theatre companies turned up uninvited and they mounted shows in smaller venues in Edinburgh such as the theatre at the YMCA in South St Andrew Street and the Little Theatre at The Pleasance (and one show at Dunfermline Abbey). They were known as 'Festival Adjuncts' and it was a relief when Robert Kemp came up with the phrase 'a fringe around the festival'. Since then the Edinburgh Fringe has burgeoned into the largest arts festival in the world, its performance spaces sprawling over the centre of Edinburgh for the month of August. It is unique and transforms the entire Edinburgh Festival into the greatest celebration of the arts anywhere.

By the mid 1950s, Scotland's traditional heavy industries were in steep decline, shedding around 10,000 jobs with each passing year. Emblematic was shipbuilding. The yards on the Clyde were being undercut by Japanese companies whose labour was cheaper and whose war-ravaged infrastructure had been rebuilt, making it more modern and more efficient. Many of the other heavy industries such as locomotive manufacture, boilermaking and steel-making also began to be hit by foreign competition.

Textile production in the Borders maintained its market share for longer with some innovative design and good marketing. Twinsets were invented and became very popular when, in 1949, the Scots-born actress, Deborah Kerr, perhaps remembering her Borders surname, supplied this gushing endorsement:

'It gives me great pleasure to tell everyone how tremendously admired my twin-sets have been here in Hollywood, not to mention how useful they have been to me personally . . . thank you for some lovely, cosy days.'

The menswear market was no doubt impressed by the well-advertised fact that Edmund Hillary had been wearing a pullover made in Hawick when he climbed Mount Everest in 1953. By the 1960s, companies in the Far East were beginning to make inroads, gaining market shares, and, by the 1970s and 1980s, they dominated production of reasonably-priced woollens.

JOE GRIMOND

The Liberal Party and its successor, the Liberal Democratic Party have long been under a powerful Scottish influence. The MP for Orkney and Shetland was personally charismatic and responsible for the rescue of the Liberal Party from electoral irrelevance but he was by no means the only Scot to lead it. Before the coalition government of Nick Clegg and David Cameron, the last Liberal to hold cabinet office was Sir Archibald Sinclair, MP for Caithness and Sutherland. He was Secretary for Air in the coalition government during the Second World War, and before that, he had been Secretary of State for Scotland in Ramsay MacDonald's National Government of 1931. But he lost his seat in the Labour landslide of 1945. In 1950, the Liberal Party returned only nine MPs, most of them in Scotland and Wales, but one was Joe Grimond, who became leader six years later. He inspired a partial revival with Liberal candidates winning by-elections at Torrington, Orpington, and Roxburgh, Selkirk and Peebles. David Steel won his Scottish seat with the help of Grimond, who toured the Borders making excellent speeches, and the young MP eventually became Liberal leader and carried on the revival. In 2005, the party won 62 seats, the highest total since the 1920s, under the leadership of Charles Kennedy, another politician in the Grimond mould. After being in coalition with the Conservatives from 2010, Kennedy, along with 50 other Liberal Democrats, lost his seat in the general election of 2015. He died, tragically young, at 55, in June, 2015.

The coronation of Elizabeth II and I in 1953 boosted television viewing tremendously and by the mid 1950s the rental market was booming. In 1955, the Conservative government approved proposals to bring commercial television into being, and on 31 August 1957 Scottish Television began broadcasting with a live programme from the stage of the Theatre Royal in Glasgow. Entitled *This Is Scotland*, it was a strange mixture of items introduced by the actor James Robertson Justice. Within a few uneasy seconds, he had forgotten his lines or was unable to read the cue cards under the camera lens and had to refer to a script. This was a sub-poetic meander around 'lusty streams', 'misty glens' and 'moist winds' read against pictures of gloomy mountains and lochs. This was not the Scotland where most Scots lived. Once the ramble around the bens and the glens had stopped, the young singer Kenneth MacKellar stood on a high podium as various figures jigged around the stage – one was dressed as a shepherd, another carried a shotgun. Perhaps some prayed that he would use it. The whole mess was sprinkled with some Hollywood names such as David Niven, Deborah Kerr (not in a twinset) and Jack Buchanan. *This Is Scotland* dragged on for an hour but it did usher in a schedule of some distinctive Scottish programming and it was different from what the BBC produced. In particular it offered a break from the BBC's unconscious middle-class bias; in 1958, the children's programme *Blue Peter* was giving advice on the correct way to groom your pony.

First known as Channel Ten, STV became what Lady Plowden, the chair of the ITV regulatory body, called 'distressingly popular'. And lucrative. The founder of the new service was Roy Thomson, a Canadian newspaper magnate who also owned *The Scotsman* for a time, and he was said to have remarked that the ownership of an ITV franchise was like a licence to print money. In any event, Scotland was eventually served by three ITV companies – Grampian was based in Aberdeen and Border TV served Galloway and the Borders from Carlisle. As successive regulators demanded more regional programming, Scotland was eventually very well served by these three contractors as they produced much more public service broadcasting than the BBC ever could.

Billed as the BBC in Scotland rather than BBC Scotland, it responded to falling ratings and, in 1958, *The White Heather Club* was launched. Presented by the singer Andy Stewart it generally began at 6.20 in the evening with Jimmy Shand on the accordion playing his own composition, 'The Six Twenty Twostep'. This was followed by the pawky Stewart singing:

> Come in, come in, it's nice to see you
> How's yersel', you're looking grand.

The conceit was that the viewer was invited to a very Scottish party, every week. It was possible to tell that it was Scottish because all men wore kilts and all the women white dresses with tartan sashes. In what always seemed a very cramped studio floor, dancing was heavily featured and the Dixie Ingram Dancers were in almost every show in its ten-year run to 1968. This nauseating version of Scottish culture, a bewildering, cringe-making mash-up of bits and pieces from the kailyard, what the producer imagined a ceilidh to be and the Victorian obsession with the Highlands, was also distressingly popular. It played across Britain on the BBC network and made Stewart and the others big stars. For some reason, expatriate Scots loved the show. What the English, the Welsh and the Irish made of it can only be imagined.

After Winston Churchill suffered a stroke in 1953 and his declining health began to impair his ability to govern (he refused to wear a hearing aid in cabinet and discussions were conducted by shouting), he was forced to resign in favour of his protégé, Anthony Eden. Despite his film-star good looks and long experience in government, his ministry was a disaster. When President Nasser of Egypt seized control of the Suez Canal which was owned by the French and the British, Eden sanctioned the dispatch of a military expedition to reclaim it. He likened Nasser to Hitler. But he did not inform the Americans and President Eisenhower was furious, exerting enough pressure to force an ignominious withdrawal. Britain had borrowed $3.5 billion from the USA in 1946 and this could have been called in at any time (it was only repaid in 2006).

The Suez debacle was a humiliating end to the notion of Britain as an imperial power and a clear sign of its relegation to the second rank of nations. India had been granted her independence in 1947, and in the 1950s and 1960s a 'wind of change' blew through Africa and most of Britain's colonies were let go. Within less than 20 years, the mighty British Empire, upon which the sun never set, had all but disappeared. At the end of the 18th century, Henry Dundas had understood how India in particular and the opportunities supplied by the Empire in general could tie ambitious Scots and eventually industrial Scotland into the Union. In the later 20th century and the early 21st, the overriding theme of Scotland's political history was to become the great question of the Union and the relationship with England.

Meanwhile there were domestic difficulties to be dealt with, and one of the most urgent continued to be housing. In 1955, the Secretary of State for Scotland designated Cumbernauld as a new town to be brought into being by the Cumbernauld Development Corporation. Two others had been created in the late 1940s at East Kilbride, to the south-west of Glasgow, and at Glenrothes, in Fife, but demand for better housing did not abate. From the outset, the concept of Cumbernauld was bold. In order to build a safe and attractive alternative to the Glasgow slums, houses were to be located in neighbourhoods clustered around the town centre. This was seen as a single, sprawling building with several elements: retail, entertainment and local administration. It was the first-ever purpose-built shopping centre in Britain. A guiding principle was the separation of traffic and people and the town was linked by a network of underpasses and paved footpaths. The initial target for Cumbernauld was a population of 50,000, making it the eighth largest urban centre in Scotland.

Industry came and the mix included electronics and chemical and food processing and part of Her Majesty's Revenue and Customs (as it later became) was devolved to the new town. And, at first, Cumbernauld was attractive. By 1960, new residential areas were identified to the north of the A80, at Castlecary, Wardpark and Westfield, and population targets were raised to 70,000. The alternatives to new towns – the vast peripheral housing estates in the two biggest cities – grew less attractive. Almost as soon as they were built, these 'schemes' around Glasgow, at Easterhouse, Drumchapel and Castlemilk, and at Craigmillar and Pilton in Edinburgh, became unpopular. Land was cheaper in those places but they were too remote from the city centre. Few facilities were included and these huge housing estates lacked shops, pubs, cinemas and other amenities. By the early 1970s, the street name signs in much of Easterhouse began to be ripped away, making the huge scheme even more anonymous. It was a powerful statement.

As time passed, enthusiasm for Cumbernauld also faded. Its stark, grey, concrete architecture seemed not to age well and, by the end of the 20th century, the town was winning unwanted awards as it was voted the most dismal town centre in the Carbuncle Awards of 2001 and 2005. But, since then, great efforts have been made and, in the 2012 Scottish Design Awards, Cumbernauld won Best Town.

When Anthony Eden was forced to resign in January 1957, after the Suez debacle, Harold MacMillan became prime minister. Although a very patrician figure, he made much of his descent from a crofting family. The closest he came to connecting with his heritage were annual visits to the grouse moors but his origins and his surname played well with voters in Scotland. In 1959, the Conservatives' famous slogan of 'You've never had it so good' also played well enough for them to defeat Labour. As often happens, no one actually uttered the sentence. What MacMillan said was 'Indeed, let us be frank about it – most of our people have never had it so good'. Hugh Gaitskell's Labour Party won seven more seats from the Conservatives in Scotland but polled a smaller percentage of the popular vote. It was a curious result and not one that was complicated by the intervention of other, smaller parties. The Liberals, the SNP, the Communists and others won only 6 per cent of the vote in what was emphatically a two-party system.

After the reforming Education Acts of 1944 and 1945, there was unfinished business. The number of young people leaving school to matriculate at universities was pitifully low at 4 per cent, half of the numbers in France and Germany and a sixth of those in the USA. And, in Scotland, the percentage of young people who wished to go to university was actually declining. The inhibition was financial. Only a privileged few could afford the tuition fees and the living costs. There were competitive bursaries available but these were sparse and inadequate. In addition, an honours degree took four years to complete in Scotland and a medical degree even longer. The Conservative government appointed the distinguished economist, Lionel Robbins, to compile a report.

Researched and written between 1961 and 1963, the Robbins Report turned out to be radical. It argued convincingly that university places 'should be available to all who were qualified by ability and attainment' and not by their parents' ability to pay. Tuition fees were to be funded by the taxpayer as were adequate maintenance grants. Robbins' arguments were economic. The Americans' performance in home and world markets was greatly enhanced by the fact that industry could rely on a steady stream of well-qualified graduates who, in turn, helped make universities into dynamic research institutions. The Education Act of 1962 put in place the necessary legislation and young Scots whose O-Grade and Higher passes were good enough began to apply for places in significantly higher numbers. These were undergraduates from all backgrounds, many of them the products of state schools, often the first members of their families to gain degrees. Although their parents had to declare their incomes – essentially be means-tested – many were willing to cooperate so that their children could 'get on' in ways that had been denied to them.

Most working-class students had attended schools which had streamed children rather than divided them by sending them to junior or senior secondaries after the results of the Control. Many were in medium-sized

Scottish towns and schools like Bell-Baxter in Cupar, The Nicolson Institute in Stornoway, Inverness Royal Academy and Berwickshire High School in Duns began to send young people to university in sizeable numbers for the first time. And the effect was cumulative. As more returned with degrees and found good jobs, more were motivated to make the same decision. To meet the demand, Strathclyde in Glasgow was elevated to the status of awarding degrees in 1964, Heriot-Watt followed in 1966, as did the new University of Stirling and, when Dundee split from St Andrews in 1967, the number of universities in Scotland had doubled in three years.

Using the elitist argument that 'more means worse', some academics argued against the changes, reflecting the deeply insular and conservative atmosphere of Scotland's universities. But Robbins's enlightened view paid dividends as a generation of young people, what he called 'a large pool of untapped talent', took advantage of the reforms. For the first time, there was social mobility in Scotland on an appreciable and consistent basis. Universities were slow to adapt and some of those faculty members who had security of tenure made little effort to teach properly, reading out lecture notes unchanged for years, and some were openly disdainful of a large intake of young people from different social backgrounds. Most academics were former public schoolboys or -girls who found themselves in contact with numbers of young people from the state sector for the first time. It made for an uneasy atmosphere and encouraged universities to entrench and remain very conservative.

However, the sensible attempts made by Robbins to mobilise Britain's greatest asset, its young people, were not to last. Maintenance grants were capped by the Conservative government in 1990 and eventually replaced by student loans. And the Labour government of 1997 to 2001 introduced the payment of tuition fees by students, initially at £1,000 a year. Now this stands at £9,000 and the universities have once again become the preserve of the middle classes and, once again, a large pool of talent is overlooked.

The Conservative Party also suddenly seemed rooted in the past. In October 1963, Harold MacMillan fell ill (although not as ill as he was first given to understand) and he decided to resign. There then followed 'the customary processes of consultation' as 'soundings' were taken amongst Tory grandees. There were at least three clear candidates: R. A. Butler, Lord Hailsham and Reginald Maudling, as well as an outsider, the Earl of Home, Alec Douglas-Home, a Scottish aristocrat who was Foreign Secretary. Four out of the five grandees who were consulted were Old Etonians, as were MacMillan and

Home, and a disappointed potential candidate, Iain Macleod, believed that there existed a conspiracy, a 'magic circle'. After all the soundings had been sounded, MacMillan advised the Queen to send for the Earl of Home. She did not appoint him Prime Minister immediately but instead asked him if he could form a government. He could and, for the first time since 1902 and the ministry of the Marquis of Salisbury, the prime minister sat in the House of Lords and not in the Commons. This was quickly remedied when Home renounced his Scottish titles and stood as a candidate in a convenient by-election in Kinross and West Perthshire. Despite the campaigning of Willie Rushton, a performer in the popular satirical TV series, *That Was The Week That Was*, Sir Alec won comfortably. But the entire episode reeked of a privileged past and, outside the town houses of Tory grandees and beyond the grouse moors, Britain and Scotland were changing.

LONNIE DONEGAN

Born in Glasgow in 1931, Lonnie and his family moved south when he was very young. But Scotland claims the 'king of skiffle', the most successful British recording artist before the phenomenon of The Beatles. With his great hits like 'Rock Island Line', Donegan brought American blues and country music to Britain but he also had success with comic numbers such as 'My Old Man's a Dustman'. He was very influential and, on his death, Mark Knopfler released a tribute, 'Donegan's Gone'.

A year before Home's by-election victory, The Beatles released 'Love Me Do', their first hit single, and they followed it, in January 1963, with 'Please Please Me'. It topped the charts and launched a cultural revolution. The Beatles became a phenomenon, the most successful band in history with 600 million records sold. But even more than that, their success and that of others spearheaded a new sense of being different, anti-establishment, as young people began to make what they saw as a clean break with the conventions of the past. In economic terms, the young also became a distinct market. Not only did they buy millions of records, they also bought clothes, especially shorter and shorter skirts and then wider and wider flares, had their hair cut differently or not cut at all and embraced new media such as pirate radio stations and alternative magazines. Against this colourful background, the government of Sir Alec Douglas-Home looked as though it came from another era – because it did.

When the general election of 1964 came, however, Home fought a robust campaign, after only a year in office. It was a remarkable achievement. He limited Labour under Harold Wilson to a majority of only 4 seats. The new government was therefore heavily dependent on its 43 Scottish MPs and the new Secretary of State for Scotland, Willie Ross, found himself in a powerful position. And he exploited it. Direct, even brusque, Ross made demands and many were included in his National Plan for Scotland, published in 1965. The whole country was designated a development area and the Scottish Development Department was founded and was well funded. New towns were brought into being at Livingston and Irvine, the new universities were given their charters and the Social Work Act for Scotland of 1967 moved to protect the less fortunate by creating a care network out of disparate elements. In a snap election called by Harold Wilson in 1966, Labour won by 96 seats and, in Scotland, the party polled 50 per cent of the vote with 46 seats.

Celebrations were, however, short-lived. In a by-election in 1967 for Glasgow Pollok, the Conservatives took the seat but, more significantly, the Scottish National Party candidate, George Leslie, came a close third behind Dick Douglas for Labour and the Conservative, Esmond Wright. No SNP candidate had stood for Pollok in the general election and, from nowhere, Leslie polled 28 per cent of the vote. This was impressive and surprising but a watershed moment was about to burst over Scotland. In the Hamilton by-election of 2 November 1967, Winnie Ewing won a sensational victory for the SNP, overturning what seemed to be an impregnable Labour majority. She was not the first SNP MP – Robert MacIntyre had held the nearby Motherwell seat for a few months in 1945. The charismatic Ewing made a tremendous and immediate impression. Her first words to the excited crowd outside the count were 'Stop the world, Scotland wants to get on.' There would be advances and reverses in the future but the victory at Hamilton showed that the SNP could be much more than a single-issue party of protest.

Meanwhile, Scotland was changing in other ways and one of the most striking was much-increased mobility. In the 1950s, Britain was the second-largest car manufacturer in the world, after the USA, and output was prodigious. By 1959, more than a million Morris Minors had been made and other popular and affordable marques such as the Ford Popular and Ford Anglia, the Standard Vanguard and the Vauxhall Velox and Cresta were also turned out in substantial numbers. The designer of the Morris Minor, Alec Issigonis, also created the British Motor Company's revolutionary Mini as a popular, reasonably-priced car and, as models began to roll off the assembly lines, it caught the public imagination immediately. Celebrities had theirs customised – the car even starred alongside Michael Caine in the film, *The Italian Job*. A consequence of the Mini's instant popularity was that it helped stimulate a growing and brisk trade in second-hand cars, the older models of the 1950s. This brought motoring within the reach of working people in Scotland and previously deserted streets in council estates were quickly lined with cars in the early 1960s. This introduced many families to their own country as they began to make day trips or go on 'touring' holidays, pulling a caravan or camping gear behind them.

Car manufacturing in Scotland was boosted by a huge new computerised plant built at Linwood, west of Glasgow, which opened in 1963. The Rootes Group of Coventry had designed the Hillman Imp as a rival for the Mini and as a second car for more affluent families. Close to a rail depot, Linwood's output could easily be distributed to dealers and showrooms all over Britain. Parts arrived from Coventry by the same means and, as production began, prospects were bright. Affordable and good-looking, available in a range of bright colours, the Imp initially sold well but it soon acquired a reputation for unreliability. Sales fell away and ultimately production ceased in 1976. But Imps are still sometimes seen on Scottish roads, highly polished and much loved.

At Bathgate in West Lothian, another vast vehicle factory was set up in the early 1960s by the British Motor Corporation (BMC). It was to produce heavy commercial vehicles, tractors, gearboxes, transmissions, diesel engines and axles. With the shrinking of shale mining and the closure of traditional industries, there was high unemployment in the area and the initiative was much welcomed. By the 1970s, the enormous factory covered 260 acres and it housed the biggest concentration of machine tools in Europe. The company became known as British Leyland, and by the end of the 1970s it was in difficulties through a mixture of poor industrial relations and pressing foreign competition. The Bathgate plant was run down and finally closed in 1986.

Scotland's traditional heavy industries were declining fast. Upper Clyde Shipbuilders (UCS) was formed in 1968 from a group of shipbuilders on the Clyde to become more competitive and achieve economies of scale. But, very quickly, in 1971, the company went into receivership after the Conservative government of Edward Heath refused a loan of £6 million. The consortium had a full order book and forecast profits for 1972. Instead of going on strike, the workforce voted to continue working and fulfil the orders. The UCS work-in was led by Jimmy Reid, Jimmy Airlie, Sammy Gilmore and Sammy Barr. All were members of the Communist Party and Reid was a gifted orator. In a speech to the workforce, he emphasised that their demeanour and image were vital. The world was watching and so 'there will be no hooliganism, there will be no vandalism, there will be no bevvying'. The work-in successfully stirred public sympathy, cash was raised and, when John Lennon of The Beatles sent a cheque for £5,000, some wag feigned amazement, 'But Lenin's deid.'

BEN CRUACHAN

Former Secretary of State for Scotland Tom Johnston never lived to see perhaps the most spectacular achievement of the North of Scotland Hydro-Electric Board in operation. Inside the beautiful Argyll mountain of Ben Cruachan there is a huge turbine hall. Work began in 1959 and the power station opened in 1965, five weeks after Johnston's death. It is a tremendous feat of engineering. In a corrie beneath the summit, a dam was built and water flowed downhill to turn the turbines and generate electricity during the day. At night, using cheap, off-peak electricity, the water was pumped back up to the reservoir so that the whole process could begin again. Around 50,000 tourists visit this technological wonder each year.

Here is the text of a speech made by Jimmy Reid two months after the work-in began when a crowd of 30,000 had gathered at Glasgow Green:

Today Scotland speaks. Not the Scotland of Edward Heath, Gordon Campbell, Sir Alec Douglas-Home – of the lairds and their lackeys. They have never represented Scotland, the real Scotland, the Scotland of the working people. No title, no rank, no establishment honour can compare with the privilege of belonging to the Scottish working class.

This is what I want to say on behalf of UCS workers to our brothers and sisters who have responded so magnificently to our call for help and solidarity. Government action has projected us into the front rank of the battle against the policies of redundancies and closure. They picked the wrong people! We stood firm and refused to retreat. We were prepared, of necessity, to stand on our own and fight alone.

But we were not alone.

Confident in our belief in our fellow workers, we told Heath and his government that this was the breaking point for the Scottish working classes . . . indeed for the Scottish people.

There were those – and they were few – who counselled against a precipitate appeal to the workers. But the shop stewards believed that time was of the very essence. That for too long the fight against redundancies and closures had been confined to the morass of high-level negotiations. Meanwhile workers whose livelihoods were at stake stood waiting outside closed doors to be told at second hand whether they might work, or whether they would sign on at the Labour Exchange. And the answer, invariably, was the dole queue.

This time the workers and the shop stewards of UCS were determined this would not happen. This time we took appropriate action and appealed over the heads of governments and institutions. We appealed to the highest authority in this land . . . to the people! Already there was pent-up anger and frustration. Hopes had been dashed. There was despair at our apparent inability to influence and determine our own destiny. There were creeping redundancies.

It needed only a spark to ignite those feelings. To give them positive expression. We suggest that the workers of UCS have themselves provided that spark. We are witnessing the eruption not of lava but of labour. The labour of working men and women.

Let Mr Heath take note. Unless he and his colleagues are prepared to meet the urgent social needs of the people then this eruption will engulf him and his government. It is incredible, but the Downing Street mentality seems to be: this government has lost confidence in the people – let's change the people.

Edward Heath, I tell you this. We are going to fight and we are not going to change. Either you will change, or we will change the government.

Mr Heath did take note and, in 1972, the government agreed to restructure the yards around two new companies – Govan Shipbuilders and Scotstoun Marine Ltd – and to inject £34 million. It was a victory and shipbuilding continued on the Clyde.

Running alongside deindustrialisation, civic society in Scotland also saw seismic change. From a peak of 1,320,000 members in 1957, the Church of Scotland found itself in spiralling decline. In a little over 50 years, its membership has fallen by 65 per cent. The Kirk supported significant ancillary institutions such as the Boys' Brigade and the Women's Guild. These allowed Scots to express their Scottishness in a non-political way in distinctive institutions that had grown and developed as part of our shared history. In 2013, the membership of the Church of Scotland stood at an all-time low of 398,389.

About 160 kilometres west of the Nigerian coast, beyond the edge of the continental shelf, where the Atlantic becomes very deep, lies a huge piece of Scotland's industrial archaeology. The *Sea Quest* semi-submersible drilling rig had been sold to Texaco and, while working in the Warri field, it suffered a blowout and tremendous fire damage. Irreparable, it was towed out into deep water and scuttled. Ten years before, the *Sea Quest* made a discovery that would change the Scottish and British economies. She discovered the huge Forties oilfield under the North Sea, about 180 kilometres east of Aberdeen. In their press release of October 1970, British Petroleum announced that the *Sea Quest* had found 'a giant oilfield' over an area of about 90 square kilometres. A year later, Shell discovered another vast field east of Shetland, what became known as the Brent oilfield. A new and unexpected industry was born. Scotland became the largest European producer, Aberdeen prospered as never before and 100,000 people, about 6 per cent of Scotland's workforce, eventually found jobs in the oil business. In 2014, the North Sea contributed £35 billion in taxation, although revenues declined sharply in 2015 as oil prices fell.

CAMERONIANS

Over a 300-year existence, the Cameronian Regiment amassed 113 battle honours and produced a remarkable number of generals. Having become the 1st Battalion The Cameronians (Scottish Rifles), they were faced with amalgamation with other regiments in the defence cuts put into action in 1967. They chose to disband. On 14 May 1968, the disbandment parade was held at the Holm at Douglas where the regiment was first mustered and it took the form of a field conventicle. A rousing sermon was given by their chaplain, the Rev. Donald MacDonald after the soldiers had marched in at the quick rifle regiment pace characteristic of the Cameronians. It was a tremendously emotional moment – a pause in Scotland's history.

In 1968, the Scottish Conservative and Unionist Party (established as an entity in 1965 when the formerly separate Unionist Party merged with the Conservative Party in England and Wales) held its conference in Perth. After defeat in the general election of 1964, Edward Heath had taken over the leadership and, at the conference, he confronted the issues raised by the SNP victory, the subsequent gains made in council elections by nationalists and Scottish constitutional issues in general. In the Declaration of Perth, he outlined his party's commitment to some form of devolution in Scotland. Ultimately, a committee, chaired by Sir Alec Douglas-Home, produced a report, 'Scotland's Government', which recommended an Assembly with 125 elected members.

At the same time, the Labour government set up the Kilbrandon Commission to look at similar issues. It appeared that momentum for change was building. When Harold Wilson called a general election in 1970, Labour had led in the opinion polls for some time, occasionally by as much as 8 per cent. But, when the votes were counted after 18 June, the Conservatives had won a workable majority of 31. In Scotland, Labour lost 2 seats but, perhaps more significantly, the SNP lost Hamilton and Winnie Ewing and gained only the Western Isles with Donald Stewart. They polled 11 per cent of the popular vote. The gains made after 1967 seemed to stall and the pressure on the two main parties to deliver some form of devolution slackened. With only 23 Scottish Conservative MPs, the Secretary of State for Scotland referred to in Jimmy Reid's speech, Gordon Campbell, was the first to hold office since 1895 without a majority of Scottish members to back him.

Politics were beginning to become the stuff of theatre. In 1971 the playwright John McGrath his wife, Elizabeth MacLennan and her brother, David MacLennan, founded the 7:84 Theatre Company. The name derived from a statistic: 7 per cent of the population of Britain was reckoned at that time to own 84 per cent of the nation's wealth. Their first and most famous production dealt with Highland history from the Clearances to the oil boom. *The Cheviot, the Stag and the Black, Black Oil* toured village halls in the north and on the islands in spring 1973, and it made a tremendous impact. Most saw the play in a TV version broadcast by BBC Scotland. Its theme was exploitation as it described how Highlanders had been cleared off the land to make way for the Cheviot sheep, then for sporting estates, and the play warned that the huge profits at stake would tempt the oil companies to despoil the land and its people further. It was an effective and impressive piece of theatre with several outstanding performances, especially from the excellent Bill Paterson.

A year before the 7:84 tour, the UCS work-in had inspired another show which starred Paterson alongside a new face, Billy Connolly. With Tom Buchan, he had written a comedy musical where instead of a shipyard, the workers had taken over a welly boot factory. Connolly played the Jimmy Reid character, the leader of the work-in, while Paterson played an American who wanted to buy the factory to make sneakers. The show's finale was a duet, 'If it Wisnae fur yer Wellies'. *The Great Northern Welly-Boot Show* premiered at the Edinburgh Festival Fringe and, in the tradition of converting unlikely venues into theatres, it was staged in the old Waverley Market. It had a glass roof and one evening it was too light to mount the show. The audience would have to wait until it grew darker for the stage lighting to have an impact and, to entertain them, Billy Connolly went on with his banjo and told stories. Bill Paterson ruefully remembered, 'The rest of the night was a wash-out; forget the rest of us trying to be funny, because we'd just seen a guy completely poleaxe an audience.'

Connolly went on to become a phenomenon, selling out large theatres everywhere, far beyond Scotland. Although his language was uncompromising, often profane, often in Scots, the stories he told were universal. At the outset of his career, he mined his Glasgow upbringing but the honesty and authenticity of his comedy appealed to everyone, regardless of whether or not they understood his accent and dialect. For many, he has become the most famous Scotsman of his generation – not because of his skill as an actor, a musician or any of the other arts but because of his Scottishness. The distinguished writer and journalist, George Rosie, was fascinated and here is part of a piece he wrote in 1975:

> In most ways Connolly is the antithesis of the Scots comic, a species usually composed of dapper little men in neat suits, with patent leather hair or a penchant for sporrans, kilts and bow ties. Connolly is big, glamorous, wears his auburn curls down to his shoulders, sports a long wizard's beard, and likes to trick himself out in gaily-coloured silks and brocades. He has all the stage arrogance of, say, the lead guitarist in a good rock and roll band. But he works hard at his stagecraft; he moves well, is an excellent banjo player, a decent guitarist, possesses a fair if unspectacular singing voice, pens a nice song, and has developed a neat way with his hecklers, 'You should get an agent, pal. Why sit there in the dark handlin' yersel''.
>
> But it is his stories that the punters pay to hear, long rambling, rude, crude, blasphemous and raw, packed with incident and character, full of the clang of the shipyards and the echoes of the back close. A running commentary

on the intricate, hot-tempered culture of the Scottish working class. Reports from a world peopled by meandering musical drunks, street-fighting heavies, slatternly mothers and snotty kids, inept teachers, no-hope scholars, whores, shipyard gaffers and wily apprentices. At its root, Connolly's work is kindly and deeply nostalgic. But it laced with a sly wit, a caustic intelligence, a sense of menace, and a cunning eye for just the right detail. It is a rich and heady mixture.

In 1971, Britain's currency changed from the ancient reckoning of farthings, halfpennies, florins and half-crowns to a new decimal system. The old imperial measurements of poles, chains, feet and inches was more slowly replaced by centimetres and kilometres as we fell into line with our European neighbours. In 1973, the link was made secure when Britain finally left her imperial past behind and embraced the future with her membership of what became the European Union. In the same year, the SNP won another extraordinary by-election when Margo MacDonald overturned a 16,000 Labour majority in Glasgow Govan. More was to come.

On 13 December 1973, the government introduced the 'Three-Day Work Order', better known as the 'Three-Day Week'. It was a drastic response to an industrial dispute. At that time, there was high inflation in Britain and wages were not keeping up with prices. The National Union of Mineworkers insisted on substantial pay rises but negotiations with Edward Heath's government broke down. In order to conserve electricity (much of it was generated by coal-fired power stations), the working week was reduced. By January 1974, the NUM membership had voted to strike and Heath called a snap election in February, using the slogan 'Who Governs Britain?'. The answer was 'Not You' and the Conservatives lost seats. Without an outright majority (and despite a huge increase in the Liberal vote that gained them only 14 seats), Labour once again took office under Harold Wilson. But in Scotland, the picture looked different. The SNP captured 7 seats, their first genuine breakthrough, and doubled their share of the popular vote. Nevertheless, Margo MacDonald lost her seat in Govan as it reverted to Labour.

When Wilson called another election for October 1974, Labour gained an overall majority but, in Scotland, the SNP took 11 seats and more than 30 per cent of the vote. As in the February election, their principal campaigning slogan was 'It's Scotland's Oil' and candidates argued that, if Scotland remained part of the United Kingdom, very little of the oil revenue would

SOMHAIRLE MACGILL-EAIN

Better known to monoglots as Sorley MacLean, he was without doubt one of the greatest Scottish poets of the 20th century. Most would accept that judgment, but they are forced to do so on trust. So few Scots (less than 50,000) have Gaelic or can even pronounce it, that it is impossible for them to appreciate fully the power and lyricism of MacLean's poems. Born at Osgaig on the island of Raasay, off the eastern coast of Skye, his first language was Gaelic, but when he began to compose poetry, he used English. All that changed when he wrote 'A' Chorra-ghritheach' ('The Heron'), his first poem is Gaelic. It was much better than his previous work and he realized that he had found his authentic voice. Much loved by his contemporaries, MacLean was famously thoughtful and meditative, taking his time to come to a view, usually talking slowly in a distinctive Hebridean drawl. At a poetry reading with his great friend, Norman MacCaig, he took the stage, opened a book of his poems and stood silent for some time, turning the pages. In a stage whisper, MacCaig said, 'I think you are meant to read aloud, Sorley.' Amongst his major works is 'Hallaig', named for a deserted village on Raasay. It takes as its theme the desolation of the Clearances. Here are its brilliant opening stanzas:

'Tha tim, am fiadh, an coille Hallaig'   'Time, the deer, is in the wood of Hallaig'

Tha buird is tairnean air an uinneig   The window is nailed and boarded
trom faca mi an Aird Iar   through which I saw the West
's tha mo ghaol aig Allt Hallaig   and my love is at the Burn of Hallaig,
'na craoibh bheithe, 's bha riamh   a birch tree, and she has always been

eadar an t-Inbhir 's Poll a' Bhainne,   between Inver and Milk Hollow,
thall 's a-bhos mu Bhaile Chuirn: here and there about Baile-chuirn:
tha i 'na beithe, 'na calltainn,   she is a birch, a hazel,
'na caorann dhirich sheang uir.   a straight, slender young rowan.

Ann an Sgreapadal mo chinnidh,   In Screapadal of my people
Far robh Tarmad 's Eachann Mor,   where Norman and Big Hector were,
Tha 'n nigheanan 's am mic 'nan coille   their daughters and their sons are a wood
A' gabhail suas ri taobh an loin   going up beside the stream.

Uaibreach a-nochd na coilich ghiuthais   Proud tonight the pine cocks
a' gairm air mullach Cnoc an Ra,   crowing on the top of Cnoc an Ra,
direach an druim ris a' ghealaich –   straight their backs in the moonlight –
chan iadsan coille mo ghraidh.   they are not the wood I love.

stay in Scotland. Aberdeen was flourishing, huge oil terminals were built at Flotta on Orkney and at Sullom Voe on Shetland and oil rig construction had created jobs onshore. UCS had found a new lease of life when the Marathon Company of Texas took it over and began building rigs on the Clyde. In addition, the Yom Kippur War between Israel and the Arab States had precipitated a huge rise in oil prices and this made the North Sea even more valuable. All of this fed the notion that Scotland could become a very wealthy country if it was not part of the Union.

Harold Wilson commissioned a White Paper on devolution but it turned out to be little more than a series of cobbled-together compromises. The issue split the Labour Party and various anomalies crept in. Even though there was to be an Assembly, the office of Secretary of State for Scotland was to retain most of its powers and the number of Westminster seats would not reduce from 71. Disagreements on devolution persuaded two west of Scotland Labour MPs, Jim Sillars and John Robertson, along with Alex Neil, the Labour Party's senior Scottish researcher, to leave and form the Scottish Labour Party. To add to the difficulties, the first Scotland Bill was talked out at Westminster and had to be redrafted. Many Labour members were unhappy and one, George Cunningham, a Scot who sat for a London constituency, introduced a condition which effectively scuppered the project. Before the Scotland Bill could be adopted, there was to be a referendum in Scotland and Cunningham proposed that the first-past-the-post system used for Westminster elections be set aside. Instead of a simple majority, 40 per cent of the electorate would have to vote Yes for the bill to become an act.

As all of this was being debated in London, a farce was being played out on the other side of the world in the summer of 1978, one that would have a profound effect. Alone of the home nations, Scotland had qualified for the football World Cup to be held in Argentina and Ally MacLeod had been appointed manager of the squad. Guided by midfielders Don Masson and Bruce Rioch and striker, Joe Jordan, the team had won the home championship of the previous season and defeated England, as well as doing well to qualify. Scotland looked to be in good form. But MacLeod made the mistake of overplaying the hype and raising expectations and, when the draw was made, the anticipation mounted even more. Scotland were in the same group as Holland, Peru and Iran. No problem. Surely they would get through to the next round and even lift the trophy. Ditties like 'Poor, poor Peru/What we're gonna do to you' became popular, and the comedian and actor Andy Cameron recorded a jaunty anthem entitled 'Ally's Tartan Army'. On the day the squad left for Argentina, they walked around Hampden Park waving to fans and waving flags and the route to Prestwick Airport was lined with cheering fans. What happened next followed a completely different script.

JOHN BYRNE

Scotland's Renaissance Man first came to notice with the production of Writer's Cramp, *a play about the fictional writer and artist, Francis Seneca McDade, that premiered on the Edinburgh Fringe in 1977 and starred Bill Paterson, Alex Norton and John Bett. A string of dramatic successes followed with* The Slab Boys *trilogy, and the TV series* Tutti Frutti, *with Robbie Coltrane, Emma Thomson and Richard Wilson, and* Your Cheatin' Heart, *starring Tilda Swinton, John Gordon Sinclair and Ken Stott. At the same time, Byrne's career as a painter burgeoned after he came to the notice of the London galleries with a series of faux-naif paintings signed Patrick. Byrne claimed they were painted by his father. Raised on the Ferguslie Park estate in Paisley, Byrne had few advantages except his immense talent – which might never have been recognised if he had not been able to attend Glasgow School of Art and have the fees paid by his local authority.*

For the first 15 minutes of the opening match against Peru, the dream looked as though it might become a reality. Joe Jordan scored first. But soon a tragedy began to unfold. Don Masson uncharacteristically missed a penalty and then the Peruvians inconsiderately scored three goals. Against Iran, clearly dazed and confused, Scotland drew 1–1. Willie Johnston failed a drugs test and was sent home. The third match looked like the last match of the tournament as Scotland faced a very good Dutch side (who would reach the final) and they needed to win by three clear goals to qualify. They played brilliantly and, in a 3–2 victory, Archie Gemmill scored one of the greatest-ever World Cup goals. But it was all too little and too late. The team arrived home in ignominy and Ally MacLeod bore the brunt of the blame, never being allowed to forget his pre-tournament claims. When the team reached Glasgow Airport, the *Daily Record* ran the headline 'Home By The Back Door'. It was all very unfair and it set a tone far beyond football.

Harold Wilson always maintained that England's success in the football World Cup in 1966 helped create an atmosphere of optimism which, in turn, persuaded voters to support Labour who marketed themselves as the party that looked to the future. The debacle of Argentina may have had an opposite effect in 1978. The date for the referendum on the Scotland Bill was set for 1 March 1979 (and there was a similar bill to be voted on in Wales) and a confused period of campaigning began. Labour refused 'to soil its hands' by joining with the SNP in running a Yes campaign while the No campaign of the Conservatives seemed self-contradictory. Lord Home announced that a No vote would actually be a vote for the creation of a better Scottish Assembly rather than none at all.

The result was a narrow victory for the Yes campaign with 32.9 per cent compared with 30.8 per cent for No. But the poll failed to meet the conditions of the Cunningham amendment and the Yes vote turned into a No even though the result translated into a clear majority of 52 per cent over 48 per cent. But Westminster deadlines quickly overtook the issues swirling around the referendum. James Callaghan had succeeded Harold Wilson as Prime Minister, and by early 1979 he was governing with Liberal support. Opinion polls showed that the Conservatives were likely to win the impending general election and matters came to a head on 28 March. The 11 SNP MPs tabled a motion of no confidence in protest at what they saw was the unfairness of the referendum result and the Liberals agreed. It was not to be the last time that issues around Scottish devolution would have a profound impact on Westminster and a general election. In any event, the leader of the opposition, Margaret Thatcher, also tabled a motion of no confidence and it trumped the others. By a single vote, it was passed and Callaghan was forced to call a general election for 3 May. In a memorable phrase, he remarked that the SNP vote against the government was 'the first time in recorded history that turkeys have been known to vote for an early Christmas'. In the ensuing poll, the SNP lost all but two of their seats and were to spend much of the following 20 years in the electoral wilderness.

Another party and its leader were to exert a determinant influence over Scottish politics and Scotland in the 1980s. Margaret Thatcher was a profoundly polarising figure, simultaneously exciting deep enmity and fervent devotion. She was not much interested in Scotland and for sound party political reasons. After her victory in the 1979 election, there were only 22 Conservative MPs in Scotland returned by a popular vote of 31 per cent. But what was striking was the contrast between her success in England and the figures in Scotland. South of the Border, the Conservatives defeated Labour by 10 clear percentage points in 1979 while, north of the Tweed, the position was exactly reversed as Labour defeated the Conservatives by 10 per cent. It was to become an apparently inexorable pattern of decline. When Mrs Thatcher won a landslide victory in 1983, her gains were all in England and Wales and her party lost a seat in Scotland and their share of the vote declined by 3 per cent. By 1987, the Conservatives were even less popular when they polled only 24 per cent of the vote and were reduced to a rump of 10 MPs. By 1997, they had lost all of their Scottish seats and the country became what opponents called a 'Tory-free zone'. Scotland and England had grown apart politically and it was this divergence that posed the most serious threat to the Union and not the activities of the SNP.

The personality of Margaret Thatcher was part of the reason for this. Her tone could be condescending and it grated on Scottish ears. Her speeches could reek of hectoring rather than be examples of persuasive oratory and there was more than a suspicion that, for her, England and Britain were synonyms. Thatcher was also unpopular in Wales, Northern Ireland and parts of the North of England. But that mattered much less than the fact that she was also a very lucky politician.

On 2 April 1982, Argentinian forces invaded sovereign British territory when they landed on the colonies of the Falkland Islands and South Georgia in the South Atlantic. For some time, there had been speculation that oil and other valuable natural resources would eventually be found in and extracted from the seas and the ice fields of Antarctica and it may be that a pre-emptive claim was being staked. The Argentinians claimed the islands as the Malvinas and the military junta that ruled in Buenos Aires calculated that the British could not or would not respond if they seized them. More than 8,000 miles to the south, the Falklands were very far distant from bases in Britain. Nevertheless, decisions were made very quickly in London and, with the backing of the House of Commons, a naval task force was sent to reclaim the crown colony. The cover of *Newsweek* magazine ran the headline 'The Empire Strikes Back'. Against some expectations, the Argentinian air force turned out to be very effective and early in the war, an Exocet missiles attack sank HMS *Sheffield* with the loss of 20 lives. Five more warships would be either sunk or very badly damaged. But when amphibious British forces were finally able to force a landing on the beaches around San Carlos Water in the west of the islands, the Falklands War began to turn and, by 14 June, the islands' capital, Stanley, had fallen and many Argentinians had been killed or taken prisoner.

It was an enormously risky and costly gamble. Britain's armed forces

452

were not equipped for such an operation – an old container ship, the *Atlantic Conveyor*, had to be converted to carry helicopters and tragically it was sunk – and the Argentinians were a spirited enemy, particularly their fighter-bomber pilots. But the mission succeeded and Margaret Thatcher's popularity soared, particularly in England. Before the Falklands War, her approval rating had been low. And victory in the South Atlantic also carried the Conservatives to a landslide victory over Michael Foot's Labour Party in 1983. Seen as a strong leader with a hefty mandate, the prime minister found herself in a very powerful position. And she was ready for another conflict.

GO ON, ALLAN!

As Allan Wells recovered from his normally slow start in the 1980 Olympic 100 metres final and began to surge for the line, his wife Margot was in the commentary box. Almost hoarse, she was roaring, 'Go on, Allan!' And he did. Although, at the time, most people thought Silvio Leonard, the Cuban, had won. The problem was that Wells had drawn the worst lane, number 8, on the outside, and Leonard was in number 1. But the photo showed that the Scot had just shaded victory as he dipped for the non-existent tape. Wells was the first Scot to win an Olympic track medal since Eric Liddell.

A staggering two million jobs in manufacturing were lost between 1979 and 1981 in the most rapid phase of deindustrialisation in Britain's history and Scotland was hit particularly hard. Headlines included the closure of the aluminium smelter at Invergordon and the Corpach Pulp Mill near Fort William and, in areas of low population, these losses had dramatic effects. All across Britain, trade unions fought the closures and, in 1981, when a list of pits thought to be uneconomic was published by the National Coal Board, a miners' strike was only narrowly averted. The Conservative government took note and began to plan for another clash. They had not forgotten Edward Heath's humiliating defeat in 1974. Resolve was stiffened by the ideological belief that trade union power was a brake on enterprise and prosperity. The National Union of Mineworkers was the most powerful and the most militant union – and it needed to be weakened and brought under control. Coal was stockpiled, several key power stations were converted to become oil-fired and road hauliers were recruited in case the railway workers struck in support of the miners. Crucially, Mrs Thatcher appointed Ian MacGregor to run the National Coal Board. He had presided over British Steel during a period when they shed half of their staff and he was seen as ruthless. The stage was set.

SUNNY PONTIFF

When the great showman John Paul II made the first-ever papal visit to Scotland in June 1982, he might have been forgiven for wondering if his advisors had mistaken the itinerary. The sun split the sky as a vast crowd of 250,000 gathered in Bellahouston Park in Glasgow to hear him deliver a sermon. Despite the sunburn and dehydration, it was a magical occasion as he began, 'It was Andrew, the heavenly patron of your beloved Scotland, who introduced Peter to Jesus . . . today we are bound to one another by a supernatural brotherhood stronger than that of blood.' Watching on a giant screen, the huge congregation was rapturous as they sang to the Pope and cheered so much that he was forced to stop many times. He beamed and waved at the crowd as he did so. The whole event seemed like a joyful affirmation, a return, a rapprochement more than 400 years after the Reformation.

On 6 March 1984, the National Coal Board announced the closure of 20 mines with the loss of 20,000 jobs. It included Polmaise near the village of Fallin in Stirlingshire. The President of the National Union of Mineworkers, Arthur Scargill, had said in 1983 that 'the policies of this government are clear – to destroy the coal industry and the NUM'. And far from closing only 20 pits, Scargill claimed that that the long-term plan was to close 70. The Conservative government and the NCB flatly denied this but the release of Cabinet Papers in 2013 revealed that it was true. In fact, it was the NCB's intention to close 75 pits. On 12 March 1984, Scargill called for strike action in all of Britain's coalfields.

What then began to unfold more resembled a class war than an industrial dispute. Mrs Thatcher called the miners 'the enemy within' and there were violent clashes. With the police acting as a national rather than a regional body, huge numbers of officers were sent to picket lines and pits. Numbers were bolstered by detachments from the Metropolitan Police who had no knowledge of and no experience of policing mining districts. Most notorious was the clash in South Yorkshire that became known as 'the Battle of Orgreave'. On 18 June, mounted police charged into crowds of pickets with their truncheons drawn and there were many casualties and arrests. Observers believed that the police ran out of control and many were injured by truncheon blows and Arthur Scargill himself was attacked. In 1987, South Yorkshire Police paid £425,000 to pickets in compensation and £100,000 for legal costs but no officers were ever disciplined.

Arthur Scargill's nagging difficulty was that he had not called for a national strike ballot and, in several coalfields, particularly in Nottinghamshire, pits were still working. In Scotland, some miners still reported for work at Polkemmet, Killoch and Barony, and there was violence at Bilston Glen in Midlothian. Miners from the Polmaise pit attempted to prevent men from working, and at Ravenscraig steelworks and Hunterston power station, pickets failed to prevent coal stocks from being moved. Scargill's other difficulty was that he had called a strike at the beginning of the summer when demand for fuel was diminishing.

By September 1984, miners had been on strike for 6 months and, with no income of any sort, they and their families were suffering. The numbers going back to work were building and, by January 1985, it was a steady flow of men known as 'the hunger scabs'. The NUM had little option but to call off the strike and it ended formally on 3 March. Nothing had been achieved except violence and privation and the near-fatal humbling of the most powerful trade union in Britain. The whole episode was nothing less than a tragedy and the Conservative government moved ahead with its plans for widespread pit closures and what became, as Scargill predicted, the destruction of not only an industry but also a way of life. The strike changed the industrial and social landscape and recast the relationship of trade unions with governments. It was the end of an era in many senses. In 2013, Britain used 60 million tons of coal and 50 million were imported. Impartial calculations reckon that Britain's untapped coal reserves remain very substantial.

While the menu of policies and attitudes – the privatisation of publically owned utilities, low taxation and political patriotism – that became known as 'Thatcherism' was not much admired in Scotland, one measure was very popular. In 1980, the Tenants' Right Act gave council house tenants the right to buy their homes on very favourable terms and many in Scotland did. It allowed those who had been tenants for three years to buy a house at a 33 per cent discount and a flat at a 44 per cent discount. Tenants of over 20 years standing got a 50 per cent discount. During the 1980s, home ownership rose from 55 per cent to 67 per cent. By the time the scheme was wound up in 2013, 455,000 Scots had bought their council houses. But, such was the depletion of housing stock, there now exists an acute shortage.

On 21 May 1988, Mrs Thatcher was invited to address the General Assembly of the Church of Scotland and her remarkable speech became known as 'the Sermon on the Mound'. As ministers and elders sat in silence, she attempted a theological justification for her policies. '"If a man will not work, he shall not eat," said St Paul' and there was more in that vein. Then she moved away from biblical quotes to her own beliefs. 'It is not the creation of wealth that is wrong but the love of money for its own sake. The spiritual dimension comes in deciding what one does with the wealth.' Several comments were more or less direct criticisms of what she saw as the Kirk's meddling in politics: 'We parliamentarians can legislate for the rule of law. You, the Church, can teach the life of faith.' Beyond the turrets of the Assembly Hall on the Mound, there were two-and-a-half million people without jobs and much of the industrial landscape of Scotland lay in ruins. It was a place where philosophical debates about what one should do with one's wealth were not often heard.

It happened that the Moderator of the General Assembly in 1988 was the Rev. Professor James A. Whyte. He had been a parish minister and Principal of St Mary's College, the divinity faculty of the University of St Andrews. When Mrs Thatcher at last finished her speech and turned to leave the dais, Professor Whyte came down from his pulpit to greet her. He was carrying two Church of Scotland pamphlets on poverty and housing. He hoped that she would find them of interest and remarked, 'Prime Minister, I do not think that you have ever been in the presence of so many people who pray for you regularly.'

A significant reaction to a decade of confrontation with the successive governments of Mrs Thatcher was the publication of *A Claim of Right for Scotland*. Brief, but carefully crafted by the Campaign for a Scottish Assembly, it harked back to history in its title for it is derived from the Claim of Right Act of 1689, which was designed as a brake on the power of the monarchy. Published in 1989, here is the text:

> We, gathered as the Scottish Constitutional Convention, do hereby acknowledge the sovereign right of the Scottish people to determine the form of Government best suited to their needs, and do hereby declare and pledge that in all our actions and deliberations their interests shall be paramount.
>
> We further declare and pledge that our actions and deliberations shall be directed to the following ends:

To agree a scheme for an Assembly or Parliament for Scotland;

To mobilise Scottish opinion and ensure the approval of the Scottish people for that scheme; and

To assert the right of the Scottish people to secure implementation of that scheme.

LOCKERBIE

On 21 December 1988, a flight from London to New York began its turn westwards over the town of Lockerbie and a bomb in its hold blew the aeroplane apart. All aboard were killed, 259 crew and passengers. And, as wreckage plunged through the little town, a further 11 people died. On one farm, between 50 and 60 bodies were found, most of them naked as the decompression tore off their clothes. The farmer, Jim Wilson, said, 'You would not know what age they were. They were battered beyond recognition. Some of them hit the earth with such force that you could almost bury them in the indentations they made in the ground.' Scotland and the world were dazed at such savagery and, as television pictures revealed the horror, Canon Kenyon Wright led the nation in prayer after that night's news.

It was signed by all of Scotland's Labour and Liberal MPs, with the exception of Tam Dalyell, ignored by the Conservative government and thought insufficiently radical by the SNP. But *A Claim of Right* was influential, appealed across society and gave rise to the Scottish Constitutional Convention. Momentum was building for what became known not as Home Rule but as devolution, a term not freighted with history and more readily acceptable to potential dissenters in the Labour Party. But events at Westminster and their impact in Scotland quickly moved centre stage.

The Adam Smith Institute was founded by three former students at St Andrews University. Madsen Pirie and the brothers Eamonn and Stuart Butler had developed their neo-conservative thinking both there and in the USA. They were later joined by another St Andrews alumnus, Douglas Mason, and, during the governments of Margaret Thatcher, their ideas on privatisation in particular became very influential. It seemed that the bolder and more radical their thinking, the more likely it was to be accepted as the Prime Minister began to act independently of her Cabinet colleagues. 'We propose things which people regard as being on the edge of lunacy. The next thing you know, they're on the edge of policy,' remarked Madsen Pirie.

Successive Conservative Secretaries of State for Scotland, George Younger and Malcolm Rifkind, had difficulty in containing local authority expenditure, especially when limits were imposed from Westminster. Douglas Mason offered a solution when he published a paper recommending a flat-rate per capita tax to replace the domestic rates. It could make local authorities more accountable to their electorate and it had the virtue of being simple and unambiguous. A duke would pay the same as a dustman. The government introduced the Community Charge in Scotland in 1989, a year before the rest of the United Kingdom, because there was a rates revaluation pending. What was quickly dubbed 'the Poll Tax' was immediately unpopular and non-payment spread across all regions. The Conservative government had calculated that local authorities would have to deal with resistance and difficulties of implementation but, instead, blame was laid squarely on the doorstep of 10 Downing Street. When it was introduced in 1990, the blatant unfairness of the Poll Tax induced unheard of rioting in the south-east of England as suburbia rebelled at what was seen as an example of extreme Thatcherism. This and her increasingly inflexible attitude to the European Union brought about the downfall of a prime minister who had won three elections as a ruthless palace coup removed her because senior Conservatives calculated that she could not win a fourth.

Margaret Thatcher did bestow one unlikely benefit on Scotland. On 18 December 1989, the Secretary of State for Scotland, Malcolm Rifkind, had a press conference hurriedly convened at St Andrew's House in Edinburgh. To the surprise of many, Rifkind announced a fund of £8 million to be spent on Gaelic language television. The ITV franchises in Scotland were up for renewal and successful applicants in the STV and Grampian regions would be required to broadcast an extra 200 hours a year of Gaelic programmes, some of them to be scheduled in peak time. The BBC were not initially involved. The figure granted was said to have been the result of a simple piece of arithmetic: £50 million was given to Welsh language TV because there were approximately 500,000 speakers, and the 80,000 Gaelic speakers, at that time, should therefore be allocated £8 million. The origins of this initiative are unclear – it possibly sprang from the interests of George Younger, Rifkind's predecessor at the Scottish Office, and was certainly encouraged by Gaelic language lobbyists. In any event, it was a tremendous success as Gaelic broke away from the dreary sterilities of the National Mod and innovative (subtitled) programmes attracted substantial audiences. They very quickly showed that the language and the culture it described could escape the clutches of quaint and become a thriving part of late 20th-century Scotland.

This welcome development was much buttressed by a musical phenomenon. In May 1990, Scottish Television broadcast *Runrig: City of Lights*, an hour-long film about a Gaelic-speaking rock band from Skye. It was scheduled in peak time at 9 p.m. and was watched by a million Scots, an unprecedented audience for a programme about Gaelic culture. With songs written in Gaelic and English by the brothers Rory and Calum Macdonald, and sung by Donnie Munro, Runrig also brought Gaelic music into the late 20th century. And, in Munro's remarkable voice, they also told snatches of Highlands and Islands history in an impressionistic and dramatic way. One of their most famous anthems concerns the Clearances and the fact that, on Skye, there did exist a 'Dance Called America':

> The landlords came
> The peasant trials
> To the sacrifice of men
> Through the past and that quite darkly
> The presence once again
> In the name of capital
> Establishment
> Improvers, it's a name
> The hidden truths
> The hidden lies
> That once nailed you
> To the pain
>
> They did a dance
> Called America
> They danced it 'round
> And waited at the turns
> For America
> They danced their ladies 'round

The revival of Gaelic can be seen as more apparent than real. While it played to the times by adding a dimension to a peculiarly Scottish sense of self that could not be more different from England, the language continues to decline with the numbers of speakers now far fewer than 80,000. But the language will not be allowed now to die even though it is unlikely ever to achieve the currency of Welsh. Its retreat has gone too far for many people to live their lives in Gaelic, using it as a first language. But it will survive as an accomplishment as much as a way of life.

The unexpected general election victory of Margaret Thatcher's successor, John Major, in April 1992 did little more than slow Conservative decline in Scotland when two seats were gained. Their share of the popular vote rose by only 1 per cent. Jim Sillars had won Govan for the SNP in a by-election in 1988 but history repeated itself when, like his wife, Margo MacDonald, he lost the seat in 1992. And the election saw the eventual resignation of Neil Kinnock, Labour's reforming leader who had dragged the party back to electoral credibility after the internal bickering of the 1980s, and the formation of the breakaway Social Democratic Party. He was replaced by John Smith, the Shadow Chancellor, a Scots advocate who was MP for Monklands East. As a minister in James Callaghan's government, he had skilfully piloted the Scotland Bill through parliament prior to the referendum of 1979. Smith was an excellent speaker, setting out arguments with lawyerly clarity, and he also had an excellent sense of fun. When he focussed on the difficulties that his opposite number, Chancellor Nigel Lawson, had with Mrs Thatcher's economic advisor, Alan Walters, he began his speech in the House of Commons by singing the theme tune to *Neighbours*, an Australian TV soap that was popular at the time.

By early 1994, Labour had gained a consistent lead in the opinion polls, sometimes of more than 20 per cent, and, with a shadow cabinet that included four other powerful Scottish figures, Gordon Brown, Robin Cook, Donald Dewar and George Robertson, it seemed that the party was on course to win the next general election. But, tragically, John Smith died suddenly of a massive heart attack on the morning of 12 May 1994. He was only 55 years old.

There followed an intense period of jockeying between the two leading candidates – Gordon Brown and Tony Blair – to take over the leadership. As Shadow Chancellor, Brown had long been seen as a preferred successor (Smith had already suffered a severe heart attack before 1994) and, while he and Blair had been close as they worked to modernise the Labour Party, Blair had been thought of as the junior partner. Some of the early discussions took place in Scotland, before and after the memorial service for John Smith at

Cluny Parish Church in Edinburgh. When *The Herald* published an article on 26 May claiming that Gordon Brown did not have the support of the majority of Scotland's 48 Labour MPs, opinion seemed to shift towards Blair. The former Labour Chancellor Denis Healey had endorsed him in a radio interview and there was also a sense that another leader who was not English might not be best for the party's prospects. However all that may be, the upshot was that Gordon Brown agreed to stand aside and Blair was elected leader of the Labour Party on 21 July 1994.

The year 1996 was an extraordinary one in Scotland – a time of arrivals and departures, of scientific advance and tragic darkness, and of the beginnings of a different political future. On 23 January, the poet Norman MacCaig died. His influence was immense as he reached across several generations of writers and readers in the course of a long and continuously productive life. Often giving public readings and being an accomplished performer with a ready sense of humour (he was once giving a reading with Sorley Maclean, the great Gaelic poet, and, as the latter stood on stage looking at his text for what seemed like a long time, MacCaig stage-whispered, 'I think you are meant to read aloud, Sorley'), he brought poetry and his sublime poetic understanding of Scotland to many. Friendly with Hugh MacDiarmid, Robert Garioch and Douglas Dunn, he also encouraged younger talents like Tom Pow and Andrew Greig. MacCaig's poetic voice was singular, fresh and clear and somehow redolent of the big skies, the wide vistas and the rich detail of Highland landscapes. The son of a Gaelic-speaking mother from Scalpay, his clarity and brevity may have come from her, since English was a second language. Most of his poems are short – when asked how long they took to compose, the reply was 'Two fags' – rarely more than two or three verses, but inside them entire landscapes and the lives lived on them can be glimpsed. The last verse of 'Praise of a Man' might also be an elegy for Norman MacCaig and an older Scotland that died with him.

> The beneficent lights dim
> but don't vanish.
> The razory edges
> dull, but still cut.
> He's gone:
> but you can see
> his tracks still, in the snow of the world.

A month after MacCaig's funeral, a very different Scotland exploded on to cinema screens. Irvine Welsh's novel, *Trainspotting*, had been published three years before but the film reached an even bigger audience. It told the tale of a group of heroin addicts from a depressed area of Edinburgh. Its portrayal of the bizarre, violent world of a drugs culture largely hidden from most Scots was very shocking. But its raw, profane dialogue and occasionally surreal storyline did include the occasional political *aperçu*. Here are the thoughts of the principal character, Mark Renton, played by Ewan McGregor, on the relationship between Scotland and England: 'It's nae good blaming it oan the English for colonising us. Ah don't hate the English. They're just wankers. We are colonised by wankers. We can't even pick a decent, vibrant, healthy culture to be colonised by. No. We're ruled by effete arseholes. What does that make us? . . . The most wretched, servile, miserable, pathetic trash that was ever shat intae creation.'

As often, fact outdid fiction and, on 13 March, a horrific, utterly tragic, evil incident took place. At 9.30 a.m., Thomas Hamilton, a 43-year-old former Scout leader, parked his van near a telegraph pole in the car park of Dunblane Primary School and, with a pair of pliers, cut the cables. Then, carrying four handguns, he entered the school by a door near the gymnasium. When confronted by Eileen Harrild, the PE teacher in charge of the primary one class, Hamilton began shooting randomly. He killed Gwen Mayor, the teacher of the P1 class as she tried to protect the children. Having wounded several, he began to shoot them at point blank range. Fifteen five-year-olds and a six-year-old died. He again began to fire randomly and stood at a fire exit from the gym to shoot at a nearby mobile classroom. Hamilton then came back into the gymnasium and shot himself. The whole incident took less than five minutes.

The journalist and columnist Fordyce Maxwell had lost his daughter, Susan, 14 years before. She was abducted and murdered by Robert Black. Better than almost anyone, Maxwell understood the pain of loss and, with all his skill, he writes heartbreakingly about the events in Dunblane:

Some parents will avoid the school. Others will haunt it. They live in two worlds – one, where they know a child is dead, the second where they still expect her to come of the school gate with a smile. Go to the school gate often enough and one day, she'll be there.

At home the crying and arguments and screaming fits will get worse. Other children in the family will be told that they are lucky to be alive, followed by instant remorse. The most difficult thing to do will be to bring them up normally, trying not to spend too much on them, trying not to panic if they are five minutes late. Parents not blaming each other, but trying to destroy themselves by taking responsibility for a horror for which no one is to blame except the man who carried it out.

Already commentators are talking about 'coming to terms' with what happened. My wife Liz said yesterday: 'If I hear coming to terms with one more time I'll scream. You never, ever come to terms with it.' All you do for the rest of your life is keep on keeping on, one of the few things I can write with certainty since our daughter, Susie, was abducted and murdered at the age of 11. She would have been 25 this month.

I write because I must. For the Dunblane parents, facing the future will be worse than they now think possible. But if they accept that, they can begin to try to live with it. There is naught for anyone's comfort in that warning, because there is no comfort to be had. Strictly speaking for the bereaved it doesn't matter what Thomas Hamilton was, or how he became like that, any more than it matters to us how Susie's murderer, Robert Black, became the twisted pervert he is.

What matters is that a child is dead and that parents will never come to terms with it, only at best learn to keep going in a world where even those of us who think we're normal live on two planes – the cheerful, hard-working outward one, and the inner one where the pain is.

Scotland and the world was shocked at this inexplicable act. Handguns were quickly banned and school security tightened but it is said that it will probably take a long time for the beautiful town of Dunblane to cease to be a byword for senseless slaughter.

The creation of life, and not the taking of it, was a headline everywhere in July. Dolly became the world's most famous sheep. She was the first mammal to be cloned. At the Roslin Institute near Edinburgh, Ian Wilmut, Keith Campbell and their colleagues succeeded in creating Dolly from an adult somatic cell using the process of nuclear transfer. The donor cell was taken from a mammary gland and the birth of the sheep proved that a cell taken from a specific part of the body could be used to create a complete individual. When Ian Wilmut was asked where the name of Dolly came from, he offered a non-PC reply, 'Dolly is derived from a mammary gland cell and we couldn't think of a more impressive pair of glands than Dolly Parton's.' Having lived her whole life at the Roslin Institute and given birth to six lambs, Dolly died in 2003. Since she was born, many other large animals, such as bulls and horses, have been successfully cloned. Once more in her history, Scotland was at the forefront of science and technology.

As John Major's government and his fractious party stumbled towards the end of their period of office and Labour rode high in the opinion polls, details of constitutional change for Scotland began to emerge. In the phrases used by John Smith, devolution was 'unfinished business' and the 'settled will of the Scottish people'. Not only was a Scottish Parliament, not an Assembly, to be one of the Labour manifesto pledges, it was also to be the subject of a referendum. Two questions would be asked of the Scottish people: did they agree that there should be a parliament and did they agree that it should have tax-varying powers? There was disappointment at what appeared to be an unnecessary vote but it was promised that, if Labour won the general election, the referendum would be held soon after the poll.

At Coldstream, an elegant bridge spans the Tweed to link England with Scotland and, on the morning of 15 November, a green army Land Rover, flanked by a platoon of soldiers and followed by two white vans, crossed it very slowly. It was raining but crowds waited on the Scottish side. Invisible inside the Land Rover was the Stone of Scone, the Stone of Destiny, returning to Scotland after a 700-year absence. Waiting to welcome it home in Coldstream, looking uncomfortable in a kilt, was Secretary of State for Scotland Michael Forsyth. It was a slightly farcical political stunt compounded by the disappointing decision to house the Stone in Edinburgh Castle and not to place it on the top of the Hill of Faith at Scone.

The trudge across the bridge availed the Conservatives little. In the 1997 general election, Michael Forsyth lost his Stirling seat and his party was completely wiped out, with all 11 of their previously held seats falling to Labour, the Liberal Democrats or the SNP. The Conservatives also lost all of their Welsh MPs. Nationally it was a Labour landslide with their largest-ever majority, of 179. After 18 years in power, the Conservatives suffered their worst result since 1906 with only 165 MPs. The new government moved quickly to enable another parliamentary election – for a Scottish Parliament.

On 11 September 1997, the devolution referendum asked its two questions. The 'Yes to Both' campaign was jointly supported by Labour, the Liberal Democrats, the SNP and the Scottish Greens. The Conservatives argued for 'No to Both' questions. The result was overwhelming: 74.9 per cent agreed that there should be a Scottish Parliament and 63.4 per cent agreed that it should have tax-varying powers. Only the canny souls of Dumfries and Galloway and Orkney voted No to the second question. The resulting Scotland Act, with its ringing first sentence, 'There shall be a Scottish Parliament', was enacted on 17 November 1998.

Its clauses set out the legislative competence of the new parliament, how many members it should have and how they should be elected. A single chamber was preferred to the Westminster model of Lords and Commons and 129 MSPs were to be elected in two ways for fixed four-year terms (although the 2011 parliament will sit for five years to avoid a clash with a UK general election, a difficulty no one anticipated in 1998). The traditional first-past-the-post system was to be used in 73 constituencies and a further 56 MSPs elected by a form of proportional representation. Seven so-called list MSPs would come from 8 electoral regions that broadly followed the boundaries for elections to the European Parliament. The other 73 MSPs shared the same boundaries as the Westminster parliament constituencies as they then were.

The PR system was new and would be used for the first time in UK elections. It attempted to deal with the inequity of parties who attracted a significant percentage of the popular vote but won few or even no seats through the first-past-the-post system. That left many people unrepresented. Parties were to nominate lists of candidates and, in each of the eight electoral regions, the total vote for each party was to be counted. The ballot papers carried two invitations to vote, one for a constituency member and the other for a party. This allowed a split vote. Using the D'Hondt method (designed by a Belgian mathematician in 1878 and used in about 40 countries across the world), the number of party votes cast in the second part of the ballot paper is divided by one plus the number of constituency seats won by each party in that electoral region. So, if a party did well in the constituencies, it did less well in the list regions. In the first Scottish parliamentary elections, ironies abounded. The Conservatives won no constituencies but were awarded 18 seats by the D'Hondt method. They had campaigned vigorously against the Scottish Parliament and the PR system they particularly disliked rescued them from political oblivion. The combination of the first-past-the-post and PR was designed to avoid overall majorities and encourage coalition.

The powers of the parliament were defined by exception. The list of 'reserved matters' which can only be dealt with by the UK parliament is long and detailed. More generally, it includes defence, international relations and import and export control. Much more is included under 11 heads and these are Home Affairs, Trade and Industry, Energy, Transport, Social Security,

Regulations of the Professions, Employment, Health and Medicines, Media and Culture and, of course, Miscellaneous. What the Scottish Parliament does oversee is nevertheless very wide-ranging: health and social work, education, local government and housing, justice and policing, agriculture, forestry and fisheries, the environment, tourism, sport and heritage, economic development and internal transport. Since 1998, these lists have been modified several times but the basic framework has remained in place.

Two years after their landslide victory in the UK general election, Labour still rode in high in the opinion polls and, in the first general election for the Scottish Parliament held on 6 May 1999, they won 56 seats, 53 of them in the constituencies. Most support came from the traditional heartlands of central Scotland. A senior Labour politician, George Robertson, had remarked in 1995 that 'devolution will kill nationalism stone dead' but, in fact, the SNP polled well in 1999, winning 35 seats to become the second most popular party by some distance and the opposition to a Labour–Liberal coalition led by Donald Dewar as first minister.

By that time, a competition to design the new building to house the parliament had been won by the Spanish architect, Enric Miralles. His concept for the preferred site at the foot of the Royal Mile was bold and flowing. 'We don't want to forget that the Scottish Parliament will be in Edinburgh, but will belong to Scotland, to the Scottish land. The Parliament should be able to reflect the land it represents. The building should arise from the sloping base of Arthur's Seat and arrive into the city almost surging out of the rock', Miralles declared.

The debating chamber is a triumph, a beautifully handled interior whose hemispherical shape was designed to avoid the confrontations of Westminster and to allow the public in the galleries above to be close to proceedings. But very soon, the project ran into tremendous difficulties. In 1997, the cost was projected to sit somewhere between £10 and £40 million but these numbers proved wildly inaccurate. By 2001, costs had spiralled to £245 million and, by completion, the bill was £414 million. It was a scandalous episode of financial mismanagement on a spectacular scale and it badly damaged perceptions of the new parliament unnecessarily.

Meanwhile, the newly elected MSPs were to use the Assembly Halls of the Church of Scotland on the Mound in Edinburgh and, with a little refurbishment, they were more than adequate. The new legislature met for the first time on 12 May 1999 and the author and journalist Ian Bell was there:

David Steel could not resist it. Five years to the day since the death of John Smith, nobody thought that he should. It was, said Sir David, the Presiding Officer of Scotland's first democratic parliament, the start of a new song. That and more.

Dr Winifred Ewing, sixty-nine, mother of the house, had already reminded us of what was being done. In the capital's grey Assembly Hall, just after 9.30 a.m., to a half-empty chamber, she uttered the simple, astonishing truth: 'The Scottish Parliament, adjourned on the 25th day of March, 1707, is hereby reconvened.'

History is memory. This moment was memory reclaimed, a right restated, a truth reaffirmed. The nation of Scotland, with all its thrawn suspicions, numberless confusions, apathy, clumsy rivalries and disparate hopes, had remembered.

We began again on a May morning in Edinburgh, high on the Mound, with thirty-five white roses, a clenched fist, 129 members sworn in with a measure of honest dissent, a Labour Party honouring John Smith's promise and a strange kind of ease. This, said the language of ritual, is what we do, ours by right, and this is how we do it. The fact was woven in neat, white letters into the very uniform of the hall's polite, patient staff: 'Scottish Parliament'.

But then, suddenly, many strands came together. The clenched fist was Tommy Sheridan's, affirming on behalf of the Scottish Socialist Party a long tradition of a democratic socialist republic. The white roses were on the lapels of the Scottish National Party. The power was with Donald Dewar's Labour, the novelty with Britain's first Green parliamentarian, the democratic question with the Liberal Democrats, the new argument with the new Scottish Tories. Whatever else home rule may come to mean, it has already given articulacy to Scotland's diversity. We have not been here, or anywhere like it, before.

Once the celebrations were over and the parliament got down to business, other journalists were distinctly unimpressed. In *New Statesman Scotland*, the popular columnist Tom Brown wrote, 'The verdict on the first batch of Scottish parliamentarians is already in: their calibre is sub-standard and the way they conduct their business is woeful. They have been written of as self-serving and more concerned with their own salary-expenses-and-holidays package than with setting Scotland to rights. Words such as "duds", "numpties", "sweetie-wives" and "skivers" have appeared in print.'

The difficulty for Brown and other commentators was that, the leadership of the parties apart, the new MSPs were seen as very much of the second or third rank, men and women dwarfed by the historic stage and the spotlights in which they found themselves. According to Brown, the new parliament was worthy of better: 'The make-up of the parliament shows that it does not represent the community. Fourteen MSPs have been full-time apparatchiks, researchers, MPs' gophers and bag-carriers and have never had a proper job. They seem to have the most to say and are the poorest at saying it. Then there are 33 former councillors, some of whom have brought with them the standard of oratory at Inversnecky Toon Cooncil.'

A giant in all senses, Donald Dewar had been appointed as the first First Minister of Scotland in May 1999. A month later, he set out an ambitious legislative programme – an Education Bill designed to raise standards, a bill to abolish feudal tenure, another to create National Parks and a problematic bill to allow access to the countryside. The 'right to roam act', as it became known, may have introduced urban dwellers to the countryside but it did not demand much of a sense of responsibility in those who left gates open, left litter and broken glass lying around and felt they had an absolute right to walk through gardens around farmhouses and cottages. Despite the lumpen numpties and sweetie wives behind and beside Dewar, his personal prestige appeared to bring democracy and their new parliament closer to Scots. In contrast to the scorn that was heaped on novice MSPs, newspapers attached the title of Father of the Nation to Donald Dewar – not something he will have enjoyed. But it turned out to be a brief moment.

In April 2000, Donald Dewar discovered that he had heart problems. Surgery for a leaking valve was carried out and, after a three-month break, he seemed recovered, if not restored to his normal vigour. But on 10 October, he tripped and fell on the steps outside Bute House, the First Minister's residence in Charlotte Square. Two hours later, he was admitted to the Western General Hospital, having suffered a brain haemorrhage. By midnight, Donald Dewar was dead, and Scotland, shocked and deeply saddened, mourned a great loss. At his funeral in Glasgow Cathedral, the Labour Chancellor, Gordon Brown, said, 'When people say what was special about Donald was his decency, they tell less than half the story. What was special was how constantly and tirelessly he pursued the logic of his decency and worked for a just and more equal society. Everyone knew someone Donald had helped.'

The journalist and broadcaster Ruth Wishart was one of a group of close friends who regularly despaired of Dewar's complete lack of interest in his appearance and clothes. His holiday wardrobe was a pair of old plimsolls instead of shoes and he owned only one ancient overcoat. When Dewar once appeared wearing a tie with YSL on it, there was amazement that he had bought something designed by Yves St Laurent. But the tie turned out to have been a gift from Yarrow Shipbuilders Limited. In the form of a well-observed sculpture of the man, a monument was erected to Donald Dewar at the top of Glasgow's Buchanan Street. The sculptor made sure the jacket was appropriately creased.

From February to late August 2001, the landscape of southern Scotland looked apocalyptic, a place of fire, smoke and ruin. Huge pyres blazed and a sickly sweet smoke blew over farms and villages. At Heddon-on-the-Wall, west of Newcastle, a farmer had fed his pigs with untreated waste and the animals developed foot-and-mouth disease. Because of the movement of livestock all over Britain and its processing at large abattoirs, it spread very quickly. At its height, in late March, 50 new cases were being reported every day. The sale of British pigs, sheep and cattle was suspended and huge tracts of northern England and southern Scotland were effectively shut down. The cure was simple, brutal and medieval. At and around infected farms, all animals were to be killed and burned. Quantities were vast with 80–90,000 slaughtered each week for two months. When the culling teams arrived at farms, the air was rent with the screams and bellows of animals that knew what was coming. Fires smouldered for days, the blackened legs of cattle clearly visible, the stench almost unbearable. There was a total ban on moving animals and, at the entrance to thousands of farms, disinfecting trays were laid down.

The cost of the outbreak was staggering, climbing to approximately £8 billion in lost revenues not only from farming and the meat trade but also tourism. Further expenditure was incurred with the involvement of the army. In Scotland, the cost to agriculture was reckoned to be £231 million and the loss in tourism even greater. In the Borders, common ridings were cancelled, the sporting calendar (especially equestrian events) was shredded and people whose passions were walking, birdwatching, rock-climbing or simply enjoying a day in the fresh air of the countryside were denied access to much of southern Scotland. And the great sadness of seeing herds and flocks they had built up with careful husbandry for generations being heaped up for burning drove some farmers to retire and much was lost. It seemed that a biblical plague had gripped the land.

The foot-and-mouth outbreak also forced the reorganisation of the political calendar. The Labour government had decided to hold a general election in 2001 on the same day as local elections and these had to be postponed. It was feared that farm workers might inadvertently spread the disease as people converged on polling places from both town and country. The elections, both local and general, were held on 7 June and the result was what became known as the 'quiet landslide' as Labour maintained its huge majority. The Conservatives gained a face-saving seat in Scotland as they defeated the SNP in Galloway and Upper Nithsdale and, under their new and dynamic leader, Charles Kennedy, the Liberal Democrats won 54 seats across Britain. This would be the last time Scotland would send 72 MPs to Westminster. Before the general election of 2005, their number would be reduced to 59.

This was, in part, a reaction to the existence of a Scottish parliament whose number of MSPs remained the same. The 2003, Scottish election showed that the system designed in the run-up to 1999 could produce a more representative result. Both Labour and SNP saw a decline in their vote and the numbers of seats won, although Labour remained the largest party and Jack McConnell was appointed first minister. But the Scottish Green Party won 7 seats by not standing in the constituencies and asking only for support in the list vote. This appears to have encouraged split voting on a significant scale. Under the leadership of their sole MSP from the 1999 parliament, Tommy Sheridan, the Scottish Socialist Party gained 6 list MSPs and 4 independents were also elected. Two were charismatic politicians who had left their parties but still retained support amongst voters – Margo MacDonald and Dennis Canavan.

The way in which politics – and, indeed, all issues of importance – was being discussed in Scotland was changing rapidly. It had long been a matter of some smugness that Scotland was a nation of avid newspaper readers, possibly the highest per capita in the world, certainly more than in England. D C Thomson's *Sunday Post* had long enjoyed a remarkable circulation, its mix of couthiness, comprehensive sports coverage and famous cartoons had been read by a staggering 60 per cent of the population over their bacon and eggs. Tabloid circulation was also high with the *Daily Record* being the most widely read and, while the so-called broadsheets had aspired to national coverage, in reality *The Herald* was seen as a Glasgow and west of Scotland paper, *The Scotsman* for Edinburgh and the south-east of Scotland, *The Courier* served Tayside and Dundee while *The Press and Journal* was most read in Aberdeen and the north-east.

The newspaper sector in Scotland looked settled, even profitable. In 2004,

Newsquest, the British arm of American publishers Gannett bought *The Herald*, the *Sunday Herald* and the Glasgow *Evening Times* from Scottish Media Group for £216 million and, a year later, Johnston Press bought *The Scotsman*, *Scotland on Sunday* and the *Edinburgh Evening News* from the Barclay Brothers for £160 million. Ten years before, the Barclays had paid only £80 million. But since then, in a very short time, the circulations of all Scottish newspapers have declined so sharply that some, especially younger people, see the purchase of a paper as a luxury item, not really necessary. The reason for this is the proliferation of news websites (some of them run by newspapers) and their easy access online, through tablets and smart phones. Fewer and fewer Scots feel the need to have their newspapers delivered or to go to a newsagent. The physical business of opening the pages of a newspaper appears to be going out of style and, when it does, that will not be a good day for newspapers. The circulation of *The Herald* is a third of what it was 20 years ago and *The Scotsman* has declined even more. This, in turn, has obviously diminished their influence. Politicians, in particular, used to worry about headlines and endorsements but what happens online, especially through social media, is now much more important.

Broadcasting in Scotland could have stepped into this growing void but the competitive landscape has changed radically since the 1980s. In return for the support of his newspapers, Margaret Thatcher allowed what became Rupert Murdoch's Sky TV to enter the market without having to pay the sort of substantial levies that the ITV companies were compelled to contribute to HM Treasury. By aggressively targeting sports rights, especially football, and taking tremendous risks, Sky built a large audience for subscription TV and simultaneously enfeebled the terrestrial broadcasters, especially ITV, as they attempted, at first, to compete. Their public service obligations were progressively run down as the ITV network centralised in London and STV (which took over Grampian TV in 1999 and remains nominally independent) is simply one more channel amongst many, its dominance long gone. It simply does not have the budgets to produce and broadcast the range of Scottish programmes it scheduled through the 1980s and 1990s. Much of the burden of reporting Scottish news (on radio as well as TV) and reflecting Scotland's culture now rests uneasily with BBC Scotland. It alone has a major responsibility to produce public service broadcasting.

The omens are not good. Professional journalism of the sort fostered by newspapers and TV and radio cannot be replaced by the chaos of the internet with all its partiality and inaccuracy as objective reporting becomes increasingly indistinguishable from comment. If newspapers begin to close in Scotland, much will be lost that is difficult to replace. Twitter is no substitute for reliable reporting.

In February 2006, a young Scottish tennis player became the British number one. At only 19 years old, Andy Murray was clearly a prodigious talent. From Dunblane (he had been at the local primary school when Thomas Hamilton entered the gymnasium), Murray began to compete with adults in the central Scotland tennis league when he was only eight years old. By 2008, he had reached his first grand slam tournament final at the US Open and he ended the year as world number four. By 2012, Murray had won the US Open and, in the same year, defeated Roger Federer in an Olympic final. But his greatest triumph came a year later. At Wimbledon, he became the first British winner of the men's single title since Fred Perry in 1936 and probably Scotland's greatest sportsman since Eric Liddell. In *The Herald*, Hugh Macdonald described the moments after victory.

> His journey to the top of world tennis ended on Centre Court yesterday afternoon with a scramble up towards the players' box. His team were hugged, with a special tribute to Ivan Lendl, his Czech-born coach who won eight grand slams, none of them at Wimbledon. All this was traditionally celebratory but, in one unScottish-like moment, he almost forgot his maw. But he was tellt.
>
> A steward pointed out that Judy Murray was sitting in the row behind the players' box. He jumped into her arms with the realisation that this was a journey shared and the fellow travellers may have been numerous, but he has only one maw.

History shifted at the 2007 Scottish parliamentary elections. By the slimmest possible margin, a single seat, the SNP became the largest party and formed a minority government with Alex Salmond as first minister. It was the culmination of a meteoric rise, from the by-election victory in 1967 at Hamilton and the advances and reverses of the 1970s, 80s and 90s, as the SNP transformed itself from a fringe party of protest that caught fire at by-elections into a responsible party of government. Of the smaller parties, only the Scottish Greens held on to win two seats while the Scottish Socialist Party lost all six. Margo MacDonald was re-elected.

One striking change from previous elections puzzled commentators. More than 7 per cent of all the votes cast, about 142,000, were declared invalid, an enormous increase from 2003 and 1999. The likely cause was a new design of the ballot papers. Instead of two pieces of paper, the list of candidates for the constituencies was printed on a single sheet along with the list of the parties for the regional vote. At the top of this single ballot paper was printed 'You Have Two Votes' and it appears that many people misunderstood. Many papers were spoiled because voters marked two crosses on the list of parties. What further confused the electorate was a new rule that allowed parties to substitute the name of their leader in the regional lists. For example, the SNP did not appear in that part of the ballot and instead their entry read 'Alex Salmond for First Minister'. A further confusion was that the local authority elections were held on the same day and, for the first time, they were conducted under the rules of the proportional representation system known as the single transferable vote.

Once it was clear that the SNP would form a minority government, approaches were made to the Liberal Democrats. A coalition would have had a majority but negotiations did not proceed. The two Scottish Greens MSPs agreed to a confidence and supply arrangement (this meant that they would support the SNP in the event of a vote of no confidence and also on the passage of money bills). Alex Salmond's government also received consistent support from the Scottish Conservative MSPs led by Annabel Goldie. They voted in favour of all four budgets in return for concessions on other issues. On 30 November, the Scottish Government published a White Paper proposing an independence referendum and, in early 2010, there was a draft bill with more detail on the form it would take. When it found no support from other parties, the government was forced to withdraw.

On 15 September 2008, the fourth largest investment bank in the USA filed for bankruptcy. Lehman Brothers had invested heavily in the subprime mortgage market, a euphemism for lending money to people who did not have the means to pay it back. So long as house prices rose and the economy was moving forward, such loans may have been sustainable. But, in 2007, the American economy began to move into recession and house prices had begun to decline as early as 2006. When Lehman Brothers was finally allowed to collapse, it was as though a thread had been pulled and the whole fabric of international finance started to unravel very quickly.

Under the leadership of Sir Fred Goodwin, the Royal Bank of Scotland had pursued an aggressive strategy of expansion by acquisition and had briefly become the largest bank in the world. It had reached into American and Chinese markets and taken stakes across a range of businesses in the financial sector. In 2005, a large and lavish new corporate RBS headquarters at Gogarburn, west of Edinburgh, had been opened by the Queen. Some commentators joked that Scotland had become a country attached to a bank.

In what was billed as the biggest bank takeover in history, RBS, in concert with Banco Santander of Spain and Fortis of Belgium, acquired ABN AMRO, a huge Dutch bank, for 70 billion euros. To outsiders the onwards march of the Royal Bank looked unstoppable and it was cheering to see a Scottish-based institution as a world player, but inside ABN AMRO, there was poison. Like all large banks, it was linked to the developing subprime crisis in America and many of its assets would turn out to be worthless. Either RBS and its partners failed to carry out due diligence as they negotiated the vast takeover deal or they knew that a large part of ABN AMRO's loan exposure was rotten and they believed they could deal with it. All of those senior executives involved, including Sir Fred Goodwin, were being paid fabulous salaries and receiving huge bonuses.

In April 2008, RBS announced the largest rights issue ever offered in Britain. The bank needed to raise £12 billion to deal with a write-down of their own assets, essentially bad loans, and also to create a substantial reserve after the acquisition of ABN AMRO. This looked to be a prudent measure and the issue was enthusiastically taken up by thousands of investors, many of them Scots, who saw RBS as a continuing success story.

When Lehman Brothers fell on 15 September 2008, assumptions began to collapse like rows of dominoes as the crash reached into other banks and became a rapidly escalating crisis. By 7 October, it became clear that ABN AMRO had been a disastrous acquisition and RBS was in serious difficulty. To the shock and dismay of all those who had taken up the rights issue only 5 months before, the share price had collapsed and dealing had been suspended twice. The bank was on the brink of collapse – but it was so large, with links to so many other financial institutions, that, if RBS had gone down, the damage to the British economy would have been immense.

The Labour chancellor, Alistair Darling, was in Luxembourg on 7 October at an EU meeting when he was telephoned by the chairman of the Royal Bank, Tom McKillop. Darling asked how long the bank could keep going. 'A couple of hours, maybe.' It was a startling statement and Darling remembered feeling 'a deep chill in [his] stomach'. Unless the government acted immediately, much of the economy would simply shut down – transactions would not be made, people would not be paid, cash machines would not work and cheques would bounce. While Alistair Darling instructed the Bank of England to inject sufficient cash into RBS to keep it afloat that day, urgent discussions began on the wider picture. On 13 October, Prime Minister Gordon Brown announced a rescue plan to invest £37 billion of new capital into not only RBS but also Lloyds TSB and HBOS. If the government had not acted immediately and emphatically, the banking system would simply have frozen – and not just in Britain but around the world. By January 2009, RBS announced a record corporate loss of £28 billion and the government stake rose to 70 per cent. But a crash on the scale of Wall Street in 1929 had been averted by decisive action.

Sir Fred Goodwin resigned as Chief Executive of RBS but he seemed to be unrepentant. A generous pension of £800,000 a year had been agreed and he attempted to justify it, as well as the cash and shares he had been paid in bonuses during his time at the bank. This may have amounted to a fortune of as much as £20 million. His pension was later cut by more than half. In common with some other high-profile bankers who had acted recklessly, Goodwin seemed not to appreciate the widespread hardship his mismanagement had caused and Alistair Darling remarked, 'To the end, he just did not get it.' Sir Fred became Fred once more as he was stripped of his knighthood although, in common with other British bankers whose actions had helped bring the world economy to the brink of ruin, Goodwin has not yet been prosecuted.

Despite their prompt and indeed visionary actions in dealing with the most severe financial crisis since the Great Depression of the 1930s, the Labour government was voted out of office in the general election of 2010. No party won an overall majority and the Conservatives went into coalition with the Liberal Democrats. In Scotland, perhaps as a result of the popularity of Gordon Brown and other senior ministers, there was a swing to Labour and a gain of two seats. Alex Salmond had set an ambitious target of 20 seats for the SNP but, in the event, they lost a seat to go down to 6 Westminster MPs. There was no hint of what was to happen in the Scottish election of 2011.

In the space of only a year, Labour was swept away in the Scottish Parliamentary elections by a tsunami of support for the SNP. Running against the electoral structure of the parliament, designed to produce coalitions, Alex Salmond led his party to an overall majority of seats. They won 69 out of a possible 129 seats, with Labour losing 16 overall and some major figures were forced out of parliament. When Alex Salmond was told that the SNP had taken the Labour heartland seat of Clydebank and Milngavie in Glasgow, his biographer, David Torrance, reported that his reaction was "'Fuck me!'" and, when he was later told that his party would form a majority government, he said, "'That's not possible.'" The Liberal Democrats were routed, losing 12 of their 17 seats and 25 candidates polling so poorly that they lost their deposits. It was a stunning unexpected victory that only seemed possible as the opinion polls swung the SNP way in the last few weeks of the campaign. It forced a clean sweep of resignations as Iain Gray, the Labour leader, left his post, as did Tavish Scott, the Liberal leader, and Annabel Goldie, the Conservative leader.

Studies have shown that Alex Salmond's remarkable victory had some unremarkable origins. After four years of minority government, the SNP was seen as competent, having performed well in parliament and handled the inevitable media scrutiny with aplomb and occasional vigour. In part, this was due to a new sense of discipline, much of it instilled by John Swinney who had led the party after Salmond's unexpected resignation in 2000. A key attribute for the voting public was the ability to 'stand up for Scotland'. When respondents were asked which party would do this most robustly, the SNP polled far ahead of its rivals. This can be attributed to at least two factors – the combative style of Alex Salmond and the fact that a Conservative–Liberal coalition was in power at Westminster. This last proved very damaging for the Liberals who were punished severely in 2011 for not only joining with Conservatives in government but also for almost immediately breaking their manifesto pledge to oppose any rise in tuition fees for students. The collapse of the Liberal vote appears to have benefitted the SNP far more than Labour. After this extraordinary election result, the constitution of Scotland and Britain would dominate political discourse for the following four years.

In contrast to their situation a year before, when they were forced to drop a bill to hold a referendum on Scottish independence, the new SNP government now had a mandate to move ahead with its plans. There was a technical difficulty to overcome in that constitutional issues were a matter reserved to the UK parliament but, in political reality, there could be no question that the Conservative–Liberal Democrat coalition would stand in the way of what was clearly the will of the majority of Scots MSPs. But the devil would be in the detail and Alex Salmond's team would prove to be the masters of it.

Skilfully brokered by the Secretary of State for Scotland, Michael Moore, the Edinburgh Agreement was signed by him, David Cameron, Alex Salmond and Nicola Sturgeon, the deputy leader of the SNP, on 15 October 2012.

Crucially it handed power to the Scottish Parliament to bring forward a bill to enable a referendum that would 'deliver a fair test and a decisive expression of the views of the people of Scotland and a result that everyone will respect'. Few could argue with that aspiration. The negotiators also agreed, after some dispute, that there should be only one question on the ballot paper rather than a series of options. But crucially the SNP government won the right to set the wording of the question to be put to voters. Their preferred wording would shape the entire campaign that followed.

The sole brake on their freedom to act was the Electoral Commission. When the Scottish Government supplied four versions of the question – which, in fact, boiled down to two – they used the market research organisation, Ipsos MORI, to test reaction. The version favoured by the SNP, 'Do you agree that Scotland should be an independent country?', was rejected because the opening three words were seen to make it a leading question. Instead, the ballot paper would carry 'Should Scotland be an independent country?' Since the answer to either for pro-independence voters would be 'Yes', a clear positive, it mattered little. The point was that, in presentational terms, it would be much better to have both the question and the answer be positive. It would be possible to persuade voters that to vote Yes would be to vote for Scotland and to vote No would obviously be negative, somehow a vote against Scotland.

In May 2012, the Yes campaign was launched and, a month later, having been forced immediately on to the back foot in the search for a title, the Better Together campaign began to make its arguments. It could not be called what it was, the No campaign, because it was by nature too negative. Other advantages had been taken. While Michael Moore was speaking in the House of Commons in January, outlining the powers that would handed to Holyrood to stage a referendum and stating that a poll would have to held before the end of 2013, Alex Salmond characteristically seized the initiative and announced outside Bute House that his government would hold a referendum in the autumn of 2014. It was to be a very long campaign, more than two years, and some feared that voter apathy was a danger. But the Scottish government's canny intervention on the timing would see the referendum held after what some would call 'the Summer of Scotland'.

In 2012, a triumphantly successful Olympic Games was mounted in London. No fewer than seven gold medals were won by Scots athletes. In addition to Andy Murray, Chris Hoy won two, Heather Stanning and Katherine Grainger picked up golds in rowing and Timothy Baillie in canoeing, while the Peebles rider, Scott Brash, won an intensely competitive showjumping competition. Commentators could not decide who would gain most political advantage. Was it Scottish excellence in winning more medals than at any other Olympic Games, a sure sign of a mature nation, further up the medal table than many larger and longer established countries? Or was it the collective ethos and preparation of Team GB that put them over the finish line? In any event, it was a glorious summer of sporting celebration. And there was more to come.

The largest sporting event ever held in Scotland was the 2014 Commonwealth Games in Glasgow, as nearly 5,000 athletes converged on the city from 71 countries across the world. Despite some awkwardness in the opening ceremony and an 'out-of-context' derogatory remark said to have been made by the great Jamaican sprinter, Usain Bolt, the games were a great success. With 19 gold medals, 53 medals of all colours and a rank of fourth in the medal table behind Canada, Australia and England, the Commonwealth Games were another huge sporting success for Scotland. This time the Saltire and not the Union Jack flew from winning flagpoles but despite the gathering pace of political events, neither side of the referendum debate attempted to make capital – a wise decision.

The date of the referendum was set for Thursday 18 September and the long-running campaigns began to wind up their efforts. Opinion polling had shown a consistent lead for the No campaign but, by August, the numbers had tightened to approximately 43 per cent for Yes and 57 per cent for No. And it was becoming clear with high levels of voter registration and the inclusion of 16- to 18-year-olds that there would be a huge turnout. On 5 August, STV broadcast the first of two televised debates between Alex Salmond and the leader of the Better Together campaign, Alistair Darling. To the surprise of many, the mild-mannered former chancellor appeared to win the argument against the combative Salmond. The key issue was uncertainty about what currency an independent Scotland would use. The incumbent Conservative chancellor, George Osborne, had ruled out a currency union with the rest of the United Kingdom in February 2014 and Alex Salmond's answers to Darling's persistence seemed vague on alternatives. By the time the second debate came around, the leader of the Yes campaign appeared to be better prepared and was thought to have bested Darling, who seemed flustered.

On 6 September, a YouGov poll reckoned that, for the first time, the Yes campaign had a lead – 47 per cent to 45 per cent for No. Other polls showed a narrow gap of between 4 per cent to 6 per cent, only just outside the margin for error. It appeared that momentum had shifted and the race to 18 September was becoming a close-run thing. The former prime minister Gordon Brown had written a book, *My Scotland, Our Britain*, that set out the historical context of the debate and the arguments for staying in the Union. By June, he had began to take a more central role, arguing that the No campaign needed to set out a much more positive vision for Scotland and reclaim the patriotic ground that had been surrendered to the SNP and their supporters. The difficulty was that the Labour-led campaign was not in a position to deliver any guarantees of what a post-referendum Scotland might look like in the event of a No vote and, therefore, he sought negotiations with David Cameron, the Conservative prime minister.

Cameron visited Edinburgh on 10 September and made a passionate speech in defence of the Union, saying that he cared far more for his country than for his party. He argued that the referendum should not be seen as a chance to 'give the effing Tories a kick'. It was much more important than that, not like a general election, he argued, but about much more lasting and profound change. Meanwhile, Alex Salmond had claimed that the No campaign was 'falling apart at the seams' and a TNS poll showed support for Yes at 38 per cent and No only a point more at 39 per cent, well within the margin for error. It seemed that the campaign had reached an absolutely critical point.

Behind the interviews, the walkabouts and the rallies, negotiations had been taking place through intermediaries between Labour, Conservatives and Liberals. Even though there was only one question on the ballot paper, Brown, Labour Party leader Ed Miliband, Cameron, Clegg and their advisors decided to answer another one. Recognising that a return to the status quo was not what the majority of Scots wanted, they came to the view that substantial change had to be offered to those thinking of voting No. There had to be a vision for a new Scotland, one different from what the Yes campaign was promoting. Accordingly, individual statements were agreed with each party leader and, crucially, a joint expression of intent was also settled on. On Tuesday, 16 September, two days before the referendum, the *Daily Record* ran the statement, signed by Cameron, Miliband and Clegg, on its front page and they called it 'The Vow'. Here is the complete text:

> The people of Scotland want to know that all three main parties will deliver change for Scotland.

WE ARE AGREED THAT:

The Scottish Parliament is permanent and extensive new powers for the Parliament will be delivered by the process and to the timetable agreed and announced by our three parties, starting on 19th September.

And it is our hope that the people of Scotland will be engaged directly as each party works to improve the way we are governed in the UK in the years ahead.

We agree that the UK exists to ensure opportunity and security for all by sharing our resources equitably across all four nations to secure the defence, prosperity and welfare of every citizen.

And because of the continuation of the Barnett allocation for resources, and the powers of the Scottish Parliament to raise revenue, we can state categorically that the final say on how much is spent on the NHS will be a matter for the Scottish Parliament.

We believe that the arguments that so powerfully make the case for staying together in the UK should underpin our future as a country. We will honour those principles and values not only before the referendum but after.

People want to see change. A No vote will deliver faster, safer and better change than separation.

THE BARNETT FORMULA

Devised in 1978 by Chief Secretary of the Treasury in the Labour government of James Callaghan, Joel Barnett, the formula was designed to adjust levels of public expenditure in Scotland, Northern Ireland and Wales in anticipation of the devolution that did not take place in 1979. It is based on population levels and adjusted according to a comparability factor. For example, if £1 billion was to be added to the budget of the National Health Service in England, then Scotland would be granted the comparable amount, approximately £103 million. This is why decisions about public expenditure taken at Westminster on what appear to be exclusively English matters should be voted on by all of the United Kingdom's members of parliament. The Barnett formula makes them interdependent.

Crucially, Gordon Brown had insisted that there be a clear timetable attached and not a series of vague assurances that promised a new Scotland some time soon. Nothing less than a calendar of firm dates would be credible at this late stage. In the event of a No vote, there would be a White

Paper on new powers for a Scottish Parliament by 30 November, St Andrew's Day. And, flowing from that, there would be draft legislation by the end of January, with Burns' Night seeming an appropriate deadline.

On the eve of the poll, many Yes campaigners gathered in Perth to hear Alex Salmond make a last, rousing speech. Despite The Vow, momentum was thought by many still to be moving towards a Yes vote and hopes were high. But no commentator was predicting the result with any certainty. On the same day in Glasgow, Gordon Brown had made the speech of his life. 'The silent majority will be silent no more,' he said. His voice quavered with emotion as he exhorted No voters to 'hold [their] heads high and have confidence' as they went to the polling booths. It was passionate, utterly sincere – and convincing. Importantly, the speech was made at midday and this allowed it to be uploaded to YouTube as well as soundbites to be run on news bulletins. Hundreds of thousands watched it before they went to the polls and Brown's clear conviction appears to have had impact.

Overnight the sunny autumn weather broke and, on 18 September, a light Scottish drizzle known by some as 'sma' rain' descended. But this discouraged very few. When the polls closed, one stunning statistic could be reported. The voter turnout had been huge at 84.59 per cent, an enormous increase on the usual 50–60 per cent for recent general elections (the 1950 election saw 83 per cent vote). Rather than producing apathy, the long two-year campaign had encouraged passionate engagement. There was no exit poll but, by midnight, YouGov was predicting a 54-per-cent-to-46-per-cent win for the No campaign. When the returning officer for tiny Clackmannanshire, formerly a Westminster seat held by the SNP and currently in nationalist hands at Holyrood, declared at 1.30 a.m., the actual numbers looked to match the predictions – 53.8 per cent voted No and 46.2 per cent voted Yes. As the night wore on, it became clear that Clackmannanshire was typical as the final count reached 55.3 per cent for No and 44.7 per cent for Yes. Four areas bucked the national trend by voting Yes – Glasgow, Dundee, North Lanarkshire and West Dunbartonshire – but the overall totals represented a convincing verdict. They were 2,001,926 for No and 1,617,989 for Yes. Despite defeat, the result was a remarkable achievement for the Scottish National Party. They had come close.

Alex Salmond accepted the clear majority for No and asked that 'all Scots follow suit in accepting the democratic verdict of the people of Scotland'. However, joy was very short-lived in the Better Together camp. Snatching a few hours sleep in a Glasgow hotel where the victory celebrations were taking place, Alistair Darling was woken at 5 a.m. with some disturbing news. David Cameron was planning a statement saying something about restricting the powers of Scots MPs at Westminster. When Darling spoke to him, the prime minister said that he would speak at 7 a.m. on the steps of Downing Street. He would welcome the decision made by the Scottish people but would also bring forward plans to curtail the voting rights of Scots MPs in the House of Commons. In an acronym known as EVEL, English Votes for English Laws, Cameron would introduce legislation that excluded Scots from voting on English-only matters. Darling implored him not to do this, pleading that it would hand the initiative straight back to the SNP only hours after their convincing defeat. Gordon Brown called Sir Jeremy Heywood, the Cabinet Secretary, to say that the statement would be nothing less than a disaster for the Union. Putting it brutally simply, Danny Alexander, Liberal Chief Secretary to the Treasury and, at the time, a Scottish MP, said, 'Talk about trying to snatch defeat from the jaws of victory. What it did was just give the nationalists a whole grievance agenda from a minute after a result was declared. It was just dreadful.' Critics claimed that Cameron was being less than statesmanlike as he attempted to both placate his backbenchers and court voters in England who might be tempted away from the Conservatives to UKIP. It appeared that the prime minister had gone back on his claim made in Edinburgh a few days before that he put country before party.

In the immediate aftermath of the result, Alex Salmond surprised many by announcing his resignation as leader of the SNP and first minister. In the early hours of Friday, 19 September, he had spoken to his deputy, Nicola Sturgeon. She recalled that 'it was a very, very emotional moment. I didn't think it was necessarily the right thing to do on that day but he had made up his mind.' It seemed that one of the giants of Scottish politics was about to leave the stage. When Salmond announced his decision at 4 p.m. at Bute House, he made an eloquent, emotional speech, saying that 'the dream shall never die'. The former Conservative Leader of the House of Lords, Lord Strathclyde, offered a summary of the first minister's efforts in fighting the referendum campaign:

> The dream that Salmond had campaigned for all his life had come to a halt. He had done everything in his power to make sure the vote went his way. He decided the date of the referendum, he decided the length of the campaign, he decided the question, he changed the franchise so that schoolchildren had got a vote, he

was wholly in control of the Scottish Government and the civil service. There was nothing more he could do. So he lost. The people have spoken. The sovereign will of the Scottish people has been heard. A once in a generation – once in a lifetime – opportunity occurred in September, and the decision is final.

Nothing in what Lord Strathclyde said is factually inaccurate and yet it does not square with the political reality. The debate appears to be far from over.

On 19 September, following Gordon Brown's timetable, David Cameron announced the appointment of Lord Smith of Kelvin, a businessman, to 'convene cross-party talks and facilitate an inclusive engagement process across Scotland to produce, by 30 November 2014, Heads of Agreement with recommendations for further devolution of powers to the Scottish Parliament.'

Ten representatives were invited from the five political parties represented at Holyrood and work began immediately as written submissions were sought from both individuals and organisations. On 27 November, three days before St Andrew's Day, these were its recommendations:

- The Scottish Parliament to have complete power to set income tax rates and bands.
- The Scottish Parliament to receive a proportion of the VAT raised in Scotland, amounting to the first 10 percentage points of the standard rate (so with the current standard VAT rate of 20 per cent, Scotland would receive 50 per cent of the receipts). However, the Scottish Parliament cannot influence the UK's overall VAT rate.
- The Scottish Parliament to have increased borrowing powers to support capital investment and ensure budgetary stability. These powers are to be agreed with the UK government.
- UK legislation to state that the Scottish Parliament and Scottish Government are permanent institutions. The parliament will also be given powers to legislate over how it is elected and run.
- The Scottish Parliament to have power to extend the vote to 16- and 17-year-olds, allowing them to vote in the Scottish Parliament general election, 2016.
- The Scottish Parliament to have control over a number of benefits including Disability Living Allowance, Personal Independence Payment, winter fuel payments and the housing elements of Universal Credit, including the under-occupancy charge (popularly known as the bedroom tax).

- The Scottish Parliament to have new powers to make discretionary payments in any area of welfare without the need to obtain prior permission from the Department for Work and Pensions.
- The Scottish Parliament to have all powers of support for unemployed people through employment programmes, mainly delivered at present through the Work Programme.
- The Scottish Parliament to have control over air passenger duty charged on passengers flying from Scottish airports.
- Responsibility for the management of the Crown Estate's economic assets in Scotland, including the Crown Estate's seabed and mineral and fishing rights, and the revenue generated from these assets, to be transferred to the Scottish Parliament.
- The licensing of onshore oil and gas extraction underlying Scotland to be devolved to the Scottish Parliament.
- The Scottish Government will have power to allow public sector operators to bid for rail franchises funded and specified by Scottish ministers.
- The block grant from the UK government to Scotland will continue to be determined via the operation of the Barnett formula. New rules to define how it will be adjusted at the point when powers are transferred and thereafter to be agreed by the Scottish and UK governments and put in place prior to the powers coming into force. These rules will ensure that neither the Scottish nor UK governments will lose or gain financially from the act of transferring a power.
- MPs representing constituencies across the whole of the UK to continue to decide the UK's budget, including income tax.
- The Scottish and UK governments to draw up and agree a memorandum of understanding to ensure that devolution is not detrimental to UK-wide critical national infrastructure in relation to matters such as defence and security, oil and gas and energy.

It was a surprisingly detailed and comprehensive list of new powers and a bill based on it was brought forward in January 2015, but enactment would have to be delayed until after the UK general election in May.

Meanwhile Nicola Sturgeon had been elected unopposed to succeed Alex Salmond. She welcomed the recommendations of the Smith Commission but believed that they did not 'deliver a modern form of home rule' or give sufficient power to a devolved Scotland. Opinion polling in November 2014 suggested that support for the SNP was rising steeply and that momentum had returned. With the resignation of Johann Lamont as leader of the Scottish Labour Party on 24 October and the subsequent election of Jim Murphy, Westminster MP for East Renfrewshire, in December, to the post, new battle lines were being drawn. With the new Fixed-term Parliaments Act of 2011 requiring that a UK general election be held on 7 May 2015, it seemed, in Scotland, that campaigning scarcely paused after the declaration of the result of the referendum.

Opinion polling continued apace and it seemed that no party looked likely to gain an overall majority and that there would be another hung parliament. In Scotland, the campaign was unlike any other. Polling put the SNP as high as 54 per cent and, with a new leader enjoying unprecedented support and coverage across Britain, the SNP appeared to be on course to win all 59 seats, making it the third largest party at Westminster. And yet, in a nation waiting for a political tsunami to hit, the campaign seemed puzzlingly low-key. Nicola Sturgeon made it clear that she would not go into government with the Conservatives under any circumstances while Ed Miliband, the Labour leader, ruled out a coalition or a deal with the SNP. It seemed that the UK election would be decided in Scotland, one way or another.

Long before it smashed its way onshore, the roar of the political tsunami that engulfed Scotland on 7 May 2015 grew louder and louder. Each successive poll put the SNP's support ever higher as Labour's and the other parties' were swamped. But, on the morning of 8 May, the electoral map still looked astonishing. Only three SNP candidates failed to win a seat in Scotland and 56 men and women, 50 of them new to Westminster, would join the new United Kingdom parliament. They ranged from 20-year-old Mhairi Black, the youngest MP for more than three centuries who defeated Douglas Alexander, a former Labour minister and campaign director, to George Kerevan, a newspaper columnist and author, as well as a large cohort of SNP local councillors.

After the tsunami hit, the landscape was devastated as Labour lost all but one seat and the Liberals were routed, down from eleven MPs to one. This only reflected their savage fate across the United Kingdom after the electorate punished them for five years of coalition. Scotland was changed utterly on 7 May with few certainties left standing as the wave swept across former Labour heartlands.

While the results in Scotland were predicted, the difficulty was credibility – no one, including the SNP, could believe them until the last vote was counted.

But what happened in England and Wales came as a complete surprise. All of the polling had predicted another hung parliament with Labour and Conservatives on a range of 250 to 290 seats. But, when the exit poll was announced after 10 p.m. on 7 May, it was jaw-dropping – the Conservatives to win 316 seats and probably a majority. There had clearly been a late, undetected surge in support. This immediately impacted in Scotland. A central element of the SNP's campaign had been their support, welcome or not, for a Labour minority government. The Conservative majority wiped out their UK role and they now claim only to represent Scottish interests.

It is not difficult to discover reasons for the huge vote for the SNP, about 50 per cent of the entire electorate, and Labour's collapse. The 45 per cent of Scots who voted Yes in 2014 appear to have moved en masse into the nationalist camp and the substitution of Nicola Sturgeon for the combative Alex Salmond attracted more support. And the Conservatives helped. Anxious that polls across England had seemed to stall, David Cameron launched a late campaigning initiative, claiming that any minority Labour government would be dominated by the SNP, needing their large bloc of seats to win a House of Commons majority. A poster showing Ed Miliband in Alex Salmond's pocket appeared. In addition to stoking anti-Scottish sentiment in England, a surprising pose for a Unionist party, the Conservatives also roused a form of English nationalism with its EVEL proposals in order to fend off the threat from the right in the shape of the UK Independence Party. Both tactics were very successful as only one UKIP MP was elected and, crucially, Labour was unable to rely on its Scottish seats. Many commentators have ascribed the late surge in support for the Conservatives to what some called 'the Scottish scare tactics'.

But, in reality, it began long before on the steps of 10 Downing Street early on the morning of 19 September 2014, when David Cameron welcomed the result of the Scottish Referendum and added his incendiary statement about English Votes for English Laws. It was no rush of blood to the head but a coldly made calculation. In the event, the Conservatives won a majority without Scotland, having neutralised Labour with the help of the SNP. This last poses the most substantial threat to the Union of 1707. From the north, the SNP will press for greater independence, regarding the new government as illegitimate, something Scots did not vote for, while from the south, the Conservatives will be diffident, knowing they can win a majority without any Scottish support. It appears that a constitutional pincer movement is under way. More change awaits.

Envoi

❊

REFLECTING ON THE immense journey that is our history, many competing interim conclusions crowd the landscape. But at least one theme is clear. Scotland was never an inevitable destination. As we approached several crossroads, our destiny might easily have turned in different directions. Scotland could have become Pictland, Alba, Norseland or Northern England. This recurring sequence of uncertainties, real enough at the time, is a useful corrective to the temptation to read history backwards.

But is difficult to resist. When Agricola watched the vast host of the Caledonian Confederacy muster to meet his legions at Bennachie or when King Bridei rode up and down the ranks of Pictish spearmen at Dunnichen, it is near-impossible for us to see those momentous days as they did. We know they won. They were uncertain. Both battles were part of the dramatic sweep of our history but neither general could know that their victories would be transient or have a profound impact. Such is political history, stories of advance and retreat, of ambition fulfilled or denied. The wars for Scotland, the unions of crowns and parliaments and the play of powerful interests, both religious and secular, all have close historical parallels across Europe and beyond.

What makes Scotland's story unique is the land, the places where it happened. It may be seen as a palimpsest, a different way of looking at history as our peoples shaped where they lived and left their marks. The matchless beauty of Scotland is often seen in rugged, even wild landscapes, the drama of mountain and flood. But, to me, it is the fields that are most beautiful and atmospheric. They are a memory of uncounted lives lived on the land, a patchwork of day-in, day-out labour somehow best seen in the evening, lit by a westering sun. Evening is best because the day's end brought rest for the numberless and nameless people who walked and worked their lives in the fields of Scotland. They can be intimate and detailed. After the harvest is home in early September, when round straw bales dot and accentuate their contours and the trees and fringing hedges are beginning to turn russet, they look at their gentle best. For all but 200 years of the 11,000 years of our continuous history, almost all Scots worked on the land in one way or another and the fields are their common monument.

Our land of Scotland is like no other – it helped form the character of the people, it determined the nature of agriculture and it directed contact and commerce. It made history. The Irish war bands who sailed the North Channel from the 5th century onwards used its character to penetrate far inland, their ships moving up the long western sea lochs to reach quickly into the heart of Scotland. It is not small-nation boastfulness to say that Scotland is unique – it is no more than the truth.

The shape of this story of Scotland has, of course, been formed by its sources and the accident of their survival. What attracted me was the possibility of writing a people's history rather than a recital of the doings of the mighty, the saintly and the notorious. But that is an ambition limited by the facts, such as they are. Prehistory and the archaeology that reveals it is necessarily about ordinary people because it does not deal with named individuals, leaders or otherwise. It is a fascinating period but anonymous. After Tacitus wrote of Calgacus, the first Scot to be named in the historical record, as he faced down the Roman legions, it is difficult to avoid dealing with elites. The sources talk almost exclusively of politics, of the deeds of great men (and very few women) and events. There are only whispers of the lives of farmers, weavers, labourers and others but no voices loud enough to be heard. Not until the second half of the 19th century is it possible to say much about the lives of ordinary Scots.

Looking out over the empty pages of the future, interconnectedness suggests itself as a new theme. Through the neon flicker of 24-hour media, through the deafening, unrelenting chatter of social media, though the constant, frenetic exchange of the markets and the ability of all of this to affect our lives directly and unexpectedly, we are pushed to define Scotland as more than just a website. We must now look outwards, offering what is uniquely attractive to the world, and also look inwards at what we can do to attract people to live, work or holiday in Scotland. Or persuade them to stay.

Scots have struggled with self-definition, often careering towards the crazier shores of parody. After Culloden, we frisked the Highlanders for their distinctive iconography – tartan, whisky, bagpipes and the Bens & Glens of the Flower that is Scotland – and applied it all to the whole nation. We did this, mostly badly, because it looked different and not English. Walter Scott has a great deal to answer for. We gamely seek alternatives but they are difficult to find because, like most nations, our identity is complex and not given to instant expression. So we put a kilt on it.

There is much uncertainty now. And, while history can teach us a great deal, the mystery of the past is also important. About a mile west of my house, there is a track that winds up to the old earthworks of a Norman motte-and-bailey castle. When I walk down to the stables to feed the horses, I can see its line clearly, shelved into the flank of the hill. I have ridden up the track once or twice and it is very old. No source has survived to say which Norman lord, if it was a Norman lord, had the track made. It fascinates me and I do not know why. Nor do I wish to.

When I was a little boy, I used to help deliver the Store milk around the streets of Kelso and, up at 5.30 a.m. six days out of seven, I saw many dawns break. As I greet another on my way to my office to write this, it seems that this moment in our history is a time of hesitation. For Scotland now, it seems that several dawns are possible.

Bibliography

✻

I have written a good deal about prehistoric and early medieval Scotland and one of the many pleasures in undertaking this project was dealing with my ignorance of our later history. No editor could have been more helpful than Rosemary Goring. Her *Scotland: The Autobiography* is a brilliant selection of key texts from the sweep of our written records, from Tacitus to the *Herald*'s reporting of Andy Murray's triumph at Wimbledon in 2013. I relied on Rosemary's work constantly and I cannot recommend her book highly enough.

Michael Lynch's *Scotland: A New History*, first published in 1991, is simply magisterial, full of insight and telling detail. For British and European contexts, one need look no further than Norman Davies' *The Isles* and his *Europe: A History*. They are unsurpassed.

This is a bibliography with a difference. It is by no means a full conspectus of everything consulted in working on this book. Nor does it attempt to be a definitive listing of what is and is not available. Nor does it restrict itself to the usual listing of non-fiction. What it does attempt to do is provide the reader with a personal listing of works that are both enjoyable and illuminating through the long flow of Scotland's story. The listing is very much for the generalist and, while there are many seminal academic works, it tends very much towards the more accessible. It also is deliberately restricted to books that are readily available – either in print or on the second-hand market. I have also used the most recent available edition as reference, as this will tend to have the most updated text. No apology is made for the fact that two publishers dominate the list. For more than twenty years Edinburgh University Press and Birlinn Ltd and its associated imprints have been at the heart of Scottish non-fiction publishing. Fiction is very much a personal selection of books with a strong historical content.

GENERAL HISTORIES

There are three main multi-volume series covering Scotland's history. The first of them is known as *The Edinburgh History* and comes in four large volumes:

Duncan, A.A.M., *The Making of the Kingdom* (Edinburgh, 1975)
Nicholson, Ranald, *The Later Middle Ages* (Edinburgh, 1978)
Donaldson, Gordon, *James V–James VII* (Edinburgh, 1965)
Ferguson, William, *1689 to the Present* (Edinburgh, 1978)

The New History of Scotland is now published by Edinburgh University Press and consists of a series of thematic histories of Scotland originally published by Edward Arnold but now revised. Katie Stevenson's and Graeme Morton's books are both new editions to the series and overlap older books. The thematic construction is often confusing but nevertheless they have been in print continuously and contain much of real interest.

Smyth, Alfred, *Warlords and Holy Men: Scotland AD 80–1000* (London, 1989)
Barrow, G.W.S., *Kingship and Unity: Scotland 1000–1306* (London, 2015)
Grant, Alexander, *Independence and Nationhood: Scotland 1306–1469* (London, 1991)
Stevenson, Katie, *Power and Propaganda: Scotland 1306–1488* (Edinburgh, 2014)
Wormald, Jenny, *Court, Kirk, and Community: Scotland 1470–1625* (London, 1991)
Mitchison, Rosalind, *Lordship to Patronage: Scotland 1603–1745* (London, 1990)
Lenman, Bruce, *Enlightenment and Change: Scotland 1746–1832* (Edinburgh, 2009)
Morton, Graeme, *Ourselves and Others: Scotland 1832–1914* (Edinburgh, 2012)
Checkland, Olive and Sydney, *Industry and Ethos: Scotland 1832–1914* (London, 1989)
Harvie, Christopher, *No Gods and Precious Few Heroes: Twentieth-Century Scotland* (London, 1998)

The New Edinburgh Histories are now published by Edinburgh University Press as well:

Fraser, James E., *From Caledonia to Pictland: Scotland to 795* (Edinburgh, 2009)
Woolf, Alex, *From Pictland to Alba, 789–1070* (Edinburgh, 2007)
Oram, Ricchard, *Domination and Lordship: Scotland, 1070–1230* (Edinburgh, 2011)
Brown, Michael, *The Wars of Scotland, 1214–1371* (Edinburgh, 2004)
Dawson, Jane, *Scotland Re-formed, 1488–1587* (Edinburgh, 2007)
Cameron, Ewen, *Impaled Upon a Thistle: Scotland Since 1880* (Edinburgh, 2010)

An excellent part series published by Birlinn in association with Historic Scotland called *The Making of Scotland* comprises the titles listed below. These are short introductions which contain a great deal of radical new thinking by leading experts. Very well illustrated and very accessible, they remain models of their kind.

Finlayson, Bill, *Wild Harvesters: The First People in Scotland* (Edinburgh, 2005)

Barclay, Gordon, *Farmers, Temples and Tombs: Scotland in the Neolithic and Early Bronze Age* (Edinburgh, 2005)

Hingley, Richard, *Settlement and Sacrifice: The Later Prehistoric Peoples of Scotland* (Edinburgh, 2005)

Maxwell, Gordon, *A Gathering of Eagles: Scenes from Roman Scotland* (Edinburgh, 2005)

Lowe, Chris, *Angels, Fools and Tyrants: Britons and Anglo-Saxons in Southern Scotland* (Edinburgh, 1999)

Campbell, Ewan, *Saints and Sea Kings: The First Kingdom of the Scots* (Edinburgh, 1999)

Carver, Martin, *Surviving in Symbols: A Visit to the Pictish Nation* (Edinburgh, 2005)

Driscoll, Stephen, *Alba: The Gaelic Kingdom of Scotland: AD 800 – 1124* (Edinburgh, 2002)

Owen, Olwyn, *The Sea Road: A Viking Voyage through Scotland* (Edinburgh, 1999)

Hall, Derek, *Burgess, Merchant and Priest: The Medieval Scottish Town* (Edinburgh, 2002)

Dixon, Piers, *Puir Labourers and Busy Husbandmen: The Medieval Countryside of Scotland* (Edinburgh, 2002)

Dodgshon, Robert, *The Age of the Clans: The Highlands from Somerled to the Clearances* (Edinburgh, 2002)

There are also a number of classic books which are generalist in their approach, deal with a number of historical periods or have thematic coverage of a particular theme over time. A number of these are listed below.

T.C. Smout's *A History of the Scottish People* is a groundbreaking classic which has stood the test of time remarkably well. Alistair Moffat's *The Scots: A Genetic Journey* is the most up-to-date account of where the people who now inhabit Scotland came from. *Sea Kingdoms* is a personal history and travelogue of the Celtic West of the country. T.M. Devine's *Scottish Nation* is a standard account of Scotland since the Union, while Christopher Fleet and his colleagues in *Scotland: Mapping the Nation* have produced a work of great beauty and absorbing interest, revealing how maps have shaped our perception of ourselves.

Devine, T.M., *The Scottish Nation* (London, 2012)
Fleet, Christopher, Wilkes, Margaret and Withers, Charles, *Scotland: Mapping the Nation* (Edinburgh, 2012)
Moffat, Alistair, *The Scots: A Genetic Journey* (Edinburgh, 2012)
Moffat, Alistair, *Sea Kingdoms* (Edinburgh, 2008)
Smout, T.C., *A History of the Scottish People 1560–1830* (London, 1998)
Sprott, Gavin, *Farming* (Edinburgh, 1995)

PREHISTORIC

Alistair Moffat's *Before Scotland* (London, 2005) provides a readable introduction to Scotland's prehistory. There is little else in print at the moment, though a new edition of Ian Armit's *Celtic Scotland* is due in 2016.

More generally, the following books are recommended:

Cunliffe, Barry, *Europe Between the Oceans* (London, 2008)
Cunliffe, Barry, *The Extraordinary Voyage of Pytheas the Greek* (London, 2002)
Cunliffe, Barry, *The Penguin Atlas of British and Irish History* (London, 2001)
Cunliffe, Barry, *The Ancient Celts* (London, 1999)
Nicolaisen, W.F.H., *Scottish Place-Names* (Edinburgh, 2011)
Watson, W.J., *The Celtic Place-names of Scotland* (Birlinn, 2011)

THE ROMAN PERIOD

Birley, Anthony, *Tacitus: Agricola and Germany* (Oxford, 1999)
Breeze, David, *Hadrian's Wall* (London, 2006) is a more archaeological perspective
Breeze, David *The Antonine Wall* (Edinburgh, 2008) is the standard account
Frere, S.S., *Britannia* (London, 1991)
Keppie, Laurence, *The Legacy of Rome* (Edinburgh, 2004) is the best single volume introduction to the Roman Empire in Scotland.
Moffat, Alistair, *The Wall* (Edinburgh, 2009) is the most recent book on Hadrian's great engineering achievement

THE DARK AGES

The Triumph Tree is an anthology of the surviving poetry of the Britons, Vikings and Scots. Including a very good translation of 'Y Gododdin', this is a marvellous book. My own book on Arthur locates him in the Borders, while *The Faded Map* is an attempt to gather up the ghostly traces of the lost Dark Age kingdoms of Central Scotland and the Borders. Sally Foster's archaeologically based study is both accessible and seminal, and the prolific Tim Clarkson provides a very good general introduction to the period in *The Makers of Scotland*, a specific history of the Picts, the standard biographical work on Columba, and two volumes on the history of the Kingdom of Strathclyde. Adomnan's *Life of St Columba* is, after the Venerable Bede, the most important text to come to us from the Dark Ages. Barbara Crawford's study is the definitive book on the Norse Earldom of Orkney. *The Orkneyinga Saga* is a wonderfully readable text about whose veracity historians wrangle endlessly. Fiona Watson's biographical study of Macbeth is an attempt to piece together the few fragments we know about this famous figure. *Alba* is a fascinating collection of essays.

Adomnan, *Life of St Columba* (*trans.* Sharpe, Richard; London, 1995)

Bede, *The Ecclesiastical History of the English People* (*ed.* Colgrave, B. and Mynors, R.A.B.; Oxford, 1991)

Clancy, Thomas (*ed.*), *The Triumph Tree* (Edinburgh, 1998)

Clarkson, Tim, *Columba* (Edinburgh, 2012)

Clarkson, Tim, *The Makers of Scotland* (Edinburgh, 2013)

Clarkson, Tim, *Men of the North* (Edinburgh, 2010)

Clarkson, Tim, *The Picts* (Edinburgh, 2013)

Clarkson, Tim, *Strathclyde and the Anglo-Saxons in the Viking Age* (Edinburgh, 2014)

Cowan, E.J. and McDonald, R.A. (*eds*), *Alba: Celtic Scotland in the Middle Ages* (Edinburgh, 2012)

Crawford, Barbara, *The Northern Earldoms* (Edinburgh, 2013)

Foster, Sally, *Picts, Gaels and Scots* (Edinburgh, 2014)

Moffat, Alistair, *Arthur and the Lost Kingdoms* (Edinburgh, 2012)

Moffat, Alistair, *The Faded Map* (Edinburgh, 2011)

The Orkneyinga Saga (*trans.* Hjaltalin, J.A. and Goudie, G.; Edinburgh, 1999)

Watson, Fiona, *Macbeth: A True Story* (London, 2010)

MEDIEVAL AND POST-MEDIEVAL

The Medieval period is sadly sparse until we reach the Wars of Independence. The following provide approachable and well-researched accounts of three key figures:

Marsden, John, *Somerled and the Emergence of Gaelic Scotland* (Edinburgh, 2008)

Oram, Richard, *Alexander II* (Edinburgh, 2012)

Oram, Richard, *David I* (Stroud, 2008)

The following provide an account respectively of the origins of what became the Lordship of the Isles and the tantalising evidence for the Kingdom of Moray:

Macdonald, R. Andrew, *The Kingdom of the Isles* (Edinburgh, 2008)
Marsden, John, *Kings, Mormaers, Rebels* (Edinburgh, 2010)

The Wars of Independence and their aftermath have spawned many works. Fisher and McNamee are by far the two best short biographies of these great figures. *The Wallace Book* is another fascinating collection of essays. *Under the Hammer* looks at the English administration of Scotland, and *The Wars of the Bruces* sets the struggle in a much broader context, including the Bruce wars in Ireland. *Bannockburn* attempts to focus on the drama and key decisions of the battle itself and give the feel of this great conflict as if we were there. E.J. Cowan examines one of the most famous documents of Scotland's history. The two key sources are Blind Harry and Barbour. Geoffrey Barrow's epoch-making biography is one of the great works of Scottish historiography.

Barbour, John, *The Bruce* (Edinburgh, 1997)
Barrow, Geoffrey, *Robert the Bruce and the Community of the Realm of Scotland* (Edinburgh, 2005)
Blind Harry, *The Wallace* (Edinburgh, 2003)
Cowan, Edward J., *For Freedom Alone: The Declaration of Arbroath* (Edinburgh, 2008)
Cowan, E.J. (*ed.*), *The Wallace Book* (Edinburgh, 2010)
Fisher, Andrew, *William Wallace* (Edinburgh, 2010)
McNamee, Colm, *Robert the Bruce* (Edinburgh, 2006)
McNamee, Colm, *The Wars of the Bruces* (Edinburgh, 2006)
Moffat, Alistair, *Bannockburn* (Edinburgh, 2014)
Watson, Fiona, *Under the Hammer* (Edinburgh, 2005)

Later Medieval Scottish history is better covered. The following are published by John Donald as part of their *Stewart Dynasty in Scotland* series, representing excellent detailed biographies of each monarch.

Penman, Michael, *David II* (Edinburgh, 2005)
Brown, Michael *James I* (Edinburgh, 2015)
McGladdery, Christine, *James II* (Edinburgh, 2015)

Macdougall, Norman, *James III* (Edinburgh, 2009)
Norman Macdougall: *James IV* (Edinburgh, 2006)
Cameron, Jamie, *James V* (Edinburgh, 2011)

Other books relating to this period include:

Boardman, Stephen, *The Campbells* (Edinburgh, 2006) focuses on the rise of a family who came to dominate Scottish politics
MacDonald, Donald, *Lewis: A History of the Island* (Edinburgh, 2004)
McCulloch, Andrew, *Galloway: A Land Apart* (Edinburgh, 2000)
Moffat, Alistair, *The Borders: A History From Earliest Times* (Edinburgh, 2002)
Olson, Ian, *Bludie Harlaw* (Edinburgh, 2014) is a major reassessment of this ferocious conflict
Reese, Peter, *Flodden* (Edinburgh, 2013) is a meticulous account of one of the most terrible days in Scottish history
Tasioulas, J. (*ed.*), *The Makars* (Edinburgh, 1996) is probably the most comprehensive and recent edition of this golden age of Scottish poetry
Thomas, Andrea, *Glory and Honour: The Renaissance in Scotland* (Edinburgh, 2013) is a sumptuously illustrated account of the Scottish Renaissance and its achievements

POST FLODDEN

Marcus Merriman's *The Rough Wooings* (East Linton, 2000) tells the story of Henry VIII and his successors' brutal attempts to marry the infant Mary Queen of Scots to the English crown through savage military oppression.

Moffat, Alistair, *The Reivers* (Edinburgh, 2008) is an account of a time both romanticised and yet terrible in the Borders when the weakness of monarchs and the endless rivalry of Scotland and England led to large areas on both sides of the border falling effectively out of central control.
Ritchie, Pamela, *Mary of Guise in Scotland 1548–1560* (East Linton, 2002) reassesses the figure of Mary of Guise.

The following biographies of Knox and Mary Queen of Scots all take different approaches but all can be recommended:

Dawson, Jane, *John Knox* (New Haven, 2015)
Fraser, Antonia, *Mary Queen of Scots* (London, 2009)
Graham, Roderick, *An Accidental Tragedy: the Life of Mary, Queen of Scots* (Edinburgh, 2009)

Guy, John, *My Heart is My Own: A Life of Mary Queen of Scots* (London, 2004)
Marshall, Rosalind, *John Knox* (Edinburgh, 2000)

THE SEVENTEENTH CENTURY

Cowan, E.J., *Montrose* (Edinburgh, 1995) is still reckoned to be the finest modern biography
Fraser, Murdo, *The Rivals* (Edinburgh, 2015) is a politician's look at the relationship of Montrose and Argyll through the story of their conflict
Mann, Alastair, *James VII* (Edinburgh, 2014) is a fine view of the King from a Scottish perspective
Prebble, John, *Glencoe* (London, 2005) is a superbly readable account of the Massacre
Stevenson, David, *Highland Warrior* (Edinburgh, 2014), compulsively readable, places Colkitto, Montrose's right-hand man at the heart of his success and shows how much the troubles of the time were seen through the prism of Campbell/Macdonald rivalry

The following three novels are wonderfully written evocations of the time. *John Splendid* is set in Munro's beloved Argyll, *Witchwood*, arguably Buchan's greatest work, in the Borders, while *John Burnet* is an exuberant romp from a writer at the start of his career. Both Buchan and Munro combine a meticulous sense of time and place with a tremendous narrative drive:

Buchan, John, *John Burnet of Barns* (Edinburgh, 2008)
Buchan, John, *Witchwood* (Edinburgh, 1998)
Munro, Neil, *John Splendid* (Edinburgh, 1994)

THE EIGHTEENTH CENTURY

For the 18th century the field begins to fill out. For those who want to read further on the Enlightenment, for instance, there are fine works by writers such as Nicholas Phillipson which are well worth reading. Buchan, Broadie and Herman all provide fine and complementary works on the Enlightenment. Michael Fry's *A Higher World* is the only conspectus of the century as a whole. *Culloden* remains a classic, although the quality of Prebble's writing and its emotional power does serve to hide a clearly one-sided interpretation and view of Scottish history. James Hunter's somewhat curiously entitled book is a solution to one of the most enduring mysteries of Scottish history: who killed Colin Campbell, in the infamous Appin Murder? *The Prisoner of St Kilda* is a tragic, moving and fascinating story of a deeply wronged wife whose husband resolved to make sure she never revealed his Jacobite plottings and much else by secreting her on the most remote place in Britain. From the fictional point of view, *Kidnapped* and *Catriona* need no introduction.

Buchan, James, *Capital of the Mind* (Edinburgh, 2007)
Broadie, Alexander, *The Scottish Enlightenment* (Edinburgh, 2007)
Fry, Michael, *A Higher World: Scotland 1707–1815* (Edinburgh, 2014)
Fry, Michael, *The Union* (Edinburgh, 2013) is the best short account
Herman, Arthur, *The Scottish Enlightenment* (London, 2003)
Hunter, James, *Culloden and the Last Clansman* (Edinburgh, 2010)
Moffat, Alistair, *The Highland Clans* (London, 2010)
Macaulay, Margaret, *The Prisoner of St Kilda* (Edinburgh, 2010)
Prebble, John, *Culloden* (London, 2002)
Prebble, John, *The Darien Disaster* (London, 2002) is again an example of Prebble at his best, telling the story of the scheme that bankrupted Scotland
Scott, Paul, *Andrew Fletcher and the Treaty of Union* (Edinburgh, 1994). There is no doubting where Paul Scott's views on the Union lie and his portrait of Andrew Fletcher is an immensely favourable one but full of detail and verve
Stevenson, Robert Louis, *Kidnapped/Catriona* (Edinburgh, 2007)
Whatley, Christopher, *The Scots and the Union* (Edinburgh, 2014) is a magisterial work which proves the consistency of principle of the Union supporters

The three great travelogues of 18th-century Scotland are listed below. Some might include Pennant's two tours as well. But Martin Martin from a Gaelic perspective, Burt from the point of view of a Hanoverian officer, and Johnson and Boswell as two of the great literary figures of the 18th century are all masterpieces.

Burt, Edmund, *Burt's Letters from the North of Scotland* (Edinburgh, 1998)
Johnson, Samuel and Boswell, James, *To the Hebrides* (Edinburgh, 2011)
Martin Martin, *Description of the Western Isles* (Edinburgh, 2014)

THE NINETEENTH AND TWENTIETH CENTURIES

Michael Fry's *New Race of Men* is a magisterial survey of 19th-century Scottish history, and his *The Scottish Empire* was the first to bring home the sheer scale of the Scottish contribution to, involvement in and shaping of the British Empire. *The Dundas Despotism* is a detailed account of the extraordinary Dundas family who dominated late 18th- and early 19th-century Scottish history and by whose support governments rose or fell. James Hunter and T.M. Devine both chronicle the extraordinary story of Scots across the world. T.C. Smout's *A Century of the Scottish People* straddles the 19th and 20th centuries and is a worthy successor to his *History of the Scottish People*.

Trevor Royle's two books look at the effect of the two great World Wars on Scotland. Catriona Macdonald's *Whaur Extremes Meet* is an award-winning conspectus of the 20th century, while Kenneth Roy's very personal look at post-war Scotland has enjoyed great acclaim.

Devine, T.M., *Scotland's Empire* (London, 2012)
Devine, T.M., *To the Ends of the Earth* (London, 2012)
Fry, Michael, *A New Race of Men* (Edinburgh, 2013)
Fry, Michael, *The Scottish Empire* (Edinburgh, 2001)
Fry, Michael, *The Dundas Despotism* (Edinburgh, 2004)
Hunter, James, *A Dance Called America* (Edinburgh, 2010)
Kelly, Stuart, *Scott-land: the Man Who Invented a Nation* (Edinburgh, 2011)
Macdonald, Catriona, *Whaur Extremes Meet* (Edinburgh, 2009)
Maclean, Sorley, *White Leaping Flame: Collected Poems* (Edinburgh, 2011)
Richards, Eric, *The Highland Clearances* (Edinburgh, 2013)
Roy, Kenneth, *The Invisible Spirit: A Life of Post War Scotland* (Edinburgh, 2014)
Royle, Trevor, *Flowers of the Forest: Scotland and the First World War* (Edinburgh, 2007)
Royle, Trevor, *A Time of Tyrants; Scotland and the Second World War* (Edinburgh, 2013)
Scott, Walter, *The Journal of Sir Walter Scott* (Edinburgh, 1999)
Smout, T.C., *A Century of the Scottish People 1830–1950* (London, 2010)

In the field of fiction Crichton Smith's *Consider the Lilies* is rightly regarded as the great novel of the Clearances. John Galt is a wonderful and humorous observer of small-town Scottish life in *The Provost* and *Annals of the Parish*, while *The Member,* on the run-up to the 1832 Reform Bill, is one of the greatest political novels ever written. Given quite how accessible and often funny a writer he is, it is deeply to be regretted that Galt is not better known. The works of Sir Walter Scott are honoured more in the breach than the observance but the *Journal* is unusually readable, indeed essential to understand early 19th-century Edinburgh. On a lighter note, the famous Para Handy stories combine great wit with superb observation of the Clyde and the Hebrides at the end of the 19th and beginning of the 20th centuries, commenting on many issues and stories of the day.

By this stage there are almost too many novels to mention, but *A Scots Quair* and its successor works remain as profound as anything in Scottish writing on the effects of war and industrial depression on a community. Often unbearably moving and powerful, Jessie Kesson writes in similar vein but at a later period. Muriel Spark's evocation of Edinburgh in the 1930s is a tour de force of observation and characterisation. Jenkins, one of the titans of Scottish writing, in *The Cone Gatherers* and *Fergus Lamont* wrote two seminal books which reach deep into the heart of 20th-century Scotland and its people. Maclean, McCaig and Macdiarmid are not simply great poets of the 20th century but of all time and for all peoples. Selections exist of them all but it is in their complete works that the full range and power of their writing is best conveyed.

Galt, John, *The Member/The Radical* (Edinburgh, 2001)
Galt, John, *The Provost/Annals of the Parish/The Ayrshire Legatees* (Edinburgh, 2002)
Gibbon, Lewis Grassic, *A Scots Quair* (Edinburgh, 2006).
Gibbon, Lewis Grassic, *Speak of the Mearns and Other Stories* (Edinburgh, 2007)
Jenkins, Robin, *The Cone Gatherers* (Edinburgh, 2012)
Jenkins, Robin, *Fergus Lamont* (Edinburgh, 1990)
Kesson, Jessie, *Another Time, Another Place* (Edinburgh, 1997)
Kesson, Jessie, *The White Bird Passes* (Edinburgh, 1996)
McCaig, Norman, *Collected Poems* (London, 1993)
Macdiarmid, Hugh, *A Drunk Man Looks at the Thistle* (Edinburgh, 2008)
Maclean, Sorley, *White Leaping Flame: Collected Poems* (Edinburgh, 2011)
Munro, Neil, *Para Handy* (Edinburgh, 2015)
Smith, Iain Crichton, *Consider the Lilies* (London, 2001)
Spark, Muriel, *The Prime of Miss Jean Brodie* (London, 2013)

A SENSE OF PLACE

Some of the finest books about Scotland are about a particular area or a short period of time. To miss them is to miss a great deal of the extraordinary variety and range of experience in the country. So here is a small selection of the finest of them.

David Kerr Cameron's trilogy are miniature masterpieces of the lives of the fermtouns of the North-east of Scotland.

Cameron, David Kerr, *The Ballad and the Plough* (Edinburgh, 2008)
Cameron, David Kerr, *The Cornkister Days* (Edinburgh, 2008)
Cameron, David Kerr, *Willie Gavin, Crofter Man* (Edinburgh, 2008)

Angus Maclellan and The Coddy are two names who would be largely unknown to us now but for the work of John Lorne Campbell. Tradition bearers, storytellers, both produced classics. Ralph Glasser's Gorbals trilogy is a sobering and powerful memoir of Glasgow

Coddy, The, *Tales from Barra* (Edinburgh, 2004)
Craig, David, *On the Crofter's Trail* (Edinburgh, 2010)
Glasser, Ralph, *Growing Up in the Gorbals* (Edinburgh, 2006)
Hunter, James, *Last of the Free* (Edinburgh, 2010)
Hutchinson, Roger, *Calum's Road* (Edinburgh, 2006)
Maclellan, Angus, *The Furrow Behind Me* (Edinburgh, 1997)
Maclellan, Angus, *Stories from South Uist* (Edinburgh, 1997)
Nicolson, Adam, *Sea Room* (London, 2002)

It is almost invidious to extend this list much further, but *Calum's Road* has become a classic of a man who would not give up, and who in his own story reflects so much of the Scottish experience. Adam Nicolson's *Sea Room* is possibly the finest book on Scottish islands – the Shiants – ever written. Craig's personal and luminous reflections on the clearances and crofting belong to travelogue, memoir and history, while Jim Hunter's passionate and personal history of the Highlands is a fusion of a lifetime's work and a deep love.

This is a small sample of the riches available. If my own history encourages you to delve further and deeper into Scotland's rich history and culture, then it has achieved its task.

Index

Note: Asterisks * denote text boxes

Abercorn, West Lothian 67
Aberdeen 156, 161, 189, 249, 362*
  King's College at 190
  Press and Journal 339
Aberdeen, George Hamilton-Gordon, Earl of 382–3
Aberdeen Angus cattle 379–80
Aberdeen Breviary (Elphinstone, W., ed.) 190
Aberdeenshire 3, 38, 93
Aberfoyle 35
Aberlemno 65–7
Aberlemno Stone 67
Abernethy 108
ABN AMRO 474
Acca, Abbot at Hexham 126
Adam, Robert 333*, 402
Adam, William 300, 333*
Adam Smith Institute 457–8
Adamson, Robert 378–9
Adamson, Willie 413
Add, River 60–61
Addinston 52
  fort at 69
Adomnan 31, 59, 60, 62, 64
Advocates, Faculty of 328
Aebudae Insulae ('Hebrides) 30
Aed, son of Boanta 86
Aed mac Ainmuirech, High King of the Ui Neill 61
Aedan mac Gabrain 53, 61, 71
Aelred of Rievaulx 118, 119, 120, 121, 141, 142
Aethelflaed, Lady of the Mercians 96
Aethelfrith 69
  Am Fleisaur ('Trickster') 53, 102
Aethelric 51

Aethelstan 96, 97, 99
  overlordship of, acceptance of 97
  victory at Brunanburgh 97–8
Africa 4, 28, 60, 190
  imperial wars in 346
  North Africa 60
Agassiz, Lake 6
Agricola 33, 34, 35, 44
  campaigns of 35
Agricola (Tacitus) 40–41
agriculture
  Anglian farmers, measurements of 74*
  beef farming, railways and development of 379–80
  common lands, division of 318–20
  courtyard steadings, fashion for 335
  crop rotation 317–18
  drainage 101
  efficient farming, Attlee's call for 429
  enclosure of lands 318–19
  Ferguson tractors ('Wee Grey Fergies') 429
  fermtouns 135–6
  foot-and-mouth disease, disaster of 469–70
  heft to the hill 137*
  medieval farming, relics of 133–4
  mixed farming 82
  pastoral society of prehistoric Britain 39–40
  plough, redesign of 324–5
  reallocation of land and ownership 319–20
  runrig system 133, 134–5, 136, 277, 317, 320

  seasons, annual challenge of 134–5
  self-sufficiency 82
  sheep flocks, hefted nature of 137*
  transhumance, ancient journey of 68
  trapping, diet supplementation by 83–4
  work in, framework of 91–2
Ahmed Aga 351*
Aikey Fair in Buchan 291–2
Ailsa Craig 4
Airlie, Jimmy 442
Alba 45–75, 144, 487
Albany, Duke of 178, 179, 199
Albany, Regent 199
Albert, Prince Consort 371
'Albion' (football teams) 58
Alcock, Charles 389–90
Ale Water 319
  valley of 132
Alexander, Danny 482
Alexander, Douglas 485
Alexander I 112
Alexander II 142, 144, 145, 146, 153
Alexander III 85, 95, 142, 144, 146, 148, 149, 151, 152
Aliens Act (1705) 287
Almond, River 14
Alnwick 130
Alt Cluith ('Rock of the Clyde') 54, 55, 56, 57, 81
Alva, Duke of 220
American War of Independence 321, 339
amphora 29
Amyatt, John 325, 328–9
anatomy 366*

Ancrum 114
Anderson, Robert 311
Aneirin 52
Angles 44, 50, 51–2, 53, 55, 66, 74, 85
farmers, measurements of 74*
Anglo-Saxon Chronicle 80, 97–8, 103
Anglo-Saxon hall at Balbridie 23–4, 25, 26
Anglo-Saxons, incursions of 16, 23–4, 52
Angus, Earl of 274
Angus, Mearns and 36, 42, 49, 62, 64*, 104
Annabel, Queen 178
Annals of Tigernach (Irish chronicle) 104
Annals of Ulster 86, 89, 94–5
Annandale 33, 118, 146
lordship of 118
Anne, Queen 285, 287, 288
last Stewart monarch 295
Anne, Princess of Denmark 226
Antonine Wall 40*, 57, 320
Antrim 239, 252
Appin 87
Applecross 73, 410
Arabic numerals 34*
Aragon, Catherine of 204
Aralt, King of Man 97
Arbroath, Declaration of 13, 166, 171, 228
archers 108, 121, 154, 157, 158–9, 163–4, 167–8, 180
architecture
achievements of James IV 189
Adam, Robert, influence of 333*
Caledonian architectural memorials 41–2
City Chambers in Glasgow 398
Cumbernauld 436
grand houses, estates and 300–301
Latin inscriptions on 47
Mackintosh, Charles Rennie 400–401
St Andrew's House 423
Victorian Glasgow 400
Ardèche Gorge 12–13
Ardnamurchan 136
Ardtornish Castle 185
Argentocoxus ('Silver Leg') 44
Argyle, Archibald Campbell, 3rd Duke of 344, 396
Argyll 53, 57, 58, 60–61, 87
Kintyre peninsula and 30–31

Argyll, Campbells of 187
Argyll, Duke of 295, 296
Argyll, Earl of 220
Argyll, Marquis of 261
Arkinholm, near Langholm 182
Arkwright, Richard 322–3, 323–4
Armagh 239
Armstrong, Johnnie of Gilnockie 203
Armstrongs 197, 240
Army Council 259
Arnold, Matthew 369
Arnott of Tongland, Rev. Samuel 262
Arran, cheese-making on 323*
Artgal, King of Strathclyde 89, 90
Arthur, Chester 240*
Ascension Island 1
Ashkirk 132
Asleifsson, Svein 143*
Asquith, H.H. 413
Assembly Halls, parliamentary use of 466–7
Atholl, Earl of 152
Atholl, John, Duke of 323
Atholl (*Ath Fotla*, 'New Ireland') 62, 70–71
Atlantic Ocean 1, 2, 4, 23, 31, 46, 73
seaboard of 3, 11, 17, 18, 19, 22, 35–6, 42, 60, 62, 74, 85, 87, 94
Attlee, Clement, optimism for government of 427–8
Auchterarder 376–7
Aud the Deep-Minded 90, 100
Augustinians 120*
Augustus, Emperor 40*
'Auld Alliance' 192, 195, 199, 209, 286
Auldhame 71*
Austria-Hungary, armaments stock-piles of 406
Austrian Succession, War Of 308
Avalonia 2, 3, 4
Avebury 26
stones at 24, 26
Aveline's Hole 21, 22
Avenels, Scoto-Norman family 147
Ayala, Pedro de 188, 195
Ayrshire 160, 240
Azores 1

Babington, Anthony 220
Babylon and Babylonians 36*
Baden Powell, Robert 398*

Bailie, Robert 243, 245, 246
Baillie, Grizel and George 299, 300, 301
Baillie, Ivan 304
Baillie, Robert 253
Baillie, Timothy 477–8
Baillie of Jerviswood, Robert 299
Baird, John Logie 415*
Balbridie Hall 23–4, 25, 26
Baldwin, Stanley 419
Balfour, A.J. 224*
Balfour, Lady Frances 396
Balfour of Kinloch, John 264, 265
de Baliol, Bernard 118
Ballantrae 4
Balliol, Edward 166, 167, 168
de Balliol, John 152, 153, 154, 166
Balmoral Estate 371
Baltic States 321
Baltica 2, 3
Bamburgh 66, 197
castle at 91
fortress at 50, 91
Bamburgh, Earl of 102
Bank of England 283, 428
Bank of Scotland 283, 307
Bannauc ('Bannock Burn') 35
Bannockburn, Battle of 160, 163–7, 170, 390
Barbados 262
Barbour, John 166
Barker, Robert 390
Barnett, Joel and Barnett formula 480*
Barr, Sammy 442
Barrie, J.M. 224*
Barvas Moor 132
Basilikon Doron (James VI) 228, 233–4
Basque language 27*
Bass of Inverurie 111, 117
Bathgate 441
Battle of the Clans 177
bawbees 40*
Bayeux Tapestry 106, 111
BBC Scotland 471
BBC Television 431
Beachy Head, Battle of 282
Beaker People 27
Beorhtric, King 80
Bearsden 39, 43
The Beatles 439, 442
Beaton, Cardinal David 200, 207
Beaton, Cardinal James 202
Beaufort, Lady Joan 179
Beaufort Sea 6

Bechuanaland 404
Bede of Jarrow 49–50, 53, 55, 57, 58, 61, 63, 66, 67, 74, 93, 151
Bedrule 102
'Beggars' Summons' 211
Bek, Antony 152
Belgium 10
Bell, Ian 466–7
Bell family 197, 240
Bell's Weekly 388
Beltane 42–3
Ben Cruachan 442*
Ben Dorian 338–9
Ben Lomond 6
Ben More 4
    extinct volcano of 30
Benedictines 120*
Bengal 385–6
Bennachie hill, near Inverurie 38
Beowulf (Anglo-Saxon tale) 23
Berchan 104
Bergen 80
Bernard, Abbot of Arbroath 13
Bernard of Kilwinning, Abbot of Arbroath 166
Bernicia and Bernicians 49, 51, 53, 91
Berwick-upon-Tweed 138, 140, 143, 154, 155, 159, 167, 183, 186, 367
    castle at 130, 153, 160
    'Pacification of Berwick' 246, 249
    port of 115, 116
    Treaty of 171
Berwickshire 3, 33, 101, 187, 232, 300, 320*324, 325, 326, 328, 356, 400, 438
Bett, John 450*
Beveridge, William 425–6
Bevin, Ernest 425
Bewcastle 48*
Bilston Glen Colliery 455
Bing, Rudolf 431–2
'Birlinn of Clanranald' 124
Birnam Wood 103–4
Black, Mhairi 485
Black, Robert 462
The Black Arrow (Stevenson, R.L.) 394
Black Cuillin 5
Black Death 168, 169, 170*
Black Douglases 182
Black Mount 10, 15
Black Rood of St Margaret 48*, 155
Black Watch *(Am Freiceadan)* 303–4, 342, 408, 409

Blackadder of Troqueer, Rev. John 262, 264
Blackfriars 120*
Blackheath Football Club 388
blackhouses 136–7
blackmail 234–5, 287
Blaeu Atlas of Scotland (1654) 101
Blair, Professor Hugh 369
Blair, Tony 460–61
Blair Castle 273, 274
Blairlomond or Beacon Field 54
Blake, William 369
Blathmac 76, 85
Blatobulgium 125
Blawearie 132
Blebo 125–6
Blebo Craigs 126
Bliadhna Thearlaich ('The Year of Charles') 336
blood eagle, ceremony of 77
Bloodstone Hill 17
Blue Peter (BBC TV) 434
'blue ring,' from fair lady 229, 230
Blythe lineage 240
BMC (British Motor Corporation) 441
Boar People 79
Boarhills 70
Bodotria (Firth of Forth) 34, 35
Boece, Hector 189, 191
Boethius 122, 122*
de Bohun, Sir Henry 161–2
de Bohun, Humphrey 153
Boleyn, Anne 204
Bolt, Usain 478
Bonar Law, Andrew 414
Bonnie Dundee *see* Graham of Claverhouse, Viscount John ('Bonnie Dundee')
Book of Common Prayer 242
The Book of the Taking of Ireland (origin legend) 13
Border ballads 370, 374
border between Scotland and England 101, 171
    raiding across 197–200, 204–5, 208–9, 235
    unfolding history of 4, 41, 45
Border Commission 235
Border Reivers 197–200, 203, 235, 238
Border Royalists 255
Border TV 434
Boswell, James 345
Botany Bay 352
Bothwell Bridge 265, 266
Boudiccan rebellion 32

Boulogne 28
Boulton, Matthew 340, 363
Bower, Walter 144–5, 158, 178
Bowes, Robert 204
box beds 140, 335
Boyd, Lord James 315
Boyd of Kilmarnock, Lord Robert 184
Boyne, Battle of 276
Boy's Brigade 398*, 443–4
Brahms, Johannes 369
Braid Hills 133
Braidwood, Thomas 322*
Bran, son of Oengus 86
Branxton Hill 193, 194, 196
Brash, Scott 478
Braxfield, Lord Justice Clerk Robert 352
Bray, Thomas 342
Brechin 373
Bretnach, Gilchrist, Gilchrist the Briton 176
Bridei, King 64*, 66, 67
Brigantes, federation of 32
Brigte, Gille 130
Britannia 32, 38, 43, 44, 48, 49–50
    'Tattoo Nation' 29*
British Council in Scotland 431
British Empire 351*
    railway developments in 384–5
    sun setting on 435
British Leyland 441
British Linen Bank 321
British Motor Company 440–41
British Pathé 416
British Petroleum 444
Britons 29, 37, 41, 44, 49, 51, 53–4, 56, 67, 74, 89
Brittany 17
Brodgar, Ring of 24
Bromborough 97
Brown, Ernest 426
Brown, George 332
Brown, Gordon 460–61, 468, 475, 479, 480, 481, 482, 483
Brown, James 332
Brown, Tom 467–8
Brown Caterthun 42
Bruce, Elizabeth 160
Bruce, Isabella 160
Bruce, Marjorie 172
Bruce, Mary 160
Bruce, Neil 160
Bruce, Robert 118, 147, 152, 153, 160, 162, 163, 164, 187, 265

Brunanburh 97
Buccleuch, Henry Scott, Duke
    of 329
Buchan, Tom 446
Buchanan, George 219, 220,
    225, 228, 327
Buchanan, Jack 434
Buchanan, James 240*
Buchanan, Thomas 321
Buckingham, Duke of 238
Buick, David Dunbar 403
Bull, Stephen 191
Bull Fort and Bull People 63
Burgess Oath 376
Burgh-on-Sands 83*
Burgher Secession Kirk 376
Burghhead 374
burghs 144
    backlands 139
    life in 138–9
Burke, William 366*
Burn, Jock and Geordie 198
Burns, Robert 240, 352–4, 358
    health of 355
    Kilmarnock edition of poems
        of 354
    tour of Scotland 354–5
    veneration for 355–6
Burntisland, Blessing of 241*
Burrell, Sir William 399–400
Burrell Collection 105–6, 400
Burt, Edward 293
Bute 54
Butler, Eamonn and Stuart
    457–8
Butler, R.A. 438
Byland Abbey 117
Byng, Admiral 290
Byrne, John 450*
Byron, George, Lord 369

Caddon Lea 154, 169
Cadell, Robert 371
Caereni ('Sheep Folk') 30–31
Caesar, Julius 28, 40
Cairngorms 3, 22*
Caithness 102
Calchvynydd, kingdom of 52
Calcutta 385–6
Calcutta Scots 350
caled, Celtic root (found in
    Kirkaldy) 34–5
Caledonia 28–44
Caledonian Forest 82
Caledonian Mercury 327, 339
Caledonians, red-gold hair of 42
Calgacus ('swordsman') 38
California 2
Caligula 28

Caliphate of Cordoba 80
Callaghan, James 451, 480*
Callendar 159
Calpurnius 48
Calvin, John 207, 236
Calvinism 223, 250
Cambuskenneth Abbey 187
Cameron, David 433*, 476–7,
    479, 486
    English Votes for English Laws
        (EVEL), statement on 482,
        486
Cameron, Richard ('Lion of the
    Covenant') 266
Cameron, Sir Donald of Lochiel
    309
Cameron, Sir Ewen of Lochiel
    272, 273
Cameron Clan 177
Cameronians 266, 274, 275, 286
    disbandment of 444*
Campbell, Archibald, Earl of
    Argyll 251, 252, 253, 268
Campbell, Archibald, Lord Ilay
    307
Campbell, Archibald, Marquis of
    Argyll 256
Campbell, Captain Robert of
    Glenlyon 280, 281, 282
Campbell, Gordon 442, 445
Campbell, John 338
Campbell, John, Duke of Argyll
    307
Campbell, Keith 463–4
Campbell, Sir Colin 280
Campbell, Sir Duncan of
    Auchinbreck 253, 254
Campbell Clan 175, 249, 251,
    252, 254
Canada 6
    emigration to 343–4, 349, 411
canal development 365–6
    Burke and Hare and 366*
Candida Casa ('White House')
    49, 50
Canmore, Malcolm ('An Ceann
    Mor') 48*, 49, 88–9, 104,
    108, 109*, 118
Cannon, Col. 275, 276
Cape Horn 283
Capellanus, John 114*
car manufacturing 440–41
Carberry Hill 218, 219
Cardean in Angus 37
Carey, Philadelphia, Lady Scrope
    228
Carey, Sir Robert 198, 228, 229,
    230
Carham, Battle of 101, 102, 103

Carham on Tweed 56
Carisbrooke Castle 255, 261
Carlenrig kirkyard 203
Carlisle 47, 48, 405*
    Bishop of 54, 199
    Carlisle Castle 110, 122, 129
    Christian Church in 48
    Luguvalium (Carlisle) 47
Carnegie, Andrew 403
Carpzov, Benedict 227
Carr, Francis 237
Carr, Robert of Ferniehurst, Earl
    of Somerset 232, 236
Carron Ironworks 321–2, 324,
    335, 340
    occupation attempt at 362
Carstares, William 299, 299*
Carter, Jimmy 240*
Carthusians 120*
Cartwright, Major John 361
Carver, Robert 213*
Carvetii (Deer People) of
    Cumbria 47, 51
Casket Letters 218
Cassius Dio 44
Catesby, Robert 232, 233
Catholic Emancipation Act
    (1829) 362
Catholic Irish, political spite
    at 420
Catholic Young Men's Society
    391
Catriona (Stevenson, R.L.) 394
Catterick, Battle of 52
Cavaliers 250, 251*
Cavan 239
'The Ceaseless Surge of the Sea'
    (MacIver, D.) 344
Cecil, Robert 228, 231, 232
Cellach, Abbot 73, 76
Cellach, Bishop of St Andrews 95
Celtic calendar 42–3
Celtic Football Club 391
Celtic order, passing in power
    elite of Scots 110
*The History of the Celtic Place-
    Names of Scotland* (Watson,
    W.J.) 62
Cenel Loairne 58, 103, 104
Cenel nGabrain of Kintyre 58,
    62, 86, 87
Cenel nOengusa 58
Census (1755) 342
Census (1861) 367–8
Census (1871) 381
Central Scotland 3, 50, 101
Cetiosaurus 5*
Chadwick Report (1842) 368
chainmail *see* mail shirts

Chalmers, Thomas 376–7, 378
Chamberlain, Neville 419, 424
Chambers, Robert 331
Chapel Royal at Holyrood Abbey 241, 242, 268
Charlemagne 80, 95
  fragmentation of empire of 105
Charles, Prince of Wales 313
Charles I 238, 240, 241, 241*, 243, 246, 248, 249, 256–7, 337, 361
Charles II 217*, 257, 258, 261, 337, 359
Charles the Simple 105
Charlotte, Queen 332
Charltons 197
Chattan, Clan 176, 177, 313
  Confederacy 270
Chaucer, Geoffrey 179
Chauvet, Jean-Marie 12–13
cheese 323*
Chepman, Walter 190
Cherbourg Peninsula 112
Chester 45, 50, 99, 101
Chester-le-Street 117
Cheviots 32, 33, 46, 94
  watershed of 143
Chichester, Arthur 239
child mortality 82
A Child's Garden of Verses (Stevenson, R.L.) 394
Cholmondley's Regiment 336
Chrestos 48
Chrichton Smith, Iain 338–9
Christianity 47, 54, 60
  development of 48–50
  Roman introduction of 44*
  savagery against Christians 76–7
Chronicle (Froissart, J.) 167, 178
Chronicle of the Kings of Alba 88
Church of Scotland 109, 109*, 326, 376
  Books of Discipline of Reformed Kirk 222–3
  'The Confession of Faith of the Kirk of Scotland' 212, 244
  Disruption of 376–8
  General Assembly (1843) 376, 377, 378
  Margaret Thatcher at General Assembly 456
  membership of, decline in 443–4
  racism of, 'The Menace of the Irish Race to our Scottish Nationality' (1923) 420
  schism, moment of 377

United Free Church and, reunion between 420
Veto Act, passing of 377
Church Penitentiary Association for the Reclamation of Fallen Women 382
Churchill, John, Duke of Marlborough 289
Churchill, Winston S. 414*, 424–5, 426–7, 431
  resignation from government of (1953) 435
Cinaed 86
cinema (pictures) 416
Cinnbelachoir 88
Cistercians 120*
Clach nam Breatann ('Stone of the Britons') 55
Claideom ('Swordland') 68
A Claim of Right for Scotland 456–7
Claish Farm 24
clan heritage 175–6
Clanranalds 124, 173, 252, 309, 313
  island of Eigg 282
Clans, Battle of the 177
Clas-gu ('Dear Family,' origin of Glasgow) 56
Claudius, Emperor 28, 29, 32
Clegg, Nick 433*, 479
Cleland, Lt. Col William 265, 274, 275
Clement VII, Pope 204
Clement XI, Pope 306
Clerisseau, Charles-Louis 333*
Cleveland, Grover 240*
climate 84
  climate flickering 9–10
  Medieval Warm Period 100–101
  winter cold, sorter and wetter summers (14th–19th centuries) 165
Clinton, Bill 240*
Cluniacs 113, 120*
Clyde, Firth of 54, 55
Clyde, Rock of the 89
Clyde Basin 155
Clyde Basin Scheme 425
Clyde Locomotive Company 385
Clyde, River 10, 11
Clyde Valley 50, 57, 112
Clydebank 385
Clydesdale heavy horses 365*
Cnut, King 102, 103
Co-operative Movement 413–14
coal-mining 363–5
  demise of (1984-5) 453–5

distribution of, heavy horses and 364–5
  expansion of 363–4
  Larkshire coalfield 365
  production, expansion of 364–5
  testimonies on young girls in 363–4
Coalbrookdale 321–2
Cobden, Richard 383
Cockburn, Henry 351
Cockburn, Mrs Alison 354
Cockburnspath 258
Coffey, Aeneas 372
coinage 40*
Coire an Lochain 22*
Colchester 28, 29, 30
Cold Snap 7, 11, 16*
Coldingham Muir 93
Coldingham Priory 187
Coldstream Guards 260
Coleraine 239
Coleridge, Samuel Taylor 370–71
Coll 3
Colmieu, Jean de 111
Colonsay 19, 20, 124, 125
colours of early Scotland 83
Coltrane, Robbie 450*
Columbus, Christopher 100, 191
comharba ('abbot' or 'heir') 60
commercial TV, beginnings of 433–4
Committee of Estates 249
Commonwealth Games (2014) 478
Communist Party 437, 442
Community Charge 458
Comyn, John 160, 166
Comyn, Walter 144, 145
Comyn family 161
Conan Doyle, Sir Arthur 405*
Confessio (St Patrick) 47
'Confession of Faith of the Kirk of Scotland' 212–13
'The Confession of Faith of the Kirk of Scotland' 212, 244
Conn of the Hundred Battles 180
Connolly, Billy 446–7
Connolly, James 413
conquest
  of Britain (Tacitus' view on) 38
  Roman strategy for 32–3, 35–8
Conservative–Liberal Democrat Coalition 476–7
Conservative Party 382–3, 384, 413, 419, 426–7

referendum (1979) 451
victory in 2015 general election
  for 486
'You've never had is so good'
  436–7
The Consolation of Philosophy
  (Boethius) 122*
Constable & Company of
  Edinburgh 360
Constantine, Emperor 47
Constantine I 65*, 70, 89, 90,
  97, 98
  army of 91
Constantine II 94, 95, 97
Constantinople 47
conventicle at East Nisbet 263–4
Conway, Lord 248
Cook, Robin 460
Cope, General Sir John 310, 311
Corbridge, Battle at 94–5
Corgarff Castle 373
Cormack, John 420
Corpach Pulp Mill 453
Corrie, Gladstone and Bradshaw
  381–2
Cotentin 112
de Coucy, Marie 145
countryside life 334–5
  atrocities of 1746 summer
    336–7, 345–6
  Battle of the Braes 392–3
  crofting, difficulties of 347–8
  crofting problems, unrest and
    392–3
  farmsteads 92–3
  glens of Highlands, emptying
    of 336, 343–4, 345–6
  grand houses, estates and
    300–301
  Higland life, 1745 and after
    335, 336, 338, 342–3,
    345–6
  kelping 347
  medieval life in 133–7
  shires 92–4
  traditional townships
    (bailtean), life in 347
  Union and changes in 299
The Courier 470
Coutts, Provost 310
Covenant, Army of the 245–6,
  248, 250, 255, 258
Covenant, Wars of the 376
Covenanters
  harsh treatment of 266–7
  see also Solemn League and
    Covenant; Wars of the
    Covenant
Craig, Archibald 375

Craig, James 331–2, 332–4, 349
Craik Forest 33
Cramond 14, 17, 161
Crane Lake, Battle at 66, 67
Creag nan Stearnan 17
Cressingham, Hugh 155, 156,
  157
Cresswell Crags 12
Cromwell, Oliver 250, 251, 255,
  256, 257, 258
  creation of eleven regions in
    Britain and Ireland 260
  Lord Protector 259, 260
Cromwell, Richard 260
crop marks at Balbridie 23
Crosd, Domhnall Ban 343–4,
  391
Crovan, Godred 124, 125
Cuillin, Isle of Skye 127
Culduthel burial, Inverness 27
Culloden, Battle of 175, 312–15,
  335–6, 336–7
  campaign medal struck for
    338
Culross monastery 55
Culross Muir 93
cultural transmission, defining
  shape of 60
Cumberland, Augustus William,
  Duke of 303, 312, 335–6,
  338
Cumbernauld 435–6
Cumbraes 55
Cumbria and Cumbrians 55,
  108, 120, 142, 143, 164
Cumming, Janet, coal mining life
  for 363–4
Cunningham, George 449
Cunningham, William, Earl of
  Glencairn 259
Cunninghame 146
Cunninghame Graham, R. B.
  397, 420
Cunobelinus, King of the
  Catuvellauni 28
curraghs 17–18, 22
Curthose, Robert 110, 112
Cymbeline (Shakespeare, W.) 28
Cynderyn, Ceann Tighearna
  ('High Lord') 55

Dacre, Lord Thomas 194, 199,
  200
Daemionologie (James VI) 226
Daiches, David 374
Daily Record 418, 450, 470,
  479–80
Dale, David 323
Dalmeny 149

Dalnaspidal 260
Dalreudians 57
Dalriada 53, 54, 68, 102–3,
  173
  fleet of, mibilisation of 61
  high kingship of 87
  kindreds of 31, 61, 67, 86
  kingdoms of 57
  kings of 60–61, 70–71
  politics of 61
  Ulster territories of 61
Dalriadan formations 3–4
Dalrymple, John, Master of the
  Stair 280
  resignation of 282
Dalyell, General Tam 261
Dalyell, Tam 457
Damian, John 188
Damnonii 54
Danish Northumbria 90
Danube, River 38, 45
Dar-Thula (Deirdre of the
  Sorrows) 370
Darby, Abraham 321–2
Darien Scheme 284–5
Dark Ages in Scotland 30, 52,
  54, 76, 93
Darling, Alistair 474–5, 478,
  481–2
Darnley, Henry Stewart, Lord
  217*, 218, 225, 305
  marriage to Mary 216–17
David, Duke of Rothesay 178
David, Earl of Huntingdon,
  Prince of Cumbria 113,
  114, 115, 116, 118, 153
David I 117, 121, 122, 129, 141,
  142, 153
David II 167, 168, 171, 172
Davis Strait 6
Davy, Sir Humphry 364–5
Day of the Seven Sleepers 103
'dean' 12*
Dearmach 58
decimalisation (1971) 447
Emperor Decius 45–6
Declaration of Arbroath 166,
  171, 228
Declaration of Breda 260
Dee, River 98
Deeside 23, 371
Defoe, Daniel 294, 297
Degsastan, Battle of 52–3, 61,
  69
deindustrialisation (1979-81)
  453–4
Deira 51–2, 53, 91
Delphi 31
Demetrius of Tarsus 31

Dempster, George 323–4
Denmark 10, 15
Denmark, Anne of 238
Dere Street 33, 94, 119, 149, 161
Description of the Isles of Orkney and Shetland (Sibbald, R.) 327
Destiny, Stone of 187
  see also Stone of Scone
destriers (war-horses) 107–8, 154, 157, 162–3, 164
Deva Victrix 98
Devil's Porridge 405*
devolution referendum (1997) 464–5
Dewar, Donald 460, 466, 467
  'Father of the Nation' 468–9
Diarmait 76
Dibdin, Rev. Dr 69
de Diceto, Ralph 120
Dickson, Rev. John of Rutherglen 262
Dilke, Sir Charles 403
Din Eidyn 54
Dinogad 84
Diocletian, Emperor 333*
diplomacy 29–30
Disarming Acts (1746) 291, 298, 359
discovery, accidental nature of 17
Disraeli, Benjamin 383
DNA research 13, 16–17, 26, 27, 56–7, 73, 77, 80, 85–6, 143*, 217*
Dogger Bank 15, 23
Dogger Hills 16
Dogger Island 23
Doggerland 15, 16, 23
dogs, domestication of 10*
Dolly the Sheep 463–4
Dominicans 120*
Domitian, Emperor 31, 34
Domna, Empress Julia 45
Donald, Clan 125, 145, 175, 176, 251
Donald, Lord of the Isles 179, 180
Donald II Ban 89, 91, 110
Donaldson, Alexander 345*
Donegal 239
Donegan, Lonnie 439*
Doon Hill 258
Dornoch 319
Douglas, Archibald 182
Douglas, David 181
Douglas, Dick 440
Douglas, Earl William 181

Douglas, George, Earl of Angus ('Red Douglas') 182
Douglas, Hugh 182
Douglas, John 182, 212
Douglas, Lord William 155
Douglas, Marquis of 274
Douglas, Rev. Thomas 265
Douglas, Sir Archibald 167
Douglas, Sir James 163, 164, 167
Douglas, William 176
Douglas-Home, Alec, Earl of Home 438–9, 442, 445, 451
  'Scotland's Government' Report by 445
Down 239, 252
de Dreux, Yolande, Countess of Montfort 149
droving, drove roads and 68, 198, 290–93, 294, 379
Druim Cett, Convention of 62
Drummond, Captain Thomas 280, 281, 284
Drummond, Lord John 313
Drummond, Lord Provost George 331–2
Drummond, Margaret 172
Drummossie Moor 312–15, 335–6
A Drunk Man Looks at the Thistle (MacDiarmid, H.) 418–19
Duart Castle 185
Dubh, Donald 185
Dublin 85
  Norsemen in 89–91
  Viking leadership in 96, 97
Dübs, Henry 384–5
Duddingston Loch 64
Dudley, Robert, Earl of Leicester 216
Dumbarton Castle 222
  siege of 91
Dumbarton Rock 54, 89, 90–91
Dumbiedykes 322*
Dumfries Courier 381
Dun Breatainn 'Fortress of the Britons' 54, 89
Dunadd 61, 68, 81, 95, 173
Dunbar 4, 88, 154
Dunbar, William 188, 189, 209*
Dunblane tragedy 462–3
Duncan, Thane of Fife 122, 123
Duncan I 89, 102, 110
Duncan II 131
Duncanson, Major Robert 281
Dundas, Henry 349–50, 435
Dundas, Henry, Viscount Melville 349–50, 351, 435
Dundas, Sir Laurence 332

Dundas of Arniston, Robert 349
Dundee
  Churchill unseated in 414*
  Irish migration to 381
  jute working in 385–6
  whaling fleet 386
Dundee Castle 156
Dundee Courier 339
Dundee University 438
Dundreggan, Grant of 336–7
Dunfermline, Abbot of 171
Dunfermline Palace 109
Dunkeld
  monastery at 86–7
  siege of 274, 275, 276, 280
Dunkeld Cathedral 279
Dunlop, cheese-making at 323*
Dunlop, William 365*
Dunn, Douglas 461
Dunnichen, Battle of 64*, 67, 92, 487
Dunnichen Hill 66, 67
Dunning, St Serf's Church at 65*
Dunnotar 97
Duns 324
Duns Castle 246
Duns Law, Covenant Army at 245–6
Dunsinane, Battle of the Seven Sleepers at 103–4
Dunsinnan Hill 104
Dunure footprint 365*
Dupplin Cross 65*
Dupplin Moor 167
Durham 53, 117, 118
  Prince Bishops of 151
  Treaty of 121
Durham Cathedral 48*, 155
Durness Limestones 3
Durward, Alan 145
Dux Macbethad 103

Eamont Bridge 96
  see also David I
Earl of Argyll 280
Earl of Bernicia 97
Earl of Crawford 182
Earl of Douglas 182
Earl of Moray 182
Earl of Morton 225
Earl of Ormonde 182
Earl of Shrewsbury 112
Earra-Ghàidhheal ('Coast of the Gaels') 58
East Barns 17, 21, 335
  prehistoric house at 14, 15
East India Company 350, 385, 403
  dissolution of 403

East Kilbride 436
East Lothian 85
East Nisbet, conventicle at 263–4
Easter Ross 31
*The Ecclesiastical History of the
    English People* (Bede) 49,
    151
Ecgfrith, King 64*, 66–7
Echline 15, 17, 21
economics
    'balance of trade,' Hume's
        concept of 329
    clearances, economics of
        348–9
    Darien Scheme, economic ruin
        and 284–5
    economic stagnation 409,
        414–15, 426
    economies of scale 441–2
    farming economy 26, 82, 101,
        114–15, 116, 338
    financial crisis (2008) 473–5
    industrial economy, growth of
        322, 334, 345–6, 398–9
    medieval economy 129,
        170–71
    money exchange 40*, 114
    North Sea oil 444
    pastoral economy 39, 68,
        336
    science and, teaching of 327
    tobacco economy 321
    trading economy 131
    Union, economic effects of
        290–91, 294
    Vikings, impact of 77
    Wall Street Crash 419
    war economies 361, 412*
    world economy, recovery of
        421
Eden, Anthony 435
    resignation of 436
Edgar the Aetheling 89, 98, 99,
    101, 108
Edinburgh 138, 140
    airport at 50
    capital city, development as
        196
    carters in 334
    City Guard 338
    fisherfolk and herring sales
        in 379
    George Street, eastern vista
        along 349
    housing 'schemes' around 436
    Lawnmarket 330–31, 332
    life in Old Town of 331
    masonry, materials and
        techniques of 334

Mound, development of area
    of 332
New Town of, development of
    331–2, 332–4
Old Town, redevelopment of
    330–31
provostship of 242
redevelopment and expansion
    of 330–31
Robertson's Land 330, 334
St Cuthbert's Co-operative
    in 413
universities in 387*
Waverley Station 339–40
Edinburgh & Glasgow Railway
    366, 367
Edinburgh Academical Football
    Club 387
Edinburgh Academy 388
Edinburgh Advertiser 345*
Edinburgh Castle 154
Edinburgh Castle Rock 81
Edinburgh Evening News 417,
    471
Edinburgh Festival 431–2
    Festival Fringe 432
Edinburgh Magazine 304
Edinburgh University Medical
    School 395
Ednam Mill 93
education
    Education Department,
        establishment of (1872) 378
    IQ testing at '11-plus' 430
    maintenance grants and
        student loans 438
    merchant company schools
        430–31
    post-war settlement 429–31
    school qualifications,
        rationalisation of 430
    tertiary education, expansion
        of 437–8
    university tuition fees 437
Education Act (1918) 420
Education Act (1962) 437
Education Acts (1944 and 1945)
    429–30, 437
Edward I 48*, 49, 83*, 149,
    151–6, 158, 159, 160
Edward II 161, 163
Edward III 167, 168, 171, 176
Edward IV 185, 186, 209
Edward the Confessor 102, 105,
    427*
Edward the Elder 96
Edward VIII 398
Eglinton, Alexander, Earl of 256
Egypt 47, 351*

Eigg 73
Eildon Hill North 42
Eilean Donan 60
Eilean Mor 173
Eilean na Comhairle ('Council
    Island') 173
Einstein, Albert 328
Elserhower, Dwight D. 435
Elcho, Lord 252
Elderslie 56–7
Eleanor of Aquitaine 130
Electoral Commission 477
Elements of Criticism (Kames,
    H.H., Lord) 326
elephants 28, 30
Elizabeth I 216, 220, 221, 224
Elizabeth II 433–4
Elliot, Walter 423
Elphinstone, William 189, 190
Emergency Hospital Service
    425
emigration, opportunities in
    381–2, 402–3, 415–16
Encyclopaedia Britannica 325,
    328–9
enechruicce ('face reddening') 174
English Channel 23, 28, 58
Enlightenment 325–6
Eoganan, son of Oengus 86
Epidii ('Horse-Kindred') 31, 34,
    35, 63
Epiphany, Feast of (1540) 206–7
Erik II 153
Erskine, John, Earl of Mar 295
Esk River 83
Eskdale 146, 147
Essie, Strathbogie 104
Estates, Committee of 249
Ettrick Forest 33, 136, 146, 203
Eutropius 29–30
Evangelicals 376–7
    Claim, Declaration and Protest
        anent the Encroachments of
        the Court of Session 377
Evening Times 471
Everest, conquest of (1953) 433
Ewing, Winnie 440, 445, 467

Factory Act (1850) 386–7
Fairfax, Thomas 255
'Faithful Congregation of Christ
    Jesus in Scotland' 210
Falaise 131
    Treaty of 130, 152
Falkirk 57
Falkland Castle 189
Falkland Palace 178
Falklands War (1982) 452–3
Falloch, Glen 55

Family Allowances Act (1945) 428

famine 71, 165–6, 278, 282, 286, 317, 380, 391
  potato blight and 380–81
  Seven Ill Years of 278

Farallon Plate 2

Farnham 238

Farquharson Clan 371

Fawkes, Guy 43, 232, 233

Fenian Cycle (fables) 121

Fenwick Weavers' Society 413

Ferdinand and Isabella of Castile and Aragon 188

Ferguslie Park, Paisley 450*

Ferguson, Adam 327

Ferguson, Harry 429

Ferguson, Professor Adam 369–70

Fergusson, Captain John 337

Fermanagh 239, 240

Fettercairn 67

feudalism 105, 108, 111, 119, 131, 152–3, 175, 468

Fflamddwyn 52

Fife 50, 101

Fife Adventurers 233*

Fife Herald 69

Findlaech's son 103

Fingal 369–70

finger numbers 34*

Finlaggan 173

Fionn mac Cumhaill 370

The First Blast of the Trumpet Against the Monstruous Regiment of Women (Knox, J.) 215

First World War 396, 405
  armaments, stock-piles of 406
  armistice, Treaty of Versailles and 409, 414
  beginnings in Sarajevo of 406
  conscription 408–9
  death toll, extent for Scotland of 409, 411–13
  economic effect on Scotland of 409, 411–13, 414
  failure of post-war ambitions 426
  Glasgow Corporation tramways in 408
  memorials to dead of 409
  munitions production 405*
  patriotic reaction in Scotland 406–7, 408
  strike for peaceful settlement in Glasgow 409
  Western Front, scale of slaughter on 408–9

Western Front, Scottish soldiers on 407–8

firsts and seconds 36*

Fisherrow 379

The Five Tables 243, 247

Fixed-term Parliaments Act (2011) 485

Flanders Moss 35, 83

Flatnose, Ketil 90

Fletcher, Andrew of Saltoun 278

Flight of Earls 239

flint, rarity in Scotland of 17

flint knapping 10

Flodden, Battle of 193–5, 357
  aftermath of 196–200, 200, 201, 205–6

Flodden Wall 195–6, 330

Floris V, Count of Holland 153

Foot, Michael 453

Football Association 387–8

football in Scotland, development of 389–90
  Hampden Park 390
  international between Scotland and England (1872) 389–90
  popularity of football 390
  sectarianism in football 390–91

football 'Wembley Wizards' (1928) 418

Forbes, Bishop 293

Forbes of Culloden, Duncan 305, 314*

de Forbin, Le Comte 290

Ford Popular 440

Fordun, John of 169

forests, royal and baronial 146–7
  see also Ettrick Forest

Forfar 66

Forfar, Loch 66

Forster, Sir John 197

Forsyth, Michael 464

Fort Augustus 336

Fort St Andrew 284

Fort William 279, 337
  An Gearasdan ('Garrison') 276

Forth, Firth of 14, 17, 34, 91, 241*

Forth and Clyde Canal 365–6

Forth valley 35

Fortriu
  centre of Pictish royal power 86
  kingdom of 64*

Fotheringhay Castle 221, 222

Fox Talbot, William Henry 378

Foyle River 239

France 16, 47, 321
  armaments, stock-piles of 406

Francis, Dauphin of France 209, 210

Francis II of France 215

Franciscans 120*

Franco-Prussion War (1870) 406

Franklin, Benjamin 329

Franks, R.H. 363–4

Franz Ferdinand, Archduke of Austria 406

Fraser, Clan 176

Frederick the Great of Prussia 307

Free Chirch of Scotland, establishment of 377–8

Freemasons' Tavern in London 387

French Revolution 351–2

French wine, disaster of *Phylloxera vastatrix* for 372

Froissart, Jean 167, 178

Fuilaidh, Mairi Nic 392

funeral arrangements 172*

furlongs, bolls and ells 74*

Furnace, HMS 337

Furness, Jocelyn of 55, 56

Gaelic language 17, 19, 31, 40, 53–8, 59*, 59–60, 62, 67, 70–71, 85
  demise of 459–60

Gaelic language TV 458–9

Gaelic lexicon 36*

Gaelic ritual, crowing and acclamation of Kings 95–6
  nation-building and 96

Gaidhealtachd 144

Gairsay 143

Gaitskell, Hugh 437

Galashiels 375–6

Galashiels and Hawick Co-operative Societies 413

Galicia 17

Gall-Gaidheil 90

Galloway 33, 50, 57, 90, 144, 161, 240
  hills of 4
  Lords of 119
  war bands of 120–21

'Gallowglasses' from Ireland 174–5

Galwegians 118, 119, 121

Gargunnock Hills 35

Garioch, Robert 461

Garmoran 172

Garry River 273

Gaul 40*, 48

Geddes, Jenny 242

Gemmill, Archie 450
General Assembly of the Church
    of Scotland 217, 223, 236,
    244
General Election (1922) 414–15
General Election (1945) 426–7
General Election (1951) 431
General Election (1959) 436–7
General Election (1964) 440
General Election (1966) 440
General Election (February, 1974)
    447
General Election (October, 1974)
    447–9
General Election (1979) 451–2
General Election (1992) 460
General Election (1997) 464
General Election (2001) 469–70
General Motors 403
General Strike (1926) 418–19
Geneva Bible 236
The Gentleman Farmer (Kames,
    H.H., Lord) 325
Gentlemen Adventurers for the
    Conquering of the Isles of
    Lewis 233*
George Heriot's school 219
George I 295, 317
George II 308, 311
George III 332
George IV 371, 372, 373
    death of (1830) 362
    visit to Edinburgh, Sir Walter
    Scott and 359–60
George V 419
gerbils and marmots, plague and
    170*
German East Africa 405
Germany 10, 15, 24, 321
    arms race with 405–6
    Nazi power in 419–20, 423
Geta, brother of Caracalla 45
Gilchrist Breatnach ('Gilchrist the
    Briton') 56
Gilmore, Sammy 442
Gilmour Barbara 323*
Gisborne, Thomas 291
Gladstone, John 381–2
Gladstone, William Ewart
    381–4, 393
de Glanvill, Ranulf 130
Glasgow 56, 362
    architecture of 399–400
    Bishop of 187
    Burrell Collection in Pollok
    Park 105–6, 400
    City Chambers 398, 399
    Edinburgh & Glasgow Railway
    366, 367

Empire, Second city of 399
Gaelic-speaking community
    in 345
Gilmorehill, University
    building on 399
Gorbals 421–2, 426
Great Western Road 399, 400
    housing 'schemes' around 436
    industry of, power of 399
    influence of 'Greek Thomson'
    on 392*
    Irish migration to 380–81
    John Paul II in Bellahouston
    Park 454*
    Loch Katrine and water supply
    for 367
    Old Firm in 391
    rent strike in (1915) 408
    Saltmarket 367, 421–2
    strike for peaceful settlement of
    Great War in 409
    tobacco trade 320–21
    trade development post-Union
    320–21
    Virginia Dons 321
    wealth of, development of
    399–400
    weavers strike in 361, 362
Glasgow Herald 339, 388–9,
    400, 420
Glasgow Locomotive Works
    384–5
Glasgow School of Art 400–401,
    402, 450*
    damage by fire (2014) 402
Glasgow University 122*
Glasser, Ralph 421–2
Glassford, John 321
Glen Orchy 338–9
Glencoe, massacre at 279–82
Glendearg 102
Glenfinnan 337
Glenlivet 372, 373–4
Glenmasan manuscript 369–70
Glenrothes 436
Glenshee, Spittal of 44*
global warming 22*
Glorious Revolution 269
Gloucester, Duke of 186, 285
Gloucester, Earl of 163
gneiss rock formation 3
Godly Commonwealth 223, 226
Gododdin, kingdom of 50–51,
    52–3, 85
Gododdin (epic poem) 35, 52, 61
Godwin, Earl of Wessex 105
Goethe, Johann Wolfgang von
    369
Goil Loch 55

Golden Royal Crown of Scotland
    160
Goldie, Annabel 473, 476
golf, development of 305–6
Golistan, Yrfai map, Lord of
    Edinburgh 51–2
Gongu-Hrolf, 'Rolf the Walker'
    105, 106
Goodwin, Fred 473–4
Gordon, Alexander, 4th Duke
    of 373
Gordon, Duke of 272
Gordon, George Hamilton 371
gospel books, iconic nature of
    59–60
Govan by-election (1973) 447
Govan Shipbuilders 443
Gow, Neil 355
Gowrie 71
Grace and Pardon, Act of (1717)
    298
Graham, James, Marquis of
    Montrose 249, 251, 252,
    253, 254, 295
Graham, Sir Robert 181
Graham of Claverhouse, Viscount
    John ('Bonnie Dundee')
    265, 272–4, 277, 279, 282,
    286, 296
Grainger, Katherine 477
Grampian Mountains 37, 63,
    64*, 68, 87
Grampian TV 434, 471
Grant, Clan 176
Grant, Archibald (son of Sir
    Francis) 316–17
Grant, Sir Francis 316–17
Grant, Ulysses S. 240*, 384
Grants of Glenmoriston 336–7
Gray, Iain 476
Great Cause, Edward I and
    adjudication of 152
Great Glen 3, 87, 253, 254
Great Harry 192
Great Heathen Army of the
    Danes 90, 91
Great Island 173
Great Lakes 6
Great Michael 190–93
*The Great Northern Welly-Boot
    Show* (Edinburgh Festival
    Fringe) 446
Great Plague of London (1665)
    170*
Great Reform Act (1832) 362
Great Seal of Scotland 154
Green, Thomas 285
Greenhead 48
Greenland 100

Greenock 362, 368
Gregor, Clan 234
Gregory, David and James,
    intellectual achievements
    of 302*
Greig, Andrew 461
Gretna, HM Factory at 405*
Grey, Prime Minister Lord 362
Greyfriars 120*
Greyfriars Kirkyard 195
Grieve, Christopher Murray
    418–19
Grimond, Joe 433*
Growing up in the Gorbals
    (Glasser, R.) 421–2
Gueldres, Mary of 182
Guisborough, Walter of 157
Guise, Mary of 204
    Queen Dowager of France 216
Guise's Regiment 337
Gulf Stream 6, 7, 11
Gunn, Clan 176
Gurness, Broch of 29
Gustavus Adolphus, King of
    Sweden 246, 247
Guthrie, Dr James 261
Guthrie, Thomas 372–3
Gwledig ('Warlord') 38
Gwyr Y Gogledd 50*

Haakon, King 144, 145
Hackston of Rathillet, David
    265, 266
Haddington ('Hoedda's Tun')
    85
Hadrian, Emperor 43
Hadrian's Wall 40*, 44–5, 46, 47,
    48, 49, 94, 110, 164
    Roman withdrawal to 43–4
Hailsham, Quintin Hogg,
    Viscount Hailsham 438
Halidon Hill 167, 168
Haliwerfolc, lands of 117*
Hall, James 320*
Halladale 348
'Hallaig' (MacLean, S.) 448*
Hallowe'en (*Samhuinn*) 43
Hallowhill 81
Haly Ruid 49
'ham' 12*
Hamilton, Duke of 256, 363,
    365
Hamilton, Ian 427*
Hamilton, James, Archbishop of
    St Andrews 218, 220, 222
Hamilton, Marquis of 244
Hamilton, Patrick 201–2
Hamilton, Thomas 462
Hamilton by-election (1967) 440

Hamilton of Bothwellhaugh,
    James 222
Hampden Clubs 361–2
'handba' games 387–8
Hannay, James, Dean of
    Edinburgh 242
Hannon, Canon Edward 391
Harcla, Sir Andrew 164
Hardie, Andrew 362
Hardie, Jamers Keir
    anti-war stance of 407
Hardie, James Keir 397–8
Hare, William 366*
Harold II 106
Harray Loch 24, 25
Harrild, Eileen 462
Harrington, William Stanhope,
    Earl of 384
Harrison, Benjamin 240*
Hartwood Burn 255
Hastings, John, Lord of
    Abergavenny 153
'haugh' 12*
Hawick 318–19, 356
    mode of speech in 224
Hawick and Wilton Cricket Club
    388
Hawley, General Henry 311,
    335–6
Hayes, Rutherford B. 384
Healey, Dennis 461
Heaney, Seamus 209, 209*
Heart of Midlothian Football
    Club 391
Heath, Edward 441–3, 444, 447
heavy industries, post-war decline
    of 432–3
Hebrides 19, 31, 40*, 61, 74, 80,
    85, 102, 140, 144, 145
heft to the hill, sheep becoming
    137*
Hegel, Georg W.F. 328
Helicourt in Picardy 160
Henderson, Alexander 243
Henri Grace à Dieu ('Great
    Harry') 192
Henrietta Maria 241, 242
Henry, Prince 228, 238
Henry I 112, 113, 142
    death of 117
    marriage to Maud 112
Henry II 130, 131
Henry III 142, 145
Henry IV 178
Henry of Anjou 129
Henry V of France 179
Henry VIII 192, 195, 199, 203,
    204, 207, 208, 209
Henryson, Robert 209, 209*

Hepburn, James , Earl of
    Bothwell 218
Hepburns 187
The Herald 461, 470–71
Herbart, Johann F. 328
Herbert, Abbot of Kelso 114
Herbert, Bishop of Glasgow
    125
Hereford, Earl of 153
Heriot, James 219
Heriot-Watt University 438
'The Heron' (MacLean, S.) 448*
Hertford, Earl of 195, 208
Hertfordshire Rangers 390
de Heselrig, William 155, 156
Hexham, Richard of 118, 119
Heywood, Sir Jeremy 482
Hibernian Football Club 390–91
hides, trade in 115–16, 170–71
High Kings
    Ireland 57
    Pictish provinces 64
High Shields 95, 104
Highland Boundary Fault 4, 225
Highland charge, facing up to
    fury of 271
Highland Clearances 175, 342,
    343–4, 347–9
    Am Bliadhna an Losgaidh
    (1814, 'Year of the Burning')
    348
    *Am Bliadhna nan Caoraich
    Mora* (1792, 'Year of the Big
    Sheep') 346–7
    brutality towards Hebridean
    emigrant families 391–2
    Cha Till Mi Tuill' ('Never
    More Shall I Return') 349
    Fuadach nan Gaidheal
    ('Driving Out of the Gael')
    349
    *Gun Bhris Mo Chridh' On
    Dh'Fhalbh Thu* ('My
    Heart Is Broken since thy
    Departure') 349
    Hebridean clearances 391–2
    Runrig and 'Dance Called
    America,' commemorations
    of 459
Highland Light Infantry 409
Highland sea-lochs 6
Highland society 369–70
Hill, Colonel John 279
Hill, David Octavius 378–9
Hill of Faith at Scone 154
Hillary, Edmund 433
hillforts 33, 42, 53, 104
Hillman Imp 441
'hirst' 12*

*The Historie and Chronicles of
    Scotland* (1436 to 1565) 191
The History of England (Hume,
    D.) 328
History of the Britons (Nennius)
    51
Hitler, Adolf 419, 423, 424, 426
HMRC 436
Hoddom 56
Hoedda 85
Hogg, James 374–5
Hogg, William 307
Holland 24, 321
'holm' 12*
Holy Tain 201*
Holyrood Abbey 155, 181
Holyroods 48*
Home, Henry Lord Kames 325
Home, Lord Alexander 194
Homer 369
Homes family 187, 197
Homo Sapiens 5, 21*
Honeyman and Leppie 400,
    401–2
Hooke, Colonel Nathaniel 289
Hope-Taylor, Brian 69
'hoppringle' 12*
Hordaland 80
House of Keys 123*
Housing (Financial Provisions)
    Act (1924) 415
housing problem 435–6
How I Found Livingstone (Stanley,
    H.M.) 404–5
Howburn Farm, South
    Lanarkshire 10–11, 15, 16*
Howden Hill 255
Howick, Northumberland 15
Hoy, Chris 477
Humber 91
Hume, David 310, 326, 327, 328,
    329, 330, 339, 345*, 369
Hume, Lord 235
Hume, Sir Patrick 300
Hume Castle, Berwickshire 356
Humes 240
Hundred Years War 175
hunger 89, 165, 278–9, 380,
    396, 418, 426, 455
hunter-gatherer populations 9,
    11, 12, 13, 14, 15, 17–18,
    19, 20–21, 22, 23, 26, 27*,
    136
    legacy of 83–4
Hunterston 455
Huntingdon, Honour of 113,
    121
Huntly 12*
Huntly, Earl of 194, 204

Huntly, Marquis of 249
Hussites 224*
Hutcheson, Francis 329
Hutchinson, John 400
Hutton, James 320*
Hutton Castle, Berwickshire 400
Hywel Dda, King of Deheubarth
    in Wales 97

Iapetus Ocean 2
Iapetus Suture 4
Iberia 13, 16
Ice Ages 5–6, 8–9, 10*, 12, 15,
    19, 22
ice cap, cracking and splintering
    of 6, 9–10
Ida, King 51
Ilomon 54
Imbolc ('Feast of St Bride') 43
immigration, problems of
    380–81
Inchgalbraith Island 56
Inchinnan 268
Inchtuthil, nails found at 38–9
Independent Labour Party
    397–8, 414
India, imperial wars in 346
Indians of Eastern United States
    22
industrial unrest, post-Waterloo
    361–2
industrialization 322–3, 340–42,
    345
    factory work, dangers of
        341–2
    heavy industry, Clyde and
        development of 385
    living conditions in cities
        367–8
    poverty in cities, abject nature
        of 368
    railways and quickening of
        pace of 367
    release of workers from grind
        of 386–7
    shipbuilding, development
        of 385
    urban development and 367
Inglis, Dr Elsie 396
Ingram, Archibald 321
'In Praise of Ben Dorian'
    (Chrichton Smith, I) 338–9
intellectual climate
    clubs, establishment of 327
    progressive thinking at
        Scotland's universities
        326–7
    publishing, printer-publishers
        and 327

Inverary Castle 252
Inverdovat 91
Inverlochy Castle 161, 253, 254
Inverness 156, 180
Iolaire disaster 410–11
Iona 3, 31, 47, 59, 61, 62, 63,
    76
    monastery on 59, 60
Iona, Abbot of 174
Iona, Sound of 73
Iona, Statutes of 234
IQ testing at '11-plus' 430
Ireland 34, 47, 58
    Easter Rising in (1916) 413
    High Kings at Tara 64
    potato famine in (and
        migration to Scotland)
        380–81
Irish Catholics, political spite
    at 420
Irish MacDonalds 252
Irish Sea 4
Irish Vikings 94
    in East Lothian 71*
iron-working 321–2
Ironsides 255
Irvine 440
Irving 240
Isbister 21
Islay 18, 19, 20, 124
    cheese-making on 323*
    peninsula of 3
    Rhinns of 11
Isle of Man 4, 102, 143, 144,
    145, 146
    sea-lord of 143
Isles, Bishop of the 174
Isles, Lordship of the 173
Issigonis, Alec 440–41
ITV 434
Ivar 89, 91
Ivory, William, Sheriff Principle
    of Inverness and Harris 393

Jackson, Alex 418
Jackson, Andrew 240*
Jacobite Rebellions
    Charles Edward Stewart (1745)
        195–6, 308–9, 310, 314*,
        332, 333*, 344, 357, 371,
        376–7
    Old Pretender (1715) 259,
        269, 291, 300–301, 302–3
James, Duke of Albany and York
    268
James Francis Edward ('The
    Pretender') 286, 289, 290,
    295, 297, 300–302, 306,
    309, 314

James I 178, 180
James II 181, 182, 183
James III 184, 186, 187
James IV 187, 188, 189, 190,
    191, 193, 194, 195, 200,
    201*
James the Fat 182
James V 200, 202, 203, 204, 205,
    206, 296*
James VI 233*, 327
James VI and I 217, 218, 221–3,
    225, 226–8, 230–31, 232,
    234, 238, 241
  bisexual nature of 236–7,
    237–8
  Border Commission 240
  dreams of union 259
  Middle Shires, concept of 232
  Robert Cecil and, account of
    meeting between 231
James VII and II 269, 273, 279,
    286, 296, 298
Jamestown 233*
Jardine Matheson, William
    Jardine and 370*
Jaun Fernandez archipelago 297*
Jedburgh 114, 117, 200, 203,
    356
  'handba'' in 387
  'Jethart Justice' 235, 240
Jedburgh Abbey 149
Jex-Blake, Sophia 395–6
Joan, Queen 181
John, King 142, 160
John, Earl of Carrick 176
John, Earl of Middleton 259
John Brown & Company 405–6
John I 153, 154, 156, 158
John of Fordun 131
John of Hexham 95
John of Islay, Lord of the Isles
    182
John Paul II, Pope 454*
John the Chaplain 113, 114*
John XXII, Pope 13, 166
Johnson, Andrew 240*
Johnson, Dr Samuel 345*, 369
Johnson, James 355
Johnston, Archibald of Warriston
    243, 246, 247, 261
Johnston, Tom 425, 426, 428,
    442*
Johnston, Willie 450
Johnston Press 471
Johnstone, James 310
Jordan, Joe 449–50
journalism, outlook for 471–2
Judaea 47
Julius II, Pope 193

Jura 18, 19, 20
  Paps of 11
Jurassic period 5*
Justice, James Robertson 434
jute working 385–6

'Kaiser' 32
Kames, Henry Home, Lord 325,
    326, 327, 329
Kant, Immanuel 328
Keigwin, L.D. 100
Keith, George 301
Keith, Sir Robert 164
Keith, Thomas 351*
Kells, Book of 61
Kells, County Meath 76
Kelso 85, 114
  Calchvynydd in Old Welsh 52
  ferrys at 277–8
Kelso Abbey 93, 115, 184, 199,
    220
  charter of (1159) 121–2, 122*
Kelso Race Course 396
Kelvin, Lord Smith of 483
Kemp, Robert 432
Kenmure, Viscount 296
Kennedy, Charles 433*, 470
Kennedy, James, Bishop of St
    Andrews 185
Kenneth, King of Scots 98
Kenneth II 99, 101
Kerevan, George 485
Kerr, Abbot Tam 199, 200
Kerr, Andrew 199
Kerr, Deborah 432–3, 434
Kerr, Thomas 199
Kerr of Cessford, Sir Robert
    198
Kerr of Ferniehurst, Dand 199
Kerrera island 144
Kerrs 197, 240
Keys, House of 123*
Kidnapped (Stevenson, R.L.)
    393–4
Kilbrandon Commission 445
Kildonan 348
  church at 60
Killiecrankie, Pass of 273, 276
Kilmarnock, Earl of 315
Kilmarnock–Troon Railway
    365–6
Kilsyth 35
kilts, big and small 304–5
Kincaid, Thomas 305
Kincardine Castle 146
Kindred of Lorne 87–8
King James Bible 236, 237*
'King of the Islands of Strangers'
    123, 125

Kingdom of the Isles 123, 124
Kinghorn 149
Kingis Quair (King James) 179
kingship by consent 166
Kinloch Glen 17
Kinnock, Neil 460
Kinross 145
Kinrymont ('St Andrews') 70
Kirk in Scotland 212–13, 214,
    215, 218–19, 223, 244, 256,
    258, 376
  see also Church of Scotland
Kirkcaldy 35
Kirkliston 158
Kirkmadrine 49
Kirkwall, 'handba' in 387
Kirkwood, David 415
knights in warfare 105–6, 107–8,
    119, 121, 123, 158, 159,
    163, 175
Knopfler, Mark 439*
Knox, Dr Robert 366*
Knox, John 207, 209, 211, 212,
    213*, 215, 222, 236, 326
kurgans 27*
Kyle of Lochalsh 410
Kyleakin ('Narrows of Haakon')
    145
Kylerhea, droving cattle at 292

Labour and Trades Councils 409
Labour Party 413, 415, 419,
    426–7, 431
  Co-operative Movement, links
    with 413–14
  devolution, split on 449
  power of Scots in 460
  referendum (1979) 451
  Scotland Bill, Cunningham
    amendment to 449, 451
The Lady of the Lake (Scott, W.)
    358, 368–9, 371
Laidlaw, Meg 374
Lairg 348
Lammermuirs 101
Lamont, Johann 485
landscape 82–3, 132–3, 134–5
  farmsteads in openness of 277
  fire forged nature of 5
  medieval landscape 136
  vocabulary for 12*
Lanercost Chronicle 148–9, 156,
    166, 167–8
Langholm 12*
  Rugby Club at 388
languages 16–17, 31, 46, 50, 53,
    55, 102
  Celtic languages 16, 31, 119,
    121

of King James Bible 237*
language shift 144
of Scotland 56, 61, 66–7, 96,
178, 180, 206, 361, 419
see also Gaelic language
Largs 145
Larkshire coalfield 365
Lascaux 8–9
Latinus Stone 48
Laud, William, Archbishop of
Canterbury 242
'Laud's Liturgy' 243, 244
Lauder 318
tollbooth at 115
Laurentia 2–3, 4
Lawrence of Lindores 224*
Lawrie, Dr W.L. 368
laws 12*, 95–6, 110, 136, 153,
174, 204, 231, 282, 345,
382
Lawson, Nigel 460
The Lay of the Last Minstrel (Scott,
W.) 358
Learmonth, James 233
Learmonth, Patrick, Provost of St
Andrews 210
*Leaves from the Journal of our Life
in the Highlands* (Queen
Victoria) 371–2
Lees of Torwoodlee, Catie 227
Lehman Brothers 473
Leigh, Sir Henry 235
Leinstermen 58
Leith Battalion, Territorial Army
407*
Lennon, John 437, 442
Lennox 35, 82
Lennox, Earl and Regent 222
Leonard, Silvio 453*
Leslie, General Alexander, Earl of
Leven 244, 245, 246, 247*,
248, 250, 251
Leslie, George 440
Leslie, Sir David 255, 256, 258
Lesmahagow 114
Leven, River 54
Lewis, Isle of 85, 233, 343
Liberal Party 383, 384, 393, 397,
413, 414*, 433*
Liddell, Eric 416–17, 453*
Liddesdale 50
life expectancy 81–2
The Life of St Columba
(Adomnan) 58–9
Lightbody, William 388
Lindisfarne 47, 51, 76, 85, 117*,
151
monastery on 71, 72, 73
siege of 52, 55

Lindsay, David, Bishop of
Edinburgh 242, 243
Lindsay of Pitscottie, Robert
190–1
linen
manufacture of 321
market for 298–9
Linklater, Eric 143*, 420
Linlithgow Palace 205
Linn nan Creach ('Age of the
Forays') 234
'Lion' bombard 183
Lionel, Duke of Clarence 171
Little Ice Age 22*, 165, 170–71,
278
Livingston 440
Livingstone, David 403–5
death of national hero 404–5
Livingstone, Sir Alexander 181,
182
'Lizzie the Lizard' 3*
Lleddiniawn, Princess of Thenu
55
Lloyd George, David 411, 413
Llywelyn Mawr, Prince of Wales
50*
Loairn, Cenel 87
Local Government Act (1929)
423
Loch Awe 68
Loch Fyne 252, 253
Loch Katrine 367, 368–9, 371
Loch Leven 218, 220
Loch Lomond 3, 35, 54, 55
Loch Lomond Stadial 7
Loch Ness 156
Loch of Drylaw, James 348
Loch Roag 343
Loch Ryan 30
Loch Tay 35
Lochaber 349
Lochiel, Cameron of 313
Lochmaben Stane 83*
Locke, James 375–6
Lockerbie disaster 457*
Lockhart, George 289
Lockhart, J.G. 358–9, 360
Lockhart, Major I.
(Cholmondley's) 336–7
logarithms, Napier and 387*
Loire Valley 47
Lollards 224*
London Bridge 159
London Missionary Society 404
London School of Medicine for
Women 396
Londonderry 239
Longnewton in Roxburghshire
319

Longton, J., of Burntisland 241*
Lord Advocate 243
Lord High Admiral of Scotland
191
Lord of the Articles 272
Lord of the Congregation 244
Lordship of the Isles 173, 174,
234, 270
Lorne 87
Kindred of 87–8
men of 121
Lothian, Earl of 319
Lothian, Marquis of (1606) 363
Lothians 41, 50, 51, 57, 101, 171
men of 121
Loudon Hill 265
Louis XII 193
Louis XIV 269, 282, 286, 289,
290, 296, 306
Louis XVI 352
Lower Largo, Fife 297*
Lowland Clearances 319–20,
342
loyalty
family and 197
importance of bonds of 68
Ludwig, George von
Braunschweig-Luneburg
285
Lughnasa ('Lammas') 43
Lugi ('Raven People') 30–31,
34, 63
Luguvalium (Carlisle) 47
Lulach 104
Lumphanan 104
Lumsdaine of Blanerne 324–5
Lundie, Richard 157
Luther, Martin 201, 204
Lyndsay, Sir David 206

mac an Ollaimh, Giolla Coluim
185–6
MacAlasdair, Iain 281
macAlasdair, Malcolm 117
macAlpin, Kenneth 85, 86, 87,
88, 90, 95, 297
MacAulays 176
MacBane, Donald 271, 274
MacBean, Gillies 313
Macbeth, 'King of Moray' 88,
103, 104, 105
Macbeth (Shakespeare, W.) 232
MacBrayne, David 393
MacCaig, Norman 448*
death of 461–2
MacColla, Alasdair 250, 251–2,
253, 254
McCombie, William at Tillyfour
379–80

McCullough, Derek 431
Maccus, King of Islands 98
MacDiarmid, Hugh 418–19, 420, 461
MacDonald, Aeneas 308
MacDonald, Alexander, Lord of the Isles 180
MacDonald, Amie 172
MacDonald, Angus Og and Islesmen 172
MacDonald, Coll, Chief of MacDonalds of Keppoch 270, 272
MacDonald, Isobel 337
Macdonald, John of Islay, High Chief of Clan Donald 172, 185
MacDonald, Margo 447, 460, 472
Macdonald, Murdo 136
MacDonald, Norman 308
MacDonald, Ramsay 415, 419, 433*
MacDonald, Rev. Donald 444*
MacDonald, Rory and Calum 459
MacDonald blood 173
MacDonald of Clanranald 309
MacDonald of Keppoch 173–4
MacDonald of Kinlochmoidart 309
MacDonald of Kintyre 173
MacDonald of Morar, Alan 309
MacDonald of Sleat, Sir Alexander 344
MacDonald regiments 313, 314
MacDonalds 336
MacDonalds of Glencoe 280, 281, 282
MacDonells of Glengarry 304, 309
MacDougall, Clan 125, 172
Macduff, brother of Earl of Fife 153
MacEacherns ('sons of the Horse Lord') 31
MacEwens 175
McGillivray, John 313
MacGillivrays 176
McGrath, John 445
MacGregor, Alasdair 234
McGregor, Ewan 462
MacGregor, Geddes 236
MacGregor, Ian 454
MacGregor, Rob Roy 301
MacGregors 234
MacIain, Alasdair, Chief of MacDonalds of Glencoe 279, 280, 281

MacIain of Ardnamurchan 173
MacIntyre, Duncan Ban 338–9
MacIntyre, Robert 440
MacIver, Donald 343–4
MacIvers 176
MacKay of Scourie, General Hugh 273, 276, 286
MacKellar, Kenneth 434
Mackenzie, Clan 233*
Mackenzie, Captain Kenneth 270
Mackenzie, Graeme 127*
MacKenzie, Henry 354
Mackenzie, Munro 391
Mackenzie River 6
McKillop, Tom 474
McKinley, William 240*
MacKinnons 174
Mackintosh, Charles Rennie 400–402
Mackintosh, Lachlan, Chief of Clan Chattan 270
MacKintosh, William of Borlum 296
Mackintoshes 176, 313
McLachlan, Margaret 267
MacLarens 175
Maclean, Alasdair 136
MacLean, John 408–9
MacLean, Sorley (Somhairle MacGill-Eain) 448*, 461
Maclean of Duart 174
Maclean of Lochbuie 174
MacLennan, David 445
MacLennan, Elizabeth 445
MacLeod, Alistair 349
MacLeod, Ally 449–50
MacLeod, Iain 439
MacLeod, John F. 411
MacLeod, Murdoch of Inverness 312
MacLeod, Neil and Murdo 233*
MacLeod of Dunvegal, Norman 344
Macleod of Harris 174
Macleod of Lewis 174
MacLeods 176
macMalcolm, David ('David FitzMalcolm') 112
macMalcolm, House of 148, 150
claims to estates in England 142
macMalcolm, Maud 109
macMalcolm Kings 109, 136
MacMhuirich, Lachlan Mor 180
MacMillan, Harold 436–7, 438, 439
McMullen, Jimmy 418
MacNeil of Barra 174

MacNeil of Gigha 174
MacPherson, James 57, 369–70
MacPhersons 176
Macquarie, Lachlan 403
McShane, Harry 406, 424
MacSweens 176
macTaggart, Farquhar 142, 144
macUilleam, Domhnall 131
MacWard, Rev Robert 266
Madeleine, daughter of Francis I of France 203
Maeatae 44
Maelrubha 60
Maeshowe tomb 24
Magic Mountain of the Caledonians 35
Magna Carta 142
Magnus Merriman (Linklater, E.) 420
Magus Moor 264, 265
mail shirts 106, 109–10, 174–5
Mainard the Fleming 115, 128
Maitland, John, Earl of Lauderdale 255, 261
Maitland, William of Lethington 216, 222
Major, John 460
end of office for 464
Makars, The Lament for the (Henryson, R.) 209*
Malaios Insula ('Mull') 30
Malcolm, King of Cumbrians 98, 99
Malcolm, son of Duncan 104
Malcolm I 98, 102
Malcolm II 56, 88, 101, 102, 103
Malcolm III *see* Canmore, Malcolm
Malcolm IV 95, 121, 122, 125, 126, 128
The Man of Feeling (MacKenzie, H.) 354
Manor Valley 93
A Man's a Man for a' That (Burns, R.) 352–4
Manufacture, Board of Trustees for 298
Maol Ruadh 270, 272, 274
Mar, Earl of 152, 180, 222, 296, 298
Marathon Company of Texas 449
Margaret, daughter of Christian I of Denmark 184
Margaret, daughter of Henry III 148
Margaret, Maid of Norway 148, 150

Marie Antionette 352
Marius, Gaius 32
Marks & Spencer 192*
Marmion (Scott, W.) 357–8
Marmoutier monastery 47, 48
Marston Moor 248, 250, 251
martyrdom, colours of 59*
Martyrs' Bay 73
Mary, Countess of Ross 180
Mary, Queen of Scots 145, 205,
  208, 221, 305
  Darnley and, marriage of
    216–17
  execution of 221
  return to Scorland of 215–16
Mary of Guise 206, 209, 212
Mary Rose 192
Mason, Douglas 457–8
Massalia 29
Masson, Don 449–50
The Master of Ballantrae
  (Stevenson, R.L.) 394
Matheson, James 370*
Matheson, Kay 427*
Matilda 113, 117
Maudling, Reginald 438
Mavorius 49
Mawr, Llywelyn, last Prince of
  Wales 51
Maxton, James 415
Maxwell, Fordyce and abduction
  and murder of daughter
  Susan 462–3
Maxwell, James 409
Maxwell, Lord Robert 205
Maxwells 197
Maynard, William 390
Mayor, Gwen 462
measurement, old imperial system
  74
medieval battles, characteristics
  of 164
Medieval Warm Period 100–101
Medium Aevum (Middle Age)
  162*
Mellerstain House 300, 301
Mellifont, Treaty of 239
Melrose 33, 136
Melrose Abbey 147, 186, 220
Melrose Chronicle 98
Melville, Andrew 223, 224, 235,
  326
*Memoirs of the Most Renowned
  James Graham, Marquis of
  Montrose* (Wishart, G.) 257
Mendelssohn, Felix 369
Mennons, John 339
Menzies, Clan 176
Merchiston 387*

Mercia 101
Merse 101
*m'eudail (Gaelic term of
  endearment)* 40
Mid-Atlantic Ridge 1–2, 4
Mid-Atlantic Rift Valley 2
middens 139–40
  dating of 19–20
Middle Ages 54, 57
Middleton, Earl of 306
Midland Valley 6
Midlothian, Gladstone elected
  for 384
Mighty Ones 31
Miliband, Ed 479, 485, 486
Military Survey of Scotland,
  1747–1755 (Roy, W.) 320
Miller, Captain and Chief
  Constable of Glasgow 367
Mini 440–41
Minstrelsy of the Scotish Border
  (Scott, W.) 358, 359
mints, setting up of 131
*Mirifici Logarithmorum Canonis
  Descriptio* 387*
Moffat, Agnes, coal mining life
  for 364
Moffat, Robert 404
Moine formations 3
Molendinar Burn 56
Moluag, Saint 60
monastic orders 120*
Monck, General George 259,
  260, 272
Mondynes 110
Monith Carno 67
Monklands Canal 365
Monmouth, Duke of 299, 307
Mons Graupius, Battle at 37–8
Mons Meg 191
monsatic orders
  dietary rules of 138
Montrose 154
Montrose, Marquis of *see*
  Graham, James
Montrose Basin 37
Monymusk, Aberdeenshire
  316–17, 318
Moore, Michael 476–7
Moorfoots 101, 146
Moot Hill, Scone 87, 95, 145,
  187
Mor macErc, Fergus 87
Theory of Moral Sentiments
  (Smith, A.) 329
Morar 17
Moravians (men from Moray)
  121
Moray 87, 131, 144

Moray, Andrew 156, 157
Moray, Earl of (Regent) 220, 222
Moray, Laigh of 374
Moray coastlands 3
Moray Firth 84, 86
Morcant Bwlc 52
Morris Minor 440–41
Morrison, Herbert 425
Morton, James Douglas, Earl
  of 222
Morvern 87
Moses, Alfred 388
Mosspaul 356
Mounth 64
Mousa on Shetland 42
Mowbray, Sir Philip 161
Muir, Thomas 352
Muirs 82
Mull 87
Mull *(Malaios Insula)* 4, 30
Mungo ('*Mwyn Gwr,* Dear One')
  56
munitions production 405*
Munro, Donny 459
Munro, Sir George 259
Murdoch, Albany's son 179
Murdoch, Rupert 471
Murphy, Jim 485
Murray, Andy 472, 477
Murray, Anne, daughter of Earl of
  Tullibardine 238
Murray, Dr Kylie 122*
Murray, Lord George 301, 310,
  311, 312, 313, 314, 323
Murrays 240
Mursell, Walter 407
My Scotland, Our Britain (Brown,
  G.) 479
Myllar, Andrew 190
Myln, Walter 210, 213

naming of the names *(sloinneadh)*
  180
Napier, John 387*
Napier, Robert 385
Napier College 387*
Napier Commission 393
Napoleon Bonaparte 32, 59, 348,
  356, 369
  threat to Britain from (and
  warning systems of) 356
Nasser, Gamal, Abdul 435
National Assistance Act (1948)
  429
National Coal Board (NCB)
  453–5
National Covenant 243, 244,
  251, 255, 257, 261, 262
National Government 419, 433*

National Health Service 425, 426
National Health Services Act
    (1947) 428–9
National Insurance Act (1947)
    428–9
National Liberals 413
National Library of Scotland 121
National Party of Scotland
    420–21
National Plan for Scotland 440
National Union of Mineworkers
    447
National Union of Women's
    Suffrage Societies 396
nationalization of key industries
    428
Neanderthals 10, 218
Nechtan, King 69, 70
    Oengus and 86, 87
Neil, Alex 449
Neilson, James 366
Neislon, Walter 384–5
Nennius 52
Ness of Brodgar 24–5, 26
Neville's Cross, Battle of 48*, 168
New Caledonia 284
New Edinburgh 284
New Lanark 323, 341
New Mains (Newbiggin) 335
New Model Army 255, 256,
    257, 258
New Park 163
New Statesman Scotland 467
New York Herald 404
Newbery, Fra 400–401
Newcastle 153, 159
    walled city of 248, 255
Newcastle, Thomas Pelham-
    Holles, 1st Duke of 336
Newcomen, Thomas 340
Newfoundland 1
Newhaven 379
newsreels 416
Newstead 147
Newsweek 452
Niall Noigiallach ('Niall of the
    Nine Hostages') 57, 58
Niarbyl 4
Ninewells near Chrinside 326
Nith, River 131
Niven, David 434
Nixon, Richard 240*
nobility of Caledonia 41–2
Norfolk, Duke of 220
Norham 117, 151–3
Norham Parish Church 151, 152
Norman Conquest 146
North America 4, 9
North Atlantic 6, 7

North Atlantic Gyre 100
North Berwick 44
North Britain 45
    notion of being North British
        361
North Channel 31, 58, 60
North Lanarkshire coalfield 397
North of Scotland Hydro-Electric
    Board 425, 442*
North Sea 16, 23, 24
    oil industry 444, 447–9
North Uist 40
North Yorkshire 53
Northallerton 119
Northern Ireland 60
Northern Isles 42, 74, 80, 140,
    145, 184
Northumberland 53, 130, 142
    coast of 49, 51
Northumbria, kingdom of 54,
    94, 108
    influence of 92
Northumbrians, Scottish
    Borderers and 102
Norton, Alex 450*
Norway 23, 85
    Norwegians' in Hebrides and
        Dublin 90
Novantae 33, 50
NUM (National Union of
    Mineworkers) 453–5

Oak Fountain 84
Oakwood Tower 33
oaths 103, 279
Oban 144
Oban Times 393
Ochil Hills 35
O'Connell, Daniel 391
Odiham Castle 171
Odin 77
O'Donnell, Hugh 239
Oengus, grandson of Lulach 116
Oengus I 68, 70
Oengus II 71
Og, Alasdair 28
Ogilvy, Marion 200
Olaf, King of Dublin 89, 90,
    91, 97
Olaf Guthfrithsson, King 71
Old English 12*
Old Red Sandstone 3
Old Welsh 31, 32
An Ollaimh Rìgh 144–5
Olympic Games (1924) 416–17
    (1980) 453*
    (2012) 477–8
O'Neill, Hugh 239
O'Neill Earls 239

Opium Wars (1839) 404
oral tradition, epic tales and
    poetry of 78–9
Orange, William of 269, 271,
    272, 273, 274, 279, 282
Orcades ('Boar Islands') 30–31
Orcadie Lake 25*
Orderic Vitalis 116
Ordnance Survey 319–20
Orgreave, 'Battle' of 454–5
Orkney 21–2, 24, 25, 26, 29, 86,
    90, 102, 105, 133, 143*,
    145, 152, 174, 184, 200,
    327, 412*, 433*, 449, 465
    kings of 29, 30, 31, 36, 64
    Norwegian Earls of 89
    Orcadian surnames 77
Orkneyinga Saga 143*
Orleans, Duke of 296
Ormistoun, Sandy 357
Oronsay 19–20, 21
Orygynale Cronykil of Scotland
    (Wyntoun, A.) 103–4
Osborne, George 478
Ossian 369–70
O'Sullivan, Colonel John 309,
    310
Otadini 33
Otterburn, Battle of 176
Ottoman Turks 192
Out Isles 123*
Overbury, Sir Thomas 237
King Owain of Rheged
    (Strathclyde) 51, 52, 56,
    71*, 97, 102

Paine, Thomas 352
Paisley 362
Paisley pattern shawls 343*
Palace of Holyroodhouse 229,
    230
palaeocontinental welding 2–3
Palladian architecture 333*
Pallinsburn, near Cornhill 54
Palmerston, Henry John Temple,
    Viscount Palmerston 383
Panama, isthmus of 283
Pangaea 4
Pankhurst, Emmeline 396
partible inheritance, legacy of 82
Pasha, Muhammad Ali 351*
Paterson, Bill 445–6
Paterson, William 283
Patrick (Patricius) 47, 49
Patronage Act (1712) 294–5, 376
Patterson, Bill 450*
Paul III, Pope 204
pecunia 40*
Peebles 85

Peel, Sir Robert 382–3
pelagic sand 23
Pelstream Burn 163, 164
Pennines 32
Penny Wheep (MacDiarmid, H.)
    419
Pentland Hills 146
People's Palace, Glasgow 321
Perche, Forest of 120
Perpetual Peace, Treaty of (1502)
    191–2, 192–3
Persians 32
Perth 85, 138, 159, 319, 336
    ferrys at 277–8
    medieval city of 192*
    Treaty of 145
Perthshire 371
Peterborough Cathedral 221
Peterloo Massacre, Manchester
    (1819) 362
Peter's Pence 204
Pettycur 149
Philip IV 168
Philiphaugh 255
photography, pioneers of 378–9
Picasso, Pablo 8
Picts 44, 49, 57, 66–7
    history of 64*
    language of 31
    old provinces of 87
    Pictland 62, 63, 66, 67, 70,
        75, 84–5, 86, 93, 96, 487
    provinces or kingdoms of 63
    symbol stones of 63–5
pilgrimage 70, 73, 103, 125,
    126–7, 128–9, 169, 201*
pioneers, gossamer traces of
    17–18
Piranesi, Giovanni Batista 333*
Pirie, Madsen 457–8
'pirn' or 'pirnie' 12*
Pitlochry 62
Pitt, William 304
Pittodrie 63
Pius, Antoninus 44
place-names 84–5, 92–3, 95,
    101–2, 124, 135, 144, 147,
    165*, 176, 225, 255, 276,
    298–9, 335
plague 168–9, 170*, 171, 231,
    259, 372, 469
Plain Indians 9
Plautius, Aulus 28
Playfair, John 320*
Plowden, Bridget Horatia, Lady
    434
Plutarch 31
*Poems, Chiefly in the Scottish
    Dialect* (Burns, R.) 354

The Poems of Ossian (MacPherson,
    J.) 369–70
Poker Club 327–8
Poland 24
politics
    discussions in Scotland on,
        change in 470–71
    international politics 141, 270
    landscape of, change in 396–8
    political future, beginnings of
        difference in (1996) 461–2
    Roman Imperial politics 28
    as stuff of theatre 445–6
Polk, James 240*
'Poll Tax' 458
Pollok by-election (1967) 440
Pollok Park 105
Polmaise Colliery 454, 455
Pons Aelius 110
Pontypridd mining disaster
    (1894) 397–8
Poor Law (1845) 382
Port Royal in Jamaica 284
Port-Vendres 402
Portsmouth 1
potato blight, famine and 380
Pottinger, Edward 282
Pow, Tom 461
'Powder Treason' 232
Praemonstratensian Canons
    120*
Praetorian Guard 28
prefabs (prefabricated homes)
    428
Presbyterianism 223, 244, 250
Press and Journal 470
Pretannikai ('People of the
    Tattoos') 29
primogeniture 88, 95, 116, 153
*The Private Memoirs and
    Confessions of a Justified
    Sinner* (Hogg, J.) 374
Privy Council 243, 247, 280
Protestant Action Society 420
Protestantism 212
    Protestant settlers 239
    rise of 209–15, 219–20
Proto-Indo-European culture 27*
Pryor, Francis 39
Ptolemy 30, 31, 33, 54, 58, 64,
    239
public life, scale of 140–41
Purging Committee 257
Pyrenees 8–9, 12
Pytheas and the Periplus 29*

Quaternary Period 5
Queen Margaret Medical College
    400

Queen's Park Football Club
    389–90
Queensbury, Duke of 287
Queensferry 109*
Quesnay, François 329
Quintinshill, rail disaster at 407*

Raeburn Place, international
    rugby between England and
    Scotland at (1871) 388–9
Ragged Schools 372
Ragman Roll 155
Ragnall 94
Ragnarsson, Halfdan 91
railway development 366–7,
    371, 372
    beginnings of 339–41
    locomotive works in Glasgow
        384–5
Ramsay, Lady Margaret 165
Ramsey, Allan 327
Randolph, Thomas, Earl of
    Moray 161, 162, 163, 167,
    212
Rangers Football Club 391
Rannoch, Loch 35
Rattray, John 305
Ravenscraig 455
Rawlinson, Thomas 304
Read, Isabella, coal mining life
    for 364
Rebellion (1745) 371
rectors 224*
Red Douglases 182, 187
Red Friars 120*
Red martyrs 59*
Redden Burn 143
Redeemer, a Son of Prophecy 52
referendum (2014)
    Better Together campaign 477,
        478, 481
    campaign by Salmond in, Lord
        Strahclyde's view on 482–3
    eve of poll 481
    referendum bill, Parliamentary
        power for 476–7
    result 481
    voter turnout 481
    Vow published in *Daily Record*
        479–80, 481
    Yes campaign 477, 478–9,
        481
Reform Act (1884) 393
Reformation 204, 213*, 325–6
    Reformation Parliament 213
Regnum Scotiae 143–4
Reid, Jimmy 442–3, 445, 446
religious life, post-Flodden
    200–201

Renfrew, Battle of 125
Rent and Mortgages Restriction
    Act (1915) 408
Renton, Mark 462
Renwick, Rev. James 267
Representation of the People Act
    (1918) 411
Reptiles, Age of 5
Rere Cross on Stainmore 99
Rerigonium, Royal Place on Loch
    Ryan 33, 34
Rerigonium (Ptolemy) 30
Restenneth Priory 66
Reuda, Irish chieftain 58
Revocation, Act of (1625) 240
Rheged
    Dark Age kings of 30
    kingdom of 50*, 51, 53
    see also Strathclyde
Rhine frontier 46
Rhinns of Galloway 30, 34
Rhun, brother of King Owain 54
Rhydderch, Hael, King, Riderch
    the Generous 55, 56
Rhymer, Thomas the 183
Ri Innse Gall 125
Riccio, David 217*
Richard, Duke of Buccleuch
    217*
Richard III 189
Richard Lionheart 129, 131
Riddell, Maria 355
Rifkind, Malcolm 458
The Rights of Man (Paine, T.) 352
Rioch, Bruce 449–50
road building, Wade and
    Highland progress 303
Robbins, Lionel (and Robbins
    Report) 437–8
Robert, Earl of Fife 176
Robert I 13, 129, 166, 175
Robert II 172, 176
Robert III 177, 178
Robertson, Anne 381–2
Robertson, George 460, 466
Robertson, John 449
Robertson, William 327
Robinson Crusoe (Defoe, D.) 294,
    297*
Rocky Mountains 2
Roebuck, John 340
Rogart 348
Rognvald Eysteinsson, Earl of
    More in Norway 105
Roman Empire 28
Roman Legion IX 36, 37
Roman year 36
Rome 45
Rona, Isle of 337

Roosevelt, Theodore 240*
Rootes Group 441
Rosebery, Archibald Primrose,
    Earl of 384
Rosie, George 446–7
Roslin Chapel 165
Roslin Institute 463–4
Ross, James of 186
Ross, Willie 440
'Rough Wooing' 208
Roundheads 251*
roundhouses, traces of 37
Row, John 212
Roxburgh 115, 138, 140
    Dukes of 121, 214
Roxburgh Castle 117, 123, 130,
    154, 160, 180, 183
Roy, William 320
Royal Bank of Scotland 307,
    332, 338, 473–4
Royal Border Bridge at Berwick-
    upon-Tweed 367
royal burghs 138
Royal College of Physicians 327
Royal Navy
    Iolaire disaster, returning sailors
        in 410–11
    shipbuilding for 405–6
Royal Scots Fusiliers 337
Rubh an Dunain 127*
Ruddiman, Thomas 327, 339
Rugby Football Union 388
rugby Grand Slam for Scotland
    (1925) 417–18
rugby union, development of
    388–9
    Scotland–England
        international match (1871)
        388–9
ruling classes, accessibility of
    141–2
Rullion Green 261, 264, 265
Rum, Island of 17, 19, 20
Rum Bloodstone 17
Rump Parliament 259
Runrig: City of Lights (Scottish
    TV) 459
Rupert, Prince of the Rhine 250
Russell, James 265
Russia 27
    armaments, stock-piles of
    406
'Ruthven Raid' 226
Ruthwell 48*
Ruttlidge, Sir Walter 308

Sabir nomads 35
St Aidan's monastery 88
St Alban 47

St Andrews 67, 81, 98, 161, 169
    Sarcophagus of 69–70
St Andrews Cathedral 128
St Andrews Cross, Saltire flag
    of 127
St Andrew's House in Edinburgh
    423
St Andrews' shrine 109, 126, 128
St Andrews University 224*, 438
St Anthony the Great 47
St Benedict, rule of 120
St Bernard of Clairvaux 120*
St Boisil's monastery at Old
    Melrose 88
St Boswells 319
St Columba, 31, 59–61, 109
    Niall Noigiallach and 60
    relics of 86–7
St Comgall 60
St Cuthbert 48, 117, 151
    monastery of 88
    shrine of 72, 73
St Cuthbert's Land 117*, 118
St Donnan 60, 73, 85
St Duthac 201*
St Germain-en-Laye 279, 289
St Giles 196
St Gordian 93
St James's Fair 115
St John the Baptist's monastery
    98
St Kilda 4
St Kentigern 55, 56
St Leger, Sir Anthony 175
St Maelrubha 59, 73
St Margaret of Scotland 48*, 109*,
    155
St Martin of Tours 46, 48
St Mary's Loch 374
St Ninian 48, 49, 93, 167
    shrine at Whithorn 167
St Oran, chapel on Iona 125
St Paulinus 53
St Peter 105
St Rule and tower 126
St Serf 54, 65
Sais (English) 51–2
Salisbury, Robert Gascoyne-Cecil,
    Marquess of 439
Salmond, Alex 472, 473, 475–6,
    476–7, 478, 479, 481, 486
    referendum campaign of, Lord
        Strathclyde's view on 482–3
    resignation as SNP leader 482
Saltcoats, salt-pans at 323*
Saltire alternative 129
Sampson, Agnes 226
Sandyknowe Farm, near Kelso
    357

Sangschaw (MacDiarmid, H.) 419
Sanna Bay 136
'Sanquhar Declaration' 266
Santiago, St James of Compostela 126
Sarajevo 406
Sargasso Sea 99
Sark, River 83
Sauchieburn, Battle of 187
le Saucier, Alexander 149
Saudi Arabia 351*
Saxonia 88
Scalacronica 166
Scandinavia 15
Scandinavian Scotland 74
Scapa Flow 412*
Scargill, Arthur 454–5
scent hounds ('rauchs') 147
Scetes desert 47
Schiehallion, peak of 34
schiltrons, spearmen in 159, 163, 164, 167–8, 334
Schleiermacher, Friedrich 328
school qualifications, rationalisation of 430
Schopenhauer, Arthur 328
Scone 95, 144, 156, 167
Scone Abbey 211, 213*
Scotch Irish 240
Scotch Whisky: Past and Present (Daiches, D.) 374
Scotia 143
Scotichronicion 144–5, 158, 169, 178
Scotland Act (1998) 465
Scotland Bill, referendum of (1979) 451
Scotland on Sunday 471
Scots Gaelic 17, 34*, 88, 225
see also Gaelic language
Scots Irish 240*
The Scots Magazine 339
Scots Musical Museum (Johnson, J., Ed.) 355
Scotsman, HMS 406
The Scotsman 339–40, 395, 434, 470, 471
Scotstoun Marine Ltd 443
Scott, Arabella 396
Scott, Captain Caroline 337
Scott, Giles Gilbert 399, 402
Scott, James, Duke of Monmouth 265, 268
Scott, Sir Walter 208, 272, 302, 350, 356–7, 368–9, 370, 374–5, 393–4
  early years (and ailments) 357
  fantasy at Abbotsford, creation of 360

financial difficulties 360–61
George IV's visit to Edinburgh and 359–60
gift for names and phrases 272
influence of 360, 361
Liddesdale excursion 358–9
politics of 361
success for 359
Scott, Tavish 476
Scott, William 388
Scotticisms 345*
Scottish Assembly, Campaign for a 456–7
Scottish Association of the Friends of the People 352
Scottish Borders 102, 113, 214, 224, 232, 240
Scottish Church 114*, 129, 130
  see also Church of Scotland
Scottish Conservative and Unionist Party 444–5
  Declaration of Perth 445
Scottish Constitutional Convention 456–7
Scottish Cooperative Wholesale Society (SCWS) 413–14
Scottish Development Department 440
Scottish Enlightenment 325–6, 326–8
Scottish Federation of Women's Suffrage Societies 396
Scottish Football Association 389–90, 391
Scottish Home Service (radio) 431
Scottish Labour Party 397, 449, 485
Scottish Media Group 471
Scottish National Party (SNP) 440, 445, 466
  election in Scotland (2011) and majority for 475–6
  foundation of (1934) 420–21
  'It's Scotland's Oil' 447–9
  political tsunami in election of 2015 for 485–6
  referendum (1979) 451
  'turkeys voting for early Christmas' 451
Scottish Office 423
Scottish Parliament (modern)
  debating chamber 466
  elections for (2003) 470
  elections for (2007) 472–3
  elections for (2011) 475–6
  first meeting of 466–7
  legislative competences 465
  powers of, definition of 465–6

proportional representation (PR) in elections for 465
referendum bill, power for 476–7
Scottish Parliament (original) 236, 249, 286
  Classes, Act of (1649) 256
  coal masters, powers for (1672) 363
  Common Lands, Act of 1695 on 318–19
  end of 287–8
  Mining, Act on (1606) 363
  Peace and War, Act Anent (1704) 286
  Rescissory, Act of (1660) 261
  Security, Act of (1704) 286
Scottish Protestant League 420
Scottish Reformation 213
Scottish Rugby Union 388–9
Scottish Special Housing Association 423
Scottish Television 434
Scottish TV 471
Scottish universities, progressive thinking in 326–7
Scottish Wardenries 197
Scotus, Marianus 103
Scout Movement 398*
Scresort, Loch at Kinloch 17
Scrymgeour, Edwin 414*
Scythia, Greater 13
Sea Quest, semi-submersible drilling rig 444
Seafield, Viscount 295
'seafloor spreading' 1–2
Seaforth, Earl of 253
Second Civil War 256
Second World War
  casualties of 427–8
  Clydebank blitz 424, 425
  declaration of hostilities 423–4
  Forth, action at Firth of 424
  Labour ministers, appointment of 424–5
  victory in Europe 426
Sedgemoor 268
Segrave, Sir John 165*
Seine River 105
A Select Collection of Original Scottish Airs for the Voice (Thomson, G.) 355
Select Society 327, 329
self-definition, Scots struggles with 488–9
Selgovae, 'the Hunters' 33
Selkirk 33, 114*, 318
  monastery founded at 113
Selkirk, Alexander 297, 297*

Selkirk Abbey 120*
Selkirk charter 113–15
  endowments under 114–15
  witnesses to 113
Sellar, Patrick 348
Selma, Alabama 369
Senchus Fer nAlban ('History
  of the Men of Scotland')
  57–8, 61, 82
Senlac Hill 108
Seton, Robert, Earl of Winton
  230
Seton, Sir Alexander 163
Settlement, Act of (1701) 285,
  286
7:84 Theatre Company 445
Severus, Septimius 44, 45
sewing, invention of art of 22
Shakespeare, William 103, 232
Shand, Jimmy 434–5
Sharp, Archbishop James of St
  Andrews 264, 265
shawls 343*
sheep flocks, hefted nature of
  137*
Shell 444
shepherd's plaid 374–5
Sheridan, Tommy 467
Sheriffmuir 93
Shetland 15, 23, 75, 86, 133,
  174, 184, 327, 412*, 433*,
  444, 449
Shinbanes Field 165*
Shinwell, Emmanuel 415, 429
Shortreed, Robert 358–9
Shrewsbury, Earl of 220
Sibbald, Robert 327
Siberia 10, 35
Siccar Point 320*
Silk Road 170
Sillars, Jim 449, 460
Silures 32
Sinclair, John 324–5
Sinclair, John Gordon 450*
Sinclair, Oliver 204, 205, 206*
Sinclair, Sir Archibald 433*
'Singing Braes,' near Morebattle
  261
Skaill, Viking hall at 77–8,
  79–80
Skara Brae 24
Skellig Michael 47
Skeoch Hill 262
skiffle 439*
Sky TV 471
Skye 4, 73, 87
Skyesaurus 5*
The Slab Boys (Byrne, J.) 450*
Slain Men's Lea 255

Slammanan Muir 93
slavery 47, 80–81, 92, 344, 382
Slezer, John 276–8, 316–17
Smailholm Tower 357
Small, James of Blackadder
  Mount 324–5, 326
Smellie, William 325, 328–9
Smith, Adam 327, 329–30, 339,
  341
  core ideas 330
Smith, Alexander 385
Smith, George 373–4
Smith, John 460
Smith, William 398*
Smith Commission
  recommendations 483–4
Smithfield Market, London 380
Smollett, Tobias 318, 321
Snechtai, Mael 104
Sobieska, Maria Clementina 306
Sochet or Succat 47
Social Insurance and Allied
  Services, Report to
  Parliament on (1942) 426
social mobility 438, 440–41
Social Work Act for Scotland
  (1967) 440
society, Beveridge's 'Giant Evils'
  of 426
Soldier's Leap 274
Solemn League and Covenant
  250, 256, 257, 261
Solway 47, 50, 83
Solway fords 83
Solway Moss 83, 83*, 205
Somerled the Viking 123, 124,
  125, 144, 172
Son of Destiny ('Y Mab
  Darogan') 50*, 51
Sophia, Electress of Hanover
  285, 287
South America 4
South Wales 32
Southern Uplands 33
  Southern Upland Fault 4
Soutra, watershed hill of 44*
Spain 13, 17
Spence, Catherine 403
spittals and wicks 44*
sporting rivalry, Union and 390
Spottiswoode, John 212
SSPCK (Scottish Society for
  Promoting Christian
  Knowledge) 342–3
Stafford, George Leveson-Fower,
  Marquis of 348
Standard, Battle of the 119, 121,
  123, 130, 140
Standard Motor Company 429

Standard Vanguard 440
Stanegate 94
Stanley, Henry Morton 404
Stanley Mills 323–4, 341
Stanning, Heather 477
Stanwick fort 32–3
Staosnaig, Colonsay 18
State Management Scheme 405*
Statutes of Iona 234
steam power, beginnings of
  340–41
Steel, David 433*, 467
Stenness, Standing Stones of
  24, 26
Stenness Loch 24, 25
Stephen de Blois 117, 130
Stephenson,.George 366
Stevenson, Robert Louis 393–5
  death on Samoa and burial
  of 394
  legacy of 395
Stewart, Clan 176
Stewart, Alexander, Duke of
  Albany ('Alexander IV') 186
Stewart, Andy 434–5
Stewart, Charles of Ardshiel 313
Stewart, Donald 445
Stewart, Esmé, Duke of Lennox
  225, 226
Stewart, James, Commendator of
  Melrose Abbey 200
Stewart, James, Earl of Moray
  216, 219
Stewart, James Edward 269
Stewart, James of Killin 338
Stewart, Margaret 222
Stewart, Prince Charles Edward
  195–6, 306, 308, 333*,
  335, 344
Stewart, Robert, Commendator
  of Holyrood Abbey 200
Stewart, Robert, Duke of Albany
  178
Stewart, Robert, Earl of Orkney
  200
Stewart, Sir John 181
Stewart, Walter, Earl of Atholl
  181
Stewart dynasty 176, 180, 237,
  252, 269, 272, 274, 276,
  285–6, 290, 306, 309,
  326–7
Stewart of Bonkyll, Sir John 217*
Stewart standard 289
Stewarts 326–7
Stirling 101, 140, 156, 159
Stirling Bridge, Battle of 56, 158
Stirling Castle 112, 146, 154,
  161

Stirling Castle Rock 53, 67
Stockton–Darlington Railway 366
Stone of Scone 48*, 87, 95, 145, 155
  Coldstream and repartiation of 464
  theft of 427*
Stonehaven 4, 63
Stonehenge 26
Stooky Bill 415*
Storegga Trench 15, 23
Storegga tsunami 23
Stornoway 233, 233*
Stornoway, *Iolaire* disaster at 410–11
Stott, Ken 450*
Stow 12*
Strabo, Walafrid 76
Stracathro 116
Strachan, Archibald 257
Stranaer *(Rerigonium)* 'Very Royal Palace' 30
The Strange Case of Dr Jekyll and Mr Hyde (Stevenson, R.L.) 394
Strathbrora 348
Strathclyde 55, 67, 68, 71*, 89
Strathclyde University 438
Strathearn 63, 64*
  Battle of 86
street names 120*
Sturgeon, Nicola 476–7, 486
  leadership of SNP, election to 484–5
Sturrock, Mary Newbery 401–2
Suez Crisis 435
suffragette movement 396–7
Suilven 3
Sullom Voe, Shetland 23
Sunday Herald 471
Sunday Post 470
sundials 43*
Supremacy, Act of (1534) 262
Surgeon's Hall, Edinburgh, riot at 395–6
Surrey, Earl of 199
Sutherland, Elizabeth, Countess of 348
Swale River 52
Sweden, *Riksråd* (State Council) in 247–8
Swettenham, Captain 309, 310
Swinton, Tilda 450*
symbol stones 62, 64, 65

Tacitus, Publius Cornelius 32, 33–4, 35–6, 37, 38, 40, 41, 488

Taliesin 51
Talorcan, brother of Oengus 68
tanistry 88–9
Tara 370
  Hill of 95
Tarvedunum at Burghead 63
taxation 130, 216, 259, 260, 444, 455
Tay, Firth of 91, 103
Tay, River 273
Tayside 49, 62, 64*
television, birth of 415*
Temperance Movement 397, 414
Temple Pyx (gilded bronze plaque) 105–6
Tenants' Right Act (1980) and effects of 455–6
Terrell, Jacques 190, 191
The Testament of Cresseid (Henryson, R.) 209*
Tetzel, Johann 200
Teudubr, King of Strathclyde 68
Teviot Valley 132, 144
  men of Teviotdale 121
Teviotdale 33
textiles
  industrial growth and development of 322–3
  production of, twinsets and 432–3
Thames River 165
Thatcher, Margaret 451–2
  Falklands War and popularity of 453
  mineworkers and 453–5
  polarising figure 451–2
  privatisation, Adam Smith Institute and influence on 457–8
  'Sermon on the Mound' 456
  'Thatcherism,' Scottish attitudes to 455–6
Theatre Royal, Glasgow 434
Theatrum Scotiae (Slezer, J.) 276, 316–17
Theodoric the Great 122*
This Is Scotland (Scottish TV) 434
Thomas, Professor Charles 47
Thompson, William 351*
Thomson, Alexander ('Greek Thomson') 392*
Thomson, Charles Wyville 1
Thomson, D.C. 414*
Thomson, Emma 450*
Thomson, George 355
Thomson, Roy 434
Thoreau, Henry D. 369
thrall 80

'Three-Day Week' 447
A Satire of the Three Estates (Lyndsay, D.) 206–7
Three Fragments (Irish chronicle) 94–5
thumbikins 299*
Thurstan, Archbishop of York 118, 119
Tibbie Shiel's 374
Tinwald in Dumfriesshire 283
Tiree 3, 11
Tiron, forest of Perche 113
Tironesians 114*, 120*
  re-founding of monastery at Kelso by 115
Titus, Emperor 33
Tod & MacGregor 385
Toleration Act (1712) 295
tolls, tolbooths and 115
Tomb of the Eagles 21–2
Tongland, Abbey of 188
Torrance, David 476
Torridon Mountains 3
Torrisdale Bay 348
A Tour Thro' the Whole Island of Great Britain (Defoe, D.) 294
Toward peninsula 54
Townshend, Charles (grandson of 'Turnip') 329
Townshend, Viscount Charles 'Turnip' 317–18
Trades Union Congress 409, 418
Trainspotting (Welsh, I.) 462
Tranent Militia Riot (1797) 352
transhumance, ancient journey of 68
trapping, diet supplementation by 83–4
Traprain Law, East Lothian 39, 85
Treasure Island (Stevenson, R.L.) 394
A Treatise on Human Nature (Hume, D.) 328
'Treaty of Engagement' (1647) 256
Treaty of Westminster-Ardtornish (1461) 185
Triennial Act (1640) 247, 249
Trimontium 33
Trinity College, Dublin 56
Tristan da Cunha 1
Troilus and Criseyde (Chaucer, G.) 179
Trossachs 367, 369, 370–71
Trotternish Peninsula 5*
Tuathalan, Abbot of Conrigh Monaid 70

Tudor, Margaret, daughter of Henry VII 191
Tullibardine, Marquis of 309
Tummel River 273
Turgot, Bishop of St Andrews 109*
Tusun Pasha 351*
Tutti Frutti (BBC TV Scotland) 450*
Tweed basin 50, 53, 56, 67, 94, 101, 112, 155
Tweed, River 33, 39, 45, 49, 55, 90, 143
early farming north of 40
near Kelso 24
Tweed valley 102
tweeds, development of production of 374–6
Tyndale, William 209
Tyne, River at Newburn 248, 249
Tyneside 2
Tyninghame 71*
Tyrone 239
Tyrrhenian Sea 13

Uallas (Welsh-speaker or Briton) 56
Uchtred 130
UCS (Upper Clyde Shipbuilders) 441–3, 445–6, 449
Uilleam Breatnach ('William the Briton') 56
Ukraine 27
Ulster 31, 53, 57, 61, 86, 239, 240
'Undertakers' in 239–40
Ulster Scots *(Ullans)* 240
unemployment 414, 415–16, 418, 419, 423, 426, 441
UNESCO 25
Union, Act of (1707) 285, 294
Church of Scotland, guarantees in 294–5
Union. Act of (1707)
Westminster Parliament, treatment in 288–9
Union, Bill of (1706) 287
Union of Parliaments (1707) 320–21, 322–3, 326
intellectual life, impact on 326
trade and industrial development following 320–21, 322–3
United Free Church 420
United Reform Church 397
United Secession Church (New Licht) 376, 378

United States, politics in 384
Universities (Scotland) Act (1892) 396
King Urien 50–51
Urquhart Castle 161
Ury, River 111
Usher, Andrew 372
Utrecht, Treaty of (1713) 288

Vale of Leven 53–4
de Valence, Sir Aymer 160
van Dyck, Anthony 241
Vauxhall Velox 440
vellum 60
Venutius 32, 33
Versailles, Treaty of (1919) 339, *409, 414
Verulamium 46
Vespasian 32, 33
Queen Victoria 375, 380, 384
golden jubilee, Queen Empress in Glasgow City Chambers 398
Scotland and 371–2
Victoria Falls 404
Vikings 16, 59*, 71–4, 85, 86
army of 91
dragion ships of, threat to Britons from 89
in East Lothian 71*
kingdom of York, break-up of 91
legacy of 73
longships of 72–3
settlement by, process of 71–5
shipyard on Skye 127
'Sons of Death' 72, 73, 79
'The Untimate Viking' 143*
Villiers, George ('Steenie') 237, 238
Vinland the Good 100
Virgil 369
Viventius 48
Votadini 33, 35, 50

Waasland in Belgium 317
Wade, Field Marshall George 302, 334, 337
Walberswick 402
Walker, Patrick 278
Wall Street Crash (1929) 419
economic recover, slowness following 421
Wallace, William 56–7, 147, 155, 156, 157, 158, 159
Walsh, Antoine 308
Walsingham, Francis 220
Walters, Nigel 460
war-horses *see* destriers

de Warenne, John, Earl of Surrey 156, 157, 158, 159
Wars of Independence 55, 56–7, 116
see also Bruce; Wallace
Wars of the Covenant 245–53, 278
Waterloo, Battle of 348
Watson, Lt Colonel David 320
Watson, W.J. 62
Watson of Keillor, Hugh 380
Watt, James 340, 363
Waverley (Scott, W.) 357, 359
An Inquiry into the Nature and Causes of the Wealth of Nations (Smith, A.) 329–30
Webster, Rev. Alexander 342
Weir of Hermiston (Stevenson, R.L.) 394
Wellington, Sheena 354
Wells, Allan 417, 453*
Welsh, Dr David 377, 423
Welsh, Irvine 462
Welsh, Rev. John (great-grandson of John Knox) 262
Welsh Triads 30
West Clerkland Farm 323*
West Cumbria 2
West of Scotland Cricket Club 389–90
Western Isles 3, 133, 411, 445
Westlothiana lizziae 3*
Westminster 155
Westminster Abbey 222, 427*
Westminster-Ardtornish, Treaty of (1461) 185
Westminster Parliament
Act of Union (1707), treatment in 288–9
Scottish representation in 288
Wheatley, John 415
Whiggamores 256, 261
whiskey production, development of 372–4
illicit distillers 372–3
White Caterthun 42
White Heather Club (BBC TV) 434–5
White martyrs 59*
Whitehall, Banqueting House in 256
Whitehall Palace 268
Whitelaw, Archibald 189
Whithorn, Galloway 48, 49, 53
Whyte, Rev. Professor James A. 456
'wick' ('outlying farm') 44*
Wightman, General Joseph 302
Wigtown Bay 267

'Wild Mountain Thyme' 140*
Wildwood 7, 13, 14, 20
Wilfred, Celtic Football Club and Brother 391
Wiliam of Normandy 106, 108
Wilkinson, John 340
William III (II of Scotland) 272, 282, 284
William IV 362
William of Orange 285
William Rufus 110, 112
William the Lion 129, 130, 131, 140, 142, 152, 153
Williams, Captain Oliver 311
Willock, John 212
Wilmut, Ian 463–4
Wilson, Agnes 267
Wilson, Gilbert 267
Wilson, Harold 440, 447
    devolution, White Paper on 449
    England World Cup victory, (1966), optimism resulting from 450–51
Wilson, James 361, 362
Wilson. Jim 457*
Wilson, John 354
Wilson, Margaret 267
Wilson, Richard 450*
Wilson, Woodrow 240*
Wimund, Bishop of the Isles 117
Windram, Major 268

Windsor Castle 380
Winram, John 212
winter of 1946–7, bitterness of 429
Wirral, Mersey shore of 97
Wishart, Rev. George 207, 257
Wishart, Robert, Bishop of Glasgow 152, 156
Wishart, Ruth 468–9
witchcraft and witch trials 215–16, 226–7, 233
The Witness 380
Wittenberg 201
wolf dogs 10*
Wolfe, General James 304, 313
Wolsey, Cardinal 199
Women's Guild 443–4
Women's Social and Political Union 396
Wood, Harvey 431–2
Wood, Sir Andrew of Largo 191
Wood, Stan 3*
wool trade 115–16, 170–71
Worcester, John of 119
Wordsworth, William 351
Wordsworth, William and Dorothy 370–71
World Cup football (1978) 449–51
    debacle of, and effects of 450–51
World Heritage status for Ness of Brodgar 24–5

Wright, Canon Kenyon 457*
Wright, Esmond 440
Writer's Cramp (Byrne, J.) 450*
Life of St Wulfstan, Bishop of Worcester 81
Wynkfield, Robert 221
Wyntoun, Andrew 103

Y Bedydd ('Baptised') 52
Y-chromosome 13, 16, 27, 56–7, 73
Y Gynt 'Gentiles' or 'Heathens') 52
Y Mab Darogan ('Son of Destiny') 50*, 51
Yarrow Valley 374
Yeavering, near Wooler 68
Yetholm 65
Yom Kippur War 449
York 44, 91, 118
    museum at 69
    Treaty of (1237) 142–3
    Viking leadership in 96
    York Danes 94
Yorkshire 11, 32
Young, Robert 377
Young Folks 394
Younger, George 458
Younger, John 319
Your Cheatin' Heart (Byrne, J.) 450*

Zambezi River 404

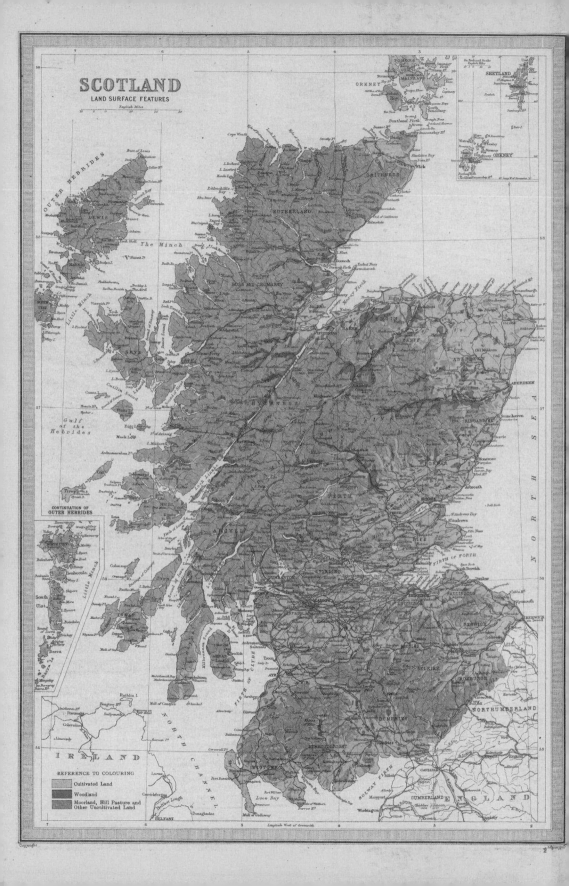

SCOTLAND

LAND SURFACE FEATURES

English Miles

REFERENCE TO COLOURING

Cultivated Land
Woodland
Moorland, Hill Pasture and
Other Uncultivated Land

CONTINUATION OF
OUTER HEBRIDES

SHETLAND

ORKNEY

OUTER HEBRIDES

LEWIS

The Minch

Little Minch

NORTH
UIST

Gulf
of the
Hebrides

SKYE

CAITHNESS

SUTHERLAND

ROSS AND CROMARTY

INVERNESS

BANFF

ABERDEEN

ABERDEEN

KINCARDINE

Stonehaven

FORFAR

PERTH

ARGYLL

MULL

JURA

ISLAY

FIRTH OF FORTH

STIRLING

DUMBARTON

GLASGOW

EDINBURGH

HADDINGTON

BERWICK

PEEBLES

SELKIRK

ROXBURGH

AYR

DUMFRIES

WIGTOWN

KIRKCUDBRIGHT

NORTHUMBERLAND

SOUTH
UIST

Barra

NORTH
CHANNEL

IRELAND

BELFAST

SOLWAY FIRTH

CUMBERLAND ENGLAND

N O R T H   S E A

Longitude West of Greenwich

LEDO NIV

Thyle insula

Medium insulæ

OCEA NVS

Orcades insulæ
triginta circiter

Dumna

Ocitis

Isys Fluvi.

Volsas sinus

Cernotes

Creones

Carnonacæ

Carini

Cornabij

Taruedrum quod et O.

Caledonia Silua

Simertę

Logi

Viruedrum promont.

Cale donij

Cante

Ripa alba

Veruuium prom.

imia

Alata cast.

Vacemagi

Varar Estuarium

Tuesis

enni cones

Celnius Flu

Tuesis estuarium

Deuana

Tæzali

Tæzalum prom.

Taua Estuarium

Diua Fluvius

Saxonum insulæ tres

O CE

3 8002 02243 014 6